M000021943

The Phenom

Sometimes the game is more than a game

To Leah, Olivia, Micah, Millie and Justine
you inspire me.

The Phenom

Sometimes the game is more than a game

JACK SHNIDERMAN
WITH BRUCE MILES

Copyright ©2020, Jack Shniderman

ALL RIGHTS RESERVED.

No part of this publication may be reproduced, stored in a
retrieval system, or transmitted in any form or by any means—
electronic, mechanical, photo-copy, recording, or any other—except for
brief quotation in reviews, without the prior permission
of the author or publisher.

ISBN: 978-1-948638-17-3 (hardcover)
978-1-948638-16-6 (paperback)

*This is a work of fiction. Names, characters, businesses, places, events and
incidents are either the products of the authors' imaginations or used in a
fictitious manner. Any resemblance to actual persons, living or dead, or actual
events is purely coincidental.*

Published by

Fideli Publishing, Inc.
119 W. Morgan St.
Martinsville, IN 46151

www.FideliPublishing.com

PREFACE

Go ahead. Talk about the "tortured history" of the Chicago Cubs.

The so-called Billy Goat and Bartman curses went bye-bye when the Cubs won their World Series in 2016. Fittingly, they won it against the team everybody should be talking about: The Cleveland Indians.

At least the Cubs had "Beautiful Wrigley Field" to market when they were holding up the rest of the National League from the bottom of the standings or falling heartbreakingly short in the postseason.

The Indians?

Ha! They played all those years in the "Mistake by the Lake," Municipal Stadium, where the mosquitoes were as big as B-52s, where "Nickel Beer Night" gave the entire city a black eye and where a decent crowd of 20,000 would get swallowed up by 60,000 empty seats.

Hell, they even made a movie, "Major League," about the ineptness of the Tribe.

Remember all those feel-good stories about Cubs fans going to cemeteries and putting team gear on their fathers' and grandfathers' graves? The Erie Street Cemetery across the street from Progressive Field should have Indians laundry piled sky high by now.

A move to shiny new Jacobs Field — later renamed Progressive Field — helped immeasurably, but the Indians never could get over the hump of winning a World Series. Their last Series win was in 1948 against the Boston Braves, well before the term "politically correct" had even been invented as it related to Chief Wahoo.

But as I imagine it, this year will be different.

Back for another season with the Tribe is first baseman Oliver Reiner. Even though "The Shark" is starting to show his age, he did hit 25 homers last year and added another Gold Glove to his trophy case.

Third baseman Terry Rovetto wants to build on his 20-homer season, and with the Shark's Gold Gloves, the Indians have a steady corner combo.

With the free agent acquisition of Wilson White from St. Louis, the Tribe added a solid everyday left fielder to the mix. Rookie Huron Southworth looks ready to shine after leading the Indians' Class AAA club to the championship last year after slugging twenty-six homers and batting .351. Huron can't wait to patrol right field at Progressive.

Second baseman Angel Rodriguez hopes to stay healthy this year. Rodriguez made headlines awhile back by coming out as openly gay. His teammates greeted the news with a shrug, and they've accepted Rodriguez for what he is: a solid fielder and a reliable teammate. If Rodriguez does suffer another nagging injury, 23-year-old Scott Michaels is waiting in the wings as a backup.

Michaels is a third-year player who was the first to befriend Rodriguez after he came out. Even though he has a ton of potential, Michaels is coming off shoulder surgery. Michaels, the Big Ten batting champion out of Indiana University was a first-round (fourth player overall) draft pick of the Tribe, and when he was selected, the comparisons were made to both Ryne Sandberg and to Indians legend Jason Kipnis.

That's a lot of hype to live up to for any youngster, but to have Kipnis' name thrown at you in Cleveland, well, you get the idea. But at this point of his young career, Michaels is sliding dangerously close from the status of "prospect" to "suspect." Time, perhaps as early as this season, will tell if Michaels can turn the corner at last.

For the last few years, hitting never was the problem for the Indians. The bad contracts and the bad karma haunted the pitching staff.

Lynn Moda did win 17 games last year while leading the team with a 3.78 ERA. Moda is a reliable innings eater, but he's never going to overpower anybody.

The Indians are banking on a Japanese import, Tak Fujimoto, the power pitcher they crave to complement Moda. With the luck they've had the last few years with pitchers, the Indians hope Fujimoto won't be more like Hidekei Kobiyashi, a Japanese fad that turned out to be a dud.

Late in spring training they finally settled a bitter and contentious contract dispute with Ollie Gonzalez, better known as Ollie G, and expect him to perform well this season.

The man on the hot seat will be manager Dave Mills. Clevelanders are running out of patience with the "vanilla" Mills.

So, baseball fans, buckle up for a wild ride with the Tribe as viewed through the all-seeing eyes of Cleveland Press baseball columnist Sam Lardner, said to be a great-great nephew of legendary writer Ring Lardner.

Lardner's colleagues call him "Zing," for the sarcastic one-liners he tosses out in the press box as the Indians stumble their way to another loss. The season at hand, with its unexpected twists and turns, would test even Sam's famous cynicism. What follows are his game-by-game columns for the Cleveland Press, covering all 162 games of the Indians' historic season.

CLEVELAND INDIANS

THE STARTING LINEUP

1B	Oliver "The Shark" Reiner	10 year veteran. "The Shark" for his poolhall abilities and what he does to rookies. Has a history of 25 homers per year.
2B	Angel Rodriguez	Gold glove caliber fielder with little power and injury prone. First openly gay player.
SS	Justin Kestino	Reliable infielder has occasional power and steady in the field.
3B	Terry Rovetto	The clubhouse leader. Does it all, gold glove, hits for power and average. Perennial all star.
LF	Wilson White	Club's big free agent acquisition. Solid everyday player.
CF	Rikki Labudda	Fastest man on the team. Lead off man, 50 stolen base potential.
RF	Huron Southworth	20 year old rookie. Led AAA team to league championship.
C	Morris Jerome	Longtime vet nearing the end of his career. Excellent at handling the pitching staff. Considered future coach.

RESERVES

!B	J.J. Kulakofski	Biggest man on the team. 6'8". Good power but not ready to unseat Reiner.
2B	Scott Michaels	3rd year player coming off shoulder surgery. First round pick in the draft and has all the tools if healthy.
IF-OF	Leo Taylor	Versatile player, can play infield or outfield. Excellent defender, good speed, little power.
INF	Bernard Harper	Switch hitting corner infielder. Steady bat, but a defensive liability.
OF	Micah Millison	Good young outfielder but still lost starting job to Southworth.
OF	Kieran Catsef	Superstitious, once asked to be pinch hit for because opposing pitcher wore number 13.
C	Iceberg Peters	Good with pitchers and fair power. Legally changed his name to Iceberg because of his large size and lack of speed.

PITCHERS

SP	Lynn Moda	Staff ace. Won 17 games last year, provides innings and leadership.
SP	Ollie Gonzalez	"Ollie G". Big imposing lefty. 15 game winner last year.
SP	Brian "Doc" Howard	Finesse pitcher who knows how to operate.
SP	Kenny Camden	Known as "The Wiz". Has a great stock portfolio and mentors young players about their finances.
SP	Tak Fujimoto	Excelled in Japan the last four years. Can he play at this level?
RP	Solly Alvarez	Long relief or spot starter.
RP	Mickey Penny	2nd year man showed a lot of promise. Made jump from AA.
RP	Buck Sterling	Local favorite with Cleveland roots. Grew up in Beechwood.
RP	Geno Milzie	Right handed knuckleball closer to compliment Zyzna.
RP	Ivan Zyzna	Last in the phone book, last in the game. Left handed closer. Great stuff, power pitcher "adonis" with his shirt off.

GAME 1

By SAM LARDNER
The Cleveland Press

ANAHEIM, April 6 — Well, so much for all of that optimism coming out of the desert. It all went up in a puff of sand Monday night at Angel Stadium.

Both the Indians and the Los Angeles Angels of Anaheim made the short trip from Arizona to Southern California at the end of spring training, but the Indians looked like they needed a stop at an oasis for some thirst quenching.

That quick-start manager Dave Mills talked about as the team broke camp? Alas, a good start was but a mirage.

The Angels struck early and often, scoring seven runs in the first inning on the way to a 15–3 shellacking of the Tribe on Opening Night. If there's any saving grace, it's that the good folks back home in Northeast Ohio turned out the lights and were in bed by the second inning.

Starting pitcher Lynn Moda, looking to build off last year's 17-win season, barely broke a sweat, as he was knocked about and finally out in the first. "I don't know what happened out there," Moda said. "I felt great warming up in the bullpen. In fact, Mo (catcher Morris Jerome) told me it was the best stuff he's seen me have all spring."

Mills had no other choice but to get the hook for Moda after Pete Warren, the Angels' big first baseman, took Moda deep with two men on base.

Albert Torres and Benji Washington singled ahead of Warren, setting the table for his blast. Warren finished with four RBIs on the night.

"You hate to do that to your bullpen in the first game of the season, but Modes (Moda) clearly didn't have it, and I didn't want him to stand out there and take it anymore," Mills said. "Everything gets magnified in the first game of the season. Every pitcher has a bad start in the middle of the season, and nobody notices. But when it happens on Opening Day, it's the end of the world."

It may not be the end of the world as we know it for the Indians, but it's certainly not the brave new world they had talked about embarking on all spring in Arizona. It's one thing to lose, it's quite another to look as uninspired as the Indians did in the opener.

"Listen," said Jerome. "Nobody feels worse about this than Modes. I know you guys are going to jump all over him, but you were all there last year in Detroit, when they beat us 16–1 and then the next night, Modes went out and stuck it up their (butts) and we won 1–0. So, let's not make too much of this, OK? It's not like anybody's losing their job or anything like that. We still have 161 to go. It's not a sprint, it's a marathon."

Nobody's losing their job, not yet anyway. Mills opens this season on the hot seat after last year's disappointing finish and if there are going to be empty seats at Progressive Field, somebody will take the fall. The Angels also got a big night from 30–30 threat Chico Gomez, who homered twice — once to the rocks beyond the center-field wall — and drove in five. His three-run homer in the third made it 10–0.

In case you went to bed early but had Oliver Reiner in the pool to hit the Tribe's first homer, you're in luck. "The Shark" was about the only thing the Indians had going for them, as he hit a two-run homer in the fifth, after the game was well out of reach. Terry Rovetto had a sacrifice fly in the seventh for the other Indians run. Rookie Huron Southworth found out that he's not in Triple-A anymore, as he struck out three times and grounded out once. Wilson White, in his first game for the Indians after signing that big deal last winter after parlaying a huge year in St. Louis, also was hitless, going 0-for-4 with a walk.

"We'll come back and do it all again tomorrow," Mills offered up. He didn't say if that was a promise or a threat.

GAME 1

CLEVELAND INDIANS AT LOS ANGELES ANGELS · APRIL 6
LOS ANGELES 15 / CLEVELAND 3

CLEVELAND INDIANS

BATTING	AB	R	H	RBI	2B	3B	HR	BB	SO	BA
RIKKI LABUDDA CF	4	1	1	0	0	0	0	0	0	.250
WILSON WHITE LF	4	0	0	0	0	0	0	1	1	.000
OLIVER REINER 1B	3	2	1	2	0	0	1	0	1	.333
TERRY ROVETTO 3B	3	0	0	1	0	0	0	0	0	.000
MORRIS JEROME C	4	0	1	0	0	0	0	0	1	.250
JJ KULAKOFSKI DH	3	0	1	0	0	0	0	1	0	.333
JUSTIN KESTINO SS	3	0	1	0	0	0	0	1	1	.333
HURON SOUTHWORTH RF	4	0	0	0	0	0	0	0	3	.000
ANGEL RODRIGUEZ 2B	3	0	0	0	0	0	0	1	0	.000

PITCHING	IP	H	R	ER	SO	BB	ERA			
LYNN MODA L (0-1)	0.3	5	5	5	0	0	150.00			
BUCK STERLING	4.6	8	5	5	1	3	9.78			
MICKEY PENNY	2	4	4	4	1	2	18.00			
SOLLY ALVAREZ	1	1	1	1	1	0	9.00			

LOS ANGELES ANGELS

BATTING	AB	R	H	RBI	2B	3B	HR	BB	SO	BA
LIM CHANG 3B	6	1	2	1	1	0	0	0	0	.333
JACOB BAKER DH	5	1	1	0	0	0	0	0	2	.200
CHICO GOMEZ CF	4	3	2	5	0	0	2	1	0	.500
BENJI WASHINGTON SS	4	1	2	0	0	0	0	1	0	.500
ALBERT TORRES 2B	4	2	3	1	1	0	0	1	0	.750
PETE WARREN 1B	5	2	2	4	0	0	1	0	0	.400
CARLOS DIAZ C	4	0	1	0	0	0	0	1	2	.250
TRENT NORRIS LF	5	2	3	0	2	1	0	0	0	.600
NOAH WILLIAMS RF	2	2	2	3	1	0	0	1	0	1.000

PITCHING	IP	H	R	ER	SO	BB	ERA			
ROBERTO COLON W (1-0)	6	7	2	2	7	4	3.00			
LEE HICKSON	2	0	1	0	1	0	0.00			
MIKE VANDENBERG	1	0	0	0	1	0	0.00			

INNING	1	2	3	4	5	6	7	8	9	TOTAL
CLEVELAND	0	0	0	2	0	0	1	0	0	3
LOS ANGELES	7	0	4	0	0	2	1	1		15

GAME 2

By **SAM LARDNER**
The Cleveland Press

ANAHEIM, April 7 — Second verse same as the first. If you're looking for moral victories for the Cleveland Indians, it's that they held the Los Angeles Angels of Anaheim to single digits in runs scored. The end result Tuesday was the second straight loss to begin the season, and now we have to say it: There doesn't seem to be much life in the Tribe.

This perplexing Indians team, with seemingly everything to play for and with jobs on the line, went out and lost 7–4 to the Angels Tuesday night at Angel Stadium, where the Santa Ana winds were blowing, but doing no favors for the Indians.

The score line doesn't sound as bad as the Opening Night 15–3 loss, but even though the difference was only three runs, the Indians weren't really in this one, either. The only spark for the Tribe was a straight steal of home in the seventh by Rikki LaBudda, but even then, it seemed the Angels were hardly paying attention to LaBudda. Truth be told, they seemed so secure in their lead that it looked like they were allowing him to have a little harmless fun.

Indians lefty Ollie Gonzalez gave up early runs just as did Lynn Moda in the opener, and Gonzalez lasted five innings, giving up nine hits and six earned runs. Manager Dave Mills put on his bravest face, but he had no answers.

"We just need to get a lead and relax a little bit," said Mills, whose stolid demeanor is difficult to discern. Is he trying not to evince panic? Or is he starting to get tight?

"Look," he said. "I know everybody back home will be unhappy about us being 0–2, but I'll say it here and I'll say it again: You can't overreact to these situations. The mood coming out of spring training was great. It was upbeat. Guys were optimistic. And it's still that way."

Gonzalez, who won 15 games last year and whose "mound presence" (in the modern parlance of the game) can be imposing, took the blame. "I didn't give us much of a chance," he said. "Mo (catcher Morris Jerome) and I were on the same page. They just hit a couple mistakes and did what good hitters are supposed to do with them. We'll be all right. There's too much talent here."

For the second straight night, the Angels' Pete Warren hit one of those mistakes, this time for a two-run homer in the first. The Angels added two in the third on singles by Albert Torres and Tim Thorsen and a two-run double by Trent Norris. In the fifth, Angels DH Jacob Baker lined a single that scored Thorsen and Gabriel Gustafson. Baker moved to third on a pair of groundouts and came home on a wild pitch by Gonzalez.

Things were out of hand by the time LaBudda stole home in the seventh. Indians DH J.J. Kulakofski crushed a 450-homer to right in the eighth but that was merely consolation. As for LaBudda, he simply took what the Angels were giving him. And they didn't seem to mind as evidenced by the somewhat amused looks on the faces on the field and on the face of Angels manager Gary Lee.

"I just saw that they weren't really watching me, and with the lefty (the Angels' Hector Lugo) on the mound, I just I'd try it and see if I could give the team a spark," LaBudda said. "Maybe it will have some carry-over effect into tomorrow. At least I hope so."

The speedy LaBudda would do better to give the Indians a spark by raising his lifetime batting average from .270 to closer to .300 and his paltry on-base percentage from about .310 to about .345 or better.

After all, you can steal home, but you can't steal first.

CLEVELAND INDIANS AT LOS ANGELES ANGELS · APRIL 7
LOS ANGELES 7 / CLEVELAND 4

CLEVELAND INDIANS

BATTING	AB	R	H	RBI	2B	3B	HR	BB	SO	BA
RIKKI LABUDDA CF	5	1	2	1	0	0	0	0	0	.333
WILSON WHITE LF	5	0	2	0	0	0	0	0	0	.222
OLIVER REINER 1B	5	0	1	0	0	0	0	0	2	.250
TERRY ROVETTO 3B	5	1	2	0	1	0	0	0	1	.250
MORRIS JEROME C	5	0	1	0	0	0	0	0	1	.222
JJ KULAKOFSKI DH	4	1	1	2	0	0	1	0	1	.286
JUSTIN KESTINO SS	3	1	2	0	1	0	0	2	0	.500
HURON SOUTHWORTH RF	4	0	0	0	0	0	0	0	0	.000
ANGEL RODRIGUEZ 2B	4	0	0	0	0	0	0	0	2	.000

PITCHING	IP	H	R	ER	SO	BB	ERA
OLLIE GONZALEZ (L)	5	9	7	6	3	6	12.60
MICKEY PENNY	2	2	0	0	1	1	9.00
BUCK STERLING	1	0	0	0	0	0	7.94

LOS ANGELES ANGELS

BATTING	AB	R	H	RBI	2B	3B	HR	BB	SO	BA
TIM THORSEN SS	3	1	1	0	0	0	0	2	0	.333
JACOB BAKER DH	4	1	1	2	0	0	0	0	0	.222
CHICO GOMEZ CF	5	1	2	0	1	0	0	0	0	.444
PETE WARREN 1B	5	1	2	2	0	0	1	0	2	.400
ALBERT TORRES 2B	3	1	1	0	0	0	0	2	1	.571
LIM CHANG 3B	4	1	1	0	0	0	0	0	1	.300
CARLOS DIAZ C	5	0	0	0	0	0	0	0	1	.111
TRENT NORRIS LF	5	0	2	2	1	0	0	0	0	.500
GABRRIEL GUSTAFSON RF	2	1	1	0	0	0	0	2	0	.500

PITCHING	IP	H	R	ER	SO	BB	ERA
HECTOR LUGO (W)	5	5	0	0	7	2	0.00
JAVIER RIVERA	2	2	1	1	1	1	4.50
LEE HICKSON	2	2	3	3	1	1	13.50

INNING	1	2	3	4	5	6	7	8	9	TOTAL
CLEVELAND	0	0	0	0	0	0	1	2	1	4
LOS ANGELES	2	0	2	0	3	0	0	0		7

GAME 3

By SAM LARDNER
The Cleveland Press

ANAHEIM, April 8 — The hot Santa Ana winds swirled across Angel Stadium on a dusty Wednesday afternoon. If you squinted really hard, you'd swear you saw tumbleweed rolling past the Cleveland Indians' first-base dugout.

Let's face it, folks. That dugout looked like a ghost town, and the Indians look like they're taking a drink at the Last Chance Saloon. It really was that bad as the Los Angeles Angels completed a three-game season-opening sweep, beating a listless Indians team 8–2.

To recap, the Tribe is 0–3 and has been outscored 30–9. The Indians dressed quickly after Wednesday's game and got out of town by sundown, but things don't seem any sunnier on the horizon, as they head for Minneapolis and three games against the Twins.

Speaking of riding off into the sunset, Indians manager Dave Mills has that look in his eyes.

"It wasn't pretty here, was it?" he asked to no one in particular after this one. "I don't know if I can tell you any more than I did the last two days. We're just not getting it done. But we will."

Mills sounded like he was having a hard time convincing himself that things are suddenly going to turn around for his beleaguered ballclub. A bright off-season has suddenly turned dark. All the optimism of spring training has faded to black.

On this bright and windswept afternoon, normally reliable Brian Howard, given the nickname "The Doctor" for the way he operates by teammate and close friend Lynn Moda, seemed to come down with whatever malady that ails the Indians as he lost his normally pinpoint control. He even got himself, perhaps mercifully, tossed from the game after giving up a grand slam to Pete Warren to put the Angels up 5–0 in the fourth.

Howard plunked the next hitter, Benji Washington, and home-plate umpire Dino Rozan gave him the heave-ho without so much as a warning.

"Anybody could see that I didn't have my control," Howard said. "There was no way I was trying to hit anybody in that situation. I should have been able to stay in there and take one for the team. Now look at it. After three games our bullpen is beat up. I thought he (Rozan) overreacted. Washington didn't seem to have a problem with it."

Howard was replaced by Buck Sterling, and he immediately gave up a homer to Trent Norris, and the rout was on. The Indians, once again, got their runs when the game was out of reach. Rikki LaBudda and Huron Southworth, the Nos. 1 and 2 hitters, reached on singles and raced home on a double by Wilson White, the club's free-agent pickup this past winter.

The Tribe will need more of that. So, who steps up? Who tries to right things before they completely spiral out of control? Do the players need to hold a players-only meeting?

"Whoa, whoa, whoa," said team leader Terry Rovetto. "It's only three games. Yeah, we've looked bad, but we're capable of going into Minnesota and doing what the Angels did to us."

For Mills, the risk now is that he'll "lose" the clubhouse, that players will begin to tune his message — vanilla as it may be — out and quit playing for him. Baseball history is full of such examples.

"It's not the manager's fault," Rovetto said. "He's not the one out there failing to come through and making mental mistakes. That's on us, the players. Millsie has the support of everybody in here, from the top guy down to the 25th man."

History is full of that kind of talk from players, too. But Mills may be looking over his shoulder this coming weekend. General manager J.D Eisner is scheduled to meet the team in Minneapolis, and that will have tongues wagging. We'll see if Mills makes it to the home opener.

My advice: Rent. Don't buy.

CLEVELAND INDIANS AT LOS ANGELES ANGELS • APRIL 8
LOS ANGELES 8 /CLEVELAND 2

CLEVELAND INDIANS

BATTING	AB	R	H	RBI	2B	3B	HR	BB	SO	BA
RIKKI LABUDDA CF	4	1	1	0	0	0	0	0	1	.308
HURON SOUTHWORTH RF	4	1	1	0	0	0	0	0	1	.083
WILSON WHITE LF	3	0	1	2	1	0	0	1	0	.250
OLIVER REINER 1B	4	0	2	0	1	0	0	0	1	.333
TERRY ROVETTO 3B	4	0	1	0	0	0	0	0	1	.250
MORRIS JEROME C	4	0	1	0	0	0	0	0	1	.231
BERNARD HARPER DH	3	0	2	0	0	0	0	1	0	.667
JUSTIN KESTINO SS	4	0	0	0	0	0	0	0	0	.300
ANGEL RODRIGUEZ 2B	3	0	0	0	0	0	0	0	1	.000
JJ KULAKOWSKI PH	1	0	0	0	0	0	0	0	0	.375

PITCHING	IP	H	R	ER	SO	BB	ERA			
BRIAN HOWARD (L)	3	5	6	6	1	2	18.00			
BUCK STERLING	3	2	1	1	2	0	5.06			
GENO MILZIE	2	3	1	1	2	0	4.50			

LOS ANGELES ANGELS

BATTING	AB	R	H	RBI	2B	3B	HR	BB	SO	BA
TIM THORSEN RF	3	1	1	2	0	0	0	0	1	.333
JACOB BAKER DH	3	1	1	0	1	0	0	0	1	.250
CHICO GOMEZ CF	3	1	1	0	0	0	0	1	1	.417
PETE WARREN 1B	4	1	1	4	0	0	1	0	1	.357
BENJI WASHINGTON SS	2	1	1	0	1	0	0	1	0	.500
TRENT NORRIS LF	4	1	1	2	0	0	1	0	1	.429
LIM CHANG 3B	3	0	1	0	0	0	0	0	1	.308
ALBERT TORRES 2B	3	1	1	0	0	0	0	0	0	.500
CARLOS DIAZ C	3	1	2	0	0	1	0	0	0	.250

PITCHING	IP	H	R	ER	SO	BB	ERA			
JACKSON WOODRUFF (W)	5	6	2	2	4	2	0.00			
HIRAM MOLINA	3	3	0	0	1	0	4.50			
MIKE VANDENBERG	1	0	0	0	0	0	13.50			

INNING	1	2	3	4	5	6	7	8	9	TOTAL
CLEVELAND	0	0	0	0	2	0	0	0	0	2
LOS ANGELES	0	0	0	7	0	0	1	0		8

GAME 4

By SAM LARDNER

The Cleveland Press

MINNEAPOLIS, April 9 — The Land of 10,000 Lakes can be a very welcoming place, with its natural beauty, late summer sunsets and charming folk.

Feeling a whole lot less than welcome on a frigid Friday night were the Cleveland Indians, who can't seem to get anything to go their way. The Tribe was well on its way to the team's first quality start of the season as Kenny "The Wiz" Camden sailed into the seventh inning with a seemingly comfortable 6–0 lead.

You probably can guess the rest. In the bottom of the seventh inning, the Twins' Bruce "Bruiser" Conklin, who is reminding many in these parts of Harmon "Killer" Killebrew, hit a three-run homer after Tony Wilders walked and Tommy Hopkins singled to put runners on the corners. Conklin's blast, to right-center, measured 461 feet.

Camden still had some room to maneuver. But he quickly painted himself into a corner by giving up back-to-back singles to Fabio Pineda and Carl Dorey.

That was enough for Indians manager Dave Mills, who played the odds and went with knuckleballer Geno Milzie to face Ralph Taylor. Before you could say "twin killing," Taylor tied the game by slicing a three-run homer down the line in right just inside the foul pole to tie the game at 6–6.

"We had it all lined up, we really did," Mills said. "Even with Camden losing his stuff so fast, our bullpen was ready. It was a knuckleball that didn't knuckle, and you saw what happened." Milzie was apologetic.

"I could not preserve a win for Wiz, and that's what hurts the most," he said. "It's hard to get a grip on the knuckler in this weather, but that's no excuse. I should have made a better pitch."

Few teams use their closer for more than one inning nowadays, but Mills had no other choice but to go with Ivan Zyzna in the 10th, and he worked a 1-2-3 inning to preserve the tie.

In the top of the 11th, the Indians had a big chance, with Wilson White doubling to lead off. But that's as far as he got, as Terry Rovetto struck out, Oliver Reiner popped out and Scott Michaels rolled back to the mound. It was Michaels' first game action of the season, and he was looking to make an impression with Angel Rodriguez nursing some aches and pains and Mills perhaps looking just to shake things up. Michaels went 0-for-2 with two walks.

Zyzna pitched too carefully to Conklin in the bottom of the inning and walked him. Pineda singled, and Dorey ended it with a gapper to right to score Conklin on what was scored a single.

Frozen, beaten and battered, the Indians trudged dejectedly off the field after giving it what they thought was their best only to end up with the loss and a record of 0–4.

The Tribe took a 3–0 lead in the second on Terry Rovetto's two-run double after Huron Southworth singled and White walked. In the fourth, Justin Kestino hit his first homer of the season, a two-run shot to left.

All that was left for Mills to do — besides thaw out — was to cite moral victories. That's the only kind the Indians are getting these days.

"The guys came out with some spark and got the lead," he said. "And nobody hung their heads after the Twins came back to tie it. They're going to be tough in our division. All we need is that one break to help us on our way."

GAME 4

CLEVELAND INDIANS AT MINNESOTA TWINS · APRIL 9
MINNESOTA 7 / CLEVELAND 6

CLEVELAND INDIANS

BATTING	AB	R	H	RBI	2B	3B	HR	BB	SO	BA	
RIKKI LABUDDA CF	6	0	2	0	1	0	0	0	1	.316	
HURON SOUTHWORTH RF	5	1	0	0	0	0	0	1	1	.059	
WILSON WHITE LF	6	1	3	0	1	0	0	0	1	.333	
OLIVER REINER 1B	6	0	2	0	0	0	0	0	0	.333	
TERRY ROVETTO 3B	5	0	1	2	0	0	0	0	3	.235	
MORRIS JEROME C	3	1	1	1	0	0	0	0	2	.250	
BERNARD HARPER DH	5	1	2	1	1	0	0	0	2	.500	
JUSTIN KESTINO SS	5	1	2	2	0	0	1	0	0	.333	
SCOTT MICHAELS 2B	2	1	0	0	0	0	0	1	0	.000	
ICEBERG PETERS PH	1	0	0	0	0	0	0	0	1	.250	

PITCHING	IP	H	R	ER	SO	BB	ERA				
KENNY CAMDEN	6	9	5	5	7	3	7.50				
GENO MILZIE	3	6	1	1	1	1	3.60				
IVAN ZYZNA (L)	0	2	1	1	0	1	0.00				

MINNESOTA TWINS

BATTING	AB	R	H	RBI	2B	3B	HR	BB	SO	BA	
TONY WILDERS 2B	4	1	1	0	0	0	0	2	0	.300	
TOMMY HOPKINS 3B	6	1	1	0	0	0	0	0	2	.222	
BRUCE CONKLIN 1B	5	2	2	3	0	0	1	1	1	.412	
FABIO PINEDA LF	6	1	4	0	1	0	0	0	0	.450	
CARL DOREY RF	4	1	2	1	0	0	0	2	1	.500	
RALPH TAYLOR CF	4	1	1	3	0	0	1	1	1	.389	
AVERY BECKER SS	5	0	2	0	1	0	0	0	0	.333	
DONNIE WALLACE DH	5	0	0	0	0	0	0	0	0	.333	
JOSE CHAVEZ C	5	0	3	0	0	0	0	0	1	.353	

PITCHING	IP	H	R	ER	SO	BB	ERA				
CLAUDIO ONTIVEROS	6	11	5	5	7	2	4.09				
HYUN SOO PARK	2	0	0	0	1	0	4.50				
SANDY GREENE (W)	2	1	1	1	1	0	13.50				
ROGER SANFORD (S)	1	1	0	0	1	0	0.00				

INNING	1	2	3	4	5	6	7	8	9	10	TOAL
CLEVELAND	1	2	0	1	1	1	0	0	1	0	6
MINNESOTA	0	0	0	0	0	0	6	0	0	1	7

GAME 5

By SAM LARDNER
The Cleveland Press

MINNEAPOLIS, April 10 — Even after getting off to an 0–4 start to the season, the Cleveland Indians were an eager bunch in the clubhouse before Saturday evening's game at Target Field against the Minnesota Twins.

They were getting their first regular-season look at pitcher Tak Fujimoto, the Indians' prize free-agent signing out of Japan.

Fujimoto didn't disappoint. The rest of the Tribe? Let's just say it was more of the same but with a different twist in a 1–0 defeat. Fujimoto tossed seven brilliant innings of two-hit shutout baseball, but even that wasn't enough to save the Indians from themselves.

The Twins scored the game's only run without benefit of a hit in the eighth against Mickey Penney, who came on in relief because the rest of the bullpen had been beaten up by short starts by the rotation.

Penney promptly hit Tommy Hopkins with his first pitch of the game. Backup catcher Iceberg Peters, playing in place of Morris Jerome, went out to settle Penney down. It appeared umpire Larry Braverman did Penney no favors as he called a close 3–2 pitch a ball to the dangerous Bruce Conklin.

Infuriated, Indians manager Dave Mills yelled choice words at Braverman, who promptly tossed him from the game. To add to the insult, Indians shortstop Justin Kestino allowed Fabio Pineda's bouncer to play him, and the ball ended up in short left field for a run-scoring error.

Mills was still fuming after the game.

"How the hell does he (Braverman) call that pitch a ball?" he said. "I mean, I know Penney is only in his second year and doesn't have a 'reputation' yet, but look at the replay here."

Mills pointed to the computer screen on his office desk. The replay of the pitch showed it clearly inside the strike-zone box.

"That's the kind of (bleeping) (bleep) that happens when you're 0–4 and not having any luck," Mills said, taking a long swig from his postgame bottle of beer. "You just can't catch a break. I'll probably get fined for saying this, but that's clearly a strike."

Fujimoto met with reporters with his translator in front of his locker. The big talk during spring training was whether Fujimoto's success the last four years in Japan would carry over to Major League Baseball. One start is not enough to judge by, but he did enjoy a strong spring in Arizona.

"Even though it was as cold of a night (45 degrees) as I've pitched in, I felt pretty good," he said through the translator. "The breaking pitches did exactly what I wanted them to do, and the fastball command was right there. I didn't feel nervous or anything like that. I'm used to pitching before some pretty loud crowds in Japan, and these fans were pretty polite."

Indians batters, who had been hitting, suddenly went cold against Twins starter Jake Maddisson and relievers Hyun-Soo Park and closer Roger Sandford, who struck out the side in the ninth.

The Tribe managed just three hits, two by Rikki LaBudda, who stole a base in the fourth and was caught stealing in the sixth. The other hit was a double by Terry Rovetto in the seventh.

When things are going bad, Rovetto is usually there to face the music.

"Tak did a hell of a job out there for us," Rovetto said. "It's a shame we couldn't have gotten him — or us — a win."

Even though Mills is an embattled manager, the players seemed to appreciate him getting tossed from the game fighting for them.

"That's all you can ask of a manager in that situation," Rovetto said. "Penney can't really say anything to the umpire at that point, so Millsie went to bat for him and got thrown out. Sometimes things like that can fire up a team."

At this rate, the Indians are going to need a bonfire.

CLEVELAND INDIANS AT MINNESOTA TWINS · APRIL 10
MINNESOTA 1 / CLEVELAND 0

CLEVELAND INDIANS

BATTING	AB	R	H	RBI	2B	3B	HR	BB	SO	BA
RIKKI LABUDDA CF	4	0	2	0	0	0	0	0	1	.348
WILSON WHITE LF	4	0	0	0	0	0	0	0	0	.273
TERRY ROVETTO 3B	4	0	1	0	0	0	0	0	0	.238
OLIVER REINER 1B	3	0	0	0	0	0	0	0	0	.286
BERNARD HARPER DH	3	0	0	0	0	0	0	0	1	.364
JUSTIN KESTINO SS	3	0	0	0	0	0	0	0	1	.278
ICEBERG PETERS PH	3	0	0	0	0	0	0	0	0	.182
ANGEL RODRIGUEZ	3	0	0	0	0	0	0	0	0	.000
HURON SOUTHWORTH RF	2	0	0	0	0	0	0	1	0	.053

PITCHING	IP	H	R	ER	SO	BB	ERA			
TAK FUJIMOTO	7	2	0	0	8	4	0.00			
MICKEY PENNY (L)	2	0	1	0	2	1	6.00			

MINNESOTA TWINS

BATTING	AB	R	H	RBI	2B	3B	HR	BB	SO	BA
TONY WILDERS 2B	3	0	0	0	0	0	0	0	2	.231
TOMMY HOPKINS 3B	2	1	0	0	0	0	0	1	0	.200
BRUCE CONKLIN 1B	3	0	0	0	0	0	0	1	1	.350
FABIO PINEDA LF	4	0	1	0	0	0	0	0	0	.417
CARL DOREY RF	3	0	0	0	0	0	0	0	1	.385
RALPH TAYLOR CF	3	0	1	0	0	0	0	0	2	.381
AVERY BECKER SS	2	0	0	0	0	0	0	1	0	.300
DONNIE WALLACE DH	2	0	0	0	0	0	0	1	0	.294
FREDERICK SWANSTROM C	2	0	0	0	0	0	0	0	2	.316

PITCHING	IP	H	R	ER	SO	BB	ERA			
JAKE MADDISON	6	2	0	0	4	1	2.65			
HYUN SOO PARK	2	1	0	0	1	0	2.25			
ROGER SANDFORD (W)	1	0	0	0	1	0	9.00			

INNING	1	2	3	4	5	6	7	8	9	TOTAL
CLEVELAND	0	0	0	0	0	0	0	0	0	0
MINNESOTA	0	0	0	0	0	0	0	0	1	1

GAME 6

By SAM LARDNER
The Cleveland Press

MINNEAPOLIS, April 11 — Forget the welcome-home committee. Cancel the rally at Hopkins International. The Cleveland Indians just may want to slink back home under cover of darkness.

The Tribe completed a thoroughly forgettable 0–6 road trip Sunday with a 6–3 loss to the Minnesota Twins at Target Field. Spring finally sprung in the Twin Cities, but the Indians' defense sprung more leaks than a sieve with three errors, leading to five unearned runs charged to starting pitcher Lynn Moda, who went 0–2 on the road trip to Anaheim and Minneapolis.

"Not much to say," Moda said. "I never blame the guys behind me in the field because they make so many good plays over the course of the year to save me from bad pitches. It all evens out. The important thing is we have to regroup and look forward to coming home and playing before our great fans. They won't be happy with us, but no one is more unhappy than we are with ourselves. Nobody has played up to expectations."

Says who? The Indians have played so badly on this disastrous road trip that bad baseball has become totally expected.

To wit:

The Indians showed some spark in the first inning with Rikki LaBudda leading off with a bunt single and stealing second base before trying to get cute and being thrown out easily while trying to steal third. LaBudda

16

might have scored since Huron Southworth and Wilson White followed with singles, but the Tribe came up empty. Spark snuffed out.

Normally sure-handed Terry Rovetto committed a two-out error in the bottom of the inning, setting the stage for Twins DH Donnie Wallace to connect on a home run. Errors by sub Scott Michaels and Justin Kestino on a botched double-play ball in the fourth allowed three more unearned runs to score.

The Indians looked utterly demoralized after that, but they did get a consolation two-run homer from Rovetto and a solo shot by Michaels in the seventh, his first of the year.

Adding it up, the Tribe was outscored 43–18 by the Angels and Twins on the road trip. And we'll leave it to others to research how many teams have started 0–6 and made the postseason. The shame of it all for the Indians is that the American League Central looks wide open, and they let the Twins get well after a slow start of their own.

"Yeah, wasted chances and errors," said embattled manager Dave Mills, who was a lot more subdued Sunday than he was after Saturday night's profanity-laced tirade against the umpires. "You never get on players for physical errors. But the mental mistakes ..."

Mills' voice trailed off at that point, and he was asked if he was talking about LaBudda's overly aggressive base-running mistake in the first inning.

"I'll talk to him about it on the plane ride home," Mills said. "That's between us."

For his part, LaBudda seemed contrite.

"I was just trying to spark the team," he said. "God knows we could use it about now. But I should have left well enough alone after the bunt and the steal of second."

So now what?

"We're going to go home, greet our fans, line up on the baseline for the home opener and play the Royals," Mills said. "The players right now need the support of the fans more than ever. They don't deserve to be booed. Boo me if you want. Our players have been busting their butts."

About that booing, something says Mills is going to get his wish.

CLEVELAND INDIANS AT MINNESOTA TWINS · APRIL 11
MINNESOTA 6 / CLEVELAND 3

CLEVELAND INDIANS										
BATTING	**AB**	**R**	**H**	**RBI**	**2B**	**3B**	**HR**	**BB**	**SO**	**BA**
RIKKI LABUDDA CF	4	0	1	0	0	0	0	0	0	.333
HURON SOUTHWORTH RF	3	0	1	0	0	0	0	1	1	.091
WILSON WHITE LF	4	0	1	0	0	0	0	0	1	.269
OLIVER REINER 1B	4	1	2	0	1	0	0	0	0	.320
TERRY ROVETTO 3B	3	1	1	2	0	0	1	1	1	.240
BERNARD HARPER DH	4	0	1	0	0	0	0	0	1	.357
JUSTIN KESTINO SS	3	0	0	0	0	0	0	0	1	.238
SCOTT MICHAELS 2B	4	1	1	1	0	0	1	0	1	.167
MORRIS JEROME C	3	0	0	0	0	0	0	0	1	.211
PITCHING	**IP**	**H**	**R**	**ER**	**SO**	**BB**	**ERA**			
LYNN MODA (L)	4	5	5	0	2	1	10.47			
BUCK STERLING	3	3	1	1	1	2	4.22			
SOLLY ALVAREZ	1	1	0	0	1	0	0.00			

MINNESOTA TWINS										
BATTING	**AB**	**R**	**H**	**RBI**	**2B**	**3B**	**HR**	**BB**	**SO**	**BA**
TONY WILDERS 2B	4	1	2	1	1	0	0	1	0	.294
TOMMY HOPKINS 3B	4	0	1	1	1	0	0	0	1	.208
BRUCE CONKLIN 1B	4	1	1	0	0	0	0	0	1	.333
DONNIE WALLACE DH	4	1	1	2	0	0	1	0	0	.393
FABIO PINEDA LF	3	0	1	0	0	0	0	1	0	.375
CARL DOREY RF	3	0	0	0	0	0	0	1	1	.375
RALPH TAYLOR CF	4	1	1	0	0	0	0	0	0	.250
AVERY BECKER SS	4	1	0	0	0	0	0	0	0	.238
JOSE CHAVEZ C	4	1	1	2	1	0	0	0	0	.304
PITCHING	**IP**	**H**	**R**	**ER**	**SO**	**BB**	**ERA**			
REINALDO ROJAS (W)	7	7	3	3	6	1	3.00			
JOAQUIN ALMEIDA	1	1	0	0	1	0	1.80			
ROGER SANDFORD (S)	1	1	0	0	0	1	6.75			
INNING	**1**	**2**	**3**	**4**	**5**	**6**	**7**	**8**	**9**	**TOTAL**
CLEVELAND	0	0	0	0	0	3	0	0	0	3
MINNESOTA	2	0	0	3	0	1	0	0	0	6

GAME 7

By SAM LARDNER

The Cleveland Press

CLEVELAND, April 12 — Opening Day went from restive to festive in a hurry Monday on a cool but sun-splashed afternoon at Progressive Field.

An 0–6 record by the hometown Indians on their season-opening road trip had the crowd of 42,798 in a skeptical mood as the player introductions were made and a huge American flag was unfurled in center field.

Most of the players received warm applause, but many in the crowd saved some lusty boos for manager Dave Mills, who gave a polite but half-hearted tip of the cap at home plate as he was introduced.

All seem to be forgiven early, though, as the Tribe hit Royals starting pitcher Taisuke Kaneko for four runs in the bottom of the third inning on the way to an easy 8–2 victory.

The big hit was a three-run homer by Oliver Reiner. The way "The Shark" saw it, the Tribe had one of these coming.

"No doubt about it," he said. "I know the record looked bad on the road trip, but we battled, especially in those games at Minnesota. A break here or there, and we're looking at taking two of three instead of getting swept in three."

An interested observer was Indians general manager J.D. Eisner, who was surrounded by writers, radio reporters and TV cameras in front of the third-base dugout late in the morning. Naturally, Eisner was asked about the status of Mills.

"I'm not getting into that," Eisner said. "Millsie has the backing of the players, certainly, and of the front office and ownership. We don't make any decisions based on a handful of games or public pressure."

If that doesn't sound like the dreaded "vote of confidence," we don't know what does. But Eisner was in Minneapolis for the weekend series, and clearly, he's keeping a close eye on the situation. The last thing the Indians can afford is to get buried in the standings in April.

The offensive explosion was a welcome one for the Tribe, with the beneficiary being starting pitcher Ollie Gonzalez, who rebounded with seven-plus strong innings to even his record at 1–1. Gonzalez worked into the eighth, when he gave up a leadoff single on his 100th pitch of the game. For the afternoon, he allowed six hits and both Royals runs. Derrek Hargrove touched Gonzalez for a two-run homer in the sixth.

"All credit to the offense," said Gonzalez, who walked one and struck out seven. "They scored those runs early and allowed me to go out, relax and just pitch. You don't know how important that is for a starting pitcher, when you don't have to worry about being too fine."

For once, the offense played like Mills drew it up. The Indians had runners aboard in each of the first two innings, but left them stranded. Finally, in the third, Rikki LaBudda led off with an infield single to deep short. After Huron Southworth and Wilson White struck out, Terry Rovetto drew a walk, seeing 10 pitches during the plate appearance. Reiner crushed his homer to deep right-center.

"I battled him (Kaneko) the whole at-bat just like Terry did, and he finally gave in to me with a fastball," Reiner said. "It felt pretty good off the bat and just kept carrying. I'll take it."

Justin Kestino followed immediately with a double and came home on Morris Jerome's single up the middle for the inning's fourth run.

Every member of the Tribe contributed a hit including Angel Rodriguez who was hitless in his previous thirteen at bats.

The Indians touched the Kansas City bullpen for two each in the fifth and sixth, with Rovetto doubling home two in the fifth and Angel Rodriguez hitting a two-run single in the sixth.

As far as Mills goes, he seemed like a guy who had the weight of the world — or at least a six-game losing streak — lifted from his shoulders.

"I told the writers on the road that we'd break out of it one of these days," he said in the postgame interview room.

Asked about the crowd response before the game, Mills just shrugged.

"I can't expect the fans to be happy with an 0–6 start. "If they want to boo me, I'd rather have that than the players getting booed. I just hope they keep supporting us."

CLEVELAND INDIANS VS KANSAS CITY ROYALS · APRIL 12
CLEVELAND 8 / KANSAS CITY 2

CLEVELAND INDIANS

BATTING	AB	R	H	RBI	2B	3B	HR	BB	SO	BA
RIKKI LABUDDA CF	4	1	1	0	0	0	0	0	0	.323
HURON SOUTHWORTH RF	3	1	1	0	0	0	0	1	1	.120
WILSON WHITE LF	4	1	1	0	0	0	0	0	1	.267
TERRY ROVETTO 3B	3	1	2	2	1	0	0	0	0	.276
OLIVER REINER 1B	4	1	1	3	0	0	1	1	1	.310
JUSTIN KESTINO SS	3	1	1	0	1	0	0	0	1	.250
MORRIS JEROME C	4	0	1	1	0	0	0	0	1	.217
BERNARD HARPER DH	3	1	2	0	1	0	0	0	1	.412
ANGEL RODRIGUEZ 2B	4	0	1	2	0	0	0	0	1	.059

PITCHING	IP	H	R	ER	SO	BB	ERA			
OLLIE GONZALEZ (W)	7	6	2	2	7	1	6.00			
GENO MILZE	2	0	0	0	1	0	7.71			

KANSAS CITY ROYALS

BATTING	AB	R	H	RBI	2B	3B	HR	BB	SO	BA
KYLE MONTGOMERY 2B	4	0	0	0	0	0	0	0	1	.238
VERNON COLEMAN CF	4	0	0	0	0	0	0	0	0	.179
OMAR BRACHO 1B	4	0	1	0	0	0	0	0	1	.321
TRUMAN GREYSTONE DH	4	0	1	0	0	0	0	0	0	.375
TODD STEPHANS LF	4	0	1	0	0	0	0	1	0	.350
ARCENIO INCIARTE C	3	1	1	0	0	0	0	1	2	.370
DEREK HARGROVE 3B	4	1	1	2	0	0	1	0	2	.250
RUGLAS SUBERO SS	3	0	1	0	1	0	0	0	1	.250
ALCIDES CASTILLO RF	3	0	0	0	0	0	0	0	1	.269

PITCHING	IP	H	R	ER	SO	BB	ERA			
TAISUKE KANEKO (L)	3	7	4	4	6	1	4.00			
AARON WESTFALL	2	5	2	2	3	1	3.86			
GLENN MARCHAND	2	3	2	2	0	0	7.50			
BRUNO LACHNER	1	0	0	0	1	1	2.70			

INNING	1	2	3	4	5	6	7	8	9	TOTAL
KANSAS CITY	0	0	0	0	0	2	0	0	0	2
CLEVELAND	0	0	4	0	2	2	0	0		8

GAME 8

By SAM LARDNER
The Cleveland Press

CLEVELAND, April 14 — Lo and behold, a winning streak!

Now, we'll not get into the semantics of whether two wins in a row constitute a "streak." Certainly, the Indians aren't splitting hairs, certainly not after a crisply played 3–1 victory over the Kansas City Royals on a chilly night at Progressive Field. The realities of the weather and the Tribe's slow start set in, as only 17,383 fans showed up, one game after Opening Day's sellout gathering.

Those who did show up — and shivered in the 38-degree cold — saw the Indians play errorless ball and starting pitcher Brian Howard work eight innings in a game that took only two hours and 22 minutes to play.

Howard gave up just three hits and the one run while walking nary a soul and striking out six, a pretty good total for a finesse pitcher.

"On a night like tonight, you want to get it and throw it," said Howard, who improved to 1–1. "I don't need all the velocity in the world if I'm moving the ball around and putting it on the hitters' hands. They can get themselves out that way. And the fielders like it when you're working fast. Keeps them on their toes."

The Tribe is now 2–6, getting a sweep of the short two-game set against the Royals. Howard got nice fielding plays behind him from Rikki LaBudda in center and from Angel Rodriguez at second. LaBudda ran to the right-center field gap in the second to snag a drive off the bat of Omar Bracho.

In the fifth, Rodriguez ranged behind the second-base bag to grab a grounder from Jared Buckner and throw him out at first. Rodriguez looked like he might have shaken himself up on the play, and he was replaced an inning later by Scott Michaels.

"Great defense," said manager Dave Mills, who seemed uncharacteristically relaxed. Amazing what two wins will do for a guy. "Those are the kinds of plays our guys are capable of. We just didn't see them in the first few games, and it hurt us. But I'm really confident you'll see more of that going forward."

The Indians got a run in the first against Ender Ramos. LaBudda walked and stole second base. He came home on a single by Wilson White. DH J.J. Kulakofski had a two-run double in the fifth after Oliver Reiner walked and Justin Kestino singled, putting runners on first and third.

"It feels good to contribute to a win," said Kulakofski, who is waiting in the wings to play first base behind Reiner but who has to settle for most of his at-bats as the designated hitter. "I know my role here. I'm not selfish. On a cold night like this, you have to take some extra swings in the batting cage in the tunnel to stay warm. No problem."

The Royals got a homer from Vernon Coleman in the eighth off a tiring Howard. Ivan Zyzna came on to nail down the save with a 1-2-3 ninth.

"Just how you draw it up," Mills said. "Get a good start, play good defense and hand the ball to your closer. It doesn't always work out that way, but when it does, you feel pretty good about it. And we're feeling pretty good about ourselves right now after that rough start. We've dug ourselves a hole, but this is the only way to dig out of it."

CLEVELAND INDIANS VS KANSAS CITY ROYALS · APRIL 14
CLEVELAND 3 / KANSAS CITY 1

CLEVELAND INDIANS

BATTING	AB	R	H	RBI	2B	3B	HR	BB	SO	BA
RIKKI LABUDDA CF	3	1	0	0	0	0	0	1	0	.294
HURON SOUTHWORTH RF	4	0	1	0	0	0	0	0	1	.103
WILSON WHITE LF	4	0	2	1	1	0	0	0	1	.235
TERRY ROVETTO 3B	3	0	0	0	0	0	0	0	0	.250
OLIVER REINER 1B	2	1	0	0	0	0	0	1	1	.290
JUSTIN KESTINO SS	3	1	1	0	0	0	0	0	0	.222
MORRIS JEROME C	3	0	1	0	0	0	0	0	0	.192
JJ KULAKOFSKI DH	3	0	1	2	1	0	0	0	1	.333
ANGEL RODRIGUEZ 2B	2	0	1	0	0	0	0	0	0	.105
SCOTT MICHAELS 2B	1	0	1	0	0	0	0	0	0	.286

PITCHING	IP	H	R	ER	SO	BB	ERA			
BRIAN HOWARD (W)	8	3	1	1	6	0	5.73			
IVAN ZYZNA (S)	1	0	0	0	0	0	9.00			

KANSAS CITY ROYALS

BATTING	AB	R	H	RBI	2B	3B	HR	BB	SO	BA
KYLE MONTGOMERY 2B	4	0	0	0	0	0	0	0	0	.200
TODD STEPHANS LF	4	0	0	0	0	0	0	0	0	.156
OMAR BRACHO 1B	3	0	0	0	0	0	0	0	1	.290
TRUMAN GREYSTONE DH	3	0	0	0	0	0	0	0	2	.343
VERNON COLEMAN CF	3	0	1	1	0	0	1	0	0	.348
ARCENIO INCIARTE C	3	0	1	0	0	0	0	0	1	.367
DEREK HARGROVE 3B	3	0	1	0	1	0	0	0	1	.258
JARED BUCKNER SS	3	0	0	0	0	0	0	0	0	.222
ALCIDES CASTILLO RF	3	0	0	0	0	0	0	0	1	.241

PITCHING	IP	H	R	ER	SO	BB	ERA			
ENDER RAMOS (L)	5	5	3	4	3	1	4.50			
JAIR MOSQUERO	2	2	0	0	1	0	3.00			
GLENN MARCHAND	1	1	0	0	0	0	6.43			

INNING	1	2	3	4	5	6	7	8	9	TOTAL
KANSAS CITY	0	0	0	0	0	0	0	1	0	1
CLEVELAND	1	0	0	0	2	0	0	0		3

GAME 9

By SAM LARDNER
The Cleveland Press

CLEVELAND, April 15 — So much for the "winning streak."

The Indians reverted to their dreary early season form Friday night with an utterly lackluster 4–0 loss to the Minnesota Twins at Progressive Field.

It was these same Twins who put a hurtin' on the Tribe last weekend in Minneapolis, sweeping a three-game set. Falling four straight times to a division rival could be damaging to a team's health, not to mention to the job health of Indians manager Dave Mills, who looked to have gotten a reprieve following a pair of wins against the Royals in the first series of the home season.

"Hey, listen, I'm not worried about any of that, like I've told you guys," said Mills, whose team fell to 2–7. "My job is to get these guys prepared to play every night."

If that's the case, Mills might as well begin drafting the press release to announce his own firing. The Tribe managed just four hits against Twins pitching, three against starter Jay Rutherford, who looked brilliant against the sleepy Indians offense.

Maybe it was the two-run top of the first by the Twins that set the Indians back on their heels. Leadoff hitter Tony Wilders, not known for his power, hit the first pitch of the game over the wall in left field against Kenny Camden. Later in the inning, Bruce "Bruiser" Conklin, made like a leadoff hitter as he beat out an infield single to score Tito Almeida, who walked, stole second base and went to third on a groundout.

"No doubt I set the bad tone," said Camden. "I tried to sneak a first-pitch fastball past Wilders, and he was waiting for it. That (ticked) me off, which led to the walk. No disrespect to those guys, but those two guys shouldn't be beating me."

Camden worked six innings. The other two runs came against reliever Buck Sterling in the eighth, when the game was still conceivably a contest. But Sterling, pitching in front of the home folks, may have been trying to overthrow the ball, as he walked Conklin and Tommy Hopkins before Jose Chavez doubled them home with a gapper to right-center."

"No excuses for the walks," Sterling said. "I've pitched in this ballpark a lot. Instead of overthrowing it, I actually might have been trying to be too fine."

Three of the Tribe's base hits were singles, two by Rikki LaBudda, but he was caught stealing in the fourth and didn't make it past first base in the seventh.

"Sometimes you've got to give the other guy credit," Mills said. "It's so easy to place blame, but Rutherford pitched well. He kept us off-balance all night. We've got Tak (Fujimoto) out there tomorrow, and he pitched well his first time out (a 1–0 loss at Minnesota). I'm not concerned about the offense at all."

GAME 9

CLEVELAND INDIANS VS MINNESOTA TWINS · APRIL 15
MINNESOTA 4 / CLEVELAND 0

CLEVELAND INDIANS

BATTING	AB	R	H	RBI	2B	3B	HR	BB	SO	BA
RIKKI LABUDDA CF	4	0	2	0	0	0	0	0	0	.316
KIERAN CATSEF RF	3	0	0	0	0	0	0	0	0	.000
WILSON WHITE LF	3	0	0	0	0	0	0	0	0	.216
TERRY ROVETTO 3B	3	0	0	0	0	0	0	0	0	.229
OLIVER REINER 1B	3	0	1	0	0	0	0	0	1	.294
JUSTIN KESTINO SS	3	0	1	0	1	0	0	0	0	.233
MORRIS JEROME C	2	0	0	0	0	0	0	0	1	.179
JJ KULAKOFSKI DH	3	0	0	0	0	0	0	0	1	.267
LEO TAYLOR 2B	1	0	0	0	0	0	0	0	1	.000

PITCHING	IP	H	R	ER	SO	BB	ERA			
KENNY CAMDEN (L)	6	5	2	2	3	2	4.76			
BUCK STERLING	2	1	2	2	0	3	4.97			
GENO MILZE	1	0	0	0	0	0	6.75			

MINNESOTA TWINS

BATTING	AB	R	H	RBI	2B	3B	HR	BB	SO	BA
TONY WILDERS 2B	5	1	1	1	0	0	1	0	0	.200
TITO ALMEIDA CF	4	1	1	0	0	0	0	1	0	.167
FABIO PINEDA LF	4	0	1	0	1	0	0	0	1	.286
BRUCE CONKLIN 1B	3	0	1	1	0	0	0	1	2	.342
TOMMY HOPKINS 3B	3	1	0	0	0	0	0	1	0	.308
JOSE CHAVEZ C	4	0	2	2	1	0	0	0	1	.382
CARL DOREY RF	2	0	0	0	0	0	0	1	0	.242
DAVE WALLACE DH	4	0	0	0	0	0	0	0	1	.194
AVERY BECKER SS	3	0	0	0	0	0	0	1	1	.219

PITCHING	IP	H	R	ER	SO	BB	ERA			
JAY RUTHERFORD (W)	8	4	0	0	5	1	3.60			
ROGER SANDFORD	2	2	0	0	1	0	2.70			

INNING	1	2	3	4	5	6	7	8	9	TOTAL
MINNESOTA	2	0	0	0	0	0	0	2	0	4
CLEVELAND	0	0	0	0	0	0	0	0	0	0

GAME 10

By SAM LARDNER

The Cleveland Press

CLEVELAND, April 16 — Reporters had an inkling something was up after 20 minutes passed and Indians manager Dave Mills did not show up in the interview room for his postgame news conference.

The scuttlebutt was that Mills and first baseman Oliver Reiner were trying to get their stories straight after a disastrous eighth inning, when it looked like Mills had lost track of the outs and failed to play his infield in with one out and the Minnesota Twins having runners on second and third in a 1–1 game.

Sure enough, a weak grounder off the bat of Avery Becker scored a run on a ball that very well could have gone for an out at the plate had the infield been in. Mills finally did bring his infield in for the next batter, Jose Chavez, but as the Indians' luck would have it, Chavez chopped the ball over Reiner's head, allowing the third run to score.

After the game, media members were prepared to pounce on those plays. But when Indians general manager J.D. Eisner entered the room and media relations chief Glenn Liss had a fistful of news releases, you could hear the collective gasp and the air go out of the room.

Eisner took to the podium and announced that Mills had been dismissed after three-plus seasons and that third-base coach Todd Stein would replace him on an interim basis. Holding up his hand as if to head off the obvious question, Eisner launch into a preamble.

"This is not about one game, today's game," he said. "As bad as it looked today, this is something that has been building and something to which we've given a lot of thought. We thank Dave Mills for his time with the Indians and wish him well. Todd Stein provides us with continuity, especially early in the season, and he will be a candidate for the permanent job."

Mills did not attend the news conference. He dressed and left Progressive Field quickly. Stein came into the interview room after Eisner took questions for 20 minutes.

"I'm honored even to have been considered to manage the club," Stein said. "First, I want to thank Dave Mills for bringing me on to the staff two years ago. It's also a special feeling to be manager of the Cleveland Indians, who made Frank Robinson the first African-American manager all those years ago. That's not lost on me. All I can tell you is that we'll play hard every night, and there will be attention to detail here."

Stein, who is black, interviewed for managerial jobs in the past with the Orioles and Padres, but those teams were in rebuilding modes, and he said he felt he wouldn't be around when those teams enjoyed success. He is known for using very unconventional lineups in his minor league stints.

The way things are going with the Indians, there are no guarantees here, either. Eisner joined the Indians on the recent road trip in Minnesota, and that set tongues to wagging. He also addressed Mills' situation before the home opener.

"I thought we should have gotten out of the gate better, especially after what we all thought was a good spring training," Eisner said. "But for whatever reason, we looked flat from the get-go, and then the team starting playing tight. I talked to ownership, and we just did not want this to spiral out of control so early in the season and with the division looking like it would be wide open. So, this felt like the right time to make a change."

Reiner, who was at the center of Saturday's confusion on the field, felt bad for Mills. "Listen, what happened out there today was my fault," he said. "I was looking across to the dugout from first base and thought I saw Millsie signal one thing. This (the firing) is on all of us as players. We didn't get the job done, and a good man is going home because of it. We're all going to give Steinie our best. He's an enthusiastic guy, and you can't help but want to play hard for him."

Saturday's game was another wasted start for Indians pitcher Tak Fujimoto, who also got no run support last weekend in a 1–0 loss at Minnesota. The Indians fell behind 1–0 in the second on DH Tucker Harris' homer. Terry Rovetto got the run back in the fourth with a homer of his own, a drive just inside the foul pole in left field.

That was it until the fateful eighth, when Geno Milzie came on in relief of Fujimoto, who gave up just four hits and the one run while walking two, one intentionally, and striking out six, while getting out of a big jam in the seventh leaving the bases loaded. Milzie's knuckleball knuckled a little too much as he walked Tommy Hopkins leading off the inning. Bruce Conklin popped out, but Harris doubled Hopkins to third setting up the bizarre sequence of events that followed.

"Tak sure deserved better than what we did to him in that inning," Milzie said. "It was all set up by the walk. You walk the leadoff batter you're just asking for trouble and we got it — big time."

No more so than did Mills, who paid for it "big time" with his job.

CLEVELAND INDIANS VS MINNESOTA TWINS · APRIL 16
MINNESOTA 3 / CLEVELAND 1

CLEVELAND INDIANS										
BATTING	AB	R	H	RBI	2B	3B	HR	BB	SO	BA
RIKKI LABUDDA CF	4	0	1	0	1	0	0	0	0	.310
KIERAN CATSEF RF	4	0	1	0	0	0	0	0	1	.143
WILSON WHITE LF	4	0	2	0	0	0	0	0	1	.244
TERRY ROVETTO 3B	4	1	1	1	0	0	1	0	1	.231
OLIVER REINER 1B	4	0	2	0	0	0	0	0	1	.316
JUSTIN KESTINO SS	4	0	1	0	0	0	0	0	0	.235
MORRIS JEROME C	4	0	0	0	0	0	0	0	1	.156
JJ KULAKOFSKI DH	3	0	0	0	0	0	0	0	2	.222
ANGEL RODRIGUEZ 2B	3	0	1	0	0	0	0	0	0	.136
PITCHING	IP	H	R	ER	SO	BB	ERA			
TAK FUJIMOTO	7	4	1	1	6	2	5.79			
GENO MILZE (L)	1	2	2	2	0	1	8.00			
IVAN ZYZNA	1	1	0	0	0	0	4.50			

MINNESOTA TWINS										
BATTING	AB	R	H	RBI	2B	3B	HR	BB	SO	BA
TONY WILDERS 2B	5	0	1	0	0	0	0	0	2	.200
TOMMIE HOPKINS	3	1	1	0	0	0	0	0	0	.241
BRUCE CONKLIN 1B	3	0	0	0	0	0	0	1	0	.317
TUCKER HARRIS DH	3	2	2	1	1	0	1	0	2	.257
AVERY BECKER SS	2	0	0	1	0	0	0	1	0	.206
JOSE CHAVEZ C	4	0	1	1	1	0	0	0	1	.368
CARL DOREY RF	4	0	1	0	0	0	0	0	1	.243
FABIO PINEDA LF	4	0	1	0	0	0	0	0	0	.179
TITO ALMEIDA CF	4	0	0	0	0	0	0	0	1	.150
PITCHING	IP	H	R	ER	SO	BB	ERA			
JAKE MADDISON	6	7	1	1	4	0	3.33			
SANDY GREEN	1	0	0	0	0	0	1.66			
OSVALDO BORGES (W)	1	1	0	0	1	0	2.87			
ROGER SANDFORD (S)	1	1	0	0	1	0	2.45			

INNING	1	2	3	4	5	6	7	8	9	TOTAL
MINNESOTA	0	1	0	0	0	0	0	2	0	3
CLEVELAND	0	0	0	1	0	0	0	0	0	1

GAME 11

By SAM LARDNER
The Cleveland Press

CLEVELAND, April 17 — The Todd Stein Era in Cleveland Indians baseball began with a bang Sunday, and forgive the fans and the most cynical members of the media if they ask: "What took you so long?"

Looking refreshed and revitalized one day after Dave Mills was fired as manager and replaced by Stein, the Indians went out and cruised past the Minnesota Twins 5–0 before 30,987 fans at Progressive Field, no doubt many of whom wanted to see the new guy operate.

As for the old guy, Mills, he has made himself scarce, but he did issue a statement through his agent thanking the Indians and their fans.

"I leave with my head held high," the statement read. "We did our best to bring a winner to Cleveland but fell short. Please join me in wishing Todd Stein and the players all the best for the rest of the season and beyond."

As for the new guy, he couldn't have scripted Sunday's game any better.

Starting pitcher Lynn Moda got off the schneid and won his first decision against two losses as he worked seven shutout innings, giving up six hits while walking one and striking out five. He might have gone another inning, but his pitch count reached 111, and Stein decided that was it. Mickey Penney came on for the final two innings and worked them without incident.

After the game, first baseman Oliver Reiner presented Stein with the lineup card, signed by all the players.

"Nice gesture," said Stein, the third-base coach under Mills. "But it's really not about me. It's about the players. They went out today and played a relaxed game, and you saw what happened."

We'll be watching for the "new-manager bump," which often occurs when a team fires one guy and brings in a fresh voice.

"It's nothing against Millsie," Reiner said. "We enjoyed playing for him. But we really wanted to go out and give a good effort and get Steinie his first win as a manager. I guess when you get good starting pitching, like Modes gave us, it's pretty easy."

Nothing has been easy for the Tribe, who have a long way to go with their 3–8 record. But this was the most complete game they played all year, and one has to wonder if the distraction of Mills' situation wasn't affecting them before Sunday.

Moda retired the first three batters of the game on eight pitches, getting a groundout and two popouts. Then, as if the hand-break had been released, Indians leadoff man Rikki LaBudda bunted to lead off the bottom of the first against Reinaldo Rojas and advanced on catcher Jose Chavez's throwing error, as it looked like Chavez rushed his throw in an effort to get the speedy LaBudda.

A new manager always wants to put his stamp on things, and it was a slight lineup change that produced the game's first run. Micah Millison replaced — at least for Sunday — the slumping Huron Southworth in the lineup, and he immediately tripled to the right-field corner to bring LaBudda home. Wilson White's sacrifice fly scored Millison.

"Don't read too much into that," Stein said. "Southworth had been pressing a little bit, so I thought that giving him a Sunday afternoon off might do him some good. You'll see plenty of him. But it was nice that Millison provided us with a little spark."

Millison singled in the fourth and stole second base. After White struck out, Terry Rovetto singled up the middle to score Millison. Iceberg Peters, getting a start behind the plate, doubled home a pair of runs in the sixth. That was all the support Moda needed.

"It was great working with Ice today, and I also enjoy pitching when Mo (Morris Jerome) is behind the plate, too," Moda said. "We've got two great catchers, but Ice put down all the right fingers today, and I let the guys behind me make the plays."

So what to make of this bunch? It's too early to tell — too small a sample size as the stat geeks like to say — but the mood in the clubhouse was decidedly different both before and after this game. And the crowd seemed a lot more energized, as if all was forgiven.

"Oh, I don't know," Stein said. "I mean, the crowd was great, don't get me wrong. But it's just one game, and we've got a tough Oakland club coming in here. But I will say this, dinner is going to taste pretty good tonight."

GAME 11

CLEVELAND INDIANS VS MINNESOTA TWINS • APRIL 17
CLEVELAND 5 / MINNESOTA 0

CLEVELAND INDIANS

BATTING	AB	R	H	RBI	2B	3B	HR	BB	SO	BA
RIKKI LABUDDA CF	5	1	2	0	0	0	0	0	0	.319
MICAH MILLISON RF	5	2	2	1	0	1	0	0	0	.400
WILSON WHITE LF	5	1	1	1	0	0	0	0	1	.239
TERRY ROVETTO 3B	5	0	2	1	0	0	0	0	1	.250
OLIVER REINER 1B	5	1	3	0	0	0	0	0	0	.349
JUSTIN KESTINO SS	3	0	1	0	0	0	0	1	1	.243
ICEBERG PETERS C	3	0	1	2	1	0	0	1	1	.214
JJ KULAKOFSKI DH	4	0	1	0	0	0	0	1	0	.227
SCOTT MICHAELS 2B	4	0	0	0	0	0	0	0	2	.182

PITCHING	IP	H	R	ER	SO	BB	ERA			
LYNN MODA (W)	7	4	0	0	6	2	5.79			
MICKEY PENNY	1	2	2	2	0	1	8.00			

MINNESOTA TWINS

BATTING	AB	R	H	RBI	2B	3B	HR	BB	SO	BA
TONY WILDERS 2B	4	0	1	0	0	0	0	0	0	.205
TOMMIE HOPKINS 3B	4	0	1	0	0	0	0	0	0	.242
BRUCE CONKLIN 1B	4	0	0	0	0	0	0	0	2	.289
TUCKER HARRIS DH	4	0	1	0	1	0	0	0	2	.256
AVERY BECKER SS	3	0	2	0	1	0	0	1	0	.243
JOSE CHAVEZ C	4	0	1	0	0	0	0	0	1	.357
CARL DOREY RF	4	0	1	0	0	0	0	0	0	.244
FABIO PINEDA LF	3	0	1	0	0	0	0	0	0	.190
TITO ALMEIDA CF	3	0	0	0	0	0	0	0	0	.140

PITCHING	IP	H	R	ER	SO	BB	ERA			
REINALDO ROJAS (L)	4.67	10	3	3	4	2	3.02			
JOAQUIN ALMEIDA	1	5	2	2	1	1	2.60			
SANDY GREEN	2.33	1	0	0	0	0	1.45			

INNING	1	2	3	4	5	6	7	8	9	TOTAL
MINNESOTA	0	0	0	0	0	0	0	0	0	0
CLEVELAND	2	0	0	1	0	2	0	0	0	5

GAME 12

By SAM LARDNER
The Cleveland Press

CLEVELAND, April 18 — During his pregame session with the media in the dugout Tuesday, new Indians manager Todd Stein was asked if he is a "players' manager." Stein tilted his head back and laughed.

"You guys," he said. "Everybody wants to label somebody as something. Yes, I'm a players' manager. But I'm really the Indians' manager and the GM's manager and the owners' manager. I'm just myself."

Stein's looser style is in stark contrast to that of recently fired manager Dave Mills, who put the "tight" into "uptight." Stein did have to put his considerable people skills to work before the game against the Oakland Athletics at Progressive Field, explaining to Huron Southworth why he was out of the lineup for a second straight game as Stein went with Micah Millison.

But there's nothing quite like a walk-off victory to salve all wounds. It was Southworth, inserted into the game as a pinch runner, who scored ahead of Wilson White as White cracked a two-run homer off A's closer Mitch Sutherland on a 3–2 pitch in the bottom of the ninth to give the Tribe a dramatic 4–2 victory, making Stein 2–0 as interim manager.

"Wow," said White, the Indians' big free-agent pickup this past winter. "They told me the crowd could get behind you here, and I sure felt that as I was rounding the bases. Even though it was cold out there, the Gatorade bath felt pretty good."

Manning the bucket was Southworth, who wore a frown early in the day after not seeing his name on the lineup card. That prompted a little talk with the manager.

"It's OK," Southworth said. "I just wanted to see where I stood, and the skipper let me know. He's great about communicating. He told me he wanted to see what Micah could do and that we could both see a lot of time, with the DH."

Stein tried his best to defuse any controversy. "I told you guys Sunday not to read too much into this," he said. "But I guess it's your job to do just that. Southy is fine. He gets it. It's all about the team here."

Southworth came on as a pinch runner for catcher Morris Jerome, who led off the bottom of the ninth with a walk. Rikki LaBudda bunted Southworth to second, but Millison struck out for the second out. No matter. White turned on a 97-mph heater from Sutherland and launched it over the high wall in left and into the bleachers.

"People always ask if you're trying to live up to the contract," White said. "I think you can press a little bit, trying to please everybody. But when Steinie met with us after he took over, he told us all to relax. That really helped a lot."

Indians starting pitcher Ollie Gonzalez came away with a no-decision, but he pitched six creditable innings, giving up both Oakland runs on seven hits. The A's big bopper, Graeme Nilson, crushed a 3–0 pitch for a two-run homer in the third to give Oakland the lead. Angel Rodriguez doubled and came home on Rikki LaBudda's single in the fourth. Justin Kestino tied the game in the fifth on a sac fly after Terry Rovetto doubled and went to third on Oliver Reiner's groundout.

The A's mounted a threat in the ninth against Ivan Zyzna, who was in the game in a non-save situation. But he reared back and struck out two batters after putting two on with one out.

The Indians are now 4–8 with two more games to go on the homestand. With the Cavs out of the NBA playoff picture, the Tribe has a chance to win back some fans if this nice little run continues.

"We've got great fans here," Stein said. "Everybody remembers when they opened this place and they had all those consecutive sellouts. Just give an effort out there, and the fans will appreciate it. That's all we're trying to give them."

And a few wins to go with it won't hurt, either.

GAME 12

CLEVELAND INDIANS VS OAKLAND ATHLETICS · APRIL 19
CLEVELAND 4 / OAKLAND 2

CLEVELAND INDIANS										
BATTING	**AB**	**R**	**H**	**RBI**	**2B**	**3B**	**HR**	**BB**	**SO**	**BA**
RIKKI LABUDDA CF	3	0	1	1	0	0	0	1	0	.320
MICAH MILLISON RF	5	0	2	0	0	0	0	0	1	.400
WILSON WHITE LF	5	1	1	2	0	0	1	0	1	.235
TERRY ROVETTO 3B	4	1	3	0	1	0	0	0	0	.292
OLIVER REINER 1B	4	0	1	0	0	0	0	0	0	.340
JUSTIN KESTINO SS	3	0	1	1	1	0	0	0	1	.250
JJ KULAKOFSKI DH	3	0	0	0	0	0	0	0	1	.200
MORRIS JEROME C	3	0	0	0	0	0	0	1	0	.143
HURON SOUTHWORTH PR	0	1	0	0	0	0	0	0	0	.103
ANGEL RODRIGUEZ 2B	4	1	1	0	1	0	0	0	0	.154
SCOTT MICHAELS 2B	1	0	0	0	0	0	0	0	0	.167
PITCHING	**IP**	**H**	**R**	**ER**	**SO**	**BB**	**ERA**			
OLLIE GONZALEZ	6	7	2	2	5	2	5.00			
SOLLY ALVAREZ	1	1	0	0	0	0	0.00			
IVAN ZYZNA (W)	1	2	0	0	2	0	3.00			

OAKLAND A'S										
BATTING	**AB**	**R**	**H**	**RBI**	**2B**	**3B**	**HR**	**BB**	**SO**	**BA**
ISIAH HUERTAS LF	5	1	1	0	0	0	0	0	1	.205
IAN BRUDERSON SS	4	0	2	0	0	0	0	0	0	.270
GRAEME NILSON 1B	4	1	1	2	0	0	1	0	1	.286
ERNESTO MENDESOTO 3B	2	0	0	0	0	0	0	2	1	.244
TRENT ATHERTON C	4	0	2	0	0	0	0	0	0	.268
ALBERT REYES RF	4	0	1	1	0	0	0	0	0	.348
MATTHEW VAN STENCEL CF	4	0	1	0	0	0	0	0	2	.244
TREMONT HARKNESS DH	4	0	1	0	0	0	0	0	1	.214
JAYSON GIVINS 2B	4	0	1	0	0	0	0	0	1	.182
PITCHING	**IP**	**H**	**R**	**ER**	**SO**	**BB**	**ERA**			
JOSH KENNELLY	5	7	2	2	2	2	3.07			
CRAIG QUINN	2	1	0	0	1	0	2.70			
JAKE RICHARDS	1	0	0	0	1	0	2.29			
MITCH SUTHERLAND (L)	0.67	1	2	2	2	1	2.94			

INNING	1	2	3	4	5	6	7	8	9	TOTAL
OAKLAND	0	0	2	0	0	0	0	0	0	2
CLEVELAND	0	0	0	1	1	0	0	0	2	4

GAME 13

By SAM LARDNER
The Cleveland Press

CLEVELAND, April 20 — Old habits are hard to break, as new Indians manager Todd Stein found out Wednesday night at Progressive Field.

The new boss witnessed some of the bad old ways that had been all too commonplace in the first week of the season as the Indians fell 6–1 to the Oakland Athletics. Tribe batters failed in the clutch, going 1-for-9 with runners in scoring position. Fielders committed two errors, and starting pitcher Brian "The Doctor" Howard might have been sued for malpractice, as he lasted just four innings, giving five runs, three of them earned.

"They aren't all going to be oil paintings," Stein said. "As we move along, we'll clean up some of these things. I just want greater awareness of situations on the field. As far as the hitting goes, I'm not worried about it. These guys have proven track records, and they've all hit in the past. And the Doc didn't have his best stuff, but the errors didn't help. Just forget this one and move on."

Howard worked out of trouble in each of the first two innings, stranding a pair each time. In the third, an error by normally sure-handed second baseman Angel Rodriguez led to two runs. Rodriguez booted an easy grounder off the bat of Renaldo Casiano with two outs. Ernesto Mendesoto made the Tribe pay with a home run on an 0–2 pitch.

"You can blame me for that, not Angel," Howard said. "He makes that play 99 times out of 100. The 0–2 pitch to Mendesoto just caught too

40

much of the plate. It was a cutter that backed up, and he did what good hitters are supposed to do with mistakes. He hit it far."

The Indians got the run right back in the bottom half of the inning on a homer by Oliver Reiner, his third, but that was it for the offense.

In the fourth, the Athletics got two more, with a throwing error by Justin Kestino proving costly. He rushed a throw trying to get Ramon Torres, and the ball ended up in the stands. Doubles by Jason Givins and Graeme Nilson brought two more in.

"Yeah, just sloppy," Stein said. "We were our own worst enemy out there tonight. That's what I meant about awareness. Justin didn't need to hurry that throw, and he knows it. No reason to say anything to him."

The short outing by Howard allowed Stein to get some long-relief work in for Solly Alvarez, who worked the next four innings before Mickey Penney mopped up in the ninth.

"Solly really saved the bullpen for tomorrow by eating up those innings," Stein said. "It may not look like much, but those kinds of outings mean a lot in the long run. It's thankless work sometimes, but I appreciate and the rest of the pitching staff appreciates it."

GAME 13

CLEVELAND INDIANS VS OAKLAND ATHLETICS · APRIL 21
OAKLAND 6 CLEVELAND 1

CLEVELAND INDIANS										
BATTING	AB	R	H	RBI	2B	3B	HR	BB	SO	BA
RIKKI LABUDDA CF	3	0	1	0	0	0	0	1	0	.321
MICAH MILLISON RF	5	0	2	0	0	0	0	0	1	.400
WILSON WHITE LF	5	1	1	0	0	0	0	0	1	.232
TERRY ROVETTO 3B	4	1	3	0	1	0	0	0	0	.327
OLIVER REINER 1B	4	0	1	1	0	0	1	0	0	.333
JUSTIN KESTINO SS	3	0	1	0	1	0	0	0	1	.256
JJ KULAKOFSKI DH	3	0	0	0	0	0	0	0	1	.179
MORRIS JEROME C	3	0	0	0	0	0	0	1	0	.132
ANGEL RODRIGUEZ 2B	4	1	1	0	1	0	0	0	0	.167
PITCHING	IP	H	R	ER	SO	BB	ERA			
BRIAN HOWARD (L)	6	7	5	3	5	2	5.00			
SOLLY ALVAREZ	4	1	0	0	0	0	0.00			
MICKEY PENNY	1	2	0	0	2	0	3.00			
OAKLAND A'S										
BATTING	AB	R	H	RBI	2B	3B	HR	BB	SO	BA
ISIAH HUERTAS LF	4	0	1	0	0	0	0	1	1	.208
ALBERT REYES RF	5	1	2	1	1	0	0	0	0	.216
RENALDO CASIANO 2B	5	1	2	1	0	0	0	0	0	.244
ERNESTO MENDESOTO 3B	5	1	2	2	0	0	1	0	1	.261
TRENT ATHERTON C	4	0	1	0	0	0	0	0	0	.267
RAMON TORRES SS	3	1	0	0	0	0	0	1	0	.271
JAYSON GIVINS DH	4	1	2	1	1	0	0	0	0	.231
GRAEME NILSON 1B	4	1	1	1	1	0	0	0	1	.283
MATTHEW VAN STENCEL CF	4	0	1	0	0	0	0	0	1	.245
PITCHING	IP	H	R	ER	SO	BB	ERA			
JERMAINE SANTOS (W)	7	6	1	1	4	1	2.87			
CRAIG QUINN	2	2	0	0	1	0	2.45			
INNING	1	2	3	4	5	6	7	8	9	TOTAL
OAKLAND	0	0	2	2	0	1	0	0	1	6
CLEVELAND	0	0	0	1	0	0	0	0	0	1

GAME 14

By SAM LARDNER

The Cleveland Press

CLEVELAND, April 21 — Maybe all it took was some bright sunshine and a cool breeze to air out the stink from the previous night. Whatever, the Indians made the quick turnaround from Wednesday night into Thursday afternoon a productive one with a 7–4 victory over the Oakland Athletics to finish the homestand with a series win, taking two of three.

This one wasn't as close as the score indicates. The Tribe had built a 7–0 lead by the fifth, with the A's scoring twice in both the eighth and ninth innings.

"Much better," said interim manager Todd Stein, who is 3–1 on the job with the team being 5–9 overall. "I thought it was important that we regroup quickly after last night. The guys did just that."

With the day game after a night game, Stein rested a few players, including second baseman Rikki LaBudda and Angel Rodriguez, who made a key throwing error the night before. That enabled Scott Michaels to get a start, and the former phenom went 1-for-2 with a homer and a pair of walks. Batting fifth in the lineup, Michaels cracked a three-run homer in the first off Kris Perkins after Micah Millison and Wilson White had singled.

"I know I'm not going to play every day, but Skip has been good on his word that everybody is going to get a shot," Michaels said, referring to Stein. "I'm doing my best to stay sharp, getting my work in the batting cage."

Michaels' career has been derailed to this point by shoulder woes, but he said he feels fine now. "Oh, yeah," he said. "There are no health issues. It's just a matter of fighting for — and earning — playing time. All I can do is perform when the manager calls on me."

With runs to work with, Indians pitcher Kenny Camden retired the first 10 batters he faced before giving up a single to Matthew Van Stencel in the fourth.

"When the guys put three on the board for you, it makes it that much easier to go out there, relax and pitch," said Camden, who notched his first victory of the season by walking two and striking out eight in seven innings. "Their hitters are aggressive, so we just tried to make them swing early, put the ball on the ground and get quick outs."

The Indians sent nine men to the plate in the fifth, scoring four runs to break it open. The big hit was a bases-loaded three-run double by Huron Southworth, who got back into the starting lineup after being benched for two games by Stein after he took over.

"I probably deserved to sit, even though I didn't see it that way," Southworth said. "I know I have to earn my way back into being an everyday player. There is still time for us to do some special things here, and I want to be part of it. Sulking about playing time isn't going to help anybody or be productive."

Reliever Buck Sterling got into trouble in the eighth and ninth, forcing Stein to go with closer Ivan Zyzna, who wound up with a save. Now, it's on to Boston to begin a tough cross-country trip that also includes stops in Oakland and Texas.

"Fenway Park is always tough," Stein said. "The Red Sox are a good team, and that crowd is right on top of you. It seems odd that we're going right back to the West Coast after opening the season in Anaheim, but I think the players will have a chance to do some real bonding on the trip. It's a tight-knit group. They've stuck together after the rough start to the season, and I'm looking forward to seeing what they can do with a little wind at their backs."

CLEVELAND INDIANS VS OAKLAND ATHLETICS · APRIL 21
CLEVELAND 7 / OAKLAND 4

CLEVELAND INDIANS										
BATTING	AB	R	H	RBI	2B	3B	HR	BB	SO	BA
MICAH MILLISON RF	5	1	3	1	0	0	0	0	0	.450
WILSON WHITE LF	4	1	2	0	0	0	0	1	1	.250
TERRY ROVETTO 3B	4	0	1	0	0	0	0	1	0	.321
OLIVER REINER 1B	5	0	1	0	0	0	0	0	0	.321
SCOTT MICHAELS	2	2	1	3	0	0	1	2	0	.214
JUSTIN KESTINO SS	4	0	1	0	0	0	0	0	1	.255
MORRIS JEROME C	4	1	1	0	0	0	0	0	1	.143
BERNARD HARPER DH	3	1	1	0	0	0	0	1	0	.400
HURON SOUTHWORTH CF	4	1	1	3	1	0	0	0	0	.121
PITCHING	IP	H	R	ER	SO	BB	ERA			
KENNY CAMDEN (W)	7	5	0	0	8	2	3.38			
BUCK STERLING	1.3	6	4	4	0	0	7.07			
IVAN ZYZNA (S)	0.67	0	0	0	1	0	2.45			
OAKLAND A'S										
BATTING	AB	R	H	RBI	2B	3B	HR	BB	SO	BA
ALBERT REYES RF	5	0	1	0	0	0	0	0	2	.196
MATTHEW VAN STENCEL CF	5	0	2	0	0	0	0	0	0	.241
ERNESTO MENDESOTO 3B	3	1	1	1	0	0	0	1	1	.224
GRAEME NILSON 1B	4	0	1	1	0	0	0	0	1	.228
TRENT ATHERTON C	3	0	0	0	0	0	0	1	0	.250
JAYSON GIVINS DH	4	0	1	0	0	0	0	0	2	.467
RAMON TORRES SS	4	1	2	1	2	0	0	0	1	.154
TREMONT HARKNESS LF	4	1	1	1	0	0	0	0	1	.217
GLENN WALLS 2B	4	0	1	1	1	0	0	0	1	.188
PITCHING	IP	H	R	ER	SO	BB	ERA			
KRIS PERKINS (L)	4.33	9	4	4	3	4	3.30			
JORGE BAREA	1.67	3	3	3	0	0	3.38			
JACK RICHARDS	1	0	0	0	0	0	2.25			
DEVON CLAVELL	1	0	0	0	1	0	1.38			
INNING	1	2	3	4	5	6	7	8	9	TOTAL
OAKLAND	0	0	0	0	0	0	0	2	2	4
CLEVELAND	3	0	0	0	4	0	0	0	0	7

GAME 15

By SAM LARDNER
The Cleveland Press

BOSTON, April 22 — The Indians' 5–1 loss to the Boston Red Sox at Fenway Park Friday night took a back seat to an ugly and disturbing incident directed at Indians second baseman Angel Rodriguez.

Rodriguez, who is openly gay, stood on the on-deck circle waiting to bat in the third inning when he apparently was the victim of verbal abuse by several fans on the third-base side. Home-plate umpire Martin Atkinson called timeout as he saw Rodriguez turn and climb atop the short fence next to the on-deck circle.

Security guards, to their credit, quickly moved in and escorted three men out of the seats and down the stairs leading to the concourse. Play resumed, and Rodriguez was given an ovation by most in the crowd of 33,947.

"You never want to see that; I thought we were past that," said Indians manager Todd Stein. "Angel has the full support of the Indians and his teammates. He has twice the courage of those cowards who heckled him from a safe distance."

Rodriguez, an outspoken advocate for LGBTQ rights, was more than willing to talk to reporters — both from Cleveland and Boston — after the game. "I'm not going to let it get me down or affect my play," he said. "But this kind of (stuff) has to be confronted head on. I'm a public figure who has a forum to talk about these issues, and I'm going to do so. I appreciate the support of my teammates, and I thank the Red Sox and their security people for moving so fast."

In the interview room on the other side of Fenway Park, Red Sox manager Jackson Miller offered an apology on behalf of the team. "In no way do we condone that kind of behavior," Miller said. "I've known Angel a long time. He competes hard, and his personal life is his own business. I'll speak to him personally on the field during batting practice tomorrow and apologize in person."

Boston has had its own checkered history of intolerance. The Red Sox were the last team to integrate, with Pumpsie Green in 1959, and the city itself has seen its share of racial incidents over the years, as have most major U.S. cities.

Police said alcohol may have played a part in Friday's ugliness. The game was delayed 55 minutes at the start because of rain, leaving fans with plenty of time to imbibe. Once order had been restored, the Red Sox owned the game, jumping out to a 4–0 lead against Indians starter Tak Fujimoto by the fourth inning.

Trace Attenberg hit a solo homer over the Green Monster in left field leading off the bottom of the third. The Red Sox got three more in the fourth, on a two-run double by Desmond Underwood and an RBI single by Stu Kennedy. Fujimoto was gone after five innings.

"You can't give them chances, especially in this ballpark," Fujimoto said through a translator. "The home run I can live with. It was a fly ball that would have been an out in most ballparks, but here, with that wall, it's a homer. But I allowed them to bunch hits in the fourth."

The Indians got their run in the sixth on a homer around the Pesky Pole in right by Bernard Harper, his first of the year. But all anybody wanted to talk about was the incident involving Rodriguez.

"That's horse (bleep)," said Terry Rovetto, the team leader. "Angel is a guy who just wants to play baseball like the rest of us. None of us in the clubhouse has ever had a problem with him, and if we don't, nobody else should. I'm not going to paint the entire city of Boston with a broad brush, but this kind of (stuff) has got to stop."

GAME 15

CLEVELAND INDIANS VS BOSTON RED SOX • APRIL 22
BOSTON 5 / CLEVELAND 1

CLEVELAND INDIANS										
BATTING	AB	R	H	RBI	2B	3B	HR	BB	SO	BA
RIKKI LABUDDA CF	4	0	1	0	1	0	0	0	0	.316
WILSON WHITE RF	4	0	1	0	0	0	0	0	1	.250
TERRY ROVETTO 3B	4	0	0	0	0	0	0	0	0	.300
OLIVER REINER 1B	4	0	0	0	0	0	0	0	1	.300
JUSTIN KESTINO SS	3	0	1	0	0	0	0	0	1	.260
MICAH MILLISON LF	3	0	1	0	0	0	0	0	0	.435
MORRIS JEROME C	3	0	1	0	0	0	0	0	0	.156
BERNARD HARPER DH	3	1	2	1	0	0	1	0	0	.435
ANGEL RODRIGUEZ 2B	3	0	1	0	0	0	0	0	1	.182
PITCHING	IP	H	R	ER	SO	BB	ERA			
TAK FUJIMOTO (L)	5	8	4	4	5	2	6.63			
SOLLY ALVAREZ	2	2	1	1	1	1	3.60			
GENO MILZIE	1	0	0	0	0	0	7.20			

BOSTON RED SOX										
BATTING	AB	R	H	RBI	2B	3B	HR	BB	SO	BA
DESMOND UNDERWOOD 3B	4	1	1	2	1	0	0	0	0	.273
TRACE ATTENBERG 1B	3	1	1	1	0	0	1	1	0	.254
STU KENNEDY SS	4	0	2	1	0	0	0	0	0	.241
JACK KINCAID DH	4	1	2	0	0	1	0	0	1	.271
WILLARD WASHINGTON CF	4	0	1	1	0	0	0	0	0	.242
OMAR PEREZ (LF)	4	0	0	0	0	0	0	0	2	.273
SALVADOR ESPINOZA RF	3	1	1	0	0	0	0	0	1	.241
SANTIAGO AVILLA 2B	4	1	1	0	0	0	0	0	0	.236
MARTY BLACKBURN C	3	1	1	0	0	0	0	1	0	.323
PITCHING	IP	H	R	ER	SO	BB	ERA			
EDUARDO SUAREZ (W)	7	5	1	1	2	0	2.71			
EDDIE MYERS	2	3	0	0	0	0	2.88			

INNING	1	2	3	4	5	6	7	8	9	TOTAL
CLEVELAND	0	0	0	0	0	1	0	0	0	1
BOSTON	0	0	1	3	0	0	1	0	0	5

GAME 16

By SAM LARDNER
The Cleveland Press

BOSTON, April 23 — The Indians picked a fine time to make their first national TV appearance.

Playing a prime-time Saturday night game on FOX, the Tribe bombed at Fenway Park, falling 10–1 to the Boston Red Sox, with No. 1 starting pitcher Lynn Moda lasting just two and two-thirds of an inning.

The only redeeming thing of the night for the Indians was that the Red Sox issued a formal apology to Indians second baseman Angel Rodriguez after he was the target of homophobic abuse Friday night. The Red Sox asked if Rodriguez would bring out the lineup card, and at home plate, they presented him with a $10,000 check for the charity of his choice.

"That was a classy gesture," said Rodriguez, who received cheers from most in the capacity crowd the first time he came to the plate. "It's good to know that this kind of abuse is not going to be tolerated. As I said last night, I just want to play baseball. I compete hard against all teams, but it's nice that an opposing team stood beside me."

Rodriguez also was interviewed during the network's pregame show, with the interview beamed on the Fenway Park videoboard.

On the field, the Indians have made a bad habit of letting games get away from them early, and Saturday's game was no exception.

The Red Sox scored two runs in each of the first three innings to grab a 6–0 lead. Interim manager Todd Stein had to go to his bullpen early, using Solly Alvarez, Mickey Penney and Buck Sterling.

"That hurts," Stein said. "We're going to be in a bit of a bind for tomorrow. Hopefully we can get some innings out of Ollie (Gonzalez). Modes has had a tough time getting out of the gate this year, and I'm not sure why. But he's working at it, I do know that."

Moda looked especially dejected after the game.

"I can't keep doing this," he said. "I think it's just a mechanical thing where I'm not getting on top of the ball and throwing it on a downward plane. Everybody knows I'm not going to blow anybody away with velocity, so it's important that I locate. We'll look at the video and work on things during the next side session before my next start."

Moda may not want to look at the video of Saturday's game. It was more like a horror show for him and the Indians. He hit Omar Perez leading off the bottom of the first and allowed a single to Stu Kennedy, putting runners at the corners. One out later Trace Attenberg doubled them both home on a drive to the deepest part of the ballpark in right-center. Moda got out of the inning but there was more trouble in the second.

Omar Perez singled with one out for the Red Sox, and he rode home on catcher Carlos Blanco's homer over the Green Monster.

The Red Sox touched each of the Indians' reliever for runs, with Desmond Underwood adding the finishing touch, a three-run homer in the eighth against Sterling.

"Hey, look, this one got away," Stein said. "It's bad that it was on national TV and all that, but that's the way it goes sometimes. You don't agonize over this one so much as you would a 2–1 loss. You just shower it off and come back tomorrow."

Stein took a moment to acknowledge the gesture the Red Sox made to Rodriguez.

"That's a great way to put this behind us," he said. "When (Red Sox manager) Billy Stone talked to both of us during BP (batting practice), he suggested the idea of Angel bringing out the lineup card. I had no idea they were going to make a presentation. I know Angel was touched, and I thought it was a neat touch having him carry out the lineup card."

GAME 16

CLEVELAND INDIANS VS BOSTON RED SOX· APRIL 23
BOSTON 10 / CLEVELAND 1

CLEVELAND INDIANS

BATTING	AB	R	H	RBI	2B	3B	HR	BB	SO	BA
RIKKI LABUDDA CF	3	1	0	0	0	0	0	1	0	.300
WILSON WHITE RF	4	0	2	0	0	0	0	0	1	.265
TERRY ROVETTO 3B	3	0	1	1	0	0	0	0	0	.302
OLIVER REINER 1B	4	0	0	0	0	0	0	0	1	.281
JUSTIN KESTINO SS	4	0	1	0	1	0	0	0	1	.259
MICAH MILLISON LF	4	0	0	0	0	0	0	0	1	.370
MORRIS JEROME C	3	0	2	0	0	0	0	0	1	.188
BERNARD HARPER DH	3	0	1	0	0	0	1	0	0	.423
ANGEL RODRIGUEZ 2B	3	0	1	0	0	0	0	0	1	.194

PITCHING	IP	H	R	ER	SO	BB	ERA			
LYNN MODA (L)	2.3	9	5	5	3	1	7.72			
SOLLY ALVAREZ	2.67	3	1	1	2	0	3.11			
MICKEY PENNY	1	2	0	0	0	0	7.00			
BUCK STERLING	3	5	3	3	3	1	8.00			

BOSTON RED SOX

BATTING	AB	R	H	RBI	2B	3B	HR	BB	SO	BA
OMAR PEREZ LF	5	2	2	1	1	0	0	0	1	.240
STU KENNEDY SS	5	1	2	1	0	0	0	0	1	.259
CARLOS BLANCO C	5	2	2	2	0	0	1	0	0	.241
TRACE ATTENBERG 1B	5	1	2	2	1	1	0	0	0	.246
JACK KINCAID DH	5	0	1	0	0	0	0	0	2	.250
DESMOND UNDERWOOD 3B	5	2	3	3	1	0	1	0	2	.271
SALVADOR ESPINOZA RF	3	1	1	0	0	2	0	0	0	.236
SANTIAGO AVILLA 2B	5	0	2	1	0	0	0	0	2	.220
VICTOR TRAGGER JR CF	5	1	2	0	1	0	0	0	1	.286

PITCHING	IP	H	R	ER	SO	BB	ERA			
RICH DORLAND (W)	6	7	1	1	4	1	3.05			
FELIX INFANTE	1	1	0	0	0	0	2.65			
NICK SPERO	1	0	0	0	1	0	3.46			

INNING	1	2	3	4	5	6	7	8	9	TOTAL
CLEVELAND	0	0	0	0	1	0	0	0	0	1
BOSTON	2	2	2	0	0	1	0	3	0	10

GAME 17

By SAM LARDNER
The Cleveland Press

BOSTON, April 24 — A couple steps forward, three steps back. That's the way it has gone all April for the Indians, and they staggered out of Fenway Park Sunday after a 3–2 loss to the Red Sox.

Lefty Ollie Gonzalez did what he had to do, gutting out eight innings on a day when the Indians needed it most because of their depleted bullpen. Gonzalez gave up all three runs, but as has been the case in the early going, an Indians offense that was supposed to be a strength looked totally lifeless once again.

The Tribe managed just five hits against Red Sox righty Scott Johnson and a pair of relievers. Micah Millison struck out with runners on first and second and two outs in the ninth against Boston closer Jose Rodriguez, who angered some on the Indians by gesticulating wildly after the final out.

But if the Indians are worried about that, they've got bigger problems. They were swept in three games at Fenway, getting outscored 18–4 and seeing their overall record fall to 5–12.

"I'm old-school, so I don't like all the theatrics, but we can't dwell on that," said interim manager Todd Stein, who is 3–4 since taking over for the fired Dave Mills. "The fact is, the game was there for us to win, in the ninth and at several other points in the game. But give Boston's pitchers some credit, too. It's on to Oakland, and we'll forget about this on the plane ride."

Gonzalez has been the Tribe's most consistent starter, and he was on again Sunday, striking out nine with two walks. Solo homers by Morgan Leifer in the third and Salvador Espinoza in the fifth gave the Red Sox a 2–0 lead. While that was going on, the Indians were leaving the bases loaded in the first and stranding one in each of the third, fourth and seventh."

"They say if you're going to give up homers, make them solo homers," Gonzalez said. "I can't complain about the pitches, Leifer went down and golfed a good pitch over the wall in left, and I think the wind might have helped Espinoza's ball."

The Indians tied the game at 2–2 in the sixth as Terry Rovetto got hold of one and knocked it into the bullpen in right-center after Justin Kestino walked. Just the third homer for Rovetto for the season. Trace Attenberg hit a sacrifice fly in the seventh, giving the Red Sox their 3–2 lead. In the top of the ninth, Morris Jerome doubled with one out and went to third on Rodriguez's wild pitch. Leo Taylor, getting a rare start, worked a walk, putting runners on first and third. The runners wound up at those bases as Rikki LaBudda popped out to the catcher and Millison went down on strikes on a high fastball.

"Yeah, he got me, but I think he got a little carried away celebrating," Millison said of Rodriguez. "Skip placed a lot of trust me with all of this playing time lately (in place of Huron Southworth), and I let us down. That high fastball looks good coming in, but it's a tough pitch to catch up to."

Stein said he expects to hear in Oakland from general manager J.D. Eisner about a possible bullpen call-up. It's possible a reliever could go on the injured list or somebody could be sent down.

"We'll be OK," Stein said. "This was just one of those series. We caught a hot ballclub, and they took it to us. We're going to be that hot ballclub one of these days really soon, and we're going to be the one sweeping somebody. There's too much talent here for that not to happen."

CLEVELAND INDIANS VS BOSTON RED SOX· APRIL 24
BOSTON 3 / CLEVELAND 2

CLEVELAND INDIANS

BATTING	AB	R	H	RBI	2B	3B	HR	BB	SO	BA
RIKKI LABUDDA CF	5	0	1	0	0	0	0	0	1	.292
MICAH MILLISON LF	5	0	1	0	0	0	0	0	2	.344
JUSTIN KESTINO SS	3	1	1	0	0	0	0	1	0	.263
TERRY ROVETTO 3B	3	1	1	2	0	0	1	1	1	.303
OLIVER REINER 1B	3	0	0	0	0	0	0	1	1	.269
WILSON WHITE RF	4	0	1	0	1	0	0	0	0	.264
JJ KULAKOFSKY DH	3	0	0	0	0	0	0	0	0	.161
SCOTT MICHAELS PH	1	0	0	0	0	0	0	0	0	.133
MORRIS JEROME C	3	0	1	0	1	0	0	1	1	.196
LEO TAYLOR 2B	3	0	0	0	0	0	0	0	0	.000

PITCHING	IP	H	R	ER	SO	BB	ERA
OLLIE GONZALEZ (L)	8	11	3	3	9	2	4.50

BOSTON RED SOX

BATTING	AB	R	H	RBI	2B	3B	HR	BB	SO	BA
OMAR PEREZ LF	4	0	2	0	1	0	0	0	1	.259
STU KENNEDY SS	4	1	2	0	0	0	0	0	1	.276
MORGAN LEIFER DH	3	1	2	1	0	0	1	1	0	.333
TRACE ATTENBERG 1B	3	1	0	1	0	0	0	0	2	.234
CARLOS BLANCO C	4	0	3	0	0	0	0	0	1	.276
DESMOND UNDERWOOD 3B	4	0	0	0	0	0	0	0	1	.250
SANTIAGO AVILLA 2B	4	2	2	0	0	0	0	0	0	.254
SALVADOR ESPINOZA RF	3	1	1	1	0	0	1	1	1	.226
VICTOR TRAGGER JR CF	3	0	0	0	0	0	0	0	1	.263

PITCHING	IP	H	R	ER	SO	BB	ERA
SCOTT JOHNSON (W)	8	5	2	2	6	2	3.13
JOSE RODRIGUEZ (S)	1	1	0	0	1	0	1.80

INNING	1	2	3	4	5	6	7	8	9	TOTAL
CLEVELAND	0	0	0	0	0	2	0	0	0	2
BOSTON	0	0	1	0	1	0	1	0	0	3

GAME 18

By SAM LARDNER
The Cleveland Press

OAKLAND, Calif., April 25 — Nobody looks forward to a long cross-country plane ride, but the Indians had to like looking across the way at the Coliseum and seeing the Oakland Athletics after they arrived in the Bay Area.

After all, the Tribe took two of three from the A's last week at Progressive Field before their lost weekend at Boston, where they were swept in three by the Red Sox.

So, it was again Monday night, as Brian "The Doctor" Howard was surgically precise during a 4–1 victory. He carved up the A's in a six-inning performance, giving up three hits and one run.

There was also another development worth watching. The game was sweet redemption for Micah Millison, who struck out to end Sunday's 3–2 loss at Fenway Park. Not only did Millison hit a three-run homer in the third inning against A's starter Mickey Vold, but manager Todd Stein confirmed what everybody already seemed to know: that Millison has supplanted the slumping Huron Southworth in the everyday starting lineup, at least for the foreseeable future.

"I think we had to make that move," said Stein, whose team improved to 6–12 on the season. "We really can't wait much longer to get the offense going. Southy is still going to play, as I told you guys a few days ago. But Micah has looked good. Even when he struck out yesterday, he had good looks at the plate. We're just going to go with it, ride it and see how it plays out."

Millison seemed to appreciate the vote of confidence.

"Yeah, especially after I let the team down yesterday," he said. "When you come into the clubhouse and see your name on the lineup card, it's always a good feeling. I don't look at it as a competition with Southy. He's a good friend, and I know he's going to contribute before this thing is all over."

Millison's homer came after Morris Jerome walked and Rikki LaBudda singled. The drive went to deep right-center, no mean feat in a stadium where fly balls go to die at night.

"It felt good off the bat," Millison said. "But I ran hard out of the box because in this place, you never know. You can crush one, and the next thing you know, the outfielder is catching it on the warning track. Tough place to hit."

As for the good doctor, Howard, he seemed to enjoy the cool conditions at the Coliseum. He retired the first six A's he faced before Ramon Torres singled. But Torres was wiped out on Graeme Nilson's double-play grounder.

The only run off Howard came when Jayson Givins doubled home Isaiah Huertas, who walked.

"They say walks get you, and that one got me," Howard said. "But no, I'm happy with how the game turned out. The guys gave me enough runs, especially in this park. I've always enjoyed pitching here, with the big foul territory and how the ball doesn't carry at night. But I am glad it carried for our guys."

The Indians added an insurance run in the ninth, on DH Bernard Harper's sacrifice fly that scored Scott Michaels, who went in at second base for Angel Rodriguez (back spasms) in the seventh and singled in the ninth.

Freshly recalled Lorry Unger pitched the eighth as he came up from Triple-A Columbus to replace Buck Sterling, who went on the injured list with "shoulder fatigue." Geno Milzie worked the bottom of the ninth for the save.

"Complete effort," Stein said. "Now we need to build on this and claw our way back to .500 and go from there. I think Millison is going to give us a shot in the arm, and if we get starting pitching like Howard gave us tonight, a lot of good things will happen."

GAME 18

CLEVELAND INDIANS VS OAKLAND ATHLETICS· APRIL 26
CLEVELAND 4 / OAKLAND 1

CLEVELAND INDIANS										
BATTING	AB	R	H	RBI	2B	3B	HR	BB	SO	BA
RIKKI LABUDDA CF	5	1	3	0	1	0	0	0	1	.314
MICAH MILLISON LF	5	1	1	3	0	0	1	0	1	.324
BERNARD HARPER DH	4	0	2	1	0	0	0	0	1	.433
TERRY ROVETTO 3B	5	0	1	0	0	0	0	0	0	.296
OLIVER REINER 1B	4	0	1	0	0	0	0	0	0	.268
WILSON WHITE RF	3	0	1	0	1	0	0	1	0	.267
JUSTIN KESTINO SS	4	0	2	0	0	0	0	0	1	.279
MORRIS JEROME C	3	1	1	0	0	0	0	1	1	.204
ANGEL RODRIGUEZ 2B	3	0	0	0	1	0	0	0	0	.179
SCOTT MICHAELS 2B	1	1	1	0	0	0	0	0	0	.250
PITCHING	IP	H	R	ER	SO	BB	ERA			
BRIAN HOWARD (W)	6	3	1	1	4	1	4.13			
BUCK STERLING	1	0	0	0	0	0	7.58			
LORRY UNGER	1	1	0	0	0	1	0.00			
GENO MILZIE (S)	1	0	0	0	0	0	6.55			
BOSTON RED SOX										
BATTING	AB	R	H	RBI	2B	3B	HR	BB	SO	BA
ISAIAH HUERTAS LF	3	1	0	0	0	0	0	1	0	.226
JAYSON GIVINS 2B	3	0	1	1	1	0	0	0	1	.263
ERNESTO MENDESOTO 3B	3	0	0	0	0	0	0	0	1	.308
TREMONT HARKNESS DH	3	0	0	0	0	0	0	0	1	.242
ALBERT REYES CF	3	0	1	0	0	0	0	0	0	.281
MATTHEW VAN STENCEL RF	3	0	1	0	0	0	0	1	0	.275
RAMON TORRES SS	3	0	1	0	0	0	0	0	1	.226
GRAEME NILSON 1B	3	0	0	0	0	0	1	0	1	.224
MARCUS THOMPSON C	3	0	0	0	0	0	0	0	1	.263
PITCHING	IP	H	R	ER	SO	BB	ERA			
MICKEY VOLD (L)	6	7	3	3	2	2	3.76			
CRAIG QUINN	1	2	0	0	2	0	3.60			
DEVON CLAVELL	1	2	0	0	1	0	2.81			
MITCH SUTHERLAND	1	2	1	1	1	0	3.00			
INNING	1	2	3	4	5	6	7	8	9	TOTAL
CLEVELAND	0	0	3	0	0	0	0	0	1	4
OAKLAND	0	0	0	1	0	0	0	0	0	1

GAME 19

By SAM LARDNER

The Cleveland Press

OAKLAND, Calif., April 27 — There's an old saying in baseball that momentum is as strong as the next day's starting pitcher. Consider any West Coast momentum for the Indians stalled because Tuesday night's starting pitcher, Kenny Camden, was not strong.

Camden hardly lived up to his nickname of "The Wiz" during a lackluster 4 and two-thirds inning performance in a 6–3 loss to the Oakland Athletics at the Coliseum. The A's jumped on Camden for three runs in the first inning and chased him with more in the fifth as they erased the Indians' good feeling from the previous night's 4–1 victory.

"You hope to build on things," said interim manager Todd Stein, whose team fell to 6–13. "After we got swept in Boston, we bounced back nicely last night and felt good about things as we try to bond on this long road trip. But I think Kenny got a little out of whack with his mechanics early, and it seemed that the A's knew what was coming. We'll look at the video on that."

Camden handled the A's well five days earlier in Cleveland when it looked like he had no-hit stuff early in the game. He also had an early cushion. In Tuesday's game, the A's made Camden a pin cushion, sticking him for three runs in the first inning. It even looked like Camden might be "tipping" his pitches, when Matthew Van Stencel hit a three-run homer.

"No, no, no, nothing like that," Camden said when asked about pitch tipping. "That's the easy fallback position when you get hit. My mechanics were a little out of whack with the first two batters. We'll look at the video and get that ironed out."

Camden walked the first two batters he faced, Ramon Torres and Albert Reyes, and he did it on eight pitches. Van Stencel looked like he knew what was coming when he crushed a first-pitch fastball over the wall in right field. With Camden having a hard time finding the plate, one might have thought Van Stencel may have taken a pitch.

"I know Camden pretty well, and I knew he would want to try to get ahead in the count, especially after he walked Ramon and Albert," Van Stencel said from the A's clubhouse. "He's normally an aggressive pitcher, and he didn't want to put anybody else on base. So I guessed right with the fastball."

The A's chased Camden with two outs in the fifth after Trent Atherton doubled home two runs after Van Stencel walked and Tim Szerlong singled to put runners on first and third. Solly Alvarez shut the inning down, and Wilson White hit a solo homer off A's starter Jack Richards in the sixth. It was the only run off Richards.

Alvarez gave up a run in the bottom of the inning, and the Tribe scored twice off Devon Clavell in the eighth on a two-run double by Oliver Reiner. Rikki LaBudda walked to lead off the inning, stole second and Micah Millison singled ahead of Reiner. But that, as they say, was that, as A's closer Mitch Sutherland worked the ninth for the save.

"Yeah, this is one we could just as easily could have won," Stein said. "We got behind the eight-ball early and just couldn't put anything together until it was too late. But the guys are plugging. I have no problem with the effort."

GAME 19

CLEVELAND INDIANS VS OAKLAND ATHLETICS· APRIL 27
OAKLAND 6 / CLEVELAND 3

CLEVELAND INDIANS										
BATTING	AB	R	H	RBI	2B	3B	HR	BB	SO	BA
RIKKI LABUDDA CF	4	1	0	0	0	0	0	1	0	.297
MICAH MILLISON LF	4	1	1	0	0	0	0	0	0	.317
OLIVER REINER 1B	4	0	1	2	1	0	0	0	1	.267
TERRY ROVETTO 3B	4	0	1	0	0	0	0	0	2	.293
WILSON WHITE RF	4	1	1	1	0	0	1	0	0	.280
BERNARD HARPER DH	2	0	0	0	0	0	0	2	0	.406
JUSTIN KESTINO SS	4	0	0	0	0	0	0	0	1	.262
MORRIS JEROME C	4	0	3	0	1	0	0	0	0	.241
LEO TAYLOR 2B	4	0	1	0	0	0	0	0	1	.100
PITCHING	IP	H	R	ER	SO	BB	ERA			
KENNY CAMDEN (L)	4.67	6	5	5	3	3	4.39			
SOLLY ALVAREZ	1.33	3	1	1	1	0	3.60			
GENO MILZE	2	1	0	0	1	0	5.54			

OAKLAND A'S										
BATTING	AB	R	H	RBI	2B	3B	HR	BB	SO	BA
RAMON TORRES SS	3	1	1	0	0	0	0	1	0	.269
ALBERT REYES CF	3	1	1	0	1	0	0	1	0	.283
MATTHEW VAN STENCEL RF	3	1	1	3	0	0	1	1	1	.278
TIM SZERLONG LF	4	1	1	0	0	0	0	0	0	.234
TRENT ATHERTON C	4	0	1	2	1	0	0	0	1	.276
ERNESTO MENDESOTO 3B	4	0	1	0	0	0	0	0	1	.304
TREMONT HARKNESS DH	4	0	1	0	0	0	0	0	1	.242
NOLAN PHILLIPS 1B	4	1	2	0	1	0	0	0	0	.237
RENALDO CASIANO 2B	3	1	1	1	0	0	0	0	0	.289
PITCHING	IP	H	R	ER	SO	BB	ERA			
JACK RICHARDS (W)	6	6	1	1	3	1	3.27			
DEVON CLAVELL	2	2	1	1	2	2	2.59			
MITCH SUTHERLAND (S)	1	1	0	0	0	0	2.70			

INNING	1	2	3	4	5	6	7	8	9	TOTAL
CLEVELAND	0	0	0	0	0	1	0	2	0	3
OAKLAND	3	0	0	0	2	1	0	0	0	6

GAME 20

By SAM LARDNER
The Cleveland Press

OAKLAND, Calif., April 28 — This is what the Indians have been waiting for.

After an underwhelming, yet hard-luck, start to his Cleveland career, Tak Fujimoto looked every bit the pitcher the Tribe thought they were getting Wednesday night in a masterful 3–0 victory over the Oakland Athletics at the Coliseum.

Fujimoto won his first major-league victory with a complete-game effort, as he threw just 97 pitches and allowed four hits while walking one and striking out eight.

Signed out of Japan in the off-season, Fujimoto has been in the spotlight since spring training as the Indians and their fans wait to see if he's the real deal. He was the victim of poor run support in his first couple of starts before getting belted around in Boston early in this road trip.

Against, the A's, however, Fujimoto was simply dominant. Oakland batters looked totally flummoxed by his array of breaking balls and could not catch up to the high fastball.

"I felt really good out there tonight," Fujimoto said through his translator. "The cool weather at night reminded me a little of pitching in Japan this time of year. I was disappointed in myself at Boston, so I wanted to show the team what I could do."

Consider his teammates and his manager impressed.

"Wow," said catcher Morris Jerome, who emphatically plopped the game ball into Fujimoto's glove after the final out, a strikeout of Nolan Phillips. "I just sat back there and put down fingers. Tak hit all the spots. My job was pretty easy."

"From the side, sometimes it's hard to tell how the ball is moving, but that was a pitching clinic out there tonight," said manager Todd Stein, whose team has taken two of the first three games of this series to run its season record to 7–13. "You could see it in the look on his face when he'd come into the dugout after every inning. The confidence seemed to grow."

Interestingly enough, Fujimoto gave up a single to the first batter of the game, Ramon Torres, before he reeled off 10 straight outs. In addition to the eight strikeouts, he recorded nine outs on the ground.

"That's important," Stein said. "You get into a rhythm like that, and the fielders are ready. And we made some nice plays out there tonight."

One of those plays was turned in by second baseman Scott Michaels, who backhanded a ball behind the bag in the fourth to throw out Renaldo Casiano.

At the plate, Michaels went 2-for-4, with his two-run single in the second driving in Micah Millison and Terry Rovetto after Millison singled and Rovetto doubled. The hit came against A's starter Maurice Waters, who gave up thirteen hits in a losing complete game effort.

"Felt good to be out there," said Michaels, who subbed again for Angel Rodriguez, whose balky back acted up again. "Just a fun game to be a part of with Fuji out there dealing the way he was."

Justin Kestino homered in the ninth, to give Fujimoto an insurance run. Stein had Ivan Zyzna up and ready in the bullpen, but he decided to stick with Fujimoto.

"If a guy is able to go long, I think it gives him confidence for the next time out," Stein said. "Fuji didn't labor at all in this game, so the 97 pitches seemed more like 77. It was cool out there, and I don't think he even broke a sweat."

CLEVELAND INDIANS VS OAKLAND ATHLETICS· APRIL 28
CLEVELAND 3 / OAKLAND 0

CLEVELAND INDIANS										
BATTING	AB	R	H	RBI	2B	3B	HR	BB	SO	BA
RIKKI LABUDDA CF	5	0	1	0	0	0	0	0	0	.291
WILSON WHITE RF	4	0	0	0	0	0	0	0	0	.266
OLIVER REINER 1B	3	0	2	0	0	0	0	1	0	.282
MICAH MILLISON LF	4	1	1	0	0	0	0	0	0	.311
TERRY ROVETTO 3B	3	1	2	0	1	0	0	1	0	.308
SCOTT MICHAELS 2B	4	0	2	2	0	0	0	0	1	.300
JUSTIN KESTINO SS	4	1	2	1	0	0	1	0	1	.275
BERNARD HARPER DH	4	0	1	0	1	0	0	0	2	.389
MORRIS JEROME C	4	0	2	0	0	0	0	0	0	.258
PITCHING	IP	H	R	ER	SO	BB	ERA			
TAK FUJIMOTO (W)	9	4	0	9	8	1	4.50			
OAKLAND A'S										
BATTING	AB	R	H	RBI	2B	3B	HR	BB	SO	BA
RAMON TORRES SS	4	0	1	0	0	0	0	0	1	.268
ALBERT REYES CF	4	0	1	0	0	0	0	0	1	.281
MATTHEW VAN STENCEL RF	3	0	1	0	0	0	0	1	0	.263
TIM SZERLONG LF	4	0	0	0	0	0	0	0	1	.216
TRENT ATHERTON C	4	0	0	0	0	0	0	0	1	.258
NOLAN PHILLIPS 1B	4	0	0	0	0	0	0	0	0	.214
ERNESTO MENDESOTO 3B	3	0	0	0	0	0	0	0	1	.288
TREMONT HARKNESS DH	3	0	1	0	0	0	0	0	1	.246
RENALDO CASIANO 2B	3	0	0	0	0	0	0	0	2	.268
PITCHING	IP	H	R	ER	SO	BB	ERA			
MAURICE WATERS (L)	9	13	3	3	7	2	3.66			

INNING	1	2	3	4	5	6	7	8	9	TOTAL
CLEVELAND	0	2	0	0	0	0	0	0	1	3
OAKLAND	0	0	0	0	0	0	0	0	0	0

GAME 21

By SAM LARDNER
The Cleveland Press

OAKLAND, Calif., April 29 — There's no truth to the rumor that the Cleveland Indians will petition Major League Baseball to move them to the American League West so they can be nearer to the Oakland Athletics.

The A's have turned into the kissin' cousins for the Indians in the early going. In Cleveland on the first homestand of the season, the Indians took two of three from the A's. On Thursday, the Tribe took their third game in four tries against the A's at the Coliseum.

After three-night games in the cool of the East Bay, the Indians basked in the afternoon sunshine and rode the pitching of Lynn Moda and the hitting of Micah Millison to a 5–2 victory, improving their season record to 8–13.

"Important win for us," said interim manager Todd Stein, who is 6–5 since taking over for the fired Dave Mills. "Our goal from here on out is to win series. That's all. If you do that, you climb back to .500, and before you know it, you can find yourself back in the race. To be able to take three of four on the West Coast, in a tough place to play, should give us a big lift. At least I hope so."

Following on the heels of Tak Fujimoto's complete-game effort of the previous night, Moda worked seven strong innings, giving up both Oakland runs and five hits. That erased the memory of his 10–1 loss at Boston last Saturday.

"It was all mechanical," Moda said. "We made the adjustments I talked about after that Boston start, and it paid off. I had a good downward plane on the ball. This is something to build on, and I can't wait to get back out there the next time."

This game was scoreless until the fourth, when a pair of players joined at the hip contributed to a three-run inning. Millison hit a two-run homer after Rikki LaBudda led off with a triple to the right-field corner. Stein has given Millison regular playing time after benching Huron Southworth because of a slow start.

It just so happened that Southworth was in Thursday's lineup as the DH because of the quick turnaround after the night game Wednesday. Southworth followed Millison's homer with a single and a stolen base. He then came home on Terry Rovetto's single up the middle, giving the Indians a 3–0 lead. All of that damage came off A's ace Josh Kennelly.

"It was good that both of us could contribute that inning," Millison said. "I know Southy has been itching to get back in there, and he'll get his chances by being DH and when other guys need a rest. It was a good day to hit here, with the ball carrying a little better during the daytime."

The Indians took a 5–0 lead in the sixth, bunching four singles from Kieran Catsef (also getting a rare start), Iceberg Peters, Leo Taylor and LaBudda. True to his reputation Stein continues to use unconventional lineups.

The A's got a pair of harmless runs in the bottom of the eighth against Mickey Penney before Geno Millzie finished up in the ninth for the save.

"We got some guys in there today," Stein said. "With this busy stretch on the road and the day game after the night game, it's important to get guys off their feet and give other guys a chance to swing the bat and stay fresh. Pinch-hitting chances don't come around as much over here in the American League as much as they do in the National because we have the DH. But I can use the DH to give guys like Southy and others a chance."

The long and winding road trip continues with four games in Texas, in the air-conditioned comfort of the Rangers' latest ballpark.

"Yeah," Stein said with a weary chuckle. "From Boston to Oakland to Texas, that's quite and itinerary. But at least we're heading back east. I think we'll remember what home looks like when we get back there, but we're eager to take care of business in Texas."

CLEVELAND INDIANS VS OAKLAND ATHLETICS· APRIL 29
CLEVELAND 5 / OAKLAND 2

CLEVELAND INDIANS										
BATTING	AB	R	H	RBI	2B	3B	HR	BB	SO	BA
RIKKI LABUDDA CF	4	1	2	1	0	1	0	0	0	.301
MICAH MILLISON RF	4	1	1	2	0	0	1	0	1	.306
HURON SOUTHWORTH DH	4	1	2	0	0	0	0	0	0	.162
TERRY ROVETTO 3B	4	0	1	1	0	0	0	0	1	.305
OLIVER REINER 1B	3	0	0	0	0	0	0	0	1	.268
SCOTT MICHAELS 2B	3	0	1	0	1	0	0	1	0	.304
KIERAN CATSEF LF	4	1	1	0	0	0	0	0	2	.182
ICEBERG PETERS C	4	1	1	0	1	0	0	0	1	.222
LEO TAYLOR SS	3	0	1	1	0	0	0	1	0	.154
PITCHING	IP	H	R	ER	SO	BB	ERA			
LYNN MODA (W)	7	5	2	2	7	2	6.17			
MICKEY PENNY	1	1	0	0	0	1	6.30			
GENO MILZIE (S)	1	1	0	0	0	0	5.14			

OAKLAND A'S										
BATTING	AB	R	H	RBI	2B	3B	HR	BB	SO	BA
RAMON TORRES SS	4	0	1	0	0	0	0	0	1	.267
ALBERT REYES CF	4	0	1	0	1	0	0	0	0	.279
MATTHEW VAN STENCEL RF	4	0	0	0	0	0	0	1	0	.246
GLENN WALLS LF	3	0	1	1	0	0	0	0	1	.222
TRENT ATHERTON C	4	1	0	0	0	0	0	0	2	.242
NOLAN PHILLIPS 1B	3	1	1	0	0	0	0	0	0	.222
ERNESTO MENDESOTO 3B	3	0	2	1	1	0	0	0	1	.306
TREMONT HARKNESS DH	3	0	0	0	0	0	0	0	1	.236
RENALDO CASIANO 2B	3	0	1	0	0	0	0	0	2	.409
PITCHING	IP	H	R	ER	SO	BB	ERA			
JOSH KENNELLY (L)	5.33	7	5	5	6	2	4.08			
JORGE BAREA	2.66	2	0	0	1	0	3.21			
CRAIG QUINN	1	1	0	0	0	1	2.50			

INNING	1	2	3	4	5	6	7	8	9	TOTAL
CLEVELAND	0	0	0	3	0	2	0	0	0	5
OAKLAND	0	0	0	0	0	0	0	2	0	2

GAME 22

By SAM LARDNER

The Cleveland Press

ARLINGTON, Texas, April 30 — For many years, playing the Rangers meant coming to Arlington and wilting in the Texas heat.

The Indians chose to lose in air-conditioned comfort Friday night.

After an inspiring series at Oakland — where the Tribe won three of four — Friday night produced a dud of a 4–1 loss at Globe Life Field. The Indians finished an eventful April with a record of 8–14.

The biggest event of the month was the firing of manager Dave Mills and replacing him with Todd Stein after 10 games.

"May brings a fresh start, and we're all looking forward to that," Stein said. "Tonight, wasn't very good. We know that. But it's just one game. I think if you ask the guys, they believe we have this thing going in the right direction."

Lefty Ollie Gonzalez was the hard-luck loser for the second straight start. He got no run support and a pair of errors behind him sealed his fate. Gonzalez wound up with a quality start as he worked six innings, giving up seven hits and all four runs, but only one earned.

"I'm not going to cry about bad luck," Gonzalez said. "If I had done my job better, we might have won. That's the bottom line. The guys behind me are busting their butts out there every game. Mistakes and errors are part of it."

Things came apart for the Tribe in the bottom of the fourth, when the Rangers scored three runs, thanks to errors by Angel Rodriguez and Justin Kestino. Rodriguez made the first of the keystone combo's errors when he fumbled a grounder by the speedy Richie Young Jr. with one out. Rodriguez also has been bothered by a bad back.

"No excuse," he said. "Young is pretty fast, and I took my eye off the ball for a split second. Shouldn't happen. I've made that play a million times."

The dangerous Miguel Beltre popped out, and the Indians breathed a little easier, but Kestino allowed Willard Chandler's grounder to go through him for the second error of the inning. Ryan Rose followed with a homer into the left-field stands for a 3–0 lead. It used to be that the wind would help balls fly out of the previous ballparks here, but this one needed no help indoors as it was hit hard.

Gonzalez gave up an RBI groundout to Frank Sowell in the sixth.

"I make a pitch to Rose, and we're out of the inning, no matter the errors," Gonzalez said. "It's as simple as that."

The Indians got their only run in the eighth. Terry Rovetto doubled, and Wilson White singled him home. Rangers closer Tino Fernandez shut down the Indians 1-2-3 in the ninth.

"A little sloppiness in one inning cost us," Stein said. "Those two guys (Rodriguez and Kestino) are dependable guys. They probably won't make errors in the same game for the rest of the season."

GAME 22

CLEVELAND INDIANS VS TEXAS RANGERS · APRIL 30
TEXAS 4 / CLEVELAND 1

CLEVELAND INDIANS

BATTING	AB	R	H	RBI	2B	3B	HR	BB	SO	BA
RIKKI LABUDDA CF	4	0	1	0	0	1	0	1	0	.299
MICAH MILLISON LF	4	0	0	0	0	0	0	0	1	.283
JJ KULAKOFSKI 1B	4	1	1	0	0	0	0	0	0	.171
TERRY ROVETTO 3B	3	0	2	0	0	0	0	0	1	.318
WILSON WHITE RF	4	0	2	1	0	0	0	0	1	.277
JUSTIN KESTINO SS	4	0	0	0	0	0	0	1	0	.260
BERNARD HARPER DH	4	0	0	0	0	0	0	0	2	.350
MORRIS JEROME C	3	0	1	0	1	0	0	0	1	.262
ANGEL RODRIGUEZ 2B	3	0	1	0	0	0	0	1	0	.190

PITCHING	IP	H	R	ER	SO	BB	ERA			
OLLIE GONZALEZ (L)	6	7	4	1	4	1	6.56			
BUCK STERLING	1	1	0	0	1	0	7.20			
IVAN ZYZNA	0	1	0	0	1	0	0.64			

TEXAS RANGERS

BATTING	AB	R	H	RBI	2B	3B	HR	BB	SO	BA
RICHIE YOUNG JR 2B	4	1	1	0	0	0	0	0	0	.267
MIGUEL BELTRE 3B	4	1	1	0	1	0	0	0	0	.279
WILLARD CHANDLER RF	4	1	2	0	0	0	0	1	0	.295
RYAN ROSE LF	4	1	1	3	0	0	1	0	1	.278
FRANK SOWELL SS	4	0	1	1	0	0	0	0	0	.273
NICK MARSANS 1B	4	0	0	0	0	0	0	0	0	.267
FERNANDO POSADA DH	4	0	1	0	1	0	0	0	0	.274
ADRIAN MOLINA CF	3	0	2	0	0	0	0	0	1	.236
JUAN CEPEDA C	3	0	1	0	0	0	0	0	2	.273

PITCHING	IP	H	R	ER	SO	BB	ERA			
DARCY EVANS (W)	8	8	8	1	6	3	2.57			
TINO FERNANDEZ (S)	1	0	0	0	0	0	1.80			

INNING	1	2	3	4	5	6	7	8	9	TOTAL
CLEVELAND	0	0	0	0	0	0	0	1	0	1
TEXAS	0	0	0	3	0	1	0	0		4

GAME 23

By SAM LARDNER
The Cleveland Press

ARLINGTON, Texas, May 1 — The Indians have had the uncanny knack this season of gaining some momentum and then frittering it all away.

It's happened again right here deep in the heart of Texas.

After losing a mistake-filled game Friday night, the Indians lost a heart-breaker Saturday evening, as Nick Marsans hit a leadoff homer off Ivan Zyzna leading off the bottom of the 10th inning to give the Rangers a 3–2 victory. The Indians had battled back from a 2–0 deficit to tie the game in the top of the ninth on a two-out double by Micah Millison.

"That's a gut punch," said Indians manager Todd Stein. "To battle back like that ..."

Stein's voiced trailed off at that point.

Zyzna came on in a non-save situation — seemingly always a trouble spot for closers — and gave up Marsans' blast to right field on a 3–2 pitch.

"Hung a slider," Zyzna said. "Just hung it. "Not much more to say than that. The guys came back and gave us a chance, and I gave it away. But I'll want the ball again tomorrow. That's the life of a closer."

The Indians got a decent start from Brian Howard, who walked away with a no-decision. He gave up single runs in each of the first two innings but sailed from there, working seven innings, giving up seven hits.

Adrian Molina singled home Richie Young Jr. in the first. DH Arthur Dahlgren homered just over the wall in the second against Howard.

"They jumped on me quick," Howard said. "After that, I was able to settle down and work the game plan with Mo (catcher Morris Jerome)."

The Indians offense did little with Rangers starter Cary Simon, getting a runner past second base only once. Simon worked eight innings, giving up two hits while walking none and striking out eight.

"He was tough," Stein said. "I think we could have been a little more patient — no walks is never a good thing. But he was all around the plate, and our guys didn't want to fall behind in the count. That's part of the reason they were so aggressive."

The top of the ninth began innocently enough against Ranger closer Tino Fernandez, on for his second straight game against the Indians and his third straight overall. No. 8 hitter Angel Rodriguez struck out on three pitches to begin the inning. Jerome singled through the hole at shortstop, and Rikki LaBudda beat out an infield chopper.

That set the stage for Millison, who picked on a first pitch from Fernandez and sent it to the gap in right center to tie the game.

"He might have lost a little bit of his stuff, having worked three days in a row," Millison said of Fernandez. "I thought he might want to come in with a first-pitch strike, and I was ready."

Geno Milzie held the Rangers in the bottom of the ninth before the Tribe went out 1-2-3 in the top of the 10th.

Marsans fouled off three pitches on 3–2 before launching his game-winner off Zyzna who's been very effective the entire season before this game.

"Ivan battled him," Stein said. "He threw the right pitch but just hung it. Credit the hitter for doing what he was supposed to do with that pitch."

GAME 23

CLEVELAND INDIANS VS TEXAS RANGERS · MAY 1
TEXAS 3 / CLEVELAND 2

CLEVELAND INDIANS											
BATTING	AB	R	H	RBI	2B	3B	HR	BB	SO	BA	
RIKKI LABUDDA CF	5	1	0	0	0	1	0	0	1	.283	
MICAH MILLISON LF	5	0	2	2	1	0	0	0	1	.293	
OLIVER REINER 1B	4	0	0	0	0	0	0	0	0	.256	
TERRY ROVETTO 3B	5	0	0	0	0	0	0	0	1	.318	
WILSON WHITE RF	4	0	0	0	0	0	0	0	1	.264	
JUSTIN KESTINO SS	4	0	0	0	0	0	0	1	0	.247	
BERNARD HARPER DH	4	0	0	0	0	0	0	0	2	.318	
ANGEL RODRIGUEZ 2B	4	0	0	0	0	0	0	0	1	.174	
MORRIS JEROME C	4	1	0	0	0	0	0	0	1	.246	
PITCHING	IP	H	R	ER	SO	BB	ERA				
BRIAN HOWARD	7	7	2	2	5	1	3.77				
GENO MILZIE	2	0	0	0	1	0	4.50				
IVAN ZYZNA (L)	0	1	1	1	0	0	1.29				
TEXAS RANGERS											
BATTING	AB	R	H	RBI	2B	3B	HR	BB	SO	BA	
RICHIE YOUNG JR 2B	5	1	2	0	1	0	0	0	0	.277	
ADRIAN MOLINA CF	5	0	2	1	1	0	0	0	0	.279	
WILLARD CHANDLER RF	4	0	0	0	0	0	0	0	2	.277	
RYAN ROSE LF	4	0	1	0	0	0	0	0	0	.276	
FRANK SOWELL SS	4	0	1	0	0	0	0	0	0	.271	
NICK MARSANS 1B	4	1	1	1	0	0	1	0	0	.265	
ARTHUR DAHLGREN DH	4	1	1	1	0	0	1	0	0	.327	
MIGUEL BELTRE 3B	4	0	0	0	0	0	0	1	1	.194	
JUAN CEPEDA C	3	0	0	0	0	0	0	0	2	.255	
PITCHING	IP	H	R	ER	SO	BB	ERA				
CARY SIMON (W)	8	8	8	1	6	3	2.57				
TINO FERNANDEZ (S)	1	0	0	0	0	0	1.59				

INNING	1	2	3	4	5	6	7	8	9	10	TOTAL
CLEVELAND	0	0	0	0	0	0	0	0	2	0	2
TEXAS	1	1	0	0	0	0	0	0	0	1	3

GAME 24

By SAM LARDNER

The Cleveland Press

ARLINGTON, Texas, May 2 — The Indians needed a breath of fresh air Sunday, and they got it at Globe Life Field — and from Globe Life Field.

The Tribe lost the first two games of this four-game set, both with the retractable roof closed. But on a bright late-Sunday afternoon, the Rangers rolled back the roof, and the Indians rolled out their power during a 7–3 victory.

Home runs by Oliver Reiner, Wilson White and hot-hitting Micah Millison routed Rangers starting pitcher Javy Oliva as the Indians had a rare big lead.

"Wow," said Indians manager Todd Stein. "They had the air conditioning turned on here the first two nights, but the natural a/c really made that ball carry today. This place is really two different ballparks depending on whether the roof is open or closed. It reminded me of the old days here, when the ball always seemed to carry.

"But, hey, the way things have been going for us, we'll take it."

Oliver Reiner hit a two-run homer in the second inning after Terry Rovetto led off with a walk. Reiner's ball got up and seemed to keep carrying as it sailed over the wall in center field.

"I thought I caught it pretty good, but not that good," Reiner said. "I kept running hard because I thought it might go off the wall. But when it went over the wall, I was able to slow down and enjoy a home run trot.

We had a couple balls knocked down here the first night, so I guess it all evens out."

Millison, who has been the talk of the club since he took over for Huron Southworth, hit a three-run homer in the fourth. Iceberg Peters, who started to give Morris Jerome a day off, doubled to lead off and Rikki LaBudda walked and stole his sixth base. Millison cranked a 2–0 pitch over the wall in right. This one might have been gone if there was a gale blowing against it.

"I was sitting on dead-red (fastball) on 2–0," Millison said. "He came in with one. That gave us a little breathing room."

The beneficiary of that breathing room was Kenny Camden. The Wiz weaved six innings of four-hit, one-run ball, giving up a harmless solo homer to Miguel Beltre in the fifth.

"I was a little worried when I saw our guys hitting them," Camden said with a laugh. "I thought it was going to be one of those days where both sides would hit about five apiece and the score would be 11–10. Fortunately, I was able to keep the ball in the park today."

White added a two-run homer in the seventh after Millison walked. The Rangers scored a pair in the bottom of the eighth against Lorry Unger, on for some mop-up work.

"It seems like every game we've played this year has been tense," Stein said. "I know that's not been the case, but when you're in the position we're in (9–15 record), every game is a battle. I know I've said it 100 times, but maybe this can relax us and start us on that roll we know is in there and that we're capable of."

GAME 24

CLEVELAND INDIANS VS TEXAS RANGERS · MAY 2
CLEVELAND 7 / TEXAS 3

CLEVELAND INDIANS										
BATTING	AB	R	H	RBI	2B	3B	HR	BB	SO	BA
RIKKI LABUDDA CF	5	1	1	0	0	1	0	0	1	.278
MICAH MILLISON LF	4	2	1	3	1	0	1	1	1	.290
WILSON WHITE RF	5	1	2	2	0	0	1	0	0	.272
TERRY ROVETTO 3B	4	1	0	0	0	0	0	1	1	.303
OLIVER REINER 1B	4	1	2	2	0	0	1	0	1	.264
JUSTIN KESTINO SS	4	0	1	0	0	0	0	1	0	.247
BERNARD HARPER DH	4	0	2	0	0	0	0	0	0	.333
ANGEL RODRIGUEZ 2B	3	0	1	0	0	0	0	0	1	.184
SCOTT MICHAELS 2B	1	0	1	0	0	0	0	0	0	.333
ICEBERG PETERS C	4	1	1	0	1	0	0	0	1	.222
PITCHING	IP	H	R	ER	SO	BB	ERA			
KENNY CAMDEN (W)	6	4	1	1	5	1	3.89			
LORRY UNGER	3	3	2	2	2	0	4.50			

TEXAS RANGERS										
BATTING	AB	R	H	RBI	2B	3B	HR	BB	SO	BA
RICHIE YOUNG JR 2B	4	0	1	0	0	0	0	0	0	.275
ADRIAN MOLINA CF	4	0	0	0	0	0	0	0	1	.264
WILLARD CHANDLER RF	4	0	1	0	1	0	0	0	2	.275
RYAN ROSE LF	4	1	1	0	0	0	0	0	0	.274
FRANK SOWELL SS	4	1	1	0	0	0	0	0	0	.270
NICK MARSANS 1B	4	0	0	0	0	0	0	0	2	.245
ARTHUR DAHLGREN DH	4	0	1	2	1	0	0	0	0	.321
MIGUEL BELTRE 3B	4	1	2	1	0	0	1	1	1	.211
JUAN CEPEDA C	3	0	0	0	0	0	0	0	1	.240
PITCHING	IP	H	R	ER	SO	BB	ERA			
JAVY OLIVA (L)	5	8	5	5	4	2	4.34			
CLEON LEFLOR	2	3	2	2	1	1	4.00			
GABE KINDER	2	2	0	0	1	0	3.32			

INNING	1	2	3	4	5	6	7	8	9	TOTAL
CLEVELAND	0	2	0	3	0	0	2	0	0	7
TEXAS	0	0	0	0	1	0	2	0	0	3

GAME 25

By SAM LARDNER

The Cleveland Press

ARLINGTON, Texas, May 3 — The road trip that seemed like it would never end finally did end for the Indians Monday night.

The dreaded wraparound series — Friday to Monday — made for a long weekend in Texas, but the Indians made the best of it with a 7–1 victory over the Rangers for a split of the four-game series.

So, the three-city 11-game trip that began in Boston with an intermediate stop in Oakland ended with the Tribe posting a 5–6 record.

Could have been better.

Could have been worse, especially since the Indians were swept in Boston to begin their wandering.

"Whew!" said manager Todd Stein. "That was some trip. The guys are tired, but give them credit for how they responded tonight. Now we get a day off and get to play at home. At the end of the year, you play 81 home and 81 on the road. Sure, you would rather not travel all over the country on a trip, but that's just how it worked out."

The Indians head home with a 10–15 record after getting off to an 0–6 start. Tak Fujimoto was the man of the moment again in the series finale with the Rangers. He posted his second straight victory and has allowed only one run in those starts.

On Monday, it was a 6 and two-thirds inning performance with the pitch count (111) finally forcing Stein to pull him in the seventh. Fujimoto gave up the Rangers' only run while walking two and striking out six.

"I was looking forward to pitching down here," Fujimoto said through his translator. "I remember (former Ranger) Yu Darvish having a lot of success at the old ballpark here. This place, with the roof closed, is a pretty good place to pitch."

Fujimoto mowed down the first nine Rangers he faced before giving up a leadoff triple to Alberto Rodriguez and an RBI groundout by Pedro Rivera.

From there, it was all Indians.

Scott Michaels, getting the start at second base over Angel Rodriguez, cracked a two-run homer in the fifth after Terry Rovetto walked. Michaels went 2-for-4 and may be giving Stein food for thought as far as playing time at second base.

"Scott is healthy, and that's the key," Stein said, referring to the shoulder problems that plagued Michaels in the past. "We want to keep him healthy. Angel has been a little beat up, so Scott is going to get some chances. We'll see how it works out." J.J. Kulakofski also got a rare start to rest Oliver Reiner and he responded with two hits today.

The Indians loaded the bases with nobody out in the sixth and scored four runs to blow the game open. Back-to-back two-run doubles by Morris Jerome and Rikki LaBudda made quick work of Rangers starter Gary Helms.

"They got us lightning quick," said Rangers manager Jimmy Degnan. "They're going to be a dangerous club if they can put things together. I'm not going to want to face them later on this summer."

Huron Southworth, getting a start at DH, added a solo homer in the eighth. The Indians got good bullpen work from Solly Alvarez and Mickey Penney, giving the back of the pen a break.

The Tribe heads home having won two straight games for the fourth time this season. The problem has been putting together a longer streak. They've not won three in a row so far.

Perhaps some home cooking can fix that.

"We'll see," said Stein, who is 8–7 as interim boss. "We've been close to busting out a few times. In a couple of games, we were our own worst enemy, with either mistakes in the field or giving up too many walks. If we can go on that run that we've talked about and get to .500, we can really take off from there. At least that's what I think.

"Let's get home and see what happens."

GAME 25

CLEVELAND INDIANS VS TEXAS RANGERS • MAY 3
CLEVELAND 7 / TEXAS 1

CLEVELAND INDIANS										
BATTING	AB	R	H	RBI	2B	3B	HR	BB	SO	BA
RIKKI LABUDDA CF	5	0	1	2	1	0	0	0	1	.275
MICAH MILLISON LF	5	0	1	0	0	0	0	0	1	.284
TERRY ROVETTO 3B	4	1	0	0	0	0	0	1	0	.290
SCOTT MICHAELS 2B	4	1	2	2	0	0	1	1	1	.357
WILSON WHITE RF	5	0	2	0	0	0	0	0	1	.278
JUSTIN KESTINO SS	4	1	1	0	0	0	0	1	0	.247
JJ KULAKOFSKI 1B	4	1	2	0	0	0	0	0	0	.205
HURON SOUTHWORTH DH	4	2	2	1	0	0	1	0	1	.195
MORRIS JEROME C	4	1	1	2	1	0	0	0	1	.247
PITCHING	IP	H	R	ER	SO	BB	ERA			
TAK FUJIMOTO (W)	6.67	3	1	1	6	2	3.89			
SOLLY ALVAREZ	1.33	2	0	0	1	0	3.18			
MICKEY PENNY	1	1	0	0	2	0	5.73			

TEXAS RANGERS										
BATTING	AB	R	H	RBI	2B	3B	HR	BB	SO	BA
ALBERTO RODRIGUEZ SS	4	1	1	0	0	1	0	0	1	.241
PEDRO RIVERA 2B	4	0	0	1	0	0	0	1	1	.262
MIGUEL BELTRE 3B	4	0	1	0	0	0	0	0	2	.213
NICK MARSANS 1B	4	0	2	0	1	0	0	0	0	.263
ARTHUR DAHLGREN DH	4	0	1	0	0	0	0	0	0	.317
WILLARD CHANDLER RF	4	0	0	0	0	0	0	1	2	.260
ADRIAN MOLINA CF	4	0	1	0	0	0	0	0	0	.263
RYAN ROSE LF	3	0	0	0	0	0	1	1	1	.264
ROGER BRIDWELL C	3	0	0	0	0	0	0	0	2	.240
PITCHING	IP	H	R	ER	SO	BB	ERA			
TERRY SHIPP (L)	6	8	6	6	4	2	4.50			
JOHAN CONCEPCION	1	1	0	0	1	1	2.84			
RUEBEN SORIANO	1	2	1	1	1	0	3.68			
GABE KINDER	1	1	0	0	0	0	3.15			

INNING	1	2	3	4	5	6	7	8	9	TOTAL
CLEVELAND	0	0	0	0	2	4	0	1	0	7
TEXAS	0	0	0	1	0	0	0	0	0	1

GAME 26

By **SAM LARDNER**
The Cleveland Press

CLEVELAND, May 4 — Attention, Cleveland Indians: It's OK. You're home. Start playing like it.

The Indians came home to Progressive Field Wednesday night on a high and left on a low. After winning their final two games at Texas to end a long road trip, the Tribe returned to a nice midweek crowd of 27,873 but sent the fans home shaking their heads after a dismal 4–0 loss to the Seattle Mariners.

So once again, the Indians were thwarted in their bid to put together their first three-game winning streak of the season.

"No excuses," said interim manager Todd Stein. "We had a day off after the road trip and should have been energized by the home crowd. They came out on a May weeknight to support us, and we didn't give them much of a show. I wish I could explain it."

We'll try for you, Skipper.

The Indians aren't getting much consistency with either their much-hyped offense or their starting pitching.

The hitters managed just four hits off Mariners starting pitcher Dino Toban and none against two relievers as they went quietly into that good night. That was on the heels of scoring a combined 13 runs in the final two games at Texas, including some good situational hitting in the series finale.

Ace pitcher Lynn Moda has had a start-and-stop beginning to his season, and it was more of the latter against the Mariners. Moda lasted five innings, giving up all four runs on nine hits and four walks. He left having thrown 102 pitches in the short outing.

"I thought I had some things figured out, but obviously not," said Moda, who posted an impressive victory at Oakland his previous time out. "Tonight, I fell behind in the count too many times. No feel for the changeup or the breaking ball. But I'm not going to get down on myself. I will climb out of this inconsistency and so will the team."

The Mariners took the starch out of the crowd with a pair of runs in the first inning. The dreaded leadoff walk came back to haunt Moda as he put leadoff man Vance Roberts on base on four pitches. Christian Romo singled, and Xavier Battle's double brought both runners home. That prompted a rare early visit to the mound by Stein, not the pitching coach.

"I just wanted to let Modes know that he couldn't let this thing get away from us early," Stein said. "He did settle down after that. Problem was, we didn't do anything to help him."

As long as we're writing memos to get the attention of the Indians, we might as well send one to Stein if he hopes to jump-start the offense: You might want to start Scott Michaels again. Michaels finished nicely at Texas but found himself on the bench again Wednesday as Angel Rodriguez played — and went 0-for-4.

The Mariners scored twice in the fifth as Charlie Dwyer touched Moda for a two-run homer. The only extra-base hit for the Indians came when Micah Millison doubled in the fourth. He was left stranded. They got widely scattered singles from Justin Kestino, Morris Jerome and Rikki LaBudda, but never seriously threatened.

"Disappointing," Stein said. "We've already made one lineup change with Millie going in for (Huron) Southworth. Angel's defense is so important to us, but we may have to look at some things there, too. We have to get this thing going, and sooner rather than later."

GAME 26

CLEVELAND INDIANS VS SEATTLE MARINERS • MAY 4
SEATTLE 4 / CLEVELAND 0

CLEVELAND INDIANS										
BATTING	AB	R	H	RBI	2B	3B	HR	BB	SO	BA
RIKKI LABUDDA CF	4	0	1	0	0	0	0	0	1	.274
MICAH MILLISON LF	4	0	1	0	1	0	0	0	1	.282
TERRY ROVETTO 3B	4	0	0	0	0	0	0	1	0	.278
OLIVER REINER 1B	4	0	0	0	0	0	0	1	0	.253
WILSON WHITE RF	4	0	0	0	0	0	0	0	1	.267
JUSTIN KESTINO SS	4	0	1	0	0	0	0	1	1	.247
BERNARD HARPER DH	4	0	0	0	0	0	0	0	0	.308
MORRIS JEROME C	4	0	1	0	0	0	0	0	1	.247
ANGEL RODRIGUEZ 2B	4	0	0	0	0	0	0	0	1	.170
PITCHING	IP	H	R	ER	SO	BB	ERA			
LYNN MODA (L)	5	9	4	4	3	4	6.35			
LORRY UNGER	2	2	0	0	1	0	3.00			
GENO MILZIE	2	1	0	0	2	0	4.00			
SEATTLE MARINERS										
BATTING	AB	R	H	RBI	2B	3B	HR	BB	SO	BA
RAUL COTA 2B	4	1	1	0	0	0	0	0	0	.276
CHRISTIAN ROMO SS	3	1	2	0	0	0	0	1	0	.241
XAVIER BATTLE 3B	4	0	2	2	1	0	0	0	0	.286
COREY GILLESPIE LF	4	0	1	0	1	0	0	0	0	.262
HUGO VENEGAS DH	3	1	2	0	0	0	0	1	1	.317
CHARLIE DWYER RF	4	1	2	2	0	0	1	1	0	.273
BILLY NEVILLE 1B	3	0	2	0	1	0	0	1	0	.278
SKYLER TOWNSEND C	4	0	0	0	0	0	0	0	1	.284
ROBERTO AGUIRRE CF	4	0	1	0	0	0	0	0	1	.250
PITCHING	IP	H	R	ER	SO	BB	ERA			
DINO TOBAN (W)	7	4	0	0	6	1	3.65			
JALEN GATES	1	0	0	0	1	1	2.70			
KELVIN BILLINGSLEY	1	0	0	0	1	0	3.52			
INNING	1	2	3	4	5	6	7	8	9	TOTAL
SEATTLE	2	0	0	0	2	0	0	0	0	4
CLEVELAND	0	0	0	0	0	0	0	0	0	0

GAME 27

By SAM LARDNER
The Cleveland Press

CLEVELAND, May 5 — Home sweet home? More like home sweep home.

The Seattle Mariners, nobody's favorite to win the American League West, got out of Progressive Field Thursday night with a 5–3 victory over the Indians and a sweep of the short two-game series.

So the Indians have fallen completely flat on their faces after winning the final two games of their long road trip at Texas.

Is it even possible that the Indians were looking past the Mariners?

"No," snapped an angry manager Todd Stein. "We don't have that right. You've seen us play. You know our record. We can't afford to look past anybody, not even a high school team. So there was none of that. The Mariners are a major-league team with a lot of pride. We know that. We just didn't get the job done."

Stein should have added "again."

Stein mixed up the lineup again tonight giving Rikki LaBudda and Angel Rodriguez a day off by playing Kieran Catsef and Leo Taylor but without much success. For the second straight night, the Indians played uninspired and uninterested baseball. They did get a two-run homer from DH Bernard Harper, but that was in the seventh inning and well after the M's had taken a 5–0 lead.

Until then, it was more of the same old, same old for the Tribe, who fell to 10–17 overall and to 8–9 under interim skipper Stein. So the new-manager "bump" has clearly worn off, and it looks like this may be who the Indians are, no matter who is at the helm.

"I don't buy into that," Stein said. "We're only in early May, and it can take time for teams to hit their stride. But that said, we need to turn it around fast."

Lefty Ollie Gonzalez has not gotten much help from his teammates so far in the early going, either at the plate or in the field. He took another loss after working six innings and giving up all five Seattle runs.

Matt Connor hit a solo homer off Gonzalez in the third, and Ed Alpert touched him for another in the fourth.

It all came apart in the top of the sixth, when the M's sent nine men to the plate and score three more runs, essentially putting the game away.

"Everybody has talked about a lack of support or whatever," Gonzalez said. "But that wasn't it tonight. I completely lost it in the sixth, when we were still in the game. I know the guys have my back. I let them down tonight."

Back-to-back walks to Charlie Dwyer and Skyler Townsend portended evil things to come for Gonzalez. The bad luck that has plagued Gonzalez in the early going reared its head again when he got Nestor Sanchez to bunt right back to him, but nobody was at third base to cover on a possible force out, and by the time Gonzalez looked to first, Sanchez had beaten the ball out.

Vance Roberts's line drive to left went for a single that scored one run and left the bases loaded. Xavier Battle then hit a single deep enough to score two more.

"Those are the kinds of things that have hurt us," Stein said. "We just can't seem to shut down the big inning, whether it's a mistake in the field or walks. Them going up 5–0 on us seemed to take the life out of the entire ballpark."

Not only that, many in the crowd of 20,065 booed the Tribe off the field when the inning ended. Harper's late homer brought little more than yawns from those who remained. They likely were lulled to sleep by Mariners starting pitcher Tyrell Bishop, who allowed three hits while striking out eight over seven innings. Tony Dos Santos pitched a perfect ninth for the save.

But hey, the Tampa Bay Rays are coming to town for the weekend, so maybe the Indians can get well against them.

"You heard what I said a minute ago," Stein said. "I'm not getting into that. The Rays are a damn good club. If we're not ready, they're going to come in here and knock our heads off."

Wouldn't be the least bit surprising.

GAME 27

CLEVELAND INDIANS VS SEATTLE MARINERS • MAY 5
SEATTLE 5 / CLEVELAND 3

CLEVELAND INDIANS										
BATTING	**AB**	**R**	**H**	**RBI**	**2B**	**3B**	**HR**	**BB**	**SO**	**BA**
LEO TAYLOR 2B	4	0	1	0	0	0	0	0	1	.176
MICAH MILLISON RF	4	0	1	0	1	0	0	0	1	.280
TERRY ROVETTO 3B	4	0	0	0	0	0	0	1	0	.267
OLIVER REINER 1B	4	0	0	0	0	0	0	1	0	.242
WILSON WHITE LF	4	0	0	0	0	0	0	0	1	.257
JUSTIN KESTINO SS	4	0	1	0	0	0	0	1	1	.247
BERNARD HARPER DH	4	0	1	2	0	0	1	0	0	.286
MORRIS JEROME C	4	0	1	0	0	0	0	0	1	.247
KIERAN CATSEF CF	4	0	0	0	0	0	0	0	1	.133
PITCHING	**IP**	**H**	**R**	**ER**	**SO**	**BB**	**ERA**			
OLLIE GONZALEZ (L)	6	9	5	5	3	4	6.99			
MICKEY PENNY	2	2	0	0	1	0	4.85			
IVAN ZYZNA	2	1	0	0	2	0	1.13			
SEATTLE MARINERS										
BATTING	**AB**	**R**	**H**	**RBI**	**2B**	**3B**	**HR**	**BB**	**SO**	**BA**
NESTOR SANCHEZ DH	5	1	1	0	0	0	0	0	0	.264
VANCE ROBERTS 2B	5	0	1	1	0	0	0	1	0	.237
XAVIER BATTLE 3B	4	0	2	2	1	0	0	0	1	.295
ED ALPERT LF	4	1	1	1	1	0	1	0	0	.262
BILLY NEVILLE 1B	4	0	1	0	0	0	0	1	1	.277
ROBERTO AGUIRRE CF	4	0	0	0	0	0	0	1	2	.232
MATT CONNOR SS	4	1	1	1	1	0	1	1	0	.280
CHARLEY DWYER RF	4	1	1	0	0	0	0	0	1	.272
SKYLER TOWNSEND C	4	1	2	0	0	0	0	0	0	.296
PITCHING	**IP**	**H**	**R**	**ER**	**SO**	**BB**	**ERA**			
TYRELL BISHOP (W)	7	3	3	3	8	2	4.38			
MYA NAGAMOTO	1	0	0	0	1	1	3.27			
TONY DOS SANTOS (S)	1	0	0	0	1	0	2.74			
INNING	**1**	**2**	**3**	**4**	**5**	**6**	**7**	**8**	**9**	**TOTAL**
SEATTLE	0	0	1	1	0	3	0	0	0	5
CLEVELAND	0	0	0	0	0	3	0	2	0	3

GAME 28

By SAM LARDNER
The Cleveland Press

CLEVELAND, May 7 — Not exactly a rousing start to your weekend, eh, Cleveland?

The way the Indians' season is going, trips to the lake or car rides to the countryside will begin in earnest well before summer kicks in.

After all, there have to be better alternatives to the Indians, who aren't exactly making their case for their share of the entertainment dollar. As it was, a disappointing Friday night crowd of 21,112 came out and left wondering what they had just watched after the Tribe fell 10–3 to the Tampa Bay Rays at Progressive Field.

Clevelanders will applaud the effort even if the end result isn't there, but they're getting neither these days from their baseball team.

"I know the guys in there care," said interim manager Todd Stein, who saw his team fall to 10–18. "This was one of those nights where things just snowballed. Once again, we were in a game for much of the way before one big blow hurt us."

That big blow was a grand slam by the Rays' Tim Stafford in the fourth inning to turn a 2–0 lead against Brian Howard to 6–0.

And as we've seen all too often, the Indians went quietly after that.

Yes, you can say it's still "early" in the season, but it's starting to get late.

"Just a couple of bad pitches, and when you're going the way we're going, you never seem to get away with them," Howard said. "We're getting punished for every mistake. When you're winning, you get away with mistakes, and nobody even remembers that you've made them. Now, everything is magnified."

General manager J.D. Eisner made a rare on-field appearance before the game and was asked if any further shakeups were in order. Eisner fired manager Dave Mills after 10 games and replaced him with Stein. Before Friday's game, the Indians activated reliever Buck Sterling off the injured list and optioned Lorry Unger back to Class AAA Columbus.

"Nobody really talks trade this early in the year," Eisner said. "We've done some things internally, with giving Micah Millison the bulk of the starts. Right now, we think the solutions are from within. I understand the fans' impatience. They deserve better, and I can tell them that we feel the need to give it to them. Sometimes, it's about guys getting back to the approaches that made them successful instead of trying to press and gain back five games in one day."

In Friday's disaster, the Rays jumped on Howard with two runs in the second. Eric Miller doubled and went to third on Paul Duffy's sharp single to left field. Both runners came home on Brett Archer's double that rattled around the left-field corner, with Wilson White having trouble picking up the ball as the runners raced around the bases.

A single, an error by Justin Kestino and a walk in the fateful fourth loaded the bases for Stafford, who deposited a hanging slider from Howard to the back of the bleachers in left field. That ended Howard's night after 3 and two-thirds innings. Sterling got three innings of long relief work, with Solly Alvarez getting some all-too-familiar mop-up work.

Once again, the Indians' runs were of the consolation variety. Scott Michaels hit an RBI single in the fifth. Millison added a two-run double in the eighth, after most of the crowd had left to finish their evenings elsewhere.

"We don't have time to get down about this," Stein said. "We have to come right back tomorrow. That's the beauty of this game. You can forget about games like this quickly."

CLEVELAND INDIANS VS TAMPA BAY RAYS • MAY 7
TAMPA BAY 10 / CLEVELAND 3

CLEVELAND INDIANS

BATTING	AB	R	H	RBI	2B	3B	HR	BB	SO	BA
RIKKI LABUDDA CF	4	1	1	0	0	0	0	0	1	.273
MICAH MILLISON LF	4	0	1	2	1	0	0	0	0	.278
TERRY ROVETTO 3B	4	0	0	0	0	0	0	1	1	.257
OLIVER REINER 1B	4	1	2	0	0	0	0	0	0	.252
WILSON WHITE LF	3	0	1	0	0	0	0	0	0	.259
JUSTIN KESTINO SS	4	0	1	0	0	0	0	1	1	.247
BERNARD HARPER DH	4	0	0	0	0	0	0	0	2	.267
MORRIS JEROME C	3	1	2	0	0	0	0	0	1	.262
SCOTT MICHAELS 2B	2	0	1	1	0	0	0	2	1	.367

PITCHING	IP	H	R	ER	SO	BB	ERA
BRIAN HOWARD (L)	3.67	7	6	4	3	2	4.41
BUCK STERLING	3.33	4	2	2	1	1	6.95
SOLLY ALVAREZ	2	1	0	0	2	0	4.73

TAMPA BAY RAYS

BATTING	AB	R	H	RBI	2B	3B	HR	BB	SO	BA
REGGIE PATTERSON CF	5	0	1	0	0	0	0	0	0	.264
RODRIGO BENITEZ SS	5	2	2	1	0	0	0	1	0	.254
BRANDON GREGERSON DH	5	1	2	2	1	0	0	0	1	.295
FRANK MORETTI C	4	1	0	0	0	0	0	0	0	.246
ERIC MILLER 2B	4	2	2	0	0	0	0	1	1	.289
TIM STAFFORD LF	4	1	2	4	0	0	1	1	2	.268
PAUL DUFFY 3B	4	1	3	1	1	0	0	1	0	.307
BRETT ARCHER 1B	4	0	1	2	0	0	0	0	1	.272
LUIS CRESPO RF	4	2	2	0	0	0	0	0	0	.296

PITCHING	IP	H	R	ER	SO	BB	ERA
LUIS DURANGO (W)	6	7	1	1	7	3	4.03
LIAM MURPHY	2	2	2	2	1	1	2.84
ADOLFO VASQUEZ	1	1	0	0	1	0	2.74

INNING	1	2	3	4	5	6	7	8	9	TOTAL
TAMPA BAY	0	2	0	4	0	2	0	1	1	10
CLEVELAND	0	0	0	0	1	0	0	2	0	3

GAME 29

By SAM LARDNER
The Cleveland Press

CLEVELAND, May 8 — Fireworks. Yeah, that'll get 'em out to the ballpark. The Indians drew a Saturday night crowd of 37,261 for the 6:05 p.m. start and postgame fireworks show. But those weren't the only fireworks.

The in-game pyrotechnics display by interim manager Todd Stein and pitcher Kenny Camden fired up the big crowd who witnessed both men being ejected by umpire Lee Mason after some high-and-tight pitching during the seventh inning of the Tribe's 6–5 victory over the Tampa Bay Rays. Whether that sparks the Indians on to better things remains to be seen, but at this point, it can't hurt.

"Sometimes you need a little of that, but I can tell you this: There was nothing calculated about it," Stein said after his team snapped a three-game losing streak and improved to 11–18.

Stein watched the final innings of the game from the comfort of his office after getting tossed. The back-and-forth game took a nasty turn in the bottom of the sixth, when Terry Rovetto hit a three-run homer to tie the game at 5–5.

No sooner had the noise died down before Oliver Reiner put the Tribe ahead on the next pitch with his fifth homer down the line in left. Reiner pumped his fist in an uncharacteristic display of emotion as he rounded first base.

That caught the eye of Rays pitcher Jose Diaz, who plunked Justin Kestino in the backside on the first pitch of the at-bat. Kestino glared out to the mound for a few seconds before heading to first base.

Camden apparently made a mental note of it and hit Rays batter Roberto Gonzalez leading off the top of the seventh. Even though no warnings were issued, Mason immediately tossed both Camden and Stein, bringing Stein out of the dugout for a prolonged display of anger directed at Mason.

"Give me a break," Stein said. "I may get fined for this, but they hit our guy after we hit two homers, and it looked pretty obvious to me. Then our guy hits a guy, and without a warning, he gets tossed. That's not how it's supposed to work. Their guy got away with one, and our guy was kicked out."

Camden was equally upset. "In a one-run game, I'm not trying to put anybody on," he said after winning his second straight decision. "That's total horse(bleep). The problem with these rules is that the umpire becomes a mind reader. I'd love to have that talent." Camden's words dripped with sarcasm, but Rays manager Thomas Brady said Camden had the ejection coming.

"Seemed pretty obvious to me," Brady said. "The ball got away from Diaz when he hit Kestino. Camden fired it right at Gonzalez' back."

When the dust cleared, the Indians got hitless relief from back-end standouts Geno Milzie and Ivan Zyzna, who picked up the save.

"Let's not forget about that bullpen work," Stein said. "Those two guys really shut down this game."

Camden wasn't his sharpest, giving up six hits and five runs. The Indians took a 2–0 lead in the first. Rikki LaBudda walked and stole second base. He scored on Millison's single. Wilson White then doubled home Millison. The Rays got two in the second against Camden on a two-run double by Randy McGee. Tampa Bay took a 5–2 lead in the third on Brett Archer's three-run homer.

Amid the clubhouse celebration, Reiner took issue with the Rays thinking he was trying to show them up. "I've been in this game 10 years, and I've never done that," he said. "I got caught up in the game situation. And if you hadn't noticed, we haven't played well, so I was happy to hit the homer. But the idea that I was trying to showboat or show them up is ridiculous. We'll see what happens tomorrow."

More fireworks? As Reiner said, we'll see.

GAME 29

CLEVELAND INDIANS VS TAMPA BAY RAYS · MAY 8
CLEVELAND 6 / TAMPA BAY 5

CLEVELAND INDIANS

BATTING	AB	R	H	RBI	2B	3B	HR	BB	SO	BA
RIKKI LABUDDA CF	5	2	2	0	0	0	0	0	1	.278
MICAH MILLISON LF	5	1	1	1	1	0	0	0	0	.274
WILSON WHITE RF	4	0	1	1	0	0	0	1	1	.259
TERRY ROVETTO 3B	4	1	2	3	0	0	1	0	0	.266
OLIVER REINER 1B	4	1	1	1	0	0	1	0	0	.252
JUSTIN KESTINO SS	4	0	0	0	0	0	0	1	1	.238
BERNARD HARPER DH	4	0	1	0	0	0	0	0	2	.266
MORRIS JEROME C	4	0	1	0	0	0	0	0	1	.261
ANGEL RODRIGUEZ 2B	3	1	1	0	0	0	0	2	1	.179
SCOTT MICHAELS 2B	1	0	0	0	0	0	0	0	1	.355

PITCHING	IP	H	R	ER	SO	BB	ERA			
KENNY CAMDEN (W)	6	6	5	5	4	1	4.43			
GENO MILZIE	2	3	0	0	2	0	3.60			
IVAN ZYZNA (S)	1	0	0	0	1	0	1.06			

TAMPA BAY RAYS

BATTING	AB	R	H	RBI	2B	3B	HR	BB	SO	BA
REGGIE PATTERSON CF	5	0	1	0	0	0	0	0	1	.259
PAUL DUFFY 3B	5	0	0	0	0	0	0	0	1	.288
BRANDON GREGERSON DH	4	0	0	0	1	0	0	0	1	.283
FRANK MORETTI C	4	0	2	1	0	0	0	0	0	.261
ERIC MILLER 2B	4	0	1	0	0	0	0	0	1	.287
TIM STAFFORD LF	4	1	1	0	0	0	1	0	2	.267
ROBERTO GONZALEZ RF	3	2	0	0	1	0	0	1	0	.233
RANDY MCGEE SS	4	1	2	2	0	0	0	0	1	.284
BRETT ARCHER 1B	4	1	2	2	0	0	1	0	0	.282

PITCHING	IP	H	R	ER	SO	BB	ERA			
JOSE DIAZ (L)	6	7	1	1	7	3	4.38			
DON DAVENPORT	2	2	2	2	1	1	3.60			
BUDDY ANDERSON	1	1	0	0	1	0	3.00			

INNING	1	2	3	4	5	6	7	8	9	TOTAL
TAMPA BAY	0	2	3	0	0	0	0	0	0	5
CLEVELAND	2	0	0	0	0	4	0	0		6

GAME 30

By SAM LARDNER
The Cleveland Press

CLEVELAND, May 9 — There were no residual fireworks Sunday at Progressive Field. You need a spark for that, and the Indians had none.

One night after tempers flared between the Indians and the Tampa Bay Ray, Sunday's game was as subdued as a leisurely stroll through the park.

Indians batters wasted a decent start by Tak Fujimoto by managing just five hits against Rays starter Laz Reeder and the Tampa Bay bullpen during a 3–1 loss. For his part, Fujimoto turned in a quality start, going six innings and giving up all three Rays runs on seven hits.

Before the game, umpires talked to each manager but issued no formal warnings in the wake of Saturday night's festivities, which included batters being hit on both sides and Indians manager Todd Stein being ejected along with Tribe starter Kenny Camden.

"It didn't affect me," Fujimoto said through his translator. "Everything was taken care of last night. I wasn't going to hit anybody and get thrown out of the game in the first inning. That wouldn't be smart. I just wanted to pitch my game."

And he did. It was a creditable effort, as Fujimoto gave up a run in the fourth and two in the fifth. But the Tribe could get only a run in the bottom of the fifth and nothing more after that.

"Give Tak credit," Stein said. "He battled. I thought his stuff was pretty good. There are a lot of good-hitting clubs in this league. I consider us one of those, but we need to be able to overcome a 3–0 deficit. But all in all, we played well in the field."

Fujimoto gave up three straight singles to score a run in the fourth, with Reggie Patterson getting the RBI after Eric Miller and Gilberto Ayarza hitting singles ahead of him.

In the fifth, Rays backup catcher Kevin Serrano hit a double to center field to score Luis Crespo and Brandon Grergerson.

"Just a mistake to Serrano," Fujimoto said. "That's a guy I shouldn't let beat me. I'm finding out over here that you can't afford to take any hitter lightly. There is much more depth to these lineups."

The Indians got a run-scoring single from their own backup catcher, Iceberg Peters, who drove in Kieran Catsef after Catsef doubled. But a double-play grounder on a hard-hit ball by the speedy Rikki LaBudda ended the inning.

"Bad break there," Stein said. "Rikki hit the (bleep) out of that ball but right at their second baseman. Nobody beats that one out."

Hard-throwing Buddy Anderson wound up with the save as he struck out two of the three Indians batters he faced in the bottom of the ninth.

"Call me crazy, but I think we're getting there," Peters said. "Tak pitched a good game today, and we couldn't catch a break. I observe a lot on the bench, and I think you're going to see this turn in our favor really soon."

CLEVELAND INDIANS VS TAMPA BAY RAYS • MAY 9
TAMPA BAY 3 / CLEVELAND 1

CLEVELAND INDIANS										
BATTING	AB	R	H	RBI	2B	3B	HR	BB	SO	BA
RIKKI LABUDDA CF	4	0	0	0	0	0	0	0	1	.269
MICAH MILLISON LF	4	0	0	0	0	0	0	0	0	.261
TERRY ROVETTO 3B	4	0	0	0	0	0	0	1	1	.257
OLIVER REINER 1B	4	0	1	0	0	0	0	0	0	.252
JUSTIN KESTINO SS	4	0	0	0	0	0	0	0	2	.229
HURON SOUTHWORTH DH	4	0	1	0	0	0	0	0	1	.200
ANGEL RODRIGUEZ 2B	3	0	1	0	0	0	0	1	0	.186
KIERAN CATSEF RF	4	1	1	0	1	0	0	0	2	.158
ICEBERG PETERS C	4	0	1	1	0	0	0	0	1	.227
PITCHING	IP	H	R	ER	SO	BB	ERA			
TAK FUJIMOTO (L)	6	7	3	3	4	1	3.98			
BUCK STERLING	3	2	0	0	1	0	6.15			

TAMPA BAY RAYS										
BATTING	AB	R	H	RBI	2B	3B	HR	BB	SO	BA
REGGIE PATTERSON CF	4	0	1	2	1	0	0	0	0	.258
PAUL DUFFY 3B	3	0	0	0	0	0	0	1	1	.277
RODRIGO BENITEZ SS	4	0	1	0	1	0	0	0	1	.254
ERNESTO JURADO 1B	4	0	0	0	0	0	0	0	0	.296
BRANDON GREGERSON DH	4	1	2	0	0	0	0	0	1	.292
LUIS CRESPO LF	4	1	1	0	0	0	0	0	1	.293
KEVIN SERRANO C	4	0	1	1	1	0	0	0	0	.243
ERIC MILLER 2B	4	1	1	0	0	0	0	0	1	.286
GILBERTO AYARZA RF	4	0	1	0	0	0	0	0	0	.243
PITCHING	IP	H	R	ER	SO	BB	ERA			
LAZ REEDER (W)	8	4	1	1	6	1	3.65			
BUDDY ANDERSON (S)	1	1	0	0	2	0	2.84			

INNING	1	2	3	4	5	6	7	8	9	TOTAL
TAMPA BAY	0	0	0	1	2	0	0	0	0	3
CLEVELAND	0	0	0	0	1	0	0	0	0	1

GAME 31

By SAM LARDNER
The Cleveland Press

CLEVELAND, May 10 — To his credit, Lynn Moda is the first to say that he has not pitched like an ace so far this season.

But in Monday night's series opener against the Baltimore Orioles at Progressive Field, Moda was dealing. He turned in a seven-inning performance, giving up five hits and two runs as the Indians cruised past the O's 7–2.

Granted, the Orioles aren't exactly off to a great start — neither are the Tribe — but Moda looked in complete command as he threw an even 100 pitches over his seven innings. He got some early help with a three-run homer by Bernard Harper in the second inning and a four-run outburst in the fifth that finished off Orioles starting pitcher Ronaldo Bucardo.

"Run support is nice, but the bottom line is I have to do my job, and that hasn't always been the case so far," said Moda, who was coming off a 4–0 loss to the Seattle Mariners. "So I felt good tonight about the stuff I had and the confidence I felt out there on the mound. I know the team is counting on me, and I want to justify their faith in me."

Interim manager Todd Stein's crew improved to 12–19 with a chance to make some hay against the lowly O's.

"We don't look at it that way," Stein said. "Anybody can come in here and beat you, and unfortunately for us, we've experienced it. But Modes was really locked in tonight. It all starts with that. Get a quality start and you really give yourself a chance to win. Of course, we put up a few runs in bursts, and something we've been lacking."

Moda got three quick groundball outs in the first inning to set the tone for the rest of the night. He was around the plate all game, and the young and aggressive Baltimore batters obliged with some first-pitch swinging in the early innings.

Terry Rovetto led off the home second with a single, and after Oliver Reiner struck out, he went to second on a walk to Scott Michaels, getting another start with Angel Rodriguez's achy back acting up again. After Justin Kestino struck out, DH Bernard Harper went deep, sending a fastball from Bucardo 444 feet out to right-center.

"Being the DH, I'm able to look at the other pitcher on the monitor," Harper said. "I had a pretty good idea of what he'd do. He's got a good arm, but he's young, and he gave in to me when the count got to 3–1."

The Indians put it away for good in the fifth, sending 10 men to the plate and chasing Bucardo with only one out. Rikki LaBudda sparked things with a bunt single to lead off and stole second base. Bucardo got his only out, a strikeout of Micah Millison, before the Indians began their hit barrage. Wilson White's single sent LaBudda to third, and Terry Rovetto doubled both runners home.

Oliver Reiner's single scored Rovetto, with Michaels hitting a single to put runners on the corners. A walk to Justin Kestino loaded the bases, and Reiner scored on Morris Jerome's high chopper that went for a single.

The Orioles got a meaningless run in the top of the sixth against Moda on an RBI double by Jules Peterson after Barbaro Castro walked.

From there, relievers Buck Sterling and Mickey Penney finished up without incident.

"This is more of what we have been expecting," Stein said. "Our offense is just too good to keep down. It wasn't all home runs, either. We kept the line moving pretty good in that one inning. I think that as the weather warms up, we'll see more of that."

CLEVELAND INDIANS VS BALTIMORE ORIOLES • MAY 10
CLEVELAND 7 / BALTIMORE 2

CLEVELAND INDIANS										
BATTING	AB	R	H	RBI	2B	3B	HR	BB	SO	BA
RIKKI LABUDDA CF	5	1	2	0	0	0	0	0	0	.274
MICAH MILLISON LF	4	0	1	0	0	0	0	1	0	.261
WILSON WHITE RF	4	1	1	0	0	0	0	1	1	.259
TERRY ROVETTO 3B	4	2	2	2	2	0	0	0	0	.265
OLIVER REINER 1B	4	0	1	1	0	0	0	0	1	.252
SCOTT MICHAELS 2B	2	2	1	0	0	0	0	2	1	.364
JUSTIN KESTINO SS	3	0	0	0	0	0	0	1	0	.222
BERNARD HARPER DH	4	1	1	3	0	0	1	0	1	.265
MORRIS JEROME C	4	0	2	1	0	0	0	0	1	.272
PITCHING	IP	H	R	ER	SO	BB	ERA			
LYNN MODA (W)	7	5	2	2	4	1	5.60			
BUCK STERLING	1	0	0	0	0	0	5.93			
MICKEY PENNY	1	1	0	0	0	0	4.50			

BALTIMORE ORIOLES										
BATTING	AB	R	H	RBI	2B	3B	HR	BB	SO	BA
BARBARO CASTRO SS	4	1	0	0	0	0	0	0	0	.293
JULES PETERSON 1B	4	0	1	1	1	0	0	1	0	.274
JORGE ESTRELLA 3B	4	0	1	0	1	0	0	0	1	.289
GREG VOIGHT 2B	4	0	0	0	0	0	0	1	0	.296
KEVIN BRADY CF	4	1	2	0	0	1	0	0	1	.292
RONALDO BUCARO DH	3	0	0	1	0	0	0	0	1	.284
LEROY CAMPBELL LF	4	0	1	0	0	0	0	0	0	.243
RODOLFO SANCHEZ RF	4	0	0	0	0	0	0	0	1	.275
TERRY SHINER C	4	0	1	0	0	0	0	0	0	.243
PITCHING	IP	H	R	ER	SO	BB	ERA			
RONALDO BUCARDO (L)	4.33	8	6	6	3	3	5.40			
JIM DECASTRO	2.67	3	1	1	2	1	3.74			
RODNEY DAVIS	1	0	0	0	0	1	4.00			

INNING	1	2	3	4	5	6	7	8	9	TOTAL
BALTIMORE	0	0	0	1	0	1	0	0	0	2
CLEVELAND	0	3	0	0	4	0	0	0		7

GAME 32

By SAM LARDNER
The Cleveland Press

CLEVELAND, May 11 — OK, now this is getting ridiculous. Just ask Ollie G. But do so at your own risk.

For what seems the umpteenth time this early season, Gonzalez was the victim of non-support by his teammates during a 3–2 loss to the Baltimore Orioles Tuesday night at Progressive Field. Over Gonzalez's last four starts, the Indians have scored a grand total of eight runs.

"There always seems to be that one guy on a staff," said manager Todd Stein. "Poor Ollie. It's been him over the first month of the season. I feel bad for him. He certainly pitched well enough to win. But he's a pro. He'll take the ball again and do his job."

You could hardly blame Gonzalez for being a little irritable in the post-game session with the media. But he wasn't throwing his teammates under the bus.

"No, no, no," he said. "I can't walk two guys in an inning, give up a home run and blame it on somebody else. That's on me. Our hitters are doing the best they can. They're going to bail me out more than I'm going to bail them out. So don't even go there."

The inning that did Gonzalez in was the fifth, and the game was score-less. It began innocently enough with an easy groundout off the bat of Orioles leadoff man Barbaro Castro. Somehow, Gonzalez lost his way and walked Greg Voight on four pitches and Jorge Estrella on a close 3–2 pitch.

He recovered to strike out Jules Peterson, but Kevin Brady jumped on a 3–0 pitch and sent it into the bleachers in left.

"That's what I was talking about," Gonzalez said. "You get behind in the count, and you ask for trouble. I got it."

The Indians didn't fold after that inning as they have so many times this season, but they didn't exactly mount a serious attack, either.

After barely touching junkballer, Ofilio Calderon, all night, they received a leadoff single by Scott Michaels in the bottom of the sixth. Michaels took second on Calderon's wild pitch and scored on Morris Jerome's one-out single.

They got another run in the bottom of the eighth on a solo homer by Micah Millison off reliever Anibal Novoa. But Orioles closer Isaac Crawford sent the Indians home in the ninth with barely a whimper.

Gonzalez wound up working six innings, giving up six hits and three walks.

"It seems like we've had a lot of these games, both for Ollie and as a team," Stein said. "But it's not for lack of effort or concentration. I can't say anything bad about either of those tonight. All Ollie has to do is hang in there, and things will turn. I know they will."

GAME 32

CLEVELAND INDIANS VS BALTIMORE ORIOLES · MAY 11
BALTIMORE 3 / CLEVELAND 2

CLEVELAND INDIANS										
BATTING	AB	R	H	RBI	2B	3B	HR	BB	SO	BA
RIKKI LABUDDA CF	4	0	1	0	0	0	0	1	0	.273
MICAH MILLISON LF	4	1	1	1	0	0	1	0	1	.260
TERRY ROVETTO 3B	4	0	0	0	0	0	0	0	2	.256
OLIVER REINER 1B	4	0	1	0	0	0	0	0	1	.252
JUSTIN KESTINO SS	4	0	2	0	1	0	0	0	0	.232
J.J.KULAKOFSKI DH	4	0	1	0	0	0	0	0	1	.209
SCOTT MICHAELS 2B	1	1	1	0	0	0	0	2	0	.382
HURON SOUTHWORTH RF	4	0	1	0	0	0	1	0	1	.204
MORRIS JEROME C	3	0	2	1	0	0	0	0	1	.284
PITCHING	IP	H	R	ER	SO	BB	ERA			
OLLIE GONZALEZ (L)	6	6	3	0	5	2	5.77			
GENO MILZIE	1.67	1	0	0	1	1	3.32			
SOLLY ALVAREZ	1.33	1	0	0	1	1	4.30			
BALTIMORE ORIOLES										
BATTING	AB	R	H	RBI	2B	3B	HR	BB	SO	BA
BARBARO CASTRO SS	4	0	1	0	0	0	0	0	0	.292
GREG VOIGHT 2B	3	1	0	0	0	0	0	2	2	.284
JORGE ESTRELLA 3B	3	1	1	0	1	0	0	1	1	.290
JULES PETERSON 1B	4	0	2	0	0	0	0	1	0	.284
KEVIN BRADY CF	4	1	2	3	0	0	1	0	1	.300
RONALDO BUCARO DH	4	0	0	0	0	0	0	0	1	.269
LEROY CAMPBELL LF	4	0	1	0	0	0	0	0	0	.244
RODOLFO SANCHEZ RF	4	0	0	0	0	0	0	0	1	.263
TERRY SHINER C	4	0	1	0	0	0	0	0	1	.243
PITCHING	IP	H	R	ER	SO	BB	ERA			
OFILIO CALDERON (W)	7	7	1	1	6	2	3.89			
ANIBAL NOVOA	1	3	1	1	0	1	3.32			
ISAAC CRAWFORD (S)	1	0	0	0	1	0	4.20			
INNING	1	2	3	4	5	6	7	8	9	TOTAL
BALTIMORE	0	0	0	0	3	0	0	0	0	3
CLEVELAND	0	0	0	0	0	1	0	1	0	2

GAME 33

By SAM LARDNER
The Cleveland Press

CLEVELAND, May 12 — Well how about this? The Cleveland Indians won themselves a series.

It took every bit of strength, resourcefulness and staying power the Indians had, but they managed to outlast the Baltimore Orioles 4–3 in 12 innings Wednesday night at Progressive Field. That enabled the Tribe to take two of three in the series. They enjoy a day off before heading to Detroit and Chicago.

Micah Millison's sacrifice fly drove in pinch runner Kieran Catsef from third base in the bottom of the 12th. Catsef went in for catcher Morris Jerome, who led off with a double. Rikki LaBudda bunted Catsef to third before Millison lifted a high fly ball into medium right field. Catsef slid home just as the throw was arriving at the plate.

"As soon as he (Orioles right fielder Wilfredo Murillo caught it), I was off," said Catsef, one of the Indians' bench players. "I put my head down and ran. I knew it was going to be close, but we were here long enough tonight, right?"

Right, Kieran. It's also right that there aren't any must-win game or series in May, but the Indians really did need this one. The victory improved their record to 13–20 overall and to 11–12 under interim manager Todd Stein.

"We did need this win," Stein said. "The thing I liked about it is that it was a real character test, and we came through with flying colors in that regard. We could have folded a couple times, but we didn't."

The Indians got a nice start from Brian Howard, who did not figure into the decision — the win went to Buck Sterling, who worked the 11th and 12th innings without giving up a hit. Howard lasted six innings, giving up six hits and two runs. He left with the game tied at 2–2.

"I'll take it," said Howard, who was on the wrong end of a 10–3 score to the Rays in his previous outing. "We had some pretty good starting pitching on this homestand, even in the games we didn't win. So I wanted to keep that going."

The Indians went up 2–0 in the third against O's starter Austin Blackwell. Bernard Harper walked and went to second on a passed ball. Jerome singled him home and went to third on Leo Taylor's single LaBudda bounced one up the middle for an RBI single.

The Orioles tied it in the fifth on a two-run homer by George Rader after Elmer Vega walked.

After the Indians went ahead in the bottom of the seventh on a solo shot by Wilson White, the Orioles tied it at 3–3 in the eighth as Geno Milzie suffered a blown save. Milzie gave up a leadoff walk to Barbaro Castro, and he came all the way around to score on Kevin Brady's double.

That was all the scoring until the 12th, as Milzie settled down and Ivan Zyzna worked the ninth before Solly Alvarez pitched the 10th.

"It stunk that I let that one get away," Milzie said. "But we pick each other up in that bullpen. Guys like Solly and Buck don't get a lot of attention, but they save us in a lot of games. That happened tonight."

Another road trip brings opportunity to the Tribe, who face two American League Central foes.

"You're always looking to take advantage of division games," Stein said. "We know a lot of our fans will make the trip to Detroit, and we'll see a few in Chicago, too. Just take care of our own business. That's all we can do."

CLEVELAND INDIANS VS BALTIMORE ORIOLES · MAY 12
CLEVELAND 4 / BALTIMORE 3

CLEVELAND INDIANS

BATTING	AB	R	H	RBI	2B	3B	HR	BB	SO	BA			
RIKKI LABUDDA CF	6	0	2	1	0	0	0	1	0	.276			
MICAH MILLISON LF	5	0	1	1	0	0	0	0	0	.257			
TERRY ROVETTO 3B	5	0	0	0	0	0	0	0	2	.246			
OLIVER REINER 1B	5	0	0	0	0	0	0	0	1	.242			
JUSTIN KESTINO SS	5	0	1	0	1	0	0	0	0	.231			
WILSON WHITE RF	4	1	1	1	0	0	1	0	1	.258			
BERNARD HARPER DH	4	1	1	0	0	0	0	2	0	.264			
MORRIS JEROME C	5	2	2	1	1	0	1	0	1	.290			
KIERAN CATSEF PR	0	0	0	0	0	0	0	0	0	.158			
LEO TAYLOR 2B	4	0	1	0	0	0	0	0	0	.176			

PITCHING	IP	H	R	ER	SO	BB	ERA						
BRIAN HOWARD	6	6	2	2	4	1	4.20						
GENO MILZIE (BS)	2	3	1	1	1	1	3.42						
IVAN ZYZNA	1	0	0	0	1	0	1.00						
SOLLY ALVAREZ	1	0	0	0	1	0	4.02						
BUCK STERLING (W)	2	0	0	0	2	0	5.52						

BALTIMORE ORIOLES

BATTING	AB	R	H	RBI	2B	3B	HR	BB	SO	BA			
BARBARO CASTRO SS	5	1	1	0	0	0	0	1	1	.287			
KEVIN BRADY CF	6	0	2	1	1	0	0	0	0	.302			
JORGE ESTRELLA 3B	5	0	0	0	0	0	0	0	2	.276			
JULES PETERSON 1B	5	0	1	0	0	0	0	0	2	.280			
ELMER VEGA LF	5	1	1	0	0	0	0	1	0	.254			
GEORGE RADER DH	5	1	2	2	1	0	1	0	1	.256			
RODOLFO SANCHEZ CF	4	0	0	0	0	0	0	0	0	.253			
WILFREDO MURILLO RF	4	0	1	0	0	0	0	0	2	.233			
TERRY SHINER C	4	0	1	0	0	0	0	0	1	.244			

PITCHING	IP	H	R	ER	SO	BB	ERA						
AUSTIN BLACKWELL	7	5	3	3	4	2	4.33						
LUIS RAUDEZ	2	1	0	0	1	0	3.86						
RODNEY DAVIS	2	1	0	0	1	1	3.60						
ISAAC CRAWFORD (L)	1	2	1	1	0	0	5.00						

INNING	1	2	3	4	5	6	7	8	9	10	11	12	TOTAL
BALTIMORE	0	0	0	0	2	0	0	1	0	0	0	0	3
CLEVELAND	0	0	2	0	0	0	1	0	0	0	0	1	4

GAME 34

By SAM LARDNER
The Cleveland Press

DETROIT, May 14 — Apparently the only way to get Kenny Camden out of a game these days is for him to get tossed out.

The Detroit Tigers could only have wished that Camden had made an early exit Friday night, but quite the opposite was the case. "The Wiz" worked eight comfortable innings and won his third straight decision as the Indians had little trouble with the Tigers in an 8–1 victory.

"Felt good to stay in almost the whole way," Camden said with a sly smile, referring to his previous start, when he was ejected as part of a set-to with the Tampa Bay Rays. "Maybe coming out of that last game early helped me. I sure felt fresh. But you guys know my feelings on that. There was nothing to the whole thing (with the Rays).

"Tonight, I came out throwing strikes and worked with Mo (catcher Morris Jerome). The guys behind me made some plays, and the hitters came through. Things are starting to feel like they're looking up for us."

Maybe. The Tribe took two of three from the Baltimore Orioles this week at Progressive Field. It may sound like no great shakes that the Indians have turned it up a notch against teams like the Orioles and Tigers, but they're not throwing any of these victories back.

"Hell no," said interim manager Todd Stein, whose team is 14–20. "You come in here (Comerica Park), and you have to play well, what with the big outfield and a crowd split between their fans and ours. Kenny was really good — again — and we played another clean game."

Camden gave up only five hits and the only Tigers run in his eight innings. That came on a harmless eighth-inning homer by Kyle Cramer on Camden's 100th pitch of the game. Camden wound up throwing 107.

His mates made it easy by scoring their runs early — two in the first, one in the second, one in the third, two in the fourth and two more in the fifth.

Scott Michaels, who is off to a scorching hot start and making the most of his chances to play, got the Tribe on the board in the first on a two-run double that scored Rikki LaBudda and Terry Rovetto. LaBudda led off the game with a walk and a stolen base. He took third on Rovetto's two-out infield single. Michaels doubled to the far reaches of right-center. He entered the game hitting .414 and got two more hits today.

"I've been trying to stay ready," said Michaels, who did not play in the series finale against the Orioles but who has four hits in his last three games, including two hits Friday. "This can be a tough park to hit homers in, but if you make good contact and go to the gaps, you can be rewarded. It's a great doubles and triples park."

Jerome hit a solo homer in the third against Tigers starter Patrick McCoy, but all he wanted to talk about was Camden.

"Wiz was fantastic," Jerome said. "I don't think he shook me off once all night. And if he did, he was probably right. We got into a real good rhythm out there and played pitch and catch. It was a lot of fun."

Oliver Reiner's two-run single in the fifth finished off McCoy. Reiner drove in Wilson White and Micah Millison after White singled and Millison doubled him to third.

From there, the Indians put it on cruise control, something they've not been able to do most of the early going.

"You need these kinds of games," Stein said. "Everybody can relax a little bit, and you don't have to go to your bullpen so early and so often. Once we get this ship righted — and we will — games like this will help us in the long run."

GAME 34

CLEVELAND INDIANS VS DETROIT TIGERS • MAY 14
CLEVELAND 8 / DETROIT 1

CLEVELAND INDIANS										
BATTING	AB	R	H	RBI	2B	3B	HR	BB	SO	BA
RIKKI LABUDDA CF	5	1	0	0	0	0	0	1	0	.266
WILSON WHITE RF	5	1	1	0	0	0	0	0	0	.256
MICAH MILLISON RF	5	2	2	0	1	0	0	1	0	.264
TERRY ROVETTO 3B	4	1	0	0	0	0	0	0	1	.238
SCOTT MICHAELS 2B	4	1	2	2	1	0	0	0	0	.395
OLIVER REINER 1B	4	0	2	3	1	0	0	0	1	.250
JUSTIN KESTINO SS	4	1	1	0	0	0	0	0	0	.231
JJ KULAKOFSKI DH	4	0	2	2	1	0	0	0	1	.234
MORRIS JEROME C	4	1	1	1	0	0	1	0	1	.288
PITCHING	IP	H	R	ER	SO	BB	ERA			
KENNY CAMDEN (W)	8	5	1	1	4	1	3.88			
MICKEY PENNY	1	0	0	0	0	0	4.20			
DETROIT TIGERS										
BATTING	AB	R	H	RBI	2B	3B	HR	BB	SO	BA
KRIS WHITE CF	4	0	0	0	0	0	0	0	1	.280
RODNEY REYNOLDS 2B	4	0	1	0	0	0	0	1	0	.292
AARON SCHUTZMAN LF	4	0	1	0	0	0	0	0	0	.301
MARLON RIVERS 1B	4	0	0	0	0	0	0	0	2	.267
KYLE CRAMER 3B	4	0	1	1	0	0	1	0	0	.257
BOBBY BENKERT SS	4	0	1	0	0	0	0	0	0	.303
ARGELIS SORIANO DH	3	0	0	0	0	0	0	0	0	.255
JESUS FRIAS RF	4	1	1	0	0	0	0	0	0	.259
RAMON GARCIA C	3	0	0	0	0	0	0	0	1	.247
PITCHING	IP	H	R	ER	SO	BB	ERA			
PATRICK MCCOY (L)	4.33	6	6	6	3	2	5.24			
DAMIEN MOORE	1.67	3	2	2	1	0	4.57			
GROVER SHEARD	1	1	0	0	1	1	3.52			
CLAUDE SHOEMAKER	1	0	0	0	0	0	4.50			
INNING	1	2	3	4	5	6	7	8	9	TOTAL
CLEVELAND	2	1	1	2	2	0	0	0	0	8
DETROIT	0	0	0	0	0	0	0	1	0	1

GAME 35

By SAM LARDNER

The Cleveland Press

DETROIT, May 15 — Normally three-game winning streaks are cause for celebration.

But leave it to the way this season has started for the Indians that a three-game winning streak comes with cause for concern.

The Tribe posted back-to-back-to-back victories for the first time all year Saturday afternoon with a 2–1 victory over the Detroit Tigers at Comerica Park.

The victory was tempered by an arm injury to closer Ivan Zyzna, who was trying to finish the victory for starting pitcher Tak Fujimoto in the bottom of the ninth inning. Zyzna, who had been off to a fantastic start to the season, with an ERA of 1.00, grabbed his right forearm after delivering a pitch to Freddie Derring after getting the first out of the inning.

Geno Milzie came on to replace Zyzna and earn the save. But this development is not a good one for the Indians, who have climbed to 15–20 as they try to completely extricate themselves from the hole they dug themselves after an 0–6 start to the season.

Forearm injuries can be tricky and can be precursors to elbow problems. However, it's too early to speculate on that, and the Indians will send Zyzna to the Cleveland Clinic for an MRI first thing Monday.

"He felt something grab," said Todd Stein, the Indians' interim manager. Mo (catcher Morris Jerome) noticed it right away, and so did we on the bench. You never want to fool with anything like that. Ivan is so important to any success we have as a team this year. We feel we have guys who can step in."

General manager J.D. Eisner did not make the short trip to Detroit, but he was on the phone with Stein in his office after Saturday's game. Zyzna will go on the injured list, and the Indians will have to call up a pitcher from Class AAA Columbus. Lorry Unger was up for Buck Sterling earlier this year, but the Indians may opt for hard-throwing right-hander Lee Hazelton, who has eight saves already for Columbus.

As for Saturday's game, Fujimoto enjoyed another solid outing. He hasn't gotten much run support lately, but he made two runs stand up over seven innings, as he gave up four hits and one run, a fourth-inning RBI single to Bobby Benkert. Fujimoto walked one and struck out eight.

"I don't worry about what the offense is doing; I just try to keep the team in the game while I'm on the mound," Fujimoto said through his translator. "You like having the 'W' next to your name, but you can't always control that, so I don't worry about it. The team won, and that's all that matters. Of course, we're concerned about Ivan, but we feel good about how we've played lately."

The Indians strung together four hits in the third inning and scored both of their runs against Tigers starter Austin Wylie. Micah Millison and Wilson White opened with singles, putting runners on the corners. Terry Rovetto doubled to score Millison and send White to third. Scott Michaels hit a single up the middle to drive in the second run.

"It's nice that we don't have to depend on the home run all the time, especially in this ballpark, where it's so hard to hit them out," Rovetto said. "Guys had good approaches up at the plate today."

A team leader, Rovetto was asked about the possible long-term loss of Zyzna, who came on after Sterling worked a 1-2-3 eighth.

"We're hopeful it's just going to be a short stint on the IL," he said. "Zyz means so much to this club. Listen, we regrouped after the 0–6 start and after Dave (former manager Mills) was fired. We've rallied around Steinie, and we'll do the same this time around, too."

With this team, it always seems to be something.

GAME 35

CLEVELAND INDIANS VS DETROIT TIGERS • MAY 15
CLEVELAND 2 / DETROIT 1

CLEVELAND INDIANS										
BATTING	AB	R	H	RBI	2B	3B	HR	BB	SO	BA
MICAH MILLISON LF	4	1	2	0	0	0	0	0	0	.273
WILSON WHITE RF	4	1	1	0	0	0	0	0	1	.256
TERRY ROVETTO 3B	4	0	1	1	1	0	0	1	1	.239
SCOTT MICHAELS 2B	5	0	1	1	0	0	0	0	2	.372
OLIVER REINER 1B	4	0	1	0	0	0	0	0	0	.250
JUSTIN KESTINO SS	4	0	1	0	0	0	0	0	0	.232
BERNARD HARPER DH	4	0	0	0	0	0	0	1	1	.250
MORRIS JEROME C	4	0	0	0	0	0	0	1	0	.278
KIERAN CATSEF CF	3	0	0	0	0	0	0	0	1	.136
PITCHING	IP	H	R	ER	SO	BB	ERA			
TAK FUJIMOTO (W)	7	4	1	1	4	2	3.59			
BUCK STERLING	1	1	0	0	0	0	5.34			
IVAN ZYZNA	0.33	0	0	0	0	0	0.98			
GENO MILZIE (S)	0.67	1	0	0	0	0	3.33			
DETROIT TIGERS										
BATTING	AB	R	H	RBI	2B	3B	HR	BB	SO	BA
KRIS WHITE CF	4	0	0	0	0	0	0	1	0	.269
RODNEY REYNOLDS 2B	4	0	0	0	0	0	0	0	1	.282
AARON SCHUTZMAN LF	4	1	2	0	1	0	0	0	0	.309
FREDDIE DERRING 1B	4	0	1	0	0	0	0	0	1	.289
KYLE CRAMER 3B	4	0	0	0	0	0	0	0	0	.243
BOBBY BENKERT SS	4	0	1	1	0	0	0	0	0	.301
ARGELIS SORIANO DH	3	0	1	0	0	0	0	1	0	.257
JESUS FRIAS RF	3	0	0	0	0	0	0	0	1	.246
RAMON GARCIA C	3	0	1	0	0	0	0	0	1	.250
PITCHING	IP	H	R	ER	SO	BB	ERA			
AUSTIN WYLIE (L)	6	6	2	2	4	2	3.62			
AARON BRISSETT	2	1	0	0	1	0	3.52			
AL ANDALMAN	1	1	0	0	1	1	4.26			
INNING	1	2	3	4	5	6	7	8	9	TOTAL
CLEVELAND	0	0	2	0	0	0	0	0	0	2
DETROIT	0	0	0	1	0	0	0	0	0	1

GAME 36

By SAM LARDNER
The Cleveland Press

DETROIT, May 16 — It didn't matter Sunday that the Indians were operating without their closer. It turns out they didn't need one in a lackluster 6–2 loss to the Detroit Tigers at Comerica Park.

The loss snapped the Tribe's modest winning streak at three games as they begin life — at least temporarily — without closer Ivan Zyzna, who left Saturday's game with a forearm injury.

As expected, the Indians formally placed Zyzna on the injured list and recalled hard-throwing right-hander Lee Hazelton from Class AAA Columbus. The team left after Sunday's game for Chicago, with Zyzna heading back to Cleveland for an MRI Monday at the Cleveland Clinic.

"We're just trying to be precautionary," Zyzna said Sunday morning. "Sure, it's a little frustrating because I had gotten off to a good start. I'm anticipating good news from the MRI. I'm not in any real pain, but there is some persistent soreness I felt it pitching Saturday."

Manager Todd Stein is expected to throw Hazelton right into the closer's role, with Geno Milzie there to back him up. Hazelton had eight saves for Columbus.

"Great opportunity," Hazelton said. "You hate for it to be under these circumstances. I got to know Ivan a little in spring training, and he was great in passing along advice about learning the hitters. I'll just do the best I can while he's out."

Stein also commented on hot-hitting Scott Michaels' condition.

"Scott sat out with a little back discomfort today, nothing serious and we expect him back in the lineup in a day or two," said Stein. "He's off to a great start this season so we're just trying to be cautious."

The Indians will need all facets of their game to be at the top without Zyzna. That includes getting length out of the starting pitchers to take some of the heat off the bullpen.

They didn't get it Sunday as ace Lynn Moda lasted just four innings, giving up eight hits and four runs. The crusher was a three-run homer off the bat of Kyle Cramer in the fourth, enabling the Tigers to turn a 1–0 lead to 4–0.

Consistency — or lack thereof — has been Moda's bugaboo for the entire season to date.

"Very disappointed in myself," he said. "Even with Ivan out, we had a chance to sweep here and build some real momentum for the first time this year, and I let us down. Solo homers early in the game you don't mind. But when you walk a couple guys, you're asking for trouble, and that's what I got in the fourth."

The solo homer came to the first batter Moda faced as he tried to sneak a first-pitch fastball past leadoff hitter Rodney Reynolds. In the fateful fourth, Moda walked Reynolds and Bobby Benkert before Kramer blasted one out to left.

Manager Todd Stein is sticking by his beleaguered ace.

"He's been through it before," said Stein, whose club fell to 15–21. "The guy won 17 ballgames last year. He tried to get a little too fine in the fourth and it ended up costing him."

The Tribe got a two-run homer from Oliver Reiner in the sixth against Tigers starter Omar Alvarado.

The Tigers added a pair of insurance runs off Mickey Penney in the seventh on a homer by Aaron Schutzman.

So the Tigers' flirtation with .500 is proving to be quite the tease.

"We just have to keep grinding, with our without our closer," Stein said. "There isn't much else we can do. Hopefully we'll get good news on Ivan tomorrow and circle the wagons in the pen."

CLEVELAND INDIANS VS DETROIT TIGERS · MAY 16
DETROIT 6 / CLEVELAND 2

CLEVELAND INDIANS										
BATTING	AB	R	H	RBI	2B	3B	HR	BB	SO	BA
MICAH MILLISON LF	4	0	1	0	0	0	0	1	0	.272
WILSON WHITE RF	4	0	1	0	0	0	0	1	1	.256
TERRY ROVETTO 3B	4	0	2	0	1	0	0	0	1	.246
BERNARD HARPER DH	4	1	0	0	1	0	0	0	2	.238
OLIVER REINER 1B	4	1	2	2	0	0	1	0	0	.257
JUSTIN KESTINO SS	4	0	1	0	0	0	0	0	0	.233
ICEBERG PETERS C	4	0	0	0	0	0	0	0	1	.192
LEO TAYLOR 2B	4	0	1	0	0	0	0	1	0	.190
HURON SOUTHWORTH CF	3	0	1	0	0	0	0	1	1	.212
PITCHING	IP	H	R	ER	SO	BB	ERA			
LYNN MODA (L)	4	8	4	4	3	2	5.95			
SOLLY ALVAREZ	2	2	0	0	1	0	3.57			
MICKEY PENNY	1.33	1	2	2	1	0	4.96			
GENO MILZIE	0.67	0	0	0	0	0	3.24			

DETROIT TIGERS										
BATTING	AB	R	H	RBI	2B	3B	HR	BB	SO	BA
RODNEY REYNOLDS 2B	5	2	2	1	0	0	0	1	0	.287
BOBBY BENKERT SS	4	1	1	0	0	0	0	0	1	.299
KYLE CRAMER 3B	4	1	2	3	1	0	1	1	0	.256
FREDDIE DERRING 1B	4	0	0	0	0	0	0	0	2	.262
AARON SCHUTZMAN LF	4	0	2	2	0	0	1	0	0	.317
PORFIRIO FIGUEROA CF	4	1	1	0	0	0	0	0	0	.255
ARGELIS SORIANO DH	4	0	0	0	0	0	0	0	0	.248
GRANT BERGSTROM RF	4	1	2	0	0	0	0	0	1	.281
RAMON GARCIA C	4	0	1	0	0	0	0	0	1	.250
PITCHING	IP	H	R	ER	SO	BB	ERA			
OMAR ALVARADO (W)	5.67	5	2	2	4	1	3.92			
DAMIEN MOORE	2.33	3	0	0	1	0	4.13			
GROVER SHEARD	1	1	0	0	2	1	3.38			

INNING	1	2	3	4	5	6	7	8	9	TOTAL
CLEVELAND	0	0	0	0	0	2	0	0		2
DETROIT	1	0	0	3	0	0	2	0		6

GAME 37

By SAM LARDNER
The Cleveland Press

CHICAGO, May 17 — The way the Indians' season has gone; they'll gladly accept the mixed bag of results they received Monday on closer Ivan Zyzna's forearm injury.

Less easy to accept was a 7–3 loss to the suddenly surging Chicago White Sox at Guaranteed Rate Field. It was the Tribe's second uninspired loss in a row, and it dropped them to 15–22 for the season.

First things first.

General manager J.D. Eisner met the team in Chicago and shared the results of the MRI Zyzna underwent Monday morning at the Cleveland Clinic. It turns out that Zyzna suffered a strain of his right forearm Saturday night but that there is no damage to the elbow or elbow ligaments.

That's the good news.

The bad news is that Zyzna will not be able to pick up a ball and throw for the next two weeks, and the earliest he could return to the bullpen is June 15 or thereabouts.

"We're pleased that there is no structural damage to the elbow," Eisner said on the field late Monday afternoon. "Ivan is in good spirits. He'll be able to do all of his cardio work to stay in shape, and we anticipate him being back at full strength once he rebuilds his arm strength and begins his throwing program."

For now, Geno Milzie and recently recalled Lee Hazelton will share the closer duties.

"Geno's been there before, and we have a lot of confidence in Lee," Eisner said. "No team goes through a season without its share of injuries."

As for Monday's loss, well, it was pretty forgettable. For all of the talk of pitcher Ollie Gonzalez's "hard luck" this season, he had nobody but himself to blame for Monday's appearance, as he lasted 5 and one-third innings, giving up eight hits and five runs. The White Sox love bashing the ball in their hitter-friendly ballpark, and they really enjoyed teeing off on Gonzalez.

They got a three-run homer from Jay Walley in the first inning after a pair of singles. They chased Gonzalez with a pair in the sixth, getting a two-run double from Travis Campbell.

"They can hurt you, especially here," said Gonzalez, who has not won since the 12th game of the season, way back on April 20 against the A's in Cleveland. "I had absolutely nothing on the ball, and their hitters did what they were supposed to do with those pitches. I just have to keep going out every fifth day thinking I'm going to pitch well."

Interim manager Todd Stein said Gonzalez is in no jeopardy of losing his spot in the rotation.

"No, no," Stein said. "Listen, tonight was a bad outing, but if you look at how he's pitched, it's been better than the results we've gotten during those games. That's not entirely his fault."

The White Sox got back-to-back one-out singles from Mark Rose and Moe Tanko in the first before Walley launched one into the left-field bleachers, setting of the pyrotechnics from the center-field scoreboard.

Tanko and Walley singled with one out in the sixth, and Campbell doubled both runners home. That was it for Gonzalez.

"Too many mistakes," he said. "I can't fault anybody but myself for this one tonight."

Scott Michaels was rested again as was Terry Rovetto with Bernard Harper getting a rare start at third but to no avail.

The Tribe got a pair in the seventh on Micah Millison's two-run homer after Wilson White walked.

Indians reliever Solly Alvarez gave up a pair in the bottom of the inning before Bernard Harper homered in the ninth for what amounted to a consolation run.

While it's "still early in the season" as the saying goes — mainly to give hope to teams in the Indians' position — it's not that early anymore. And with no top closer on the roster, things could be getting late soon.

"No panic," said Stein. "Look, I've said it before, things are going to turn for a pitcher like Gonzalez. He's just too good to be getting these results. And the rest of it will fall into place. I'm confident of that."

CLEVELAND INDIANS VS CHICAGO WHITE SOX • MAY 17
CHICAGO 7 / CLEVELAND 3

CLEVELAND INDIANS										
BATTING	AB	R	H	RBI	2B	3B	HR	BB	SO	BA
RIKKI LABUDDA CF	5	0	1	0	0	0	0	0	0	.264
WILSON WHITE RF	4	1	1	0	0	0	0	0	1	.255
MICAH MILLISON LF	4	1	1	2	1	0	1	0	1	.271
OLIVER REINER 1B	4	0	2	0	1	0	0	0	1	.264
JUSTIN KESTINO SS	4	0	1	0	0	0	0	0	0	.233
J.J. KULAKOFSKI DH	4	0	0	0	0	0	0	0	2	.216
BERNARD HARPER 3B	4	1	1	1	0	0	1	0	1	.238
ICEBERG PETERS C	4	0	1	0	0	0	0	1	1	.200
LEO TAYLOR 2B	3	0	1	0	0	0	0	1	0	.208
PITCHING	IP	H	R	ER	SO	BB	ERA			
OLLIE GONZALEZ (L)	5.33	8	5	5	6	2	6.13			
SOLLY ALVAREZ	2.67	2	0	0	1	0	3.10			

CHICAGO WHITE SOX										
BATTING	AB	R	H	RBI	2B	3B	HR	BB	SO	BA
FRANCISCO MOLINA CF	5	0	0	0	0	0	0	0	2	.278
MARK ROSE 2B	5	1	2	0	0	0	0	1	1	.296
MOE TANKO 3B	4	3	3	0	0	0	0	0	0	.282
JAY WALLEY LF	4	2	2	3	0	0	1	0	1	.333
TRAVIS CAMPBELL SS	4	1	1	2	0	0	0	1	0	.297
MIKE ISENMESSER 1B	4	0	2	2	1	0	0	0	0	.277
JACKIE WINER CF	4	0	2	0	0	0	0	0	0	.269
JASON NAKAMURA DH	4	0	0	0	0	0	0	0	1	.234
ENRIQUE FUENTES C	4	0	0	0	0	0	0	0	2	.238
PITCHING	IP	H	R	ER	SO	BB	ERA			
WILTON BERRIOS (W)	7.67	7	2	2	6	2	3.57			
CARL WOLDMAN	1.33	2	1	1	1	0	3.66			

INNING	1	2	3	4	5	6	7	8	9	TOTAL
CLEVELAND	0	0	0	0	0	0	2	0	1	3
CHICAGO	3	0	0	0	0	2	2	0		7

GAME 38

By SAM LARDNER
The Cleveland Press

CHICAGO, May 18 — As far as Indians manager Todd Stein saw it, a little shakeup was in order for his team.

That little shakeup led to big results Tuesday night with a 10–3 victory over the Chicago White Sox at Guaranteed Rate Field. The Tribe stunned the Sox with 17 hits, and everyone getting at least one hit.

After looking like they might be on their way following a three-game winning streak, the Indians reverted back to their old form and dropped a couple games, looking utterly uninterested in the process. So Stein reinstated Scott Michaels at second base, Kieran Catsef in center field and Iceberg Peters behind the plate.

The most interesting one is the hot-hitting Michaels, who continues to fill in for Angel Rodriguez. Michaels, after resting his back for a couple of days, responded by going 1-for-2 with a homer and three walks. Catsef and Peters looked to be getting one-game shots to give a breather to both Rikki LaBudda and Morris Jerome.

"We had to do something," Stein said. "And you have to give guys playing time to keep them fresh or else they're not going to come through when you need them to pinch hit or go into a game late. We'll see how it goes. Angel has been banged up a little, and Scott has a world of potential and has been playing great in spot duty this season. We'll just see how it goes."

Michaels hit a three-run homer in the first inning against White Sox starter Juri Tateyama, and from that point forward, the rout was on.

"I got one I could drive," Michaels said. "Like everybody else here, I've just got to be ready when my name is called. I don't think about expectations or any of that kind of stuff. I just think about playing well and contributing."

The Indians looked like they might waste their first-inning chance. Catsef singled to lead off and went to third on Micah Millison's single to right. Wilson White and Terry Rovetto both struck out before Michaels lofted a high drive to left for the homer, his fourth.

"That's what we've been needing, both the clutch hit and for a guy to come up and pick up his teammates," Stein said. "Instead of leaving two on base, we got three in and gave Doc some early cushion."

Stein was referring to Brian "The Doctor" Howard, who worked seven innings of three-hit, three-run ball.

"Yeah, it's always good to get that run support early," Howard said. "I know the guys might have been pressing up at the plate a little bit. That can happen when you're not scoring runs or hitting with guys on. They made it pretty easy for me to go out there and just relax and pitch."

The Tribe chased Tateyama with a four-spot in the third. Michaels drew a leadoff walk and went to third on Justin Kestino's double to the right-field corner. Oliver Reiner struck out but Peters drove them both home with a single. One out later, Catsef tripled, and Millison singled him home.

The Sox got three on a homer by Mike Isenmesser in the bottom of the sixth, but it didn't matter as Oliver Reiner got all three back with a bases-loaded double in the seventh."

Buck Sterling and Mickey Penney mopped up the final two innings.

"We've got a chance to win another series," Stein said. "That's how you climb back to .500, and that's how you climb back into contention."

CLEVELAND INDIANS VS CHICAGO WHITE SOX • MAY 17
CLEVELAND 10 / CHICAGO 3

CLEVELAND INDIANS										
BATTING	AB	R	H	RBI	2B	3B	HR	BB	SO	BA
KIERAN CATSEF CF	5	2	3	1	1	0	0	0	0	.222
MICAH MILLISON LF	5	1	2	1	0	0	0	0	1	.276
WILSON WHITE RF	4	1	2	0	1	0	0	1	1	.262
TERRY ROVETTO 3B	4	1	1	0	0	0	0	1	0	.246
SCOTT MICHAELS 2B	2	3	1	3	0	0	1	3	0	.378
JUSTIN KESTINO SS	4	1	2	0	1	0	0	0	0	.241
OLIVER REINER 1B	4	0	2	3	0	0	0	0	1	.271
BERNARD HARPER DH	4	0	2	0	0	0	0	0	0	.250
ICEBERG PETERS C	4	1	2	2	0	0	0	0	1	.235
PITCHING	IP	H	R	ER	SO	BB	ERA			
BRIAN HOWARD (W)	7	3	3	3	5	2	4.15			
BUCK STERLING	1	1	0	0	0	0	5.17			
MICKEY PENNY	1	1	0	0	0	0	4.67			

CHICAGO WHITE SOX										
BATTING	AB	R	H	RBI	2B	3B	HR	BB	SO	BA
FRANCISCO MOLINA CF	4	0	0	0	0	0	0	0	0	.269
MARK ROSE 2B	4	0	0	0	0	0	0	0	1	.284
MOE TANKO 3B	3	1	1	0	0	0	0	1	0	.284
JAY WALLEY LF	4	0	0	0	0	0	0	0	2	.304
TRAVIS CAMPBELL SS	4	1	1	0	0	0	0	1	0	.295
MIKE ISENMESSER 1B	4	1	1	3	0	0	1	0	0	.275
JACKIE WINER CF	4	0	1	0	0	0	0	0	0	.269
JASON NAKAMURA DH	4	0	0	0	0	0	0	0	1	.221
ENRIQUE FUENTES C	4	0	1	0	0	0	0	0	1	.239
PITCHING	IP	H	R	ER	SO	BB	ERA			
JURI TATEYAMA (L)	2.66	7	7	7	3	2	5.13			
FELIX VALERO	3.33	3	0	0	1	1	2.91			
RANDY ROSELLI	2	5	3	3	0	2	4.82			
BRAD HUTCHINSON	1	2	0	0	0	0	4.00			

INNING	1	2	3	4	5	6	7	8	9	TOTAL
CLEVELAND	3	0	4	0	0	0	3	0	0	10
CHICAGO	0	0	0	0	0	3	0	0	0	3

GAME 39

By SAM LARDNER
The Cleveland Press

CHICAGO, May 19 –There are baptisms by fire, and there are baptisms by bonfire. Lee Hazelton experienced the latter in stunningly hot fashion Wednesday night.

Called on to protect a 3–2 lead in the bottom of the ninth inning and have a chance at earning his first major league save in his first major league game, Hazelton suffered both a blown save and a loss as the Chicago White Sox stunned him and the Indians 4–3 with a pair of home runs.

First it was Mike Isenmesser, who homered yesterday, hit a two-out game-tying homer, a ball that just cleared the left-field wall near the foul pole.

The smoke from the fireworks hadn't even cleared with Mo Tanko delivered the walk-off game-winner, a drive over the center field wall. Indians center fielder Rikki LaBudda made a leaping attempt, but the ball ticked off his glove and skimmed over the fence. Welcome to the big leagues, kid.

"I don't know what to say," said Hazelton, called up a couple days ago to take the place of injured closer Ivan Zyzna. "I got the first two outs so quickly that I thought it was going to be easy to finish them off. But there's nothing easy about anything up here. That's why it's called the big leagues.

"On the first one, he went down and golfed a good pitch out. I actually thought it was going foul, but the wind might have pushed it back fair. On the second one, he hit it pretty good. Rikki made a hell of an attempt on it. It's tough, but I've waited for this a long time, and I'll get over it."

The Indians thought they were well on their way to a victory in the game and a series win as well, but instead, they find themselves back to seven games under .500 at 16–23.

They also wasted a fine pitching performance by Kenny Camden. The Wiz limited the Sox to four hits over seven effortless innings.

"Wow, that is a tough one," said interim manager Todd Stein. "But I told the players in there, especially Lee, not to hang their heads. We're going to go right back to him if the opportunity presents itself. He'll come through."

It was all set up so perfectly for the Indians. Geno Milzie worked a 1-2-3 eighth with the Tribe up 3–2, setting things up for Hazelton, who garnered high praise from the White Sox.

"Man, that kid has some good stuff," said Isenmesser from the celebratory Chicago clubhouse. "I really had to work to stay with him."

Tanko was still soaked in Gatorade from his reception at home plate. "That kid can bring it," he said. "I knew he'd want to come right in there, so I was looking dead red. What did he throw, 95–96 miles an hour? It was every bit of that. I caught it good and let it ride."

Both teams played good, errorless, ball all night before a crowd of 15, 202. The Indians got a two-run homer from Terry Rovetto, his fifth, in the second against Jim Zechman. Wilson White singled ahead of the homer. The Sox tied it in the third on a two-run double by Isenmesser. The Indians took their 3–2 lead in the fourth on a sacrifice fly by Micah Millison, who's eight-game hitting streak came to an end, to score LaBudda, who tripled to lead off the inning.

Both teams made good defensive plays, with the Indians White running down Tanko's drive to the gap in the fifth. Justin Kestino was robbed by third baseman Tanko's backhand snag of his liner in the seventh.

The clubhouse after the game was dead quiet. Players such as Oliver Reiner and catcher Morris Jerome made sure to give Hazelton more than a few words of encouragement.

"I'd call for the same pitches again," Jerome said. "Sometimes you have to give credit to the hitters. They were both good pitches. Sometimes you get beat. But this kid is going to bounce back strong. I like the fact that he's not afraid of coming right at guys and challenging them."

The Indians get a much-needed day off Thursday before opening a long homestand, with the Tigers coming in Friday night.

"This will be our chance to make some hay, and we have to take advantage," Stein said. "I almost wish we were playing tomorrow so I could give the ball to Lee again right away. But he'll be able to clear his head and be ready to close things out Friday."

CLEVELAND INDIANS VS CHICAGO WHITE SOX • MAY 97
CHICAGO 4 / CLEVELAND 3

CLEVELAND INDIANS

BATTING	AB	R	H	RBI	2B	3B	HR	BB	SO	BA
RIKKI LABUDDA CF	4	1	1	0	0	1	0	0	0	.264
MICAH MILLISON LF	4	0	0	1	0	0	0	0	0	.268
WILSON WHITE RF	4	1	1	0	1	0	0	0	0	.262
TERRY ROVETTO 3B	4	0	1	2	0	0	1	1	0	.247
OLIVER REINER 1B	4	0	0	0	0	0	0	0	2	.264
JUSTIN KESTINO SS	4	0	1	0	1	0	0	0	0	.241
BERNARD HARPER DH	4	0	1	0	0	0	0	0	1	.250
MORRIS JEROME C	4	0	0	0	0	0	0	0	0	.268
ANGEL RODRIGUEZ 2B	3	0	1	0	0	0	0	0	1	.194
SCOTT MICHAELS PH	1	0	0	0	0	0	0	0	0	.370

PITCHING	IP	H	R	ER	SO	BB	ERA			
KENNY CAMDEN	7	4	2	2	5	1	3.72			
GENO MILZIE	1	1	0	0	0	0	3.12			
LEE HAZELTON (BS)(L)	0.67	1	2	2	0	0	26.87			

CHICAGO WHITE SOX

BATTING	AB	R	H	RBI	2B	3B	HR	BB	SO	BA
FRANCISCO MOLINA CF	4	1	1	0	0	0	0	0	0	.268
MARK ROSE 2B	4	0	0	0	0	0	0	0	0	.274
MIKE ISENMESSER 1B	4	1	2	3	1	0	1	0	1	.291
MO TANKO 3B	4	1	1	1	0	0	1	0	2	.282
JAY WALLEY LF	4	0	0	0	0	0	0	1	0	.280
JACKIE WINER CF	4	0	1	0	0	0	0	0	1	.268
TRAVIS CAMPBELL SS	4	0	0	0	0	0	0	0	1	.284
JASON NAKAMURA DH	4	0	0	0	0	0	0	0	0	.208
ENRIQUE FUENTES C	3	1	1	0	0	0	0	0	0	.242

PITCHING	IP	H	R	ER	SO	BB	ERA			
JIM ZECHMAN	6	4	3	3	3	1	3.66			
CARL WOLDMAN	2	2	0	0	1	0	3.32			
DOUR GORHAM (W)	1	0	0	0	0	0	2.04			

INNING	1	2	3	4	5	6	7	8	9	TOTAL
CLEVELAND	0	2	0	1	0	0	0	0	0	3
CHICAGO	0	0	2	0	0	0	0	0	2	4

GAME 40

By SAM LARDNER
The Cleveland Press

CLEVELAND, May 21 — Media members were politely asked to leave the Indians' clubhouse at 4 p.m. Friday after just 25 minutes of pregame access.

The reason? Players-only meeting.

The Indians and their season might not be in crisis yet, but the players apparently felt the need to head off something after a few days of lackluster play and Wednesday's heartbreaking walk-off loss at Chicago. The Tribe then went out and posted a convincing 6–0 victory over the Detroit Tigers at Progressive Field.

Coincidence? Who knows?

We'll know more after a few days. Interim manager Todd Stein did not seem to mind that neither he nor his coaching staff were part of the meeting. Instead, he seemed heartened the players took the initiative on their own.

"I'm glad they had the meeting," Stein said during his pregame chat with reporters. "They hear from me and from the coaches enough. Sometimes you have to air things out among your peers."

The players weren't sharing what was said. But one veteran said there was no finger pointing.

"If we wanted to tell you what was said, we'd have invited you in," team leader Terry Rovetto said with a sly smile. "What's said in here stays in here.

But the tone was positive, and we're all pulling in the same direction. We haven't gotten off to the start we wanted, so guys wanted to speak their minds. Everybody had a chance to say something, from the young guys to us old guys."

With Friday night's victory, the Indians improved to 17–23, meaning they still have a long way to go before they can be taken seriously as contenders in the American League Central. But there were plenty of positive things in the game, starting with pitcher Tak Fujimoto, who tossed seven shutout innings, allowing five hits while walking one and striking out 10.

"This was something new from me," the veteran of Japanese baseball said through his translator. "Players have a lot of freedom here, and it was interesting for me to watch the players address everything. But on the mound, I wasn't thinking about that. I was just trying to get us a win."

Fujimoto retired the first 10 batters he faced, striking out the side in the first inning to set the tone. Indians batters jumped on Tigers starter Austin Wylie for three runs in the third. Rikki LaBudda got things going with a leadoff bunt single and a stolen base. He went to third on Micah Millison's infield single. Wilson White singled LaBudda home, sending Millison to third. Millison scored on a wild pitch, and Rovetto singled home White home. Wylie left after the fifth, and the Indians put it away on Oliver Reiner's three-run homer off reliever Grover Sheard in the sixth.

"I think it's like Terry was saying," Reiner said. "We just wanted to grab this thing before it spun out of control. That wasn't happening, but sometimes you have to nip things in the bud. But you can talk all you want. We still have to go out there and execute. That's what we did tonight."

Solly Alvarez pitched the eighth for the Tribe, and Stein gave rookie Lee Hazelton a chance to pitch the ninth with little pressure on him. That came on the heels of Hazelton giving up two homers in the bottom of the ninth Wednesday as he suffered both a blown save and a loss.

"Just get him an inning and let him pitch and air it out a little," Stein said. "Even if it was a save situation, I would have gone to him. But this was a nice opportunity to get him back on the horse again."

CLEVELAND INDIANS VS DETROIT TIGERS • MAY 21
CLEVELAND 6 / DETROIT 0

CLEVELAND INDIANS

BATTING	AB	R	H	RBI	2B	3B	HR	BB	SO	BA
RIKKI LABUDDA CF	4	1	1	0	0	0	0	1	0	.263
MICAH MILLISON LF	4	2	2	0	0	0	0	0	0	.275
WILSON WHITE RF	4	2	2	1	0	0	0	0	0	.268
TERRY ROVETTO 3B	4	0	1	1	0	0	0	0	0	.247
OLIVER REINER 1B	4	1	1	3	0	0	1	0	1	.263
JUSTIN KESTINO SS	4	0	0	0	0	0	0	0	0	.234
BERNARD HARPER DH	4	0	1	0	0	0	0	0	1	.250
MORRIS JEROME C	4	0	0	0	0	0	0	0	0	.259
SCOTT MICHAELS 2B	3	0	1	0	0	0	0	0	1	.367

PITCHING	IP	H	R	ER	SO	BB	ERA			
TAK FUJIMOTO (W)	7	5	0	0	10	1	3.13			
SOLLY ALVAREZ	1	1	0	0	0	0	2.95			
LEE HAZELTON	1	0	0	0	0	1	10.78			

DETROIT TIGERS

BATTING	AB	R	H	RBI	2B	3B	HR	BB	SO	BA
RODNEY REYNOLDS 2B	4	0	1	0	0	0	0	0	1	.271
BOBBY BENKERT SS	4	0	1	0	1	0	0	0	0	.292
KYLE CRAMER 3B	4	0	0	0	0	0	0	0	2	.261
FREDDIE DERRING 1B	4	0	1	0	0	0	1	0	1	.271
AARON SCHUTZMAN LF	4	0	2	0	0	0	0	1	0	.300
PORFIRIO FIGUEROA RF	4	0	0	0	0	0	0	0	2	.259
ARGELIS SORIANO DH	4	0	1	0	0	0	0	0	2	.275
GRANT BERGSTROM CF	3	0	0	0	0	0	0	1	0	.239
RAMON GARCIA C	3	0	0	0	0	0	0	0	2	.231

PITCHING	IP	H	R	ER	SO	BB	ERA			
AUSTIN WYLIE (L)	5	6	3	3	2	1	3.94			
GROVER SHEARD	2	3	3	3	1	0	4.95			
CLAUDE SHOEMAKER	1	0	0	0	0	0	3.24			

INNING	1	2	3	4	5	6	7	8	9	TOTAL
DETROIT	0	0	0	0	0	0	0	0	0	0
CLEVELAND	0	0	3	0	0	3	0	0		6

GAME 41

By SAM LARDNER
The Cleveland Press

CLEVELAND, May 22 — Looks like that team meeting is continuing to pay dividends. The Indians got their second straight victory after Friday's confab, this time beating the Detroit Tigers 5 to 1 behind ace Lynn Moda Saturday evening.

The victory did come with somewhat of a price, though. Second baseman Angel Rodriguez limped off the field in the fifth inning with an apparent hamstring injury. Manager Todd Stein said the club would not know the extent of Rodriguez's injury until Sunday at the earliest.

Now for the good news for the Tribe. Moda mowed down the men from Motown over seven innings, giving up five hits and one run, a sixth-inning homer to Marlon Rivers. That was on the heels of a four-inning stinker in his previous start, against the Tigers in Detroit. As downcast as Moda was after that game, he was equally upbeat after Saturday's gem.

"That's definitely more like it," he said. "I've struggled with my mechanics and getting a consistent release point all season. We made some tweaks in my side sessions after the last start, and I really felt it tonight. Mo (catcher Morris Jerome) didn't have to come out to the mound once, and I don't think he shook me off once. It's something to build on."

The Indians got going right away against Tigers starter Omar Alvarado. Rikki LaBudda, who seems as energized as anybody, slapped a single to right leading things off. After Micah Millison bounced out to move LaBudda to second, Wilson White picked on a 3–2 pitch and drove it over the high wall in left field for his sixth home run of the season.

"I think the team is feeling pretty good," White said. "The attitude has always been good, but I think the meeting cleared the air a bit. We're going to be fine."

Rodriguez, who has suffered nagging injuries since spring training, started the Indians' three-run fifth inning with a bunt single, but he grabbed the back of his hamstring after he ran through the bag. He hobbled down the right-field line and came out in favor of Leo Taylor. If Rodriguez does have to go on the injured list, the Tribe could turn to Scott Michaels at second base. Michaels was the DH Saturday.

"I don't know," Stein said. "We got ice on it right away. Hamstrings are funny. Angel is such a good fielder, but he's been kind of snakebit with injuries. If we had to go with Scott at second, we'd be perfectly comfortable with that."

Jerome followed Rodriguez's hit with a double that sent Taylor to third. LaBudda hit a sacrifice fly to score Taylor and move Jerome to third. Millison followed with his sixth homer of the season to give the Indians a 50 lead.

"We're starting to get the kind of timely hitting we were lacking early on," said Millison, who has been the starter in right field lately, having replaced Huron Southworth, who got off to a terrible start at the plate. "I'm just going to ride it as long as I can."

Buck Sterling and Mickey Penney finished with scoreless relief for the Indians, who are back to within five games of .500 at 18 and 23.

"It's getting close to Memorial Day, and that's kind of the first big milepost of the season," Stein said. "We've had our share of ups and downs so far, but there's a long way to go and a lot of opportunity out there for us."

CLEVELAND INDIANS VS DETROIT TIGERS • MAY 22
CLEVELAND 5 / DETROIT 1

CLEVELAND INDIANS										
BATTING	**AB**	**R**	**H**	**RBI**	**2B**	**3B**	**HR**	**BB**	**SO**	**BA**
RIKKI LABUDDA CF	4	1	1	1	0	0	0	1	0	.263
MICAH MILLISON LF	4	1	2	2	0	0	1	1	0	.281
WILSON WHITE RF	4	1	1	2	0	0	1	0	1	.268
TERRY ROVETTO 3B	4	0	2	0	0	0	0	0	0	.253
OLIVER REINER 1B	3	0	0	0	0	0	0	0	1	.258
JUSTIN KESTINO SS	4	0	1	0	0	0	0	0	0	.235
SCOTT MICHAELS DH	4	0	1	0	0	0	0	1	1	.358
ANGEL RODRIGUEZ 2B	2	1	1	0	0	0	0	0	0	.203
LEO TAYLOR 2B	2	0	0	0	0	0	0	0	1	.192
MORRIS JEROME C	4	1	1	0	1	0	0	0	1	.258
PITCHING	**IP**	**H**	**R**	**ER**	**SO**	**BB**	**ERA**			
LYNN MODA (W)	7	5	1	1	6	1	5.24			
BUCK STERLING	1	1	0	0	1	0	5.01			
MICKEY PENNY	1	1	0	0	0	0	4.42			

DETROIT TIGERS										
BATTING	**AB**	**R**	**H**	**RBI**	**2B**	**3B**	**HR**	**BB**	**SO**	**BA**
RODNEY REYNOLDS 2B	4	0	1	0	0	0	0	0	1	.271
BOBBY BENKERT SS	4	0	1	0	1	0	0	0	0	.291
KYLE CRAMER 3B	4	0	0	0	0	0	0	0	2	.247
MARLON RIVERS 1B	4	0	1	1	0	0	1	0	1	.263
AARON SCHUTZMAN LF	4	0	2	0	0	0	0	1	0	.315
PORFIRIO FIGUEROA RF	4	0	0	0	0	0	0	0	2	.250
ARGELIS SORIANO DH	4	0	1	0	0	0	0	0	2	.274
GRANT BERGSTROM CF	3	0	0	0	0	0	0	1	0	.230
RAMON GARCIA C	3	0	0	0	0	0	0	0	2	.223
PITCHING	**IP**	**H**	**R**	**ER**	**SO**	**BB**	**ERA**			
OMAR ALVARADO (L)	4.33	8	5	5	4	2	4.40			
AARON BRISSET	2.66	2	0	0	1	0	3.48			
DAMIEN MOORE	1	1	0	0	0	1	3.24			

INNING	1	2	3	4	5	6	7	8	9	TOTAL
DETROIT	0	0	0	0	0	1	0	0	0	1
CLEVELAND	2	0	0	0	3	0	0	0		5

GAME 42

By SAM LARDNER
The Cleveland Press

CLEVELAND, May 23 — The Indians got some more bad injury news before Sunday's game, but that seemed to be all forgotten in the postgame celebration following their 8–2 victory over the Detroit Tigers at Progressive Field.

Before the game, the Tribe put infielder Angel Rodriguez on the injured list with a strained right hamstring. They recalled Willie Bartlett from Class AAA Columbus.

But it was all smiles — and even a beer shower for pitcher Ollie Gonzalez — after the Indians completed a three-game sweep of the Tigers to pull within four games of .500 at 19–23.

Gonzalez had not won a decision since the seventh game of the season, and the Indians had not won a game in which he started since Game 12. The big lefty has been the victim of poor run support most of the season, but his teammates poured it on with three homers Sunday and later poured the beer on him as teams often do when pitchers win a milestone victory.

"That was good of the guys," said Gonzalez, who worked seven innings of five-hit ball. "They appreciated the fact that I hadn't badmouthed them about not scoring runs. So they decided to have a little fun, and I appreciate that."

It's been all fun and games since the players-only meeting before the start of this series. The Indians outscored the Tigers 19–3 in this series.

"Yeah, well, sometimes you gotta do these things," said third baseman and team leader Terry Rovetto, who chaired the meeting Friday. "We felt bad for having not scored any runs for Ollie, so the beer shower was our way of letting him know how we feel about him."

Rovetto hit a three-run homer off Elvis Reich in the second inning to stake Gonzalez to a 3–0 lead. That seemed to relax Gonzalez, who cruised most of the way. It helped again in the fifth when Scott Michaels, who is off to a great start and is hitting at a torrid pace, launched a two-run homer after Rovetto walked to lead off.

"I think so," Gonzalez said. "It was fun to just go out there and pitch and relax a little. The runs really helped. I can't say enough about the guys."

The Indians chased Reich in the fifth. Bernard Harper hit a two-run homer in the sixth after Michaels was hit by a pitch from reliever Claude Shoemaker. Iceberg Peters doubled home Kieran Catsef after Catsef singled to lead off the bottom of the seventh.

Gonzalez was charged with two runs, both coming on a two-run double by Kris Whyte in the seventh. Geno Milzie and Buck Sterling pitched the final two innings for the Indians.

As far as Rodriguez's situation is concerned, general manager J.D. Eisner said the stint on the injured list could be for up to three weeks.

"You know how hamstrings are," he said. "And Angel has battled some things all year. We're not going to rush things. Michaels has shown he deserves more playing time anyway, so this give us a chance to look at him for an extended period. Who knows? He could continue his hot hitting and really spark us. Willie Bartlett gives us some speed and versatility. He can play second, short and third, and we won't be afraid to play him in the outfield, either."

GAME 42

CLEVELAND INDIANS VS DETROIT TIGERS • MAY 23
CLEVELAND 8 / DETROIT 2

CLEVELAND INDIANS

BATTING	AB	R	H	RBI	2B	3B	HR	BB	SO	BA
RIKKI LABUDDA CF	5	0	0	0	0	0	0	0	2	.255
MICAH MILLISON LF	5	1	1	0	0	0	0	0	0	.279
OLIVER REINER 1B	4	1	3	0	1	0	0	1	0	.270
TERRY ROVETTO 3B	4	2	2	3	1	0	1	0	0	.259
SCOTT MICHAELS 2B	3	2	1	2	0	0	1	0	0	.357
BERNARD HARPER DH	4	1	2	2	0	0	1	0	0	.260
JUSTIN KESTINO SS	4	0	0	0	0	0	0	1	0	.229
KIERAN CATSEF LF	4	1	2	0	0	0	0	0	2	.258
ICEBERG PETERS C	4	0	2	1	1	0	0	0	1	.263

PITCHING	IP	H	R	ER	SO	BB	ERA			
OLLIE GONGALEZ (W)	7	5	2	2	4	1	5.44			
GENO MILZIE	1	1	0	0	1	0	5.01			
BUCK STERLING	1	0	0	0	1	0	4.42			

DETROIT TIGERS

BATTING	AB	R	H	RBI	2B	3B	HR	BB	SO	BA
RODNEY REYNOLDS 2B	4	0	1	0	0	0	0	0	1	.270
BOBBY BENKERT SS	4	0	1	0	1	0	0	0	0	.289
KYLE CRAMER 3B	4	0	0	0	0	0	0	0	2	.234
FREDDIE DERRING 1B	4	0	1	0	0	0	0	0	1	.270
AARON SCHUTZMAN LF	4	0	2	0	0	0	0	1	0	.328
KRIS WHYTE RF	4	0	0	2	0	0	0	0	2	.233
ARGELIS SORIANO DH	4	0	1	0	0	0	0	0	2	.274
GRANT BERGSTROM CF	3	0	0	0	0	0	0	1	0	.221
ANTONIO FLORIO C	3	0	0	0	0	0	0	0	2	.250

PITCHING	IP	H	R	ER	SO	BB	ERA			
ELVIS REICH (L)	4	8	5	5	2	2	4.08			
CLAUDE SHOEMAKER	2.67	4	2	2	1	0	3.72			
GROVER SHEARD	1	2	1	1	0	1	5.14			
SILVIO SEVERINO	1	0	0	0	1	0	3.00			

INNING	1	2	3	4	5	6	7	8	9	TOTAL
DETROIT	0	0	0	0	0	0	2	0	0	2
CLEVELAND	0	3	0	0	2	2	1	0		8

GAME 43

By SAM LARDNER
The Cleveland Press

CLEVELAND, May 24 — The Indians are officially on a roll.

By beating the Chicago White Sox 3–1 Monday night at Progressive Field, the Tribe achieved its longest winning streak of the season at four as they pulled within three games of .500 at 20–23. Coming off a weekend sweep of the Tigers, things are suddenly looking up for the Indians, who continue to play crisp and clean baseball in the wake of a players-only meeting last Friday.

"Yeah, it's encouraging to see," said interim manager Todd Stein, whose easygoing grip on the throttle seems to be resonating with his players. "All the credit goes to the players. I had no problem with them having that meeting. If it cleared the air, fine. But I just think the talent of this team is starting to come to the fore."

"We're just too good of a baseball team to have played the way we did early in the season. So I'm going to just let them keep playing, and we'll see where it takes us."

The Indians got another strong start from Brian "The Doctor" Howard, who won his second straight decision — he got a no-decision in an Indians win before that — and another strong contribution from second baseman Scott Michaels, who hit a two-run homer in the second inning, going 2-for-4 overall. Howard has been a constant in the rotation, but

Michaels is getting a chance make his mark as he takes over for the injured Angel Rodriguez.

"I'm just trying to fit in," said Michaels, a onetime phenom who may just need to stay healthy to see his potential blossom. "It's nice that they've had the faith in me to give me a clear shot while Angel is out. I know some people were starting to have their doubts about me, and with some justification. So it's up to me to prove that I belong."

The Indians went out 1-2-3 in the first before Terry Rovetto led off the bottom of the second with a walk. Michaels, who has been batting fifth in the order when he plays, picked on a first-pitch fastball from Sox starter Juri Tateyama and sent it over the high wall in left field for a homer that put the Tribe up 2–0.

"I figured he'd want to come in after walking Terry," Michaels said. "So I was looking fastball all the way. I kind of ran into one there (laughing). It's always good to get out to an early lead, and The Doc did the rest on the mound for us."

Howard worked seven innings, giving up four hits and a fifth-inning homer to Jay Walley. The Indians got an insurance run with an eighth-inning homer from Oliver Reiner. Geno Milzie pitched the eighth, with fireballer Lee Hazelton earning the save with a 1-2-3 ninth. It was Hazelton's first major league save.

"Feels really good, especially after a tough outing," said Hazelton, who had the ball from the final out at his locker. "I never lost any confidence. I know I can pitch at this level. I'm just trying to hold down a spot here until Ivan (injured closer Zyzna) gets back."

Howard, for one, was happy for the kid. "This is how we draw it up," Howard said. "It's been a long time coming for us, but we've never lost belief in ourselves. Steinie deserves a lot of credit for just allowing us to go out and play. It was good to see Haze get the save, too. With Ivan hurt, we need everybody to step up. I can't wait for my next start to roll around. It's starting to get fun again."

CLEVELAND INDIANS VS CHICAGO WHITE SOX • MAY 24
CLEVELAND 3 / CHICAGO 1

CLEVELAND INDIANS

BATTING	AB	R	H	RBI	2B	3B	HR	BB	SO	BA
RIKKI LABUDDA CF	4	0	0	0	0	0	0	1	0	.248
MICAH MILLISON RF	4	0	0	0	0	0	0	1	0	.271
WILSON WHITE LF	4	0	0	0	0	0	0	0	0	.261
TERRY ROVETTO 3B	3	1	0	0	0	0	0	1	0	.255
SCOTT MICHAELS 2B	4	1	2	2	0	0	1	0	1	.367
OLIVER REINER 1B	4	1	2	1	0	0	1	0	0	.276
JUSTIN KESTINO SS	4	0	0	0	0	0	0	0	0	.223
J.J. KULAKOFSKY DH	4	0	1	0	0	0	0	0	2	.218
MORRIS JEROME C	4	0	1	0	0	0	0	0	0	.258

PITCHING	IP	H	R	ER	SO	BB	ERA			
BRIAN HOWARD (W)	7	4	1	1	6	0	3.79			
GENO MILZIE	1	0	0	0	0	0	4.86			
LEE HAZELTON (S)	1	0	0	0	1	0	6.74			

CHICAGO WHITE SOX

BATTING	AB	R	H	RBI	2B	3B	HR	BB	SO	BA
FRANCISCO MOLINA CF	4	0	0	0	0	0	0	0	1	.266
MARK ROSE 2B	4	0	0	0	0	0	0	0	0	.281
MO TANKO 3B	4	0	1	0	0	0	0	0	0	.320
JAY WALLEY LF	4	1	1	1	0	0	1	0	1	.258
TRAVIS CAMPBELL SS	4	0	0	0	0	0	0	0	0	.241
MIKE ISENMESSER 1B	4	0	1	0	1	0	0	0	2	.272
JACKIE WINER RF	4	0	1	0	0	0	0	0	1	.274
JASON NAKAMURA DH	4	0	0	0	0	0	0	0	0	.225
ENRIQUE FUENTES C	3	0	0	0	0	0	0	0	1	.250

PITCHING	IP	H	R	ER	SO	BB	ERA			
JURI TATEYAMA (L)	6	5	2	2	2	2	3.35			
FELIX VALERO	2	1	1	1	1	1	3.38			

INNING	1	2	3	4	5	6	7	8	9	TOTAL
CHICAGO	0	0	0	0	1	0	0	0	0	1
CLEVELAND	0	2	0	0	0	0	0	1		3

GAME 44

By SAM LARDNER
The Cleveland Press

CLEVELAND, May 25 — Thud.

That was the sound of the end of the Indians' four-game winning streak. The Tribe reverted to old form Tuesday night in a stinker of a 6–0 loss to the Chicago White Sox at Progressive Field.

Starting pitcher Kenny Camden was rocked for five of the six Sox runs in five innings, but he wasn't alone in the ballpark needing a good fumigating.

The Indians managed just four hits off White Sox starting pitcher Jim Zechman over seven innings and just one more off the bullpen as their record fell to 20 and 24. Indians fielders also committed three errors, with a pair of miscues leading to four unearned runs in the third inning.

Just as the Indians keep climbing that mountain toward .500, they seem to slip back.

"It's just one game," said interim manager Todd Stein. "You're going to have these. We've been playing so well of late that it's kind of a shocker now to see us play this poorly. We have too much going for us now for this to get us down. We still have a chance to win the series, and that's been our goal as we've tried to climb back into this thing."

Camden couldn't be blamed for everything, especially the errors, but he walked five and could not pitch his team past the mistakes in the field.

"You just throw this one in the garbage and forget about it," said Camden, who pitched well against the White Sox at Chicago in his previous start but came away a no-decision. "The guys in the field have bailed me out so many times that I wouldn't dare say a word about errors. They're part of the game. Physical errors are going to happen. I have a feeling we're just going to shake this thing off and come out and start another winning streak."

There was a whole lot of shaky fielding going on in the third. Scott Michaels fumbled a grounder by slow-footed catcher Enrique Fuentes to start the proceedings. Camden walked Mark Rose and Travis Campbell to load the bases, and Moe Tanko's grounder to third got through Terry Rovetto for another error and bounded into the left-field corner to score all three runners. Jay Walley singled home Tanko.

Indians catcher Morris Jerome's throwing error led to another run in the sixth, and Jackie Winer homered off Buck Sterling in the eighth to complete the scoring.

Rikki LaBudda had two of the Tribe's four hits (both singles), with Rovetto contributing a double and Justin Kestino adding another single.

"It was kind of a mess out there tonight, and I sure did my part in making that mess," Rovetto said. It's been awhile since we played that poor of a game. I don't think you'll see too many more of these."

His manager agreed.

"Back at it tomorrow," he said as he took a final swig of a postgame beer. "Not much else to say. We're better than this, and you'll continue to see that."

CLEVELAND INDIANS VS CHICAGO WHITE SOX •MAY 25
CHICAGO 6 / CLEVELAND 0

CLEVELAND INDIANS										
BATTING	AB	R	H	RBI	2B	3B	HR	BB	SO	BA
RIKKI LABUDDA CF	4	0	2	0	0	0	0	0	0	.254
MICAH MILLISON RF	4	0	0	0	0	0	0	0	2	.264
WILSON WHITE LF	4	0	1	0	0	0	0	0	1	.261
TERRY ROVETTO 3B	4	0	1	0	1	0	0	1	0	.255
SCOTT MICHAELS 2B	4	0	0	0	0	0	0	0	0	.344
OLIVER REINER 1B	4	0	0	0	0	0	0	0	1	.269
JUSTIN KESTINO SS	3	0	1	0	0	0	0	0	1	.225
BERNARD HARPER DH	3	0	0	0	0	0	0	0	2	.252
MORRIS JEROME C	3	0	0	0	0	0	0	0	0	.252
PITCHING	IP	H	R	ER	SO	BB	ERA			
KENNY CAMDEN (L)	5	6	5	0	3	5	3.41			
BUCK STERLING	3	3	1	1	1	0	4.22			
LEE HAZELTON	1	0	0	0	0	0	4.90			

CHICAGO WHITE SOX										
BATTING	AB	R	H	RBI	2B	3B	HR	BB	SO	BA
MARK ROSE 2B	4	1	1	0	0	0	0	1	0	.280
TRAVIS CAMPBELL SS	3	2	0	0	0	0	0	2	0	.230
MO TANKO 3B	4	1	2	0	0	0	0	1	0	.325
JAY WALLEY LF	4	0	1	1	0	0	0	0	1	.258
MIKE ISENMESSER 1B	4	0	2	0	0	0	0	1	0	.280
JACKIE WINER RF	4	1	2	1	1	0	1	0	1	.281
JASON NAKAMURA DH	4	0	0	0	0	0	0	0	1	.217
VLADIMIR JANAKOWSKI CF	4	0	1	0	0	0	0	0	1	.222
ENRIQUE FUENTES C	4	1	0	0	0	0	0	0	0	.236
PITCHING	IP	H	R	ER	SO	BB	ERA			
JIM ZECHMAN (W)	7	4	0	0	5	1	3.42			
CARL WOLDMAN	2	1	0	0	0	0	2.61			

INNING	1	2	3	4	5	6	7	8	9	TOTAL
CHICAGO	0	0	4	0	0	1	0	1	0	6
CLEVELAND	0	0	0	0	0	0	0	0	0	0

GAME 45

By SAM LARDNER
The Cleveland Press

CLEVELAND, May 26 — For fans of the Indians, following their team must seem a lot like tracking the stock market day after day.

After victories, euphoria sets in and happy days are here again.

After losses, the sky is falling.

It was back to the latter after Wednesday night at Progressive Field following a 4 to 2 loss to the Chicago White Sox. If there's any consolation for the Indians, it's that they at least played a cleaner game than the sloppy mess they turned in the previous night in a 6 to 0 loss to the Sox.

"I suppose," said interim manager Todd Stein. "But we're beyond moral victories at this point. We have to start stringing together real victories, which we did until we hit this little speed bump. And I still that that's all this is."

After reeling off a four-game winning streak to come within three games of .500, the Indians dropped two of three to the White Sox to fall to 20 and 25 with the tough Boston Red Sox coming to town this weekend.

It was another creditable pitching performance by Tak Fujimoto, who seems to have found a comfort zone after a shaky beginning to his career in Major League Baseball. The 28-year-old righty out of Japan turned in a quality start with six innings of six-hit, three-run ball.

One mistake in the fourth led to a three-run homer off the bat of Mike Isenmesser to erase a 2–0 Tribe lead. The Sox added an insurance run in the top of the ninth with a double by Mo Tanko driving in Travis Campbell.

"One bad pitch," Fujimoto said through his translator. "I feel like I've been pitching well the last couple of weeks. The support system here is great. I'm happy working with both catchers (Morris Jerome and Iceberg Peters), and the fans here have been great. I wish I could have given them a better end result today."

The Indians took their lead in the second on a two-run homer by Justin Kestino. Terry Rovetto singled against Wilton Berrios to start the inning, and Scott Michaels struck out. Kestino took a slider from Berrios over the wall in left.

"He's tough," Kestino said of Berrios. "He just happened to hang one in that spot, and I was fortunate enough to get it all. We just couldn't get anything else going the rest of the way."

Berrios danced in and out of trouble through six innings, with the Indians leaving the bases loaded in the sixth, with Huron Southworth, getting a rare start striking out on a checked swing.

"Man, that was a tough call," Southworth said. "I don't think I went, but what are you going to do? They don't have replay for that. But we had our chances. I didn't come through there."

The Sox bullpen of Brad Hutchinson, Randy Roselli and Doug Gorham shut the Tribe down the rest of the way.

"It's a tough one to lose, but we get a day off before Boston comes in," Stein said. "We have some good things to reflect on and some things we have to improve on. I like the challenge coming up. They (the Red Sox) are tough, but I think that's going to bring out the best in us. We've been through so much early that I think we're pretty well battle tested."

Time will tell whether it's wise now to buy low on the Indians or to sell that stock.

Stay tuned.

CLEVELAND INDIANS VS CHICAGO WHITE SOX • MAY 26
CHICAGO 4 / CLEVELAND 3

CLEVELAND INDIANS										
BATTING	**AB**	**R**	**H**	**RBI**	**2B**	**3B**	**HR**	**BB**	**SO**	**BA**
RIKKI LABUDDA CF	4	0	0	0	0	0	0	0	0	.249
HURON SOUTHWORTH RF	4	0	1	0	0	0	0	0	2	.214
WILSON WHITE LF	4	0	0	0	0	0	0	0	1	.255
OLIVER REINER 1B	4	1	2	0	1	0	0	1	0	.275
TERRY ROVETTO 3B	4	1	1	0	0	0	0	0	0	.254
SCOTT MICHAELS 2B	3	0	0	0	0	0	0	1	1	.328
JUSTIN KESTINO SS	3	1	2	2	0	0	1	0	1	.233
BERNARD HARPER DH	3	0	1	0	0	0	0	0	0	.255
MORRIS JEROME C	3	0	1	0	0	0	0	0	0	.254
PITCHING	**IP**	**H**	**R**	**ER**	**SO**	**BB**	**ERA**			
TAK FUJIMOTO (L)	6	6	3	3	5	1	3.26			
MICKEY PENNY	2	1	0	0	1	0	3.98			
SOLLY ALVAREZ	1	2	1	1	0	0	3.22			

CHICAGO WHITE SOX										
BATTING	**AB**	**R**	**H**	**RBI**	**2B**	**3B**	**HR**	**BB**	**SO**	**BA**
MARK ROSE 2B	4	1	1	0	0	0	0	1	0	.279
TRAVIS CAMPBELL SS	4	1	0	0	0	0	0	0	1	.215
MO TANKO 3B	4	1	2	1	1	0	0	0	0	.329
JAY WALLEY LF	4	0	0	0	0	0	0	0	0	.247
MIKE ISENMESSER 1B	4	1	2	3	0	0	1	0	1	.288
JACKIE WINER RF	4	0	1	0	1	0	0	0	0	.280
JASON NAKAMURA DH	4	0	1	0	0	0	0	0	1	.218
VLADIMIR JANAKOWSKI CF	4	0	1	0	0	0	0	0	2	.224
ENRIQUE FUENTES C	4	0	1	0	0	0	0	0	1	.237
PITCHING	**IP**	**H**	**R**	**ER**	**SO**	**BB**	**ERA**			
WILTON BERRIOS (W)	6	5	3	3	4	1	3.98			
BRAD HUTCHINSON	1	2	0	0	0	0	3.05			
RANDY ROSELLI	1	2	0	0	0	1	2.95			
DOUG GORHAM (S)	1	0	0	0	1	0	2.20			
INNING	**1**	**2**	**3**	**4**	**5**	**6**	**7**	**8**	**9**	**TOTAL**
CHICAGO	0	0	0	3	0	0	0	0	1	4
CLEVELAND	0	2	0	0	0	0	0	0	0	2

GAME 46

By SAM LARDNER
The Cleveland Press

CLEVELAND, May 28 — In the old days, they used to say that "the Jake was jumpin'." That was back when Progressive Field was called Jacobs Field and the Indians would routinely sell out their games.

On Friday night, you might say that the Prog was rockin'.

The Indians welcomed the Boston Red Sox to town on a late spring evening, and lo and behold, a sellout crowd of 35,041 showed up to cheer the Tribe on to a 5–3 victory.

The last time these two teams met, the Red Sox were taking two of three at Fenway Park back in April. The crowds then were raucous, and at one point, things got out of hand in Boston when Indians infielder Angel Rodriguez, who is openly gay, was the subject of homophobic abuse at the hands of some Red Sox fans.

Friday night, the crowd at Progressive Field showered the Indians with nothing but cheers as the team snapped a mini two-game losing skid and improved to 21 and 25 for the season.

"How about that crowd?" said interim manager Todd Stein. "We had a beautiful Friday night, and the fans came out in full force for us. I think it gave our guys a big lift."

Doing much of the heavy lifting for the Tribe was ace starting pitcher Lynn Moda, who worked seven strong innings, giving up seven hits and three runs while throwing 110 pitches. The pitch count was the only thing keeping him from going longer.

Moda, the ace of the staff, has begun to pitch like it. He earned his second straight victory, going seven innings for a second time in two starts to even his record at five and five.

"It was hard not to get fired up by that crowd," Moda said. "When they're behind you like that, there's nothing quite like it. I've felt a special responsibility for getting us back on track, considering how I started the season."

Moda's mates made it comfortable for him as they jumped on Red Sox starter Eduardo Suarez with three runs in the first inning. The big blow was a bases-loaded double by Justin Kestino. The Indians loaded the bases on a leadoff single by Rikki LaBudda, a walk to Micah Millison and an infield hit by Wilson White.

It looked like the Indians might not capitalize, as Terry Rovetto struck out and Scott Michaels popped out, but Kestino came through, much to the delight of the crowd.

"With the crowd noise, I just wanted to slow things down, relax and try to drive the ball," Kestino said. "There's no doubt the crowd can lift you up, but you've got to be careful not to get too amped up."

Kestino's double was a gapper to right-center on a 3–2 pitch with the runners off, making it easy for all three to score.

Moda walked a pair in the third but worked out of that trouble. Millison hit a solo homer in the bottom of the fourth to give the Indians a 4–0 lead. The Red Sox got a two-run homer from Morgan Leifer in the fifth and an RBI double from Desmond Underwood in the sixth to make it 4–3.

A sacrifice fly by Morris Jerome in the bottom of the sixth gave the Indians a two-run cushion. Moda gutted out one more inning before Geno Milzie and Lee Hazelton finishing up, with Hazelton striking out two of the three batters he faced in the ninth to earn his second save. The crowd was on its feet for the final two outs.

"Quite a rush," said Hazelton, who was recalled from Class AAA Columbus to fill in for injured closer Ivan Zyzna. I'm getting more comfortable every time out there. I felt like I was walking on air as we came off the field at the end."

GAME 46

CLEVELAND INDIANS VS BOSTON RED SOX• MAY 28
CLEVELAND 5 / BOSTON 3

CLEVELAND INDIANS										
BATTING	AB	R	H	RBI	2B	3B	HR	BB	SO	BA
RIKKI LABUDDA CF	5	1	2	0	0	1	0	0	0	.253
MICAH MILLISON RF	5	2	2	1	0	0	1	0	1	.268
WILSON WHITE LF	4	1	1	0	0	0	0	0	1	.254
TERRY ROVETTO 3B	4	0	0	0	0	0	0	1	0	.249
SCOTT MICHAELS 2B	5	0	1	0	0	0	0	0	0	.319
JUSTIN KESTINO SS	4	1	1	3	1	0	0	0	1	.234
OLIVER REINER 1B	4	0	2	0	0	0	1	0	1	.280
BERNARD HARPER DH	4	0	1	0	1	0	0	0	0	.255
MORRIS JEROME C	4	0	1	1	0	0	0	0	0	.254
PITCHING	IP	H	R	ER	SO	BB	ERA			
LYNN MODA (W)	7	7	3	3	4	2	5.06			
GENO MILZIE	1	1	0	0	0	0	4.72			
LEE HAZELTON (S)	1	0	0	0	2	0	3.85			
BOSTON RED SOX										
BATTING	AB	R	H	RBI	2B	3B	HR	BB	SO	BA
OMAR PEREZ LF	4	0	1	0	0	0	0	0	0	.279
STU KENNEDY SS	3	0	1	0	0	0	0	1	0	.234
CARLOS BLANCO C	3	1	0	0	1	0	0	1	2	.318
MORGAN LEIFER 1B	4	1	2	2	0	0	1	0	0	.268
DESMOND UNDERWOOD 3B	4	1	1	1	0	0	0	0	0	.279
TRACE ATTENBERG DH	4	0	1	0	1	0	0	0	1	.280
SANTIAGO AVILLA 2B	4	0	0	0	0	0	0	0	0	.238
SALVATORE ESPINOSA RF	4	0	2	0	0	0	0	0	2	.237
VICTOR TRAGGER JR CF	4	0	0	0	0	0	0	0	1	.224
PITCHING	IP	H	R	ER	SO	BB	ERA			
EDUARDO SUAREZ (L)	5	6	4	4	2	0	4.22			
FELIX INFANTE	2	3	1	1	1	1	2.91			
EDDIE MYERS	1	2	0	0	0	1	2.75			

INNING	1	2	3	4	5	6	7	8	9	TOTAL
BOSTON	0	0	0	0	2	1	0	0	0	3
CLEVELAND	3	0	0	1	0	1	0	0		5

GAME 47

By SAM LARDNER
The Cleveland Press

CLEVELAND, May 29 — There's nothing quite like a laugher to keep everybody happy.

The Indians got just that Saturday night with a nationally televised 9–1 victory over the Boston Red Sox before 35,202 fans at Progressive Field with the Tribe pounding out 16 hits.

The blowout may have had TV fans tuning out of the FOX broadcast early, but the locals didn't mind. Nary a soul seemed to have left the park as the suddenly resurgent Indians won their second straight and their sixth out of their last eight games to improve to 22 and 25.

The Indians got home runs from Scott Michaels, his seventh, Oliver Reiner, his eighth, and Terry Rovetto, his seventh, with the first two coming off Boston starter Scott Johnson.

Getting the biggest chuckle of all was Indians starting pitcher Ollie Gonzalez, who is beginning to get the benefit of run support after being the Tribe's hard-luck starter early in the season. Today he was dealing pitching 6 innings and only allowing 4 hits.

"That's why I never said a word about it early," Gonzalez said with a laugh. "You just know that with a lineup like ours, the runs are going to come for me. That was just a coincidence early I wasn't exactly throwing it lights-out when the team overall was going bad. But I'll take this."

This was no contest from the get-go. Rikki LaBudda led off the bottom of the first inning with a single and a stolen base. Two outs later, Terry Rovetto walked and both runners rode home on Michaels' homer to left field.

"It was good to get us off to that start," Michaels said. "Things have been going pretty well for me and the team. I had a couple rough games here (1-for-17 over his last three), but I just stuck with it."

A healthy and productive Michaels could go a long way toward getting the Indians back to .500 and beyond. He has taken over at second base for the injured Angel Rodriguez. Michaels does possess more power than does Rodriguez even though his fielding may not be quite as slick. But in the middle of this lineup, he is doing damage.

"We like Scott a lot in the middle of the order," said manager Todd Stein. "He's always had the stroke. It's just been a matter of keeping him healthy and now, getting him some regular at-bats."

Reiner hit a two-run homer in the third, and Rovetto's three-run blast in the fifth chased Johnson. From there, the Indians coasted.

Gonzalez went six easy innings, giving up a harmless solo homer to Trace Attenberg in the fifth. Solly Alvarez got some work by pitching the final three innings.

Late in the game, Stein went with some subs, giving Kieran Catsef, Willie Bartlett and Leo Taylor some time on the field.

"With the day game coming up (Sunday), it was good to get a few guys off their feet," said Stein, who may start one or two of his subs in the series finale. "We haven't had too many of these games this year in our favor, so it was nice to sit back and watch a ballgame."

CLEVELAND INDIANS VS BOSTON RED SOX • MAY 29
CLEVELAND 9 / BOSTON 1

CLEVELAND INDIANS										
BATTING	**AB**	**R**	**H**	**RBI**	**2B**	**3B**	**HR**	**BB**	**SO**	**BA**
RIKKI LABUDDA CF	5	2	2	0	0	0	0	0	0	.257
MICAH MILLISON RF	5	2	2	0	1	0	0	0	1	.272
WILSON WHITE LF	3	0	2	0	0	0	0	0	0	.262
KIERAN CATSEF LF	2	0	1	1	0	0	0	1	0	.273
TERRY ROVETTO 3B	3	2	1	3	0	0	1	0	0	.250
WILLIE BARTLETT 3B	2	0	0	0	0	0	0	0	0	.000
SCOTT MICHAELS 2B	4	1	2	3	0	0	1	0	0	.329
JUSTIN KESTINO SS	3	1	2	0	1	0	0	0	0	.241
LEO TAYLOR SS	2	0	1	0	0	0	0	0	0	.214
OLIVER REINER 1B	4	1	1	2	0	0	1	0	0	.279
BERNARD HARPER DH	4	0	1	0	0	0	0	0	0	.254
MORRIS JEROME C	4	0	1	0	0	0	0	0	0	.254
PITCHING	**IP**	**H**	**R**	**ER**	**SO**	**BB**	**ERA**			
OLLIE GONZALEZ (W)	6	4	1	1	4	0	4.99			
SOLLY ALVAREZ	3	1	0	0	1	0	2.84			

BOSTON RED SOX										
BATTING	**AB**	**R**	**H**	**RBI**	**2B**	**3B**	**HR**	**BB**	**SO**	**BA**
OMAR PEREZ LF	4	0	0	0	0	0	0	0	0	.270
STU KENNEDY SS	4	0	1	0	0	0	0	0	1	.235
CARLOS BLANCO C	4	0	1	0	0	0	0	0	0	.317
MORGAN LEIFER 1B	4	0	1	0	0	0	0	0	1	.267
DESMOND UNDERWOOD 3B	4	0	0	0	0	0	0	0	0	.270
TRACE ATTENBERG DH	4	1	1	1	0	0	1	0	1	.279
SANTIAGO AVILLA 2B	4	0	0	0	0	0	0	0	0	.229
SALVATORE ESPINOSA RF	4	0	0	0	0	0	0	0	0	.225
VICTOR TRAGGER JR CF	3	0	1	0	0	0	0	0	2	.228
PITCHING	**IP**	**H**	**R**	**ER**	**SO**	**BB**	**ERA**			
SCOTT JOHNSON (L)	3	9	5	5	0	1	4.56			
SANDY BENCOMO	3	5	3	3	1	0	3.57			
NICK SPERO	2	2	1	0	0	1	2.61			
INNING	**1**	**2**	**3**	**4**	**5**	**6**	**7**	**8**	**9**	**TOTAL**
BOSTON	0	0	0	0	1	0	0	0	0	1
CLEVELAND	3	0	2	0	3	0	0	1		9

GAME 48

By SAM LARDNER

The Cleveland Press

CLEVELAND, May 30 — Home sweep home.

Home was certainly where the heart — and the near heart attacks — were Sunday as the Indians completed a three-game sweep of the Boston Red Sox at Progressive Field with a 3–2 walk-off victory in the bottom of the ninth inning.

Unlike Saturday night's romp for the Tribe, Sunday's game was a taut affair played out under bright blue late-May skies with a hint of summer in the air.

Rookie closer Lee Hazelton gave up a two-out game-tying homer to the Red Sox' Desmond Underwood in the top of the ninth inning with the crowd of 37,358 on its feet.

But the shock barely had time to wear off as Indians DH Bernard Harper led off the home half with a first-pitch homer to left against Jose Rodriguez.

"I haven't had too many big moments this year, but this is one I'll remember for a long time," said Harper, fresh off a reception at home plate that included baths in various flavors of Gatorade. "I try to get some swings in between innings in the cage behind the dugout. I felt pretty loose and fresh. I figured he would try to get ahead in the count with a fastball, and I guessed right."

The victory sends the Indians to a brief road trip to Yankee Stadium with a record of 23–25 as they try to reach the .500 mark for the first time this season and then go from there.

"This was really a big series for us," said interim manager Todd Stein, who is 21–17 since taking over for the fired Dave Mills after the team got off to a 2–8 start. "You don't want to say that this is a season-defining series or anything like that because tomorrow is a new day. But this is certainly going to make the ride to New York a lot more fun. You can still hear the guys celebrating in the clubhouse. This means a lot to them."

Stein rested both Micah Millison and Oliver Reiner, giving starts to both Huron Southworth and J.J. Kulakofski.

It meant a lot to starting pitcher Brian "The Doctor" Howard even though he didn't come away with the "W" next to his name in the box score. As a 30-year-old veteran, Howard has seen a few things.

"In the end, it doesn't matter who gets the win as long as it's the team," said Howard, who pitched seven innings, giving up six hits and a first-inning sacrifice fly to Willard Washington. "I've sort of sat back and watched. We had a team meeting not too long ago. I spoke my piece, but I wanted to listen and observe. I like what I'm seeing."

Stein has done some re-crafting of the roster, partly because of performance and partly because of injury. Scott Michaels, who has won the position because of his bat has been getting more playing time because of the hamstring injury to second baseman Angel Rodriguez. Michaels went 2-for-5 Sunday with a two-run double in the fourth inning against Rich Dorland that scored Wilson White and Terry Rovetto, both of whom singled ahead of him. That hit gave the Indians a 2–1 lead that held up until the ninth.

"Scott is an interesting player," Stein said. "I know the team thought he would be a star when they drafted him. But he had the shoulder surgery and other nagging injuries. I'm not going to put any extra pressure on him. I'm just going to write his name on the lineup card and let him play."

Neither team got much going after that. Buck Sterling pitched the eighth inning for the Indians before giving way to Hazelton in the ninth. Hazelton got Stu Kennedy looking on strikes to open the inning. Omar Perez then popped out to Oliver Reiner at first base before Underwood homered after fouling off three straight fastballs.

"I came with a slider and probably sped up his bat," said Hazelton, who got the win despite the blown save. "I should not have given in there. That's part of learning in the big leagues. I'm just glad Harp picked me up in the bottom of the inning. I was the first guy out of the dugout to greet him at the plate."

GAME 48

CLEVELAND INDIANS VS BOSTON RED SOX• MAY 30
CLEVELAND 3 / BOSTON 2

CLEVELAND INDIANS										
BATTING	AB	R	H	RBI	2B	3B	HR	BB	SO	BA
RIKKI LABUDDA CF	5	0	2	0	0	0	0	0	0	.261
HURON SOUTHWORTH RF	4	0	1	0	1	0	0	1	1	.217
WILSON WHITE LF	4	1	2	0	0	0	0	1	0	.267
TERRY ROVETTO 3B	4	1	1	0	0	0	0	1	0	.250
SCOTT MICHAELS 2B	5	0	2	2	0	0	0	0	0	.333
JUSTIN KESTINO SS	3	0	0	0	0	0	0	2	1	.237
JJ KULAKOFSKI 1B	4	0	1	0	0	0	0	0	1	.220
BERNARD HARPER DH	4	1	2	1	1	0	1	0	0	.263
ICEBERG PETERS C	4	0	1	0	0	0	0	0	2	.262
PITCHING	IP	H	R	ER	SO	BB	ERA			
BRIAN HOWARD	7	6	1	1	5	2	3.50			
BUCK STERLING	1	1	0	0	0	0	4.03			
LEE HAZELTON (BS) (W)	1	1	1	1	2	0	4.76			

BOSTON RED SOX										
BATTING	AB	R	H	RBI	2B	3B	HR	BB	SO	BA
STU KENNEDY SS	4	1	1	0	0	0	0	1	1	.236
OMAR PEREZ 2B	3	0	1	0	0	0	0	1	0	.271
DESMOND UNDERWOOD 3B	4	1	1	1	0	0	1	0	0	.269
WILLARD WASHINGTON CF	4	0	1	1	0	0	0	0	1	.287
MORGAN LEIFER 1B	4	0	0	0	0	0	0	0	2	.257
TRACE ATTENBERG DH	4	0	2	0	0	0	0	0	1	.286
SANTIAGO AVILLA 2B	4	0	1	0	0	0	0	0	1	.229
SALVATORE ESPINOSA RF	4	0	0	0	0	0	0	0	0	.214
MARTY BLACKBURN C	3	0	1	0	0	0	0	0	1	.238
PITCHING	IP	H	R	ER	SO	BB	ERA			
RICH DORLAND	8	11	2	2	5	5	3.61			
JOSE RODRIGUEZ (L)	0	1	1	1	0	0	2.55			

INNING	1	2	3	4	5	6	7	8	9	TOTAL
BOSTON	1	0	0	0	0	0	0	0	1	2
CLEVELAND	0	0	0	2	0	0	0	0	1	3

GAME 49

By SAM LARDNER
The Cleveland Press

NEW YORK May 31 — The bright lights of Broadway proved to be too much for the Indians Monday night.

After completing an emotional three-game sweep of the Red Sox in Cleveland over the weekend, the Indians looked a bit wide-eyed in a 4-1 loss to the New York Yankees at Yankee Stadium.

Pitcher Kenny Camden fell behind early and Tribe batters couldn't get anything going against Yankees starter Ty Goodman who tossed a complete game.

"I give the credit to them rather than blaming us," said Indians manager Todd Stein, whose team fell to 23–26. "It always looks like your lifeless or whatever you want to call it when you don't have anybody on base. But Goodman had our number tonight, and we just couldn't get anything going. This can be an intimidating place to play, but our guys have been through a few things, and they've all played in New York before. If we can string a couple hits together here and there for the rest of the series, we'll be OK."

The Indians have not won a game Camden started since he beat the Tigers in Detroit more than two weeks ago. They also have scored just one run in his last two starts.

"I kind of got us behind the eight-ball early," Camden said. "You get behind 3–0 early, and the way Goodman was pitching, well, I didn't give

153

us much of a chance. But I was happy with how we limited the damage after that."

The Yankees took their 3–0 lead in the third when Gary Ashcroft dropped a three-run homer just over the short porch in right field. That came after Camden walked Jake Koenig and gave up a single to Chris Hansen.

"You can say it was a pop-fly homer if you want," Camden said. "But the walk set up the whole inning. The ballpark is what it is. I'm sure we'll get one or two like that before it's over."

The Yankees' Rick Steinberg had an RBI single in the fifth before Micah Millison's double in the sixth drove in Rikki LaBudda, who led off with a single and a stolen base.

Yankees manager Craig Whitehead had some words that should be encouraging for Indians fans.

"We've seen how they've been playing," Whitehead said. "This is a dangerous ballclub. Just ask the Red Sox. Their pitching is solid, and their lineup is just too good to hold down for too long. They're going to be in the Central race all year once they get over the hump. I just hope they get out of town before that happens here."

Camden lasted six innings with Mickey Penney and Solly Alvarez finishing up.

"This has been a big stretch for us, with games against Boston and the Yankees," Stein said. "If they provide a measuring stick, I'd say we're standing pretty tall."

GAME 49

CLEVELAND INDIANS VS NEW YORK YANKEES • MAY 31
NEW YORK 4 / CLEVELAND 1

CLEVELAND INDIANS										
BATTING	AB	R	H	RBI	2B	3B	HR	BB	SO	BA
RIKKI LABUDDA CF	4	1	2	0	0	0	0	0	0	.266
MICAH MILLISON RF	4	0	2	1	1	0	0	0	0	.278
WILSON WHITE LF	3	0	1	0	0	0	0	1	1	.268
TERRY ROVETTO 3B	4	0	1	0	0	0	0	0	1	.245
SCOTT MICHAELS 2B	4	0	0	0	0	0	0	0	2	.318
OLIVER REINER 1B	4	0	0	0	0	0	0	0	2	.273
BERNARD HARPER DH	4	0	1	0	0	0	0	0	1	.262
MORRIS JEROME C	4	0	1	0	1	0	1	0	0	.254
LEO TAYLOR SS	3	0	1	0	0	0	0	1	1	.226
PITCHING	IP	H	R	ER	SO	BB	ERA			
KENNY CAMDEN (L)	6	9	4	4	4	2	3.64			
MICKEY PENNY	1	1	0	0	1	0	3.80			
SOLLY ALVAREZ	1	0	0	0	1	1	2.73			

NEW YORK YANKEES										
BATTING	AB	R	H	RBI	2B	3B	HR	BB	SO	BA
MARK STRANTON CF	4	0	1	0	0	0	0	1	0	.237
WILLIE ROBINSON 3B	4	0	1	0	0	0	0	1	0	.271
RAIDEL MEDINA DH	4	1	2	0	1	0	0	0	0	.276
GUILLERMO CRUZ 1B	4	0	0	0	0	0	0	0	1	.276
RICK STEINBERG C	4	0	1	1	0	0	0	0	1	.257
JAKE KOENIG SS	4	1	0	0	0	0	0	1	1	.277
CHRIS HANSEN 2B	4	1	2	0	1	0	0	0	1	.239
GARY ASHCROFT LF	4	1	2	3	0	0	1	0	0	.227
RODNEY BRINKMAN RF	4	0	0	0	0	0	0	0	2	.224
PITCHING	IP	H	R	ER	SO	BB	ERA			
TY GOODMAN (W)	9	9	1	1	8	2	3.64			

INNING	1	2	3	4	5	6	7	8	9	TOTAL
CLEVELAND	0	0	0	0	0	1	0	0	0	1
NEW YORK	0	0	3	0	1	0	0	0		4

GAME 50

By SAM LARDNER
The Cleveland Press

NEW YORK, June 1 — It's not often that an opposing player gets an ovation, much less at Yankee stadium.

But that's what the Indians Tak Fujimoto experienced Tuesday night when Bronx cheers were really cheers of the sincere kind.

Fujimoto was the hard-luck loser as the Tribe fell 1–0 to the Yankees in an exquisite pitcher's duel between Fujimoto and Yankees ace Gregg Sterney, each pitcher only allowing three hits. The loss was the Tribe's second straight in this three-game series to drop to 23 and 27 for the season as June gets underway.

As for Fujimoto, he retired the first 15 New York batters he faced before giving up a leadoff homer to Nick Wright leading the sixth inning. That was it for the scoring. When manager Todd Stein came out to remove Fujimoto from the game in the eighth, many in the crowd applauded, some standing.

Part of that is due to history. The Yankees have a strong heritage of bringing in quality Japanese players, from Hideki Matsui to Masahiro Tanaka. That enabled the Yankees to cultivate a following of Japanese-American fans as well as natives of Japan who feel the need to catch a ballgame while in the Big Apple.

"I was somewhat surprised," Fujimoto said through his translator. "I know the Yankees had some interest in me when I was a free agent. It didn't

156

work out, but it was nice to hear that from the fans. They are really knowledgeable about baseball here."

Fujimoto teamed with backup catcher Iceberg Peters to handcuff the Bronx Bombers for most of the night. After getting a pair of groundouts in the first inning, Fujimoto struck out the side in the second. The home run by Wright was a no-doubter, as the ball landed in the second deck in left field.

"Man, he was tough," Wright told the New York media in the Yankees clubhouse. "You can see why a lot of teams, including ours, wanted him last winter. He moves the ball around, and his velocity gets that ball on top of you in a hurry."

Fujimoto gave up three hits total in 7 and one-third innings as he threw 115 pitches. All the while, though, Indians batters got nothing going against Sterney, who lasted seven innings, giving way to relievers Sherwin Caisman and Pete Snow.

Scott Michaels got as far as third base in the fourth when he doubled and went to third on Justin Kestino's groundout to the right side of the infield. But he died on third when Harper and Peters struck out.

The Indians really didn't mount much of a threat after that.

"Hats off to both starting pitchers," said Indians manager Todd Stein. "Our guy, I thought, was fabulous, and we've run into a pair of pretty-well-pitched games by the Yankees. We've got to salvage something tomorrow before the off-day and a weekend at home. But I'll take a pitching performance like that all the time and take my chances on the result."

CLEVELAND INDIANS VS NEW YORK YANKEES · JUNE 1
NEW YORK 1 / CLEVELAND 0

CLEVELAND INDIANS

BATTING	AB	R	H	RBI	2B	3B	HR	BB	SO	BA
RIKKI LABUDDA CF	4	0	1	0	0	0	0	0	0	.265
MICAH MILLISON RF	4	0	0	0	0	0	0	0	1	.271
WILSON WHITE LF	4	0	1	0	0	0	0	0	0	.268
TERRY ROVETTO 3B	3	0	1	0	0	0	0	1	1	.246
SCOTT MICHAELS 2B	4	0	1	0	1	0	0	0	0	.315
JUSTIN KESTINO SS	4	0	0	0	0	0	0	0	1	.232
BERNARD HARPER DH	4	0	0	0	0	0	0	0	2	.254
ICEBERG PETERS C	4	0	0	0	0	0	0	0	0	.239
J.J. KULAKOFSKI 1B	4	0	0	0	0	0	0	0	1	.206

PITCHING	IP	H	R	ER	SO	BB	ERA
TAK FUJIMOTO (L)	7.33	3	1	1	3	0	3.04
LORRY UNGER	0.67	1	0	0	0	0	2.70

NEW YORK YANKEES

BATTING	AB	R	H	RBI	2B	3B	HR	BB	SO	BA
MARK STRANTON CF	4	0	1	0	0	0	0	0	0	.225
WILLIE ROBINSON 3B	4	0	0	0	0	0	0	0	0	.255
RAIDEL MEDINA DH	4	0	0	0	0	0	0	0	0	.252
GUILLERMO CRUZ 1B	4	0	1	0	0	0	0	0	1	.284
RICK STEINBERG C	4	0	1	0	0	0	0	0	1	.257
JAKE KOENIG SS	4	0	0	0	0	0	0	0	1	.270
NICK WRIGHT RF	4	1	1	1	0	0	1	0	0	.303
GARY ASHCROFT LF	4	0	0	0	0	0	0	0	0	.196
CHRIS HANSEN 2B	3	0	0	0	0	0	0	0	0	.224

PITCHING	IP	H	R	ER	SO	BB	ERA
GREG STERNEY (W)	7	3	0	0	4	1	3.61
SHERWIN CAISMAN	1	1	0	0	1	0	2.33
PETE SNOW (S)	1	0	0	0	1	0	1.89

INNING	1	2	3	4	5	6	7	8	9	TOTAL
CLEVELAND	0	0	0	0	0	0	0	0	0	0
NEW YORK	0	0	0	0	0	1	0	0		1

GAME 51

By SAM LARDNER
The Cleveland Press

NEW YORK, June 2 — If your ace can do it, so can ours.

That was the mantra emanating out of the Indians clubhouse Wednesday night after their ace starting pitcher, Lynn Moda, came through with an ace-like performance in a 7–2 victory over the Yankees at Yankee Stadium.

One night after watching Yankees ace Gregg Sterney handcuff his teammates, Moda went out and shut down the Bronx Bombers over 6 and two-thirds innings, allowing four hits and one run as the Tribe salvaged the final game of this three-game set to improve to 24–27 for the season.

After the Indians swept the Red Sox in Cleveland over this past weekend, they would have found that getting swept in New York to be deflating if not devastating.

Enter Moda.

The ace of the Indians staff turned it up a notch and came through with his third straight solid start at a time when he needed it most.

He struck out five and walked no one, leaving only after his pitch count reached 110. Of course, it helped that the Tribe's offense staked him to a big lead early, getting a grand slam from Scott Michaels in the first inning against Yankees No. 2 starter Carlos Morejon.

"I feel like I've found a rhythm these last three or four starts," Moda said. "We really needed to win this game tonight, and I felt I needed to do my part. The hitters certainly did theirs. We just couldn't afford to give back all the gains we made against the Red Sox last weekend."

The Indians will enjoy a Thursday off before welcoming in another legendary club, the Chicago Cubs, into Progressive Field for a weekend series that's sure to be sold out.

They got down to business quickly, with Rikki LaBudda starting the game with a bunt single that seemed to catch the Yankees napping. Micah Millison singled LaBudda to third base. Wilson White walked to load the bases. A fly ball by Terry Rovetto to left field was not deep enough to score even the fleet-footed LaBudda, but Michaels' drive to left-center — to the deepest part of the park — was plenty deep enough as it cleared the wall by plenty and shocked the big Bronx crowd of 40,098.

"I just put my head down and kept running hard," said Michaels, who went 2-for-5 with a single in addition to the slam. "The way this ballpark plays, I had no idea the ball was going out. I thought I had a double. But when I heard the crowd go silent, I looked up and saw that the ball had cleared the wall. It was a great feeling, and I kind of floated on air the rest of the way around the bases."

The Indians got a two-run homer from Oliver Reiner in the fifth, his tenth, and as solo job from Bernard Harper in the sixth.

"Yeah, I sneaked one over the short wall in right," Harper said. "It happened to us the other night, so it was nice to return the favor. We needed this one."

With the day off coming up, manager Terry Stein got some work in for ace setup man Geno Milzie and new closer Lee Hazelton.

The schedule now sets up favorably for the Indians, with six home games coming up against the Cubs and Brewers of the National League.

"We're looking forward to it," Stein said. "The Cubs will bring their fans with them. I know both of these teams have been struggling, so we'll have to be ready. But we're hoping our fans will turn out and give our guys a boost."

GAME 51

CLEVELAND INDIANS VS NEW YORK YANKEES · JUNE 2
CLEVELAND 7 / NEW YORK 2

CLEVELAND INDIANS

BATTING	AB	R	H	RBI	2B	3B	HR	BB	SO	BA
RIKKI LABUDDA CF	5	1	2	0	0	0	0	0	0	.269
MICAH MILLISON RF	4	1	1	0	0	0	0	1	0	.271
WILSON WHITE LF	5	1	0	0	0	0	0	0	0	.261
TERRY ROVETTO 3B	4	1	0	0	0	0	0	1	1	.241
SCOTT MICHAELS 2B	5	1	2	4	0	0	1	0	0	.319
OLIVER REINER 1B	4	1	2	2	0	0	1	0	1	.278
JUSTIN KESTINO SS	4	0	1	0	0	0	0	0	0	.232
BERNARD HARPER DH	4	1	2	1	0	0	1	0	0	.262
MORRIS JEROME C	4	0	0	0	0	0	0	0	1	.260

PITCHING	IP	H	R	ER	SO	BB	ERA			
LYNN MODA (W)	6.67	4	1	1	5	0	4.65			
GENO MILZIE	1.33	2	1	1	1	0	4.80			
LEE HAZELTON	1	0	0	0	1	0	4.05			

NEW YORK YANKEES

BATTING	AB	R	H	RBI	2B	3B	HR	BB	SO	BA
MARK STRANTON CF	4	2	2	2	1	0	0	0	0	.238
WILLIE ROBINSON 3B	4	0	0	0	0	0	0	0	0	.248
RAIDEL MEDINA DH	4	0	0	0	0	0	0	0	2	.244
GUILLERMO CRUZ 1B	4	0	1	0	0	0	0	0	1	.283
RICK STEINBERG C	4	0	0	0	0	0	0	0	0	.248
JAKE KOENIG SS	4	0	0	0	0	0	0	0	2	.262
NICK WRIGHT RF	4	0	0	0	0	0	0	0	0	.290
GARY ASHCROFT LF	3	0	2	0	0	0	0	0	1	.211
LEONARD LEE 2B	3	0	1	0	0	0	0	0	0	.271

PITCHING	IP	H	R	ER	SO	BB	ERA			
CARLOS MOREJON (L)	4.67	8	6	6	0	2	4.84			
HERNAN ROCHA	2.33	2	1	1	1	0	3.42			
STEPH PERLOW	1	0	0	0	2	0	2.84			

INNING	1	2	3	4	5	6	7	8	9	TOTAL
CLEVELAND	4	0	0	0	2	1	0	0	0	7
NEW YORK	0	0	0	0	0	1	1	0	0	2

GAME 52

By SAM LARDNER
The Cleveland Press

CLEVELAND, June 4 — There is always a roiling of emotions when the Chicago Cubs come to Cleveland to play the Indians.

There's the raucous band of Cubs fans who seem to make as much noise as the home crowd in any ballpark they invade.

There's the interleague rivalry between two charter members of their respective leagues.

And, oh yeah, there's that whole World Series thing of a few years back, when the Cubs got what some believe was some divine help in the form of a rain delay to win the World Series at Progressive Field.

All of the raw emotions were on display Friday night, and this time, fans of the Indians had the first laugh of the weekend as their team came away with a 5–2 victory before a standing-room-only crowd of 36,001.

"The Cubbies, man," said Indians manager Todd Stein with an admiring slow whistle and shake of the head. "They bring it, them and their fans. But you know what? It's great for baseball. Seeing and hearing all that back-and-forth going on in the stands gets both teams going. It was fun tonight, and it's going to be a fun weekend here."

Having the fun for the Indians were lefty Ollie Gonzalez and right fielder Micah Millison. Gonzalez spun six solid innings, giving up both runs and six hits. Millison, a bench player when the season started, continued to show why moving him into the starting lineup was the right move, hit a three-run homer in the fourth inning to break a scoreless tie and send the Indians on their way. It was Millison's eighth home run of the season. They're within two games of .500 again at 25–27.

"Good team effort," said Gonzalez, who has turned his season around (and gotten some run support) just as the team has. "I think I had another inning left in me, but Skip is thinking long term. He wants us all fresh for the end of the first half and the stretch run. I know we're going to be in this thing."

Millison's homer came off Cubs starting pitcher Jimmy Fox. No. 9 hitter Morris Jerome singled and went to second on a balk by Fox. Rikki LaBudda walked. Millison then drove one over the wall in right field.

"That kind of quieted their fans down," Millison said. "Until then, the Cubs fans had been making most of the noise. But our fans kind of took over from there. You always want your crowd behind you. It kind of gets on your nerves when you hear so much noise from the other team's fans."

The Cubs came within 3–2 in the fifth when Troy Carney took Gonzalez over the wall in left with a man on. It took Gonzalez 34 pitches to get through the inning, hastening his departure from the game.

"We're not holding anybody back, but you've got to be prudent with these guys," Stein said. "We wouldn't do it if we didn't have confidence in our bullpen. They've been pretty good despite a couple of hiccups. But that's the case with any pen."

The Indians got an inning each out of relievers Mickey Penney, Geno Milzie and Lee Hazelton, who got the save. Justin Kestino provided Hazelton a little breathing room with a two-run double in the bottom of the eighth scoring Oliver Reiner and Bernard Harper who got a rare start at third base giving Terry Rovetto a day off.

"Good way to start the homestand," Stein said. "For a while it almost felt like a road game, but we got the home crowd back into it with Micah's homer. I'm sure this place will be jumping all weekend."

Count on it.

CLEVELAND INDIANS VS CHICAGO CUBS · JUNE 4
CLEVELAND 5 / CHICAGO 2

CLEVELAND INDIANS										
BATTING	AB	R	H	RBI	2B	3B	HR	BB	SO	BA
RIKKI LABUDDA CF	4	1	0	0	0	0	0	0	0	.263
MICAH MILLISON RF	4	1	2	3	0	0	1	1	0	.276
WILSON WHITE LF	4	0	0	0	0	0	0	1	0	.255
BERNARD HARPER 3B	4	1	1	0	0	0	0	0	1	.261
SCOTT MICHAELS 2B	4	0	1	0	0	0	1	0	0	.316
OLIVER REINER 1B	4	1	2	0	0	0	0	0	1	.283
JUSTIN KESTINO SS	4	0	1	2	1	0	0	0	0	.232
J.J. KULAKOFSKI DH	4	0	1	1	0	0	0	0	1	.209
MORRIS JEROME C	4	1	2	0	0	0	0	0	1	.267
PITCHING	IP	H	R	ER	SO	BB	ERA			
OLLIE GONZALEZ (W)	6	6	2	2	5	1	4.78			
MICKEY PENNY	1	0	0	0	0	1	3.63			
GENO MILZIE	1	1	0	0	0	0	4.66			
LEE HAZELTON (S)	1	0	0	0	1	1	5.87			
CHICAGO CUBS										
BATTING	AB	R	H	RBI	2B	3B	HR	BB	SO	BA
JOSE PINTO CF	4	0	1	0	0	0	0	0	0	.298
JERRY ARMSTRONG 2B	3	0	0	0	0	0	0	1	0	.264
COLE JOHNSON 1B	4	0	1	0	0	0	0	1	0	.297
RAFAEL CINCOTTA 3B	4	0	2	0	0	0	0	0	1	.292
BO AUSTIN C	4	1	1	0	0	0	0	0	2	.265
FRANCO SUAREZ DH	4	0	0	0	0	0	0	0	1	.262
TROY CARNEY RF	4	1	1	2	0	0	1	0	0	.280
PABLO MENDEZ LF	4	0	0	0	0	0	0	0	1	.235
BROCK LAMARCA SS	3	0	1	0	0	0	0	0	1	.271
PITCHING	IP	H	R	ER	SO	BB	ERA			
JIMMY FOX (L)	6	7	3	3	3	1	4.05			
HARLEY KAPLAN	2	3	2	2	1	1	3.81			

INNING	1	2	3	4	5	6	7	8	9	TOTAL
CHICAGO	0	0	0	0	2	0	0	0	0	2
CLEVELAND	0	0	0	3	0	0	0	2		5

GAME 53

By SAM LARDNER
The Cleveland Press

CLEVELAND, June 5 — The contrast in moods between the two club-houses at Progressive Field Saturday could not have been starker.

A unified and happy bunch of Cleveland Indians reveled in their 6–3 victory over the Chicago Cubs.

A sniping and unhappy bunch of Cubs spat out pointed words while pointing fingers after a wild game that took nearly four hours to play on a bright and sunny afternoon.

The game was tied at 3–3 in the bottom of the eighth inning when Cubs third baseman Rafael Cincotta picked up a slow roller by speedy Willie Bartlett, in for Justin Kestino, with runners and first and second and threw wildly down the first-base line and into right field, allowing both runners to score. The Indians added one more on a single by Morris Jerome to earn their third straight victory, moving them to within a game of .500 at 26–27.

The best choice probably would have been for Cincotta to hold the ball — at least Cubs manager Perry Tasky thought so — but the Indians weren't asking questions.

"We'll take it," said manager Todd Stein. "I know what it feels like to be on the other end of one of those. It's bang-bang all the way, but in the end, the throw went awry and we caught a break."

On the other side, Tasky was lamenting his team's poor play.

"Damn, Raffy has got to eat the ball right there," he said. "Who knows what might have happened after that, but at least the game would still be tied. Look, I'm not blaming our guy. It's a tough play. But these kinds of plays have been killing us."

Apprised of his manager's words, Cincotta fired back.

"Tell Tasky I'd do it all over again," he said.

Well, then.

The Indians have had their share of problems this year, but things seem to be coming around, and they've managed to stick together through the good times and bad.

The teams traded three-run homers in the third inning, with Brock Lamarca crushing one against Indians starter Brian Howard.

Not to be outdone, Scott Michaels rifled a line-drive homer over the wall in left against Lydon Neuman in the bottom of the inning to tie it. That was Michaels' first of three hits in five at-bats on the afternoon and his ninth home run

"Whew," Michaels said. "I think that's everybody's emotion today. If you stay with it, you'll make your own breaks."

The speed of Bartlett no doubt forced the wild throw in the fateful eighth. Bartlett is a recent call-up in the wake of the hamstring injury to Angel Rodriguez.

"I topped the ball, and I knew if it stayed fair, I'd have a chance to either beat it out or that they'd eat the ball," Bartlett said. "I forced the throw, and it was a bad one. Sometimes speed comes in handy, I guess."

Neither starting pitcher was around for a decision. Howard was done after five innings. Neuman went 6.

"It was fun sitting on the bench and watching that one unfold in the eighth," Howard said. "That was two good-hitting ballclubs going at it. I made too many pitches early, and when you're up around the 100 mark in the fifth, you know you're not going back out. But the pen shut them down again."

Solly Alvarez and Buck Sterling held the Cubs at bay, and Lee Hazelton overcame a leadoff walk in the ninth to earn the save, his second in two games. Stein knows he may have to get creative with the pen for Sunday's finale.

"We'll see," he said. "Haze was lights-out. I know he had that walk, but the stuff was so good. I'll talk to him in the morning to see how he feels. He's done all we've asked from a rookie. We have a chance — finally — to get to .500. I'm sure Haze will tell me he's ready if we have to call on him. But we're just happy to get the heck out of here with a 'W' today and let the dust settle."

CLEVELAND INDIANS VS CHICAGO CUBS · JUNE 5
CLEVELAND 6 / CHICAGO 3

CLEVELAND INDIANS										
BATTING	**AB**	**R**	**H**	**RBI**	**2B**	**3B**	**HR**	**BB**	**SO**	**BA**
RIKKI LABUDDA CF	5	1	2	0	1	0	0	0	1	.267
MICAH MILLISON RF	5	1	0	0	0	0	0	0	1	.268
WILSON WHITE LF	4	0	2	0	1	0	0	1	0	.260
OLIVER REINER 1B	4	0	2	0	0	0	0	1	2	.287
SCOTT MICHAELS 2B	5	2	3	3	0	0	1	0	0	.330
TERRY ROVETTO 3B	4	1	1	0	0	0	0	1	0	.241
BERNARD HARPER DH	4	0	0	0	0	0	0	1	1	.254
WILLIE BARTLETT SS	4	0	1	0	0	0	0	0	1	.250
MORRIS JEROME C	4	0	2	0	0	0	0	0	2	.273
PITCHING	**IP**	**H**	**R**	**ER**	**SO**	**BB**	**ERA**			
BRIAN HOWARD	5	5	3	3	3	1	3.65			
SOLLY ALVAREZ	1	1	0	0	0	0	3.63			
BUCK STERLING (W)	2	1	0	0	0	0	3.70			
LEE HAZELTON (S)	1	0	0	0	0	1	5.20			

CHICAGO CUBS										
BATTING	**AB**	**R**	**H**	**RBI**	**2B**	**3B**	**HR**	**BB**	**SO**	**BA**
JOSE PINTO CF	4	0	1	0	0	0	0	0	0	.295
JERRY ARMSTRONG 2B	4	0	0	0	0	0	0	0	0	.257
COLE JOHNSON 1B	3	0	1	0	0	0	0	1	0	.298
RAFAEL CINCOTTA 3B	4	0	0	0	0	0	0	0	2	.282
BO AUSTIN C	4	0	1	0	0	0	0	0	0	.265
FRANCO SUAREZ DH	4	1	0	0	0	0	0	0	0	.255
TROY CARNEY RF	4	1	1	0	1	0	0	0	0	.278
PABLO MENDEZ LF	3	0	1	0	0	0	0	1	1	.239
BROCK LAMARCA SS	4	1	2	3	0	0	1	0	0	.284
PITCHING	**IP**	**H**	**R**	**ER**	**SO**	**BB**	**ERA**			
LYDON NEUMAN	6	8	3	3	4	2	3.98			
JOHNNY GOODWIN	1	2	0	0	3	2	3.24			
VITO BONICCI (L)	1	3	3	1	1	0	4.26			

INNING	1	2	3	4	5	6	7	8	9	TOTAL
CHICAGO	0	0	3	0	0	0	0	0	0	3
CLEVELAND	0	0	3	0	0	0	0	3		6

GAME 54

By SAM LARDNER
The Cleveland Press

CLEVELAND, June 6 — The Indians know by now how that mytholog-
ical figure Sisyphus must have felt, even if he was a little before their time.

In Greek mythology, Sisyphus was doomed to rolling a boulder up a
hill only to have it roll back down once he reached the top. Then he had
to do it all over again.

Just when the Indians thought they were ready to reach the .500 mark;
another setback befell them. Such was the case in Sunday's series finale
against the Chicago Cubs at Progressive Field.

The Tribe got off to a 2–0 start only to fritter it away on the way to
a 4–2 loss. A victory would have evened the Indians' record to 27–27.
Instead, they fell to 26–28 as their season reached its one-third point.

"We're going to get there, I can tell you that," said Indians manager
Todd Stein. "We won the series, and if we keep doing that, it's just a matter
of time, and not a long time, either."

Another sellout crowd (36,021) got itself revved up in the second when
Terry Rovetto led off with a single against Rick Hoffman and rode home
on Oliver Reiner's home run to center field, his tenth. But the Indians went
quietly after that, getting only five hits for the game. Hoffman got the win
and Albert Weiss, the Cubs closer got a rare two inning save.

"We were feeling pretty good about ourselves at that point," Reiner said. "The crowd was into it. But give the Cubs credit. They could have packed it in and quit, but they didn't."

Hoffman worked seven innings to get the win. Indians starter Kenny Camden was sailing along until the fifth, when the Cubs blitzed him for all four of their runs. The first three batters reached base before Javon Claypool doubled home two and Bo Austin singled home two more.

"It happened so fast," said Camden, who has been on a minor skid of late. "I felt pretty good out there. I just left some balls up over the plate, and they got hit. I feel bad about that because we had a chance to get back to .500 and finally dig ourselves out of that hole we dug for ourselves at the start of the season.

"But the funny thing is, we all feel that some special things are in front of us. Steinie has come in here and really set a positive tone. Some of the guys like (Scott) Michaels and (Micah) Millison have grown into starting roles and really sparked this team. The weather is starting to warm up for good now, and that should help us all and make for a fun summer."

The Indians had to use their bullpen more than they would have liked again, and general manager J.D. Eisner may have to call up a reliever for Tuesday's game against Milwaukee at Progressive Field. Buck Sterling and Geno Milzie finished up for Camden on Sunday.

"The off-day (Monday) comes at a good time," Eisner said. "We have guys at Columbus who are throwing well and can come up and give the pen a bit of a break here. We'll talk about it tomorrow and see which way we're inclined to go."

GAME 54

CLEVELAND INDIANS VS CHICAGO CUBS · JUNE 6
CHICAGO 4 / CLEVELAND 2

CLEVELAND INDIANS									
BATTING	**AB**	**R**	**H**	**RBI**	**2B**	**3B**	**HR**	**BB**	**SO**	**BA**
RIKKI LABUDDA CF	4	0	0	0	0	0	0	1	0	.262
MICAH MILLISON RF	4	0	1	0	0	0	0	0	1	.268
TERRY ROVETTO 3B	4	1	1	0	0	0	0	0	0	.241
OLIVER REINER 1B	4	1	1	2	0	0	1	0	1	.286
SCOTT MICHAELS 2B	4	0	0	0	0	0	0	0	1	.318
BERNARD HARPER DH	4	0	1	0	1	0	0	0	0	.254
KIERAN CATSEF LF	4	0	0	0	0	0	0	0	1	.243
MORRIS JEROME C	4	0	0	0	0	0	0	0	0	.266
LEO TAYLOR SS	3	0	1	0	0	0	0	0	2	.235

PITCHING	**IP**	**H**	**R**	**ER**	**SO**	**BB**	**ERA**			
KENNY CAMDEN (L)	4.66	7	4	4	3	1	3.91			
BUCK STERLING	2.3	1	0	0	0	1	3.38			
GENO MILZIE	2	1	0	0	1	0	4.43			

CHICAGO CUBS									
BATTING	**AB**	**R**	**H**	**RBI**	**2B**	**3B**	**HR**	**BB**	**SO**	**BA**
JOSE PINTO CF	4	1	1	0	0	0	0	0	0	.293
JERRY ARMSTRONG 2B	4	1	2	0	0	0	0	0	0	.264
COLE JOHNSON 1B	4	1	1	0	0	0	0	0	0	.297
JAVON CLAYPOOL 3B	4	1	1	2	1	0	0	0	1	.278
BO AUSTIN C	4	0	1	2	0	0	0	0	1	.264
FRANCO SUAREZ DH	3	0	0	0	0	0	0	1	0	.250
TROY CARNEY RF	4	0	1	0	0	0	0	0	1	.277
PABLO MENDEZ LF	4	0	0	0	0	0	0	0	1	.228
BROCK LAMARCO SS	3	0	2	0	0	0	0	1	0	.299

PITCHING	**IP**	**H**	**R**	**ER**	**SO**	**BB**	**ERA**			
RICK HOFFMAN (W)	7	4	2	2	5	1	3.41			
ALBERT WEISS (S)	2	1	0	0	1	0	1.29			

INNING	**1**	**2**	**3**	**4**	**5**	**6**	**7**	**8**	**9**	**TOTAL**
CHICAGO	0	0	0	0	4	0	0	0	0	4
CLEVELAND	0	2	0	0	0	0	0	0	0	2

GAME 55

By SAM LARDNER
The Cleveland Press

CLEVELAND, June 8 — The Indians spent Monday's off-day at their annual charity golf outing. By the looks of things Tuesday night, their heads were buried in a green-side bunker.

Or perhaps the 19th hole took its toll.

Whatever the case, the Indians carded the equivalent of a triple bogey in an 8–1 loss to the National League's Milwaukee Brewers at Progressive Field.

Starting pitcher Tak Fujimoto hardly looked like the same guy who spun a masterful 1–0 game in a heartbreaking loss last week at New York.

"It wasn't good in any sense," said interim manager Todd Stein, whose team fell back to three games under .500 at 26–29. "It wasn't all on Fuji. We didn't hit. We didn't field. We didn't pitch. I wish I could explain it. We played so well to get within a game of .500, and now we've dropped a pair."

Stein was quick to dismiss notions that Monday's revelry had anything to do with Tuesday's lackluster effort.

"No, no, no," he said. "Let's not even go there. The guys were out having a good time — and for a great cause, I might add. Who can begrudge them that? This is just a bad game. Of course, we're not happy about it, but let's not read too much into it."

Stein also gave Micah Millison a day off and started forgotten man Huron Southworth in right field who went 1 for 3.

The only stroke of good luck for the Indians was that they fortified their bullpen before the game when they recalled Lorry Unger from Class AAA Columbus and sent infielder Willie Bartlett down. Unger looked sharp in his 4 plus innings of work allowing no runs on two hits. The bullpen has been beat up of late, and Fujimoto's 3 and two-thirds inning stinker didn't help matters Tuesday.

Fortunately for the Tribe, Unger was well rested, and he was able to go 4.1 innings of long relief, with position player Kieran Catsef finishing up for some, well, comic relief in the ninth.

"You never like to use a position to pitch, but we've used our pen a lot lately," Stein said. "At least it gave the guys a chuckle at the end of a blow-out. It might make this one easier to forget."

Forgettable is the only way to describe Fujimoto's performance. He gave up eight hits and six runs (four earned) in his short outing.

The Brew Crew's Jonathan Vega hit a three-run homer with two outs in the third after an error by Justin Kestino at shortstop.

Milwaukee scored four more in the fourth, chasing Fujimoto. A throwing error by catcher Morris Jerome and a three-run double by Keith Brooks proved fatal to Fujimoto and the Indians.

The Indians got a solo homer from Terry Rovetto, his eighth, off Brewers starter Pedro Da Silva in the fifth. Da Silva worked six innings, giving up five hits striking out four and walking four.

"I don't know what to say," Fujimoto said through his translator. "I did throw a lot of pitches in my last start, but with the off-day yesterday, I had plenty of time to recover. It just got out of hand in that one inning. I'm sorry to have made Lorry work so hard. The bullpen already has pitched too much lately."

Unger was up earlier this season. With closer Ivan Zyzna on the injured list, the Indians will have to muddle through somehow."

"We're always looking for help," said general manager J.D. Eisner, who added that no trades were imminent. "Unger has done a nice job for us, and (Lee) Hazelton is holding his own. We do have some organizational depth. You never rule anything out, but we don't have any irons in the fire right now."

GAME 55

CLEVELAND INDIANS VS MILWAUKEE BREWERS • JUNE 8
MILWAUKEE 8 / CLEVELAND 1

CLEVELAND INDIANS

BATTING	AB	R	H	RBI	2B	3B	HR	BB	SO	BA
RIKKI LABUDDA CF	4	0	1	0	0	0	0	1	0	.261
SCOTT MICHAELS 2B	5	0	1	0	0	0	0	0	0	.313
TERRY ROVETTO 3B	4	1	2	1	0	0	1	1	0	.246
OLIVER REINER 1B	4	0	2	0	0	0	0	1	0	.291
WILSON WHITE LF	4	0	1	0	0	0	0	0	1	.260
JUSTIN KESTINO SS	4	0	0	0	1	0	0	0	0	.228
BERNARD HARPER DH	3	0	1	0	0	0	0	1	0	.255
MORRIS JEROME C	4	0	0	0	0	0	0	0	1	.259
HURON SOUTHWORTH RF	3	0	1	0	0	0	0	0	1	.222

PITCHING	IP	H	R	ER	SO	BB	ERA			
TAK FUJIMOTO (L)	3.66	8	6	4	2	0	3.39			
LORRY UNGER	4.33	2	0	0	3	1	1.74			
KIERAN CATSEF	1	3	1	1	0	0	9.00			

MILWAUKEE BREWERS

BATTING	AB	R	H	RBI	2B	3B	HR	BB	SO	BA
DIEGO ALVAREZ 2B	5	2	2	0	0	1	0	0	0	.301
ISAAC DE JESUS SS	5	0	0	0	0	0	0	0	2	.248
KEITH BROOKS LF	5	1	2	3	1	0	0	0	0	.303
EMERSON KEENE 1B	4	1	2	0	1	0	0	1	1	.289
CAM HELTON 3B	5	1	2	1	0	0	0	0	0	.270
MARTIN PULLIDO RF	4	1	2	1	1	0	0	0	1	.261
JOHNATHAN VEGA DH	4	1	2	3	0	0	1	0	0	.287
FERNANDO MONTED C	4	0	0	0	0	0	0	0	1	.261
EMMET BRIGGS CF	4	1	1	0	0	0	0	0	0	.256

PITCHING	IP	H	R	ER	SO	BB	ERA			
PEDRO DA SILVA (W)	6	5	1	1	3	4	3.20			
ALDO QUEVEDO	2	3	0	0	0	0	3.81			
CYRUS BELLO	1	1	0	0	0	0	4.95			

INNING	1	2	3	4	5	6	7	8	9	TOTAL
MILWAUKEE	0	0	3	4	0	0	0	0	1	8
CLEVELAND	0	0	0	0	1	0	0	0	0	1

GAME 56

By SAM LARDNER
The Cleveland Press

CLEVELAND, June 9 — The Cleveland Indians and the Milwaukee Brewers used to have quite the thing going when both were in the American League Central. The Brewers moved to the National League in 1998 — "We're taking this thing National" was their catchphrase — and after Wednesday, the Indians might hope never to see them again.

For the second straight night, the Brewers completely outclassed the Indians, this time shutting them out 5–0 at Progressive Field. Stop us if you've heard this one before: After yet another flirtation with .500, the Indians are now back to four games under break-even at 26–30.

"It's been a roller coaster, that's for sure," said interim manager Todd Stein, whose team has lost three straight. "We get close, and then we fall back. The disappointing thing is we're doing this at home. We had some nice crowds here over the weekend. People were really excited. We don't want to keep teasing them. We want to show them we're for real."

Not even ace pitcher Lynn Moda could save the Tribe on this night. Moda, who has pitched well of late, took a step backward against the Brewers, giving up all five runs and nine hits in five innings.

"I warmed up pretty well in the bullpen before the game, and we had a good game plan," Moda said. "I just didn't execute it when it counted. It's nothing mechanical like it was at the beginning of the season. I'm actually feeling pretty good, and the ball is coming out of my hand well. This is just one night."

Once again, an early big inning by the opposition doomed the Indians. Moda walked the first two batters of the game and had some words for home-plate umpire Gary Koppel after the second base on balls. He regrouped to strike out Cam Helton, but a passed ball charged to Morris Jerome set the stage for a two-run single by Vince Lazaro and a run-scoring single by Keith Brooks.

"I thought the strike zone was a little tight from the get-go," Moda said. "That's no excuse. But I pride myself on having good control, and if those pitches missed, they didn't miss by much.

You'll notice their guy (Brewers starter Corey Matthews Jr.) didn't walk anybody. You just want consistency."

By the time Moda faced Emmett Briggs in the fifth, he ran his pitch count to 100.

The Indians did little with Matthews, getting four hits against him in seven innings. Solly Alvarez, Buck Sterling and Mickey Penney finished up in relief of Moda. The good news, if there is any, for the bullpen, is that Geno Millie and Lee Hazelton should be ready to roll for Wednesday's series finale and beyond.

"Back at it tomorrow," Stein said. "That's all you can do. We're just going to keep rolling it out there and keep plugging away. There's no panic here."

We've heard that before.

GAME 56

CLEVELAND INDIANS VS MILWAUKEE BREWERS • JUNE 9
MILWAUKEE 5 / CLEVELAND 0

CLEVELAND INDIANS

BATTING	AB	R	H	RBI	2B	3B	HR	BB	SO	BA
RIKKI LABUDDA CF	3	0	0	0	0	0	0	1	0	.258
MICAH MILLISON RF	4	0	2	0	0	0	0	0	1	.273
TERRY ROVETTO 3B	4	0	0	0	0	0	0	0	1	.242
OLIVER REINER 1B	3	0	1	0	0	0	0	1	0	.291
SCOTT MICHAELS 2B	4	0	0	0	0	0	0	0	1	.302
WILSON WHITE LF	4	0	0	0	0	0	0	0	2	.255
JUSTIN KESTINO SS	4	0	1	0	1	0	0	0	1	.228
BERNARD HARPER DH	3	0	0	0	0	0	0	1	0	.250
MORRIS JEROME C	3	0	1	0	0	0	0	0	2	.261

PITCHING	IP	H	R	ER	SO	BB	ERA
LYNN MODA (L)	5	9	5	5	2	2	4.98
SOLLY ALVAREZ	2	2	0	0	0	0	3.33
BUCK STERLING	1.33	1	0	0	1	0	3.22
MICKEY PENNY	0.67	1	0	0	0	0	3.53

MILWAUKEE BREWERS

BATTING	AB	R	H	RBI	2B	3B	HR	BB	SO	BA
DIEGO ALVAREZ 2B	4	1	1	0	0	1	0	0	0	.299
ISAAC DE JESUS SS	3	1	2	0	0	0	0	1	1	.257
CAM HELTON 3B	3	0	0	0	0	0	0	1	0	.264
VINCE LAZARO 1B	4	1	2	2	1	0	0	1	1	.314
KEITH BROOKS LF	4	0	3	1	0	0	0	0	0	.317
MARTIN PULLIDO RF	4	0	1	0	0	0	0	0	1	.261
JOHNATHAN VEGA DH	4	1	2	0	1	0	0	0	0	.295
FERNANDO MONTED C	4	0	0	0	0	0	0	0	0	.250
EMMET BRIGGS CF	4	1	2	2	0	0	1	0	2	.268

PITCHING	IP	H	R	ER	SO	BB	ERA
COREY MATTHEWS JR (W)	7	4	0	0	7	2	2.91
RAYMOND HURTADO	2	1	0	0	1	1	3.46

INNING	1	2	3	4	5	6	7	8	9	TOTATL
MILWAUKEE	3	0	0	0	2	0	0	0	0	5
CLEVELAND	0	0	0	0	0	0	0	0	0	0

GAME 57

By SAM LARDNER
The Cleveland Press

CLEVELAND, June 10 — Who knew? Who could have known? Just chalk it up to baseball.

Earlier this season, Indians lefty Ollie Gonzalez couldn't catch a break. Indians batters weren't scoring for him, and the team wasn't winning the games he started.

Sometimes ya just gotta give it time.

Gonzalez has gone from hard-luck pitcher to Mr. Dependable of late. Thursday night's 8–3 victory over the Milwaukee Brewers couldn't have come at a better time for the Tribe.

Not only was Gonzalez good, but he got a lot of help from his friends as the Indians snapped a three-game losing streak and upped their record to 27 and 30, heading into a weekend series down the road at Cincinnati.

"That's a big relief," said Indians manager Todd Stein. "Ollie hung in there early when things weren't going great, and now he's pitching like an ace of the staff. And the bats came alive a little bit tonight, too."

Gonzalez went seven innings and gave up six hits and all three Brewers runs. The pitch count reached 118, but he was more than willing to go another inning in the wake of a busy spell for the bullpen.

"Whatever we need," he said. "The guys really stepped up for me tonight. We got contributions from everybody. I felt pretty fresh out there even after seven innings. I was half-expecting to go back out for one more, but Skip made the right call."

The Indians got a two-run homer from Scott Michaels, his ninth, in the second inning, a three-run bomb from little-used Huron Southworth in the fourth and a bases-loaded double from Justin Kestino in the fifth. They roughed up Brewers starting pitcher Nolan Sheffield for 10 hits over five innings.

With a big lead, Gonzalez relaxed and "pitched to the score." He gave up a three-run homer to Malcolm Adkidson in the sixth, but the game was well in hand by then.

"Yeah, I was just out there playing catch with Iceberg," he said, referring to backup catcher Iceberg Peters. "If you're going to give up homers, make sure they're solo homers or that they come when you're way ahead in the game."

General manager J.D. Eisner will make the short trip to Cincinnati with the ballclub. He said injured closer Ivan Zyzna is progressing well and could begin a minor league rehab assignment as early as next Monday.

Eisner also said infielder Angel Rodriguez is "coming along steadily" from his hamstring injury but that the Indians would not rush him back, given Rodriguez's injury history and Scott Michaels' good play filling in for Rodriguez.

Michaels has been a pleasant surprise. Early results of all-star balloting are out, but Michaels will need write-in help. His name is not even on the ballot. Third baseman Terry Rovetto is fourth in American League balloting among third basemen, and Oliver Reiner is third among first basemen.

"We're not worried about the All-Star Game," Eisner said. "We're worried about getting fully healthy and playing up to our capabilities. It should be a fun weekend at Cincinnati."

GAME 57

CLEVELAND INDIANS VS MILWAUKEE BREWERS • JUNE 10
CLEVELAND 8 / MILWAUKEE 3

CLEVELAND INDIANS										
BATTING	AB	R	H	RBI	2B	3B	HR	BB	SO	BA
RIKKI LABUDDA CF	4	1	2	0	1	0	0	1	0	.262
HURON SOUTHWORTH RF	4	1	1	3	0	0	1	0	1	.224
TERRY ROVETTO 3B	4	1	2	0	1	0	0	0	0	.246
OLIVER REINER 1B	4	1	2	0	0	0	0	1	0	.295
SCOTT MICHAELS 2B	4	2	2	2	0	0	1	0	0	.308
WILSON WHITE LF	3	1	2	0	0	0	0	1	0	.261
JUSTIN KESTINO SS	4	0	2	3	1	0	0	0	0	.234
BERNARD HARPER DH	4	1	1	0	0	0	0	0	0	.250
ICEBERG PETERS C	3	0	1	0	0	0	0	0	1	.245
PITCHING	IP	H	R	ER	SO	BB	ERA			
OLLIE GONZALEZ (W)	7	6	3	3	5	2	4.68			
GENO MILZIE	1	1	0	0	1	0	4.31			

MILWAUKEE BREWERS										
BATTING	AB	R	H	RBI	2B	3B	HR	BB	SO	BA
DIEGO ALVAREZ 2B	4	0	0	0	0	0	0	0	0	.287
ISAAC DE JESUS SS	4	1	1	0	0	0	0	0	1	.256
CAM HELTON 3B	3	1	1	0	0	0	0	1	0	.266
VINCE LAZARO 1B	4	0	2	0	1	0	0	0	1	.321
MALCOLM ADKIDSON LF	4	1	2	3	0	0	1	0	1	.296
MARTIN PULLIDO RF	4	0	0	0	0	0	0	0	0	.255
JOHNATHAN VEGA DH	4	0	0	0	0	0	0	0	2	.284
FERNANDO MONTED C	4	0	1	0	0	0	0	0	0	.250
EMMET BRIGGS CF	3	0	0	0	0	0	0	1	1	.259
PITCHING	IP	H	R	ER	SO	BB	ERA			
NOLAN SHEFFIELD (L)	4.66	10	8	8	0	1	4.00			
ALDO QUEVEDO	2.33	4	0	0	1	0	3.49			
NACY ALLSWANG	1	1	0	0	1	0	4.71			

INNING	1	2	3	4	5	6	7	8	9	TOTAL
MILWAUKEE	0	0	0	0	0	3	0	0	0	3
CLEVELAND	0	2	0	3	3	0	0	0		8

GAME 58

By SAM LARDNER
The Cleveland Press

CINCINNATI, June 11 — A trip to southern Ohio to meet up with their kissin' cousins always seems to do the Indians some good.

Such was the case Friday night at the hitter's haven known as the Great American Ball Park, where Indians batters put the "launch" into "launching pad" during a 7–1 victory over the Cincinnati Reds.

The Tribe got homers from Scott Michaels, Micah Millison and Morris Jerome as they pulled within two games of .500 at 28–30. That gives Michaels 11, Millison nine and Jerome five.

While the Indians have been a pretty respectable franchise over the last several decades, the Reds have had their moments but have had trouble gaining serious traction in a division that includes the Chicago Cubs and the St. Louis Cardinals.

The Indians also had their fair share of fans in the stands for the opener of this intrastate weekend series.

"Yeah, we heard all those Cubs fans at our place last weekend, so it was nice to go on the road and hear our great fans well represented," said Indians manager Todd Stein. "This is as good an interleague series as it gets. Two passionate fan bases from the same state. They draw from Dayton. We draw from Akron and Youngstown, and I'm sure Columbus is pretty well split. We're expecting a fun weekend."

It was fun for Michaels, who may be embarking on a quixotic write-in campaign for an all-star spot. He has been among the Indians' most dependable hitters since taking over for the injured Angel Rodriguez. Friday night, Michaels hit a three-run homer in the third inning on the way to a 3-for-4 night.

"This is a good place to hit," he said. "It's a good hitter's background and the ball really carries. As far as all that other (all-star) stuff, I don't even think about it. You guys and the fans can have fun with it. I just want to play every day for this team."

Michaels' blast came against Reds starter Johan Herrera after Wilson White walked and Terry Rovetto reached on an error.

Millison's homer was a solo blast in the fifth, Wilson White doubled home Oliver Reiner in the seventh and Jerome added a two-run shot in the ninth to put the game well out of reach.

Benefiting from the offensive outburst was Indians starting pitcher Brian Howard. "The Doctor" coasted through seven innings, giving up five hits. He's been on a roll of late himself, pitching well even if he doesn't always get the "W" next to his name in the box score. The hitters made sure he got the winning decision Friday.

"They made it easy for me to go out there and throw to Mo (Jerome)," he said. "All you can do as a starting pitcher is give your team a chance to win. Things like personal wins and losses take care of themselves. I take pride in a good ERA and trying to reach 200 innings every year."

Howard gave up a meaningless homer to Justyn Simmons in the sixth. Buck Sterling and Mickey Penney finished up.

Stein said recently recalled Lorry Unger should be able to go as early as Saturday after getting stretched out in his first appearance since getting the call from Columbus. That should help the pen, as should the continued offensive outbursts.

"They hit the ball well over there, too," Stein said of the Reds. "So we're going to need every available arm in this ballpark. When you get a start like Doc gave us tonight, it makes a lot of things easier."

GAME 58

CLEVELAND INDIANS VS CINCINNATI REDS • JUNE 11
CLEVELAND 7 / CINCINNATI 1

CLEVELAND INDIANS

BATTING	AB	R	H	RBI	2B	3B	HR	BB	SO	BA
RIKKI LABUDDA CF	5	0	2	0	0	0	0	0	0	.265
MICAH MILLISON RF	4	1	1	1	0	0	1	0	1	.272
TERRY ROVETTO 3B	4	1	0	0	0	0	0	0	0	.242
OLIVER REINER 1B	4	1	2	0	0	0	0	0	0	.299
WILSON WHITE LF	4	2	2	1	1	0	0	1	0	.265
SCOTT MICHAELS 2B	4	1	3	3	0	0	1	0	0	.323
JUSTIN KESTINO SS	4	0	0	0	0	0	0	0	1	.229
MORRIS JEROME C	4	1	2	2	0	0	1	0	0	.266
BRIAN HOWARD P	2	0	0	0	0	0	0	0	1	.000
BERNARD HARPER PH	1	0	0	0	0	0	0	0	0	.248

PITCHING	IP	H	R	ER	SO	BB	ERA			
BRIAN HOWARD (W)	7	5	1	1	4	1	3.42			
BUCK STERLING	1	1	0	0	1	0	3.21			
MICKEY PENNY	1	1	0	0	1	0	3.38			

CINCINNATI REDS

BATTING	AB	R	H	RBI	2B	3B	HR	BB	SO	BA
ALEX JIMENEZ CF	4	0	1	0	0	0	0	0	0	.266
MARCO PINEDA 1B	4	0	1	0	0	0	0	0	2	.267
RICH AMEND 3B	4	0	1	0	0	0	0	0	2	.264
ANGEL PULIDO C	4	0	2	0	1	0	0	0	0	.330
DIANDRE SPIERS LF	4	0	0	0	0	0	0	0	1	.278
JUSTYN SIMMONS RF	4	1	1	1	0	0	1	1	0	.261
LANDON WILSON 2B	4	0	1	0	0	0	0	0	0	.275
ERICK GUZMAN SS	4	0	0	0	0	0	0	0	0	.240
JOHAN HERRERA P	2	0	0	0	0	0	0	0	1	.000
CORNELL CALLOWAY PH	1	0	0	0	0	0	0	0	0	.283
MILLER WINN JR PH	1	0	0	0	0	0	0	0	0	.270

PITCHING	IP	H	R	ER	SO	BB	ERA			
JOHAN HERRERA P (L)	6	5	4	4	3	1	3.44			
DENZEL KENDRICK	1.67	3	1	1	0	0	4.76			
AMARI DAWKINS	1.33	2	2	2	1	0	4.28			

INNING	1	2	3	4	5	6	7	8	9	TOTAL
CLEVELAND	0	0	3	0	1	0	1	0	2	7
CINCINNATI	0	0	0	0	0	1	0	0	0	1

GAME 59

By SAM LARDNER
The Cleveland Press

CINCINNATI, June 12 — Kenny Camden isn't called "The Wiz" for nothing.

A very smart dude and also known for his talent in the stock market, Camden has been around long enough to know that sometimes all it takes is a little patience.

The 32-year-old crafty left-hander won his first decision in nearly a month Saturday night as the Indians edged the Cincinnati Reds 4–3 at the Great American Ball Park. Camden had replaced fellow pitcher Ollie Gonzalez as the Tribe's hard-luck pitcher lately, but like Gonzalez, Camden kept his head down, his mouth shut and pitched.

He finally got a winning decision Saturday, as his teammates staked him to a 4–0 lead, with the bullpen holding on to give the Indians (29–30) their third win in a row.

"You've just got to stay true to yourself and trust that things are going to bounce your way eventually," Camden said. "I don't put any extra pressure on myself. Heck, I've been around too long for that. The main goal is to give us innings and try to shut the other team down."

Playing in a National League park, Camden got to bat, and he surprised everyone ending up with a sacrifice bunt and a single to right field.

"I thought I was going to get thrown out by their right fielder on that hit," Camden said with a laugh. "We've been taking a lot of batting practice lately, so I felt pretty good up there with the stick in my hand. You get so used to having a DH, but the National League game is fun."

Camden engaged Reds starter Jose Cordova in a scoreless duel until the Indians got two in the fourth and two more in the fifth. Rikki LaBudda led off the fourth with a bunt single and promptly stole second base, his fourteenth of the season. Micah Millison walked, and both runners came home on Wilson White's double to the corner in right field.

In the fifth, Scott Michaels led off with a single. Justin Kestino doubled Michaels to third, and Morris Jerome singled them both home.

"It's surprising that we didn't homer tonight, but we'll take it," White said. "The big thing is that we strung together a few hits. You can't always rely on the long ball."

Camden worked 6 and one-third innings, giving up seven hits. He was charged with two runs in the seventh after putting two aboard and watching as reliever Lorry Unger gave up a three-run homer to Landon Wilson. Geno Milzie relieved Unger and worked the eighth, with Lee Hazelton pitching a 1-2-3 ninth for the save.

"This might have been a game we lost earlier this year," said interim manager Todd Stein. "I was hoping not to use Unger, but he said he was ready to go. Fortunately, we were able to shut the door and nail this one down."

Once again, the Indians have a chance to reach the elusive .500 mark in Sunday's series finale.

"That's been the goal since we got off to that 0–6 start, or whatever it was," Camden said. "It seems like we take a step forward and then a step or two back, but if you look at it since that start, we've played pretty well overall. We'll get there."

CLEVELAND INDIANS VS CINCINNATI REDS · JUNE 12
CLEVELAND 4 / CINCINNATI 3

CLEVELAND INDIANS

BATTING	AB	R	H	RBI	2B	3B	HR	BB	SO	BA
RIKKI LABUDDA CF	5	1	1	0	0	0	0	0	0	.264
MICAH MILLISON RF	4	1	1	0	0	0	0	2	1	.272
WILSON WHITE LF	4	0	2	2	1	0	0	1	0	.270
TERRY ROVETTO 3B	4	0	0	0	0	0	0	1	1	.237
OLIVER REINER 1B	5	0	2	0	1	0	0	0	0	.301
SCOTT MICHAELS 2B	5	1	0	0	0	0	0	0	0	.318
JUSTIN KESTINO SS	4	1	1	0	1	0	0	0	1	.229
MORRIS JEROME C	4	0	1	2	0	0	0	0	0	.266
KENNY CAMDEN P	3	1	1	0	0	0	0	0	1	.333
BERNARD HARPER PH	1	0	1	0	0	0	0	0	0	.253

PITCHING	IP	H	R	ER	SO	BB	ERA			
KENNY CAMDEN (W)	6.3	7	2	2	4	2	3.83			
LORRY UNGER	0.67	1	1	1	1	0	2.45			
GENO MILZIE	1	1	0	0	1	1	4.21			
LEE HAZELTON	1	0	0	0	1	0	4.66			

CINCINNATI REDS

BATTING	AB	R	H	RBI	2B	3B	HR	BB	SO	BA
ALEX JIMENEZ CF	4	0	1	0	0	0	0	1	0	.265
MARCO PINEDA 1B	4	0	1	0	1	0	0	0	1	.266
RICH AMEND 3B	4	0	1	0	0	0	0	0	2	.263
ANGEL PULIDO C	3	1	2	0	1	0	0	1	0	.340
DIANDRE SPIERS LF	4	1	1	0	0	0	0	0	0	.277
JUSTYN SIMMONS RF	4	0	1	0	0	0	0	1	1	.261
LANDON WILSON 2B	4	1	1	3	0	0	1	0	0	.274
ERICK GUZMAN SS	4	0	0	0	0	0	0	0	0	.231
JOSE CORDOVA P	2	0	0	0	0	0	0	0	2	.000
CORNELL CALLOWAY PH	1	0	0	0	0	0	0	0	1	.278
MILLER WINN JR PH	1	0	0	0	0	0	0	0	0	.263

PITCHING	IP	H	R	ER	SO	BB	ERA			
JOSE CORDOVA (L)	4.6	6	4	4	1	3	4.02			
LEE HEE CHAN	2.3	3	0	0	2	1	3.22			
GABRIEL QUINTERO	2	2	0	0	1	0	3.54			

INNING	1	2	3	4	5	6	7	8	9	TOTAL
CLEVELAND	0	0	0	2	2	0	0	0	0	4
CINCINNATI	0	0	0	0	0	0	3	0	0	3

GAME 60

By SAM LARDNER
The Cleveland Press

CINCINNATI, June 13 — The quest will have to wait — again.

Seemingly poised to reach the .500-mark Sunday, the Indians gave one back by giving one away to the Cincinnati Reds in a 6–4 loss at the Great American Ball Park.

Starting pitcher Tak Fujimoto wasn't as bad as he was last week against the Brewers, but he wasn't sharp, either.

Indians fielders committed three errors on a wet field with the game played during intermittent rain. When it all shook out in the slop, the Indians headed home and into a Monday off-day with a record of 29–31 as they get set to open a seven game homestand, with Oakland and Seattle coming to town.

"I haven't fretted too much about the whole .500 thing, as you guys know, but this one was disappointing," said Indians manager Todd Stein. "Look, I know the conditions weren't great out there, but we can't throw the ball around like that. There were both mental and physical errors out there today."

Fujimoto somehow got through five innings, as he gave up eight hits and five runs, four of them unearned.

"It's been a couple rough starts in a row for me," Fujimoto said through his translator. "I know we didn't play our best game out there, but I've got to be better, too. It was hard for me to get a good grip on the ball, so I'm sure it was tough for our fielders to get a good grip, too."

Things were looking good early for a series sweep when Oliver Reiner hit a two-run homer, number 12, in the first inning against Eli Batt, one out after Rikki LaBudda walked and stole a base.

Fujimoto, with no help from his fielders, couldn't stand the prosperity. He put the first two batters on in the bottom of the inning before Diondre Spiers grounded one to Justin Kestino at short. Kestino bobbed the ball for one error and then threw the ball away at first for a second error, allowing both baserunners to score as the ball bounded down the right-field line.

"I should have eaten it right there," Kestino said. "That's what Skip was talking about with mental and physical errors. It was a mental error on my part when I threw that ball away."

An error by Scott Michaels at second base opened the gates to three runs in the third, with Erick Guzman making Fujimoto and the Tribe pay with a three-run double.

The Indians got a two-run double from Iceberg Peters in the sixth to come within 5–4, but Rich Amend gave the Reds a big insurance run with a solo homer off Mickey Penney in the eighth.

"The game was there for us to take all day, but instead we gave it away," Stein said. "We're trying to flush these kinds of game out of our system for good. Hopefully one of these days. We've got a big homestand ahead of us. It will be important for us take advantage."

CLEVELAND INDIANS VS CINCINNATI REDS · JUNE 13
CINCINNATI 6 / CLEVELAND 4

CLEVELAND INDIANS										
BATTING	AB	R	H	RBI	2B	3B	HR	BB	SO	BA
RIKKI LABUDDA CF	4	1	0	0	0	0	0	1	0	.259
MICAH MILLISON RF	4	0	1	0	0	0	0	1	1	.271
WILSON WHITE LF	5	0	1	0	0	0	0	0	0	.268
OLIVER REINER 1B	4	1	1	2	0	0	1	1	0	.300
TERRY ROVETTO 3B	4	1	2	0	1	0	0	0	0	.242
SCOTT MICHAELS 2B	5	0	1	0	0	0	0	0	0	.313
JUSTIN KESTINO SS	4	1	1	0	0	0	0	0	1	.230
ICEBERG PETERS C	4	0	1	2	1	0	0	0	0	.245
TAK FUJIMOTO P	3	0	0	0	0	0	0	0	2	.000
BERNARD HARPER PH	1	0	0	0	0	0	0	0	0	.252
LEO TAYLOR PH	1	0	1	0	0	0	0	0	0	.257
PITCHING	IP	H	R	ER	SO	BB	ERA			
TAK FUJIMOTO (L)	5	8	5	1	3	1	3.29			
BUCK STERLING	1	0	0	0	0	0	3.10			
MICKET PENNY	2	2	1	1	1	0	3.46			
CINCINNATI REDS										
BATTING	AB	R	H	RBI	2B	3B	HR	BB	SO	BA
ALEX JIMENEZ CF	5	1	2	0	0	0	0	0	0	.269
MARCO PINEDA 1B	4	1	2	0	1	0	0	0	1	.272
RICH AMEND 3B	4	1	1	1	0	0	1	0	0	.263
ANGEL PULIDO C	4	0	0	0	1	0	0	0	0	.327
DIONDRE SPIERS LF	4	1	0	0	0	0	0	0	0	.267
JUSTYN SIMMONS RF	3	1	1	0	0	0	0	1	1	.262
LANDON WILSON 2B	4	1	1	0	0	0	1	0	0	.274
ERICK GUZMAN SS	4	0	2	3	1	0	0	0	0	.241
ELI BATT P	3	0	0	0	0	0	0	0	2	.000
CORNELL CALLOWAY PH	1	0	1	0	0	0	0	0	0	.291
PITCHING	IP	H	R	ER	SO	BB	ERA			
ELI BATT (W)	7	6	4	4	4	2	3.69			
ARMANI DAWKINS	1	2	0	0	0	0	3.95			
BRIAN SPECTOR (S)	1	0	0	0	0	0	4.05			

INNING	1	2	3	4	5	6	7	8	9	TOTAL
CLEVELAND	2	0	0	0	0	2	0	0	0	4
CINCINNATI	2	0	3	0	0	0	0	1		6

GAME 61

By SAM LARDNER
The Cleveland Press

CLEVELAND, June 15 — The last time the Indians faced the Oakland Athletics, they were in quite a different place, both literally and figuratively.

It was in late April when the Indians and A's played in the Bay Area. The Indians were getting used to a new manager and trying to climb out of the season-opening hole they had dug for themselves.

The two teams renewed acquaintances again Tuesday night at Progressive Field, and the arrow continues to be pointing upward for the Indians, especially after a 4–1 victory that once again brought them to within a game of .500 at 30–31.

The author of Tuesday's story was Indians ace pitcher Lynn Moda, who rebounded from last week's clunker against the Brewers. The Athletics could do little with Moda over seven innings, as he gave up the one run on six hits while walking one and striking out five for his seventh win.

"Much better," Moda said. "It was more like what I expect out of myself. I forgot about the last start the minute it was over. That was more of an oddity. If you look at my starts over the last month or so, you'll see that they've been pretty good."

Both manager Todd Stein and the Indians bullpen appreciated the innings out of their ace. The bullpen has been overtaxed of late.

"That's why he's an ace," Stein said of Moda. "He stepped up when we needed to give our guys down in the pen a little bit of a break. Modes isn't going to overpower anybody, but he kept the hitters off-balance tonight and had them chasing pitches out of the zone."

Moda matched up with the A's Josh Kennelly, who was pretty good himself in the early going. Things didn't get going offensively for either side until the bottom of the fourth, when Scott Michaels hit a two-run homer after Terry Rovetto singled on the ninth pitch of the plate appearance. Rovetto fouled off four straight pitches at one point.

"Believe it or not, that allowed me to draw a bead on Kennelly," Michaels said. "You get a good look from the on-deck circle, and with Terry seeing that many pitches, I was able to get a better idea of what to look for. He came with a slider that hung just a little bit, and I was able to drive it out."

The A's came within a run on Graeme Nilson's homer in the sixth, but the Indians got it right back and one more in the bottom of the inning. Michaels (3-for-5) doubled and went to third on Justin Kestino's single. Catcher Morris Jerome singled to score Michaels, sending Kestino to third. Leo Taylor then singled up the middle to score Kestino.

Geno Milzie worked the eighth inning, and Lee Hazelton pitched the ninth for a save. Hazelton appears to have gotten his feel firmly on the ground since filling in for the injured Ivan Zyzna.

"The kid looks good," Stein said of Hazelton. "He's got a great arm, that's for sure. Facing big league hitters is quite a bit different than facing hitters in Triple-A. But he's made the adjustment nicely. We'll see what happens when Zyzna gets back, but we're going to need to close down games no matter who is in that spot."

CLEVELAND INDIANS VS OAKLAND ATHLETICS • JUNE 15
CLEVELAND 4 / OAKLAND 1

CLEVELAND INDIANS

BATTING	AB	R	H	RBI	2B	3B	HR	BB	SO	BA
RIKKI LABUDDA CF	5	0	2	0	0	0	0	1	0	.262
MICAH MILLISON RF	4	0	0	0	0	0	0	0	1	.266
WILSON WHITE LF	4	0	1	0	0	0	0	0	1	.268
OLIVER REINER 1B	4	0	1	0	1	0	0	0	0	.300
TERRY ROVETTO 3B	4	1	2	0	0	0	0	0	0	.247
SCOTT MICHAELS 2B	5	2	3	2	1	0	1	0	1	.324
JUSTIN KESTINO SS	4	1	2	0	0	0	0	0	1	.235
MORRIS JEROME C	4	0	1	1	0	0	0	1	0	.266
LEO TAYLOR DH	4	0	2	1	0	0	0	0	0	.282

PITCHING	IP	H	R	ER	SO	BB	ERA			
LYNN MODA (W)	7	6	1	1	5	1	4.63			
GENO MILZIE	1	1	0	0	0	0	4.10			
LEE HAZELTON (S)	1	0	0	0	1	0	4.22			

OAKLAND A'S

BATTING	AB	R	H	RBI	2B	3B	HR	BB	SO	BA
ISIAH HUERTAS LF	5	0	0	0	0	0	0	0	1	.293
IAN BRUDERSON SS	4	0	1	0	0	0	0	0	0	.266
GRAEME NILSON 1B	4	1	1	1	0	0	1	0	1	.263
ERNESTO MENDESOTO 3B	3	0	0	0	0	0	0	1	1	.305
TRENT ATHERTON C	4	0	2	0	0	0	0	0	0	.284
ALBERT REYES RF	4	0	1	0	0	0	0	0	0	.260
MATTHEW VAN STENCEL CF	4	0	1	0	0	0	0	0	0	.274
TREMONT HARKNESS DH	4	0	0	0	0	0	0	0	1	.278
JAYSON GIVINS 2B	4	0	0	0	0	0	0	0	1	.270

PITCHING	IP	H	R	ER	SO	BB	ERA			
JOSH KENNELLY (L)	5	7	2	2	2	2	3.66			
CRAIG QUINN	2	1	0	0	1	0	3.82			
JAKE RICHARDS	1	0	0	0	1	0	4.00			

INNING	1	2	3	4	5	6	7	8	9	TOTAL
OAKLAND	0	0	0	0	0	1	0	0	0	1
CLEVELAND	0	0	0	0	2	0	2	0		4

GAME 62

By SAM LARDNER

The Cleveland Press

CLEVELAND, June 16 — Ollie Gonzalez's luck ran out in a big way Wednesday night, and it ran out to the tune of that unluckiest of numbers. The Oakland Athletics pounded Gonzalez for eight runs over 4 and one-third innings on the way to a 13–5 romp at Progressive Field.

The Indian's staff got rocked for 18 hits as every player in the A's lineup got at least one hit. Gonzalez began the season as the Indians' hard-luck starter, but until Wednesday, the team hadn't lost one of his starts since May 17. The A's nickel-and-dimed Gonzalez to death during the first three innings of the game before unloading in the fifth, when they scored six runs.

"There was no luck about it, good or bad," Gonzalez said. "I just sucked. I was bad. We had another chance to get to .500, and I let us down. I feel bad about it."

Yes, the Indians fell back to two games under .500 (30–32), squandering yet another chance to even their record for the first time this season.

The only good news the Indians got was the closer Ivan Zyzna should be ready to come off the injured list in time for this weekend's series against Seattle. Zyzna tossed a perfect inning Wednesday afternoon in a rehab appearance for Class AAA Columbus and reported that his forearm felt fine. General manager J.D. Eisner said Zyzna would be examined by the team doctor Thursday, and if that goes well, he could be activated by Friday.

"We're encouraged by that," Eisner said. "The bullpen has held it's own since Ivan has been on the IL. We'll have a decision to make about the roster, but we like our depth."

It could well be that the Indians keep hard-throwing rookie Lee Hazelton on the roster when Zyzna comes back, giving the Tribe a 1–2 setup-man duo of Hazelton and Geno Milzie.

But first things first.

Gonzalez looked just fine in the first inning against the A's, going 1-2-3 with two strikeouts. But the Athletics pinged him for a run in the second, two in the third, one in the fourth and the coup de grâce, six in the fifth.

The big blow in the fifth was a grand slam off the bat of Matthew Van Stencel in the fifth, sending Gonzalez to an early exit. Van Stencel had a career high 6 RBIs in the game.

"Gonzo just couldn't find it after the first inning," said manager Todd Stein. "He's pitched so well for us lately that I can't really say too much about it. Let's not forget, too, that the A's can swing the bats a little bit. They're patient, they get runners on base, and when you do that, you have a chance at big innings. That's one of the things we're striving for ourselves."

Reliever Lorry Unger gave up three runs over three innings of relief. He could be sent back to Columbus once Zyzna comes off the IL. Solly Alvarez finished up for the Tribe.

Offensively, the Indians got a three-run homer from Bernard Harper in the bottom of the fifth against starter Mickey Vold. Justin Kestino and Micah Millison each added RBI singles late, but all was too little.

"You know, we never did quit battling," Stein said. "That's one thing I look for. If you get behind by a lot of runs, like we did tonight, you can either give up or keep playing. We kept playing."

CLEVELAND INDIANS VS OAKLAND ATHLETICS · JUNE 16
OAKLAND 13 / CLEVELAND 5

CLEVELAND INDIANS										
BATTING	AB	R	H	RBI	2B	3B	HR	BB	SO	BA
RIKKI LABUDDA CF	4	1	2	0	1	0	0	0	0	.266
MICAH MILLISON RF	4	0	1	1	0	0	0	1	1	.266
WILSON WHITE LF	4	1	2	0	0	0	0	0	1	.272
OLIVER REINER 1B	4	1	1	0	1	0	0	0	1	.299
TERRY ROVETTO 3B	4	1	3	0	0	0	0	0	1	.255
SCOTT MICHAELS 2B	4	0	0	0	0	0	0	0	1	.315
JUSTIN KESTINO SS	4	0	2	1	0	0	0	0	1	.240
BERNARD HARPER DH	4	1	1	3	0	0	1	0	0	.252
MORRIS JEROME C	3	0	0	0	0	0	0	1	0	.261

PITCHING	IP	H	R	ER	SO	BB	ERA
OLLIE GONZALEZ (L)	4.3	12	8	8	2	1	5.43
LORRY UNGER	3.67	4	3	3	0	0	3.68
SOLLY ALVAREZ	1	2	2	2	1	1	3.91

OAKLAND A'S										
BATTING	AB	R	H	RBI	2B	3B	HR	BB	SO	BA
ISIAH HUERTAS LF	6	2	2	1	2	0	0	0	0	.295
IAN BRUDERSON SS	6	1	3	2	0	1	0	0	2	.274
GRAEME NILSON 1B	5	2	1	0	1	0	0	1	1	.261
ERNESTO MENDESOTO 3B	5	1	2	1	0	0	0	0	0	.309
TRENT ATHERTON C	5	2	2	0	0	0	0	0	0	.289
TONY DAMICO RF	4	3	2	1	1	0	0	1	0	.250
MATTHEW VAN STENCEL CF	4	1	3	6	1	0	1	0	0	.289
TREMONT HARKNESS DH	4	0	2	2	1	0	0	0	0	.286
JAYSON GIVINS 2B	4	1	1	0	1	0	0	0	1	.269

PITCHING	IP	H	R	ER	SO	BB	ERA
MICKEY VOLD (W)	6	7	3	3	4	2	3.97
JORGE BAREA	2	5	2	2	2	0	3.77
DEVON CLAVELL	1	0	0	0	0	0	4.15

INNING	1	2	3	4	5	6	7	8	9	TOTAL
OAKLAND	0	1	2	1	6	1	0	2	0	13
CLEVELAND	0	0	0	0	3	0	1	1	0	5

GAME 63

By SAM LARDNER
The Cleveland Press

CLEVELAND, June 17 — The timing was all right for the Indians Thursday night.

The real man of the moment was Scott Michaels, whose walk-off solo homer in the bottom of the 10th inning lifted the Tribe to a 5–4 victory over the Oakland Athletics at Progressive Field. Lucky number 13 for the hot-hitting Michaels.

Equally as fortuitous for the Indians was that closer Ivan Zyzna came off the injured list a day early and wound up getting the victory by pitching the top of the 10th inning. Zyzna reported back 100 percent after being on the IL since May 16 with a forearm injury, and not a minute too soon for the Indians, who've seen their bullpen beat up and beleaguered. Zyzna's ERA is now a miniscule .093.

Zyzna's return was the big news online before the game, but he didn't mind being relegated to old-news status after Michaels continued his hot hitting with a blast to left field in the 10th against Mitch Sutherland.

"I felt great, but how about Scottie?" Zyzna said. "I was able to talk them into activating me. There was no reason to wait another day. I know they'll take it easy on me for the first little bit, but I was champing at the bit."

Michaels not only was the man of the minute for the Indians, but he's been their man of the month since taking over for injured second baseman

Angel Rodriguez. The homer was his second hit of the game in five at-bats. He also drove in a run with a fifth-inning double.

"Getting Ivan back is kind of like getting the band back together," Michaels said. "I still feel like I'm a bit player and that Angel is still going to contribute a lot when he gets back. We talk all the time. But I've been feeling pretty good out there. You hate to get your chance because a team-mate — especially a great guy like Angel — gets hurt, but all I can do is try to produce when Skip (manager Todd Stein) puts me out there."

The Indians (31–32) got another good start from Brian Howard. The Doc worked 6 and two-thirds innings, getting a no-decision. He gave up six hits and three runs, two coming in the second on a homer by Tremont Harkness and one in the sixth, when Jayson Givins' run-scoring single tied the game at 3 to 3.

"Yeah, not bad," Howard said. "This had a little bit of an off feel to it tonight. But we hung in there as a team."

The A's went ahead 4–3 in the seventh when Ernesto Mendesoto homered off Buck Sterling. Oliver Reiner's clutch RBI single in the eighth tied it at 4–4, setting the stage for the big finish.

"The team never stops, even in a blowout like last night," said manager Todd Stein, referring to Wednesday night's 13–5 loss to the A's. "It didn't pay off last night, but it said something about our character. It came through in the end tonight."

Way back at the beginning of this game, the Indians staked Howard to a 2–0 lead in the first on Terry Rovetto's two-run double. Michaels' double in the fifth made it 3–0. The Indians gave the lead away, but instead of folding as they did often in April and May, they didn't let things snowball.

"That's the difference right there," Stein said. "I really liked the response. The A's had all the momentum, but we shut it down."

GAME 63

CLEVELAND INDIANS VS OAKLAND ATHLETICS • JUNE 17
CLEVELAND 5 / OAKLAND 4

CLEVELAND INDIANS										
BATTING	AB	R	H	RBI	2B	3B	HR	BB	SO	BA
RIKKI LABUDDA CF	5	2	2	0	1	0	0	0	0	.269
MICAH MILLISON RF	4	1	1	0	0	0	0	0	0	.265
WILSON WHITE LF	4	0	0	0	0	0	0	0	2	.267
OLIVER REINER 1B	4	0	1	1	0	0	0	0	0	.298
TERRY ROVETTO 3B	2	1	2	2	0	0	0	2	0	.262
SCOTT MICHAELS 2B	5	1	2	2	1	0	1	0	0	.318
JUSTIN KESTINO SS	4	0	1	0	0	0	0	0	0	.240
J.J. KULAKOFSKI DH	4	0	0	0	0	0	0	0	1	.197
MORRIS JEROME C	4	0	0	0	0	0	0	1	0	.255
PITCHING	IP	H	R	ER	SO	BB	ERA			
BRIAN HOWARD	6.67	6	3	3	7	1	3.47			
BUCK STERLING	2.33	3	1	1	0	0	3.16			
IVAN ZYZNA (W)	1	0	0	0	0	0	0.93			

OAKLAND A'S										
BATTING	AB	R	H	RBI	2B	3B	HR	BB	SO	BA
ISIAH HUERTAS LF	5	0	1	0	0	0	0	0	0	.292
IAN BRUDERSON SS	4	0	0	0	0	1	0	1	2	.268
GRAEME NILSON 1B	4	0	2	0	1	0	0	0	2	.267
ERNESTO MENDESOTO 3B	4	1	2	1	0	0	1	0	1	.315
TRENT ATHERTON C	4	0	0	0	0	0	0	0	1	.280
TONY DAMICO RF	4	1	1	0	1	0	0	0	1	.250
MATTHEW VAN STENCEL CF	4	1	1	0	1	0	0	0	1	.288
TREMONT HARKNESS DH	4	1	1	2	0	0	1	0	0	.284
JAYSON GIVINS 2B	4	0	1	1	0	0	0	0	1	.269
PITCHING	IP	H	R	ER	SO	BB	ERA			
KRIS PERKINS	6.33	5	3	3	2	1	4.08			
JAKE RICHARDS	1.67	1	0	0	1	0	3.63			
CRAIG QUINN	1	2	1	1	1	0	4.18			
MITCH SUTHERLAND (L)	0.67	1	1	1	0	0	2.89			

INNING	1	2	3	4	5	6	7	8	9	10	TOTAL
OAKLAND	0	2	0	0	0	1	1	0	0	0	4
CLEVELAND	2	0	0	0	1	0	0	1	0	1	5

GAME 64

By SAM LARDNER

The Cleveland Press

CLEVELAND, June 18 — There's nothing quite like Friday night fireworks at the old ballpark.

Making the pyrotechnics all the more enjoyable for the Indians fans at Progressive Field was an 8–2 victory over the Seattle Mariners, propelling their team, at long last, to the .500 mark at 32–32, hammering out 17 hits with everyone in the lineup contributing.

It's the first time all year the Indians have been at break-even, as they began the season 0–6, setting the stage for manager Dave Mills being fired.

So why not? Go ahead and set off a couple more Roman candles and pinwheels.

"Yippee ki yay," said Todd Stein, the man who replaced Mills at the top of the dugout steps after the 10th game of the season. "We had so many false starts in getting back to .500 that it seemed like maybe we'd never get here. But here we are.

"That's only the immediate goal, though. We want to get way beyond .500."

The heroes were many on this 80-degree night that felt like the perfect prelude to summer. Starting pitcher Kenny Camden won his sixth game and second straight decision, working seven innings and giving up six hits and both Seattle runs.

"I don't know what to tell you," Camden said. "After all that trial and tribulation, we finally got back to a place where we can work from. You can't talk about contending unless you at first get to .500 and then build on that. That's what we're going to try to do."

The Indians had a couple of big innings. They sent 10 men to the plate in the third, scoring four runs and knocking Mariners starter Miguel Reyes out of the game. Scott Michaels had a three-run triple in the inning. He scored on Justin Kestino's single, with Kestino coming home on a double by Kieran Catsef.

The M's Skyler Townsend homered off Camden in the fourth with one on, but that was it against the crafty left-hander.

Michaels batted twice in the Indians' four-run sixth, hitting an RBI single and walking. The other two runs in that inning came off the bat of Rikki LaBudda, who singled home a pair."

"It's good to come up to the plate that often in a game," Michaels said. "We've had some pretty good offensive games this year, but two outbursts in one game make it a fun night."

The Indians got good relief work from Solly Alvarez and Buck Sterling. With the weather heating up, expect more fireworks this weekend.

"We've got to come right back tomorrow, so we can enjoy this one for a few hours and get right back at it," Stein said. "It's been a long uphill climb to get to .500. We don't want to backslide now."

CLEVELAND INDIANS VS SEATTLE MARINERS · JUNE 18
CLEVELAND 8 / SEATTLE 2

CLEVELAND INDIANS

BATTING	AB	R	H	RBI	2B	3B	HR	BB	SO	BA
RIKKI LABUDDA CF	6	0	2	2	1	0	0	1	0	.270
MICAH MILLISON RF	6	1	2	0	0	0	0	1	0	.267
OLIVER REINER 1B	6	2	2	0	0	0	0	1	2	.299
TERRY ROVETTO 3B	5	1	2	0	1	0	0	2	1	.265
SCOTT MICHAELS 2B	7	1	3	4	0	1	0	0	0	.323
JUSTIN KESTINO SS	6	1	1	1	0	0	0	0	0	.238
KIERAN CATSEF LF	5	0	2	1	1	0	0	0	0	.262
BERNARD HARPER DH	5	1	1	0	0	0	0	1	0	.250
MORRIS JEROME C	5	1	2	0	0	0	0	1	0	.259

PITCHING	IP	H	R	ER	SO	BB	ERA			
KENNY CAMDEN (W)	7	6	2	2	5	2	3.72			
SOLLY ALVAREZ	1	0	0	0	0	1	3.76			
BUCK STERLING	1	1	0	0	1	1	3.00			

SEATTLE MARINERS

BATTING	AB	R	H	RBI	2B	3B	HR	BB	SO	BA
COREY GILLESPIE CF	4	0	0	0	0	0	0	1	2	.288
DIEGO GONZALEZ LF	4	0	0	0	0	0	0	0	1	.268
PHIL BORNTRAGER 3B	3	0	1	0	1	0	0	1	0	.262
BILLY NEVILLE 1B	3	1	2	0	0	0	0	1	0	.317
HUGO VENEGAS DH	4	1	0	0	0	0	0	0	1	.280
VANCE ROBERTS 2B	4	0	1	0	1	0	0	0	0	.250
JAMIE BROCKER SS	3	0	1	0	1	0	0	0	1	.290
BRENDON KAHN RF	4	0	1	0	0	0	0	0	0	.284
SKYLER TOWNSEND C	4	0	1	2	0	0	0	1	1	.269

PITCHING	IP	H	R	ER	SO	BB	ERA			
MIGUEL REYES (L)	2.67	8	5	5	0	4	4.59			
JOAQUIN TORRES	2.33	2	0	0	1	1	3.57			
KELVIN BILLINGSLEY	0.67	4	3	3	0	1	4.88			
JALEN GATES	2.33	3	0	0	2	0	3.54			

INNING	1	2	3	4	5	6	7	8	9	TOTAL
SEATTLE	0	0	0	2	0	0	0	0	0	2
CLEVELAND	0	0	5	0	0	3	0	0		8

GAME 65

By SAM LARDNER
The Cleveland Press

CLEVELAND, June 19 — As memorable as Saturday's victory was for the Indians, the day was totally unforgettable for infielder Angel Rodriguez, and he didn't even play in the 3–1 victory over the Seattle Mariners at Progressive Field.

The Indians went over the .500 mark (33–32) for the first time all season behind the pitching of Tak Fujimoto.

In addition to that, Saturday was Pride Day in Cleveland, making it a special day for Rodriguez, who is openly gay.

During a pregame ceremony at home plate and shown on the ballpark's video boards, the Indians honored Rodriguez by making several charitable donations in his name. The Cleveland chapter of the Baseball Writers also presented Rodriguez with its annual Good Guy Award. Doing the honors were Burt Reiter of the Akron Daily Journal and Karl Cauffmann, sports editor of the Cleveland Press. Cauffmann is active in the local LGBTQ community.

Earlier in the day, Rodriguez served as the grand marshal of Cleveland's Pride Parade.

Just a few weeks earlier, he received homophobic abuse by a handful of fans at Boston's Fenway Park. But there was nothing but good vibes on Saturday at Progressive Field.

"This means so much to me," Rodriguez told the crowd. "All I want to is be accepted for who I am, and all of you here in Cleveland have done that. I thank you very much."

Rodriguez is on the injured list with a hamstring injury, but he gave the fans a little tease.

"I'll be back soon," he said.

As for the game, it was Rodriguez's replacement, Scott Michaels, who complemented Fujimoto's work on the mound. Michaels' two-run double in the fifth inning broke a scoreless tie. Micah Millison's RBI groundout in the sixth made it 3–0.

Even though Michaels has supplanted Rodriguez on the field, the two remain friends. Was Michaels thinking of his buddy when he got the big hit?

"Oh, yeah," he said. "Angel was always supportive of me when I was going through my struggles with my shoulder. All he wants to do is play baseball, just like the rest of us. So I'm glad I could get the hit and dedicate it to him. And I'm even more glad that we won the game."

Fujimoto rebounded from a pair of poor starts to work seven innings and give up four hits while walking one and striking out eight. The Mariners scored their only run on a homer in the seventh by Phil Borntragger on Fujimoto's 105th pitch. He wound up throwing 111 for the game.

"This was an important game for me," Fujimoto said through his translator. "I feel I let the team down in my last two starts, so I wanted to make right today."

Geno Milzie pitched the eighth, and Lee Hazelton got the save as manager Todd Stein gave No. 1 closer Ivan Zyzna a break. Zyzna has pitched twice since coming off the injured list.

"I told you we had good bullpen depth and that we would use everybody in save situations," Stein said. "Geno will close some games, too. It's a nice situation."

Speaking of nice, Stein was asked about the entire day at the ballpark.

"How about that; we're all so proud of Angel," he said. "The turnout was great, and the reception he got was even nicer. And getting the win and going above .500 was a nice topper."

GAME 65

CLEVELAND INDIANS VS SEATTLE MARINERS · JUNE 19
CLEVELAND 3 / SEATTLE 1

CLEVELAND INDIANS

BATTING	AB	R	H	RBI	2B	3B	HR	BB	SO	BA
RIKKI LABUDDA CF	4	1	2	0	0	1	0	0	0	.274
MICAH MILLISON RF	4	0	1	1	0	0	0	0	0	.267
WILSON WHITE LF	4	0	0	0	0	0	0	0	1	.263
OLIVER REINER 1B	3	1	1	0	1	0	0	2	1	.299
TERRY ROVETTO 3B	4	0	1	0	1	0	0	0	0	.264
SCOTT MICHAELS 2B	4	0	2	2	0	0	0	0	0	.327
JUSTIN KESTINO SS	4	0	0	0	0	0	0	0	1	.234
BERNARD HARPER DH	4	0	1	0	0	0	0	1	1	.250
ICEBERG PETERS C	4	0	0	0	0	0	0	1	2	.228

PITCHING	IP	H	R	ER	SO	BB	ERA			
TAK FUJIMOTO (W)	7.33	4	1	1	8	1	3.11			
GENO MILZIE	0.67	1	0	0	1	1	4.04			
LEE HAZELTON (S)	1	1	0	0	1	0	3.86			

SEATTLE MARINERS

BATTING	AB	R	H	RBI	2B	3B	HR	BB	SO	BA
COREY GILLESPIE CF	4	0	1	0	0	0	0	1	1	.287
DIEGO GONZALEZ LF	4	0	0	0	0	0	0	0	2	.262
PHIL BORNTRAGER 3B	4	1	1	1	0	0	1	0	0	.262
BILLY NEVILLE 1B	3	0	1	0	0	0	0	0	2	.318
HUGO VENEGAS DH	3	0	1	0	0	0	0	1	0	.281
VANCE ROBERTS 2B	4	0	0	0	1	0	0	0	1	.243
JAMIE BROCKER SS	4	0	1	0	1	0	0	0	0	.289
BRENDON KAHN RF	4	0	0	0	0	0	0	0	2	.275
SKYLER TOWNSEND C	4	0	1	0	0	0	0	1	2	.268

PITCHING	IP	H	R	ER	SO	BB	ERA			
ADRIAN CRUZ (L)	7	7	3	3	5	2	4.16			
MAYA NAGATOMO	1	1	0	0	1	0	3.82			

INNING	1	2	3	4	5	6	7	8	9	TOTAL
SEATTLE	0	0	0	0	0	0	1	0	0	1
CLEVELAND	0	0	0	0	2	1	0	0		3

GAME 66

By SAM LARDNER

The Cleveland Press

CLEVELAND, June 20 — The Indians gave new meaning to the term "ace in the hole" Sunday.

That's just where pitcher Lynn Moda and his mates put themselves during a 6–2 loss to the Seattle Mariners at Progressive Field.

After breathing the rarefied air of being above .500 for one day, the Tribe sunk back to the break-even mark at 33–33 with one more game to play Monday night in this wrap-around weekend series.

The Mariners hit Moda and infielders with four runs in the first inning, well before the 35,657 fans could get settled into their seats on this first day before the start of summer.

An error by Scott Michaels on the first play of the game and a passed ball charged to Iceberg Peters later in the frame set the tone for another sloppy game, something the Indians are desperately try to leave in the past.

"It's disappointing that we took our own fans out of the game in the first inning," said interim manager Todd Stein. "The ball to Scottie might have taken a bad hop, so I can't completely fault him. Modes tried to pitch around it, but there was too much stuff going on."

Moda, who has had an up-and-down season to date, took the blame.

"I'm supposed to be the leader of the staff, so yeah, it's up to me to stop the bleeding, and I didn't do that," he said. "I think we're on the right track overall. We do have to tighten some things up if we're going to make the run we think we can make. Today, it started with me."

That's the kind of accountability that endears Moda to his teammates. Others followed his lead Sunday.

"I have to catch that groundball," Michaels said. "That opened the floodgates to a big inning for them. I've got to be better. It's a two-way game, not just offense."

The first inning began with Michaels booting Vance Roberts's grounder. Moda got two quick outs before he contributed to the mess by walking Jamie Brocker and Brendan Kahn to load the bases.

Given the invitation to cause trouble, the Mariners gladly accepted. First baseman, Billy Neville tripled to the gap in right-center, and Peters' momentary lapse of concentration behind the plate allowed the fourth run of the inning to score on the passed ball.

"There was a cross-up, and that was my doing," said Peters, the Indians' venerable backup catcher. Modes wanted one pitch, and I thought we were on the same page. Looking at the video, it was pretty clear my glove was in the wrong spot."

Moda gave up two more runs in the fifth on a homer by Corey Gillespie and was gone after working 4 and two-thirds innings.

The Indians got their runs in the sixth on a homer by Micah Millison after Rikki LaBudda walked and stole second base. That came against M's starter Dino Toban, who went seven strong innings.

Solly Alvarez and Buck Sterling pitched what were essentially mop-up innings for the Tribe.

So the Indians will have one more at home before embarking on road trip to Toronto and Kansas City.

"We want to get out of here on a good note," Stein said. "We certainly don't want to fall back to under .500 after we worked so hard to bring ourselves to a winning record. It does feel odd having one of these series that will end on a Monday, but we'll deal with it."

GAME 66

CLEVELAND INDIANS VS SEATTLE MARINERS • JUNE 20
SEATTLE 6 / CLEVELAND 2

CLEVELAND INDIANS

BATTING	AB	R	H	RBI	2B	3B	HR	BB	SO	BA
RIKKI LABUDDA CF	3	1	0	0	0	0	0	1	0	.271
MICAH MILLISON RF	4	1	1	2	0	0	1	0	0	.267
WILSON WHITE LF	4	0	0	0	0	0	0	0	1	.258
J.J. KULAKOFSKI 1B	3	0	2	0	1	0	0	1	0	.216
TERRY ROVETTO 3B	4	0	1	0	1	0	0	0	0	.264
SCOTT MICHAELS 2B	4	0	0	0	0	0	0	0	2	.319
LEO TAYLOR SS	4	0	1	0	0	0	0	0	0	.279
BERNARD HARPER DH	4	0	1	0	0	0	0	0	1	.250
ICEBERG PETERS C	4	0	1	0	0	0	0	0	1	.230

PITCHING	IP	H	R	ER	SO	BB	ERA			
LYNN MODA (L)	4.67	7	6	2	4	2	4.58			
SOLLY ALVAREZ	2.33	1	0	0	1	0	3.46			
BUCK STERLING	2	1	0	0	2	0	2.81			

SEATTLE MARINERS

BATTING	AB	R	H	RBI	2B	3B	HR	BB	SO	BA
COREY GILLESPIE CF	4	1	1	2	0	0	1	0	0	.286
PHIL BORNTRAGER 3B	4	0	2	0	1	0	0	0	1	.268
VANCE ROBERTS 2B	4	1	1	0	0	0	0	0	1	.244
JAMIE BROCKER SS	3	1	1	0	0	0	0	1	0	.290
BRENDON KAHN RF	3	1	1	0	0	0	0	1	1	.276
BILLY NEVILLE 1B	4	1	2	3	1	1	0	0	1	.323
HUGO VENEGAS DH	4	0	0	0	0	0	0	0	1	.273
ROBERTO AGUIRRE RF	4	1	0	0	0	0	0	0	0	.233
SEBASTIAN MACIAS C	4	0	1	0	0	0	0	0	2	.268

PITCHING	IP	H	R	ER	SO	BB	ERA			
DINO TOBAN (W)	7	6	2	2	5	1	4.03			
JOAQUIN TORRES	1	1	0	0	0	1	3.47			
TONY DOS SANTOS	1	0	0	0	0	0	2.54			

INNING	1	2	3	4	5	6	7	8	9	TOTAL
SEATTLE	4	0	0	0	2	0	0	0	0	6
CLEVELAND	0	0	0	0	0	2	0	0	0	2

GAME 67

By SAM LARDNER
The Cleveland Press

CLEVELAND, June 21 — When Todd Stein used the term "wasted opportunity," he could have been referring to Monday night's 4–3 loss to the Seattle Mariners at Progressive Field.

Or he could have been referring to this four-game series, in which the Indians won the first two games only to fritter away a chance at a series victory, only to settle for a split.

Or Stein could just as well have been referring to the entire season, which has turned into one of fits and starts for the Indians.

The phrase is one-size-fits-all. And it certainly fits how the Indians have played all year long.

After taking a 3–0 lead in the fifth inning, the Tribe watched as the Mariners beat them by a steady drip-drip-drip of four single runs over four innings to snatch the victory.

"It's a wasted opportunity because we're back under .500 (33–34) when we had a chance to really take off," Stein said. "I get tired of saying it, and you guys get tired of hearing it, but as much as you have to give credit to the other team at times, we have to do our job to hold leads when we get them, especially at our home ballpark."

It was smooth sailing — or so it appeared — for Indians starting pitcher Ollie Gonzalez, who rebounded nicely from last week's 13–5 drubbing at the hands of the Oakland Athletics.

Staked to a 3–0 lead by DH Bernard Harper's three-run homer in the fifth, his eighth, Gonzalez hardly looked fazed when the Mariners scored in the top of the sixth on Billy Neville's solo blast.

Gonzalez appeared to tire in the seventh, when he was pulled in favor of Geno Milzie after Xavier Battle's one-out double. A single by Roberto Aguirre tightened the game at 3–2.

"I might have lost a little something there in the seventh, so I can't blame Steinie for taking me out there," Gonzalez said. "Our bullpen has been doing the job lately, but I put a man in scoring position there. You can't expect guys to come in out of the pen with men on all the time and not give up any hits."

Lee Hazelton took over for Milzie in the eighth and promptly walked the first two men he faced before Vance Roberts tied the game with a groundball single up the middle.

Stein declined to go with closer Ivan Zyzna with the score tied and not a save situation in the ninth, Instead, he stuck with youngster Hazelton, who yielded a leadoff homer to Jamie Brocker.

"Had we gone ahead in the bottom of the eighth, I would have gone to Zyzna," Stein said. "But we're still trying to be careful with him. He's not that far removed from being on the IL (injured list). And Hazelton got beat on a good pitch. Brocker squared up a 95-mile-an-hour fastball and hit it out."

Now the Indians are tasked with trying to re-establish a winning record on a road trip that will take them to Toronto and Kansas City in a season that is inexorably heading toward its halfway point.

In other words, it's not early anymore.

"We have to get this thing going in the right direction for good, not just for a day or two," Stein said. "Everybody here knows that. The Twins and the White Sox aren't going to wait for us at the top, and the Tigers and Royals play everybody tough. It will be important for us to have a good road trip."

CLEVELAND INDIANS VS SEATTLE MARINERS · JUNE 21
SEATTLE 4 / CLEVELAND 3

CLEVELAND INDIANS

BATTING	AB	R	H	RBI	2B	3B	HR	BB	SO	BA
KIERAN CATSEF CF	4	0	1	0	0	0	0	1	0	.261
MICAH MILLISON RF	4	0	1	0	1	0	0	0	2	.266
WILSON WHITE LF	3	0	0	0	0	0	0	1	0	.255
OLIVER REINER 1B	3	0	1	0	0	0	0	1	0	.300
TERRY ROVETTO 3B	4	1	1	0	1	0	0	0	1	.264
SCOTT MICHAELS 2B	4	0	1	0	0	0	0	0	1	.317
JUSTIN KESTINO SS	4	1	0	0	0	0	0	0	1	.230
BERNARD HARPER DH	4	1	2	3	0	0	1	0	0	.256
MORRIS JEROME C	3	0	1	0	0	0	0	1	2	.260

PITCHING	IP	H	R	ER	SO	BB	ERA			
OLLIE GONZALEZ	6.33	5	1	1	4	0	5.09			
GENO MILZIE	1.67	3	2	2	0	2	4.30			
LEE HAZELTON (L)	1	1	1	1	1	0	4.27			

SEATTLE MARINERS

BATTING	AB	R	H	RBI	2B	3B	HR	BB	SO	BA
COREY GILLESPIE CF	3	1	1	0	0	0	0	1	0	.287
PHIL BORNTRAGER 3B	3	0	1	0	1	0	0	1	0	.269
BILLY NEVILLE 1B	4	1	2	1	0	0	1	0	1	.328
VANCE ROBERTS 2B	4	0	1	1	0	0	0	0	0	.244
BRENDON KAHN RF	4	0	0	0	0	0	0	0	2	.268
XAVIER BATTLE DH	4	1	1	0	1	0	0	0	1	.244
ROBERTO AGUIRRE RF	4	0	1	1	0	0	0	0	0	.233
JAMIE BROCKER SS	4	1	2	1	0	0	0	0	0	.296
SKYLER TOWNSEND C	4	0	0	0	0	0	0	0	1	.259

PITCHING	IP	H	R	ER	SO	BB	ERA			
TYRELL BISHOP	6	5	3	3	3	2	3.57			
KELVIN BILLINGSLEY	1	1	0	0	1	1	4.71			
JALEN GATES (W)	1	2	0	0	1	0	3.38			
TONY DOS SANTOS (S)	1	0	0	0	2	1	2.42			

INNING	1	2	3	4	5	6	7	8	9	TOTAL
SEATTLE	0	0	0	0	0	1	1	1	1	4
CLEVELAND	0	0	0	0	3	0	0	0	0	3

GAME 68

By SAM LARDNER
The Cleveland Press

TORONTO, June 22 — Indians general manager J.D. Eisner hooked up with his ballclub as it began a road trip against the Toronto Blue Jays.

But to hear Eisner tell it, he almost didn't make it.

"Border patrol threatened to keep me out of Canada," joked Eisner, a member of the Blue Jays front office before the Indians snapped him up a couple years back. "Something about me abandoning club and country. Actually, they were quite nice. I have a lot of fond memories here, and the people are always so welcoming."

The border folks might wish they had kept the Indians out instead after the Tribe thrashed the Jays 9–3 Tuesday night at Rogers Centre.

The game was pretty much a rout from the get-go as the Indians got a three-run homer from Wilson White in the first inning against Hank O'Brien. White finished the game with four hits including his seventh home run.

Scott Michaels added a solo shot in the third, his fourteenth, and Oliver Reiner hit a three-run homer in the fifth, his thirteenth.

Benefiting from the outburst was starting pitcher Brian Howard. The Doc kept his recent run of success going by eeking out the quality start, giving up all three Jays runs in six innings.

"I've been pretty lucky with all the support lately," Howard said. "This is a great place to hit and a tough place to pitch. I gave up that three-run bomb (to Jermaine Brown in the fifth), so you know things can turn in a hurry up here."

As for the Indians as a whole, they're the epitome of mediocrity with a record of 34–34. Eisner said he doesn't see it that way.

"Remember, we started out 0–6," he said, as if anyone could forget. "We've done a good job clawing our way back and into contention, even though we still have a ways to go."

Eisner praised the job interim manager Todd Stein has done since taking over for the fired Dave Mills after the 10th game of the season. However, Eisner added that now is not the time to talk about taking the "interim" tag off Stein's title.

"There will be plenty of time to talk about that, either at the all-star break, late in the year or even in the fall," Eisner said. "We think the world of Todd. He's done a remarkable job keeping things on an even keel here."

Eisner will be with the team on the entire seven-game road trip, which includes three games in Toronto and four in Kansas City.

Although the July 31 trading deadline is still over a month away, there are some rumblings. No doubt the Indians will look to augment their bullpen and bench if they can get above the .500 mark and make a run at the American League Central crown or a wild-card spot.

Outfielder Huron Southworth has voiced his unhappiness about losing playing time to Micah Millison after a slow start. He's quoted as saying, "I know I'm an everyday player and I proved it last year in Triple-A. I don't make up the lineup cards. It's skip's call but I'm frustrated being on the bench."

He eventually could be moved to bring back an arm or a backup infielder.

"Huron has been a pro about it," Eisner said. "Of course, he wants to play more. All players do. They have pride. But while he's not happy about the loss of playing time, he's not been a disruptive force. Todd will work him in there, and you never know when an injury might come up."

For his part, Stein said he appreciates the nice words from the boss.

"All that contract stuff will take care of itself," he said. "I just worry about getting the team ready to play every day and writing out the lineup card. I'm sure we'll talk later in the season."

CLEVELAND INDIANS VS TORONTO BLUE JAYS • JUNE 22
CLEVELAND 9 / TORONTO 3

CLEVELAND INDIANS										
BATTING	AB	R	H	RBI	2B	3B	HR	BB	SO	BA
RIKKI LABUDDA CF	4	2	2	0	1	0	0	1	0	.274
MICAH MILLISON RF	5	1	1	0	1	0	0	0	0	.265
WILSON WHITE LF	5	3	4	3	0	0	1	0	0	.266
OLIVER REINER 1B	5	1	1	3	0	0	1	0	1	.298
TERRY ROVETTO 3B	5	0	2	1	1	0	0	0	0	.267
SCOTT MICHAELS 2B	4	1	1	1	0	0	1	1	1	.316
JUSTIN KESTINO SS	4	1	3	0	0	0	0	0	0	.238
BERNARD HARPER DH	4	0	2	1	0	0	0	0	0	.261
MORRIS JEROME C	4	0	0	0	0	0	0	0	1	.255
PITCHING	IP	H	R	ER	SO	BB	ERA			
BRIAN HOWARD (W)	6	6	3	3	3	1	3.54			
SOLLY ALVAREZ	2	1	0	0	1	0	3.23			
BUCK STERLING	1	0	0	0	0	0	2.73			
TORONTO BLUE JAYS										
BATTING	AB	R	H	RBI	2B	3B	HR	BB	SO	BA
CARLOS ARNALDO CF	4	0	2	0	0	0	0	0	0	.291
JEFF STEPHENS DH	4	1	1	0	1	0	0	0	0	.268
ANDY TENZER 3B	4	1	0	0	0	0	0	0	0	.314
RAMON ORTIZ SS	3	0	1	0	0	0	0	1	1	.277
JERMAINE BROWN LF	4	1	1	3	0	0	1	0	1	.276
RAYMOND BALKMAN 1B	4	0	0	0	0	0	0	0	1	.236
RICO ESPINOSA C	4	0	1	0	0	0	0	0	1	.233
JOEL NISSALKE 2B	4	0	0	0	0	0	0	0	0	.281
ROYCE MANFRED RF	3	0	1	0	0	0	0	0	0	.270
PITCHING	IP	H	R	ER	SO	BB	ERA			
HANK O'BRIEN (L)	4.33	9	6	6	1	1	4.07			
JAMIE SHEDLER	1.67	3	1	1	0	0	4.59			
OMAR MELENDEZ	2	3	2	2	1	0	4.04			
MIKE KILCRAN	1	1	0	0	1	1	2.42			
INNING	1	2	3	4	5	6	7	8	9	TOTAL
CLEVELAND	3	0	1	0	3	0	1	1	0	9
TORONTO	0	0	0	0	3	0	0	0	0	3

GAME 69

By SAM LARDNER
The Cleveland Press

TORONTO, June 23 — Nothing doing.

That about sums up everything surrounding the Cleveland Indians these days. It certainly was an apt description of Wednesday night's sleepy 4–0 loss to the Toronto Blue Jays in the dead quiet of Rogers Centre.

Nothing to see here. The Tribe managed just five hits against Blue Jays starting pitcher Armando Ojeda and the Toronto bullpen as their wheel-spinning continued. Ojeda battled some wildness and walked six but managed to wiggle out of trouble each time as the Tribe failed to capitalize on the free passes.

The loss dropped the Indians back to one game under .500 at 34–35, making one wonder if this is how it's going to all year long.

General manager J.D. Eisner watched stone-faced from his box along press row. Indians fans can only hope that Eisner's cell phone is working because the Indians look like they can use an infusion of energized blood.

As he did Tuesday, Eisner reiterated that nothing was doing on that front — at least not yet –either.

"We aren't going rush or panic into anything," Eisner said. "Look, I know, the fans are impatient and you guys (media) are going to take your shots. But we have a good core here, and we're confident they're going to get the job done in the end.

"That won't preclude us from making moves. But it takes two to get a deal done, and not a lot of teams are motivated to talk about trades at this point. That's all I can tell you."

Indians starting pitcher Kenny Camden might be seen in provincial court in the morning suing for non-support. The Wiz pitched creditably, but the crafty left-hander got no help from his friends. Camden worked six innings, giving up five hits and three runs. Mickey Penney gave up one more in the seventh.

Camden did not want to hear about getting the quality start. "Only one thing matters, and that's getting the win," he said. "And I'm not going to say anything about the offense. If I had done my job earlier and kept us in it, maybe we could have rallied. We're all frustrated we can't get over this hump. But all we can do is keep going out there every day. It's not for lack of effort, and you can see by guys' expressions in here that we care. So let's not make a big deal out of all this."

Camden gave up a solo homer to Andy Tenzer in the bottom of the first after the Indians went meekly on 11 pitches in a 1-2-3 top of the inning. A two-run double by Joel Nissalke in the fourth basically finished Camden and the Tribe.

"Hard to figure, especially in a great hitters park like this," said Indians manager Todd Stein. "I wish I could explain it. We're working at this, but we're not pressing. At the same time, the sense of urgency is there."

GAME 69

CLEVELAND INDIANS VS TORONTO BLUE JAYS · JUNE 23
TORONTO 4 / CLEVELAND 0

CLEVELAND INDIANS

BATTING	AB	R	H	RBI	2B	3B	HR	BB	SO	BA
RIKKI LABUDDA CF	4	0	0	0	0	0	0	1	0	.270
MICAH MILLISON RF	4	0	0	0	0	0	0	1	1	.261
WILSON WHITE LF	4	0	1	0	0	0	0	1	1	.266
OLIVER REINER 1B	4	0	1	0	0	0	0	1	0	.297
TERRY ROVETTO 3B	4	0	1	0	0	0	0	1	0	.266
SCOTT MICHAELS 2B	3	0	0	0	0	0	0	0	0	.310
JUSTIN KESTINO SS	4	0	2	0	1	0	0	0	0	.243
BERNARD HARPER DH	4	0	0	0	0	0	0	0	2	.255
MORRIS JEROME C	3	0	0	0	0	0	0	1	0	.251

PITCHING	IP	H	R	ER	SO	BB	ERA			
KENNY CAMDEN (L)	6	5	3	3	5	0	3.77			
MICKEY PENNY	2	2	1	1	0	1	3.54			

TORONTO BLUE JAYS

BATTING	AB	R	H	RBI	2B	3B	HR	BB	SO	BA
CARLOS ARNALDO CF	4	1	1	0	0	0	0	0	0	.290
JEFF STEPHENS DH	4	0	0	0	0	0	0	0	1	.261
ANDY TENZER 3B	4	1	2	1	0	0	1	0	0	.319
RAMON ORTIZ SS	3	0	0	1	0	0	0	0	1	.272
JERMAINE BROWN LF	4	1	1	0	1	0	0	0	0	.275
RAYMOND BALKMAN 1B	4	1	1	0	0	0	0	0	1	.236
RICO ESPINOSA C	4	0	1	0	0	0	0	0	0	.233
JOEL NISSALKE 2B	4	0	1	2	1	0	0	0	0	.281
ROYCE MANFRED RF	3	0	0	0	0	0	0	1	2	.263

PITCHING	IP	H	R	ER	SO	BB	ERA			
ARMANDO OJEDA (W)	8	5	0	0	5	4	3.34			
RICK SANTORI	1	0	0	0	0	0	2.49			

INNING	1	2	3	4	5	6	7	8	9	TOTAL
CLEVELAND	0	0	0	0	0	0	0	0	0	0
TORONTO	1	0	0	2	0	0	1	0		4

GAME 70

By SAM LARDNER
The Cleveland Press

TORONTO, June 24 — With the clock going tick-tock, Tak took one for the team.

That's Tak as in Indians starting pitcher Tak Fujimoto.

Although he didn't come away with a quality start Thursday night, Fujimoto got the more important stat — the "W" — as he gutted out seven innings in a 5–4 victory over the Toronto Blue Jays at Rogers Centre.

The Tribe needed a starting pitcher to go deep, and Fujimoto did just that throwing 118 pitches and giving up seven hits while watching on the bench as his teammates scored just enough runs for a victory that sent the Indians back to .500 at 35–35.

"I could have even gone one more," Fujimoto said through his translator. "I knew this was an important game because we needed to win this series. I'm happy to do my part."

The respect for Fujimoto was readily apparent in the eyes of his teammates and in their words.

"Huge," said first baseman and team leader Oliver Reiner. "Our pen has been beat up, and even though it was a bit of a struggle for Fuji, he kept going out there and battling. We heard about his guts when he signed here (last winter) from Japan. And we've seen it. The results aren't always there for all of us, but all you can ask of your teammates is that they go out and compete. He did that tonight."

This was a back-and-forth battle from the start. The teams each scored two runs in the first inning, with Reiner's two-run homer driving in Rikki LaBudda, who walked to open the game against Dean Pinto.

Fujimoto gave up a two-out single to Ramon Ortiz in the bottom of the inning before Raymond Balkman homered into the third deck.

"If you're going to give one up, give it up big," said Indians manager Todd Stein, who could afford to smile. "I really liked the way Fuji battled out there. He didn't have quite his best stuff, but he kept going out there inning after inning."

The Indians got a two-run double from Scott Michaels in the fourth and a solo homer from little-used Huron Southworth (in a possible trade showcase) in the fifth, giving Fujimoto a 5–2 lead.

Things got a little tight in the seventh, when the pitch count went up and Rico Espinosa hit a single through the middle with runners on second and third to score two. Stein allowed Fujimoto to finish the inning before Geno Milzie and Ivan Zyzna finished, with Zyzna getting the save with two strikeouts in the ninth and lowered his ERA to a ridiculous .089.

From here, it's off to Kansas City for another wrap-around weekend series.

"I'm sure it's going to be hot down there, in more ways than one," Stein said. "We should be able to get a big lift from this game. What Tak did for us tonight is almost immeasurable."

CLEVELAND INDIANS VS TORONTO BLUE JAYS • JUNE 24
CLEVELAND 5 / TORONTO 4

CLEVELAND INDIANS										
BATTING	AB	R	H	RBI	2B	3B	HR	BB	SO	BA
RIKKI LABUDDA CF	4	1	1	0	0	0	0	1	0	.270
HURON SOUTHWORTH RF	4	1	1	1	0	0	1	1	0	.225
WILSON WHITE LF	5	1	2	0	0	0	0	0	1	.268
OLIVER REINER 1B	5	2	2	2	1	0	1	0	0	.299
TERRY ROVETTO 3B	4	0	0	0	0	0	0	0	0	.262
SCOTT MICHAELS 2B	5	0	2	2	1	0	0	0	0	.313
JUSTIN KESTINO SS	4	0	2	0	0	0	0	0	0	.247
J.J. KULAKOFSKI DH	4	0	1	0	0	0	0	0	2	.218
ICEBERB PETERS C	4	0	0	0	0	0	0	0	0	.215
PITCHING	IP	H	R	ER	SO	BB	ERA			
TAK FUJIMOTO (W)	7	7	4	4	6	3	3.26			
GENO MILZIE	1	1	0	0	0	0	4.20			
IVAN ZYZNA (S)	1	0	0	0	2	0	0.89			

TORONTO BLUE JAYS										
BATTING	AB	R	H	RBI	2B	3B	HR	BB	SO	BA
CARLOS ARNALDO CF	4	1	1	0	0	0	0	0	0	.289
ANDY TENZER 3B	4	0	0	0	0	0	0	0	1	.310
RAMON ORTIZ SS	4	1	2	1	0	0	1	0	0	.277
RAYMOND BALKMAN 1B	3	0	0	1	0	0	0	0	1	.231
JERMAINE BROWN LF	4	1	1	0	1	0	0	0	0	.274
JEFF STEPHANS DH	4	1	1	0	0	0	0	0	1	.261
JOEL NISSALKE 2B	4	0	1	0	0	0	0	0	0	.280
ROYCE MANFRED RF	4	0	1	2	1	0	0	0	0	.262
RICO ESPINOSA C	3	0	0	0	0	0	0	1	2	.230
PITCHING	IP	H	R	ER	SO	BB	ERA			
DEAN PINTO (L)	3.67	5	4	4	1	1	4.39			
BUDDY HARKNESS	2.33	3	1	1	0	1	4.22			
JAMIE SHEDLER	2	2	0	0	1	0	4.32			
LARRY BRAVERMAN	1	1	0	0	1	0	3.22			

INNING	1	2	3	4	5	6	7	8	9	TOTAL
CLEVELAND	2	0	0	2	1	0	0	0	0	5
TORONTO	2	0	0	0	0	0	2	0	0	4

GAME 71

By SAM LARDNER
The Cleveland Press

KANSAS CITY, Mo., June 25 — Friday was a make-good night all around for the Indians.

Ace pitcher Lynn Moda bounced back from this past Sunday's sloppy 6–2 loss to the Mariners in Cleveland.

An error by Scott Michaels in that game set the Tribe on the way to a loss, but it was Michaels who also made good Friday, going 3-for-5 with a homer and four RBIs as the Indians made a winner of Moda with a 7–3 victory over the Kansas City Royals at Kauffman Stadium. The victory inched the Indians back over .500 at 36–35.

"All is good," said Moda, who went seven innings, giving up six hits and three runs. "You know that sooner or later, your teammates are going to pick you up. I forgot all about Scottie's error in that last game until you guys brought it up. He's been a big part of our better play lately, and we're going to count on him from here on out."

Michaels, who has established himself as the everyday second baseman with Angel Rodriguez on the injured list, hit a two-run homer, his fifteenth, in the second off Royals starter Yusmeiro Morales after Terry Rovetto opened the inning with a single to right.

"I felt bad about the way Modes' last start went — I put him in a hole in the very first inning," Michaels said. "It was nice to return the favor, so to speak, in a good way tonight. The ball doesn't always carry here, but it was a warm night, and I think that helped my ball carry out of here."

General manager J.D. Eisner traveled with the Indians from Toronto to KC, as he continues to evaluate the team well ahead of the July 31 trading deadline. Eisner said Rodriguez would be heading out on a minor-league rehab assignment as early as Sunday as he recovers from a hamstring injury.

When Rodriguez returns, that will present the Indians with a roster crunch.

"We'll cross that bridge when we come to it," Eisner said before the game. "These things have a way of sorting themselves out. Angel can help us in a lot of ways, with his glove and his speed, so he'll see plenty of action even if he doesn't start."

One guy on the bubble could be infielder Leo Taylor, who started at short in place of Justin Kestino, who deals with a sore wrist that will keep him out a day or two, according to Eisner.

The light-hitting Taylor made his case by driving in two in the fifth as his grounder down the first base line went all the way to the wall and rattled around in the right-field corner for a triple.

The Royals came within 4–2 in the bottom of the inning on a two-run double by Derrek Hargrove. Michaels hit a two-run single in the seventh, taking second on the throw home and going to third on a wild pitch. He then scored on a perfectly executed squeeze bunt by Taylor.

"I just do what I can," Taylor said. "I can bunt and use my speed. We have enough other guys here who can drive the ball."

Solly Alvarez pitched the final two innings as the Indians won their second straight.

"It's good to get contributions from some other guys," said manager Todd Stein. "Taylor doesn't play a lot, but you do have to get these guys in there so they stay fresh. With Justin being banged up just a bit, this was a good night to do it. We'll get him in there tomorrow, too."

CLEVELAND INDIANS VS KANSAS CITY ROYALS · JUNE 25
CLEVELAND 7 / KANSAS CITY 3

CLEVELAND INDIANS

BATTING	AB	R	H	RBI	2B	3B	HR	BB	SO	BA
RIKKI LABUDDA CF	4	0	1	0	0	0	0	1	0	.270
MICAH MILLISON RF	4	1	1	0	1	0	0	0	1	.260
WILSON WHITE LF	5	1	2	0	0	0	0	0	0	.271
OLIVER REINER 1B	4	1	1	0	1	0	0	1	0	.298
TERRY ROVETTO 3B	5	2	2	0	0	0	0	0	1	.265
SCOTT MICHAELS 2B	5	2	3	4	0	0	1	0	1	.321
LEO TAYLOR SS	4	0	2	3	0	1	0	0	0	.298
BERNARD HARPER DH	4	0	0	0	0	0	0	0	2	.250
MORRIS JEROME C	3	0	2	0	0	0	0	1	1	.257

PITCHING	IP	H	R	ER	SO	BB	ERA			
LYNN MODA (W)	7	6	3	3	5	3	4.52			
SOLLY ALVAREZ	2	1	0	0	0	0	3.04			

KANSAS CITY ROYALS

BATTING	AB	R	H	RBI	2B	3B	HR	BB	SO	BA
KYLE MONTGOMERY 2B	4	1	1	0	0	0	0	0	0	.289
NELSON QUARRELS RF	3	0	0	0	0	0	0	1	0	.313
JARED BUCKNER SS	4	2	2	0	0	1	0	0	0	.277
ALCIDES CASTILLO LF	4	0	1	1	0	0	0	0	1	.237
DERREK HARGROVE 3B	3	0	0	2	1	0	0	1	0	.269
TRUMAN GREYSTONE DH	3	0	1	0	0	0	0	1	1	.262
LEQUAN BROWN 1B	4	0	0	0	0	0	0	0	1	.273
ARCENIO INCIARTE C	4	0	1	0	1	0	0	0	1	.262
VERNON COLEMAN CF	3	0	1	0	0	0	0	1	1	.235

PITCHING	IP	H	R	ER	SO	BB	ERA			
YUSMEIRO MORALES (L)	6.33	10	6	6	5	2	4.48			
AARON WESTFALL	1.67	3	1	1	1	0	4.31			
BRUNO LACHNER	1	1	0	0	1	0	3.22			

INNING	1	2	3	4	5	6	7	8	9	TOTAL
CLEVELAND	0	2	0	0	2	0	3	0	0	7
KANSAS CITY	0	0	0	0	2	0	1	0	0	3

GAME 72

By SAM LARDNER
The Cleveland Press

KANSAS CITY, Mo., June 26 — Ollie Gonzalez hasn't always gotten the run support this season. So the Indians' big left-hander took things into his own left hand Saturday night.

Runs were hard to come by for both the Indians and the Kansas City Royals at Kauffman Stadium, with Gonzalez and Royals starter Ender Ramos matching each other pitch for pitch.

The game was scoreless until the sixth, when hot-hitting Scott Michaels hit a two-run double off Ramos. Gonzalez gave one back in the bottom of the inning on a homer by Laquan Brown, but he and the Indians bullpen shut things down for a 2–1 victory before 39,009 fans on a perfect summer night.

Indians manager Todd Stein went with setup man Geno Milzie in the eighth and with closer Ivan Zyzna, who continues to be near perfect, in the ninth. Those two were perfect, and the Indians went two games above .500 (37–35) for the first time this season. They have beaten the Royals all four times they have played them this season, including in the home-opening series in Cleveland back in April.

"You got to win these kinds of games, too," said Indians manager Todd Stein. "You don't see many low-scoring pitchers duels anymore but both starters were dealing. We played good defense, and most important, I don't think we walked anybody."

Gonzalez did walk one, Kyle Montgomery, with one out in the fourth, but Montgomery was quickly erased on a double-play grounder to short-stop Leo Taylor, playing his second straight game as Justin Kestino (wrist) gets a rest.

"I know you guys talked about run support earlier, but the guys can support you on defense, too," said Gonzalez, who bounced back from a 4–3 loss to the Mariners in his previous start, a game in which the Indians gave up the lead. "We forget sometimes that it's up to us pitchers to go out and put up zeroes. Their guy was doing that tonight, and it was my challenge to go out there and do it for us. We made a lot of nice plays out there in the field."

In addition to Taylor turning a double play, Rikki LaBudda ran down a fly ball in this ballpark's spacious center field in the fifth. Terry Rovetto made a nifty backhand snag of Vernon Coleman's hot shot in the seventh.

"It's amazing what can happen when you play good defense and don't walk people," Stein said. "We're capable of that on a nightly basis. I think the warmer weather has helped. Earlier in the year, it was pretty cold, and that can make it hard to get a grip on the ball and play good defense. And let's not forget the bullpen. Geno and Ivan were lights-out again. That's a pretty good combination all around."

CLEVELAND INDIANS VS KANSAS CITY ROYALS · JUNE 26
CLEVELAND 2 / KANSAS CITY 1

CLEVELAND INDIANS										
BATTING	AB	R	H	RBI	2B	3B	HR	BB	SO	BA
RIKKI LABUDDA CF	4	0	2	0	0	0	0	0	0	.273
MICAH MILLISON RF	3	0	1	0	1	0	0	1	0	.261
WILSON WHITE LF	3	1	0	0	0	0	0	0	1	.268
OLIVER REINER 1B	4	0	0	0	0	0	0	0	1	.294
TERRY ROVETTO 3B	4	1	2	0	0	0	0	0	0	.268
SCOTT MICHAELS 2B	4	0	2	2	1	0	0	0	1	.324
LEO TAYLOR SS	4	0	0	0	0	0	0	0	1	.275
BERNARD HARPER DH	4	0	0	0	0	0	0	0	2	.245
MORRIS JEROME C	4	0	0	0	0	0	0	0	0	.252
PITCHING	IP	H	R	ER	SO	BB	ERA			
OLLIE GONZALEZ (W)	7	4	1	1	6	2	4.77			
GENO MILZIE	1	0	0	0	0	0	4.11			
IVAN ZYZNA (S)	1	0	0	0	0	0	0.84			

KANSAS CITY ROYALS										
BATTING	AB	R	H	RBI	2B	3B	HR	BB	SO	BA
KYLE MONTGOMERY 2B	3	0	0	0	0	0	0	1	0	.285
NELSON QUARRELS RF	4	0	1	0	0	0	0	0	1	.311
JARED BUCKNER SS	4	0	0	0	0	0	0	0	2	.271
ALCIDES CASTILLO LF	4	0	1	0	0	0	0	0	0	.237
DERREK HARGROVE 3B	4	0	0	0	0	0	0	0	2	.261
TRUMAN GREYSTONE DH	4	0	1	0	0	0	0	0	0	.262
LEQUAN BROWN 1B	4	1	1	1	0	0	1	0	0	.272
ARCENIO INCIARTE C	4	0	0	0	1	0	0	0	1	.254
VERNON COLEMAN CF	3	0	0	0	0	0	0	1	0	.231
PITCHING	IP	H	R	ER	SO	BB	ERA			
ENDER RAMOS (L)	8	6	2	2	5	2	3.86			
AARON WESTFALL	1	1	0	0	1	0	4.18			

INNING	1	2	3	4	5	6	7	8	9	TOTAL
CLEVELAND	0	0	0	0	0	2	0	0	0	2
KANSAS CITY	0	0	0	0	0	1	0	0	0	1

GAME 73

By SAM LARDNER
The Cleveland Press

KANSAS CITY, Mo., June 27 — Oftentimes during the summer, a drenching afternoon downpour brings sweet relief to these parts of the country.

But a two-hour rain delay wrought havoc with the Indians' relief corps Sunday during a 10–3 loss to the Kansas City Royals. The loss snapped an Indians winning streak at three and dropped them to 37–36.

Ominous clouds began gathering in the distance as early as the second inning with the Indians up 2–0 and Brian Howard on the mound. By the time the fourth inning rolled around, the heavens opened with the game tied at 2–2.

Once play resumed, the Indians bullpen let things get out of hand, with Solly Alvarez, Buck Sterling, Mickey Penny and Lee Hazelton all giving up runs.

"It's a shame things played out that way," said Tribe manager Todd Stein. "The Doc (Howard) looked pretty sharp out there, but you can't send a guy back out there after two hours. This puts us in a little bit of a bind again with our bullpen, so we'll see if we have to do anything for tomorrow night's game. We've had (Lorry) Unger up here before, so it's not out of the question we could get him here for tomorrow's game."

When things were nice and sunny — in the first inning — the Indians looked on their way to their fourth straight victory. Rikki LaBudda came out of the box bunting for a single. He stole second base and came home on a single by Micah Millison. Wilson White promptly doubled to score Millison, but Royals starting pitcher Taisuke Kaneko shut things down from there.

Royals DH Truman Greystone hit a two-run homer off Howard in the bottom of the third, the first two of his five RBIs. The Royals were batting in the fourth with two outs and nobody on when the rain hit.

"Yeah, it's one of those things," Howard said. "I should be plenty fresh for my next start. You could even smell the rain coming. I was just hoping to get through the inning and for us to take the lead with the game being official. It didn't work out that way. But I felt pretty good out there, with good stuff and location. The rain delay changed the whole dynamic of the game and of the day."

When play resumed, Alvarez promptly gave up a homer to Arcenio Inciarte, giving the Royals a 3–2 lead. He gave up two more in the fifth.

Sterling allowed one in the sixth, Penney two in the seventh and Hazelton two in the eighth. The Indians got a consolation run in the seventh on Justin Kestino's homer.

"It was like two different games out there," Stein said. "The whole flow was interrupted, but that's what you deal with. You're going to get weather from time to time. They (the Royals) had to deal with it, too. Fortunately, with a night game tomorrow, we've got a lot of time to recover and regroup."

Off the field, there was more balloting news for the All-Star Game. Oliver Reiner remains a distant third at first base, and Terry Rovetto is fourth among third baseman. A write-in campaign for second baseman Scott Michaels has him fourth.

CLEVELAND INDIANS VS KANSAS CITY ROYALS • JUNE 27
KANSAS CITY 10 / CLEVELAND 3

CLEVELAND INDIANS

BATTING	AB	R	H	RBI	2B	3B	HR	BB	SO	BA
RIKKI LABUDDA CF	4	1	1	0	0	0	0	0	0	.272
MICAH MILLISON RF	3	1	1	1	1	0	0	1	0	.262
WILSON WHITE LF	3	0	2	1	1	0	0	1	0	.272
OLIVER REINER 1B	4	1	2	0	0	0	0	0	2	.297
TERRY ROVETTO 3B	4	0	2	0	0	0	0	0	0	.272
SCOTT MICHAELS 2B	4	0	0	0	0	0	0	0	2	.318
JUSTIN KESTINO SS	4	0	1	1	0	0	1	0	0	.247
BERNARD HARPER DH	3	0	2	0	0	0	0	1	0	.251
MORRIS JEROME C	3	0	0	0	0	0	0	1	1	.249

PITCHING	IP	H	R	ER	SO	BB	ERA
BRIAN HOWARD	3	6	2	2	1	0	3.62
SOLLY ALVAREZ (L)	2	4	3	3	2	2	3.64
BUCK STERLING	1	2	1	1	2	0	2.91
MICKEY PENNY	1	4	2	2	0	1	4.03
LEE HAZELTON	1	2	2	2	0	1	5.27

KANSAS CITY ROYALS

BATTING	AB	R	H	RBI	2B	3B	HR	BB	SO	BA
KYLE MONTGOMERY 2B	6	1	2	0	1	0	0	1	0	.286
NELSON QUARRELS RF	6	0	1	1	0	0	0	0	1	.305
JARED BUCKNER SS	6	2	2	0	0	0	0	0	1	.273
ALCIDES CASTILLO LF	5	2	2	0	1	0	0	1	0	.243
DERREK HARGROVE 3B	5	2	3	1	0	0	0	1	0	.273
TRUMAN GREYSTONE DH	5	1	3	5	0	0	1	0	1	.272
LEQUAN BROWN 1B	5	1	1	0	0	0	0	0	0	.270
ARCENIO INCIARTE C	5	1	2	2	1	0	0	0	2	.260
VERNON COLEMAN CF	4	0	2	1	0	0	0	1	0	.237

PITCHING	IP	H	R	ER	SO	BB	ERA
TAISUKE KANEKO (W)	5	7	2	2	4	3	3.90
JAIR MOSQUERA	2	2	1	1	1	0	4.32
GLENN MARCHAND	2	2	0	0	0	1	3.38

INNING	1	2	3	4	5	6	7	8	9	TOTAL
CLEVELAND	2	0	0	0	0	0	1	0	0	3
KANSAS CITY	0	0	2	1	2	1	2	2		10

GAME 74

By SAM LARDNER
The Cleveland Press

KANSAS CITY, Mo., June 28 — The Indians spent another long weekend making it a lost weekend.

For the second week in a row, the Tribe had a chance to win a weekend wrap-round series. And for the second week in a row, they gummed it up.

As a result of Monday night's 4–1 loss to the Kansas City Royals, this maddening Cleveland ballclub is yet again back to .500 at 37–37.

The silence in the postgame Indians clubhouse was telling. One can only imagine how quiet the plane ride home was after the Indians lost the final two games of this series after winning the first two.

"Same old story," said Indians manager Todd Stein. "It's disappointing, that's for sure. It seemed like that long rain Sunday delay took something out of us. That's no excuse, and really, it's unacceptable. But I know the guys will take this to heart as we head home."

Waiting for them when they do get home will be the Minnesota Twins who happen to lead the American League Central by three games over the Chicago White Sox and a full seven ahead of the Indians.

"(Bleep), this really sucks," said starting and losing pitcher Kenny Camden. "We keep doing this to ourselves. I got us behind the eight-ball early, making it difficult on our guys. Their pitcher (Madison Behrens) was good, but you get tired of giving credit to the other side. We've got to grab this thing and run with it. We're almost at the all-star break. We did a good job of crawling out of that 0–6 hole, but then we can't extricate ourselves from the .500 mark."

The Indians did make one roster move before the game, as had been expected. They placed reliever Solly Alvarez on the injured list with shoulder fatigue and once again called up Lorry Unger from Class AAA Columbus to help out in the bullpen.

"Solly has been used a lot lately, and he's feeling it," general manager J.D. Eisner said before the game. Eisner beat a hasty retreat out of his GM box and onto the team bus without even stopping in the clubhouse after the game.

One could hardly blame Eisner for heading out early. He might have said something he'd regret later.

As it was, the Indians fell behind 2–0 in the first inning. Nelson Quarrels chopped a double over the third-base bag with one out. He went to third on Camden's wild pitch and scored on Jared Buckner's single. Buckner stole second base and came home on a single by Alcides Castillo.

"We got nickel-and-dimed or pecked to death, whatever you want to call it, in that first inning," Stein said. "But we've got to shut things down. The wild pitch kind of threw us off. It always seems to be something when we lose games like this."

Camden went five innings, giving up two more in the fifth on a homer by Todd Steffans. The Indians got their lone run on Bernard Harper's ninth home run in the sixth against Behrens, who lasted eight innings.

Unger pitched two innings in his first game back with the big club, with Geno Milzie finishing up.

"Our pen has been stretched pretty thin, so I had to use Geno," Stein said. "It seems like we've been in Kansas City forever. It will be good to get the heck out of here and go home."

GAME 74

CLEVELAND INDIANS VS KANSAS CITY ROYALS • JUNE 28
KANSAS CITY 4 / CLEVELAND 1

CLEVELAND INDIANS										
BATTING	AB	R	H	RBI	2B	3B	HR	BB	SO	BA
RIKKI LABUDDA CF	4	0	1	0	0	0	0	0	0	.272
MICAH MILLISON RF	3	0	2	0	1	0	0	1	0	.267
WILSON WHITE LF	4	0	1	0	0	0	0	0	1	.272
OLIVER REINER 1B	3	0	0	0	0	0	0	1	0	.293
TERRY ROVETTO 3B	3	0	0	0	0	0	0	1	0	.269
SCOTT MICHAELS 2B	3	0	1	0	0	0	0	0	1	.318
JUSTIN KESTINO SS	3	0	1	0	0	0	0	0	2	.248
BERNARD HARPER DH	3	1	1	1	0	0	1	0	1	.253
MORRIS JEROME C	3	0	0	0	0	0	0	0	1	.245
PITCHING	IP	H	R	ER	SO	BB	ERA			
KENNY CAMDEN (L)	3	6	2	2	1	0	3.62			
LONNY UNGER	2	4	3	3	2	2	3.64			
GENO MILZIE	1	2	1	1	2	0	2.91			
KANSAS CITY ROYALS										
BATTING	AB	R	H	RBI	2B	3B	HR	BB	SO	BA
KYLE MONTGOMERY 2B	4	0	0	0	0	0	0	1	0	.281
NELSON QUARRELS RF	4	1	1	0	1	0	0	0	0	.304
JARED BUCKNER SS	4	1	1	1	0	0	0	0	0	.272
ALCIDES CASTILLO LF	4	0	3	1	0	0	0	0	1	.257
DERREK HARGROVE 3B	4	1	1	0	0	0	0	0	1	.272
TODD STEFFANS DH	4	1	2	2	1	0	1	0	1	.273
LEQUAN BROWN 1B	3	0	0	0	0	0	0	1	0	.265
ARCENIO INCIARTE C	4	1	0	0	0	0	0	0	0	.252
VERNON COLEMAN CF	3	0	1	0	0	0	0	0	1	.238
PITCHING	IP	H	R	ER	SO	BB	ERA			
MADISON BEHRENS (W)	8	7	1	1	6	3	3.76			
DERWIN RENTERIA (S)	1	1	0	0	0	0	3.34			

INNING	1	2	3	4	5	6	7	8	9	TOTAL
CLEVELAND	0	0	0	0	0	1	0	0	0	1
KANSAS CITY	2	0	0	0	2	0	0	0		4

GAME 75

By SAM LARDNER
The Cleveland Press

CLEVELAND, June 29 — The Indians came home Tuesday night to a heaping helping of skepticism.

Only 16,324 showed up at Progressive Field to watch the Indians beat the Minnesota Twins 6–3 on a lovely early summer night.

Let's face it: That skepticism is well earned. The Indians have been baseball's biggest teases this season. Yes, they've recovered nicely from their 0–6 start (which included three losses at Minnesota) to move to one game over .500 at 38–37. But given the talent on this Cleveland club, the inconsistency is utterly confounding.

"We have to earn the fans back to our side," said interim manager Todd Stein, who took over after a pair of losses to the Twins at Progressive Field in the ninth and 10th games of the season. "We're hoping to have a nice run to the all-star break and then a big second half. Tonight's win against the first-place club in our division is a good start. We need to keep that going."

Give credit once again to pitcher Tak Fujimoto for being the stopper. The big free-agent signing out of Japan has battled his own consistency issues this season, but he came out big Tuesday after two uninspired losses at Kansas City to even his record to seven and seven.

Fujimoto went six innings, giving up six hits and all three Minnesota runs. He was perfect through three innings before walking Avery Becker to start the fourth. That walk hurt, as Becker scored on Bruiser Conklin's booming homer. But the Indians had a 3–0 lead at the time and added on later. Fujimoto gutted out seven innings in his previous start at Toronto, a 5–4 Tribe victory.

"It was good to have that kind of performance after two losses," Fujimoto said through his translator. "The manager wanted to be a little cautious with me after I threw so many pitches (118) in Toronto. So we limited it to 90 today, and I think that was a good plan."

Stein paired Fujimoto with backup catcher Iceberg Peters, who may be the best pitch framer in the league. The two seemed to have clicked.

"Fuji is easy to catch even though his ball moves a lot," Peters said. "If you know that ahead of time, you can position yourself back there and be ready for anything. The guy is a pleasure to work with."

The offensive story for the Indians continues to be onetime phenom Scott Michaels, who is finally enjoying good health.

Michaels went 3-for-4 with a first-inning three-run homer, number sixteen, off Jake Maddisson to get the Indians on the board. Micah Millison singled with one out and went to third on Wilson White's base hit to left. Terry Rovetto's fly ball was not deep enough to score Millison, but Michaels' drive to left was certainly deep enough, as it cleared the high wall easily.

"It's been a nice little run here," said Michaels, who has 11 hits in his last six games. "I'm seeing it pretty good, and the warmer weather certainly helps. The shoulder feels better than it ever has, so we'll ride it as long as we can,"

Oliver Reiner hit a two-run homer in the sixth, number sixteen, driving in Terry Rovetto, who led off with a walk. That made it 5–2. The teams traded single runs in the seventh, with the Twins scoring off reliever Mickey Penney. Geno Milzie and Ivan Zyzna finished for the Tribe out of the bullpen.

"That's about how you draw it up," Stein said. "Good start, some timely hitting and solid bullpen work. We need to gain some ground on the Twins. They beat us up pretty good early and were a big reason we got into that hole. They're leading the division for a reason. But we think we can play with them."

GAME 75

CLEVELAND INDIANS VS MINNESOTA TWINS • JUNE 29
CLEVELAND 6 / MINNESOTA 3

CLEVELAND INDIANS										
BATTING	AB	R	H	RBI	2B	3B	HR	BB	SO	BA
RIKKI LABUDDA CF	4	0	3	0	0	0	0	1	0	.279
MICAH MILLISON RF	4	1	2	0	1	0	0	0	0	.271
WILSON WHITE LF	3	1	1	0	0	0	0	1	0	.273
TERRY ROVETTO 3B	3	1	1	0	0	0	0	0	1	.270
SCOTT MICHAELS 2B	4	1	3	3	0	0	1	0	1	.327
OLIVER REINER 1B	4	1	0	2	1	0	1	0	0	.289
JUSTIN KESTINO SS	4	1	2	0	0	0	0	0	0	.252
BERNARD HARPER DH	4	0	1	0	1	0	0	0	1	.252
ICEBERG PETERS C	3	0	1	1	0	0	0	0	1	.221
PITCHING	IP	H	R	ER	SO	BB	ERA			
TAK FUJIMOTO (W)	6	6	3	3	5	2	3.34			
MICKEY PENNY	1	1	0	0	2	2	3.90			
GENO MILZIE	1	2	1	1	2	0	3.09			
IVAN ZYZNA (S)	1	0	0	0	0	0	0.81			
MINNESOTA TWINS										
BATTING	AB	R	H	RBI	2B	3B	HR	BB	SO	BA
TONY WILDERS 2B	4	0	2	0	0	0	0	1	0	.290
TOMMY HOPKINS 3B	4	1	0	0	0	0	0	0	2	.297
AVERY BECKER SS	4	1	1	0	0	0	0	0	0	.272
BRUCE CONKLIN 1B	4	0	2	2	0	0	1	0	1	.250
RALPH TAYLOR CF	4	1	0	0	0	0	0	0	2	.265
FABIO PINEDA LF	4	1	1	0	1	0	0	0	1	.266
CARL DOREY RF	3	0	2	1	0	0	0	1	0	.277
MIKE HANSEN DH	4	1	0	0	0	0	0	0	2	.252
JOSE CHAVEZ C	3	0	1	0	0	0	0	0	1	.238
PITCHING	IP	H	R	ER	SO	BB	ERA			
JAKE MADDISSON (L)	6	9	5	5	4	2	4.43			
SANDY GREENE	0.67	2	1	0	1	0	3.38			
JOAQUIN ALMEDA	0.33	1	0	0	1	0	3.27			
OSWALDO BORGES	1	2	0	0	1	0	3.30			
INNING	1	2	3	4	5	6	7	8	9	TOTAL
MINNESOTA	0	0	0	2	0	0	1	0	0	3
CLEVELAND	3	0	0	0	0	2	1	0		6

GAME 76

By SAM LARDNER
The Cleveland Press

CLEVELAND, June 30 — The ace and the phenom dealt the Indians a winning hand Wednesday night at Progressive Field.

Starting pitcher Lynn Moda turned in one of the best performances of the season as he went eight innings, giving up one run as the Indians won their second in a row over the Minnesota Twins, 5–1.

Onetime phenom Scott Michaels took care of things on the other end, going 2-for-4 with a three-run homer that broke a scoreless tie in the fourth inning.

The only thing missing from that winning hand was a full house, as only 16,543 turned out at Progressive on a perfect summer night. Apparently, the public is not convinced that the Indians are for real despite a 16–11 June that moved them to 39–37 overall and to within five games of the first-place Twins in the American League Central.

"They'll come out," said Moda, who has had his own ups and downs this season. "This city has a great history of supporting a winning ballclub. You saw it years ago when this ballpark opened, all those sellouts in a row. We have to give them a reason to come out. I think we're starting to do that."

This was the second straight game for Moda that he got help from Michaels, who went 40-for-118 (.339) in June, bringing his season batting average to .330. The All-Star Game is coming up, and Michaels wasn't even on the fan ballot, the result of his past injury woes and limited play-ing time. He'll have to wait to be selected by Major League Baseball or be placed on the final Internet fan ballot.

"No matter what happens with the All-Star Game, it's pretty satisfy-ing," Michaels said. "To be honest, I have not given that any thought at all. I've just been focused on staying healthy and making the most of my playing time."

Moda retired the first 10 Twins he faced before giving up a walk to Tony Wilders and a single to Avery Becker in the fourth. But he managed to work out of trouble by getting a pair of groundball outs.

In the home half of the inning, Oliver Reiner and Terry Rovetto sin-gled, setting up Michaels' homer, a drive to left-center against Reinaldo Rojas.

"Scottie has been a pleasant surprise, that's for sure," said manager Todd Stein, who put Michaels into the lineup when Angel Rodriguez went on the injured list. "I think it's safe to say that he's going to be in there from now on. We'll get plenty of work for Angel when he gets back in a day or two. But Scottie has opened a lot of eyes around here and around the league."

Twins manager Archie Knowles agreed.

"I'm sure a lot of teams are rethinking their scouting reports on Michaels," Knowles said. "You knew his pedigree coming up, but when you miss so much time with injury, you can kind of sneak back in under the radar. He's not under the radar anymore."

Moda gave up a solo homer to Tommy Hopkins in the fifth, but that was it. The Indians got a two-run triple from Micah Millison in the sev-enth after Morris Jerome walked and Rikki LaBudda singled. Lorry Unger finished up out of the bullpen for the Indians.

"If we're going to get back in this thing, the Twins are the team we have to beat," Stein said. "We played a pretty complete game tonight. We're looking to head into July with some momentum and finish strong going into the break."

CLEVELAND INDIANS VS MINNESOTA TWINS · JUNE 30
CLEVELAND 5 / KANSAS CITY 1

CLEVELAND INDIANS										
BATTING	AB	R	H	RBI	2B	3B	HR	BB	SO	BA
RIKKI LABUDDA CF	4	1	1	0	0	0	0	0	0	.278
MICAH MILLISON RF	4	0	2	2	1	1	0	0	0	.274
WILSON WHITE LF	3	0	0	0	0	0	0	1	1	.270
OLIVER REINER 1B	4	1	2	0	0	0	0	0	1	.292
TERRY ROVETTO 3B	4	1	2	0	0	0	0	0	0	.273
SCOTT MICHAELS 2B	4	1	2	3	1	0	1	0	0	.330
JUSTIN KESTINO SS	4	0	1	0	0	0	0	0	2	.252
BERNARD HARPER DH	4	0	2	0	1	0	0	0	0	.257
MORRIS JEROME C	3	1	1	0	0	0	0	1	0	.247
PITCHING	IP	H	R	ER	SO	BB	ERA			
LYNN MODA (W)	8	5	1	1	7	1	4.22			
LORRY UNGER	1	1	0	0	0	0	3.53			

MINNESOTA TWINS										
BATTING	AB	R	H	RBI	2B	3B	HR	BB	SO	BA
TONY WILDERS 2B	3	0	1	0	0	0	0	1	0	.291
TOMMY HOPKINS 3B	4	1	1	1	0	0	1	0	1	.296
AVERY BECKER SS	4	0	1	0	0	0	0	0	2	.272
BRUCE CONKLIN 1B	4	0	0	0	0	0	0	0	0	.243
RALPH TAYLOR CF	4	0	0	0	0	0	0	0	1	.258
FABIO PINEDA LF	4	0	0	0	0	0	0	0	1	.258
CARL DOREY RF	4	0	2	0	0	0	0	0	0	.283
MIKE HANSEN DH	4	0	1	0	0	0	0	0	1	.252
JOSE CHAVEZ C	4	0	1	0	0	0	0	0	1	.239
PITCHING	IP	H	R	ER	SO	BB	ERA			
REINALDO ROJAS (L)	6	9	3	3	3	2	4.15			
HYUN-SOO PARK	2	4	2	2	1	0	3.78			

INNING	1	2	3	4	5	6	7	8	9	TOTAL
MINNESOTA	0	0	0	0	1	0	0	0	0	1
CLEVELAND	0	0	0	3	0	0	2	0		5

GAME 77

By SAM LARDNER
The Cleveland Press

CLEVELAND, July 1 — Don't look now, but as July dawns, the Cleveland Indians find themselves in an honest-to-goodness pennant race.

Who woulda thunk it, even a few days ago?

But that's where the Indians are after Thursday night's 4–3 victory over the Minnesota Twins at Progressive Field. The Indians pulled off an improbable three-game sweep of the Twins and now are third in the American League Central, four games behind the first-place Twins and two behind the second-place Chicago White Sox.

"That's how fast it can turn around," said an elated Indians manager Todd Stein. "This could be a huge three-game swing. Just think if things had gone the other way. I know we still have to be more consistent, but you can't beat the intensity we played with in these three games. And we had to hold on to win this one. There was no folding."

The Indians are now a season-best three games over .500 at 40–37, and they have a good chance to add to that this weekend when the last-place Kansas City Royals come to town. After that, the Indians will be tested with a three-game set in Minneapolis.

"We're not getting ahead of ourselves," Stein warned. "We're not going to take the Royals lightly, and we certainly know how tough the Twins are at home. We'll enjoy this one and get ready for a big weekend. Hopefully the fans will come out."

A respectable crowd of 24,109 came out on a warm Thursday night. Those folks witnessed lefty Ollie Gonzalez again working his magic once again in a tight game. Gonzalez went six innings, giving up two runs on six hits. Gonzalez beat the Royals 2–1 in his previous start.

"I don't know where we'd be without Ollie G," Stein said. "He didn't get much support early, and he never complained. He always seems to be in a tight game. All the credit to him."

The Twins took a 1–0 lead in the first inning on a two-out solo homer by Bruce "Bruiser" Conklin, a longtime Indians tormentor. The Indians got two runs right back in the bottom half. Rikki LaBudda slapped a single to left field and stole second base, his nineteenth steal of the year. He scored on Micah Millison's single to center, with Millison taking second on the throw home. Wilson White doubled home Millison.

The Indians made it 4–1 in the fourth on a two-run homer by Morris Jerome. He scored behind Justin Kestino, who walked on 10 pitches against Twins starter Elliott Brown.

All Jerome wanted to talk about was Gonzalez.

"He was the real story, that and our bullpen," Jerome said. "I can't tell you what a pro Ollie G is. He works quick and doesn't shake me off. He's a pleasure."

Gonzalez gave up a sacrifice fly to Fabio Pineda after Jay Rosenthal doubled and went to third on a groundout in the sixth. Stein went with relievers Lee Hazelton, Geno Milzie and Ivan Zyzna to finish, with Zyzna giving up a homer to Carl Dorey in the ninth to make it a one-run game.

"It's nice to get the 'W' next to my name, but look how this team has been playing," Gonzalez said. "That Twins team is relentless. Ivan came right after Dorey, and he happened to hit one out. But you'd rather have that than giving up a walk. Ivan's been almost perfect ever since he came back from injury."

Zyzna earned the save by striking out Pineda to end the game with the crowd on its feet.

"That was some kind of noise they made with a big threat up," Zyzna said. "That's the kind of support that we need and that can help us down the stretch. It's fun to be pitching in meaningful games again."

GAME 77

CLEVELAND INDIANS VS MINNESOTA TWINS · JULY 1
CLEVELAND 4 / MINNESOTA 3

CLEVELAND INDIANS

BATTING	AB	R	H	RBI	2B	3B	HR	BB	SO	BA
RIKKI LABUDDA CF	4	1	2	0	0	0	0	0	0	.281
MICAH MILLISON RF	4	1	2	0	1	1	0	0	0	.278
WILSON WHITE LF	4	0	2	2	0	1	0	0	1	.273
OLIVER REINER 1B	4	0	0	0	0	0	0	0	1	.288
TERRY ROVETTO 3B	3	0	2	0	0	0	0	1	0	.277
SCOTT MICHAELS 2B	4	0	0	0	1	0	0	0	0	.324
J.J. KULAKOFSKI DH	3	0	1	0	0	0	0	1	1	.222
JUSTIN KESTINO SS	3	1	0	0	1	0	0	0	0	.249
MORRIS JEROME C	3	1	2	2	0	0	1	0	1	.252

PITCHING	IP	H	R	ER	SO	BB	ERA			
OLLIE GONZALEZ (W)	6	6	2	2	6	1	4.65			
LEE HAZELTON	1	1	0	0	0	0	4.91			
GENO MILZIE	1	0	0	0	0	1	3.00			
IVAN ZYZNA (S)	1	1	1	1	1	0	1.16			

MINNESOTA TWINS

BATTING	AB	R	H	RBI	2B	3B	HR	BB	SO	BA
TONY WILDERS 2B	4	0	1	0	0	0	0	0	0	.290
TOMMY HOPKINS 3B	3	0	1	0	0	0	0	1	0	.297
BRUCE CONKLIN 1B	3	1	2	1	0	0	1	1	0	.252
AVERY BECKER SS	4	0	0	0	0	0	0	0	2	.266
JAY ROSENTHAL C	4	1	1	0	1	0	0	0	2	.284
CARL DOREY RF	4	1	2	1	0	0	1	0	0	.288
FABIO PINEDA LF	3	0	0	1	0	0	0	0	1	.252
RALPH TAYLOR CF	4	0	0	0	0	0	0	0	1	.252
MIKE HANSEN DH	4	0	0	0	0	0	0	0	1	.245

PITCHING	IP	H	R	ER	SO	BB	ERA			
ELLIOTT BROWN (L)	6	10	4	4	4	2	4.28			
STU SPEAR	2	2	0	0	1	0	3.24			

INNING	1	2	3	4	5	6	7	8	9	TOTAL
MINNESOTA	1	0	0	0	0	1	0	0	1	3
CLEVELAND	2	0	0	2	0	0	0	0		4

GAME 78

By SAM LARDNER
The Cleveland Press

CLEVELAND, July 2 — Payback was sweet relief for Brian Howard.

The veteran Indians pitcher no doubt felt he had one coming Friday night after Sunday's rain-drenched loss at Kansas City, where the relievers let one get out of hand as the Royals took an 8–3 decision.

Howard was in complete control Friday as he held those same Royals to four hits over 6 and one-third innings in an 8–1 Tribe victory at Progressive Field. The Indians improved to 41–37 for the season with their fourth win in a row and remained four games behind the Minnesota Twins in the American League Central.

"It's kind of ironic that we scored eight tonight," Howard said. "The guys came through with a lot of hits when they counted. There was nothing we could do about the rain last Sunday. Those things are part of the game. I think I mentioned after that game that the rain might make me fresher for this start, and I think it did. I was really itching to get back out there, and I felt really good."

The Friday night crowd of 33,098 got a show from the offense. Scott Michaels, who went 0-for-4 in the series finale against the Twins on Thursday, was 2-for-4, with a two-run double in the third inning and a run scoring single in the fourth. Stein rested both Justin Kestino and Terry Rovetto today trying to keep everyone fresh.

The Indians then torched Royals reliefer Glenn Marchand for four runs in the fifth, and the rout was on.

"Yeah, things just seemed to be clicking for us," Michaels said. "We were glad to get one for the Doc (Howard) after he kind of got railroaded by the rain last week. We know how hard he competes and how much he cares."

Howard gave up a homer to Todd Steffans. His night ended in the top of the seventh after an even 100 pitches. He looked a little reluctant to give up the ball but said he understood.

"I probably could have finished the inning, but I understand," Howard said. "Skip (manager Todd Stein) doesn't want things to get out of hand with the pitch counts. The bullpen has been pretty much lights-out during this little run that we've been on the last few weeks or so."

Mickey Penney and Buck Sterling finished up for the Indians, giving the big bullpen guns a rest in the wake of Thursday's one-run victory over the Twins.

"Guys are starting to feel it a little bit, but we don't to get too cocky, or cocky at all," Stein said. "I give the guys all the credit in the world for this turnaround after we got off to an 0–6 start. I know a lot of people — some here in Cleveland — left us for dead, but here we are. Let's see how high we can go."

CLEVELAND INDIANS VS KANSAS CITY ROYALS · JULY 2
CLEVELAND 8 / KANSAS CITY 1

CLEVELAND INDIANS

BATTING	AB	R	H	RBI	2B	3B	HR	BB	SO	BA
RIKKI LABUDDA CF	5	1	2	0	0	0	0	1	0	.280
MICAH MILLISON RF	4	1	2	0	0	1	0	1	0	.281
WILSON WHITE LF	4	2	2	0	0	0	0	0	0	.270
OLIVER REINER 1B	4	1	1	0	0	0	0	0	1	.295
BERNARD HARPER 3B	4	1	2	1	0	0	0	0	1	.262
SCOTT MICHAELS 2B	4	0	2	3	1	0	0	0	0	.336
LEO TAYLOR SS	4	2	2	2	0	0	0	0	0	.291
J.J. KULAKOFSKI DH	4	0	1	1	1	0	0	0	1	.221
MORRIS JEROME C	3	0	1	1	1	0	0	0	1	.249

PITCHING	IP	H	R	ER	SO	BB	ERA			
BRIAN HOWARD (W)	6.3	5	1	1	5	2	3.47			
MICKEY PENNY	0.67	0	0	0	0	0	3.81			
BUCK STERLING	2	1	0	0	1	0	2.75			

KANSAS CITY ROYALS

BATTING	AB	R	H	RBI	2B	3B	HR	BB	SO	BA
KYLE MONTGOMERY 2B	4	0	0	0	0	0	0	0	0	.286
NELSON QUARRELS RF	3	0	1	0	1	0	0	1	0	.287
JARED BUCKNER SS	4	0	0	0	0	0	0	0	0	.268
ALCIDES CASTILLO LF	3	0	1	0	0	0	0	1	1	.253
DERREK HARGROVE 3B	4	0	2	0	0	0	0	0	1	.287
TODD STEFFANS DH	4	1	1	1	0	0	1	0	1	.257
LEQUAN BROWN 1B	4	0	0	0	0	0	0	0	1	.265
ARCENIO INCIARTE C	4	0	0	0	0	0	0	0	0	.262
VERNON COLEMAN CF	3	0	1	0	0	0	0	0	2	.241

PITCHING	IP	H	R	ER	SO	BB	ERA			
TOMMY KOVACS (L)	3.33	7	4	4	1	2	4.08			
GLENN MARCHAND	1.67	6	3	3	1	0	4.42			
BRUNO LACHNER	2	2	1	1	2	0	3.78			
JAIR MOSQUERA	1	1	0	0	0	0	3.72			

INNING	1	2	3	4	5	6	7	8	9	TOTAL
KANSAS CITY	0	0	0	0	1	0	0	0	0	1
CLEVELAND	0	0	2	1	4	0	0	1		8

GAME 79

By SAM LARDNER
The Cleveland Press

CLEVELAND, July 3 — Well, that was fun while it lasted for the Indians.

After a spate of baseball that was crisp and clean, the Tribe managed to find a way of throwing in one of their stinkers Saturday in a 7–1 loss to the Kansas City Royals before a disappointed crowd of 36,021 at Progressive Field.

Many of those fans have stayed away for much of this season because of the very crimes the Indians committed Saturday: errors by their fielders, walks issued by their pitchers and general sloppy play.

The loss snapped a season-best four-game winning streak and dropped the Indians' record to 41–38. They're now five games behind the first-place Minnesota Twins in the suddenly competitive American League Central.

"We hadn't seen one of those in a while," sighed manager Todd Stein. "Let's hope we don't see another one for a long time to come. The guys have been getting after it this last month or so, really. I'm not going to worry too much about it. It's just a shame that a big crowd had to watch this. They deserved better."

Indians starting pitcher Kenny Camden could not get out of the fourth inning, as he left with one out and the Tribe down 7–1, although all 7 runs were unearned. This was the second straight clunker for Camden and his third straight losing decision. Early trouble has been the big bugaboo.

"It's something I have to correct," The Wiz said. "It has nothing to do with fatigue or any of that (B.S.). I don't want to hear about that. And I'm not going to point fingers at the fielders, either. They didn't walk those four or five guys. I did."

If you can believe it, the Indians actually took the lead in this game. Rikki LaBudda led off the bottom of the first against Madison Behrens and legged out a double to short center field, sliding in ahead of a tag attempt. LaBudda now has a ten-game hitting streak. After Micah Millison grounded out, sending LaBudda to third. Wilson White's sacrifice fly to the warning track allowed LaBudda to trot home.

And that was that for the Indians as Behrens pitched his first career complete game striking out seven and walking two.

An error by Scott Michaels with two outs in the top of the second prolonged the inning, and Taylor Lawson homered to give the Royals a 2–1 lead. Michaels' calling card has been his hitting. With Angel Rodriguez due to come off the injured list, as early as Sunday, it's possible Michaels can be subbed out for defense late in games.

"That's on me," he said. "Wiz should have been in the dugout by then. It was a ball I should have had."

Camden lost all semblance of control in the fourth, walking the first two batters he faced before an error by Justin Kestino loaded the bases. Kyle Montgomery walked to force in a run before Derrek Hargrove delivered the crushing blow, a grand slam to right.

The only saving grace was the Indians got good mop-up relief work from Mickey Penney, Lorry Unger and Buck Sterling, saving the pen for another day.

"All that action early, and then nothing," Stein said. "We couldn't mount a comeback. Their pitcher (Behrens) was pretty good. The Royals have given us fits, and part of that is a credit to them. Let's remember that. But we'll get after it again tomorrow."

GAME 79

CLEVELAND INDIANS VS KANSAS CITY ROYALS • JULY 3
KANSAS CITY 7 / CLEVELAND 1

CLEVELAND INDIANS									
BATTING	AB	R	H	RBI	2B	3B	HR	BB	SO	BA
RIKKI LABUDDA CF	4	1	1	0	1	0	0	0	0	.279
MICAH MILLISON RF	4	0	0	0	0	0	0	0	0	.277
WILSON WHITE LF	3	0	0	1	0	0	0	0	0	.267
OLIVER REINER 1B	4	0	1	0	0	0	0	0	2	.294
TERRY ROVETTO 3B	4	0	1	0	0	0	0	0	0	.276
SCOTT MICHAELS 2B	4	0	1	0	0	0	0	0	1	.326
JUSTIN KESTINO SS	3	0	1	0	0	0	0	1	1	.257
BERNARD HARPER DH	3	0	0	0	0	0	0	1	1	.258
MORRIS JEROME C	4	0	1	0	1	0	0	0	2	.249

PITCHING	IP	H	R	ER	SO	BB	ERA
KENNY CAMDEN (L)	4.33	8	7	0	0	3	3.45
MICKRY PENNY	1.67	2	0	0	0	1	3.69
LORRY UNGER	2	2	0	0	0	1	3.34
BUCK STERLING	1	1	0	0	1	0	2.68

KANSAS CITY ROYALS									
BATTING	AB	R	H	RBI	2B	3B	HR	BB	SO	BA
KYLE MONTGOMERY 2B	4	1	1	1	0	0	0	2	0	.286
DERREK HARGROVE 3B	5	1	2	4	1	0	1	0	0	.290
JARED BUCKNER SS	4	0	1	0	0	0	0	1	0	.268
ALCIDES CASTILLO LF	4	0	0	0	0	0	0	0	1	.247
NELSON QUARRELS RF	4	0	1	0	0	0	0	0	0	.286
TODD STEFFANS DH	4	0	2	0	0	0	0	0	0	.263
LEQUAN BROWN 1B	3	2	2	0	0	0	0	1	0	.272
ARCENIO INCIARTE C	3	1	1	0	0	0	0	1	0	.264
TAYLOR LAWSON CF	4	2	2	2	0	0	1	0	0	.254

PITCHING	IP	H	R	ER	SO	BB	ERA
MADISON BEHRENS (W)	9	6	1	1	7	2	3.71

INNING	1	2	3	4	5	6	7	8	9	TOTAL
KANSAS CITY	0	2	0	5	0	0	0	0	0	7
CLEVELAND	1	0	0	0	0	0	0	0	0	1

GAME 80

By SAM LARDNER

The Cleveland Press

CLEVELAND, July 4 — Maybe we can hold off on that parade.

No, not the nice Fourth of July parade they held downtown Sunday. We're talking about that parade for the supposedly resurgent Cleveland Indians.

There was no striking up the band or much of anything else during a 3–0 loss to the Kansas City Royals in front of 36,767 fans at Progressive Field.

The Indians' second straight loss dropped them to 41–39 and to six games behind the Minnesota Twins in the American League Central. The Twins have responded well to being handled by the Indians while the Tribe can't seem to stand prosperity.

It was hard to fault the effort of Indians starting pitcher Tak Fujimoto, who went seven innings, giving up all three runs on five hits. It was the long ball that did Fujimoto in. Will Guerra's two-run homer followed by Dimitri Demos' solo shot in the fifth provided a stunning and ultimately fatal 1-2 punch.

"Sometimes, you can lose a game in one moment," Fujimoto said through his translator. "That's what happened today. I gave up a walk and then made two bad pitches. It was 3–0 in just a few seconds."

Tribe batters did nothing at all with Royals starter Kris Steiner, who went six innings before giving way to a bullpen that locked down the victory.

"We just couldn't get it going today," said Indians manager Todd Stein. "It wasn't like yesterday, where we played a poor game. This was just baseball today. There's no other way for me to explain it."

The Indians mounted a couple of rallies, but couldn't cash in on the opportunities. Oliver Reiner struck out with runners on second and third and two outs in the fourth. In the sixth, Scott Michaels popped out with the bases loaded. Michaels, the Indians' hottest hitter, went 0-for-5 after hitting in both of his previous two games and five of his previous six. Rikki LaBudda's 10-game streak also came to an end.

"Start a new hitting streak tomorrow, I guess," Michaels said with a sheepish grin. "I'm feeling pretty good at the plate despite having an 0-fer today. I feel like I can go on another tear."

Stein added that Michaels will be the everyday second baseman even with Angel Rodriguez coming off the injured list Sunday after recovering from a hamstring injury. To make room, Kieran Catsef was placed on the IL with an ankle injury.

"No, Scott has earned his way into the everyday lineup," Stein said. "We need the offense more than anything. Angel will get his time filling in at second, short and third. His glove is too valuable. But Scottie is coming into his own, and he can be a real leader the rest of the way."

GAME 80

CLEVELAND INDIANS VS KANSAS CITY ROYALS · JULY 4
KANSAS CITY 3 / CLEVELAND 0

CLEVELAND INDIANS

BATTING	AB	R	H	RBI	2B	3B	HR	BB	SO	BA
RIKKI LABUDDA CF	3	0	0	0	0	0	0	2	0	.277
MICAH MILLISON RF	4	0	1	0	0	0	0	0	1	.276
WILSON WHITE LF	4	0	2	0	1	0	0	1	0	.271
OLIVER REINER 1B	4	0	1	0	0	0	0	1	1	.293
TERRY ROVETTO 3B	4	0	1	0	0	0	0	1	0	.275
SCOTT MICHAELS 2B	5	0	0	0	0	0	0	0	2	.318
JUSTIN KESTINO SS	4	0	1	0	0	0	0	0	1	.256
BERNARD HARPER DH	4	0	0	0	0	0	0	0	0	.253
ICEBERG PETERS C	4	0	1	0	0	0	0	0	1	.222

PITCHING	IP	H	R	ER	SO	BB	ERA			
TAK FUJIMOTO (L)	4.33	8	7	0	0	3	3.20			
GENO MILZE	1.67	2	0	0	0	1	2.87			
LEE HAZELTON	2	2	0	0	0	1	4.32			

KANSAS CITY ROYALS

BATTING	AB	R	H	RBI	2B	3B	HR	BB	SO	BA
KYLE MONTGOMERY 2B	4	0	1	0	0	0	0	0	0	.285
DERREK HARGROVE 3B	5	0	2	0	1	0	0	1	0	.293
JARED BUCKNER SS	4	0	1	0	0	0	0	0	1	.267
MAURICE MORSE LF	4	0	0	0	0	0	0	0	1	.301
NELSON QUARRELS RF	4	1	1	0	1	0	0	0	0	.285
TODD STEFFANS DH	4	0	2	0	0	0	0	0	1	.269
WILL GUERRA 1B	4	1	2	2	0	0	1	0	0	.277
DIMITRI DEMOS C	4	1	1	1	0	0	1	0	0	.263
TAYLOR LAWSON CF	4	0	2	0	0	0	0	0	1	.261

PITCHING	IP	H	R	ER	SO	BB	ERA			
KRIS STEINER (W)	6	5	0	0	6	4	4.18			
AARON WESTFALL	2	1	0	0	0	1	3.13			
DERWIN RENTERIA (S)	1	1	0	0	0	0	2.48			

INNING	1	2	3	4	5	6	7	8	9	TOTAL
KANSAS CITY	0	0	0	0	3	0	0	0	0	3
CLEVELAND	0	0	0	0	0	0	0	0	0	0

GAME 81

By SAM LARDNER
The Cleveland Press

CLEVELAND, July 5 — The Indians are halfway there. Whether it's halfway home, halfway to the postseason or halfway to oblivion remains to be seen.

With this team, there is absolutely no telling. The Indians wasted another opportunity against a lowly team Monday night, falling meekly to the Kansas City Royals 4–1 at Progressive Field.

After sweeping the first-place Minnesota Twins and winning the first game of this series, the Indians dropped the next three games to the Royals, getting outscored 14–3 in those three games.

So when the story of this season is fully written after another half-season, it shouldn't be the 0–6 start that gets remembered. It should be the frittering away of chances against teams like the Royals.

General manager J.D. Eisner joined manager Todd Stein in his office after this game and sat slumped on the couch. The two men alternated in answering the media's questions.

"It's frustrating, that's for sure," Eisner said. "We're not giving up on this group by any means, but we need to show more consistency."

The all-star break will be here soon, and the July 31 trading deadline is not far behind. There are rumors about the Indians trading forgotten man Huron Southworth, who lost his job to Micah Millison early this season, but Eisner insists there are no irons in the fire.

"No, it's been pretty quiet," he said. "I'm sure we'll make a move, or two, by the 31st, but there's nothing now, and you know that I won't discuss specific players. But we can win with this group. We're close to the wild card and we were closing in on the Twins in the division."

Monday's loss dropped the Indians to seven games behind Minnesota in the American League Central.

Ace pitcher Lynn Moda, who has come through several times in his own inconsistent season, gave up three runs in 5 and two-third innings against the Royals. The other run came in the ninth against Lee Hazelton.

The Indians struck first, as Scott Michaels doubled home Terry Rovetto in the second inning against Yusmeiro Morales.

Moda gave it back and then some in the top of the third, when DH Truman Greystone hit a bases-clearing three-run double. That came after a single by Kyle Montgomery and a pair of walks.

"I've got to bear down a little better there," Moda said. "I've let a few games get away. We can't let that happen as a team."

Especially not with a three-game series coming up at Minnesota, where the Twins will have a little blood in their eye.

"They'll be laying in the weeds for us," Stein said. "The guys know what's at stake. We beat them at our place, but their fans will be out in full force. We need to show up."

Both for the next game and the entire second half.

GAME 81

CLEVELAND INDIANS VS KANSAS CITY ROYALS • JULY 5
KANSAS CITY 4 / CLEVELAND 1

CLEVELAND INDIANS

BATTING	AB	R	H	RBI	2B	3B	HR	BB	SO	BA
RIKKI LABUDDA CF	4	0	1	0	0	0	0	0	0	.276
MICAH MILLISON RF	4	0	0	0	0	0	0	0	0	.272
WILSON WHITE LF	3	0	1	0	1	0	0	1	0	.271
TERRY ROVETTO 3B	3	1	1	0	0	0	0	0	1	.276
OLIVER REINER 1B	3	0	0	0	0	0	0	0	1	.290
SCOTT MICHAELS 2B	3	0	1	1	1	0	0	0	1	.318
LEO TAYLOR SS	3	0	0	0	0	0	0	0	1	.276
J. J. KULAKOFSKI DH	3	0	1	0	0	0	0	0	1	.225
MORRIS JEROME C	3	0	0	0	0	0	0	0	0	.246

PITCHING	IP	H	R	ER	SO	BB	ERA			
LYNN MODA (L)	5.67	6	3	3	4	2	4.25			
BUCK STERLING	1.33	1	0	0	1	2	3.23			
LEE HAZELTON	2	2	1	1	0	0	4.34			

KANSAS CITY ROYALS

BATTING	AB	R	H	RBI	2B	3B	HR	BB	SO	BA
KYLE MONTGOMERY 2B	4	1	1	0	0	0	0	0	1	.284
DERREK HARGROVE 3B	3	1	0	0	0	0	0	1	0	.288
JARED BUCKNER SS	3	2	1	0	0	0	0	1	0	.268
TRUMAN GREYSTONE DH	4	0	2	3	1	0	0	0	2	.307
NELSON QUARRELS RF	3	0	0	0	0	0	0	1	1	.280
MAURICE MORSE RF	4	0	2	1	0	0	0	0	0	.306
WILL GUERRA 1B	4	0	1	0	0	0	0	0	1	.277
DIMITRI DEMOS C	3	0	0	0	0	0	0	1	0	.258
TAYLOR LAWSON CF	4	0	2	0	0	0	0	0	0	.268

PITCHING	IP	H	R	ER	SO	BB	ERA			
YUSMEIRO MORALES (W)	8	4	1	1	5	1	4.36			
DERWIN RENTERIA (S)	1	1	0	0	0	0	2.40			

INNING	1	2	3	4	5	6	7	8	9	TOTAL
KANSAS CITY	0	0	3	0	0	0	0	0	1	4
CLEVELAND	0	1	0	0	0	0	0	0	0	1

GAME 82

By SAM LARDNER
The Cleveland Press

MINNEAPOLIS, July 6 — Are this year's Cleveland Indians going to be remembered as one of those teams that plays "to the level of its competition?"

It certainly seems so of late.

After doing their best to stumble all over themselves in games against the last-place Kansas City Royals, the Indians have looked like world beaters against the first-place Minnesota Twins.

The Indians won their fourth straight of recent vintage against the Twins, this time a thrilling 6–5 victory in 10 innings Tuesday night at Target Field.

Scott Michaels smashed a double down the left-field line against Roger Sandford to drive in the go-ahead run in the 10th, scoring Micah Millison, who opened the inning with a walk and wound up on third after a ground-out by Wilson White and a flyout by Terry Rovetto.

The victory moved the Indians (42–40) within six games of the Twins in the American League Central. It also snapped a three-game losing streak, suffered at home against the aforementioned Royals.

"That's a show of character right there," said Indians manager Todd Stein, who watched the Twins tie the game in the bottom of the ninth inning on Donnie Wallace's homer off closer Ivan Zyzna, who suffered the rare blown save. "It would have been easy to get deflated, especially after the way the homestand ended, but our guys kept fighting. Scottie has been doing it all year for us.

"And I think the energy here in this park and the fact that the Twins are in first place gave us a lift, too. It's a great atmosphere."

Neither starting pitcher figured in the decision. Indians lefty Ollie Gonzalez labored through five innings, giving up seven hits and three runs. The Indians looked well on their way to a fourth straight loss after a shaky first inning, when Gonzalez gave up a three-run blast to Tommy Hopkins. But he bore down after that and made it through the next four innings.

"You hate to fall behind like that," Gonzalez said. "But you can't panic, either. The offense is more than good enough to come back, and that's what they did. I didn't have my best stuff out there, but somehow you find a way to reach back and find a little something extra."

The Indians got Gonzalez back in it in the fifth, when Michaels (2-for-3 with a walk) singled and went to second on a wild pitch by Stu Spear. Oliver Reiner walked, and both runners scored on Justin Kestino's double to the gap in right-center.

Spear exited in the sixth when the Indians scored two more, on White's two run homer. That made it 4–3 Indians, but the Twins got a run against Mickey Penney in the sixth on an RBI single by Frederick Swanstrom.

Things quieted down until the eighth, when the Indians' Rikki LaBudda manufactured the go-ahead run with a walk and stolen base number 20. He then caught the Twins napping as he scored all the way from second on Rovetto's groundout from first baseman Bruce Conklin to pitcher Sandy Greene.

"I just kept running," LaBudda said. "The play took a long time to develop. Greene is a big lumbering guy, and I figured his momentum would carry him past the first-base bag. I took a chance even though (third-base coach) Eddie (Walker) was waving me."

Zyzna gave up the homer to Wallace with two outs in the ninth, and Lee Hazelton pitched the bottom of the 10th to earn the win.

"We made it interesting," Stein said. "I think that play by Rikki really charged us up. That's what speed and intelligence together can do. And we were able to bounce back after that homer. My heart is still racing."

GAME 82

CLEVELAND INDIANS VS MINNESOTA TWINS · JULY 6
CLEVELAND 6 / MINNESOTA 5

CLEVELAND INDIANS

BATTING	AB	R	H	RBI	2B	3B	HR	BB	SO	BA	
RIKKI LABUDDA CF	4	1	0	0	0	0	0	0	0	.273	
MICAH MILLISON RF	4	2	2	0	0	0	0	1	0	.276	
WILSON WHITE LF	5	1	2	2	1	0	1	0	1	.273	
TERRY ROVETTO 3B	4	0	0	1	0	0	0	0	2	.272	
SCOTT MICHAELS 2B	3	1	2	1	1	0	0	2	1	.323	
OLIVER REINER 1B	4	1	3	1	0	1	0	0	0	.296	
JUSTIN KESTINO SS	4	0	1	1	1	0	0	0	2	.256	
BERNARD HARPER DH	4	0	2	0	0	0	0	0	0	.258	
MORRIS JEROME C	4	0	0	0	0	0	0	0	2	.241	

PITCHING	IP	H	R	ER	SO	BB	ERA				
OLLIE GONZALEZ	5	7	3	3	3	3	4.69				
MICKEY PENNY	3	1	1	1	1	1	3.63				
IVAN ZYZNA (BS)	1	1	1	1	0	0	1.48				
LEE HAZELTON (W)	1	0	0	0	2	0	4.12				

MINNESOTA TWINS

BATTING	AB	R	H	RBI	2B	3B	HR	BB	SO	BA	
TONY WILDERS 2B	5	1	1	0	0	0	0	1	0	.283	
DONNIE WALLACE DH	5	2	2	1	0	0	1	0	0	.297	
BRUCE CONKLIN 1B	4	0	0	0	0	0	0	0	2	.262	
TOMMY HOPKINS 3B	4	1	2	3	1	0	1	0	0	.307	
FABIO PINEDA LF	4	0	0	0	0	0	0	0	1	.263	
CARL DOREY RF	3	0	1	0	0	0	0	2	0	.285	
AVERY BECKER SS	4	1	2	0	1	0	0	0	1	.294	
RALPH TAYLOR CF	3	0	0	0	0	0	0	1	0	.258	
FREDERICK SWANSTROM C	4	0	1	1	0	0	0	0	2	.261	

PITCHING	IP	H	R	ER	SO	BB	ERA				
ELLIOTT BROWN	5.33	7	2	2	4	2	4.58				
OSWALDO BORGES	1.67	2	2	2	2	0	2.93				
SANDY GREENE	1	1	1	1	1	0	3.86				
ROGER SANDFORD (L)	2	2	1	1	1	0	2.40				

INNING	1	2	3	4	5	6	7	8	9	10	TOTAL
CLEVELAND	0	0	0	0	2	2	0	1	0	1	6
MINNESOTA	3	0	0	1	0	0	0	0	1	0	5

GAME 83

By SAM LARDNER
The Cleveland Press

MINNEAPOLIS, July 7 — Nobody could realistically expect the Minnesota Twins to lie down for the Cleveland Indians, not forever anyway.

Most of all the Twins couldn't expect that of themselves.

"We have a lot of pride, and we're in first place for a reason," said Twins manager Archie Knowles Wednesday night after a convincing 9–2 victory over the Indians at Target Field. "They had beat us up pretty good here in the last week or so. They're a good ballclub, but so are we. We pride ourselves on playing well at home and bouncing back from tough losses. You saw that tonight."

Did we ever.

Less than 24 hours after the Indians scored an emotional 10-inning, 6–5 victory, the Twins roared back with a vengeance, pummeling the Indians and pitcher Brian Howard 9–2. Howard didn't make it through the fourth inning, as the Twins took a 7–0 lead and didn't look back.

Howard was the beneficiary of an Indians offensive outburst in an 8–3 victory over the Royals on July 2, but he was on the receiving end this time. The Twins (49–34) roughed him up for eight hits and six runs in 3 and two-third innings as they set the third-place Indians (42–41) seven games back of them in the American League Central.

"That's just an ass-whupping," Howard said, mincing no words. "You feel good when you're on the winning side of games like this, but man, it hurts to be on the receiving end. "That club can hit. At the same time, I have to execute better pitches."

This one was never in doubt. The Twins scored twice in the first inning on a two-run homer by Donnie Wallace who hit for the cycle and drove in four. They added three more in the third and two more in the fourth, sending Howard to an early exit.

"I'm not going to fret too much about this one," said Indians manager Todd Stein. "We just got beat. That's baseball. The Doc (Howard) didn't have his best stuff, and a good-hitting team like the Twins is going to take advantage."

The Indians finally got on the board in the sixth on Scott Michaels' two-run single off Claudio Ontiveros. The usual mop-up crew of Mickey Penney, Buck Sterling and Lorry Unger finished up on the mound for the Tribe, who get one more shot at the Twins and a chance to win the series before heading home again.

"We just have to stay within striking distance, both of the division and the wild card," Stein said. "Playing the Twins gives us that opportunity. We've taken advantage lately. Tonight, it wasn't to be."

The Twins boss reiterated that his team isn't going anywhere anytime soon.

"We have respect for the Indians, but we have a lot of confidence in our guys, too," Knowles said. "I know they (the Indians) were probably feeling it a little bit after beating us a few games. But they have to catch us, not the other way around."

GAME 83

CLEVELAND INDIANS VS MINNESOTA TWINS • JULY 7
MINNESOTA 9 / CLEVELAND 2

CLEVELAND INDIANS

BATTING	AB	R	H	RBI	2B	3B	HR	BB	SO	BA
RIKKI LABUDDA CF	4	0	1	0	0	0	0	0	0	.273
MICAH MILLISON RF	3	0	2	0	0	0	0	1	0	.280
WILSON WHITE LF	4	1	1	0	0	0	0	0	1	.273
TERRY ROVETTO 3B	4	1	1	0	0	0	0	0	1	.272
OLIVER REINER 1B	3	0	0	0	0	0	0	1	0	.294
SCOTT MICHAELS 2B	4	0	1	2	0	0	0	0	1	.322
JUSTIN KESTINO SS	4	0	1	0	1	0	0	0	0	.256
BERNARD HARPER DH	4	0	0	0	0	0	0	0	2	.253
MORRIS JEROME C	4	0	1	0	0	0	0	0	2	.242

PITCHING	IP	H	R	ER	SO	BB	ERA			
BRIAN HOWARD (L)	5	7	3	3	3	3	4.69			
MICKEY PENNY	3	1	1	1	1	1	3.63			
BUCK STERLING	1	1	1	1	0	0	3.38			
LORRY UNGER	1	0	0	0	2	0	4.12			

MINNESOTA TWINS

BATTING	AB	R	H	RBI	2B	3B	HR	BB	SO	BA
TONY WILDERS 2B	5	2	2	2	0	0	0	0	0	.286
DONNIE WALLACE DH	5	2	4	4	1	1	1	0	0	.311
BRUCE CONKLIN 1B	4	0	1	2	0	0	0	0	1	.262
TOMMY HOPKINS 3B	4	0	0	0	1	0	0	0	2	.301
FABIO PINEDA LF	4	1	1	0	0	0	0	1	0	.263
CARL DOREY RF	5	0	2	1	1	0	0	0	0	.288
AVERY BECKER SS	4	1	1	0	0	0	0	0	1	.293
RALPH TAYLOR CF	4	2	2	0	0	0	0	0	0	.264
FREDERICK SWANSTROM C	4	1	1	0	0	0	0	0	1	.260

PITCHING	IP	H	R	ER	SO	BB	ERA			
CLAUDIO ONTEVEROS (W)	6	5	2	2	4	1	4.05			
HYUN SOO PARK	2	2	0	0	2	1	2.32			
JOAQUIN ALMEIDA	1	1	0	0	1	0	3.63			

INNING	1	2	3	4	5	6	7	8	9	TOTAL
CLEVELAND	0	0	0	0	0	2	0	0	0	2
MINNESOTA	2	0	3	2	0	0	1	1		9

GAME 84

By SAM LARDNER
The Cleveland Press

MINNEAPOLIS, July 8 — Kenny Camden has become the Indians' new hard-luck pitcher. Earlier this season, that dubious honor went to Ollie Gonzalez.

Camden is the guy now. He dropped his fourth straight decision Thursday night in a well-pitched 3–2 loss to the Minnesota Twins at Target Field.

As disappointing as the result was for Camden, it was more damaging for the Indians as a team. They fell back to .500 at 42–42 after their second straight loss to the Twins in this three-game series.

Now it's home to face the Cincinnati Reds three times leading up to the all-star break. The third-place Indians now trail the division-leading Twins by eight games in the American League Central.

"We can't seem to extricate ourselves from that .500 mark," said Indians manager Todd Stein. "We got to four games over (41–37) and thought we had it permanently in the rear-view mirror. But it's back to the drawing board, so to speak, I guess. Hopefully we can get some momentum at home heading into the break."

Camden turned in the quality start, going six innings and giving up three runs on seven hits. He hasn't won since June 18, and back then, it was a happy time as the Indians reached .500 for the first time this season.

"That's no longer good enough," Camden said. "We can't keep putting ourselves in this position. We had a chance there to make a real run at first place. So now, we go home, regroup and try to get it going again. I know we will."

Camden and Twins starter Jay Rutherford both started off well, retiring the sides in order in the first two innings. Indians catcher Morris Jerome led off the third with a solo homer, but the Twins got it back in the bottom half as Fabio Pineda singled and Carl Dorey walked. Avery Becker and Ralph Taylor each followed with RBI singles to give the Twins a 2–1 lead. They made it 3–1 in the fourth on a homer by Bruce "Bruiser" Conklin, who has done his best to bruise the Tribe this season.

"A little bit of everything," Camden said. "I kind of got pinged to death that one inning, and then Conklin crushed one. We've had trouble with him all year. But overall, I felt good out there. If I can keep pitching like that, the results will come. That's why sometimes the won-loss record can be a little misleading."

The Indians made it close in the seventh on Scott Michaels' sacrifice fly. He also walked, going 1-for-2 overall as he extended his hitting streak to four games.

But that was it, as Twins closer Roger Sandford retired the Indians with barely a whimper in the top of the ninth.

"Their pitching was pretty good tonight," Stein said. "But so was ours. Wiz (Camden) was outstanding. Our bullpen was pretty good, too with Haze (Lee Hazelton) and (Geno) Milzie finishing nicely for us."

Hazelton and Milzie each had one perfect inning in relief of Camden.

"Let's get the heck out of here and get home," Stein said. "That club (the Twins) is a good one, but our guys battled them. We won't see them again this year, so we'll need some help if we're going to catch them."

CLEVELAND INDIANS VS MINNESOTA TWINS · JULY 8
MINNESOTA 3 / CLEVELAND 2

CLEVELAND INDIANS										
BATTING	AB	R	H	RBI	2B	3B	HR	BB	SO	BA
RIKKI LABUDDA CF	4	0	0	0	0	0	0	0	0	.269
MICAH MILLISON RF	3	0	0	0	0	0	0	1	0	.277
KIERAN CATSEF LF	4	0	1	0	0	0	0	0	2	.260
TERRY ROVETTO 3B	4	1	1	0	0	0	0	0	2	.272
OLIVER REINER 1B	4	0	0	0	0	0	0	0	0	.290
SCOTT MICHAELS 2B	2	0	1	1	0	0	0	1	1	.323
JUSTIN KESTINO SS	4	0	2	0	1	0	0	0	0	.260
BERNARD HARPER DH	4	0	0	0	0	0	0	0	1	.249
MORRIS JEROME C	4	1	2	1	0	0	1	0	0	.246
PITCHING	IP	H	R	ER	SO	BB	ERA			
KENNY CAMDEN (L)	6	7	3	3	7	2	3.51			
LEE HAZELTON	1	0	0	0	0	0	3.92			
GENO MILZIE	1	0	0	0	0	0	2.79			
MINNESOTA TWINS										
BATTING	AB	R	H	RBI	2B	3B	HR	BB	SO	BA
TONY WILDERS 2B	4	0	1	0	0	0	0	1	0	.285
DONNIE WALLACE DH	4	0	1	0	1	0	0	0	1	.309
BRUCE CONKLIN 1B	4	1	1	1	0	0	1	0	1	.262
TOMMY HOPKINS 3B	4	0	0	0	0	0	0	0	1	.294
FABIO PINEDA LF	4	1	1	0	0	0	0	0	2	.263
CARL DOREY RF	3	1	1	0	0	0	0	1	0	.289
AVERY BECKER SS	4	0	1	1	0	0	0	0	0	.292
RALPH TAYLOR CF	4	0	1	1	0	0	0	0	0	.264
FREDERICK SWANSTROM C	4	0	0	0	0	0	0	0	2	.253
PITCHING	IP	H	R	ER	SO	BB	ERA			
JAY RUTHERFORD (W)	6	5	2	2	4	1	4.05			
ROGER SANDFORD (S)	2	2	0	0	2	1	2.25			

INNING	1	2	3	4	5	6	7	8	9	TOTAL
CLEVELAND	0	0	1	0	0	0	1	0	0	2
MINNESOTA	0	0	2	1	0	0	0	0		3

GAME 85

By SAM LARDNER
The Cleveland Press

CLEVELAND, July 9 — You couldn't blame the Indians if they rolled out a red carpet for the Cincinnati Reds.

And if things keep going the way they went Friday; the Tribe won't let the Reds out of town.

The Indians scored their biggest victory of the year, and they did it in a big way, as they pummeled the Reds 16–4 at Progressive Field.

Tribe batters pounded out 22 hits, getting home runs from Scott Michaels, Oliver Reiner, Micah Millison and Bernard Harper, whose grand slam in the fourth highlighted an eight-run inning that chased Reds starting pitcher Bruce Robinson.

The outburst delighted the Indians fans in the sellout crowd of 36,337 and sent the many Reds fans for an early Friday night at the surrounding downtown establishments.

"We had one of those coming," said Indians manager Todd Stein, whose club has beaten their Ohio National League rivals three times out of four this year. "We were kind of stymied the last couple games at Minnesota, so I think guys took out their frustrations a little bit tonight."

Michaels extended his hitting streak to five games with a three-run homer in the first inning. Michaels is 8-for-16 during the mini-streak.

"It was good to get us off on the right foot," he said. "I said when I had that 0-fer the other day that I felt I could go on a little run. I've been seeing the ball well for quite some time. Hopefully Skip keeps writing my name on the card every day and I can keep going."

There's no doubt about that. Michaels supplanted Angel Rodriguez earlier this season when Rodriguez went on the injured list. Rodriguez replaced Michaels at second base late in the game when Stein took several players out of the game.

Benefiting from the largess was starting pitcher Tak Fujimoto, who lost the only game the teams played against each other last month in Cincinnati. Fujimoto went six innings, giving up five hits and two runs for his eighth win. Lorry Unger worked the final three innings and by official-scoring rules, was credited with a save even though the game was a blowout.

Fujimoto got exactly zero runs in his previous start, a 3–0 loss to the Royals.

"I appreciate all the runs," Fujimoto said through his translator. "It looked like my teammates were having a good time hitting today. It made me want to get a bat. All I can do is pitch. I did not change my approach even with the big lead."

Reiner hit his homer, a three-run blast in the third. Millison had a two-run homer in the sixth, and Harper piled on with a three-run shot in the seventh.

Rikki LaBudda was on base four times and stole two more bases, numbers 21 and 22. In addition to Rodriguez getting into the game, Stein gave some playing time to rarely used Huron Southworth and to Leo Taylor.

With the DH in use, Reds manager Jack Constantine let his bullpen take the hit and did not resort to using a position player to pitch.

"We had some fresh arms, and I don't normally like to do that," Constantine said. "This was just one of those nights. I just feel bad for our fans who drove up here to see this. I hope we can make the rest of the weekend fun for them."

GAME 85

CLEVELAND INDIANS VS CINCINNATI REDS • JULY 11
CLEVELAND 16 / CINCINNATI 4

CLEVELAND INDIANS

BATTING	AB	R	H	RBI	2B	3B	HR	BB	SO	BA
RIKKI LABUDDA CF	5	2	3	2	1	0	0	1	0	.274
MICAH MILLISON RF	4	2	2	2	0	0	1	0	0	.280
HURON SOUTHWORTH RF	2	0	1	0	0	0	0	0	1	.233
WILSON WHITE LF	6	2	2	0	1	0	0	1	1	.274
TERRY ROVETTO 3B	5	1	2	2	1	0	0	0	0	.274
SCOTT MICHAELS 2B	4	2	3	3	0	0	1	0	0	.331
ANGEL RODRIGUEZ 2B	2	0	1	0	0	0	0	0	1	.212
OLIVER REINER 1B	5	2	2	3	1	0	1	1	0	.260
JUSTIN KESTINO SS	4	2	2	0	0	0	1	0	1	.263
LEO TAYLOR SS	2	0	1	0	0	0	0	0	0	.283
BERNARD HARPER DH	5	2	2	4	0	0	1	0	0	.252
ICEBERG PETERS C	5	1	1	0	1	0	0	0	1	.221

PITCHING	IP	H	R	ER	SO	BB	ERA			
TAK FUJIMOTO (W)	6	5	2	2	5	2	3.19			
LORRY UNGER	3	2	2	2	2	1	4.37			

CINCINNATI REDS

BATTING	AB	R	H	RBI	2B	3B	HR	BB	SO	BA
ALEX JIMENEZ CF	4	1	1	0	0	0	0	1	0	.284
MARCO PINEDA 1B	4	0	1	0	0	0	0	0	1	.292
RICH AMEND 3B	4	0	1	2	0	0	0	0	2	.267
ANGEL PULIDO C	3	1	2	2	0	0	0	1	0	.309
DIONDRE SPIERS LF	4	1	1	0	0	0	0	0	0	.268
JUSTYN SIMMONS RF	4	0	1	0	0	0	0	1	1	.283
LANDON WILSON 2B	4	1	0	0	0	0	0	0	0	.282
ERICK GUZMAN SS	4	0	0	0	0	0	0	0	2	.256
VIRGIL SANDQUIST DH	3	0	0	0	0	0	0	0	1	.255

PITCHING	IP	H	R	ER	SO	BB	ERA			
BRUCE ROBINSON (L)	2.67	10	6	6	1	1	5.12			
DENZEL HENDRICK	2.33	6	6	6	1	2	4.86			
GABRIEL QUINTERO	2	4	3	3	1	1	2.40			
AMARI DAWKINS	1	2	1	1	0	0	4.35			

INNING	1	2	3	4	5	6	7	8	9	TOTAL
CINCINNATI	0	0	0	2	0	0	2	0	0	4
CLEVELAND	3	0	3	2	2	2	3	1		16

GAME 86

By SAM LARDNER

The Cleveland Press

CLEVELAND, July 10 — No, the Indians aren't going to score 16 runs every day, not even against the Cincinnati Reds. But five proved to be more than enough Saturday afternoon in a 5–1 victory over the Reds before 35,908 at Progressive Field.

Ace pitcher Lynn Moda kept the Reds at bay through seven innings, and the Tribe got homers from Justin Kestino and Oliver Reiner. Second baseman Scott Michaels went 2-for-4 with an RBI single, extending his hitting streak to six games.

"Sixteen was sweet, but we've got to win the lower-scoring games," said Indians manager Scott Stein, whose team is 44–42 with one more game to go until the all-star break. "This was a solid performance by Modes and the offense. And the fact that we played well in the field is a big plus. Regardless of how things go tomorrow, we know we're going into the break above .500, and that's really something since we started 0–6 and had to struggle just to get to .500."

Moda got just one run of support, in his previous start, a 4–1 loss to the Royals. But he was dominant on this bright Saturday, limiting the Reds to five hits and a harmless solo homer to DH Denny Carnehl in the fifth inning.

"I've thrown it pretty well lately," Moda said. "I talked after the last start about bearing down a little better. I focused on that today. Mo (catcher

Morris Jerome) put down all the right fingers. All I had to do was hit the glove."

Indians batter hit the ball early against Reds starter Eli Batt. Terry Rovetto singled with two outs in the bottom of the first and rode home on Reiner's home run to left field. Michaels' double in the third drove in Reiner, who had walked.

"If we get that middle of the order going, we're going to be dangerous," Reiner said. "With Scottie hitting so well, that makes it tough to pitch around any of us. He's really added a dimension to this lineup that we didn't have before, and that's taking nothing away from Angel."

Reiner was referring to Angel Rodriguez, who lost his starting job to Michaels when he went on the injured list in late May with a hamstring injury. During his hitting streak, Michaels is 10-for-20."

"It's nice because Angel has been my biggest backer," Michaels said. "It's almost kind of a partnership because he'll go in for me in the ninth sometimes for his defense, which is second to none in this league."

Kestino finished the scoring with a two-run homer in the seventh. Geno Milzie and Lee Hazelton finished for Moda out of the bullpen, with Hazelton stranding a pair of runners in the ninth after a two-out walk and a single got him into minor trouble. Stein resisted going to closer Ivan Zyzna in that situation.

"It was good for Lee to finish in somewhat of a pressure situation, and we gave Ivan another day of rest," Stein said. "The days of the complete game are almost completely over, so it's important to have four or five guys in that pen you can feel confident closing a game with. We've got to keep the concentration for one more game before the guys get a well-deserved break."

CLEVELAND INDIANS VS CINCINNATI REDS • JULY 10
CLEVELAND 5 / CINCINNATI 1

CLEVELAND INDIANS										
BATTING	AB	R	H	RBI	2B	3B	HR	BB	SO	BA
RIKKI LABUDDA CF	4	0	1	0	0	0	0	1	0	.274
MICAH MILLISON RF	4	0	0	0	0	0	0	0	1	.276
TERRY ROVETTO 3B	4	2	2	0	0	0	0	0	0	.276
OLIVER REINER 1B	2	2	2	2	0	0	1	2	0	.265
SCOTT MICHAELS 2B	4	0	2	1	1	0	0	0	0	.333
JUSTIN KESTINO SS	4	1	2	2	0	0	1	0	0	.266
KIERAN CATSEF LF	4	0	1	0	0	0	0	0	1	.259
BERNARD HARPER DH	3	0	0	0	0	0	0	1	2	.249
MORRIS JEROME C	4	0	2	0	0	0	0	0	0	.250
PITCHING	IP	H	R	ER	SO	BB	ERA			
LYNN MODES (W)	6	5	1	1	4	1	4.09			
GENO MILZIE	2	1	0	0	0	1	2.66			
LEE HAZELTON	1	1	0	0	1	1	3.74			
CINCINNATI REDS										
BATTING	AB	R	H	RBI	2B	3B	HR	BB	SO	BA
ALEX JIMENEZ CF	3	0	2	0	0	0	0	1	0	.289
MARCO PINEDA 1B	3	0	0	0	0	0	0	1	0	.287
RICH AMEND 3B	4	0	1	0	0	0	0	0	0	.267
ANGEL PULIDO C	4	0	1	0	0	0	0	0	1	.308
DIONDRE SPIERS LF	4	0	0	0	0	0	0	0	1	.263
JUSTYN SIMMONS RF	3	0	1	0	0	0	0	1	2	.284
LANDON WILSON 2B	4	0	0	0	0	0	0	0	0	.276
ERICK GUZMAN SS	4	0	0	0	0	0	0	0	1	.250
DENNY CARNEHL DH	4	1	2	1	0	0	1	0	1	.286
PITCHING	IP	H	R	ER	SO	BB	ERA			
ELI BATT (L)	6.33	9	3	3	3	3	4.10			
LEE HEE CHAN	2.33	3	2	2	1	1	3.89			

INNING	1	2	3	4	5	6	7	8	9	TOTAL
CINCINNATI	0	0	0	0	1	0	0	0	0	1
CLEVELAND	2	0	1	0	0	0	2	0		5

GAME 87

By SAM LARDNER
The Cleveland Press

CLEVELAND, July 11 — The Indians scattered to the wind Sunday as 23 players headed home for the all-star break after a 6–3 victory over the Cincinnati Reds for a three-game sweep at Progressive Field.

First baseman Oliver Reiner and closer Ivan Zyzna took off for Anaheim and the all-star festivities after playing parts in Sunday's victory.

Reiner hit a three-run double in the fourth inning, and Zyzna worked a 1-2-3 ninth to earn the save and preserve the victory for starter Ollie Gonzalez, who went six innings of seven-hit, two-run ball.

Unbelievably left off the American League all-star team was hot-hitting second baseman Scott Michaels, who extended his hitting streak to seven games with a run-scoring single in the second inning against Travis Chase to put the Tribe on the board 1–0.

Michaels is batting .340 for the season and suddenly finds himself in the hunt for a batting title. But he's not an all-star.

"That's baffling to me," said manager Todd Stein, whose team is 45–42 heading into the break. "Maybe our team's slow start and Scottie not becoming an everyday player until late May had something to do with it — or the fact that he wasn't on the ballot. Either way, the few days off will do him good, and in our minds, he's certainly an all-star."

Greg Voight, the second baseman for the Baltimore Orioles was selected as their sole representative instead of Michaels. Michaels shrugged off the snub.

"It would have been nice, but I haven't played this much since the minor leagues, so the rest will do me good," he said. "We have two pretty deserving guys going to Anaheim, and I'm happy with them. I'm more interested in how we do as a team and helping us get to the playoffs."

The Indians are seven games behind the first-place Minnesota Twins and three behind the Chicago White Sox in the American League Central. The playoffs are not out of the question, but the Indians will have to continue playing as they did over the last several weeks.

One of the keys over this time has been Ollie G. The Indians won their fourth straight game that the big lefty has started. Staked to a 4–0 lead, Gonzalez worked through the Reds lineup, giving up a two-run homer to Rich Amend in the fifth and reaching the 100-pitch mark in the sixth, finishing with 105.

"I've felt really good all year," Gonzalez said. "Things weren't breaking my way early in the season, but they're certainly going my way now. Ice (backup catcher Iceberg Peters) and I had it going pretty good. A couple of walks in the fifth and sixth happened because I was trying to be too fine. That's what ran up the pitch count."

Peters added a two-run single in the bottom of the sixth to give the Indians a 6–2 lead before reliever Buck Sterling allowed a solo homer to Justyn Simmons in the seventh. Geno Milzie and Zyzna closed out from there.

The post-break schedule opens with a series at Pittsburgh and features nine games on the road in their next 11.

"You almost hate to see the break come because we have some momentum," Stein said. "But the rest will do everybody some good. I know we'll be charging out of the gate in the second half. I can't wait."

GAME 87

CLEVELAND INDIANS VS CINCINNATI REDS · JULY 11
CLEVELAND 6 / CINCINNATI 3

CLEVELAND INDIANS										
BATTING	**AB**	**R**	**H**	**RBI**	**2B**	**3B**	**HR**	**BB**	**SO**	**BA**
RIKKI LABUDDA CF	4	1	1	0	0	0	0	1	0	.274
HURON SOUTHWORTH RF	4	0	1	0	0	0	0	0	1	.234
WILSON WHITE LF	4	1	2	0	0	0	0	0	0	.277
TERRY ROVETTO 3B	3	1	0	0	0	0	0	1	0	.274
OLIVER REINER 1B	4	1	2	3	1	0	0	0	0	.268
SCOTT MICHAELS 2B	4	0	1	1	0	0	0	0	2	.332
JUSTIN KESTINO SS	4	1	2	0	0	0	1	0	0	.269
J.J. KULAKOFSKI DH	3	1	1	0	1	0	0	1	0	.228
ICEBERG PETERS C	4	0	1	2	0	0	0	0	0	.222
PITCHING	**IP**	**H**	**R**	**ER**	**SO**	**BB**	**ERA**			
OLLIE GONZALEZ (W)	6	7	2	0	5	1	4.41			
BUCK STERLING	1	1	1	1	0	0	3.51			
GENO MILZIE	1	0	0	0	0	0	2.59			
IVAN ZYZNA (S)	1	0	0	0	0	0	1.42			

CINCINNATI REDS										
BATTING	**AB**	**R**	**H**	**RBI**	**2B**	**3B**	**HR**	**BB**	**SO**	**BA**
ALEX JIMENEZ CF	4	0	1	0	0	0	0	0	0	.289
MARCO PINEDA 1B	3	1	1	0	0	0	0	1	0	.288
RICH AMEND 3B	4	1	2	2	0	0	1	0	1	.271
ANGEL PULIDO C	4	0	0	0	0	0	0	0	1	.301
DIONDRE SPIERS LF	4	0	0	0	0	0	0	0	2	.258
JUSTYN SIMMONS RF	4	1	1	1	0	0	0	0	0	.283
LANDON WILSON 2B	4	0	0	0	0	0	0	0	1	.270
ERICK GUZMAN SS	4	0	1	0	0	0	0	0	0	.250
DENNY CARNEHL DH	4	0	2	0	0	0	0	0	1	.292
PITCHING	**IP**	**H**	**R**	**ER**	**SO**	**BB**	**ERA**			
TRAVIS CHASE (L)	5.67	8	6	6	2	2	4.39			
GABRIEL QUINTERO	1.33	2	0	0	1	1	2.28			
AMARI DAWKINS	1	1	0	0	0	0	4.15			

INNING	1	2	3	4	5	6	7	8	9	TOTAL
CINCINNATI	0	0	0	0	2	0	1	0	0	3
CLEVELAND	0	1	0	3	0	2	0	0		6

GAME 88

By SAM LARDNER
The Cleveland Press

PITTSBURGH, July 15 — The unofficial second half of the season for the Cleveland Indians began not with a bang but with a thud.

In fact, the Indians who took the field Thursday night at beautiful PNC Park looked a lot like the bunch who spent most of the first half wallowing at or below mediocrity during a 4–0 loss to the Pittsburgh Pirates. Maybe the all-star break had something to do with sapping the momentum the Tribe had built during a weekend sweep of the Cincinnati Reds at Progressive Field.

Whatever, it was a decidedly flat effort put out by the Indians, who played this game before a good number of their own fans in the crowd of 20,172. They also played it in front of general manager J.D. Eisner, who also made the short trip to the confluence of the Three Rivers.

The GM is going to have plenty of decisions to make, chief among them whether to buy or sell as the July 31 trading deadline fast approaches.

"I think you'll see things heat up over the next week or 10 days," Eisner said before the game. "We still feel we're in the race, both in the division and for one of the two wild-card spots. This stretch of road games (nine away from Cleveland over the next 11) will tell us a lot. But we're operating on the premise that we're going to be in the race and looking to strengthen our ballclub."

Eisner could not have liked what he saw from his box high atop PNC Park. The Indians managed just five hits against Pirates starting pitcher Al Greco over seven innings and one against the Pittsburgh bullpen.

About the only bright spot was that second baseman Scott Michaels extended his hitting streak to eight games, going 1-for-4, a fifth-inning single.

Indians starting pitcher Brian Howard probably deserved a better fate. He worked 5 and two-thirds innings, giving up seven hits and all four runs three of them earned. Howard suffered his second straight defeat.

"I could have been sharper," The Doctor said. "I don't know if I felt too strong, having not pitched in awhile (his previous start was July 7). But the sinker stayed up instead of sinking, and that got me into trouble. Most of us sinkerballers like to feel a little tired so that the ball stays down. We'll get it back on track."

Howard gave up a pair of runs in the first. Sheridan McCall walked with one out, and Chad Jackson followed by taking a sinker that didn't sink and depositing into the Allegheny River beyond the right-field wall. Ernesto Galavan had an RBI double in the third.

An error by Michaels in the sixth led to an unearned run in the sixth. His throwing error with two outs put Galavan on second base, and Galavan scored on a single by Rueben Zanders.

"This was a little disappointing," said Indians manager Todd Stein, whose team fell to 45–43. "For whatever reason, we came out a little lethargic. I'm sure that will shock us back to life a little bit."

Stein's boss, Eisner, watched stone-faced with his cell phone pressed against his ear much of the night.

"I'm not privy to a lot of the trade talks," Stein said. "J.D. continues to work the phones. He wouldn't be doing his job otherwise. But like I've said before, we have the talent here to get it done. We'll see what happens, but I don't expect it to be a distraction."

CLEVELAND INDIANS VS PITTSBURGH PIRATES · JULY 15
PITTSBURGH 4 / CLEVELAND 0

CLEVELAND INDIANS										
BATTING	AB	R	H	RBI	2B	3B	HR	BB	SO	BA
RIKKI LABUDDA CF	4	0	0	0	0	0	0	1	0	.271
MICAH MILLISON RF	4	0	1	0	0	0	0	1	1	.309
WILSON WHITE LF	4	0	0	0	0	0	0	0	1	.274
TERRY ROVETTO 3B	3	0	1	0	0	0	0	1	0	.274
OLIVER REINER 1B	4	0	1	0	1	0	0	0	1	.267
SCOTT MICHAELS 2B	4	0	1	0	0	0	0	0	0	.331
JUSTIN KESTINO SS	4	0	1	0	0	0	0	0	0	.269
MORRIS JEROME C	4	0	0	0	0	0	0	0	0	.246
BRIAN HOWARD P	2	0	0	0	0	0	0	0	2	.000
BERNARD HARPER PH	1	0	0	0	0	0	0	0	1	.248
J.J. KULAKOFSKI PH	1	0	1	0	0	0	0	0	0	.237
PITCHING	IP	H	R	ER	SO	BB	ERA			
BRIAN HOWARD (L)	5.67	7	4	3	4	1	4.70			
LORRY UNGER	1.33	1	0	0	1	0	4.13			
MICKEY PENNY	1	1	0	0	0	1	3.53			
PITTSBURGH PIRATES										
BATTING	AB	R	H	RBI	2B	3B	HR	BB	SO	BA
RODERICK HENRIQUEZ CF	4	0	1	0	0	0	0	0	0	.259
SHERIDAN MCCALL 2B	3	1	1	0	0	0	0	1	1	.305
CHAD JACKSON LF	4	1	2	2	0	0	1	0	0	.271
ANDREW CARRINGTON 1B	3	0	1	0	0	0	0	1	1	.309
VALENTIN MACHADO SS	4	0	0	0	0	0	0	0	0	.263
ANIBAL PEREZ RF	4	1	2	0	0	0	0	0	1	.288
ERNESTO GALAVAN 3B	4	1	2	1	1	0	1	0	1	.287
RUEBEN ZANDERS C	4	0	1	1	0	0	0	0	0	.256
AL GRECO P	2	0	0	0	0	0	0	0	0	.000
MARTIN TEJADA PH	1	0	0	0	0	0	0	0	0	.250
MASON PHIBBS PH	1	0	0	0	0	0	0	0	0	.251
PITCHING	IP	H	R	ER	SO	BB	ERA			
AL GRECO (W)	7	5	0	0	5	2	3.80			
MAX WALLER	1	1	0	0	0	0	2.96			
LOGAN EDWARDS	1	0	0	0	1	0	2.49			
INNING	1	2	3	4	5	6	7	8	9	TOTAL
CLEVELAND	0	0	0	0	0	0	0	0	0	0
PITTSBURGH	2	0	1	0	0	1	0	0		4

GAME 89

By SAM LARDNER
The Cleveland Press

PITTSBURGH, July 16 — All back to normal now? The Indians seem to think so.

Kenny Camden couldn't agree more. After beginning post-all-star break play with a lackluster 4–0 loss to the Pittsburgh Pirates on Thursday, the Indians sharpened things up considerably Friday in a well-played 3–1 victory over the Bucs at PNC Park.

And, oh, yes, Camden picked up a victory for the first time since June 18, when the Tribe reached the .500 mark for the first time this season.

"Feels good," Camden said. "I had kind of forgotten that feeling. No, seriously, it was just good to get back on the winning track, for me and more importantly, for the team. We built such good momentum heading into the break and then kind of fell asleep last night. For me and at my age (32), the extra rest from the break was a good thing."

Camden went a cool seven innings, giving up five hits and one run, a fifth-inning homer to Andrew Carrington. He got all the run support he needed when Scott Michaels hit a three-run homer in the fourth after Terry Rovetto walked and Oliver Reiner singled against Blake Simpson. The homer was number 19 for Michaels and ties him for the club lead with Reiner.

From there, Camden cruised, and relievers Geno Milzie and Ivan Zyzna provided the kind of tidy relief work the Indians had become accustomed to late in the first half of the season.

"That's more like it," said Indians manager Todd Stein, whose ballclub improved to 46–43. "The Wiz (Camden) had it going today. He kept them off-balance by mixing his pitches. And Michaels? What more can I say about him? He's locked in pretty good right now. Maybe there's a chip on his shoulder from that all-star snub. I don't know. And I really don't care as long as he keeps it going."

Michaels has it going as well as anybody in Major League Baseball. He went 2-for-4, extending his hitting streak to nine games. Equally as impressive, he waited out Simpson, fouling off four straight pitches on a 3–2 count for his home run.

"He wasn't going to give in to me, that's for sure," Michaels said. "I think three of the pitches I fouled off were sliders. Finally, he hung one, and I was able to put a good swing on it."

Michaels' hot streak has gained the attention of the Pirates.

"That kid is something," said manager Gerardo Suarez. "He's not going to sneak up on anybody anymore. We don't see them much, being in the other league. But our scouts liked him an awful lot. You saw the way we pitched him. All credit to him for battling Simpson out and hitting the home run."

For the Indians, a healthy Michaels could go a long way toward determining if they make a postseason push.

"It's everybody, Stein said. "We've all got to come together and play well. But no question Scott is a big part of that. I'm not sure we would have or could have said that in April or May. But we're sure saying it now."

CLEVELAND INDIANS VS PITTSBURGH PIRATES • JULY 16
CLEVELAND 3 / PITTSBURGH 1

CLEVELAND INDIANS

BATTING	AB	R	H	RBI	2B	3B	HR	BB	SO	BA
RIKKI LABUDDA CF	3	0	1	0	0	0	0	1	0	.271
MICAH MILLISON RF	4	0	0	0	0	0	0	0	0	.305
WILSON WHITE LF	3	0	1	0	1	0	0	1	0	.274
TERRY ROVETTO 3B	3	1	0	0	0	0	0	1	0	.272
OLIVER REINER 1B	4	1	2	0	1	0	0	0	1	.270
SCOTT MICHAELS 2B	4	1	2	3	0	0	1	0	1	.333
JUSTIN KESTINO SS	4	0	1	0	0	0	0	0	1	.269
MORRIS JEROME C	4	0	1	0	0	0	0	0	0	.246
KENNY CAMDEN P	2	0	0	0	0	0	0	0	1	.000
BERNARD HARPER PH	1	0	0	0	0	0	0	0	1	.247
KIERAN CATSEF PH	1	0	0	0	0	0	0	0	0	.255

PITCHING	IP	H	R	ER	SO	BB	ERA			
KENNY CAMDEN (W)	7	5	1	1	4	2	3.36			
GENO MILZE	1	1	0	0	0	0	2.53			
IVAN ZYZNA (S)	1	0	0	0	1	0	1.37			

PITTSBURGH PIRATES

BATTING	AB	R	H	RBI	2B	3B	HR	BB	SO	BA
RODERICK HENRIQUEZ CF	4	0	1	0	1	0	0	0	0	.259
SHERIDAN MCCALL 2B	4	0	0	0	0	0	0	0	1	.301
CHAD JACKSON LF	4	0	0	0	0	0	0	0	1	.266
ANDREW CARRINGTON 1B	4	1	1	1	0	0	1	0	1	.308
VALENTIN MACHADO SS	3	0	0	0	0	0	0	1	0	.259
ANIBAL PEREZ RF	4	0	1	0	0	0	0	0	1	.287
ERNESTO GALAVAN 3B	3	0	1	0	0	0	0	1	0	.288
RUEBEN ZANDERS C	4	0	2	0	0	0	0	0	0	.262
BLAKE SIMPSON P	2	0	0	0	0	0	0	0	2	.000
ARMANDO CARMARGO PH	1	0	0	0	0	0	0	0	0	.249
CHET BAKER PH	1	0	0	0	0	0	0	0	0	.250

PITCHING	IP	H	R	ER	SO	BB	ERA			
BLAKE SIMPSON (L)	5	6	3	3	4	2	4.12			
JAIRO MONTES	2	1	0	0	0	1	3.18			
KIM YOUNG	2	1	0	0	1	0	4.76			

INNING	1	2	3	4	5	6	7	8	9	TOTAL
CLEVELAND	0	0	0	3	0	0	0	0	0	3
PITTSBURGH	0	0	0	0	1	0	0	0	0	1

GAME 90

By SAM LARDNER
The Cleveland Press

PITTSBURGH, July 17 — There's always an adaptability factor for players coming to the major leagues from Japan. More than halfway into this season, Indians pitcher Tak Fujimoto seems to be getting more comfortable by the day.

Of course, it helps when your team is scoring runs for you. Fujimoto's Tribe mates did that once again Saturday during a 7–4 victory over the Pittsburgh Pirates at PNC Park. That came on the heels of the Indians scoring 16 for Fujimoto in his previous start, a 16–4 victory over the Cincinnati Reds.

"The support from my teammates has been tremendous," Fujimoto said through his translator.

Presumably, Fujimoto was talking about moral support. But the run support is even more welcome.

"It helps to have such good teammates, and it helps when they're scoring runs for you," he said with a smile, flashing some of the humor that has become more apparent as the season has worn on. "I was welcomed here from the beginning, and my teammates stood by me early on when I was trying to settle in and get comfortable. I will try to do my part to repay them."

Fujimoto worked six innings against the Bucs, giving up six hits and three runs. Indians batters belted out 11 hits, eight against Pirates starting pitcher Luke Pollard and three relievers.

Once again, the story was hot-hitting second baseman Scott Michaels, who went 3-for-5 with a three-run double in the third that put the Indians up 3–0. Michaels' hitting streak now is in double figures at 10 games, during which he has gone 17-for-37 (.459).

"I don't think I ever went more than seven or eight games in a row in the minor leagues," Michaels said. "This is definitely new territory. Actually, so is playing every day in the big leagues. I'm really enjoying it."

So is his manager.

"The hitting streak is nice, but the fact that he's helping us win ballgames is really heartening," said Todd Stein. "I said I was going to write him in there every day once he took the job and ran with it. I have no plans on changing that."

Michaels singled and scored on a two-run single in the fifth by Bernard Harper, who was in today subbing for Terry Rovetto. The Indians chased Pollard in the sixth, when they scored twice. Rikki LaBudda doubled and then went to third on Micah Millison's groundout. Wilson White walked and Oliver Reiner brought them both home on a triple.

Fujimoto gave up a three-run homer to Anibal Perez in the bottom of the sixth to make the game somewhat interesting. Lorry Unger gave up a run in the seventh before Mickey Penney and Lee Hazelton finished without incident.

So the Indians got out of Pittsburgh winning two of three and improving to 47–43 before heading to Houston.

"That's a good way to start the second half," Stein said. "It's a totally different feeling from being 0–6 to start the season. If we can get through this road-heavy portion of the schedule okay, it sets up well for us going forward."

CLEVELAND INDIANS VS PITTSBURGH PIRATES · JULY 17
CLEVELAND 7 / PITTSBURGH 4

CLEVELAND INDIANS

BATTING	AB	R	H	RBI	2B	3B	HR	BB	SO	BA
RIKKI LABUDDA CF	5	1	1	0	1	0	0	0	0	.270
MICAH MILLISON RF	4	0	0	0	0	0	0	1	0	.301
WILSON WHITE LF	4	2	2	0	1	0	0	1	0	.277
OLIVER REINER 1B	5	1	2	2	0	1	0	0	1	.272
SCOTT MICHAELS 2B	5	1	3	3	1	0	0	0	1	.339
JUSTIN KESTINO SS	4	1	1	0	1	0	0	0	0	.269
BERNARD HARPER 3B	4	1	2	2	0	0	0	0	1	.251
ICEBERG PETERS C	3	0	0	0	0	0	0	1	0	.214
TAK FUJIMOTO P	3	0	0	0	0	0	0	0	1	.000
LORRY UNGER P	1	0	0	0	0	0	0	0	0	.000
MICKEY PENNY P	1	0	0	0	0	0	0	0	0	.000

PITCHING	IP	H	R	ER	SO	BB	ERA
TAK FUJIMOTO (W)	6	6	3	3	6	2	3.26
LORRY UNGER	1	1	1	1	0	0	4.32
MICKEY PENNY	1	0	0	0	1	1	3.44
LEE HAZELTON (S)	1	1	0	0	0	0	3.57

PITTSBURGH PIRATES

BATTING	AB	R	H	RBI	2B	3B	HR	BB	SO	BA
RODERICK HENRIQUEZ CF	4	1	2	0	1	0	0	0	0	.262
SHERIDAN MCCALL 2B	4	0	0	0	0	0	0	0	1	.297
CHAD JACKSON LF	3	1	1	1	0	0	0	1	0	.267
ANDREW CARRINGTON 1B	3	1	2	0	0	0	0	1	1	.314
VALENTIN MACHADO SS	4	0	1	0	0	0	0	0	0	.259
ANIBAL PEREZ RF	3	1	2	3	0	0	1	1	0	.293
ERNESTO GALAVAN 3B	4	0	1	0	0	0	0	1	2	.287
RUEBEN ZANDERS C	4	0	0	0	0	0	0	0	0	.256
LUKE POLLARD P	2	0	0	0	0	0	0	0	2	.000
ARMANDO CARMARGO PH	1	0	0	0	0	0	0	0	0	.248
CHET BAKER PH	1	0	0	0	0	0	0	0	1	.249

PITCHING	IP	H	R	ER	SO	BB	ERA
LUKE POLLARD (L)	5.3	9	5	5	3	2	4.28
NICK RANDOLPH	0.67	1	0	0	1	0	3.33
MAX WALLER	2	2	2	2	0	1	3.38
JAIRO MONTES	1	1	0	0	1	0	3.07

INNING	1	2	3	4	5	6	7	8	9	TOTAL
CLEVELAND	0	0	3	0	2	2	0	0	0	7
PITTSBURGH	0	0	0	0	0	3	1	0	0	4

GAME 91

By SAM LARDNER
The Cleveland Press

HOUSTON, July 18 — Indians manager Todd Stein has done his best this year to keep his starting rotation fresh, mostly by limiting pitch counts.

Ace pitcher Lynn Moda may have been a little overripe Sunday during an 8–3 loss to the Houston Astros at Minute Maid Park.

Moda lasted 4 and two-thirds innings, giving up eight hits and four runs as the Indians fell to 47–44 but stayed within seven games of first-place Minnesota and three of second-place Chicago in the American League Central.

Moda had not worked since July 10, and with the all-star break intervening, he got extra rest rather than have his turn moved up in the rotation.

Did that plan backfire?

"No, no, not at all," Moda said. "Most of the time I would prefer the work. You have heard a lot of us veterans say that our stuff works better — sinks more — when we're a little tired. But look, that would be an excuse, and you know that I don't make excuses. It was just a (lousy) day out there today."

Stein also wasn't second-guessing himself.

"We talked before the break," the manager said. "Everybody knew the plan and was on board with it. Guys like Modes and The Doc (Brian Howard) have some innings on their arms, and we're trying to protect them. Modes will bounce back, and so will we."

This one began innocently enough, with Moda mowing down the Astros 1-2-3 in the first and giving up a hit in a scoreless second.

The retractable roof fell in — figuratively, of course — in the third, when the Astros went rapid-fire to score four runs.

Ted Shaughnessy clanked a leadoff double off the metal scoreboard in left field. Kal Schoor promptly singled Shaughnessy home, taking second base on center fielder Rikki LaBudda's throw home. Moda lost control and walked Dan Olsen and Ken Ritter before Barry Sidell's double to center cleared the bases.

"That happened kind of fast," Moda said. "The hits weren't the problem. The walks were. That's not my game. I was asking for trouble, and I got it."

The Indians got two back in the fifth on Scott Michaels' single off Samee Greenlee, scoring LaBudda and Micah Millison. That extended Michaels' hitting streak to 11 games and was about the only bright spot for the Tribe all day.

Given how hot Michaels has been, Stein has moved him up to third in the order. That's a far cry from the start of the season, when the former phenom was lucky to get any kind of playing time.

"Trying to strike when the iron is hot," Stein said. "You want your No. 3 hitter to be your best hitter, and Scottie certainly is that now. We've been riding him the last couple of months, and we'll ride him in this spot in the order until further notice."

The Indians got a solo homer from Terry Rovetto in the sixth. The Astros picked up a pair of runs off Lorry Unger and two more off Buck Sterling.

"They're tough," Stein said of the Astros. "When the roof is closed here, this place holds noise, too. We'll run the same look out there tomorrow and expect better results."

CLEVELAND INDIANS VS HOUSTON ASTROS · JULY 18
HOUSTON 8 / CLEVELAND 3

CLEVELAND INDIANS

BATTING	AB	R	H	RBI	2B	3B	HR	BB	SO	BA
RIKKI LABUDDA CF	4	1	2	0	1	0	0	0	0	.273
MICAH MILLISON RF	3	1	2	0	0	0	0	1	0	.304
SCOTT MICHAELS 2B	4	0	1	2	1	0	0	0	1	.337
TERRY ROVETTO 3B	4	1	2	1	0	0	1	0	1	.275
WILSON WHITE LF	4	0	0	0	0	0	0	0	0	.274
JUSTIN KESTINO SS	4	0	1	0	1	0	0	0	0	.268
BERNARD HARPER DH	3	0	1	0	0	0	0	1	0	.252
J.J. KULAKOFSKI 1B	4	0	1	0	0	0	0	0	1	.237
MORRIS JEROME C	3	0	0	0	0	0	0	0	2	.243

PITCHING	IP	H	R	ER	SO	BB	ERA			
LYNN MODES (L)	4.67	8	4	4	3	3	4.25			
LORRY UNGER	2.33	4	2	2	1	0	4.61			
BUCK STERLING	1	3	2	2	0	1	3.86			

HOUSTON ASTROS

BATTING	AB	R	H	RBI	2B	3B	HR	BB	SO	BA
KEN RITTER RF	4	2	2	0	0	0	0	1	0	.275
BARRY SIDELL C	5	0	1	3	1	0	0	0	0	.299
JOE BANKHEAD SS	4	1	1	0	0	0	0	1	0	.266
ALBERT CHEVEZ 2B	5	0	2	2	0	1	0	0	2	.311
DAVEY JAMPOLIS DH	5	1	2	0	1	0	0	0	0	.292
LUKE BARLOW LF	4	1	2	0	0	0	0	1	0	.276
TED SHAUGHNESSY 1B	5	1	2	2	2	0	0	0	0	.270
KAL SCHOOR 3B	4	1	1	1	0	0	0	0	1	.262
DAN OLSEN CF	3	1	2	0	0	0	0	1	1	.252

PITCHING	IP	H	R	ER	SO	BB	ERA			
SAMEE GREENLEE (W)	8	9	3	3	5	2	3.80			
TOMMY HURST	1	1	0	0	0	0	2.63			

INNING	1	2	3	4	5	6	7	8	9	TOTAL
CLEVELAND	0	0	0	0	2	1	0	0	0	3
HOUSTON	0	0	4	0	0	2	0	2		8

GAME 92

By SAM LARDNER
The Cleveland Press

HOUSTON, July 19   There's no other way to put it: Ollie Gonzalez has been the goods for the Indians.

For the last month, whenever Gonzalez has tossed his glove out there, the results have been golden. Such was the case Monday night as the Tribe engaged in a rare pitcher's duel with the Houston Astros.

But never fear, Ollie G was near. Gonzalez made his first start since the all-star break, and the big lefty dominated. He worked seven innings, limiting the Astros to four hits as the Indians came away with a 2–1 victory at Minute Maid Park, improving his record to 9 and 7.

The Indians improved to 48–44 and pulled to within six games of the first-place Twins and to within two of the second-place White Sox in the suddenly rugged American League Central.

And, oh yes, second baseman Scott Michaels had a hand in this one. The new No. 3 hitter in the Cleveland lineup went 3-for-4 with a two-run homer in the fifth, his 20th, extending his hitting streak to 12 games.

"That guy is something," Gonzalez said, referring to his teammate and downplaying his own performance. "Honestly, I don't know where we'd be without him."

Manager Todd Stein praised both of the game's stars. "We got great pitching from Ollie and just enough offense, thanks to Scottie," Stein said.

"They both deserve a lot of credit. This little run that we've made has been in large part due to both of them."

Gonzalez has not been part of an Indians loss since June 21, and back then, the bullpen blew a game for him. Against the Astros, Gonzalez was perfect through the first three innings. The Astros got a one-out single from Albert Chevez in the fourth, but Gonzalez struck out Kal Schoor and Luke Barlow. Michaels' homered in the fifth after Micah Millison walked against Astros starting pitcher Arthur Brashler. Michaels took a 2–0 pitch and launched it onto the railroad tracks atop the wall in left field.

"It's been a lot of fun lately," Michaels said. "The most fun of all is winning. You're going to have to remind me about the hitting streak. I don't keep track. Twelve? OK. Twelve. Let me know when it gets to 56."

That drew a big laugh from the Cleveland and Houston media, with Michaels referring to Joe DiMaggio's seemingly untouchable 56-game hitting streak.

The Astros got their lone run when Davey Jampolis homered off Gonzalez in sixth. Stein allowed Gonzalez to run the pitch count to 115 before opting for reliable relievers Geno Milzie and Ivan Zyzna for the final two innings.

"Ollie was pretty well-rested," Stein said. "There are different ways of getting to 100 or 115 pitches, and Ollie got there with a minimum of stress. You saw how free and easy he was throwing it. We keep tabs on the pitch counts, but we're also aware of how hard or not a guy is working. He was dealing and Ivan pitched a perfect ninth to seal the win."

CLEVELAND INDIANS VS HOUSTON ASTROS • JULY 19
CLEVELAND 2 / HOUSTON 1

CLEVELAND INDIANS										
BATTING	AB	R	H	RBI	2B	3B	HR	BB	SO	BA
RIKKI LABUDDA CF	4	0	2	0	1	0	0	0	1	.275
MICAH MILLISON RF	3	1	0	0	0	0	0	1	0	.302
SCOTT MICHAELS 2B	4	1	3	2	0	0	1	0	0	.343
TERRY ROVETTO 3B	4	0	1	0	0	0	0	0	1	.274
OLIVER REINER 1B	4	0	1	0	0	0	0	0	0	.272
WILSON WHITE LF	3	0	1	0	1	0	0	1	0	.274
JUSTIN KESTINO SS	4	0	0	0	0	0	0	0	1	.265
BERNARD HARPER DH	4	0	0	0	0	0	0	0	1	.248
MORRIS JEROME C	4	0	1	0	0	0	0	0	1	.243
PITCHING	IP	H	R	ER	SO	BB	ERA			
OLLIE GONZALEZ (W)	7	4	1	1	7	2	4.21			
GENO MILZIE	1	1	0	0	0	0	2.47			
IVAN ZYZNA (S)	1	0	0	0	1	0	1.32			

HOUSTON ASTROS										
BATTING	AB	R	H	RBI	2B	3B	HR	BB	SO	BA
KEN RITTER RF	4	0	1	0	0	0	0	0	0	.275
BARRY SIDELL C	4	0	0	0	0	0	0	0	2	.295
DAVEY JAMPOLIS DH	3	1	2	1	0	0	1	1	1	.298
ALBERT CHEVEZ 2B	4	0	1	0	0	0	0	0	0	.309
KAL SCHOOR 3B	4	0	0	0	0	0	0	0	0	.256
LUKE BARLOW LF	4	0	0	0	0	0	0	0	2	.270
TED SHAUGHNESSY 1B	3	0	1	0	1	0	0	1	0	.271
PORFI PADILLA SS	4	0	0	0	0	0	0	0	2	.264
DAN OLSEN CF	4	0	0	0	0	0	0	0	1	.243
PITCHING	IP	H	R	ER	SO	BB	ERA			
ARTHUR BRASHLER (L)	7	7	2	2	4	2	3.96			
MAURY WYNN	2	2	0	0	1	0	3.18			

INNING	1	2	3	4	5	6	7	8	9	TOTAL
CLEVELAND	0	0	0	0	2	0	0	0	0	2
HOUSTON	0	0	0	0	0	1	0	0	0	1

GAME 93

By SAM LARDNER
The Cleveland Press

HOUSTON, July 20 — The Cleveland Indians suddenly have a pitching problem. Maybe more than one.

Brian Howard was lit up for all six runs Tuesday night in a 6–2 loss to the Houston Astros at Minute Maid Park. The Indians (48–45) lost two of three in this series, getting outscored 15–7 in the three games.

Howard's struggles, however, might be the least of the Tribe's problems at this point. Before the game, manager Todd Stein announced that Monday's starter, Ollie G, is suffering from left-shoulder "fatigue" and that he may miss his next start.

The Indians rotation has been dependable and healthy, if not spectacular, for most of the season, so a long-term injury to No. 2 starter Gonzalez could be a serious blow to the team's chances for a postseason bid.

General manager J.D. Eisner was not in Houston, but he's expected to address the situation when the Indians return home Wednesday to face the Toronto Blue Jays for the start of a short two-game series and two-game homestand.

If Gonzalez has to go on the injured list, the Indians may have to make a minor-league call-up or go with a spot starter or an "opener" to fill that spot in the rotation. A long-term injury may put extra pressure on Eisner to make a deal for a starting pitcher before the July 31 trading deadline.

Gonzalez is expected to have an MRI performed at the Cleveland Clinic.

"Right now it's all speculation," Stein said. "We'll know more once we get home and see what the doctors say. Ollie will probably miss at least one start. Beyond that, I don't know. But yes, it would leave a big hole in our rotation. The guy is a horse."

The Indians already have Solly Alvarez on the IL, but he's completing a minor-league rehab stint with Class AAA Columbus. He's a possibility for a spot start, or the Indians could go with Mickey Penney, Buck Sterling or Lorry Unger as a spot starter or opener.

As for Tuesday's game, Howard was in trouble from the get-go, as he gave up a pair of runs in the first inning on Kal Schoor's two run single.

After settling down in the second, Howard allowed two more in the third and two in the fourth, as he lasted just 3 and two-thirds innings.

"The Doc just didn't have it," Stein said of Howard. "Luckily, Ollie was able to go seven last night, so the bullpen was able to pick up the slack."

There may have been some irony in those words, with Gonzalez coming up lame, but Unger, Sterling, Penney and Lee Hazelton were able to work the rest of the game and not give up any more runs.

Veteran Howard was contrite.

"I put us in a bad spot," he said. "Who knows how long Ollie is going to be out? We're going to need to step up as a starting staff and make sure we don't kill the bullpen. I made a few bad pitches tonight and walked some guys. I need to get back on track."

The Indians have lost the last three games that Howard has started. Their only bright spot in this game was that Scott Michaels extended his hitting streak to 13 games by going 2-for-5 with a two-run triple in the fourth that knocked in Rikki LaBudda and Micah Millison. LaBudda walked against Leon Higgins, and Millison singled him to third. Justin Kestino also contributed three hits in the losing cause.

"You'd like to do that in a winning effort," said Michaels, who is 23-for-45 during the streak. "But that's the way it goes sometimes."

CLEVELAND INDIANS VS HOUSTON ASTROS · JULY 20
HOUSTON 6 / CLEVELAND 2

CLEVELAND INDIANS										
BATTING	AB	R	H	RBI	2B	3B	HR	BB	SO	BA
RIKKI LABUDDA CF	4	1	0	0	0	0	0	1	0	.272
MICAH MILLISON RF	4	1	1	0	0	0	0	0	0	.301
SCOTT MICHAELS 2B	5	0	2	2	0	1	0	0	0	.344
TERRY ROVETTO 3B	4	0	0	0	0	0	0	0	2	.271
OLIVER REINER 1B	3	0	0	0	0	0	0	1	0	.270
WILSON WHITE LF	3	0	0	0	0	0	0	1	0	.272
JUSTIN KESTINO SS	4	0	3	0	0	0	0	0	0	.271
BERNARD HARPER DH	4	0	0	0	0	0	0	0	1	.244
MORRIS JEROME C	4	0	1	0	0	0	0	0	2	.243
PITCHING	IP	H	R	ER	SO	BB	ERA			
BRIAN HOWARD (L)	3.67	7	6	6	1	1	5.05			
LORRY UNGER	1.33	1	0	0	1	0	4.40			
BUCK STERLING	2	1	0	0	2	1	3.68			
LEE HAZELTON	1	0	0	0	1	0	2.73			
HOUSTON ASTROS										
BATTING	AB	R	H	RBI	2B	3B	HR	BB	SO	BA
KEN RITTER RF	5	1	2	1	1	0	0	0	0	.277
BARRY SIDELL C	4	0	0	0	0	0	0	1	0	.292
DAVEY JAMPOLIS DH	4	2	2	0	0	0	0	0	0	.301
KAL SCHOOR 3B	4	1	2	2	1	0	0	0	1	.261
ALBERT CHAVEZ 2B	4	0	1	2	0	0	0	0	1	.308
LUKE BARLOW LF	4	1	1	0	0	0	0	0	0	.270
TED SHAUGHNESSY 1B	4	0	0	0	0	0	0	0	1	.265
PORFI PADILLA SS	3	1	0	0	0	0	0	1	0	.255
JOE BANKHEAD SS	1	0	0	0	0	0	0	0	0	.265
DAN OLSEN LF	4	0	1	1	0	0	0	0	2	.243
PITCHING	IP	H	R	ER	SO	BB	ERA			
LEON HIGGINS (W)	7	6	2	2	4	2	4.08			
HARMON KUROWSKI	2	1	0	0	1	1	3.49			

INNING	1	2	3	4	5	6	7	8	9	TOTAL
CLEVELAND	0	0	0	2	0	0	0	0	0	2
HOUSTON	2	0	2	2	0	0	0	0		6

GAME 94

By SAM LARDNER

The Cleveland Press

CLEVELAND, July 21 — The way this season has been going for the Indians, Wednesday's mixed bag of news should come as no surprise to anybody who has been following the team.

First, the good news for the Indians and their fans: The Tribe beat the Toronto Blue Jays 5–3 at Progressive Field behind the pitching of Kenny Camden and the exquisitely hot hitting of second baseman Scott Michaels, who went 4-for-5 with a three-run homer extend his hitting streak to 14 games.

Now for the bad news: Indians No. 2 starting pitcher Ollie Gonzalez went on the injured list with what was termed "left-shoulder fatigue." The Indians activated reliever Solly Alvarez off the IL, and he may get a spot start or be the "opener" in Gonzalez's next scheduled start.

Gonzalez will have an MRI performed at the Cleveland Clinic on Thursday. As to how long Gonzalez might be out, general manager J.D. Eisner said he didn't want to speculate.

"Let's get the result of the MRI back," he said. "Ollie is a big strong guy, and he even said he's feeling a little better today. But we're not going to take any chances, and we're not going to jump to any conclusions. Our rotation is a good one, and we have a number of options to fill Ollie's spot on a temporary basis."

Is one of those options a trade, with the July 31 deadline to make a deal fast approaching?

"That's always a possibility," Eisner said. "There's nothing in the works right now, but we've been in contact with a lot of teams, even before this (injury to Gonzalez) came about."

Gonzalez, who was not available to the media, worked seven innings in Monday's 2–1 victory at Houston.

Camden gave the Tribe a much-need solid start against the Blue Jays, working 6 and one-third innings and giving up six hits and three runs. His only sin was yielding a three-run double to Jermaine Brown in the sixth, a hit that hastened his exit. Mr. Reliable, Ivan Zyzna pitched a perfect ninth for his ninth save.

"We've all got to chip in, and we're all capable," Camden said. "Losing Ollie could be a big blow, but injuries are part of the game. We've all been there. The good teams find a way to overcome."

As for Michaels, he wasted no time getting the Indians on the board with his first-inning three-run blast off Armando Ojeda. Rikki LaBudda started the inning with a walk and went to third on Micah Millison's single to right field and both scored on the home run.

Michaels singled in the third and scored on a double by Terry Rovetto. Oliver Reiner added a solo home run in the seventh. As for Michaels, he added an infield single in the sixth and a double in the eighth. During the streak, Michaels is an otherworldly 27-for-50.

"Yeah, it's been something," he said. "I joked about starting a hitting streak a couple weeks ago, but I had no idea it would be getting this out of hand."

If it does, that's quite OK with his manager.

"Oh, yeah, I'll take it, said Todd Stein with a smile. "Honestly, with all the ups and downs we've had — and now with Ollie's injury — I don't know where we'd be without Scottie. Let him stay as hot as he wants."

CLEVELAND INDIANS VS TORONTO BLUE JAYS · JULY 21
CLEVELAND 5 / TORONTO 3

CLEVELAND INDIANS										
BATTING	AB	R	H	RBI	2B	3B	HR	BB	SO	BA
RIKKI LABUDDA CF	4	1	1	0	0	0	0	1	0	.272
MICAH MILLISON RF	4	1	1	0	0	0	0	0	0	.300
SCOTT MICHAELS 2B	5	0	4	3	1	0	1	0	0	.353
TERRY ROVETTO 3B	4	1	1	1	1	0	0	0	0	.271
OLIVER REINER 1B	3	1	1	1	0	0	1	0	0	.270
WILSON WHITE LF	3	0	0	0	0	0	0	0	0	.269
LEO TAYLOR SS	4	0	1	0	0	0	0	0	0	.281
BERNARD HARPER DH	3	0	1	0	0	0	0	1	1	.245
MORRIS JEROME C	4	0	0	0	0	0	0	0	2	.240
PITCHING	IP	H	R	ER	SO	BB	ERA			
KENNY CAMDEN (W)	6.33	7	3	3	6	2	3.41			
LORRY UNGER	1.67	1	0	0	1	0	4.15			
IVAN ZYZNA (S)	1	1	0	0	2	0	1.27			

TORONTO BLUE JAYS										
BATTING	AB	R	H	RBI	2B	3B	HR	BB	SO	BA
CARLOS ARNALDO CF	4	1	1	0	0	0	0	0	0	.293
ANDY TENZER 3B	4	1	0	0	0	0	0	0	2	.306
RAMON ORTIZ SS	4	1	2	0	0	0	0	0	0	.257
RAYMOND BALKMAN 1B	3	0	0	0	0	0	0	1	2	.302
JERMAINE BROWN LF	4	0	1	3	1	0	0	0	0	.285
JEFF STEPHANS DH	4	0	0	0	0	0	0	0	1	.272
JOEL NISSALKE 2B	4	0	0	0	0	0	0	0	2	.284
ROYCE MANFRED RF	4	0	1	0	1	0	0	0	0	.237
RICO ESPINOSA C	3	0	0	0	0	0	0	1	2	.268
PITCHING	IP	H	R	ER	SO	BB	ERA			
ARMANDO OJEDA (L)	5.33	6	4	4	1	1	3.50			
JAMIE SHEDLER	1.67	3	0	0	1	0	3.67			
LARRY BRAVERMAN	1	1	0	0	1	0	3.14			

INNING	1	2	3	4	5	6	7	8	9	TOTAL
TORONTO	0	0	0	0	0	3	0	0	0	3
CLEVELAND	3	0	1	0	0	0	1	0		5

GAME 95

By SAM LARDNER
The Cleveland Press

CLEVELAND, July 22 — The mantra with the Indians' pitching staff is now "next man up."

It's going to be that way for a while with Thursday's news that left-hander Ollie Gonzalez will be on the injured list for at least three weeks with a left-shoulder strain.

That news came a couple hours before Tak Fujimoto took the "next man up" motto to heart and pitched the Tribe to a 4–1 victory over the Toronto Blue Jays at Progressive Field.

The Indians improved to 50–45, with their best man up at the plate, Scott Michaels, who continues to crush it extending his hitting streak to 15 games. Michaels went 2-for-4 with a two-run homer off Dean Pinto in the third to stake Fujimoto to a 2–0 lead.

The Blue Jays came to within 2–1 on Julian Gomez's RBI double in the fourth driving in Royce Manfred, but that was it. The Indians got two more in the sixth on a two-run single by backup catcher Iceberg Peters.

So where do the Indians go from here? First, they head to New York for a big weekend series against the Yankees.

As far as the pitching goes, ace Lynn Moda is lined up to start the first game of the series, with reliever Solly Alvarez acting as the "opener" for Saturday's game. Manager Todd Stein said he would allow Alvarez to go one or two innings before matching up with the bullpen after that.

"It's the situation we're in," Stein said after the Indians wrapped up a short two homestand. "Everybody is going to need to step up, and I think they will. The rotation has been pretty solid, for the most part, all year. We chose Solly for Saturday because he's fresh off the IL and has been champing at the bit. He's started earlier in his career and understands what's being asked of him."

Indians general manager J.D. Eisner said an MRI performed on Gonzalez showed no structural damage to the shoulder.

"That's about the best we could have hoped for," Eisner said. "We're going to have Ollie not pick up a ball for a about a week. After that, we'll see. He can probably begin a throwing program before going out on a rehab stint."

Does this put pressure on Eisner to make a deal?

"Not necessarily," the GM said. "We're talking. You can never have too much pitching depth. But we'll need five starters long term, and we're not averse to going with six for a time once Ollie gets back. So the short answer is we'd be interested in adding if the right deal is out there."

One guy who won't be moved is Michaels. He is now 29-for-54 during the hitting streak.

"I'm not used to talking to you guys every day," he said to the media. "But this is a lot of fun. I'm enjoying it. How long can it go? I don't know. I don't want to jinx it, but you guys keep reminding me of it every day. So, we'll see."

Fujimoto worked seven innings, giving up six hits before Geno Milzie and Ivan Zyzna worked the eighth and ninth, respectively. Nominally the fifth starter, he doesn't see it that way.

"I feel like I'm a No. 1 starter ever time I'm out there," Fujimoto said through his translator. "That's what I was in Japan. I know we have an injury situation now, so each of us is going to have to pitch like a No. 1. I like that challenge."

GAME 95

CLEVELAND INDIANS VS TORONTO BLUE JAYS · JULY 22
CLEVELAND 4 / TORONTO 1

CLEVELAND INDIANS										
BATTING	AB	R	H	RBI	2B	3B	HR	BB	SO	BA
RIKKI LABUDDA CF	4	1	2	0	0	1	0	1	1	.274
MICAH MILLISON RF	4	0	0	0	0	0	0	0	1	.297
SCOTT MICHAELS 2B	4	1	2	2	0	0	1	0	1	.355
TERRY ROVETTO 3B	3	0	0	0	0	0	0	1	1	.269
OLIVER REINER 1B	3	0	0	0	0	0	0	1	1	.268
WILSON WHITE LF	4	1	2	0	1	0	0	0	0	.272
JUSTIN KESTINO SS	3	0	0	0	0	0	0	0	1	.269
BERNARD HARPER DH	3	1	2	0	0	0	0	1	1	.250
ICEBERG PETERS C	4	0	1	2	0	0	0	0	1	.216
PITCHING	IP	H	R	ER	SO	BB	ERA			
TAK FUJIMOTO (W)	7	6	1	1	7	2	3.14			
GENO MILZIE	1	1	0	0	0	0	2.42			
IVAN ZYZNA (S)	1	0	0	0	1	0	1.23			

TORONTO BLUE JAYS										
BATTING	AB	R	H	RBI	2B	3B	HR	BB	SO	BA
CARLOS ARNALDO CF	4	0	2	0	0	0	0	0	0	.296
ANDY TENZER 3B	3	0	0	0	0	0	0	1	1	.302
RAMON ORTIZ SS	3	0	0	0	0	0	0	1	0	.254
RAYMOND BALKMAN 1B	4	0	1	0	0	0	0	0	2	.302
JERMAINE BROWN LF	4	0	1	0	1	0	0	0	2	.285
JEFF STEPHANS DH	4	0	1	0	0	0	0	0	1	.271
JOEL NISSALKE 2B	4	0	0	0	0	0	0	0	1	.279
ROYCE MANFRED RF	4	1	1	0	1	0	0	0	0	.237
JULIAN GOMEZ C	3	0	1	1	1	0	0	0	1	.269
PITCHING	IP	H	R	ER	SO	BB	ERA			
DEAN PINTO (L)	6	8	4	4	7	4	3.66			
BUDDY HARKNESS	2	1	0	0	0	1	3.12			

INNING	1	2	3	4	5	6	7	8	9	TOTAL
TORONTO	0	0	0	1	0	0	0	0	0	1
CLEVELAND	0	0	2	0	0	2	0	0		4

GAME 96

By SAM LARDNER
The Cleveland Press

NEW YORK, July 23 — The Big Apple is neither too big nor too bright for a couple of Cleveland Indians players.

Ace pitcher Lynn Moda won his second straight start at Yankee Stadium, an impressive 3–1 decision Friday night before 52,124 fans who were in the game from start to finish. Moda went 6 and two-thirds innings and gave up five hits and was charged with the New York run. The other ready-for-prime-time player is second baseman Scott Michaels.

He didn't shrink under the bright lights as he extended his hitting streak to 16 games by going 2-for-5 with a single and an RBI double. Most important for the Indians, they won their third straight to improve to 51–45 and pulled within five games of the first-place Minnesota Twins in the American League Central and into a tie for second place with the Chicago White Sox.

They did it in most impressive fashion. Moda matched Yankees ace Gregg Sterney pitch for pitch, tiring in the seventh, when the Yankees got to within 2–1 on Bobby Faulhaber's single off reliever Lee Hazelton after Moda put a pair of runners aboard. Wilson White got the run back in the eighth with a homer off of Steve Salinas that curled around the foul pole in left field.

This wasn't the first time Moda came up big in the Big Apple. He and the offense kept the Indians from getting swept here in early June.

"Oh, it's fun pitching here," Moda said. "The crowd is always loud. Some guys might be intimidated by that, but I feed off it. With the game being close, I was bearing down on every pitch. I made a little bit of a mess in the seventh by giving up a walk and a hit. I put Haze in a bad spot. Those relievers don't have much margin for error when they come in. But we got the result in the end."

Hazelton settled down to work the eighth inning before Ivan Zyzna closed it out in the ninth.

Michaels got his first taste of the New York media both before and after the game. He extended his streak in the first inning with a two-out single to center field. He doubled home Micah Millison in the third after Millison walked and went to second on Sterney's wild pitch.

"Whoa, coming from Versailles, Ohio, I'm not used to this," said Michaels, who is 31-for-59. "Now I know what they say about New York. But hey, I'm just a baseball player. I love playing the game. To play in Yankee Stadium is any kid's dream."

The Indians might be drawing more attention, with them suddenly in contention and Michaels hitting every baseball in sight.

"That's OK," said manager Todd Stein, who took over as interim boss after 10 games of the season. "I didn't expect to be in this position, either, at the start of the year. This is all kind of new to me, too. But this is what you live for, and what better stage than Broadway?"

CLEVELAND INDIANS VS NEW YORK YANKEES · JULY 23
CLEVELAND 3 / NEW YORK 1

CLEVELAND INDIANS										
BATTING	AB	R	H	RBI	2B	3B	HR	BB	SO	BA
RIKKI LABUDDA CF	3	0	0	0	0	0	0	2	0	.272
MICAH MILLISON RF	4	1	1	0	0	0	0	1	0	.296
SCOTT MICHAELS 2B	5	0	2	1	1	0	0	0	1	.356
TERRY ROVETTO 3B	4	0	1	0	0	0	0	1	0	.268
OLIVER REINER 1B	4	1	1	0	0	0	0	0	2	.268
WILSON WHITE LF	4	1	1	1	0	0	1	0	1	.272
JUSTIN KESTINO SS	4	0	0	0	0	0	0	0	1	.265
BERNARD HARPER DH	4	0	1	1	1	0	0	0	0	.250
MORRIS JEROME C	4	0	0	0	0	0	0	0	2	.236

PITCHING	IP	H	R	ER	SO	BB	ERA			
LYNN MODA (W)	6.67	5	1	1	5	2	4.08			
LEE HAZELTON	1.33	2	0	0	1	0	2.61			
IVAN ZYZNA (S)	1	0	0	0	0	0	1.19			

NEW YORK YANKEES										
BATTING	AB	R	H	RBI	2B	3B	HR	BB	SO	BA
MARK STRANTON CF	4	1	2	0	1	0	0	0	0	.298
WILLIE ROBINSON 3B	4	0	0	0	0	0	0	0	0	.306
BOBBY FAULHABER DH	4	0	1	1	0	0	0	0	2	.277
GUILLERMO CRUZ 1B	3	0	1	0	0	0	0	1	1	.302
RICK STEINBERG C	4	0	0	0	0	0	0	0	2	.280
JAKE KOENIG SS	4	0	0	0	0	0	0	0	0	.267
NICK WRIGHT RF	4	0	0	0	0	0	0	0	0	.275
GARY ASHCROFT LF	4	0	2	0	1	0	0	0	0	.241
LEONARD LEE 2B	3	0	1	0	0	0	0	1	1	.270

PITCHING	IP	H	R	ER	SO	BB	ERA			
GREG STERNEY (L)	7	6	3	3	6	3	2.63			
STEVE SALINAS	2	1	0	0	1	1	3.27			

INNING	1	2	3	4	5	6	7	8	9	TOTAL
CLEVELAND	0	0	1	0	0	1	0	1	0	3
NEW YORK	0	0	0	0	0	0	1	0	0	1

GAME 97

By SAM LARDNER
The Cleveland Press

NEW YORK, July 23 — For openers, not bad.

Actually, it was very good Saturday for Indians pitcher Solly Alvarez. Indians manager Todd Stein was hoping to get an inning or two out of Alvarez as the "opener" against the New York Yankees at Yankee Stadium.

Perhaps taking advantage of the late-afternoon shadows for this 4:35 p.m. start, Alvarez worked three scoreless innings of one-hit ball as the Indians crushed the Bronx Bombers 9–4.

Alvarez, a 35-year-old lefty who has been around the block a few times, was the emergency starter in place of Ollie Gonzalez, who went on the injured list this week with left-shoulder fatigue.

Having just finished his own stint on the IL, Alvarez looked rested and ready.

"I wanted to go nine," he joked afterward. "I'm not used to this 'opener' stuff. I was really amped up about pitching. I was worried about being too amped up and keeping the ball up in the strike zone, but that didn't happen. Iceberg (catcher Peters) was really good about keeping me grounded. I'm just happy to contribute after missing some time myself this year."

Will manager Todd Stein run Alvarez back out there the next time this turn in the rotation rolls around?

"We'll see," said Stein, whose team improved to 52–45 with its fourth straight victory. "Solly surprised me, actually. Not that I didn't have confidence in him, but he was dealing out there. I told him he must have drunk from the fountain of youth down there on his minor-league rehab stint in Florida."

Whatever, Alvarez stepped up big time in a season for obscurity for him. He began the season as a long- to middle-reliever to mop-up man in the bullpen before going on the IL. He got six groundball outs and struck out two in his three innings of work. After that, the Indians got decent relief work from Buck Sterling, Mickey Penny, Lorry Unger and Lee Hazelton.

Those pitchers also had a comfy cushion with which to work, thanks largely to the hottest hitter in the land: second baseman Scott Michaels, who extended his hitting streak to 17 games by going 4-for-5 with a three-run homer in the first inning against Manuel Acuna. Michaels also hit a run-scoring double in the third before adding a pair of singles, one against reliever Carl Grey and one off of Steph Perlow.

During the streak, Michaels is an ungodly 35-for-64.

"Just having fun out there," he said. "I know I've said it before, but I can't explain it other than being 100 percent healthy and doing what I've always known I could do. I think we were all pumped up for Solly out there. He was really enthused about making this start, and I'm glad I could give him that little bit of a lead in the first inning."

The Indians also got a three-run homer from Bernard Harper in the sixth. The Yankees scored single runs in every inning from the fifth through the eighth but were no threat to the Indians. Little-used Leo Taylor hit a two-run homer in the top of the ninth, scoring another little-used player, Huron Southworth. Both players entered the game late.

"As the summer wears on, we need to get guys some playing time," Stein said. "Iceberg got a start today. Huron and Leo have been biding their time, and I know Huron is not happy about losing his job. But as I told you and as I told the team, everybody is going to contribute if we're going to win."

Alvarez was living proof of that Saturday.

GAME 97

CLEVELAND INDIANS VS NEW YORK YANKEES • JULY 23
CLEVELAND 9 / NEW YORK 4

CLEVELAND INDIANS

BATTING	AB	R	H	RBI	2B	3B	HR	BB	SO	BA
RIKKI LABUDDA CF	5	1	2	0	1	0	0	0	0	.274
MICAH MILLISON RF	4	2	2	0	0	0	0	1	0	.299
SCOTT MICHAELS 2B	5	1	4	4	1	0	1	0	0	.363
TERRY ROVETTO 3B	4	1	2	0	0	0	0	1	0	.271
OLIVER REINER 1B	5	1	1	0	0	0	0	0	1	.267
WILSON WHITE LF	4	0	1	0	0	0	0	0	0	.271
HURON SOUTHWORTH LF	1	1	1	0	0	0	0	0	0	.244
JUSTIN KESTINO SS	4	0	1	0	0	0	0	0	0	.265
LEO TAYLOR SS	1	1	1	2	0	0	1	0	0	.295
BERNARD HARPER DH	4	1	1	3	0	0	1	0	1	.250
ICEBERG PETERS C	4	0	0	0	0	0	0	0	1	.204

PITCHING	IP	H	R	ER	SO	BB	ERA
SOLLY ALVAREZ	3	1	0	0	2	0	3.35
BUCK STERLING (W)	2	2	1	1	1	1	3.72
MICKEY PENNY	2	2	2	2	1	0	3.73
LORRY UNGER	1	2	1	1	0	1	4.31
LEE HAZELTON	1	1	0	0	1	0	2.73

NEW YORK YANKEES

BATTING	AB	R	H	RBI	2B	3B	HR	BB	SO	BA
MARK STRANTON CF	3	0	0	0	0	0	0	1	0	.295
WILLIE ROBINSON 3B	4	1	1	0	0	0	0	0	0	.305
BOBBY FAULHABER DH	3	0	0	1	0	0	0	1	0	.275
GUILLERMO CRUZ 1B	4	1	1	0	0	0	0	0	1	.301
RICK STEINBERG C	4	1	2	0	0	0	0	0	1	.283
JAKE KOENIG SS	4	0	2	2	1	0	0	0	2	.271
NICK WRIGHT RF	3	1	1	0	0	0	0	1	0	.276
GARY ASHCROFT LF	4	0	0	1	0	0	0	0	0	.237
LEONARD LEE 2B	4	0	1	0	0	0	0	0	1	.269

PITCHING	IP	H	R	ER	SO	BB	ERA
MANUAL ACUNA (L)	5.33	8	6	6	3	2	4.49
CARL GREY	.167	4	1	1	0	0	3.86
STEPH PERLOW	2	3	3	3	0	0	3.97

INNING	1	2	3	4	5	6	7	8	9	TOTAL
CLEVELAND	3	0	1	0	0	3	0	0	2	9
NEW YORK	0	0	0	0	1	1	1	1	0	4

GAME 98

By SAM LARDNER

The Cleveland Press

NEW YORK, July 25 — Long ago, a wise old scribe dubbed New York as the "city that never sweeps."

On Sunday, the Big Apple got swept.

The surging Cleveland Indians waltzed into Yankee Stadium with their brooms and beat the New York Yankees 7–3 to complete a three-game sweep of this weekend series.

The Indians won their fifth in a row to improve to 53–45 and remain five games behind the first-place Minnesota Twins and remain tied for second place in the division with the Chicago White Sox.

And, oh yes, that kid from Ohio, Indians second baseman Scott Michaels, extended his hitting streak to 18 games by going 3-for-5 with a two-run homer in the first inning to get the Tribe going against Yankees starting pitcher Ty Goodman. Home run number 24 was his fifth in the last eight games.

For Indians starter, Brian "The Doctor" Howard, the day was almost as clean as an operating room as he worked 7 and one-third innings, giving up five hits and only one run while striking out five.

As the Indians head home, life is suddenly very good. They just went 8–3 during a stretch of nine road games in a stretch of 11 overall.

"No complaints," said manager Todd Stein, who is 51–37 since taking over for the fired Dave Mills after 10 games. "I'm really proud of the way the guys have stepped up here. We've made a few tweaks here and over-come some injuries, but basically, it's the same group that we opened the season with."

One of those tweaks was making Michaels the second baseman after Angel Rodriguez was hobbled much of the first half. During his 18-game hitting streak, Michaels is a sizzling 38-for-69. His first-inning home run was a drive to the second deck in left field.

"It's little crazy, yeah," he said. "I can't honestly say I expected anything like this. I'm sure teams will start pitching me a lot more carefully now. I don't think I'm doing anything differently at the plate. I just feel good, I'm seeing the ball well and I'm driving it."

The rest of the Indians joined Michaels in chasing Goodman during a four-run fourth inning. Michaels contributed "only" a single that inning, and he rode home on Justin Kestino's three-run homer. That came after Oliver Reiner's sacrifice fly.

Speedy Kieran Catsef tripled in the seventh and scored on a groundout by Morris Jerome.

After Saturday's bullpen day (featuring "opener Solly Alvarez), Howard stretched it out to 111 pitches. He gave up a run-scoring double to Randy Nadell in the seventh. Geno Milzie yielded a two-run homer to Bobby Faulhaber in the eighth before Lee Hazelton worked a 1-2-3 ninth.

"It was good for me to bounce back, but I had a lot of support today," said Howard, who lost to the Astros in his previous start. "I didn't help us at all in that last one, so I wanted to go as long as I could. It'll be good to get home and see how our fans support us. I would think that the joint would be jumpin' now."

GAME 98

CLEVELAND INDIANS VS NEW YORK YANKEES • JULY 25
CLEVELAND 7 / NEW YORK 3

CLEVELAND INDIANS										
BATTING	AB	R	H	RBI	2B	3B	HR	BB	SO	BA
RIKKI LABUDDA CF	5	1	3	0	1	0	0	0	0	.278
MICAH MILLISON RF	4	0	0	0	0	0	0	1	0	.295
SCOTT MICHAELS 2B	5	2	3	2	0	0	1	0	1	.367
TERRY ROVETTO 3B	4	1	2	0	0	0	0	1	0	.273
OLIVER REINER 1B	4	1	2	1	0	0	0	0	0	.269
JUSTIN KESTINO SS	4	1	2	3	0	0	1	0	1	.268
BERNARD HARPER DH	4	0	1	0	0	0	0	0	1	.250
KIERAN CATSEF LF	4	1	1	0	0	1	0	0	0	.254
MORRIS JEROME C	4	0	0	1	0	0	0	0	0	.233
PITCHING	IP	H	R	ER	SO	BB	ERA			
BRIAN HOWARD (W)	7.33	5	1	1	5	0	4.80			
GENO MILZIE	0.67	1	2	2	0	1	2.78			
LEE HAZELTON	1	0	1	0	1	0	2.64			

NEW YORK YANKEES										
BATTING	AB	R	H	RBI	2B	3B	HR	BB	SO	BA
RANDY NADELL CF	4	1	2	1	1	0	0	0	0	.298
WILLIE ROBINSON 3B	4	0	0	0	0	0	0	0	2	.300
BOBBY FAULHABER DH	4	1	2	2	0	0	1	0	0	.277
GUILLERMO CRUZ 1B	4	0	0	0	0	0	0	0	1	.297
RICK STEINBERG C	3	0	1	0	0	0	0	1	1	.284
JAKE KOENIG SS	4	0	0	0	0	0	0	0	1	.267
NICK WRIGHT RF	4	0	0	0	0	0	0	0	0	.271
GARY ASHCROFT LF	4	0	0	0	0	0	0	0	0	.234
LEONARD LEE 2B	4	1	1	0	0	0	0	0	1	.269
PITCHING	IP	H	R	ER	SO	BB	ERA			
TY GOODMAN (L)	3.67	8	6	6	1	0	4.10			
JEFF KRIEZELMAN	1.33	2	0	0	1	0	3.58			
PETE SNOW	2	2	1	1	0	2	3.44			
STEPH PERLOW	2	2	0	0	1	0	3.75			

INNING	1	2	3	4	5	6	7	8	9	TOTAL
CLEVELAND	2	0	0	4	0	0	1	0	0	7
NEW YORK	0	0	0	0	0	0	1	2	0	3

GAME 99

By SAM LARDNER
The Cleveland Press

CLEVELAND, July 26 — There was the buildup. And then there was the letdown.

The Indians came home to Progressive Field Monday night and were greeted by a midsummer night's crowd of 36,022.

Sudden hitting sensation Scott Michaels was surrounded at his locker before the game by local newspaper, website, TV and radio reporters, and the Dayton Times even sent a reporter to cover the boy from Versailles, Ohio.

Oh, and then the Indians went out and lost 6–0 to the lowly Detroit Tigers. The only good news for the Tribe was that Michaels extended his hitting streak to 19 games by going 2-for-4, with a fourth-inning double and a seventh-inning single. Angel Rodriguez did come in to pinch run and finish the game at second base.

That was about it, though.

"It's too bad we disappointed our fans like that, especially when they came out in droves on a Monday night," said manager Todd Stein, whose team's winning streak was snapped at five. "I know there was a lot of hype before the game, both about Scottie and about how well we've played lately. But I don't think there was any loss of focus or anything like that. We just didn't have a good game. Those are going pop up from time to time."

As for Michaels, the onetime phenom has handled his newfound celebrity with aplomb. He entertained reporters for 20 minutes at his locker as soon as the clubhouse opened to the media at 3:35 p.m. Michaels took some good-natured ribbing from his teammates for being a "moth," or someone who's attracted to the bright lights.

"Would you look at that?" said first baseman and team leader Oliver Reiner. "Guy gets a couple hits and it's like the rest of us are chopped liver. Hey, Scottie, can I be your agent?"

Third baseman Terry Rovetto even grabbed a notebook and a pencil and shouted out a question.

"Ah, it's OK," Michaels said. "I see it as a sign of acceptance. It's been a rough go the last couple years with the shoulder injury. If the guys are giving me the business, well, that's better than them ignoring me."

It was only this game that was worthy to be ignored by Indians fans. Starting pitcher Kenny Camden didn't make it out of the fifth inning, as the Tigers scored four runs, sending 10 men to the plate. The big blow was a bases-loaded double by Aaron Schutzman. That was followed by single to center by Kris Whyte scoring Schutzman.

"That sucked," Camden said. "We had all this excitement in the ballpark, and I took the air right out of the place. I just couldn't keep the ball down. With my stuff, that's just asking for trouble. They gave it to me. No excuses."

Buck Sterling gave up a two-run homer to Kyle Cramer in the seventh, as he and Mickey Penney finished up.

Indians batters managed just five hits off Tigers starter Scott Kreiss, who went seven innings. Wilson White had a double in the sixth, but was stranded there, as the Tribe was 0-for-6 with men in scoring position.

General manager J.D. Eisner was not available before the game. He no doubt was working the phones in an effort to get something done by the July 31 trading deadline. Eisner may meet the media before Tuesday night's game for a quick update.

"I know what you guys know," Stein said. "But as I've told you, I'm very confident moving forward with the group we have. But if J.D. does something, I'm sure it will help the ballclub."

GAME 99

CLEVELAND INDIANS VS DETROIT TIGERS • JULY 26
DETROIT 6 / CLEVELAND 0

CLEVELAND INDIANS										
BATTING	AB	R	H	RBI	2B	3B	HR	BB	SO	BA
RIKKI LABUDDA CF	4	0	0	0	0	0	0	0	0	.275
HURON SOUTHWORTH RF	4	0	1	0	0	0	0	0	0	.244
SCOTT MICHAELS 2B	4	0	2	0	0	0	0	0	1	.369
ANGEL RODRIGUEZ 2B	0	0	0	0	0	0	0	0	0	.212
TERRY ROVETTO 3B	3	0	0	0	0	0	0	1	0	.271
OLIVER REINER 1B	4	0	0	0	0	0	0	0	0	.263
WILSON WHITE LF	4	0	1	0	1	0	0	0	1	.271
LEO TAYLOR SS	4	0	0	0	0	0	0	0	1	.277
BERNARD HARPER DH	3	0	1	0	0	0	0	0	0	.251
MORRIS JEROME C	3	0	1	0	0	0	0	0	0	.234
PITCHING	IP	H	R	ER	SO	BB	ERA			
KENNY CAMDEN (L)	4.33	8	4	4	2	2	3.60			
BUCK STERLING	2.67	2	2	2	1	1	3.88			
MICKEY PENNY	2	1	0	0	0	0	3.54			

DETROIT TIGERS										
BATTING	AB	R	H	RBI	2B	3B	HR	BB	SO	BA
RODNEY REYNOLDS 2B	5	0	1	0	0	0	0	0	0	.300
BOBBY BENKERT SS	4	2	2	0	1	0	0	1	0	.309
KYLE CRAMER 3B	3	1	1	2	0	0	1	1	0	.278
FREDDIE DERRING 1B	4	1	2	0	0	0	0	0	0	.305
AARON SCHUTZMAN LF	4	1	3	3	1	0	0	0	0	.287
KRIS WHYTE DH	4	0	1	1	0	0	0	0	1	.267
PORFIRIO FIGUEROA CF	4	0	0	0	0	0	0	0	1	.271
GRANT BERGSTROM RF	3	0	0	0	0	0	0	0	1	.238
RAMON GARCIA C	4	1	1	0	0	0	0	1	1	.269
PITCHING	IP	H	R	ER	SO	BB	ERA			
SCOTT KREISS (W)	7	5	0	0	4	1	3.49			
DAMIEN MOORE	2	1	0	0	1	0	3.18			

INNING	1	2	3	4	5	6	7	8	9	TOTAL
DETROIT	0	0	0	0	4	0	2	0	0	6
CLEVELAND	0	0	0	0	0	0	0	0	0	0

GAME 100

By SAM LARDNER
The Cleveland Press

CLEVELAND, July 27 — There were more media members in the clubhouse Tuesday both before and after the Indians beat the Detroit Tigers 5–2 at Progressive Field.

After all, Tak Fujimoto was pitching — and pitching well — for the Indians, and he has his own contingent of about 15 media members from Japan with him.

Then there's the phenomenon — the longer version of the word "phenom," by the way — known as Scott Michaels. Major League Baseball's newest sensation extended his hitting streak to 20 games by going 2-for-5 with a two-run homer in the third inning against Austin Wylie.

After the game, the Indians' media-relations staff opted to use the interview room for both Fujimoto and Michaels as well as Fujimoto's translator, Ryuji Sato. It made for quite the postgame scene with questions being shouted out in all languages and answers being translated back.

"Hey, where's my translator?" quipped Michaels, flashing a wry sense of humor that is just now becoming apparent.

"Why don't you go get Angel?" Fujimoto shot back in perfect English, referring to Angel Rodriguez, the man Michaels supplanted at second base.

That one brought the house down, with Sato saying he might now be out of a job.

It's that way when you're winning, and the Indians have been doing just that lately. Tuesday's victory was their sixth in their last seven games, upping their record to 54–46 after an even 100 games.

All comedy aside, this is one of the Indians' better all-around efforts of the season. Fujimoto continued his strong pitching, as he looks to be justifying the big free-agent deal the Indians gave up last winter. He went seven innings and gave up five hits and both Tigers runs, on a two-run homer by Mike Wolf in the fourth inning.

That tied the game at 2–2, but the Indians got the runs back in the fifth on Iceberg Peters' two-run double. Rikki LaBudda added a rare inside-the-park homer in the seventh as Tigers outfielders Kris Whyte and Jesus Frias collided in right-center chasing his drive to the gap.

"That was fun," said Indians manager Todd Stein. "The boys are having a good time, and I'm glad of that. That's one of the things I wanted to create here, not that things were uptight under Millsie (former manager Dave Mills), but I just told them to relax and play and that things would take care of themselves."

LaBudda, known more for his speed than his power, joked about the home run.

"That's about the only way I can hit one," he said. "When I saw the outfielders collide, I just kept running. I never saw a stop sign. Maybe I can tell the grandkids one day that it was a 440-foot drive over the wall in center."

The Indians got perfect relief work from Geno Milzie and Ivan Zyzna. During the postgame news conference, general manager J.D. Eisner popped his head in.

"Oh, (bleep), am I traded?" Michaels said.

Eisner had no new updates for the media as the July 31 trading deadline is upon us.

But no, Mr. Michaels, you are not being traded.

GAME 100

CLEVELAND INDIANS VS DETROIT TIGERS · JULY 27
CLEVELAND 5 / DETROIT 2

CLEVELAND INDIANS										
BATTING	AB	R	H	RBI	2B	3B	HR	BB	SO	BA
RIKKI LABUDDA CF	5	1	2	1	0	0	1	0	0	.277
MICAH MILLISON RF	5	1	2	0	1	0	0	0	0	.297
SCOTT MICHAELS 2B	5	1	2	2	0	0	1	0	1	.370
TERRY ROVETTO 3B	4	0	1	0	0	0	0	0	1	.271
BERNARD HARPER 1B	4	0	0	0	0	0	0	0	0	.247
WILSON WHITE LF	3	1	2	0	0	0	0	1	0	.275
JUSTIN KESTINO SS	4	1	1	0	1	0	0	0	1	.268
J.J. KULAKOFSKI DH	3	0	1	0	0	0	0	1	0	.240
ICEBERG PETERS C	4	0	1	2	1	0	0	0	1	.206
PITCHING	IP	H	R	ER	SO	BB	ERA			
TAK FUJIMOTO (W)	7	5	2	2	5	1	3.11			
GENO MILZE	1	0	0	0	1	0	2.72			
IVAN ZYZNA (S)	1	0	0	0	1	0	1.15			

DETROIT TIGERS										
BATTING	AB	R	H	RBI	2B	3B	HR	BB	SO	BA
RODNEY REYNOLDS 2B	4	0	0	0	0	0	0	0	0	.296
BOBBY BENKERT SS	4	1	1	0	1	0	0	0	0	.308
KYLE CRAMER 3B	3	0	0	0	0	0	0	0	1	.275
MIKE WOLF 1B	4	1	1	2	0	0	1	0	0	.312
AARON SCHUTZMAN LF	4	0	0	0	0	0	0	0	1	.283
KRIS WHYTE DH	4	0	1	0	0	0	0	0	1	.267
PORFIRIO FIGUEROA CF	3	0	1	0	0	0	0	0	1	.271
GRANT BERGSTROM RF	2	0	0	0	0	0	0	1	0	.236
RAMON GARCIA C	3	0	1	0	0	0	0	0	1	.270
PITCHING	IP	H	R	ER	SO	BB	ERA			
AUSTIN WYLIE (L)	6	7	4	4	3	2	3.85			
AARON BRISSETT	2	5	1	1	1	0	3.49			

INNING	1	2	3	4	5	6	7	8	9	TOTAL
DETROIT	0	0	0	2	0	0	0	0	0	2
CLEVELAND	0	0	2	0	2	0	1	0		5

GAME 101

By SAM LARDNER

The Cleveland Press

CLEVELAND, July 28 — Three days before the July 31 trading deadline, Indians general manager J.D. Eisner struck.

Before the Indians went out and lost 4–2 Wednesday night to the Detroit Tigers at Progressive Field, Eisner traded disgruntled outfielder Huron Southworth and first baseman J.J. Kulakofski to the Cincinnati Reds for right-handed pitcher Eli Batt and two minor league prospects, Frank Mynard and Larry Reiner, Oliver Reiner's kid brother. Both Mynard and Reiner will go to AA ball in Akron.

The Indians rotation has been solid most of the year, but it has shown signs of fraying around the edges as the summer has worn on. Batt, 30, will take the rotation spot of Ollie Gonzalez, who is on the injured list with left-shoulder fatigue. Gonzalez could be out two more weeks.

Thursday is an off-day in the schedule, and Eisner said he expects Batt to be in Cleveland in time to start Friday night's big game against the Chicago White Sox, who come to town for a three-game weekend series. The two American League Central rivals are battling for a wild-card spot.

"We're happy with our rotation, but we feel the addition of Eli Batt will really give us some depth," Eisner said on the field before the game. "We've had a busy run of games since the all-star break. Couple that with Ollie's injury and we felt we could use an extra arm."

Gonzalez's last start was filled by reliever Solly Alvarez, who pitched well as an "opener." Alvarez will go back to the bullpen as a long man/middle reliever.

Eisner said he and manager Todd Stein will get together to discuss what the Indians do when Gonzalez comes back. They can go with a six-man rotation — which many teams started using at various points of the season early this century — or they could move one of the starters to the bullpen.

"There's no hurry on any of that," Eisner said. "Ollie will have to go on a rehab assignment. Either way, it will be a nice problem to have going down the stretch."

Batt is 8–5 with a 3.89 ERA in 15 starts with the Reds, for whom he was the No. 3 starter. Southworth lost his starting job to Micah Millison early in the season and found it difficult to find playing time and Kulakofski has been the forgotten man on the bench.

"No hard feelings," Southworth said as he packed up at his locker. "I understand. I started slow, and Micah was playing well. This will be a new lease on life for me. I know a couple guys with the Reds, and they have a good hitter's ballpark."

As for Wednesday's game, Indians ace Lynn Moda didn't pitch poorly even though he took the loss and gave up all four Detroit runs in five innings of work. A three-run homer to Aaron Schutzman in the third broke a scoreless tie. Rodney Reynolds added a run-scoring single in the fifth.

"It wasn't awful," Moda said. "Just that one bad pitch to Schutzman and that was pretty much it."

Asked about the acquisition of Batt, Moda offered: "The more the merrier. You can never have too much pitching and always look to your front office to add when you're in a pennant race. J.D. certainly stepped up with that one. We'll miss Southy, though, He was a good teammate and a lot of fun to be around. I know he was unhappy, but he didn't let it bring the clubhouse down."

The good news for the Indians, and lost amid the trade news, was that second baseman Scott Michaels extended his hitting streak to 21 games despite going "only" 1-for-5, a fourth-inning single. Otherwise it was a mostly quiet night at the plate for Michaels and the Indians.

Millison hit a two-run homer in the seventh, scoring behind Rikki LaBudda, who opened the inning with a walk and another stolen base, his 24th. The homer came off Tigers starter Omar Alvarado, whose night ended with that hit.

As for Michaels (43-for-83 during the streak), he's scheduled to appear on the TV news show "Wake Up Cleveland" Thursday morning.

"After that, I'll head home and try to get some rest," he said. "It's been quite a rush lately. Maybe I can share a recipe or two with the TV people tomorrow. I'm not sure what else I can offer."

CLEVELAND INDIANS VS DETROIT TIGERS · JULY 28
DETROIT 4 / CLEVELAND 2

CLEVELAND INDIANS										
BATTING	AB	R	H	RBI	2B	3B	HR	BB	SO	BA
RIKKI LABUDDA CF	4	1	1	0	0	0	0	1	0	.277
MICAH MILLISON RF	5	1	1	2	1	0	1	0	0	.295
SCOTT MICHAELS 2B	5	0	1	0	0	0	0	0	1	.367
TERRY ROVETTO 3B	4	0	0	0	0	0	0	1	0	.268
OLIVER REINER 1B	4	0	2	0	0	0	0	0	2	.265
WILSON WHITE LF	4	0	0	0	0	0	0	0	1	.271
JUSTIN KESTINO SS	4	0	1	0	1	0	0	0	2	.267
BERNARD HARPER DH	3	0	2	0	0	0	0	1	0	.252
MORRIS JEROME C	3	0	0	0	0	0	0	0	1	.231
PITCHING	IP	H	R	ER	SO	BB	ERA			
LYNN MODA (L)	5	5	4	4	2	2	4.21			
MICKEY PENNY	2	1	0	0	1	1	3.73			
BUCK STERLING	1	0	0	0	0	0	3.46			
LEE HAZELTON	1	0	0	0	1	0	2.56			

DETROIT TIGERS										
BATTING	AB	R	H	RBI	2B	3B	HR	BB	SO	BA
RODNEY REYNOLDS 2B	5	0	2	1	0	0	0	0	0	.298
BOBBY BENKERT SS	4	1	2	0	1	0	0	1	0	.311
KYLE CRAMER 3B	4	0	0	0	0	0	0	0	2	.272
MIKE WOLF 1B	3	1	1	0	0	0	0	1	0	.312
AARON SCHUTZMAN LF	4	1	4	3	0	0	1	0	0	.294
KRIS WHYTE DH	4	0	0	0	0	0	0	0	0	.263
PORFIRIO FIGUEROA CF	4	0	0	0	0	0	0	0	1	.267
GRANT BERGSTROM RF	3	0	0	0	0	0	0	1	1	.234
RAMON GARCIA C	4	1	0	0	0	0	0	0	0	.266
PITCHING	IP	H	R	ER	SO	BB	ERA			
OMAR ALVARADO (W)	6.3	5	2	2	5	2	3.75			
CLAUDE SHOEMAKER	1.67	2	0	0	1	1	3.37			
SILVIO SEVERINO (S)	1	1	0	0	1	0	2.54			

INNING	1	2	3	4	5	6	7	8	9	TOTAL
DETROIT	0	0	3	0	1	0	0	0	0	4
CLEVELAND	0	0	0	0	0	2	0	0	0	2

GAME 102

By SAM LARDNER
The Cleveland Press

CLEVELAND, July 30 — Maybe just the oldsters in the Progressive Field crowd of 36,222 "got it" when organist Jimmy Lee pounded out "Eli's Comin'" as newly acquired Indians pitcher Eli Batt warmed up before Friday night's game against the Chicago White Sox.

As it turned out, Eli came. He saw. He conquered. Pitching for his new team two days after his trade from the Cincinnati Reds, Batt made a sparkling Indians debut in a 6–1 victory over the Chicago White Sox in the opener of a key three-game weekend series.

Batt worked seven innings, giving up five hits and one run as the Indians (55–47) moved into sole possession of second place in the American League Central, one game ahead of the White Sox.

"It feels good to be thrust right in the middle of a pennant race," said Batt, acquired Wednesday for outfielder Huron Southworth and first baseman J.J. Kulakofski. "I had been here with the Reds, so I know the passion for the team the fans have here. It was great to have them on my side. It took Mo (catcher Morris Jerome) and me about all of two batters to get on the same page. It was just pitch and catch after that."

That was one of the big news items of the day. Second baseman Scott Michaels extended his hitting streak to 22 games by going 3-for-5 with a two-run double in the third inning and a pair of singles. Michaels is 46-for-88 during the streak.

"That's some kind of sizzling," marveled White Sox manager David Echt. "We walked into a buzz saw here tonight, what with the crowd, Batt's debut and that Michaels kid. Whew. Maybe we'll just have to walk him every time up."

The only run Batt allowed came on a third-inning homer off the bat of Moe Tanko, who leads the majors with 34. Michaels' double put the Indians ahead for good in the bottom of the inning. Wilson White touched Sox starter Mitch Mosel for a three-run homer in the sixth. Micah Millison drove in Rikki LaBudda with a sacrifice fly in the seventh. Interestingly. Reliever Solly Alvarez worked the final two innings for the Indians. He made a start as an "opener" last Saturday in place of the injured Ollie Gonzalez.

"So I go from the opener to the closer," Alvarez joked. "Hey, whatever it takes. I was ready to start again tonight and go nine if they needed me. But when you can add a guy like Batt to the rotation … well, I'm just happy to help out in any role. Maybe they'll want me to be the DH tomorrow."

That probably won't be necessary the way the Indians have been hitting the ball lately, but you never know. Manager Todd Stein and general manager J.D. Eisner seem to be pushing all the right buttons lately.

"It's all the players," Stein said. "It's taken us awhile, but we've finally hit somewhat of a stride, despite the injury problems we've had. The good teams find ways to overcome that kind of stuff. We're doing that now."

With the trade of Southworth, the Indians are carrying an extra pitcher on the roster, something Eisner said they can do for the short term, at least.

"We've got Angel (Rodriguez), Leo (Taylor), Bernard (Harper) and Iceberg (Peters), all of whom can play multiple positions," Eisner said. "Kieren (Catsef) is due to come off the IL soon, so we have plenty of options there, and Willie Bartlett has been playing well in Triple-A after we sent him back. In the American League, with the DH, there is less urgency for that extra position guy. But we'll see how it goes."

GAME 102

CLEVELAND INDIANS VS CHICAGO WHITE SOX • JULY 30
CLEVELAND 6 / CHICAGO 1

CLEVELAND INDIANS

BATTING	AB	R	H	RBI	2B	3B	HR	BB	SO	BA
RIKKI LABUDDA CF	5	2	2	0	0	0	0	0	0	.278
MICAH MILLISON RF	4	0	1	1	1	0	0	1	0	.295
SCOTT MICHAELS 2B	5	0	3	2	1	0	0	0	1	.371
TERRY ROVETTO 3B	5	1	1	0	0	0	0	0	0	.267
OLIVER REINER 1B	4	1	1	0	0	0	0	1	0	.265
WILSON WHITE LF	4	1	2	3	0	0	1	1	0	.274
JUSTIN KESTINO SS	4	0	1	0	1	0	0	0	2	.267
BERNARD HARPER DH	4	0	0	0	0	0	0	1	0	.248
MORRIS JEROME C	4	1	1	0	0	0	0	0	0	.232

PITCHING	IP	H	R	ER	SO	BB	ERA
ELI BATT (W)	7	5	1	1	6	1	1.29
SOLLY ALVAREZ	2	1	0	0	1	0	3.18

CHICAGO WHITE SOX

BATTING	AB	R	H	RBI	2B	3B	HR	BB	SO	BA
MARK ROSE 2B	4	0	1	0	0	0	0	1	0	.299
TRAVIS CAMPBELL SS	4	0	0	0	0	0	0	0	2	.304
MO TANKO 3B	4	1	2	1	0	0	1	0	0	.294
JAY WALLEY LF	4	0	0	0	0	0	0	0	1	.309
MIKE ISENMESSER 1B	4	0	2	0	0	0	0	0	1	.291
JACKIE WINER RF	4	0	1	0	1	0	0	0	0	.285
JASON NAKAMURA DH	4	0	0	0	0	0	0	0	1	.266
VLADIMIR JANAKOWSKI CF	4	0	0	0	0	0	0	0	2	.235
ENRIQUE FUENTES C	3	0	0	0	0	0	0	0	0	.266

PITCHING	IP	H	R	ER	SO	BB	ERA
MITCH MOSEL (L)	5.33	8	4	4	2	2	4.11
BRAD HUTCHINSON	1.67	3	2	2	2	0	3.70
RANDY ROSELLI	1	1	0	0	1	0	3.75

INNING	1	2	3	4	5	6	7	8	9	TOTAL
CHICAGO	0	0	1	0	0	0	0	0	0	1
CLEVELAND	0	0	2	0	0	3	1	0		6

GAME 103

By SAM LARDNER
The Cleveland Press

CLEVELAND, July 31 — Indians general manager J.D. Eisner arrived in the press box at 4:01 p.m. Saturday, just as the Indians were about to bat in the bottom of the eighth inning against the Chicago White Sox.

Uh oh. Was there a deal going down?

Nope.

"All clear," Eisner said as reporters glanced up from their laptops.

The Indians did not make a deadline deal, but then again, they probably didn't have to after obtaining pitcher Eli Batt from the Reds a few days ago.

And why mess with the chemistry that has been nothing but positive for the last several weeks?

The good times kept rolling Saturday afternoon as Brian Howard pitched and Scott Michaels hit the Indians to a 3–1 victory over the White Sox in front of 36,776 screaming spectators at Progressive Field.

Howard is known to his teammates as "The Doctor," and he sounded like he had a PhD in chemistry after this one.

"It seems funny that we're talking like this now, considering how we started, but why mess with success?" he said. "The way this club has played, really, for a couple of months, has been the way we envisioned it all when we broke camp out of spring training. The slow start could have buried us, but we didn't let it. It's a nice show of faith by J.D. in all of us. And let's not forget the job Steinie has done."

Howard was referring to interim manager Todd Stein, who took over after the Indians were 2–8. They're 56–47 now and within five games of the first-place Minnesota Twins in the American League Central. They hold the wild-card lead by two games over the White Sox.

It's not like the Indians haven't made changes throughout the season. Micah Millison replaced Huron Southworth in the lineup early this year, and Southworth and Kulakofski were traded for Batt.

And, oh yes, there's that Michaels kid. He extended his hitting streak to 23 games Saturday by going 2-for-4, with an RBI single in the fourth inning and a leadoff double in the seventh. He is 48-for-92 in the streak. He ended July with an eye-popping .372 batting average.

"Let's talk about The Doc's pitching," the modest Michaels said. "He was the reason we won the game today. "I did my small part. I don't feel like I have a hitting streak going. Maybe that's my way of blocking it out. But to me, it's just trying to hit the ball hard each game, if that makes any sense."

The game was a scoreless duel between Howard and Sox starter Juri Tateyama when Rikki LaBudda led off the bottom of the fourth with a single. He promptly stole second base. After Micah Millison struck out, Michaels stroked a solid single to center field to score the speedy LaBudda easily.

Terry Rovetto hit a solo homer in the sixth. The Sox came within a run in the seventh on Travis Campbell's single that scored Mark Rose, who opened the inning with a triple that chased Howard after 100 pitches. Lee Hazelton gave up the hit to Campbell, but after a mound visit by Stein, he settled down and struck out two batters before Mike Isenmesser popped out to end the inning.

The Tribe got back one the seventh as Michaels doubled and rode home on Wilson White's single. The usual duo of Geno Milzie and Ivan Zyzna closed the deal for the Indians lowering his ERA to a miniscule 1.11.

"I just wanted to settle Haze down," Stein said of his mound visit to Hazelton. "He's a young guy with a lot of ability, but sometimes he doubts himself. I just wanted to remind him that we have all the faith in the world in him."

As far as the deadline passing without another deal, Eisner was straightforward.

"There was nothing out there we liked," he said, neglecting to mention the change in managers. "Our roster and our lineup aren't the same as they were early in the season, and that's as it should be. We feel pretty comfortable going forward with this group. The final two months are going to be very interesting."

Buckle up.

GAME 103

CLEVELAND INDIANS VS CHICAGO WHITE SOX • JULY 31
CLEVELAND 3 / CHICAGO 1

CLEVELAND INDIANS										
BATTING	AB	R	H	RBI	2B	3B	HR	BB	SO	BA
RIKKI LABUDDA CF	4	1	2	0	0	0	0	0	0	.280
MICAH MILLISON RF	3	0	0	0	1	0	0	1	0	.292
SCOTT MICHAELS 2B	4	1	2	1	1	0	0	0	0	.372
TERRY ROVETTO 3B	4	1	1	1	0	0	1	0	2	.267
OLIVER REINER 1B	4	0	2	0	0	0	0	0	0	.268
WILSON WHITE LF	4	0	2	1	0	0	0	0	1	.276
LEO TAYLOR SS	4	0	1	0	1	0	0	0	0	.275
BERNARD HARPER DH	4	0	2	0	0	0	0	0	2	.252
MORRIS JEROME C	4	0	0	0	0	0	0	0	0	.228

PITCHING	IP	H	R	ER	SO	BB	ERA			
BRIAN HOWARD (W)	6.33	5	1	1	6	1	4.62			
LEE HAZELTON	0.67	1	0	0	0	0	2.50			
GENO MILZE	1	1	0	0	0	0	2.66			
IVAN ZYZNA (S)	1	0	0	0	1	0	1.11			

CHICAGO WHITE SOX										
BATTING	AB	R	H	RBI	2B	3B	HR	BB	SO	BA
MARK ROSE 2B	3	1	1	0	0	1	0	1	0	.300
TRAVIS CAMPBELL SS	4	0	1	1	0	0	0	0	1	.303
MO TANKO 3B	4	0	1	0	0	0	0	0	1	.293
JAY WALLEY LF	4	0	0	0	0	0	0	0	1	.305
MIKE ISENMESSER 1B	4	0	2	0	0	0	0	0	0	.294
JACKIE WINER RF	4	0	2	0	1	0	0	0	1	.288
JASON NAKAMURA DH	4	0	0	0	0	0	0	0	0	.262
VLADIMIR JANAKOWSKI CF	4	0	0	0	0	0	0	0	2	.231
ENRIQUE FUENTES C	4	0	0	0	0	0	0	0	1	.261

PITCHING	IP	H	R	ER	SO	BB	ERA			
JURI TATEYAMA (L)	6.67	10	3	3	4	1	3.73			
CARL WOLDMAN	1.33	2	0	0	1	0	3.03			

INNING	1	2	3	4	5	6	7	8	9	TOTAL
CHICAGO	0	0	0	0	0	0	1	0	0	1
CLEVELAND	0	0	0	1	0	1	1	0		3

GAME 104

By SAM LARDNER
The Cleveland Press

CLEVELAND, August 1 — A weekend that began with a lot of questions for the Cleveland Indians ended with an exclamation point.

The Indians emphatically completed a three-game sweep of the Chicago White Sox Sunday with a 9–3 victory at Progressive Field. That put the Tribe four games behind the first-place Minnesota Twins in the American League Central. They now lead both the White Sox and the Boston Red Sox by three games for the top wild-card spot. The Indians just happen to travel to Fenway Park for a three-game series beginning Monday night.

Another milestone was reached as the Indians went 10 games above .500 (57–47) for the first time this season.

The big story continues to be second baseman Scott Michaels. He went 3-for-4 to extend his hitting streak to 24 games. He is 51-for-96 during the streak and his batting .377 for the season.

Michaels also experienced something new: a curtain call. He hit a grand slam in the Indians' five-run fourth inning to knock Sox starting pitcher Jim Zechman out of the game and give the Indians a 7–0 lead.

At that point, the crowd of 37,001 stood as one and wouldn't stop until Michaels emerged from the dugout to tip his batting helmet. He was pushed to the top step by the man he replaced, Angel Rodriguez, who went in for Michaels at second base in the top of the ninth inning.

"That was something," Michaels said. "I don't think I ever experienced anything like that in high school or college. To get that from this kind of crowd gave me goose bumps. And for Angel to do that, well, that shows a lot of class on his part."

The Indians got all the pitching they needed from Kenny Camden, who worked six innings and gave up six hits and one run. Buck Sterling gave up two runs in the seventh on a home run by Mo Tanko before Lorry Unger and Mickey Penney worked the final two innings, respectively.

"The offense, especially Scottie, made my job easy," said Camden, who bounced back from a poor start against the Tigers his previous time out. "You're seeing what we can do when everybody contributes and pulls in the same direction. To get a sweep was something we didn't expect, especially against the White Sox. We've been chasing them all year. Now they're looking up at us."

Michaels got things going in the first with a single. Rikki LaBudda led off with a walk, and Micah Millison struck out ahead of Michaels. Terry Rovetto salvaged the inning with a double to the gap in right-center to score both runners.

Bernard Harper homered to get the big fourth inning going as the Indians then loaded the bases, setting the stage for Michaels' slam. Oliver Reiner and Wilson White hit back-to-back homers in the seventh to complete the scoring.

"Our lineup is pretty potent right now," said manager Todd Stein. "It's that kind of explosiveness that can do so much damage. And it's everybody, one through nine in the batting order."

Yet another test awaits the Indians. The last time they went to Boston, they got swept out of Fenway Park in a three-game series, during which Rodriguez was the object of homophobic abuse. The Red Sox apologized for that, but they weren't at all sorry about sweeping the Indians.

"We've got our work cut out for us," Stein said. "That's one hell of a tough place to play. But I like the way our guys are swinging it right now, and the weather is much warmer than it was the last time we were there. It should be fun."

GAME 104

CLEVELAND INDIANS VS CHICAGO WHITE SOX • AUGUST 1
CLEVELAND 9 / CHICAGO 3

CLEVELAND INDIANS

BATTING	AB	R	H	RBI	2B	3B	HR	BB	SO	BA
RIKKI LABUDDA CF	4	2	2	0	0	0	0	1	0	.282
MICAH MILLISON RF	4	1	1	0	0	0	0	0	1	.292
SCOTT MICHAELS 2B	4	2	3	4	0	0	1	1	0	.377
ANGEL RODRIGUEZ 2B	0	0	0	0	0	0	0	0	0	.212
TERRY ROVETTO 3B	5	0	1	2	1	0	0	0	2	.266
OLIVER REINER 1B	5	1	2	1	0	0	1	0	1	.269
WILSON WHITE LF	4	1	2	1	1	0	1	1	0	.279
JUSTIN KESTINO SS	4	0	0	0	0	0	0	1	2	.264
BERNARD HARPER DH	4	1	2	1	0	0	1	0	1	.255
MORRIS JEROME C	4	1	2	0	0	0	0	0	0	.232

PITCHING	IP	H	R	ER	SO	BB	ERA			
KENNY CAMDEN (W)	6	6	1	1	7	2	3.49			
BUCK STERLING	1	2	2	2	1	1	3.80			
LORRY UNGER	1	1	0	0	0	0	4.18			
MICKEY PENNY	1	0	0	0	0	0	3.66			

CHICAGO WHITE SOX

BATTING	AB	R	H	RBI	2B	3B	HR	BB	SO	BA
MARK ROSE 2B	4	0	0	0	0	0	0	0	1	.296
TRAVIS CAMPBELL SS	4	1	1	0	0	0	0	0	0	.302
MO TANKO 3B	4	1	2	2	0	0	1	0	1	.296
JAY WALLEY LF	3	0	1	0	0	0	0	1	0	.305
MIKE ISENMESSER 1B	4	1	2	0	1	0	0	0	2	.297
JACKIE WINER RF	4	0	1	1	0	0	0	0	1	.287
JASON NAKAMURA DH	3	0	0	0	0	0	0	1	0	.259
VLADIMIR JANAKOWSKI CF	4	0	1	0	0	0	0	0	2	.232
ENRIQUE FUENTES C	3	0	1	0	0	0	0	1	1	.262

PITCHING	IP	H	R	ER	SO	BB	ERA			
JIM ZECHMAN (L)	3.33	8	4	4	2	1	4.05			
FELIX VALERO	1.67	3	4	3	1	2	3.93			
BRAD HUTCHINSON	2	4	2	2	1	2	3.95			
RANDY ROSELLI	1	0	0	0	0	1	3.65			

INNING	1	2	3	4	5	6	7	8	9	TOTAL
CHICAGO	0	0	1	0	0	0	2	0	0	3
CLEVELAND	2	0	0	5	0	0	2	0		9

GAME 105

By SAM LARDNER
The Cleveland Press

BOSTON, August 2 — If the Indians are going to play the Boston Red Sox in the American League wild-card game, they'll want to avoid playing that game at Fenway Park.

The ballpark in the Back Bay has been a chamber of horrors for the Indians on so many levels this season. The Tribe dropped its fourth straight at Fenway Monday night, falling meekly to the Red Sox 8–0.

The last time the Indians were here, they were swept in a weekend series, and infielder Angel Rodriguez was the subject of homophobic abuse.

Maybe as an act of defiance, Indians manager Todd Stein gave Rodriguez the start at shortstop Monday night in place of Justin Kestino, who has looked in need of a rest.

"Don't read too much into that," said Stein, whose team fell to 57–48. "Angel deserves some time, and Kestie needed a breather."

The lineup change resulted in the interesting pairing of Rodriguez at shortstop, playing alongside the man who replaced him at second base: Scott Michaels.

Speaking of Michaels, he kept his hitting streak alive — barely. It took a ninth-inning infield single to allow Michaels to extend the streak to 25 games. Michaels was 1-for-5 on a night when nobody did much of anything for the Cleveland offense. He is now 52-for-101 in the streak. He saw his season batting average fall from .377 to .374.

"You need some luck sometimes to keep something like that going," said Michaels, who was besieged by both Boston and Cleveland reporters before and after the game. "But again, that's not my main focus. I'm here to help us get to the playoffs. The rest of it will take care of itself."

The Indians trail the Minnesota Twins by five games for first place in the American League Central. They lead Boston and Chicago by two games for the top wild-card spot.

Starting pitcher Tak Fujimoto didn't give them much of a chance Monday. He gave up a three-run homer to Jack Kincaid in the bottom of the first inning. Kincaid's drive went over the Green Monster in left field, but it was no cheapie. It soared high into the Boston night and cleared the 37-foot-high wall by plenty.

The Red Sox got two more in the third and another in the fourth, knocking Fujimoto from the game after just 3 and one-third innings.

"I don't think I had a very good plan tonight," Fujimoto said through translator Ryuji Sato. "If you don't come inside against their right-handed hitters, they're going to hit you hard. That's what happened tonight."

Fujimoto was paired with starting catcher Morris Jerome instead of backup Iceberg Peters, with whom Fujimoto has a rapport.

"It's not that," Fujimoto protested. "Mo and I get along well. I'm not going to ask for a 'personal catcher.' Mo didn't make those pitches. I did. I could have shaken him off, but I didn't. I take responsibility."

Red Sox starter Mark Castleberg worked eight innings, giving up just five hits. Only a pitch count of 110 kept Boston manager Billy Stone from allowing Castleberg to finish. Solly Alvarez, Lorry Unger and Mickey Penney picked up the burden out of the pen for the Indians, who have two more games to play at Fenway.

"We've got to solve it somehow," Stein said. "They've had our number here, that's for sure."

GAME 105

CLEVELAND INDIANS VS BOSTON RED SOX · AUGUST 2
BOSTON 8 / CLEVELAND 0

CLEVELAND INDIANS

BATTING	AB	R	H	RBI	2B	3B	HR	BB	SO	BA
RIKKI LABUDDA CF	5	0	0	0	0	0	0	0	0	.279
MICAH MILLISON RF	4	0	0	0	0	0	0	1	1	.288
SCOTT MICHAELS 2B	5	0	1	0	0	0	0	0	2	.374
TERRY ROVETTO 3B	4	0	0	0	1	0	0	1	0	.263
OLIVER REINER 1B	4	0	1	0	0	0	0	0	0	.269
WILSON WHITE LF	3	0	0	0	1	0	0	1	0	.277
ANGEL RODRIGUEZ SS	4	0	1	0	0	0	0	0	1	.214
BERNARD HARPER DH	4	0	1	0	0	0	0	0	0	.255
MORRIS JEROME C	4	0	1	0	0	0	0	0	2	.232

PITCHING	IP	H	R	ER	SO	BB	ERA			
TAK FUJIMOTO (L)	3.33	8	6	6	4	3	3.44			
SOLLY ALVAREZ	2.67	1	0	0	1	0	2.98			
LORRY UNGER	1	4	2	2	0	0	4.59			
MICKEY PENNY	1	0	0	0	1	0	3.59			

BOSTON RED SOX

BATTING	AB	R	H	RBI	2B	3B	HR	BB	SO	BA
OMAR PEREZ LF	5	1	1	0	0	0	0	0	0	.298
STU KENNEDY SS	5	1	2	0	1	0	0	0	1	.310
CARLOS BLANCO C	4	2	2	0	0	1	0	1	0	.294
MORGAN LEIFER 1B	4	0	0	1	0	0	0	0	1	.309
JACK KINCAID DH	3	2	3	4	0	0	1	1	0	.296
DESMOND UNDERWOOD 3B	4	1	2	1	1	0	0	0	1	.288
SANTIAGO AVILLA 2B	3	0	0	0	0	0	0	1	0	.267
SALVATORE ESPINOSA RF	4	1	1	2	1	0	0	0	1	.238
VICTOR TRAGGER JR CF	4	0	1	0	0	0	0	0	2	.269

PITCHING	IP	H	R	ER	SO	BB	ERA			
MARK CASTLEBERG (W)	8	5	0	0	6	3	3.14			
NICK SPERO	1	0	0	0	0	0	2.81			

INNING	1	2	3	4	5	6	7	8	9	TOTAL
CLEVELAND	0	0	0	0	0	0	0	0		0
BOSTON	3	0	2	1	0	0	2	0		8

GAME 106

By SAM LARDNER
The Cleveland Press

BOSTON, August 3 — Stop the presses, or whatever they say in this day of web-based story-breaking.

In the case of the Cleveland Indians, maybe the better cry Tuesday night was, "stop the pressing." The Indians finally overcame their Fenway Park jitters with a 4–3, 10-inning victory over the Boston Red Sox.

The man of the moment for the Indians was none other than Scott Michaels, who homered to lead off the top of the 10th to break a 3–3 tie. That was Michaels' second hit in five at-bats, and most important, it extended his hitting streak to a now-attention-getting 26 games.

"That's not the most important thing," Michaels corrected one intrepid reporter. "The most important thing was that we got a win that we really needed."

Were the Indians pressing in an effort to do too much at Fenway?

"I can't really say," Michaels said. "I wasn't playing a whole lot the last time we were here. Speaking for myself, I can say that I approach things the same way day in and day out, and I'm sure the rest of the guys would tell you that as well."

OK, then, important things first: The Indians improved to 58–48 and stayed within five games of the Minnesota Twins for the top spot in the American League Central. They are two ahead of Chicago and three ahead of Boston for the top wild-card spot.

As for that secondary little matter, Michaels is now 54 for 106 in the streak, and he's batting .375 for the season. His other hit was a two-out single in the first inning against Eduardo Suarez. That kept the inning alive for Terry Rovetto, who homered over the Green Monster in left field for a 2–0 Indians lead.

The Indians got a much-needed solid start from their ace, Lynn Moda, who worked seven innings giving up seven hits and two runs while walking nobody and striking out five.

"It's never easy to pitch here, but I was able to make their hitters use the big part of the ballpark," Moda said. "I've been in some tight ballgames lately, so maybe that helps me to bear down out there a little more."

Moda gave up a game-tying single to Carlos Blanco in the fifth after a single by Omar Perez and a double by Andre Banks.

The Indians went ahead 3–2 in the seventh. Terry Rovetto doubled off the Monster, and Oliver Reiner singled to right, scoring Rovetto.

Geno Milzie worked a flawless eighth for the Indians, but closer Ivan Zyzna suffered a rare blown save as he gave up a one-out single in the ninth to Morgan Leifer, who advanced to second on Zyzna's wild pitch. Desmond Underwood hit a single to short right, and Leifer scored when Micah Millison bobbled the ball.

But Michaels silenced the Fenway crowd in the 10th when he hit a 2–0 fastball from Jose Rodriguez over the Green Monster. Lee Hazelton pitched a perfect 10th for the win.

"We really needed that," said Indians manager Todd Stein. "Who better to do that than Scottie? How about that? I don't think this place (Fenway) had gotten into our heads. They just beat us up here a few times. I'd be more worried if we came in here and lost a bunch of one-run games. But yeah, it does feel good to get one at last."

CLEVELAND INDIANS VS BOSTON RED SOX · AUGUST 3
CLEVELAND 4 / BOSTON 3

CLEVELAND INDIANS											
BATTING	AB	R	H	RBI	2B	3B	HR	BB	SO	BA	
RIKKI LABUDDA CF	5	0	1	0	0	0	0	0	1	.278	
MICAH MILLISON RF	5	0	0	0	0	0	0	0	2	.285	
SCOTT MICHAELS 2B	5	2	2	0	0	0	1	0	0	.375	
TERRY ROVETTO 3B	5	2	2	1	1	0	0	0	0	.265	
OLIVER REINER 1B	4	0	2	2	0	0	0	1	1	.271	
WILSON WHITE LF	4	0	2	1	1	0	0	1	0	.279	
JUSTIN KESTINO SS	4	0	0	0	0	0	0	1	2	.261	
BERNARD HARPER DH	4	0	2	0	0	0	0	0	0	.258	
MORRIS JEROME C	3	0	1	0	0	0	0	1	1	.233	
PITCHING	IP	H	R	ER	SO	BB	ERA				
LYNN MODA	7	7	2	2	7	2	4.12				
GENO MILZIE	1	0	0	0	0	0	2.61				
IVAN ZYZNA (BS)	1	2	1	1	0	0	1.35				
LEE HAZELTON (W)	1	0	0	0	1	0	2.43				
BOSTON RED SOX											
BATTING	AB	R	H	RBI	2B	3B	HR	BB	SO	BA	
OMAR PEREZ LF	5	1	1	0	0	0	0	0	1	.297	
STU KENNEDY SS	5	1	2	1	1	0	0	0	1	.312	
CARLOS BLANCO C	4	0	1	1	0	0	0	1	1	.293	
MORGAN LEIFER 1B	5	1	1	0	0	0	0	0	0	.307	
JACK KINCAID DH	4	0	0	0	0	0	0	1	1	.291	
DESMOND UNDERWOOD 3B	4	0	2	1	1	0	0	0	0	.291	
SANTIAGO AVILLA 2B	3	0	1	0	0	0	0	0	2	.268	
SALVATORE ESPINOSA RF	4	0	0	0	1	0	0	0	1	.235	
VICTOR TRAGGER JR CF	4	0	1	0	0	0	0	0	1	.269	
PITCHING	IP	H	R	ER	SO	BB	ERA				
EDUARDO SUAREZ	7	8	3	3	5	3	3.43				
EDDIE MYERS	2	2	0	0	2	1	3.09				
JOSE RODRIGUEZ (L)	1	2	1	1	0	0	3.09				
INNING	1	2	3	4	5	6	7	8	9	10	TOTAL
CLEVELAND	2	0	0	0	0	0	1	0	0	1	4
BOSTON	0	0	0	0	2	0	0	0	1	0	3

GAME 107

By SAM LARDNER

The Cleveland Press

BOSTON, August 4 — Welcome to Fenway Park, Eli Batt.

The Cleveland Indians' newcomer got his first look at Fenway Wednesday night, and one could hardly blame him if he never wants to come back.

It wasn't that Batt pitched poorly as the 7–2 loss to the Boston Red Sox might indicate. It's just that he fell victim to Fenway's quirks, nooks and crannies.

The Red Sox's Trace Attenberg dropped a three-run homer just over the Green Monster in the first inning. In the fourth, Omar Perez curled one around the Pesky Pole, some 302 feet from home plate down the right-field line. That put the Red Sox up 5–0, and that was pretty much that, except for the Indians' Scott Michaels extending his hitting streak to 27 games by going 1 for 5, a fourth-inning single.

Batt came to the Indians last week in a trade with the Cincinnati Reds for outfielder Huron Southworth and J.J. Kulakofski. He sparkled in his Indians debut against the Chicago White Sox in a 6–1 victory. Even though he is a veteran and interleague play has been in effect since 1997, Batt had never pitched in Fenway.

"Of course, I've been here, but my turn in the rotation didn't come up when we were here," he said. "You know what you're up against here. But I seemed to get it all in one game. Those would not have been home runs anywhere else. No excuses. It is what it is. But I did feel kind of snakebit out there."

The Indians lost their fifth game in six tries at Fenway this season, and they dropped to 58–46 on the season. They trail the first-place Minnesota Twins by 5 games in the American League Central and lead the White Sox by one game and the Red Sox by two for the top wild-card spot. The three-city road trip continues Friday at Tampa Bay.

"They're all going to be tough," said manager Todd Stein. "We'll get a day off, but it's been a road-heavy schedule for us since the all-star break. Eli didn't get hit around tonight. He got dinged up a bit — nickel-and-dimed — but that's going to happen here. You tend to see some crazy things at this ballpark It can benefit both teams. Tonight, it helped the home team."

The Indians got their runs in the fifth, when Justin Kestino banged a double off the top of the Monster to score Terry Rovetto and Oliver Reiner, both of whom had singled against Red Sox starter Scott Johnson.

Batt managed to make it through 5 and one-third innings, giving up seven hits. Buck Sterling gave up the final two Boston runs in the seventh. Mickey Penney finished for the Indians.

As for Michaels, he struck out twice, popped out and grounded out in addition to his single. His season average fell from .375 to .372, and he is 55 for 111 in the streak.

"They pitched me pretty tough tonight," he said. "You're not going to hit every game."

With Michaels, it only seems that way.

CLEVELAND INDIANS VS BOSTON RED SOX · AUGUST 4
BOSTON 7 / CLEVELAND 2

CLEVELAND INDIANS

BATTING	AB	R	H	RBI	2B	3B	HR	BB	SO	BA
RIKKI LABUDDA CF	4	0	2	0	0	0	0	1	0	.280
MICAH MILLISON RF	5	0	0	0	0	0	0	0	1	.281
SCOTT MICHAELS 2B	5	0	1	0	0	0	0	0	2	.372
TERRY ROVETTO 3B	4	1	2	0	1	0	0	0	0	.268
OLIVER REINER 1B	4	1	2	0	0	0	0	0	0	.274
WILSON WHITE LF	4	0	0	0	0	0	0	0	2	.276
JUSTIN KESTINO SS	4	0	1	2	1	0	0	0	0	.261
BERNARD HARPER DH	4	0	1	0	0	0	0	0	1	.258
MORRIS JEROME C	4	0	1	0	0	0	0	0	1	.234

PITCHING	IP	H	R	ER	SO	BB	ERA
ELI BATT (L)	5.33	6	5	5	3	2	4.38
BUCK STERLING	1.67	4	2	2	1	1	4.06
MICKEY PENNY	1	1	0	0	0	0	3.52

BOSTON RED SOX

BATTING	AB	R	H	RBI	2B	3B	HR	BB	SO	BA
OMAR PEREZ LF	4	1	2	2	0	0	1	1	1	.299
STU KENNEDY SS	5	1	0	0	0	0	0	0	0	.306
CARLOS BLANCO C	5	1	2	0	0	0	0	0	0	.295
MORGAN LEIFER 1B	4	1	0	0	0	0	0	1	1	.303
TRACE ATTENBERG DH	4	0	1	3	0	0	1	1	1	.269
DESMOND UNDERWOOD 3B	4	1	2	0	1	0	0	0	0	.294
SANTIAGO AVILLA 2B	4	1	1	0	0	0	0	0	1	.268
SALVATORE ESPINOSA RF	4	0	2	2	1	0	0	0	0	.239
VICTOR TRAGGER JR CF	4	1	1	0	0	0	0	1	0	.268

PITCHING	IP	H	R	ER	SO	BB	ERA
SCOTT JOHNSON (W)	7	7	0	0	6	1	3.57
SANDY BENCOMO	2	3	2	2	1	0	3.94

INNING	1	2	3	4	5	6	7	8	9	TOTAL
CLEVELAND	0	0	0	0	0	0	2	0	0	2
BOSTON	3	0	0	2	0	0	2	0		7

GAME 108

By SAM LARDNER
The Cleveland Press

TAMPA, August 6 — The Indians got their first look at Piniella-Maddon Field, the brand-new home of the Tampa Bay Rays.

The reviews after Friday night's 2–1 loss to the Rays were decidedly mixed.

On one hand, anything has to be better than Tropicana Field, that gloomy old edifice in St. Pete.

On the other hand, the Indians could get nothing going under the retractable roof of the new place, which is named for two of the most famous managerial names in Rays (and Devil Rays) history: Lou Piniella and Joe Maddon.

"Nice place," said Indians manager Todd Stein, whose team has lost two in a row and three of four to fall to 58–50. "The hitters came back to the dugout saying the background was a little tough. But maybe it was just their pitcher."

Rays starter Johnny Dixon stymied the Indians all night, limiting them to four hits in seven innings. Dixon was not able to halt the hitting streak of Scott Michaels, who went 1 for 4, a sixth-inning single, to extend the streak to 28 games.

Just because the math is obvious, that's halfway to Joe DiMaggio's record 56-game hitting streak.

"Oh, I'm not even thinking about that," said Michaels, who is 56 for 115 during the streak. His batting average for the season dipped from .372 to .371. "I don't keep track of all that stuff. I feel like I'm scuffling just a bit right now."

For Michaels, "scuffling" means going 2 for 9 over his last two games. In Friday's series opener against the Rays, he struck out on a checked-swing in the first inning, flied out in the third and took a called third strike in the ninth.

"Just kind of in-between the last couple days," he said. "There's no pressure or anything like that. I've kind of gotten used to the attention and have had fun with it. But you're not going to swing it good every game. That's me right now."

He wasn't alone. The Indians didn't get a run until the eighth, when they were down 2–0.

Indians starter Brian Howard matched Dixon pitch for pitch until running into trouble in the fifth, when the Rays got both of their runs. Howard walked Tom Donnelly Jr. leading off before Randy McGee's single sent Donnelly to third. A double off the top of the center-field wall by Rueben Portugal scored both runners.

"The only thing I can't live with is the walk," said Howard, who went 6 and two-thirds innings, giving up seven hits with two walks and five strikeouts. "You're just asking for trouble there. But overall, I thought I threw it pretty well. You just try to keep your team in it, and except for that one inning, I feel I did that."

The Indians scored with two outs in the eighth. Morris Jerome doubled with two outs against Rays setup man Adolfo Vasquez. Rikki LaBudda hit a chopper to second baseman Donnelly, who may have rushed his throw in an effort to get the speedy LaBudda. The ball wound up hitting the netting down the right-field line, and Morris came home.

But that was it, as the Indians went down 123 against Tampa Bay closer Buddy Anderson in the ninth.

"We had our guys up there," Stein said. "He made some tough pitches. Those sliders are hard to lay off of, and I think Scottie just got fooled a little bit there. But he's the last guy I'm going to complain about these days with what he's been doing."

GAME 108

CLEVELAND INDIANS VS TAMPA BAY RAYS • AUGUST 6
TAMPA BAY 2 / CLEVELAND 1

CLEVELAND INDIANS										
BATTING	AB	R	H	RBI	2B	3B	HR	BB	SO	BA
RIKKI LABUDDA CF	4	0	1	1	0	0	0	0	0	.280
MICAH MILLISON RF	4	0	0	0	0	0	0	0	0	.278
SCOTT MICHAELS 2B	4	0	1	0	0	0	0	0	2	.371
TERRY ROVETTO 3B	3	0	1	0	1	0	0	1	0	.268
OLIVER REINER 1B	4	0	1	0	0	0	0	0	1	.273
WILSON WHITE LF	4	0	0	0	0	0	0	0	0	.273
JUSTIN KESTINO SS	4	0	0	0	0	0	0	0	1	.258
BERNARD HARPER DH	4	0	1	0	0	0	0	0	1	.258
MORRIS JEROME C	4	1	1	0	1	0	0	0	1	.234

PITCHING	IP	H	R	ER	SO	BB	ERA			
BRIAN HOWARD (L)	6.67	7	2	2	5	2	4.51			
GENO MILZIE	1.33	1	0	0	1	0	2.54			

TAMPA BAY RAYS										
BATTING	AB	R	H	RBI	2B	3B	HR	BB	SO	BA
TIM CLARK LF	4	0	2	0	0	0	0	0	0	.299
TOM DONNELLY JR 2B	3	1	0	0	0	0	0	1	1	.309
RANDY MCGEE SS	3	1	1	0	0	0	0	0	1	.293
RUEBEN PORTUGAL 3B	4	0	2	2	1	0	0	0	0	.310
ERNESTO JURADO 1B	3	0	0	0	0	0	0	1	2	.266
TIM STAFFORD RF	4	0	1	0	0	0	0	0	0	.291
FRANK MORETTI C	4	0	2	0	0	0	0	0	1	.272
BRANDON GREGERSON DH	4	0	0	0	0	0	0	0	0	.232
REGGIE PATTERSON CF	4	0	0	0	0	0	0	0	1	.264

PITCHING	IP	H	R	ER	SO	BB	ERA			
JOHNNY DIXON (W)	7	4	0	0	6	1	3.46			
ADOLFO VASQUEZ	1	2	1	1	0	0	3.77			
BUDDY ANDERSON	1	0	0	0	1	0	2.81			

INNING	1	2	3	4	5	6	7	8	9	TOTAL
CLEVELAND	0	0	0	0	0	0	0	1	0	1
TAMPA BAY	0	0	0	0	2	0	0	0		2

GAME 109

By SAM LARDNER

The Cleveland Press

TAMPA, August 7 — Scott Michaels broke out of his "mini-slump" Saturday night, and it came at the perfect time for the Cleveland Indians.

After going 2-for-9 in his previous two games, Michaels led the attack Saturday by going 3 for 5, teaming with pitcher Kenny Camden, who pitched seven shutout innings in a 5–0 whitewash of the Tampa Bay Rays.

Michaels hit a two-run homer in the fourth inning and an RBI double in the sixth as he extended his hitting streak to 29 games. One more will tie the onetime phenom for 37th place all time.

"It sounds funny to say, but I felt better out there tonight," Michaels said. "I was able to scratch out some hits the last couple of games, but tonight, I was able to square up some balls."

During his streak, Michaels is 59-for-120 (.492), and he raised his season batting average from .371 to .374.

"This is really fun to watch," said manager Todd Stein, whose team snapped a two-game skid and improved to 59–50. "When you get near 30 (games), people start to take notice. If we're winning games, I'm all for the attention the kid can get. He's earned it, especially after the injury problems he's had."

Not to be overlooked in this game was Camden. "The Wiz" was a wonder to the Tampa hitters, as he allowed only five hits, with just one runner making it as far as second base. The veteran lefty struck out five and walked nobody.

"Five is a lot of strikeouts for me," he said. "That probably ran my pitch count up. From what the guys were saying last night, this is a pretty good place to pitch, or at least it seems it is. I was able to locate pretty well, which is pretty important if you don't have velocity — which I don't have. So this one felt pretty good."

Rays starter Tyler Harrison retired the first 10 batters he faced before Micah Millison singled with one out in the top of the fourth. Michaels wasted no time, picking on a first-pitch fastball and sending it over the wall in left field.

"We need to have a better game plan against him," fumed Rays manager Harry Morgan. "The kid is on fire and just sitting dead red. You can't give him a fastball on the first pitch. Live and learn, I guess. We'll figure it out by tomorrow — or at least I hope we do."

Michaels' double drove in Rikki LaBudda, who singled and stole second base. The Indians got a pair of insurance runs in the eighth on Bernard Harper's two-run homer.

Solly Alvarez and Lee Hazelton finished up out of the pen, giving Geno Milzie and Ivan Zyzna a break.

"We're carrying the extra pitcher, so we do have that luxury," said Stein. "At this time of the year, with arms being a little tired, I'm not so sure it's a luxury as much as it's a necessity."

CLEVELAND INDIANS VS TAMPA BAY RAYS • AUGUST 7
CLEVELAND 5 / TAMPA BAY 0

CLEVELAND INDIANS										
BATTING	AB	R	H	RBI	2B	3B	HR	BB	SO	BA
RIKKI LABUDDA CF	4	1	1	0	0	0	0	1	0	.280
MICAH MILLISON RF	5	1	2	0	0	0	0	0	0	.279
SCOTT MICHAELS 2B	5	1	3	3	1	0	1	0	1	.374
TERRY ROVETTO 3B	4	0	1	0	1	0	0	0	1	.268
OLIVER REINER 1B	4	0	0	0	0	0	0	0	2	.271
KIERAN CATSEF LF	3	1	1	0	0	0	0	1	0	.258
LEO TAYLOR SS	4	0	0	0	0	0	0	0	1	.260
BERNARD HARPER DH	4	1	2	2	0	0	1	0	1	.261
MORRIS JEROME C	3	0	2	0	1	0	0	1	0	.238

PITCHING	IP	H	R	ER	SO	BB	ERA			
KENNY CAMDEN (W)	7	5	0	0	5	0	3.31			
SOLLY ALVAREZ	1	0	0	0	0	0	2.91			
LEE HAZELTON	1	0	0	0	0	0	2.36			

TAMPA BAY RAYS										
BATTING	AB	R	H	RBI	2B	3B	HR	BB	SO	BA
TIM CLARK LF	5	0	0	0	0	0	0	0	1	.295
TOM DONNELLY JR 2B	4	1	2	0	1	0	0	1	0	.311
RANDY MCGEE SS	5	0	1	0	0	0	0	0	0	.292
RUEBEN PORTUGAL 3B	4	1	2	0	0	0	0	0	0	.312
ERNESTO JURADO 1B	4	1	0	0	0	0	0	1	1	.263
TIM STAFFORD RF	4	1	1	0	1	0	0	1	1	.290
FRANK MORETTI C	4	1	0	0	0	0	0	0	0	.268
BRANDON GREGERSON DH	4	1	2	0	0	0	0	0	1	.235
REGGIE PATTERSON CF	4	0	1	0	0	0	0	0	0	.264

PITCHING	IP	H	R	ER	SO	BB	ERA			
TYLER HARRISON (L)	5.67	8	3	3	4	3	5.67			
OMAR MELENDEZ	1.3	2	0	0	1	0	3.45			
MIKE KILCRAN	2	2	2	2	1	0	3.27			

INNING	1	2	3	4	5	6	7	8	9	TOTAL
CLEVELAND	0	0	0	2	0	1	0	2	0	5
TAMPA BAY	0	0	0	0	0	0	0	0	0	0

GAME 110

By SAM LARDNER
The Cleveland Press

TAMPA, August 8 — Normally it's cause for celebration when a ballplayer's name is mentioned in the same breath with a passel of Hall of Famers.

But neither Scott Michaels nor the rest of the Cleveland Indians were in the mood to celebrate Sunday despite Michaels' hitting streak reaching 30 games.

That's because the Tribe turned in a lackluster performance reminiscent of early this season, when the often could not get out of their own way.

The result was a 6–1 loss to the Tampa Bay Rays at Piniella-Maddon Field on a sticky Sunday afternoon.

Indians starting pitcher Tak Fujimoto lost his second straight, lasting only four innings and giving up all six Rays runs. His fielders didn't help him. They committed three errors, including one by Michaels in the Rays' four-run third inning.

"I can't really feel too good about things right now," said Michaels, who was 1-for-4, a first-inning single. "I didn't play a great game and we lost. I've never been comfortable with all the hitting-streak talk, and maybe after a game like today, you'll understand why. It's not about me."

For the record, the 23-year-old Michaels moved into a tie for 37th place all time by extending the streak to 30 games. He joins such luminaries as Stan Musial, George Brett, Albert Pujols, Charlie Grimm and Tris Speaker. The last Indians hitter to hit in 30 straight was Sandy Alomar Jr., in 1997.

During the streak, Michaels is 60-for-124 (.484). He is batting .372.

"It's a nice thing; I just wish he would have reached that number in a victory," said Indians manager Todd Stein, whose team has lost four of its last six and has fallen to 59–51. "Scottie is focused on all the right things. I'm sure he'll tell you the same thing. For a young kid, he has his head screwed on straight."

Fujimoto didn't have much of a chance in this one. The Rays broke on top 2–0 in the first on Rueben Portugal's two-run homer. That came with one out after shortstop Justin Kestino threw one away for an error.

The wheels came completely off in the third, thanks to a pair of walks and Michaels' error, when he bobbed what looked to be a double-play grounder off the bat of Frank Moretti.

"I can blame no one but myself," Fujimoto said through translator Ryuji Sato. "The home run and the walks are my fault. The fielders have played well behind me all year. I cannot put that on them."

Fujimoto even had his preferred catcher, backup Iceberg Peters, behind the plate. In his previous start, an 8–0 loss to the Red Sox, Fujimoto threw to starter Morris Jerome.

"I told you that makes no difference," Fujimoto said. "End of story."

All the while, Indians batters managed a grand total of three hits off Rays starter Laz Reeder, who worked seven innings.

The Indians got a consolation run in the eighth when pinch hitter Leo Taylor doubled and came home on a double by Micah Millison. Lorry Unger, Mickey Penny and Lee Hazelton mopped up out of the pen for the Tribe, who pack up and travel to Anaheim, where this crazy season started.

"I remember it well," said Stein, who was a coach on the staff of then-manager Dave Mills at the time. "We got our asses swept. We've had a couple of these long three-city trips. I don't know how they figure that, but it is what it is. The schedule says we have to go from Cleveland to Boston to Tampa to Anaheim, so we do it."

GAME 110

CLEVELAND INDIANS VS TAMPA BAY RAYS • AUGUST 8
TAMPA BAY 6 / CLEVELAND 1

CLEVELAND INDIANS

BATTING	AB	R	H	RBI	2B	3B	HR	BB	SO	BA
RIKKI LABUDDA CF	3	0	0	0	0	0	0	0	0	.278
LEO TAYLOR PH	1	1	1	0	1	0	0	0	0	.270
MICAH MILLISON RF	4	0	1	1	1	0	0	0	0	.279
SCOTT MICHAELS 2B	4	0	1	0	0	0	0	0	1	.372
TERRY ROVETTO 3B	3	0	0	0	0	0	0	1	0	.266
OLIVER REINER 1B	4	0	1	0	0	0	0	0	1	.271
WILSON WHITE LF	3	0	0	0	0	0	0	1	0	.271
JUSTIN KESTINO SS	4	0	0	0	0	0	0	0	1	.255
BERNARD HARPER DH	3	0	1	0	0	0	0	1	1	.262
ICEBERG PETERS C	4	0	0	0	0	0	0	0	2	.198

PITCHING	IP	H	R	ER	SO	BB	ERA			
TAK FUJIMOTO (L)	4	7	6	1	2	3	3.41			
LORRY UNGER	2	1	0	0	1	0	4.33			
MICKEY PENNY	1	1	0	0	0	0	3.46			
LEE HAZELTON	1	0	0	0	1	0	2.29			

TAMPA BAY RAYS

BATTING	AB	R	H	RBI	2B	3B	HR	BB	SO	BA
TIM CLARK LF	5	0	0	0	0	0	0	0	1	.294
TOM DONNELLY JR 2B	4	1	2	2	1	0	0	1	0	.307
RANDY MCGEE SS	5	0	1	0	0	0	0	0	0	.291
RUEBEN PORTUGAL 3B	4	1	2	2	0	0	1	0	0	.308
ERNESTO JURADO 1B	4	1	0	0	0	0	0	1	1	.263
TIM STAFFORD RF	4	1	1	0	1	0	0	1	1	.290
FRANK MORETTI C	4	1	0	0	0	0	0	0	0	.265
BRANDON GREGERSON DH	4	1	2	2	0	0	0	0	1	.236
REGGIE PATTERSON CF	4	0	1	0	0	0	0	0	0	.261

PITCHING	IP	H	R	ER	SO	BB	ERA			
LAZ REEDER (W)	7	3	0	0	5	2	3.46			
DON DAVENPORT	2	2	1	1	1	0	3.66			

INNING	1	2	3	4	5	6	7	8	9	TOTAL
CLEVELAND	0	0	0	0	0	0	0	1	0	1
TAMPA BAY	2	0	4	0	0	0	0	0		6

GAME 111

By SAM LARDNER
The Cleveland Press

ANAHEIM, Calif., August 9 — What's changed for the Cleveland Indians since they opened the baseball season at Angel Stadium?

Just about everything.

The last time the Indians were here, Dave Mills was the manager, Huron Southworth and Angel Rodriguez were starters and Scott Michaels was a benchwarmer hoping that his status in the game had not been downgraded from "phenom" to "prospect" to "suspect."

An Opening Day loss was the first of six in a row for the Indians, setting the wheels in motion for Mills to be fired. Southworth has been traded, and Rodriguez has been supplanted by Michaels, whose status has risen to that of "sensation."

The changes were all quite apparent Monday night in a 4–2 victory over the Angels. Michaels extended his hitting streak to 31 games by going 2 for 4, with a single and a double. Southworth's replacement, Micah Millison, had three hits and scored on Michaels' third-inning double.

There was one similarity from the season opener for the Indians. Staff ace Lynn Moda started for the Tribe, but his result from Opening Day was quite a bit different, too. Moda was thrashed about in a 14–3 loss in the opener, but on Monday, he was in total control with a seven-inning, five-hit, two-run performance.

All of that pleased interim manager Todd Stein, who replaced Mills after 10 games.

"A little bit different visit to Disneyland this time, at least for this night," Stein said. "That seemed like an eternity ago, when we were here the last time. A win like tonight will help us put that start out of our minds."

For no one is that more true than for Moda.

"I had it in the back of my mind, to be honest with you," he said. "That was a nightmare of a start, both for me and the team. We're at a totally different place now. I can't begin to tell you the difference in feeling."

Now on to that Michaels fellow. He flied out in the first inning against Roberto Colon but was in the right spot in the third, after Millison singled. Michaels hit a drive to the opposite-field gap in right-center. The speedy Millison scored easily, and Michaels came home on Wilson White's single, putting the Tribe up 2–0.

The 31-game hitting streak ties him for 26th all time with the likes of Cleveland Naps Hall of Famer Nap Lajoie, Rogers Hornsby, Ed Delahanty and Vladimir Guerrero.

During the streak, Michaels is 62-for-128 (.484). For the season, he is batting .374. All this not too far from Hollywood.

"All I remember about the last time here was how comfortable the bench in the dugout was," he joked. "I was just hoping to stick, honestly. So yeah, this is a little bit of storybook stuff, but I'll let you guys write those stories. I'm having too much fun playing baseball and helping the team try to win and get into the postseason."

The Tribe got their other two runs in the seventh when Morris Jerome singled home Justin Kestino and Bernard Harper.

Moda, who reached the 100-pitch mark in the seventh, gave up a two-run homer to Trent Norris in that inning. Stein allowed him to finish, and Moda shut it down from there, winding up with 112 pitches. Gene Milzie earned a hold, and closer Ivan Zyzna got the save by striking out the side in the ninth.

The victory also erased the memory of Sunday's stinker at Tampa Bay, a 6–1 loss, and it improved the Indians to 60 and 51 for the season. They crept to within six games of the first-place Minnesota Twins in the American League Central. They're a game ahead of the White Sox and two ahead of Boston for the top wild-card spot.

"We've been pretty good about putting those bad games behind us," Stein said. "We played a good game in the field tonight, and when you get innings out of your starter and have Scottie going as hot as he is, you have a chance."

GAME 111

CLEVELAND INDIANS VS LOS ANGELES ANGELS · AUGUST 9
CLEVELAND 4 / LOS ANGELES 2

CLEVELAND INDIANS

BATTING	AB	R	H	RBI	2B	3B	HR	BB	SO	BA
RIKKI LABUDDA CF	4	0	1	0	0	0	0	0	0	.277
MICAH MILLISON RF	3	1	3	0	1	0	0	1	0	.285
SCOTT MICHAELS 2B	4	1	2	1	1	0	0	0	1	.374
TERRY ROVETTO 3B	3	0	0	0	0	0	0	1	0	.264
OLIVER REINER 1B	4	0	0	0	0	0	0	0	2	.268
WILSON WHITE LF	4	0	2	1	0	0	0	1	0	.273
JUSTIN KESTINO SS	3	1	2	0	0	0	0	0	1	.259
BERNARD HARPER DH	4	1	2	0	1	0	0	0	0	.265
MORRIS JEROME C	4	0	1	2	0	0	0	0	1	.238

PITCHING	IP	H	R	ER	SO	BB	ERA			
LYNN MODA (W)	7	7	2	2	6	2	4.04			
GENO MILZE	1	1	0	0	0	0	2.49			
IVAN ZYZNA (S)	1	1	0	0	3	0	2.36			

LOS ANGELES ANGELS

BATTING	AB	R	H	RBI	2B	3B	HR	BB	SO	BA
TIM THORSEN RF	4	0	1	0	0	0	0	0	1	.298
JACOB BAKER DH	4	0	0	0	1	0	0	0	1	.300
CHICO GOMEZ CF	3	0	1	0	0	0	0	1	1	.278
PETE WARREN 1B	4	0	0	0	0	0	0	0	2	.281
BENJI WASHINGTON SS	3	1	1	0	1	0	0	1	0	.267
TRENT NORRIS LF	4	1	1	2	0	0	1	0	1	.290
LIM CHANG 3B	3	0	1	0	0	0	0	0	2	.269
ALBERT TORRES 2B	3	0	0	0	0	0	0	0	0	.230
CARLOS DIAZ C	3	0	0	0	0	0	1	0	1	.258

PITCHING	IP	H	R	ER	SO	BB	ERA			
ROBERTO COLON (L)	6.33	9	4	4	4	2	3.79			
HIRAM MOLINA	1.67	3	0	0	1	1	3.98			
MIKE VANDENBERG	1	1	0	0	0	0	3.41			

INNING	1	2	3	4	5	6	7	8	9	TOTAL
CLEVELAND	0	0	2	0	0	0	2	0	0	4
LOS ANGELES	0	0	0	0	0	0	2	0	0	2

GAME 112

ANAHEIM, Calif. August 10 — This stuff is starting to get serious, isn't it?

If you couldn't stay up and watch an Indians game that began at 10:05 p.m. EDT, here is what you missed:

The Indians pounded out 16 hits in an 8–3 victory over the Los Angeles Angels at Angel Stadium.

The hottest hitter on the planet, the Indians' Scott Michaels, extended his hitting streak to 32 games, going 2 for 5 with a first-inning triple and a sixth-inning single.

Recently acquired starting pitcher Eli Batt won his second game in three decisions for the Tribe as he worked 6 and two-thirds innings, giving up six hits and two runs.

Neither Batt nor Michaels were in the picture for the Indians at the start of this season, but both could be key factors if the Tribe is going to make a run at the postseason and a run into late October and early November.

"You never know how a season is going to unfold," said interim manager Todd Stein, whose team won its second straight to improve to 61 and 51. "You have to give some credit to J.D. (general manager Eisner) and the rest of the front office for picking up Eli and having the faith in Scottie. Eli has been a big shot in the arm, and I don't have to tell you about Scottie."

They say a triple is the most exciting play in baseball, and Michaels made it so in the first inning, when his drive to the right-field corner scored Rikki LaBudda, who led off the game with a single. Michaels stumbled and fell rounding second base but picked himself up and staggered into third base.

"Not the most graceful thing you've ever seen," he said with a self-deprecating laugh. "I thought they were going to make a play on me, so I kind of got my feet tangled up. Lucky, I didn't break my leg."

For the record — and Michaels' record is growing — the 32-game hitting streak ties him for 24th all-time with Tigers Hall of Famer Harry Heilmann and Cincinnati's Hal Morris. Both of those players compiled their streaks over two seasons.

Michaels is 64-for-133 (.481). His batting average for the season held at .374. Asked by a Los Angeles reporter if he was "feeling the pressure," Michaels responded with: "No, this is fun. Pressure is thinking you might be cut and sent packing at the beginning of this season. I'm just a guy from a small town. I'd be just as happy if nobody talked to me before or after games. No offense to you guys, but that's how I am."

This game was all Indians, who jumped on Angels pitcher Hector Lugo for three more in the second, making it 4–0. The big hit was a three-run bases loaded double by catcher Morris Jerome.

DH Bernard Harper hit a three-run homer off Angels reliever Lee Hickson in the seventh and Oliver Reiner hit a solo homer in the eighth, his 20th.

Batt was masterful after getting banged up in his last start, at Boston. His only bad inning was the fifth, and even then, it was only a two-run single by Jacob Baker that accounted for the runs. Reliever Lorry Unger gave up a meaningless run in the ninth.

"This park allows you a lot more room for error than Fenway does," Batt said. "This place is a lot like Dodger Stadium in that the ball tends to die at night. I pitched here once in interleague play before and liked it. I'm glad I was traded over here in time to let me pitch here again."

GAME 112

CLEVELAND INDIANS VS LOS ANGELES ANGELS · AUGUST 10
CLEVELAND 8 / LOS ANGELES 3

CLEVELAND INDIANS										
BATTING	AB	R	H	RBI	2B	3B	HR	BB	SO	BA
RIKKI LABUDDA CF	5	1	2	0	0	0	0	0	0	.279
MICAH MILLISON RF	5	0	1	0	0	0	0	0	1	.284
SCOTT MICHAELS 2B	5	0	2	1	0	1	0	0	1	.374
TERRY ROVETTO 3B	4	0	1	0	0	0	0	1	0	.264
OLIVER REINER 1B	5	2	2	1	0	0	1	0	0	.270
WILSON WHITE LF	4	2	2	0	1	0	0	0	1	.276
JUSTIN KESTINO SS	4	1	2	0	0	0	0	0	1	.261
BERNARD HARPER DH	4	2	2	3	0	0	1	0	0	.268
MORRIS JEROME C	4	0	2	3	1	0	0	0	0	.241
PITCHING	IP	H	R	ER	SO	BB	ERA			
ELI BATT(W)	6.67	6	2	2	7	1	3.79			
BUCK STERLING	1.33	0	0	0	0	0	3.94			
LORRY UNGER	1	2	1	1	1	0	4.46			
LOS ANGELES ANGELS										
BATTING	AB	R	H	RBI	2B	3B	HR	BB	SO	BA
TIM THORSEN RF	4	1	1	0	0	0	0	0	0	.298
JACOB BAKER DH	4	0	2	2	0	0	0	0	2	.302
CHICO GOMEZ CF	3	0	0	0	0	0	0	1	0	.275
PETE WARREN 1B	4	0	0	0	0	0	0	0	1	.278
BENJI WASHINGTON SS	4	1	2	0	1	0	0	0	1	.270
TRENT NORRIS LF	4	0	1	1	1	0	0	0	1	.289
LIM CHANG 3B	4	0	0	0	0	0	0	0	0	.265
ALBERT TORRES 2B	4	0	0	0	0	0	0	0	1	.227
CARLOS DIAZ C	3	1	2	0	0	1	0	0	2	.263
PITCHING	IP	H	R	ER	SO	BB	ERA			
HECTOR LUGO(L)	4	7	4	4	3	1	3.87			
JAVIER RIVERA	2	5	0	0	1	0	3.94			
LEE HICKSON	2	4	4	4	0	0	4.50			
GRAHAM PINDER	1	0	0	0	0	0	2.90			
INNING	1	2	3	4	5	6	7	8	9	TOTAL
CLEVELAND	1	3	0	0	0	0	3	1	0	8
LOS ANGELES	0	0	0	0	2	0	0	1	0	3

GAME 113

By SAM LARDNER

The Cleveland Press

ANAHEIM, Calif. August 11 — Depending on your point of view, there were two ways to look at the Indians game at Angel Stadium Wednesday night and into Thursday morning: Whew, that was close. Damn, that was close.

The Indians and Scott Michaels chose option B after a 6–5 loss to the Angels in 11 innings. For those who chose option A, there was a big sigh of relief after Michaels waited until the top of the 11th to get his first hit of the game, an infield single that went to replay, before those monitoring the screens upheld the call by first-base umpire Sandy Gold that Michaels indeed had beaten the throw of Angels shortstop Benji Washington.

The appreciative crowd of 39,234 applauded the opposing player. That barely extended Michaels' hitting streak to 33 games as he went 1 for 6.

"I would have traded it for a win," he said. "I had some chances earlier but left a couple guys on base. If it had ended tonight and we would have won, I would have been perfectly OK with it. I was glad I was called safe because it gave us a chance to win, not because it extended any streak. You guys know that by now."

The modest Michaels seems totally unimpressed with himself, but he's opened up eyes around the league with a streak that ties him for 19th all-time with a cast of characters that includes "Prince" Hal Chase, Rogers Hornsby, Heinie Manush and Dan Uggla.

"I was scared to death every time that kid came up," said Angels manager Gary Lee. "He's hitting the hell out of the ball. Maybe it's in the cards for him to keep going, especially with that last hit. I can smile about that now because we won the ballgame."

Michaels is 65-for-139 (.468) during the streak. Overall, his batting average took a dip, from .374 to .371.

The Indians had plenty of chances for a three-game series sweep. They jumped on Angels starter Don Zega for a pair of runs in the first. Rikki LaBudda was the table-setter again, as the leadoff man opened with a bunt single. He went to third on Micah Millison's single to right.

After Michaels struck out, Terry Rovetto doubled to score LaBudda and put Millison on third. Oliver Reiner drove Millison home with a sacrifice fly. Staked to a 2–0 lead, Indians starting pitcher Brian Howard cruised through the first two innings before giving up a leadoff single to Tim Thorsen in the bottom of the third. DH Jacob Baker then cracked a two-run homer down the line in left, as White made a leaping attempt for the ball at the short fence.

The Angels went up 5–2 in the fifth on a bases-clearing double by Lim Chang. The Indians tied it in the sixth on a three-run homer by DH Bernard Harper, who homered for the second day in a row. Indians closer Ivan Zyzna sent the game into extra innings by working out of a jam in the bottom of the ninth. Mickey Penney held the Angels at bay in the 10th, and the Indians could not capitalize on Michaels' hit in the 11th. In the bottom half, Lee Hazelton walked in the winning run with the bases loaded.

"Tough way to go," said Indians manager Todd Stein, whose team fell to 61–52. "You have to trust your bullpen. Mickey got into trouble at the start of the 11th, and I went to Haze thinking he could get a strikeout or two. But he just didn't have the control. That's going to happen with young pitchers."

The Indians have Thursday off, and they'll have a throng of fans and media waiting for them Friday, when the Baltimore Orioles come to Progressive Field. Indians media-relations chief Glenn Liss says media credentials have topped 50, with Michaels' hometown paper from Versailles,

Ohio, coming along with newspapers from Dayton and Bloomington, Ind., where Michaels attended Indiana University.

"It's well deserved, and I know Scottie is going to handle it well," Stein said. "The team as a whole deserves the attention, too, for the way they've played. I'm looking forward to it."

GAME 113

CLEVELAND INDIANS VS LOS ANGELES ANGELS · AUGUST 11
LOS ANGELES 6 / CLEVELAND 5

CLEVELAND INDIANS												
BATTING	AB	R	H	RBI	2B	3B	HR	BB	SO	BA		
RIKKI LABUDDA CF	5	1	2	0	0	0	0	1	0	.280		
MICAH MILLISON RF	6	1	2	0	0	0	0	0	2	.284		
SCOTT MICHAELS 2B	6	0	1	0	0	1	0	0	1	.371		
TERRY ROVETTO 3B	5	0	2	1	1	0	0	1	0	.265		
OLIVER REINER 1B	4	0	0	1	0	0	0	0	1	.267		
WILSON WHITE LF	5	1	2	0	1	0	0	0	2	.277		
JUSTIN KESTINO SS	4	1	2	0	0	0	0	1	0	.264		
BERNARD HARPER DH	5	1	2	3	0	0	1	0	1	.270		
MORRIS JEROME C	4	0	1	0	1	0	0	1	1	.241		
PITCHING	IP	H	R	ER	SO	BB	ERA					
BRIAN HOWARD	8	9	5	5	5	1	4.58					
IVAN ZYZNA	1	1	0	0	0	0	2.29					
MICKEY PENNY	1.33	2	0	0	1	1	3.38					
LEE HAZELTON (L)	0.33	1	1	1	0	1	2.52					
LOS ANGELES ANGELS												
BATTING	AB	R	H	RBI	2B	3B	HR	BB	SO	BA		
TIM THORSEN RF	6	1	2	0	1	0	0	0	0	.298		
JACOB BAKER DH	5	1	1	2	0	0	1	1	1	.301		
CHICO GOMEZ CF	5	0	0	0	0	0	0	1	2	.271		
PETE WARREN 1B	6	1	3	0	0	0	0	0	0	.282		
BENJI WASHINGTON SS	5	2	1	0	1	0	0	0	0	.269		
TRENT NORRIS LF	5	1	2	0	1	0	0	0	1	.291		
LIM CHANG 3B	5	0	2	3	1	0	0	0	0	.268		
ALBERT TORRES 2B	4	0	2	0	0	0	0	0	0	.231		
CARLOS DIAZ C	4	0	0	1	0	0	0	1	2	.259		
PITCHING	IP	H	R	ER	SO	BB	ERA					
DON ZEGA	5.33	6	4	4	4	2	3.76					
LEE HICKSON	1.67	3	1	1	1	1	4.55					
MIKE VANDENBERG	4	4	0	0	2	1	3.00					
GRAHAM PINDER (W)	1	1	0	0	1	0	2.81					
INNING	1	2	3	4	5	6	7	8	9	10	11	TOTAL
CLEVELAND	0	0	2	0	3	0	0	0	0	0	0	5
LOS ANGELES	2	0	0	0	0	3	0	0	0	0	1	6

GAME 114

By SAM LARDNER
The Cleveland Press

CLEVELAND, August 13 — The Scott Michaels story has gotten so big that the Indians moved his pregame availability into the interview room to accommodate about 75 reporters from all types of media.

The club's media-relations director, Glenn Liss, said Michaels would do a pregame session with reporters at the start of each series as long as his hitting streak continues.

Michaels indeed kept the streak alive Friday night during a 7–1 victory over the lowly Baltimore Orioles at Progressive Field. Michaels' first-inning single extended the streak to 34 games. He added another single in the seventh, going 2 for 4 with a walk to raise his season average to .372.

The 34-game hitting streak is tied for 16th longest all time with George McQuinn, Benito Santiago and Dom DiMaggio, whose brother Joe holds the record at 56.

Most of the evening's game was nondescript, as the Indians moved to 62 and 52. Most of the entertainment came during Michaels' pregame media session. Reporters from around the state — including Michaels' hometown of Versailles, Ohio -- were present.

For a 23-year-old, Michaels handled the questions with aplomb. Asked by a Maryland reporter about his hometown, Michaels corrected him by saying it's pronounced "ver-sales," and not like the French city for which it's named. "I don't even speak French," he quipped.

Favorite food? "Skyline Chili in Cincinnati."

Favorite team growing up? "I plead the Fifth," he said before admitting it was the Indians' cross-state rivals, the Cincinnati Reds.

Favorite player growing up? "Kyle Schwarber. He's from Middletown, Ohio (55 miles due south of Versailles), and we both went to Indiana."

Does he know who Joe DiMaggio was? "Yeah, he could hit a little."

As far as Friday's game, the Indians jumped on the hapless Orioles and their starting pitcher, Renato Vasquez, for three runs in the first inning. Micah Millison and Michaels singled, and both rode home on Terry Rovetto's home run.

In the fourth, Terry Rovetto walked, and Oliver Reiner homered to make it 50. In the sixth the Tribe strung together 4 straight hits for their final two runs. That gave starting pitcher Kenny Camden plenty of cushion, and "The Wiz" was wizardly, inducing 10 groundball outs while striking out two in seven innings of five-hit, one-run ball. Solly Alvarez worked the final two innings as the Indians pulled within six games of first-place Minnesota in the American League Central. They remained tied with Chicago and two games ahead of Boston for the top wild-card spot.

"It's great to have that kind of support," Camden said. "My approach was to throw it over and let them hit it. When they put it on the ground, I feel I've done my job. We've got a real chance here this weekend to make some hay, both within the division and in the wild-card race."

GAME 114

CLEVELAND INDIANS VS BALTIMORE ORIOLES AUGUST 15
CLEVELAND 7 / BALTIMORE 1

CLEVELAND INDIANS

BATTING	AB	R	H	RBI	2B	3B	HR	BB	SO	BA
RIKKI LABUDDA CF	5	0	0	0	0	0	0	0	1	.277
MICAH MILLISON RF	4	1	2	0	0	0	0	1	0	.286
SCOTT MICHAELS 2B	4	1	2	0	0	0	0	0	1	.372
TERRY ROVETTO 3B	3	2	3	3	1	0	1	1	0	.271
OLIVER REINER 1B	4	1	2	2	0	0	1	0	0	.269
WILSON WHITE LF	4	1	1	0	1	0	0	0	2	.277
JUSTIN KESTINO SS	3	1	1	0	0	0	0	1	0	.264
BERNARD HARPER DH	4	0	1	1	0	0	0	0	1	.269
MORRIS JEROME C	4	0	1	1	1	0	0	0	1	.242

PITCHING	IP	H	R	ER	SO	BB	ERA
KENNY CAMDEN (W)	7	5	1	1	2	1	3.20
SOLLY ALVAREZ	2	1	0	0	1	0	2.78

BALTIMORE ORIOLES

BATTING	AB	R	H	RBI	2B	3B	HR	BB	SO	BA
BARBARO CASTRO SS	4	1	2	0	0	0	0	0	0	.272
KEVIN BRADY CF	4	0	1	1	1	0	0	0	0	.283
JORGE ESTRELLA 3B	4	0	0	0	0	0	0	0	1	.268
JULES PETERSON 1B	4	0	1	0	0	0	0	0	0	.281
ELMER VEGA LF	4	0	0	0	0	0	0	0	1	.265
GEORGE RADER DH	4	0	1	0	1	0	0	0	0	.290
RODOLFO SANCHEZ CF	4	0	1	0	0	0	0	0	1	.268
WILFREDO MURILLO RF	3	0	0	0	0	0	0	1	0	.228
TERRY SHINER C	3	0	0	0	0	0	0	0	0	.256

PITCHING	IP	H	R	ER	SO	BB	ERA
RENATO VASQUEZ (L)	4	7	5	5	3	1	3.88
ANIBAL NOVOA	2	3	2	2	0	1	4.78
RODNEY DAVIS	2	3	0	0	1	1	3.19

INNING	1	2	3	4	5	6	7	8	9	TOTAL
BALTIMORE	0	0	0	0	0	1	0	0	0	1
CLEVELAND	3	0	0	2	0	2	0	0		7

GAME 115

By SAM LARDNER
The Cleveland Press

CLEVELAND, August 14 — Under normal circumstances, Tak Fujimoto would have been the guy getting all the attention Saturday after he and the Indians beat the Baltimore Orioles 6–1 at Progressive Field.

Ah, but these are not normal times for the Tribe.

Fujimoto did his part and then some as he stymied the Birds for eight innings in what might have been his best performance as member of the Indians. Of course, that's what you expect when you pay a guy $103 million over six years to come over from Japan and pitch for you.

But the unexpected has upstaged everything around these parts. We're talking again of Scott Michaels (who else?), the nearly failed phenom, who is now an international sensation, thanks to the large contingent of Japanese media following Fujimoto. They, too, have turned their attention to Michaels.

They were just as curious to talk with Michaels after Saturday afternoon's performance: a 3 for 4 day at the plate with a two-run homer that extended his hitting streak to 35 games. Five other players have reached 35: Fred Clarke, Ty Cobb, George Sisler, Luis Castillo and Chase Utley. Clarke, Cobb and Sisler are Hall of Famers.

During the streak, Michaels is 70-for-147 (.476). Saturday's performance raised his season batting average from .372 to .376.

Reporters covering Fujimoto wanted to know if Michaels could say something to address the fans back in Japan.

"Wait a minute," he said. "I told everybody yesterday I don't speak French. I sure as heck can't speak Japanese."

Michaels went on to say — in English — that he appreciates the attention but that he doesn't want to upstage Fujimoto.

Impossible. Even Orioles manager Ray Rotstin was effusive in praise for Michaels.

"I don't know that I've seen anything like this," he said. "He was barely a factor for almost two months of this season, but hats off to him. I just hope we can quiet him down a little bit before we leave town tomorrow."

The game started out as a nice stroll in the park for Fujimoto and Orioles starter Austin Blackwell. Believe it or not, Baltimore took the early lead, when Greg Voight touched Fujimoto for a solo homer in the top of the fourth.

Michaels got two right back in the bottom half, picking on a first-pitch fastball — when will teams learn? — and sending it over the high wall in left field.

"I was sitting on that pitch," he said. "The scouting report says he likes to get ahead, so I was ready."

And about "the streak?"

"Nah, same old stuff," he replied. "You guys have at it. I've got to get to dinner with my parents and my girlfriend."

The Indians made quick work of Blackwell in the bottom of the sixth, scoring four times and revving up the sellout crowd of 37,317. Michaels had a single that inning, and he was one of three runners who scored on Justin Kestino's double. Backup catcher Iceberg Peters (behind the plate again for Fujimoto) singled in Kestino.

Fujimoto ran the pitch count to 120 or he might have finished. Instead, manager Todd Stein allowed Lee Hazelton close it out in a non-save situation.

"Don't you guys want to talk to Scottie some more," Fujimoto asked in mock indignation through translator Ryuji Sato. "He was something again. I had not even heard of him until I came here, but he was one of the first players to say hello to me when I arrived at spring training. He reported with the pitchers and catchers to get ready for the season early. You have to admire that."

GAME 115

CLEVELAND INDIANS VS BALTIMORE ORIOLES AUGUST 14
CLEVELAND 6 / BALTIMORE 1

CLEVELAND INDIANS										
BATTING	AB	R	H	RBI	2B	3B	HR	BB	SO	BA
RIKKI LABUDDA CF	5	0	2	0	0	0	0	0	0	.278
MICAH MILLISON RF	4	1	1	0	0	0	0	1	0	.286
SCOTT MICHAELS 2B	4	2	3	2	0	0	1	0	1	.376
TERRY ROVETTO 3B	4	0	0	0	0	0	0	0	1	.268
OLIVER REINER 1B	4	1	2	0	0	0	0	0	0	.271
KIERAN CATSEF LF	3	1	2	0	1	0	0	1	0	.277
JUSTIN KESTINO SS	3	1	2	3	1	0	0	1	0	.268
BERNARD HARPER DH	4	0	0	0	0	0	0	0	1	.266
ICEBERG PETERS C	4	0	1	1	0	0	0	0	0	.200
PITCHING	IP	H	R	ER	SO	BB	ERA			
TAK FUJIMOTO (W)	8	5	1	1	6	1	3.28			
LEE HAZELTON	1	0	0	0	0	0	2.45			

BALTIMORE ORIOLES										
BATTING	AB	R	H	RBI	2B	3B	HR	BB	SO	BA
BARBARO CASTRO SS	4	0	1	0	0	0	0	0	1	.271
KEVIN BRADY CF	3	0	0	0	0	0	0	1	0	.280
JORGE ESTRELLA 3B	4	0	1	0	1	0	0	0	0	.268
JULES PETERSON 1B	4	0	1	0	0	0	0	0	1	.281
ELMER VEGA LF	4	0	0	0	0	0	0	0	0	.262
GREG VOIGHT DH	4	1	1	1	0	0	1	0	2	.290
RODOLFO SANCHEZ CF	4	0	0	0	0	0	0	0	0	.264
WILFREDO MURILLO RF	4	0	1	0	0	0	0	0	1	.229
TERRY SHINER C	4	0	0	0	0	0	0	0	1	.252
PITCHING	IP	H	R	ER	SO	BB	ERA			
AUSTIN BLACKWELL (L)	5.67	8	4	4	2	2	3.90			
JIM DECASTER	1.33	3	2	2	1	0	3.89			
LUIS RAUDEZ	1	2	0	0	0	0	3.30			

INNING	1	2	3	4	5	6	7	8	9	TOTAL
BALTIMORE	0	0	0	1	0	0	0	0	0	1
CLEVELAND	0	0	0	2	0	4	0	0		6

GAME 116

By SAM LARDNER
The Cleveland Press

CLEVELAND, August 15 — An already newsworthy late season became even more so Sunday.

Reporters walking into the Indians clubhouse three hours before the afternoon's 6–2 victory over the Baltimore Orioles noticed a lot of hugging, handshakes and back-slapping between interim manager Todd Stein and his players.

Make that no-longer-interim manager Todd Stein.

The Indians' media-relations staff rounded up reporters and directed them to the interview room, where Stein and general manager J.D. Eisner emerged to announce that Stein not only had the "interim" tag removed, but that he had been given a two-year contract extension beyond this season. One of the reasons Eisner cited was the sudden development of second baseman Scott Michaels, who then went out and extended his hitting streak to 36 by going 3 for 5 against the Orioles.

"That's just one of the reasons we decided now was the perfect time to extend Todd," Eisner said before a packed throng in the interview room. "The entire team has fed off Todd's energy and enthusiasm. He rallied the team after a slow start, and almost immediately, we started playing better baseball, even if the wins weren't always there.

"When Angel (Rodriguez) went down with his injury in May, Todd did not hesitate to put Scott Michaels in at second base, and he stuck with

359

him. You've seen the results. But it's an overall assessment that led to this decision."

Stein was promoted from Dave Mills' coaching staff after 10 games of the season, when Mills was fired. The Indians were lauded for promoting an African-American coach to the top spot in the dugout even though Eisner said the move was totally merit based.

The Indians started the season 0–6 and they were 2 and 8 when Stein took over. After Sunday's victory, they're 64 and 52. They hold the top wild-card spot by one game over the Chicago White Sox and by three over the Boston Red Sox. The Indians also say they have designs on winning the American League Central, where they trail the first-place Minnesota Twins by five games.

Stein seemed touched by getting the extension during the stretch drive of a season. "I really appreciate the faith J.D placed in me, but most of all, I have to thank the players, who have busted their butts to get us back into contention," he said. "It's a great day for my family and me, and I hope we can have a lot of great moments here in Cleveland."

Veteran pitcher Lynn Moda, who started and won Sunday's game, praised the move. "You couldn't ask for any better manager to play for than Steinie," he said. "I haven't always been at my best this year, but he stuck with me. You want to go out there and play hard every day for a guy like that." Moda pitched six innings of four-hit, one-run ball Sunday walking no one and striking out six.

But once again, Michaels was the story of the day, upstaging even his own manager. He hit two singles and an RBI double. The 36-game hitting streak ties him for 10th all-time with Gene DeMontreville, who did it over the 1896-97 season for the Washington Senators of the National League. During the streak, Michaels is 73 for 152, and his season batting average went from .376 to .379. He is 20 games shy of Joe DiMaggio's record-56-game hitting streak.

"I'm just glad family and friends were able to drive up from Versailles (Ohio)," to see it," said Michaels, whose parents, Tom and Jennifer, and his girlfriend, Kristen Williams, were among those on the guest-pass list this weekend. "They've stuck with me through the injuries and the bad times. I'm just trying to play baseball, but I'm glad they're getting to enjoy this."

The victory gave the Indians a three-game sweep of the Orioles, last in the AL East. Michaels singled in the first inning against Ronaldo Bucardo and came home on Wilson White's two-run homer, who was back in the lineup after a day's rest. Terry Rovetto made it back-to-back shots, and the Indians never looked back. Bernard Harper, playing first today giving Oliver Reiner a much need day off, hit a three-run homer in the sixth to complete the scoring.

In his office after the game, Stein sipped on a celebratory glass of red wine, courtesy of his players. "Feels good," he said. "They're the ones who deserve all this attention, but I'll gladly accept the vino."

The Indians face a tough test this coming week, when the tough Texas Rangers come to town. The Rangers currently lead the AL West.

"No rest," Stein said. "They're going to bring their best, so we have to bring ours. But I like where we sit right now." With that, he poured himself another glass. Why not?

GAME 116

CLEVELAND INDIANS VS BALTIMORE ORIOLES AUGUST 15
CLEVELAND 6 / BALTIMORE 2

CLEVELAND INDIANS										
BATTING	AB	R	H	RBI	2B	3B	HR	BB	SO	BA
RIKKI LABUDDA CF	5	0	0	0	0	0	0	0	1	.275
MICAH MILLISON RF	5	0	2	0	0	0	0	0	0	.287
SCOTT MICHAELS 2B	5	1	3	0	1	0	0	0	0	.379
WILSON WHITE LF	4	2	2	2	0	0	1	1	0	.284
TERRY ROVETTO 3B	4	2	2	1	0	0	1	0	1	.266
BERNARD HARPER 1B	4	1	1	3	0	0	1	0	1	.266
JUSTIN KESTINO SS	3	0	1	0	1	0	0	1	0	.268
LEO TAYLOR DH	3	0	1	0	0	0	0	1	0	.273
MORRIS JEROME C	4	0	1	0	0	0	0	0	1	.242
PITCHING	IP	H	R	ER	SO	BB	ERA			
LYNN MODA (W)	6	4	1	1	6	0	3.93			
BUCK STERLING	2	1	1	1	1	0	3.96			
MICKEY PENNY	1	0	0	0	0	1	3.32			

BALTIMORE ORIOLES										
BATTING	AB	R	H	RBI	2B	3B	HR	BB	SO	BA
BARBARO CASTRO SS	4	0	0	1	0	0	0	0	0	.268
KEVIN BRADY CF	4	0	1	0	0	0	0	0	2	.279
JORGE ESTRELLA 3B	4	0	0	0	0	0	0	0	1	.265
JULES PETERSON 1B	3	1	1	0	0	0	0	1	0	.281
ELMER VEGA LF	4	0	2	0	0	0	0	0	0	.265
GREG VOIGHT DH	4	0	1	1	1	0	0	0	2	.289
RODOLFO SANCHEZ CF	4	0	0	0	0	0	0	0	0	.260
WILFREDO MURILLO RF	3	0	0	0	0	0	0	0	1	.227
TERRY SHINER C	4	1	0	0	0	0	1	0	1	.248
PITCHING	IP	H	R	ER	SO	BB	ERA			
RONALDO BUCARDO (L)	5.33	7	4	4	3	2	3.91			
RODNEY DAVIS	1.67	4	2	2	1	1	3.58			
LUIS RAUDEZ	1	2	0	0	0	0	3.19			

INNING	1	2	3	4	5	6	7	8	9	TOTAL
BALTIMORE	0	0	0	0	0	1	0	1	0	2
CLEVELAND	0	0	0	2	0	4	0	0		6

GAME 117

By SAM LARDNER
The Cleveland Press

CLEVELAND, August 16 — Scott Michaels heard something he had never heard before in his career: "MVP, MVP, MVP."

The sellout crowd of 37,056 Monday night at Progressive Field serenaded the Indians second baseman with chants of "MVP, MVP, MVP" all four times he came to bat during the Tribe's 3–0 loss to the Texas Rangers.

With those chants of "MVP," does Michaels actually have a chance at winning the Most Valuable Player Award in the American League this year?

"Oh, I don't know, and I'm not thinking about that," he said after going 2-for-4 in the loss to extend his hitting streak to 37 games. Michaels had a pair of singles, extending the streak in the first inning. "It didn't bother me not making the all-star team, and I'm certainly not focused on the MVP. But it was nice for the crowd to do that. It means a lot."

The 37-game winning streak ties Tommy Holmes of the Boston Braves (1945) for ninth all time. During the streak, Michaels is 75-for-156 (.481). For the season, he is batting .381 with 29 homers and 113 RBIs. Those are certainly MVP-type numbers.

"I think you have to more than consider Scottie," said manager Todd Stein, whose team had its three-game winning streak snapped and fell to 64 and 53. "He's done everything that an MVP does: hit, hit for power and drive in runs. And this streak is something else. I just wish we could have given the fans more to cheer about tonight."

Aside from a pair of singles from Michaels, there wasn't much going on for the Indians against Rangers starting pitcher Sammy Delgado and two relievers. They managed just six hits all night in dropping six games behind the Minnesota Twins in the American League Central. The Indians are now tied with the Chicago White Sox for the top wild-card spot, two games ahead of the Boston Red Sox.

The Rangers (70–50) are solidly in front in the AL West.

"I told you guys this was going to be a tough series," Stein said. "These four games are going to be a big test, even though we're at home. We were lucky to salvage a split in Arlington early in the season."

Recently acquired Eli Batt started for the Indians and pitched creditably, going six innings and giving up seven hits and all three Texas runs.

Miguel Beltre hit a two-run homer against Batt in the first inning one pitch after it looked like Batt had Beltre struck out a curveball. Richie Young Jr. added a run-scoring single in the fourth, and that was that for the scoring.

"Sometimes the umpire can give up on a curveball just like a hitter does," Batt said. "No excuses. I still had a chance to get him out, and I didn't. They have a tough lineup over there, and it was good to shut them down for the most part the rest of the way."

Solly Alvarez and Lorry Unger finished up with scoreless relief for the Indians, who got two hits from Justin Kestino and a double from Wilson White.

"I thought Eli pitched well," Stein said. "He's been a big shot in the arm for us. But when you don't hit, it doesn't matter. That's a team nobody is going to want to face in the postseason if they hold on."

GAME 117

CLEVELAND INDIANS VS TEXAS RANGERS • AUGUST 16
TEXAS 3 / CLEVELAND 0

CLEVELAND INDIANS

BATTING	AB	R	H	RBI	2B	3B	HR	BB	SO	BA
RIKKI LABUDDA CF	4	0	1	0	0	0	0	0	0	.275
MICAH MILLISON RF	4	0	0	0	0	0	0	0	1	.285
SCOTT MICHAELS 2B	4	0	2	0	0	0	0	0	0	.381
TERRY ROVETTO 3B	3	0	0	0	1	0	0	1	0	.264
OLIVER REINER 1B	3	0	0	0	0	0	0	1	0	.269
WILSON WHITE LF	4	0	1	0	0	0	0	0	1	.284
JUSTIN KESTINO SS	4	0	2	0	0	0	0	0	0	.270
BERNARD HARPER DH	4	0	0	0	0	0	0	0	2	.263
MORRIS JEROME C	3	0	0	0	0	0	0	1	0	.240
ANGEL RODRIGUEZ PR	0	0	0	0	0	0	0	0	0	.214

PITCHING	IP	H	R	ER	SO	BB	ERA			
ELI BATT (L)	6	7	3	3	5	2	3.96			
SOLLY ALVAREZ	2	2	0	0	1	0	2.66			
LORRY UNGER	1	1	0	0	1	0	4.34			

TEXAS RANGERS

BATTING	AB	R	H	RBI	2B	3B	HR	BB	SO	BA
ALBERTO RODRIGUEZ SS	4	1	1	0	0	0	0	0	1	.298
RICHIE YOUNG JR 2B	4	0	1	1	0	0	0	0	1	.300
MIGUEL BELTRE 3B	4	1	2	2	0	0	1	0	0	.286
NICK MARSANS 1B	4	0	0	0	1	0	0	0	1	.299
ARTHUR DAHLGREN DH	3	0	2	0	0	0	0	1	0	.272
WILLARD CHANDLER RF	4	0	1	0	0	0	0	0	2	.290
ADRIAN MOLINA CF	3	0	1	0	0	0	0	1	0	.269
RYAN ROSE LF	4	0	0	0	0	0	0	0	1	.257
ROGER BRIDWELL C	3	1	2	0	0	0	0	0	1	.263

PITCHING	IP	H	R	ER	SO	BB	ERA			
SAMMY DELGADO (W)	7	5	0	0	5	1	3.55			
GABE KINDER	1	1	0	0	1	0	3.86			
TINO FERNANDEZ (S)	1	0	0	0	0	0	2.91			

INNING	1	2	3	4	5	6	7	8	9	TOTAL
TEXAS	2	0	0	1	0	0	0	0	0	3
CLEVELAND	0	0	0	0	0	0	0	0	0	0

GAME 118

By SAM LARDNER
The Cleveland Press

CLEVELAND, August 17 — It looks like the Indians are going to do this again: being the big teases.

Playing their second straight home game against the top team in the American League West, the Indians went quietly into another good night Tuesday during a dreary 8 to 1 loss to the Texas Rangers.

The only redeeming factor on the night was that Scott Michaels kept his hitting streak going, salvaging it with an eighth-inning single to extend the streak to 38 games, tying him for eighth all time with Jimmy Rollins, who hit in 38 straight with the Phillies over 2005–06.

For the first time in a long time, Michaels did not address the media after the game, citing family needs.

The Indians have bigger concerns. With the loss, they dropped to 64–54 and fell one game behind the Chicago White Sox for the top-wild card spot. The Boston Red Sox crept within one game of the Indians for the second and last wild-card spot.

"No disrespect to Baltimore," manager Todd Stein said, referring to the lowly Baltimore Orioles, whom the Indians swept over the weekend. "But we've got to step it up against these top teams. If we make the postseason, those are the teams we're going to be facing. There are no easy touches in October. We've got two more chances here at home to get this right. We're certainly capable."

Indians starting pitcher Brian "The Doctor" Howard accused himself of malpractice after going only four innings and giving up six runs in this stinker and was rocked for the second game in a row.

The Rangers got three in the first inning and three more in the fourth to put this one to bed early.

"I just sucked tonight," the 30-year-old Howard said. "I had nothing from the get-go. Just no feel for any of my pitches. In this park against that team when it's hot at night, look out. They did exactly what they should have done with those (lousy) pitches."

Rangers first baseman Nick Marsans touched Howard for a three-run homer in the first inning. In the fourth, Howard loaded the bases on singles by Ryan Rose, Roger Bridwell and a walk to Alberto Rodriguez, who has drawn all of six bases on balls all year. A double to the gap in right-center by Richie Young Jr cleared the bases. The Rangers added single runs in the sixth and seventh.

"I got The Doc out of there after the inning because we're going to need him down the stretch," Stein said. "He's been a warrior for us and I know he wanted to take one for the team. I told him I appreciated that, but we've got Mickey (Penney) and Buck (Sterling) in the pen. Might as well let them finish and keep Doc as fresh as we can keep anybody this time of the year."

The Indians got a solo homer from Micah Millison in the fifth against starting pitcher Dwight Billingham and Cleon Leflor finished up by pitching a perfect ninth.

As far as Michaels goes, he is 76 for 160 (475) during the streak. For the season, his average fell from .381 to .379.

"There's no way I'm going to rest him, but he might be dragging a little bit right now," Stein said. "He hasn't played this much baseball in a long time, what with his history of injury. As long as he's healthy, we're going to keep running him out there. He's only 23 and didn't play a whole lot early in the year. You saw I got him out of there in the ninth inning tonight to give him a breather and give Angel (Rodriguez) a little work. We may do that more often if we're in one-sided games, one way or the other."

GAME 118

CLEVELAND INDIANS VS TEXAS RANGERS • AUGUST 17
TEXAS 8 / CLEVELAND 1

CLEVELAND INDIANS										
BATTING	AB	R	H	RBI	2B	3B	HR	BB	SO	BA
RIKKI LABUDDA CF	4	0	0	0	0	0	0	0	0	.273
MICAH MILLISON RF	4	1	1	1	0	0	1	0	0	.284
SCOTT MICHAELS 2B	4	0	1	0	0	0	0	0	2	.379
ANGEL RODRIGUEZ 2B	0	0	0	0	0	0	0	0	0	.214
TERRY ROVETTO 3B	3	0	1	0	1	0	0	1	0	.264
OLIVER REINER 1B	3	0	2	0	0	0	0	0	0	.272
WILSON WHITE LF	4	0	1	0	0	0	0	0	1	.283
JUSTIN KESTINO SS	3	0	0	0	0	0	0	1	0	.268
BERNARD HARPER DH	4	0	0	0	0	0	0	0	0	.260
MORRIS JEROME C	4	0	1	0	0	0	0	0	1	.240
PITCHING	IP	H	R	ER	SO	BB	ERA			
BRIAN HOWARD (L)	4	7	6	6	3	1	4.84			
BUCK STERLING	3	3	2	2	1	0	3.45			
MICKEY PENNY	2	1	0	0	1	0	3.81			
TEXAS RANGERS										
BATTING	AB	R	H	RBI	2B	3B	HR	BB	SO	BA
ALBERTO RODRIGUEZ SS	4	2	1	0	0	0	0	1	0	.297
RICHIE YOUNG JR 2B	5	0	1	3	1	0	0	0	0	.298
MIGUEL BELTRE 3B	4	2	2	0	1	0	0	0	2	.288
NICK MARSANS 1B	5	1	2	3	1	0	1	0	1	.300
ARTHUR DAHLGREN DH	4	1	1	1	0	0	0	1	0	.272
WILLARD CHANDLER RF	4	0	1	0	0	0	0	0	0	.290
ADRIAN MOLINA CF	4	0	0	1	0	0	0	0	0	.265
RYAN ROSE LF	4	1	2	0	1	0	0	0	1	.261
ROGER BRIDWELL C	3	1	1	0	0	0	0	0	1	.264
PITCHING	IP	H	R	ER	SO	BB	ERA			
DWIGHT BILLINGHAM (W)	8	7	1	1	4	2	3.59			
CLEON LEFLOR	1	0	0	0	1	0	3.31			

INNING	1	2	3	4	5	6	7	8	9	TOTAL
TEXAS	3	0	0	3	0	1	1	0	0	8
CLEVELAND	0	0	0	0	1	0	0	0	0	1

GAME 119

By SAM LARDNER
The Cleveland Press

CLEVELAND, August 18 — How do you balance celebrating a possible historic achievement against the need to win baseball games?

That's something the Cleveland Indians are wrestling with now.

On one hand, Indians second baseman Scott Michaels extended his hitting streak to 39 games Wednesday night at Progressive Field, drawing loud cheers from the crowd of 36,998.

On the other hand, Michaels' fourth-inning double came during a frustrating 3–2 loss to the Texas Rangers. The loss was the Tribe's third in a row against the Rangers, and it dropped them a game behind the Chicago White Sox for the top wild-card spot and into a tie with Boston for the second and last spot.

Michaels has made his position abundantly clear on the subject: He'd rather talk about the team than "the streak."

That was the case again Wednesday.

"Look, I had a chance in the ninth to tie the game and didn't get the job done," he said a few minutes after striking out with a man on second base and one out. The game ended a minute later on Terry Rovetto's groundout. "The streak is great and everything, and most days, I don't even know where it is. Thirty-nine? Great. But there are 24 other guys in this room, and they're more important than any individual achievement. I haven't earned that attention yet."

Whether Michaels and the Indians like it or not, the attention is only going to intensify if things keep going. At 39 games, Michaels' streak is tied for seventh all-time with Paul Molitor, who did it with the Milwaukee Brewers (then in the American League) in 1987. Michaels went 1 for 5 Wednesday, and he's hitting .467 (77for165) during the streak. His season average fell from .379 to .377.

"It's something I think Scottie and the team are handling well," said manager Todd Stein, whose team is 64–55 with one more game against the Rangers to go. "We understand it's a big deal. I don't think there's any resentment in the clubhouse. Scottie has set the tone well and said all the right things about it being about the team first. And he's sincere about that."

Actually, Michaels might be doing the rest of the team a favor by garnering the attention, especially after losses. On Wednesday, starting pitcher Kenny Camden let a 2–0 lead get away in the fifth inning, when the Rangers scored three — two coming on a double by Arthur Dahlgren, with Dahlgren scoring on Willard Chandler's single.

"Just one bad inning," said Camden, who had been on a good run lately. "You can't make a mistake against this team. They got a couple guys on in that inning, and I think I might have rushed things a little."

Camden dismissed any notions that Michaels' streak had become a distraction.

"No, how could it be?" answered the 32-year-old veteran. "This kid has helped us win a lot of ballgames. It's bringing attention to the whole team, and it's bringing people out to the ballpark. I hope he keeps it going as long as he can."

Camden pitched well and wound up working seven innings, with Lorry Unger and Geno Milzie finishing. The Indians got their two runs in the third against Javy Oliva, when Justin Kestino walked and went to third on Bernard Harper's double. Morris Jerome's single up the middle scored both runners and brought the crowd to its feet. But the Indians wound up stranding 11 men on the night thanks to five walks but went 1-for-9 with runners in scoring position. They had Rangers closer Tino Fernandez on the ropes in the ninth, but couldn't put him away.

"They've had our number this week," Stein said. "We've got to salvage one tomorrow. We've got Tak (Fujimoto) going, and he's been good. I like our chances."

GAME 119

CLEVELAND INDIANS VS TEXAS RANGERS •AUGUST 18
TEXAS 3 / CLEVELAND 2

CLEVELAND INDIANS										
BATTING	AB	R	H	RBI	2B	3B	HR	BB	SO	BA
RIKKI LABUDDA CF	5	0	1	0	0	0	0	0	0	.272
MICAH MILLISON RF	4	0	0	0	0	0	0	1	0	.282
SCOTT MICHAELS 2B	5	0	1	0	1	0	0	0	1	.377
TERRY ROVETTO 3B	4	0	1	0	1	0	0	1	1	.264
OLIVER REINER 1B	4	0	1	0	0	0	0	1	1	.272
WILSON WHITE LF	4	0	0	0	0	0	0	0	0	.281
JUSTIN KESTINO SS	3	1	1	0	0	0	0	1	1	.269
BERNARD HARPER DH	3	1	2	0	0	0	0	1	0	.264
MORRIS JEROME C	4	0	1	2	0	0	0	0	1	.240
PITCHING	IP	H	R	ER	SO	BB	ERA			
KENNY CAMDEN (L)	7	8	3	3	4	2	3.23			
LORRY UNGER	1	1	0	0	1	0	4.23			
GENO MILZIE	1	0	0	0	0	0	2.44			
TEXAS RANGERS										
BATTING	AB	R	H	RBI	2B	3B	HR	BB	SO	BA
ALBERTO RODRIGUEZ SS	4	0	0	0	0	0	0	0	0	.294
RICHIE YOUNG JR 2B	3	1	1	0	1	0	0	1	0	.299
MIGUEL BELTRE 3B	4	1	2	0	0	0	0	0	0	.291
NICK MARSANS 1B	3	0	0	0	0	0	0	1	1	.297
ARTHUR DAHLGREN DH	4	1	2	2	1	0	0	0	0	.275
WILLARD CHANDLER RF	4	0	1	1	0	0	0	0	1	.289
ADRIAN MOLINA CF	4	0	1	0	0	0	0	0	2	.265
RYAN ROSE LF	4	0	1	0	1	0	0	0	1	.260
ROGER BRIDWELL C	4	0	1	0	0	0	0	0	0	.264
PITCHING	IP	H	R	ER	SO	BB	ERA			
JAVY OLIVA (W)	8	6	2	2	4	5	3.48			
TINO FERNANDEZ (S)	1	2	0	0	1	0	2.83			

INNING	1	2	3	4	5	6	7	8	9	TOTAL
TEXAS	0	0	0	0	3	0	0	0	0	3
CLEVELAND	0	0	2	0	0	0	0	0	0	2

GAME 120

By SAM LARDNER

The Cleveland Press

CLEVELAND, August 19 — Amazing how a victory will have everyone stepping a little easier. And if there were an elephant in the Cleveland Indians clubhouse, it's amazing how one little win made that disappear, too.

All was right again — and all subjects were open for comfortable discussion — Thursday night after the Indians beat the Texas Rangers 4–1 to salvage the finale of this four-game set at Progressive Field.

And after a few days of having to downplay his own individual accomplishments, second baseman Scott Michaels was happy to talk about extending his hitting streak to a now-eye-popping 40 games.

Michaels went 2-for-4, with a first-inning double and a fifth-inning single.

"It feels good to talk about it tonight," said Michaels, who tied the legendary Ty Cobb for sixth all time with the 40-game streak. The Georgia Peach had his streak in 1911.

"When you're not winning games, you shouldn't feel comfortable talking about yourself. At least I don't. We felt our backs were against the all a little bit tonight after they beat us the first three games. But Fuji (starting pitcher Tak Fujimoto) came out and was dealing. He's the guy you should be talking to."

Fujimoto, who went eight innings against the Orioles in his previous start, went six against the Rangers as manager Todd Stein was mindful of the pitch count after the long performance last Saturday.

"I've been feeling more comfortable lately, both on and off the field," Fujimoto said through translator Ryuji Sato. "I knew we had to win tonight, and I wanted to keep going. But I understand the manager's position."

Once again, Stein said he was looking at the big picture. Stein used Solly Alvarez, Geno Milzie and Ivan Zyzna in relief of Fujimoto.

"Our bullpen guys have been good all year, and they're not overworked," the manager said. "We've been mindful of all our starters' workloads, especially Fuji coming over here (from Japan) for his first year. He went eight the last time, and we've got a long way to go yet."

Michaels doubled with two outs in the bottom of the first against Cary Simon after Simon got two quick outs. Terry Rovetto then homered to left field to give the Tribe a 2–0 lead.

Super subs Leo Taylor and Iceberg Peters (once again, the "personal catcher" for Fujimoto), combined for two more runs in the fifth. Taylor singled and stole second base. Peters doubled home Taylor and then scored on Rikki LaBudda's triple.

"Just shake it up a little," Stein said. "We've got a road trip coming up, and Ice has caught Fuji well. We wanted to give Micah (Millison) a bit of a blow, and Leo always brings a lot of energy. So, it worked out."

Now it's on to Seattle and another long-distance road trip, with a stop after that in Oakland.

"We've piled up the frequent-flier miles," Stein said. "That's OK. I'm sure our fans won't mind staying up late to watch Scottie hit and see us contend for the postseason. Let's go."

GAME 120

CLEVELAND INDIANS VS TEXAS RANGERS • AUGUST 19
CLEVELAND 4 / TEXAS 1

CLEVELAND INDIANS										
BATTING	**AB**	**R**	**H**	**RBI**	**2B**	**3B**	**HR**	**BB**	**SO**	**BA**
RIKKI LABUDDA CF	4	0	1	1	0	1	0	0	1	.272
WILSON WHITE LF	4	0	0	0	0	0	0	0	0	.278
SCOTT MICHAELS 2B	4	1	2	0	1	0	0	0	0	.378
TERRY ROVETTO 3B	4	1	2	2	0	0	1	0	2	.266
OLIVER REINER 1B	3	0	2	0	0	0	0	1	1	.275
JUSTIN KESTINO SS	4	0	1	0	0	0	0	0	0	.269
BERNARD HARPER DH	3	0	0	0	0	0	0	1	1	.261
LEO TAYLOR RF	4	1	2	0	0	0	0	0	0	.284
ICEBERG PETERS C	4	1	1	1	1	0	0	0	0	.202
PITCHING	**IP**	**H**	**R**	**ER**	**SO**	**BB**	**ERA**			
TAK FUJIMOTO (W)	6	5	1	1	6	1	3.21			
SOLLY ALVAREZ	1	0	0	0	1	0	2.61			
GENO MILZIE	1	1	0	0	0	1	2.39			
IVAN ZYZNA (S)	1	0	0	0	1	0	2.23			
TEXAS RANGERS										
BATTING	**AB**	**R**	**H**	**RBI**	**2B**	**3B**	**HR**	**BB**	**SO**	**BA**
ALBERTO RODRIGUEZ SS	4	0	1	0	0	0	0	0	0	.293
RICHIE YOUNG JR 2B	3	0	0	0	0	0	0	1	0	.296
MIGUEL BELTRE 3B	4	0	1	0	0	0	0	0	1	.290
NICK MARSANS 1B	4	0	0	0	0	0	0	0	2	.294
ARTHUR DAHLGREN DH	3	1	2	0	1	0	0	1	0	.278
WILLARD CHANDLER RF	4	0	1	0	0	0	0	0	1	.289
ADRIAN MOLINA CF	4	0	0	1	0	0	0	0	1	.261
RYAN ROSE LF	4	0	1	0	1	0	0	0	1	.260
ROGER BRIDWELL C	3	0	0	0	0	0	0	0	2	.261
PITCHING	**IP**	**H**	**R**	**ER**	**SO**	**BB**	**ERA**			
CARY SIMON (L)	6.33	8	4	4	5	2	3.65			
JOHAN CONCEPCION	1.67	3	0	0	1	0	3.32			

INNING	1	2	3	4	5	6	7	8	9	TOTAL
TEXAS	0	0	0	0	0	1	0	0	0	1
CLEVELAND	2	0	0	0	2	0	0	0	0	4

GAME 121

By SAM LARDNER

The Cleveland Press

SEATTLE, August 20 — If Scott Michaels and the Indians thought they would escape the hype and the hoohah by traveling to the great Pacific Northwest, they were wrong.

Not that that's necessarily a bad thing.

Michaels met the media before Friday night's 6–4 victory over the Seattle Mariners at Starbucks Field, a.k.a., "The Coffee Grounds." He was genial as usual, and then he went out and extended his historic hitting streak to 41 games by going 2-for-4.

The Indians had their usual media contingent with them, and they were greeted by a large Seattle throng. Both sets of media were bolstered by the traveling crews from Japan, on hand to chronicle the exploits of Indians pitcher Tak Fujimoto (who will not pitch in this series) and Mariners reliever Maya Nagatomo.

"I joked about not speaking Japanese a few days ago, but maybe I better start learning," said Michaels, who has captured the fancy of the media and fans in Japan as well as in the United States and Canada. "I hope the fans back home in Cleveland are going to be able to stay up and watch these games. I'm actually kind of boring, so maybe I'll just help them get to sleep faster."

No chance. Not only is Michaels making history with his hitting streak, the 23-year-old from tiny Versailles, Ohio, is proving to be quite the charmer in most interview sessions.

On the field, his streak tied Hall of Famer George Sisler for fifth all time at 41 games. Sisler did it in 1922 with the old St. Louis Browns. Michaels came up with a pair of singles, one in the fifth inning and another in the ninth. He scored two runs, including the go-ahead run in the ninth to break a 4–4 tie against Mariners closer Tony Dos Santos.

The Indians also are getting an idea why Lynn Moda is their ace pitcher. He turned in another quality start by going six innings and giving up three runs. The Indians have not lost a game Moda has started since July 28.

"Just doing what I can to keep us in games," the 28-year-old righty said. "This is a good place to pitch. It's a fairly big park, and like a lot of parks out west, the ball doesn't seem to carry at night. I've always enjoyed coming here. I love the new name of this place. It's fitting."

Neither team got much going until the fourth, when Indians catcher Morris Jerome got hold of one and sent it out over the left-field wall. That came after Justin Kestino singled off the M's starter Dino Toban.

"I run into one every now and then," Jerome said. "Toban likes to come in aggressively, especially with men on base. I guessed fastball and got one."

Michaels singled with one out in the fifth and went to second on Toban's wild pitch. He came home on an Oliver Reiner double. The Indians had a 3–0 lead at that point. Moda had problems in the bottom of the inning as he loaded the bases on two singles and a walk. Russ Granzow made him pay with a two-run double, and Phil Borntragger followed with a sacrifice fly to tie the ballgame.

The teams traded runs in the seventh. Micah Millison singled to lead off and Michaels struck out. Terry Rovetto's grounder to the right side moved Millison to second base and Oliver Reiner singled over the second-base bag to score Millison and give the Indians a 4–3 lead. But Indians reliever Lee Hazelton gave up a game-tying homer to Billy Neville in the home half to tie the score.

In the decisive ninth, Michaels and Rovetto singled to put runners on the corners with nobody out. Oliver Reiner's sacrifice fly scored Michaels to give the tribe the lead, and Wilson White doubled in Rovetto for an insurance run.

Todd Stein put in Angel Rodriguez to replace Michaels for defense at second base in the bottom of the inning, and Rodriguez made a diving catch in short right-center to snag Vance Roberts's pop fly and preserve the save for Ivan Zyzna. Rodriguez was supplanted by Michaels early in the season when Rodriguez went on the injured list with a hamstring injury.

"Hey, I thought you guys forgot about me," Rodriguez said to reporters who asked about his catch. "No, this is great for Scottie. He has supported me on and off the field. And Steinie (manager Todd Stein) said I would get my chances. Those come mostly later in games, but he's been good to his word. I'm cheering as hard as anybody for Scottie to keep that streak going."

GAME 121

CLEVELAND INDIANS VS SEATTLE MARINERS · AUGUST 20
CLEVELAND 6 / SEATTLE 4

CLEVELAND INDIANS

BATTING	AB	R	H	RBI	2B	3B	HR	BB	SO	BA
RIKKI LABUDDA CF	4	0	1	0	0	0	0	0	0	.272
MICAH MILLISON RF	3	1	1	0	0	0	0	1	0	.282
SCOTT MICHAELS 2B	4	2	2	0	0	0	0	0	0	.379
ANGEL RODRIGUEZ 2B	0	0	0	0	0	0	0	0	0	.214
TERRY ROVETTO 3B	4	1	2	0	0	0	0	0	1	.268
OLIVER REINER 1B	3	0	2	3	1	0	0	1	0	.277
WILSON WHITE LF	4	0	2	1	0	0	0	0	0	.280
JUSTIN KESTINO SS	4	1	1	0	0	0	0	0	1	.268
BERNARD HARPER DH	2	0	0	0	0	0	0	2	0	.260
MORRIS JEROME C	4	1	1	2	1	0	1	0	1	.240

PITCHING	IP	H	R	ER	SO	BB	ERA
LYNN MODA	6	7	3	3	5	2	3.95
LEE HAZELTON (W)	2	3	1	1	2	0	2.56
IVAN ZYZNA (S)	1	0	0	0	0	0	2.17

SEATTLE MARINERS

BATTING	AB	R	H	RBI	2B	3B	HR	BB	SO	BA
VANCE ROBERTS 2B	5	0	2	0	0	0	0	0	0	.303
BILLY NEVILLE 1B	4	2	2	1	0	0	1	0	0	.286
RUSS GRANZOW LF	4	1	2	0	1	0	0	0	0	.291
PHIL BORNTRAGGER 3B	3	1	1	0	1	0	0	0	0	.275
JAMIE BROCKER SS	4	0	1	2	0	0	0	1	1	.281
HUGO VENETAS DH	3	0	0	1	0	0	1	1	1	.241
BRENDAN KAHN RF	4	0	1	0	1	0	0	1	0	.253
SKYLER TOWNSEND C	3	0	1	0	0	0	0	0	1	.274
ROBERTO AGUIRRE CF	4	0	0	0	0	0	0	0	1	.278

PITCHING	IP	H	R	ER	SO	BB	ERA
DINO TOBAN	5	7	3	3	2	1	4.11
JALEN GATES	3	3	1	1	1	2	3.20
TONY DOS SANTOS (L)	1	3	2	2	0	0	2.75

INNING	1	2	3	4	5	6	7	8	9	TOTAL
CLEVELAND	0	0	0	2	1	0	1	0	2	6
SEATTLE	0	0	0	0	3	0	1	0	0	4

GAME 122

By SAM LARDNER

The Cleveland Press

SEATTLE, August 21 — On any other day, the biggest news in this beautiful city would be that it didn't rain.

After what the locals said were endless hours of gloom, the sun broke through on a glorious Saturday afternoon at Starbucks Field ("The Coffee Grounds").

That itself brought much rejoicing among those in the crowd of 30,097, who cheered when the retractable roof of this palace opened to reveal blue skies and sunshine.

For the Cleveland Indians, these are no ordinary days, though, and a 4–1 victory over the Seattle Mariners.

The Indians got a masterful pitching performance from recently acquired Eli Batt, whose run of good form is going to spark serious discussion when Ollie Gonzalez comes off the injured list. More on that later.

The bigger news was that Indians second baseman Scott Michaels continues to rise in rarefied air as he went 2-for-4 to extend his hitting streak to 42 games. That ties him for fourth all time with Bill Dahlen of the 1894 Chicago Cubs. Next up is Pete Rose's 44-gamer.

Michaels raised his season average from .379 to .381, and during the streak, he is 83 for 177 (.469). He singled in the first inning and doubled in the third.

"Quite honestly, I don't feel any different, either at the plate or with all the things surrounding the streak," Michaels said. "I think the reason for that is we have a good support system here with Steinie (manager Todd Stein) and the veterans on this team. That's allowed me to relax and just play baseball. They kid me about it from time to time, but that keeps things fun."

Like other managers around baseball, M's boss Wes Malone is marveling at what he sees.

"Since we don't see them a whole lot, being in the American League West, I wasn't sure what to expect," said Malone, a former veteran of 17 big-league seasons as a player. "I don't give out praise lightly, but you can see that this kid was a top draft pick. I guess it's just a matter of being able to stay healthy. And to think they might have been on the verge of getting rid of this kid."

Amid all this, the Indians won their third straight to improve to 67–55 for the season. They remain six games behind the stubbornly good Minnesota Twins for the top spot in the AL Central. The Indians lead the Chicago White Sox by one game and the Boston Red Sox by two for the top wild-card spot.

Playing a day game after a night game, the Indians gave a start to Leo Taylor in center field and Angel Rodriguez (whom Michaels supplanted at second base) at shortstop who responded with two hits.

The speedy Taylor led off the game with a triple and scored on a high-chopper groundout by Micah Millison. Michaels ended the suspense over the streak with a single to left field but was erased on a double-play grounder off the bat of Terry Rovetto.

The Indians scored twice more in the fourth as DH Bernard Harper doubled home Oliver Reiner, and Wilson White both of whom singled.

Batt gave up a run in the fifth on a homer by Phil Borntragger. A sac fly by Indians catcher Iceberg Peters, scoring Wilson White who doubled and went to third on Bernard Harper's groundout made it 4–1 in the seventh.

For his part, Batt worked seven innings, giving up six hits. Obtained from the Reds before the trading deadline, he has given the Indians a much-needed shot of veteran calm and cool. Geno Milzie finished up the last six outs to get his third save.

Gonzalez is due off the IL any day, and after that, the Indians are going to have some decisions to make: move Gonzalez to the bullpen or go with a six-man rotation.

General manager J.D. Eisner is on the trip, and he addressed the situation Saturday.

"We have a lot of options, and all of them are good," he said. "On top of that, rosters will expand on September 1, and we'll have even more flexibility. Ollie understands. We don't want to rush him back or give him too big of a workload when he comes back. But Eli has certainly shown he belongs."

As for Batt, he's going with the flow.

"I got traded into a great situation," he said. "I'm not going to complain. Look at all the things going on with this club right now."

CLEVELAND INDIANS VS SEATTLE MARINERS · AUGUST 21
CLEVELAND 4 / SEATTLE 1

CLEVELAND INDIANS										
BATTING	AB	R	H	RBI	2B	3B	HR	BB	SO	BA
LEO TAYLOR CF	4	1	1	0	0	0	0	0	2	.282
MICAH MILLISON RF	3	0	0	1	0	0	0	1	0	.280
SCOTT MICHAELS 2B	4	0	2	0	1	0	0	0	1	.381
TERRY ROVETTO 3B	4	0	2	0	0	0	0	0	0	.270
OLIVER REINER 1B	3	1	1	0	0	0	0	1	0	.278
WILSON WHITE LF	4	2	2	0	1	0	0	0	0	.282
BERNARD HARPER DH	3	0	1	2	1	0	0	1	0	.261
ICEBERG PETERS C	4	0	1	1	0	0	0	0	1	.204
ANGEL RODRIGUEZ SS	3	0	2	0	0	0	0	0	0	.233
PITCHING	IP	H	R	ER	SO	BB	ERA			
ELI BATT (W)	7	6	1	1	5	2	3.38			
GENO MILZIE (S)	2	2	0	0	0	0	2.31			
SEATTLE MARINERS										
BATTING	AB	R	H	RBI	2B	3B	HR	BB	SO	BA
VANCE ROBERTS 2B	4	0	2	0	0	0	0	0	0	.305
BILLY NEVILLE 1B	4	0	1	0	0	0	0	0	0	.286
RUSS GRANZOW LF	3	0	1	0	1	0	0	1	0	.291
PHIL BORNTRAGGER 3B	4	1	1	1	0	0	1	0	1	.275
JAMIE BROCKER SS	4	0	1	0	0	0	0	0	1	.281
HUGO VENETAS DH	4	0	0	0	0	0	1	0	1	.238
BRENDAN KAHN RF	3	0	1	0	1	0	0	1	0	.253
SKYLER TOWNSEND C	4	0	0	0	0	0	0	0	1	.271
ROBERTO AGUIRRE CF	4	0	0	0	0	0	0	0	1	.275
PITCHING	IP	H	R	ER	SO	BB	ERA			
TYRELL BISHOP (L)	6.67	9	4	4	4	3	3.95			
MAYA NAGAMOTO	1.33	2	0	0	0	0	3.58			
JOAQUIN TORRES	1	1	0	0	0	0	2.97			

INNING	1	2	3	4	5	6	7	8	9	TOTAL
CLEVELAND	1	0	0	2	0	0	1	0	0	4
SEATTLE	0	0	0	0	1	0	0	0	0	1

GAME 123

By SAM LARDNER
The Cleveland Press

SEATTLE, August 23 — The rain returned to the Pacific Northwest Sunday and washed away a lot of the good feelings surrounding the Cleveland Indians.

However, the retractable roof at "The Coffee Grounds" functioned just fine, forcing a game to be played, a game that was a source of great frustration to the Indians, who dropped a 5–3 decision to the Seattle Mariners.

The only bright spot for the Tribe was that second baseman Scott Michaels eked out a fourth-inning single to extend his hitting streak to 43 games, moving him into sole possession of fourth place all time, one behind Pete Rose's 44-game streak in 1978.

As for the rest of this day, the Indians would just as soon forget it, especially starting pitcher Brian Howard, who was shown the door in the fifth inning by home-plate umpire David Nyren. It seems the two didn't see eye-to-eye much of the day over the definition of the strike zone.

After Howard walked switch-hitting Vance Roberts to force in a run, Howard peered in at Nyren for several seconds and appeared to gesture that the umpire could use a pair of spectacles.

That will get you "run," in player parlance, in a blink of an eye.

"How the (bleep) does that happen?" Howard fumed afterwards. "You've got to be (bleeping) me. I had the guy (Roberts) set up perfectly, the slider bites downward at the knees and he (Nyren) misses it. Unacceptable. We're fighting for our lives here. I have to be good. So should he."

Indians manager Todd Stein also got the rest of the afternoon off after going out to defend his pitcher.

"Doc was in the right there," Stein said of Howard. "Look, we can't see pitches perfectly from the dugout, but when the batter thought he was struck out, there might be a problem. The umpires have the toughest job of all, but my goodness, you've got to stay with the pitch there. The Doc is a veteran, and he deserved a better effort than that."

The loss was damaging to the Indians, who had their winning streak snapped at three and fell to 67–56. They dropped to seven games back of the Twins for first place in the American League Central. The White Sox tied them for the top wild-card spot, and the Red Sox crept to within a game.

Making things worse for the Indians is that they took a 2–0 lead in the second on Oliver Reiner's two-run homer, a drive to left that scored Terry Rovetto, who walked ahead of him.

Howard looked fidgety on the mound for much of his short stay. He walked six in the day, including two in the first inning and one in the second. He was able to work out of trouble in those innings but not in the fifth, when the M's went ahead 4–2.

Billy Neville made Howard pay for a walk to Phil Borntragger with a two-run homer. A walk and a pair of singles brought Roberts to the plate, and the controversial walk on a 3–2 pitch ended Howard's afternoon. Solly Alvarez — the Indians' valuable swing man — came in for Howard and gave up a run on a perfectly executed squeeze bunt by Jamie Brocker.

"They might have caught us a little unawares there," Stein said. "That's my fault. I was trying to cool myself off going down the dugout runway to the clubhouse, and the next thing you know, I'm hearing the crowd roar because of that bunt. That one is on me. I should have slowed things down before leaving."

The Mariners added one more off Alvarez in the seventh before the Tribe came within two in the eighth on a solo homer by Micah Millison. Lee Hazelton and Lorry Unger finished for the Tribe, with Tony Dos Santos getting the save for Seattle.

As for Michaels, he politely waved off reporters wanting to talk to him after the game.

"Not today, guys," he said. "I wasn't a factor today, and there were too many other things going on. It's a little heated in here. We'll talk tomorrow."

GAME 123

CLEVELAND INDIANS VS SEATTLE MARINERS · AUGUST 21
SEATTLE 5 / CLEVELAND 3

CLEVELAND INDIANS

BATTING	AB	R	H	RBI	2B	3B	HR	BB	SO	BA
RIKKI LABUDDA CF	4	0	0	0	0	0	0	1	0	.270
MICAH MILLISON RF	4	1	1	1	0	0	1	1	0	.280
SCOTT MICHAELS 2B	5	0	1	0	0	0	0	0	1	.378
TERRY ROVETTO 3B	3	1	2	0	0	0	0	1	0	.273
OLIVER REINER 1B	4	1	2	2	0	0	1	0	0	.279
WILSON WHITE LF	4	0	1	0	1	0	0	0	1	.282
JUSTIN KESTINO SS	4	0	0	0	0	0	0	0	1	.266
BERNARD HARPER DH	4	0	0	0	0	0	0	0	2	.258
MORRIS JEROME C	4	0	1	0	0	0	0	0	1	.240

PITCHING	IP	H	R	ER	SO	BB	ERA			
BRIAN HOWARD (L)	4.33	6	4	4	2	6	4.95			
SOLLY ALVAREZ	1.67	3	1	1	1	0	2.70			
LORRY UNGER	1	2	0	0	1	0	4.12			
BUCK STERLING	1	1	0	0	0	0	3.39			

SEATTLE MARINERS

BATTING	AB	R	H	RBI	2B	3B	HR	BB	SO	BA
VANCE ROBERTS 2B	2	1	2	1	0	0	0	2	0	.308
BILLY NEVILLE 1B	2	0	1	1	0	0	1	1	0	.287
RUSS GRANZOW LF	4	0	1	1	1	0	0	1	1	.291
PHIL BORNTRAGGER 3B	4	1	1	0	0	0	0	1	0	.274
JAMIE BROCKER SS	4	1	2	2	0	0	0	0	0	.283
HUGO VENETAS DH	4	0	0	0	0	0	0	0	1	.236
BRENDAN KAHN RF	4	1	1	0	1	0	0	1	0	.253
SKYLER TOWNSEND C	4	1	2	0	0	0	0	0	1	.274
ROBERTO AGUIRRE CF	4	0	2	0	0	0	0	0	0	.277

PITCHING	IP	H	R	ER	SO	BB	ERA			
CESAR NAVARRO (W)	8	8	3	3	6	3	3.85			
TONY DOS SANTOS	1	0	0	0	0	0	2.70			

INNING	1	2	3	4	5	6	7	8	9	TOTAL
CLEVELAND	0	2	0	0	0	0	0	1	0	3
SEATTLE	0	0	0	0	4	0	1	0		5

GAME 124

By SAM LARDNER
The Cleveland Press

SEATTLE, August 23 — Being mentioned in the same breath as Pete Rose can be a mixed bag for any baseball player. Indians second baseman Scott Michaels was more than happy to be compared with Charlie Hustle for at least one day after Monday night's 6–0 victory over the Seattle Marines at "The Coffee Grounds."

Michaels went 3-for-5, including a first-inning three-run homer that gave the Indians a 3–0 lead and helped them to their third win in four games in this series.

The 23-year-old Michaels, a native of Versailles, Ohio, deep in the heart of Cincinnati Reds country in the southwest part of the state, also singled twice to extend his improbable hitting streak to 44 games, tying him with Rose for third longest all time. Rose did it in 1978 with the Reds.

"Pretty cool," said Michaels, who is normally reticent to talk about the streak or his own accomplishments. "I never got to see Pete Rose play, but my parents did, and plenty of people in my area of the state did, too, and they have strong feelings about Pete."

Rose, of course, is baseball's all-time hits leader. But he gained infamy with his permanent ban from the game because of his betting on baseball.

"That's a tough one for all of us," Michaels said. "I know there are plenty of people on both sides of the fence — those who want him in the game and in the Hall of Fame, and those who don't. I don't know enough about the off-field stuff or the politics of all of it. I just know what kind of a player he was. He played all-out every game and gave it everything he had. That's what I try to do."

Next up on the streak chase is Wee Willie Keeler's 45-gamer, set with the old Baltimore Orioles over 1896-97. The big one, still a long way off, is Joe DiMaggio's record 56-game streak, set in 1941.

Michaels said he didn't want to look ahead to any of that, saying the Indians have more important things to focus on, such as trying to catch the Minnesota Twins in the American League Central while at the same time holding off Chicago and Boston in the wild-card hunt.

Monday night's victory gave the Indians a record of 68–56 and brought them within six games of the Twins in the Central. They are one game ahead of both the White Sox and Red Sox for the top wild-card spot.

Michaels' hitting and the pitching of Kenny Camden were the stories of this game. Michaels' first-inning homer came off Miguel Reyes, who walked Rikki LaBudda to start the game and gave up a single to Micah Millison. Michaels then ripped a line-drive homer to left field. It was his 30th of the season, and the three RBIs gave him 116 for the season.

"That really got us going," said Indians manager Todd Stein. "Between that and what 'The Wiz' (Camden) did on the mound, it was huge."

Camden tossed the rare complete game as he gave up only six hits in pitching the shutout. He got insurance in the form of a bases-loaded double from Bernard Harper in the sixth.

"Just cruisin' out there," Camden said. "This is a good park to pitch in, and with that kind of run support, all you have to do is throw strikes and try to make them hit it to the big part of the ballpark."

So ends another of those ever-popular four-game wrap-around weekend series. From here, it's off to Oakland for a pair of games before the Indians come home for the weekend. The last time the Indians were in Oakland in the early days of the season and the early days of Stein's managerial tenure, they won three of four.

"That seems like an eternity ago," Stein said. "We're taking nothing for granted. That's a tough park to hit in, so it will be tough to see if Scottie can keep it going, but our focus is on winning as a team."

CLEVELAND INDIANS VS SEATTLE MARINERS · AUGUST 23
CLEVELAND 6 / SEATTLE 0

CLEVELAND INDIANS

BATTING	AB	R	H	RBI	2B	3B	HR	BB	SO	BA
RIKKI LABUDDA CF	4	1	2	0	0	0	0	1	0	.271
MICAH MILLISON RF	5	1	1	0	0	0	0	1	0	.279
SCOTT MICHAELS 2B	5	1	3	3	0	0	1	0	2	.381
TERRY ROVETTO 3B	4	0	2	0	0	0	0	1	1	.275
OLIVER REINER 1B	4	1	1	0	0	0	0	0	0	.279
WILSON WHITE LF	4	1	1	0	1	0	0	0	1	.282
JUSTIN KESTINO SS	3	1	1	0	0	0	0	1	0	.266
BERNARD HARPER DH	4	0	2	3	1	0	0	0	1	.260
MORRIS JEROME C	3	0	1	0	0	0	0	1	0	.241

PITCHING	IP	H	R	ER	SO	BB	ERA			
KENNY CAMDEN (W)	4.33	6	4	4	2	6	4.95			

SEATTLE MARINERS

BATTING	AB	R	H	RBI	2B	3B	HR	BB	SO	BA
VANCE ROBERTS 2B	4	0	1	0	0	0	0	0	1	.308
BILLY NEVILLE 1B	4	0	0	0	0	0	0	0	0	.284
RUSS GRANZOW LF	4	0	1	0	1	0	0	0	1	.290
PHIL BORNTRAGGER 3B	4	0	1	0	0	0	0	0	0	.274
JAMIE BROCKER SS	3	0	1	0	0	0	0	1	2	.284
HUGO VENETAS DH	3	0	1	0	0	0	0	1	0	.237
BRENDAN KAHN RF	4	0	0	0	0	0	0	0	2	.251
SKYLER TOWNSEND C	4	0	1	0	0	0	0	0	1	.273
ROBERTO AGUIRRE CF	4	0	0	0	0	0	0	0	1	.274

PITCHING	IP	H	R	ER	SO	BB	ERA			
MIGUEL REYES (L)	5.33	9	6	6	4	3	4.12			
JALEN GATES	1.67	3	0	0	0	1	3.08			
JOAQUIN TORRES	1	1	0	0	1	0	2.90			
KELVIN BILLINGSLEY	1	1	0	0	0	1	3.56			

INNING	1	2	3	4	5	6	7	8	9	TOTAL
CLEVELAND	3	0	0	0	0	3	0	0	0	6
SEATTLE	0	0	0	0	0	0	0	0	0	0

GAME 125

By SAM LARDNER
The Cleveland Press

OAKLAND, Calif., August 24 — Scott Michaels hit a couple of 'em where they ain't — or where they weren't — Tuesday night.

That helped him extend his hitting streak to 45 games and, equally as important, it helped the Indians beat the Oakland Athletics 4–3 at the Coliseum.

The Michaels phenomenon brought a crowd of 32,592 out to the Coliseum for a weeknight game. The crowd alternated between cheering for their hometown A's and the hottest sensation in baseball. The Bay Area press — from Oakland and San Francisco — was out in full force to try to capture the moment and perhaps the essence of the 23-year-old Michaels, who keeps that sort of thing pretty close to the vest.

As far as the streak goes, Michaels is tied for second all-time with Wee Willie Keeler, who hit in 45 straight for the old National League Baltimore Orioles over the 1896-97 seasons. The diminutive Keeler's key to success was to "hit 'em where they ain't."

"I did not know that," said Michaels before flashing some more of his understated humor. "Did any of you guys cover him?"

That brought a collective "ouch" from the more senior members of the media corps, both from Cleveland and the Bay Area.

But seriously, Michaels has only one more man to catch: Joe DiMaggio, who holds the all-time record at 56 consecutive games with a hit, set in 1941.

"Him I've heard of," Michaels quipped. "We're still a long way from that. You guys from Cleveland have been around me long enough to know that I'm not getting caught up in any of that. Sorry I can't give you something more colorful."

Michaels brought the crowd to its feet with a two-out single in the first inning off Maurice Waters. The Oakland fans stood and cheered the visiting player as they would one of their own. Unsure of what to do, Michaels gave a shy wave of his right hand.

"That was pretty nice of them," Michaels said. "I didn't want to tip my cap or anything like that because this isn't our home ballpark. But I hope the fans out here know I appreciate it very much.

Michaels came home on a double down the right-field line by Terry Rovetto to give the Indians a 1–0 lead.

They made it 2–0 in the second on a solo homer by Justin Kestino. Michaels' second hit was another single, in the seventh. He is hitting .466 during the streak and .382 for the season. Angel Rodriguez was brought in for Michaels in the ninth.

Indians starting pitcher Tak Fujimoto continued his run of good pitching as he worked seven innings, giving up six hits and two runs while walking one and striking out seven. The A's tied the game at 22 in the fourth. Albert Reyes led off with a single. A double by Matthew Van Stencel scored Reyes, and Ernesto Mendesoto's single scored Van Stencel.

But that was all Fujimoto gave up.

"It was nice and cool out there tonight," he said through translator Ryuji Sato. "The ball doesn't do much here in the air, so you can throw it over and let them hit it. Ice (catcher Iceberg Peters) and I were on the same page all night, as we have been every time he has caught me."

The Indians knocked Waters out of the game in the sixth, scoring twice. Justin Kestino singled and made it to third on Peters' bloop double down the left-field line. Given an RBI chance, leadoff man Rikki LaBudda came through with a solid single up the middle.

Setup man Geno Milzie allowed a solo homer to Tremont Harkness in the eighth, but Indians closer Ivan Zyzna struck out the side in the bottom of the ninth.

"Real important," said Indians manager Todd Stein, whose team is 69–56 and now within five games of the Minnesota Twins for the top spot in the American League Central. The Indians lead the White Sox by one game and the Red Sox by two for the top wild-card spot. "We're putting ourselves into a good position here, but we've got a few days of August left and then a whole month-plus of baseball to play. One more to go here, and then we go home. It's going to be quite a ride."

GAME 125

CLEVELAND INDIANS VS OAKLAND ATHLETICS · AUGUST 24
CLEVELAND 4 / OAKLAND 3

CLEVELAND INDIANS										
BATTING	AB	R	H	RBI	2B	3B	HR	BB	SO	BA
RIKKI LABUDDA CF	3	0	1	2	0	0	0	1	0	.272
MICAH MILLISON RF	4	0	0	0	0	0	0	0	1	.276
SCOTT MICHAELS 2B	4	1	2	0	0	0	0	0	0	.382
ANGEL RODRIGUEZ 2B	0	0	0	0	0	0	0	0	0	.233
TERRY ROVETTO 3B	4	0	1	1	1	0	0	0	1	.275
OLIVER REINER 1B	3	0	1	0	0	0	0	1	0	.280
WILSON WHITE LF	3	0	0	0	0	0	0	1	0	.280
JUSTIN KESTINO SS	4	2	2	1	0	0	1	0	0	.269
BERNARD HARPER DH	4	0	0	0	0	0	0	0	2	.257
ICEBERG PETERS C	4	0	1	0	1	0	0	0	1	.205
PITCHING	IP	H	R	ER	SO	BB	ERA			
TAK FUJIMOTO (W)	7	6	2	2	7	1	3.18			
GENO MILZE	1	1	1	1	0	0	2.43			
IVAN ZYZNA (S)	1	0	0	0	3	0	2.11			

OAKLAND A'S										
BATTING	AB	R	H	RBI	2B	3B	HR	BB	SO	BA
ALBERT REYES RF	4	1	1	0	0	0	0	0	1	.308
MATTHEW VAN STENCEL CF	4	1	1	1	0	0	0	0	0	.286
ERNESTO MENDESOTO 3B	4	0	1	1	0	0	0	0	2	.290
GRAEME NILSON 1B	3	0	0	0	0	0	0	1	1	.272
TRENT ATHERTON C	4	0	2	0	0	0	0	0	2	.286
JAYSON GIVINS DH	4	0	1	0	0	0	0	0	0	.263
RAMON TORRES SS	3	0	0	0	0	0	0	0	1	.251
TREMONT HARKNESS LF	4	1	1	1	0	0	1	0	0	.273
GLENN WALLS 2B	4	0	0	0	0	0	0	0	2	.259
PITCHING	IP	H	R	ER	SO	BB	ERA			
MAURICE WATERS (L)	5.67	6	4	4	3	2	3.30			
JORGE BAREA	2.33	2	0	0	1	1	3.38			
JACK RICHARDS	1	1	0	0	0	0	2.25			

INNING	1	2	3	4	5	6	7	8	9	TOTAL
CLEVELAND	1	1	0	0	0	2	0	0	0	4
OAKLAND	0	0	0	2	0	0	0	1	0	3

GAME 126

By SAM LARDNER
The Cleveland Press

OAKLAND, Calif., August 25 — Day games at the Coliseum in Alameda County are always lots of fun.

The sun shines brightly, making the Oakland Athletics' white uniforms seem even brighter than usual. And the baseball travels much better than it does here in the oppressive night air.

True to form, the A's and Indians engaged in a wild one Wednesday afternoon, with the Indians pulling out an 8–7 victory in the ninth.

The circumstances of the victory were both thrilling and a little bit chilling for the Indians. Second baseman Scott Michaels went 3-for-4 with an RBI double to extend his hitting streak to 46 games, putting him 10 behind all-time leader Joe DiMaggio.

The chill came in the seventh when Michaels slid hard into second base, appearing to turn his right ankle. He was replaced in the game by Angel Rodriguez, the man Michaels supplanted in May, when Rodriguez lost his job because of a hamstring injury.

As fate would have it, Rodriguez laid down a perfect squeeze bunt in the top of the ninth inning to score Rikki LaBudda with the go-ahead and eventual game-winning run by breaking a 7–7 tie.

Indians closer Ivan Zyzna then worked out of a bases-loaded jam of his own making — with two walks — to earn the save and get the Tribe out of town with a two-game sweep and a three-game winning streak overall.

As for Michaels, he'll get a day of rest with an off-day Thursday and be evaluated ahead of the Indians' weekend series at home against the Tampa Bay Rays.

Michaels was getting treatment on the ankle after the game and did not meet with reporters.

"We think he just tweaked it," said manager Todd Stein, whose team improved to 70-56 and crept to within four games of the first-place Minnesota Twins in the American League Central. The Indians lead the White Sox by one and the Red Sox by three in the race for the top wild-card spot.

"Those bags don't give, and it looked like he might have slid a little late," added Stein. "We're not going to take any chances with him or any other player. The streak isn't as important to him as it maybe is to you guys. We need him to win games so we make the postseason, and that's where our focus is.

"That said, it was good for Angel to get in there and 'drive in' the game-winner like that."

Rodriguez often fills in at the end of games for Michaels, and he spells Justin Kestino at shortstop from time to time. He has expressed no bitterness about losing his starting job.

"Scott is a friend of mine, and he has supported me through some tough times," Rodriguez said. "I saw him in the training room a few minutes ago, and he was in good spirits. He told me congrats on my 27-foot game-winning bunt. I'll take that. If I know him, he'll be back out there Friday night and in the starting lineup."

Indians starting pitcher Lynn Moda couldn't stand the prosperity of a 4–0 lead, given to him by Terry Rovetto's three-run double and Oliver Reiner's RBI single in the first inning. Michaels singled as the third batter of the inning to end any suspense about the streak.

But the A's scored five times in the fourth to chase Moda. The big blow was a grand slam off the bat off Ernesto Mendesoto. From there, the Indians used relievers Solly Alvarez, Mickey Penney, Buck Sterling and Zyzna.

Michaels hit his run-scoring double in the seventh as part of a three-run inning. He raised his season average to .386 (can the whispers of .400 be far behind?), and he's batting .472 during the streak.

Sterling gave up the tying runs in the bottom of the eighth, setting the stage for Rodriguez's bunting heroics in the ninth. LaBudda led off against Devon Clavell. LaBudda stole second base and went to third on Micah Millison's groundout. Rodriguez took a strike before pushing a bunt between the pitcher and the first-base line to score the speedy LaBudda.

Zyzna got a quick out in the ninth before giving up a single to Jayson Givins and walks Ramon Torres and Trent Atherton. But he struck out Glenn Walls and got Albert Reyes to pop out to Rodriguez, ending the game.

"We always make it interesting," Stein said. "I'm just glad we escaped this place with the win. We'll rest up and see how Scottie is for Friday night. I'm not betting against him."

GAME 126

CLEVELAND INDIANS VS OAKLAND ATHLETICS · AUGUST 25
CLEVELAND 8 / OAKLAND 7

CLEVELAND INDIANS										
BATTING	AB	R	H	RBI	2B	3B	HR	BB	SO	BA
RIKKI LABUDDA CF	5	3	3	0	0	0	0	0	0	.275
MICAH MILLISON RF	5	2	2	0	0	0	0	0	1	.278
SCOTT MICHAELS 2B	4	2	3	1	0	0	0	0	0	.386
ANGEL RODRIGUEZ 2B	1	0	1	1	0	0	0	0	0	.243
TERRY ROVETTO 3B	4	1	2	3	1	0	0	1	0	.277
OLIVER REINER 1B	4	0	1	1	0	0	0	1	1	.279
WILSON WHITE LF	5	0	2	2	0	0	0	0	1	.281
JUSTIN KESTINO SS	4	0	0	0	0	0	0	1	1	.266
BERNARD HARPER DH	4	0	2	0	0	0	0	0	0	.260
MORRIS JEROME C	4	0	2	0	1	0	0	0	1	.244

PITCHING	IP	H	R	ER	SO	BB	ERA			
LYNN MODA	3.33	7	4	4	3	1	4.11			
SOLLY ALVAREZ	1.67	2	1	1	1	1	2.79			
MICKEY PENNY	2	1	0	0	2	0	3.66			
BUCK STERLING (W)	1	2	2	2	0	1	4.46			
IVAN ZYZNA (S)	1	1	0	0	1	2	2.06			

OAKLAND A'S										
BATTING	AB	R	H	RBI	2B	3B	HR	BB	SO	BA
ALBERT REYES RF	4	1	0	0	0	0	0	1	1	.305
MATTHEW VAN STENCEL CF	5	1	2	0	1	0	0	0	1	.288
ERNESTO MENDESOTO 3B	5	1	2	4	0	0	1	0	0	.292
GRAEME NILSON 1B	5	1	1	0	1	0	0	0	1	.271
TRENT ATHERTON C	4	2	2	0	0	0	0	1	0	.288
JAYSON GIVINS DH	5	0	2	1	0	0	0	0	0	.265
RAMON TORRES SS	4	0	1	1	1	0	0	1	1	.251
TREMONT HARKNESS LF	4	0	0	1	0	0	0	1	1	.270
GLENN WALLS 2B	4	1	2	0	0	0	0	1	2	.262

PITCHING	IP	H	R	ER	SO	BB	ERA			
LEANDRO TORO	5	9	4	4	2	2	4.22			
CRAIG QUINN	2	5	3	3	1	1	4.40			
JORGE BAREA	1	2	0	0	0	0	3.24			
DEVON CLAVELL (L)	1	3	1	1	1	0	3.65			

INNING	1	2	3	4	5	6	7	8	9	TOTAL
CLEVELAND	4	0	0	0	0	0	3	0	1	8
OAKLAND	0	0	0	5	0	0	0	2	0	7

GAME 127

By SAM LARDNER
The Cleveland Press

CLEVELAND, August 27 — The running joke the last couple days was that when Scott Michaels sprained his ankle the other day in Oakland, all of Ohio developed a limp.

Michaels' status was just one of many story lines on a busy Friday at Progressive Field, where the Indians returned home and lost 2–1 to the Tampa Bay Rays.

The good news for Michaels and Indians fans was that the 23-year-old second baseman was able to play, and he singled in four at-bats to extend his hitting streak to 47 games, nine shy of Joe DiMaggio's all-time record.

"I'm good," he said. "Just a little sore. I hit the bag hard (Wednesday) in Oakland and kind of jarred the ankle. They wound up doing an X-ray, and it showed nothing, maybe a broken blood vessel or two. But I had it wrapped pretty good during the game and didn't have any trouble.

"It's certainly not going to affect my speed because I don't have any to begin with."

Michaels' gimpy ankle was the top story, but there were others.

Indians general manager J.D. Eisner met with the media horde in the interview room — he usually entertains reporters on the field, but with the Michaels phenomenon growing exponentially, the Indians opted for the big room.

Eisner said starting pitcher Ollie Gonzalez would finish his minor league rehab stint Saturday and be activated on Sept. 1, when rosters may expand. At that time, the Indians will go with a six-man rotation, something they may stick with for the rest of the regular season.

Gonzalez's rotation replacement, Eli Batt, pitched well Friday night but took the loss, as he gave up a two-run homer to Rueben Portugal in the sixth inning as the Rays erased a 10 deficit.

"Our guys aren't overworked by any stretch, but Eli has given us a real boost, and if you have six good arms, you might as well use them all," Eisner said.

In addition to Gonzalez being activated on Sept. 1, the Indians will call up infielder-outfielder Willie Bartlett from Class AAA Columbus to provide an element of speed. Also coming up with be reliever Alex Barsky, also from Columbus, where he has 24 saves, catcher Sam Traub and corner infielder Steve Skeevers.

The Indians could not get much going against Rays starting pitcher John Dixon, who worked seven innings and gave up six hits and one run, a run-scoring single by Morris Jerome to score Justin Kestino, who doubled with one out in the third. Rays setup man Adolfo Vasquez and closer Buddy Anderson held the Indians at bay after that.

Michaels struck out in the first inning but lined a single to left in the fourth to extend the streak. That brought the sellout crowd of 37,098 to its feet.

"You know me," Michaels said. "It's nice, but we didn't win the game, so that takes a little of the fun out of it. Their pitching was tough tonight."

Michaels' season batting average fell from .386 to .384, putting a temporary halt to the building speculation about Michaels not only catching DiMaggio, but also hitting .400 for the season.

More important for the Indians as a team, they fell back to five games behind first-place Minnesota in the American League Central. The Chicago White Sox tied the Indians for the top wild-card spot while the Boston Red Sox moved to within two games of the Indians and White Sox.

"I told you all these games are important," said manager Todd Stein. "We just got outpitched tonight, nothing more, nothing less. Their guy was dealing, and Eli made only one bad pitch on the night. We'll take that kind of performance out of him every night."

With sellout crowds expected all weekend, how does Stein think Michaels and the team are responding to the attention?

"Very well," he said. "Just watch. Scottie and the rest of the guys are embracing this. We're not shying away from anything or anybody."

CLEVELAND INDIANS VS TAMPA BAY RAYS · AUGUST 27
TAMPA BAY 2 / CLEVELAND 1

CLEVELAND INDIANS

BATTING	AB	R	H	RBI	2B	3B	HR	BB	SO	BA
RIKKI LABUDDA CF	4	0	0	0	0	0	0	0	0	.273
MICAH MILLISON RF	4	0	1	0	0	0	0	0	0	.278
SCOTT MICHAELS 2B	4	0	1	0	0	0	0	0	1	.384
TERRY ROVETTO 3B	4	0	1	0	1	0	0	0	1	.276
OLIVER REINER 1B	4	0	1	0	0	0	0	0	0	.279
WILSON WHITE LF	4	0	0	0	0	0	0	0	2	.279
JUSTIN KESTINO SS	4	1	1	0	1	0	0	0	1	.266
KIERAN CATSEF DH	4	0	0	0	0	0	0	0	1	.261
MORRIS JEROME C	4	0	1	1	1	0	0	0	1	.244

PITCHING	IP	H	R	ER	SO	BB	ERA			
ELI BATT (L)	8	7	2	2	6	1	3.15			
GENO MILZE	1	1	0	0	0	1	2.38			

TAMPA BAY RAYS

BATTING	AB	R	H	RBI	2B	3B	HR	BB	SO	BA
TIM CLARK LF	4	1	2	0	0	0	0	0	0	.295
TOM DONNELLY JR 2B	3	0	0	0	0	0	0	1	1	.286
RANDY MCGEE SS	4	0	1	0	0	0	0	0	1	.291
RUEBEN PORTUGAL 3B	4	1	2	2	1	0	1	0	0	.273
ERNESTO JURADO 1B	3	0	0	0	0	0	0	1	0	.286
TIM STAFFORD RF	4	0	1	0	0	0	0	0	0	.265
FRANK MORETTI C	4	0	1	0	0	0	0	0	1	.251
BRANDON GREGERSON DH	4	0	0	0	0	0	0	0	2	.267
REGGIE PATTERSON CF	4	0	1	0	0	0	0	0	1	.262

PITCHING	IP	H	R	ER	SO	BB	ERA			
JOHNNY DIXON (W)	7	6	1	1	5	0	3.62			
ADOLFO VASQUEZ	1	0	0	0	1	0	3.77			
BUDDY ANDERSON	1	0	0	0	1	0	3.38			

INNING	1	2	3	4	5	6	7	8	9	TOTAL
TAMPA BAY	0	0	0	0	0	2	0	0	0	2
CLEVELAND	0	0	1	0	0	0	0	0	0	1

GAME 128

By SAM LARDNER
The Cleveland Press

CLEVELAND, August 28 — Some 50 people from Scott Michaels' home-town of Versailles, Ohio, came out to watch their local boy play for the Cleveland Indians on a sultry late-summer day at Progressive Field.

"That's more than half the town," Michaels said before the game. "I hope somebody turned the lights out and that at least the police department stayed home."

Versailles is small, but it's not quite that small (population 2,700). Either way, Michaels is the biggest thing to come out of that small town in southwest-central Ohio.

Those friends and family who came out to see Michaels Saturday came away with mixed emotions. The local lad extended his hitting streak to 48 games with a fourth-inning double, but it came in a 5–2 loss to the Tampa Bay Rays.

Michaels is now only eight games shy of Joe DiMaggio's all-time record of hitting in 56 consecutive games. However, his bid to become the first .400 hitter since Ted Williams in 1941 took a hit as his season batting average fell to .382. It will take some doing for Michaels to reach .400 as Tony Gwynn, George Brett and Rod Carew will attest after making their own runs at the magical mark years ago.

The Indians and Michaels both have bigger fish to fry, and they don't want this one to get away. Saturday's loss was the team's second in a row, dropping them to 70–58 for the season.

With the Twins losing at Kansas City, the Indians remain five games behind Minnesota for first place in the American League West. But they fell one game behind the Chicago White Sox for the top wild-card spot. They continue to lead the Red Sox by two for the second and final wild-card spot.

"We can't afford to lose our focus," said manager Todd Stein. "One minute we're talking about winning the division, and the next we could be finding ourselves on the outside looking in altogether."

Michaels looked somewhat hobbled by the right-ankle injury he suffered sliding into second base Wednesday at Oakland. He might have gone for third on his double, but he pulled up at second base.

"I don't want to push it, even though I probably could," he said. "If it had been 100 percent, I might have showed off for my parents and friends, but I can't be foolish about things. A couple more days and it should be fine."

Michaels is 2-for-9 during the last two games, and the Indians' bats as a whole have gone cold in the first two games of this series, scoring only three runs.

That provided little support for starting pitcher Brian Howard, who hasn't been part of a win since July 31. "The Doctor" pitched five innings, giving up seven hits and four runs. The Indians got a first-inning homer from Micah Millison as they took a 1–0 lead against Tyler Harrison.

The Rays roared back with three in the second, on a two-run double by Pete Douglas and an RBI single by Bobby Theer.

"I've been a little off," said Howard. "Maybe going to a six-man (rotation) once Ollie (Gonzalez) comes off the IL will help. The pitches just haven't been as crisp as they were earlier."

Tampa Bay got one more off Howard in the fifth and one off Lee Hazelton in the seventh. The Indians got a sacrifice fly from Bernard Harper in the bottom of the seventh. Mickey Penney pitched the final two innings for the Tribe.

"They can throw it," Stein said of the Rays pitching staff. "We've just got to shorten up on the approaches at the plate a little bit, and I think we'll be fine. I don't know if we've been sitting back and waiting for Scottie to do something, but I don't think so. I don't know when or if that hitting streak will ever end, but we've got nine guys in the lineup who can get it done. It will come."

GAME 128

CLEVELAND INDIANS VS TAMPA BAY RAYS • AUGUST 28
TAMPA BAY 5 / CLEVELAND 2

CLEVELAND INDIANS										
BATTING	**AB**	**R**	**H**	**RBI**	**2B**	**3B**	**HR**	**BB**	**SO**	**BA**
RIKKI LABUDDA CF	5	0	1	0	0	0	0	0	0	.272
MICAH MILLISON RF	4	1	2	1	0	0	1	1	1	.279
SCOTT MICHAELS 2B	5	0	1	0	1	0	0	0	2	.382
TERRY ROVETTO 3B	4	0	0	0	0	0	0	1	0	.274
OLIVER REINER 1B	4	0	0	0	0	0	0	0	1	.277
WILSON WHITE LF	4	1	1	0	0	0	0	1	0	.278
JUSTIN KESTINO SS	4	0	2	0	1	0	0	0	1	.268
BERNARD HARPER DH	2	0	0	1	0	0	0	1	1	.259
MORRIS JEROME C	3	0	1	0	0	0	0	1	2	.245
PITCHING	**IP**	**H**	**R**	**ER**	**SO**	**BB**	**ERA**			
BRIAN HOWARD (L)	5	7	4	4	5	2	5.03			
LEE HAZELTON	2	2	1	1	1	1	2.66			
MICKEY PENNY	2	1	0	0	1	0	3.52			

TAMPA BAY RAYS										
BATTING	**AB**	**R**	**H**	**RBI**	**2B**	**3B**	**HR**	**BB**	**SO**	**BA**
TIM CLARK LF	5	1	1	0	0	0	0	0	0	.294
TOM DONNELLY JR 2B	3	0	0	0	0	0	0	2	1	.284
RANDY MCGEE SS	5	1	2	1	0	0	0	0	1	.293
RUEBEN PORTUGAL 3B	5	0	2	1	1	0	0	0	0	.275
ERNESTO JURADO 1B	4	1	1	0	0	0	0	1	1	.285
TIM STAFFORD RF	5	1	1	0	0	0	0	0	2	.264
PETE DOUGLASS C	4	1	2	2	1	0	0	0	0	.279
BOBBY THEER DH	4	0	1	1	0	0	0	0	0	.272
REGGIE PATTERSON CF	4	0	0	0	0	0	0	0	2	.259
PITCHING	**IP**	**H**	**R**	**ER**	**SO**	**BB**	**ERA**			
TYLER HARRISON (W)	7	6	1	1	5	0	3.62			
LIAM MURPHY	1	1	0	0	1	0	3.38			
BUDDY ANDERSON (S)	1	0	0	0	1	0	3.27			

INNING	1	2	3	4	5	6	7	8	9	TOTAL
TAMPA BAY	0	3	0	0	1	0	1	0	0	5
CLEVELAND	1	0	0	0	0	0	1	0	0	2

GAME 129

By SAM LARDNER
The Cleveland Press

CLEVELAND, August 29 — Sunday was a nice bounce-back day for both the Indians and second baseman Scott Michaels.

After losing the first two games of this three-game series to the Tampa Bay Rays, the Indians took out their frustrations in a 10–1 victory before 37,765 fans at Progressive Field blasting five home runs.

Among those in the sellout crowd again were family and friends of Michaels, who saw him go 2-for-5 to extend his hitting streak to 49 games, just seven shy of Joe DiMaggio's all-time record. DiMaggio did it in 1941 with the New York Yankees.

Speaking of crowds, the press box continued to get even more crowded as writers from The New York Times, The New York Post, The New York Daily News and Newsday have joined the ever-expanding press corps. The Boston Glove and Chicago Tribune are expected in Monday.

As for Michaels' immediate family, they'll be along for the rest of the ride — home or away. The Angels come in Monday and then the Tribe hits the road for games at Baltimore, Texas and Chicago.

"Dad's a retired firefighter and Mom's a substitute teacher, so they won't have to rearrange their schedules too much," Michaels said to the media throng after the game. "My girlfriend (Kristen Williams) might have to use a few vacation days. She's an admissions officer at Indiana (University). But I'm sure they'll understand."

As for his own performance Sunday, Michaels hit his 31st home run of the season in the first inning, a two-run shot that was immediately followed by a solo blast from Terry Rovetto. He added a single in the sixth. His season batting average held at .382, and he's hitting .459 (96-for-209) during the streak.

For the first time, he admitted to being a little excited about it.

"Seeing all you guys here, it's hard to ignore," he said. "Yeah, I know where the streak is, and I'm as shocked as anybody about it. But if we hadn't won the game today, I don't know how much I'd want to talk about it. In talking things over with Steinie (manager Todd Stein) and my teammates, we've just decided to have fun with it and focus on winning the games. The rest of it will take care of itself, one way or another."

In salvaging the series finale, the Indians improved to 71–58, and they remained five games behind the Twins for first place in the American League Central. They're now tied with the White Sox for the top wild-card spot and two games ahead of the Red Sox.

The ten-run output was welcome news for starting pitcher Kenny Camden, who worked six innings, giving up six hits and one run. Lorry Unger, Mickey Penney and Buck Sterling each picked up an inning of relief.

The Indians chased Rays starter Jose Diaz with five runs in the fourth. The big blow was a grand slam by Oliver Reiner. Wilson White and Justin Kestino added back to back long balls in the eighth.

"We're almost to September, so it's pretty much crunch time now," Stein said. "I think all the guys are responding well to both the playoff race and what's been going on with Scottie. We'll welcome the Angels in here and see what happens."

GAME 129

CLEVELAND INDIANS VS TAMPA BAY RAYS · AUGUST 29
CLEVELAND 10 / TAMPA BAY 1

CLEVELAND INDIANS

BATTING	AB	R	H	RBI	2B	3B	HR	BB	SO	BA
RIKKI LABUDDA CF	4	0	2	0	1	0	0	1	0	.274
MICAH MILLISON RF	5	2	2	0	0	0	0	0	0	.281
SCOTT MICHAELS 2B	5	2	2	2	0	0	1	0	0	.382
TERRY ROVETTO 3B	5	2	3	1	0	0	1	0	0	.277
OLIVER REINER 1B	4	1	1	4	0	0	1	1	1	.277
WILSON WHITE LF	5	1	1	1	0	0	1	0	1	.277
JUSTIN KESTINO SS	4	2	2	1	1	0	1	1	0	.270
BERNARD HARPER DH	4	0	1	1	0	0	0	0	1	.259
MORRIS JEROME C	3	0	2	0	0	0	0	1	0	.248

PITCHING	IP	H	R	ER	SO	BB	ERA			
KENNY CAMDEN (W)	6	6	1	1	4	1	4.81			
LORRY UNGER	1	1	0	0	1	1	4.02			
MICKEY PENNY	1	0	0	0	1	0	3.46			
BUCK STERLING	1	1	0	0	1	0	3.92			

TAMPA BAY RAYS

BATTING	AB	R	H	RBI	2B	3B	HR	BB	SO	BA
TIM CLARK LF	4	0	2	0	0	0	0	0	1	.296
TOM DONNELLY JR 2B	4	0	0	0	0	0	0	0	0	.281
RANDY MCGEE SS	4	0	1	0	0	0	0	0	1	.292
RUEBEN PORTUGAL 3B	4	0	1	0	0	0	0	0	1	.275
ERNESTO JURADO 1B	3	0	0	0	0	0	0	1	1	.283
TIM STAFFORD RF	4	0	0	0	0	0	0	0	2	.261
PETE DOUGLASS C	3	1	2	0	1	0	0	1	0	.281
BOBBY THEER DH	4	0	1	0	0	0	0	0	1	.272
REGGIE PATTERSON CF	3	0	1	1	0	0	0	0	0	.260

PITCHING	IP	H	R	ER	SO	BB	ERA			
JOSE DIAZ (L)	3.33	7	5	5	0	2	4.05			
DON DAVENPORT	1.67	5	3	3	1	2	3.88			
GIANCARLO MAZZERI	2	1	0	0	1	0	3.18			
ADOLFO VASQUEZ	1	3	2	2	1	0	4.22			

INNING	1	2	3	4	5	6	7	8	9	TOTAL
TAMPA BAY	0	0	1	0	0	0	0	0	0	1
CLEVELAND	3	0	0	5	0	0	0	2	0	10

GAMES 130 and 131
(Doubleheader)

By SAM LARDNER
The Cleveland Press

CLEVELAND, August 30 — Sit up, kids. Watch and listen. You might learn something.

You might learn a little math. And you're certainly going to learn a little history. And you're going to like it.

The Indians and Major League Baseball tried something different Monday as a way to win kids back with a day-night doubleheader with a "Baseball goes back to school" theme.

Kids around Cleveland and the suburbs will be back in the classroom Wednesday, but the Indians and the Anaheim Angels put on a nice clinic for them Monday in a split. The Indians took the first game 3–2 behind the pitching of spot starter Solly Alvarez, and the Angels bested Tak Fujimoto and the Tribe 6–4 in the nightcap.

As far as the math and history go, Indians second baseman Scott Michaels went a combined 5-for-9 in the doubleheader to extend his hitting streak to 51 games, just five behind Joe DiMaggio's all-time record.

The .400 watch might be back on, too, as Michaels' season average rose from .382 to .386. Manager Todd Stein gave Michaels somewhat of a break in the second game, using him as the DH and putting Angel Rodriguez at second base.

Michaels said the biggest thrill of the long day and night was hearing all those kids yelling "Scottie, Scottie" when he came to the plate.

"Yeah, that was cool," he said. "That made me happier than anything else. I'm not too far removed from being a kid and playing ball for the fun of it. It's important to get those kids interested in baseball, and overall, we gave them a pretty good show. Maybe they can talk about it with their friends when they head back to school Wednesday."

Michaels went 3-for-5 in the first game and 2-for-4 in the second. He brought the kids to their feet right away, with a two-out solo homer in the bottom of the first inning of the day game to give the Indians a quick 1–0 lead. It was his 32nd homer of the season.

Alvarez, who worked five innings, gave up two in the third inning on Carlos Diaz's two-run single. The Indians made him the winner by getting two in the bottom of the fifth. Terry Rovetto and Oliver Reiner singled, and both came home on Justin Kestino's double. Lee Hazelton, Lorry Unger, Geno Milzie and Ivan Zyzna each picked up an inning of relief, with Zyzna earning the save.

Stein changed things in the second game, once again pairing backup catcher Iceberg Peters with Fujimoto and putting Rodriguez in the Field. Leo Taylor and Kieran Catseff also got starts.

Fujimoto wasn't as sharp as he had been as he gutted out six innings, giving up nine hits and five runs. It was the first time since August 8 that the Indians hadn't won a game he started.

"They hit me around a little," he said through translator Ryuji Sato. "We had a pretty good game plan going in, Ice and me, but their hitters must have had a good plan, too. They hit some good pitches, but that happens."

The Angels pinged Fujimoto with single runs in each of the first three innings before piling on with three in the sixth, when Fujimoto's pitch count reached 105. A solo homer by Pete Warren and a two-run single in the sixth by Trent Norris were the hits that finally did Fujimoto in.

Michaels picked up a single in the fourth inning and had an RBI double in the seventh, driving in Taylor and getting the Indians on the board. Oliver Reiner's single drove in Michaels. The Indians made it close with two in the bottom of the eighth on an RBI single by Rodriguez and a run-scoring double by Peters.

Angels closer Graham Pinder shut down the Indians in the bottom of the ninth.

"Long day," said Stein whose team is 72–59 and 5.5 games behind the Twins in the American League Central. The Indians are a half-game behind the White Sox for the top-wild card spot.

"It's tough to win a doubleheader, so we'll take this. You have to be happy with what Solly did in that spot start. Glad he got the 'W' next to his name. We'll get Ollie G back in a couple days and some more call-ups. Time to rock 'n' roll."

GAME 130

CLEVELAND INDIANS VS LOS ANGELES ANGELS ·AUGUST 30
CLEVELAND 3 / LOS ANGELES 2

CLEVELAND INDIANS										
BATTING	AB	R	H	RBI	2B	3B	HR	BB	SO	BA
RIKKI LABUDDA CF	5	0	2	0	1	0	0	0	0	.275
MICAH MILLISON RF	4	0	0	0	0	0	0	1	0	.278
SCOTT MICHAELS 2B	5	0	3	1	0	0	1	0	1	.385
TERRY ROVETTO 3B	4	1	1	0	0	0	0	1	0	.277
OLIVER REINER 1B	4	1	1	0	0	0	0	0	1	.276
WILSON WHITE LF	4	1	0	0	0	0	0	0	1	.275
JUSTIN KESTINO SS	3	0	2	2	1	0	0	1	0	.273
BERNARD HARPER DH	4	0	1	0	0	0	0	0	2	.258
MORRIS JEROME C	4	0	1	0	0	0	0	0	1	.248

PITCHING	IP	H	R	ER	SO	BB	ERA			
SOLLY ALVAREZ (W)	5	4	2	2	3	1	2.86			
LEE HAZELTON	1	1	0	0	0	0	2.59			
LORRY UNGER	1	1	0	0	1	0	3.92			
GENO MILZE	1	1	0	0	1	1	2.34			
IVAN ZYZNA (S)	1	1	0	0	1	0	2.01			

LOS ANGELES ANGELS										
BATTING	AB	R	H	RBI	2B	3B	HR	BB	SO	BA
TIM THORSEN RF	4	0	0	0	0	0	0	0	0	.293
JACOB BAKER DH	4	0	0	0	1	0	0	0	0	.283
CHICO GOMEZ CF	4	0	1	0	0	0	0	0	0	.291
PETE WARREN 1B	3	0	1	0	0	0	0	1	2	.274
BENJI WASHINGTON SS	4	0	2	0	1	0	0	0	0	.288
TRENT NORRIS LF	3	0	1	0	0	0	0	1	2	.265
LIM CHANG 3B	4	1	2	0	0	0	0	0	0	.279
ALBERT TORRES 2B	4	1	0	0	0	0	0	0	0	.269
CARLOS DIAZ C	4	0	1	2	0	0	0	0	1	.261

PITCHING	IP	H	R	ER	SO	BB	ERA			
HECTOR LUGO (L)	5	6	2	2	4	2	3.13			
JAVIER RIVERA	3	3	0	0	1	0	3.86			
LEE HICKSON	1	0	0	0	0	0	4.19			

INNING	1	2	3	4	5	6	7	8	9	TOTAL
LOS ANGELES	0	2	0	0	0	0	0	0	0	2
CLEVELAND	1	0	0	0	2	0	0	0		3

GAME 131

CLEVELAND INDIANS VS LOS ANGELES ANGELS · AUGUST 31
LOS ANGELES 6 CLEVELAND 4

CLEVELAND INDIANS										
BATTING	AB	R	H	RBI	2B	3B	HR	BB	SO	BA
LEO TAYLOR SS	4	1	1	0	1	0	0	0	1	.281
MICAH MILLISON RF	4	0	1	0	0	0	0	0	1	.278
SCOTT MICHAELS DH	4	1	2	1	1	0	0	0	1	.386
TERRY ROVETTO 3B	3	0	0	0	0	0	0	1	0	.276
OLIVER REINER 1B	3	0	2	1	0	0	0	1	0	.279
WILSON WHITE LF	4	1	2	0	0	0	0	0	0	.277
KIERAN CATSEF CF	4	0	0	0	0	0	0	0	2	.247
ANGEL RODRIGUEZ 2B	4	1	1	1	0	0	0	0	0	.244
ICEBERG PETERS C	4	0	1	1	1	0	0	0	1	.207
PITCHING	IP	H	R	ER	SO	BB	ERA			
TAK FUJIMOTO (L)	5.67	9	5	5	3	1	3.35			
BUCK STERLING	1.33	0	0	0	2	1	3.80			
MICKEY PENNY	2	2	1	1	0	0	3.49			
LOS ANGELES ANGELS										
BATTING	AB	R	H	RBI	2B	3B	HR	BB	SO	BA
TIM THORSEN RF	5	0	0	0	0	0	0	0	1	.290
JACOB BAKER DH	4	1	1	0	0	1	0	1	0	.283
CHICO GOMEZ CF	3	1	0	1	0	0	0	0	0	.288
PETE WARREN 1B	4	2	2	1	1	0	1	0	0	.276
BENJI WASHINGTON SS	3	1	2	0	0	0	0	1	0	.291
TRENT NORRIS LF	4	0	2	2	0	0	0	0	1	.267
LIM CHANG 3B	4	0	2	1	0	0	0	0	0	.281
ALBERT TORRES 2B	4	1	1	0	0	0	0	0	2	.269
CARLOS DIAZ C	4	0	1	1	1	0	0	0	1	.261
PITCHING	IP	H	R	ER	SO	BB	ERA			
JACKSON WOODRUFF (W)	6	3	0	0	5	2	3.10			
HIRAM MOLINA	2	6	4	4	0	0	3.96			
GRAHAM PINDER (S)	1	1	0	0	1	0	2.93			
INNING	1	2	3	4	5	6	7	8	9	TOTAL
LOS ANGELES	1	1	1	0	0	2	0	1	0	6
CLEVELAND	0	0	0	0	0	0	2	2	0	4

GAME 132

By SAM LARDNER
The Cleveland Press

CLEVELAND, August 31 — Now that August is over, Indians ace Lynn Moda says it's "go time."

As far as Indians second baseman Scott Michaels goes, there's just no stopping him.

The Indians ended August with a 5–0 shutout of the Los Angeles Angels Tuesday night at Progressive Field behind Moda's masterful pitching and Michaels extending his historic hitting streak to 52 games. He's now within tasting distance of Joe DiMaggio's all-time record of 56.

And with that, the Indians sail intrepidly into September with a record of 73-59 and with postseason hopes high.

They're only 4.5 games behind the Minnesota Twins for the top spot in the American League Central. They lead Chicago by one-half game for the top wild-card spot, and they're 1.5 ahead of Boston.

"This is what we play for," said Moda, who had his game face on even after pitching seven shutout innings. "It really is go time. We had a (crappy) start to the season and now we're right in the thick of the postseason hunt. We would have signed up for that in early April. Now it's on us to finish this (bleeping) thing off."

As for Michaels, he had a pair of singles in five at-bats to keep his season batting average at .386 as he also takes aim at becoming the first .400 hitter since Ted Williams in 1941, the year of DiMaggio's streak.

"One thing at a time," he said, laughing. "No, I have not thought about .400 one time, not once. The streak thing is kind of fun, and I'm kind of bewildered by that, to tell you the truth. I've been lucky a few times, and you need that. And I think it's great my family is here to enjoy it. But let's keep the focus on the team. We're all thrilled to be going into September with a chance to go to the postseason."

Moda is the ace of the staff, and he pitched like it, going seven innings and giving up five hits while walking none and striking out six.

The Angels never got a runner past second base. The Indians have not lost a game Moda has started since July 28.

"He's a horse, and we've ridden his performances this whole second half," said manager Todd Stein. "Your No. 1 guys always seem to prove why they're just that when it comes to crunch time. He was in total command here tonight."

Moda and Roberto Colon pitched scoreless ball until the fourth, when Michaels extended his streak with a solid single to left field, bringing the crowd of 37,898 to its feet for an extended ovation. Michaels finally gave a sheepish wave to get things quieted down.

From there, Terry Rovetto singled Michaels to second (he's still nursing a sore ankle). Oliver Reiner doubled both runners home, and Wilson White's single scored Rovetto.

The Indians put it away in the seventh. Bernard Harper singled and went to third on Morris Jerome's double. Rikki LaBudda singled them both home.

Lee Hazelton and Mickey Penney finished up for the Indians, who will get some bench and bullpen reinforcements when rosters expand Wednesday.

"Our guys are excited going into September, but they've battled hard to get to this point after that rough start," said Stein, who took over from Dave Mills after the 10th game of the season. "So the more guys we have here, the merrier. With Scottie's streak and us being in contention, I promise you that you won't want to miss a minute."

GAME 132

CLEVELAND INDIANS VS LOS ANGELES ANGELS •AUGUST 31
CLEVELAND 5 / LOS ANGELES 0

CLEVELAND INDIANS										
BATTING	AB	R	H	RBI	2B	3B	HR	BB	SO	BA
RIKKI LABUDDA CF	5	0	1	2	0	0	0	0	0	.274
MICAH MILLISON RF	4	0	1	0	0	0	0	1	0	.278
SCOTT MICHAELS 2B	5	1	2	0	1	0	0	0	1	.386
TERRY ROVETTO 3B	5	1	1	0	0	0	0	0	2	.275
OLIVER REINER 1B	3	1	1	2	1	0	0	2	0	.279
WILSON WHITE LF	4	0	1	1	0	0	0	0	2	.277
JUSTIN KESTINO SS	3	0	2	0	0	0	0	1	0	.276
BERNARD HARPER DH	4	1	1	0	0	0	0	0	1	.258
MORRIS JEROME C	3	1	1	0	1	0	0	0	1	.249
PITCHING	IP	H	R	ER	SO	BB	ERA			
LYNN MODA (W)	7	5	0	0	6	0	3.92			
LEE HAZELTON	1	1	0	0	0	0	2.53			
MICKEY PENNY	1	0	0	0	0	0	3.43			

LOS ANGELES ANGELS										
BATTING	AB	R	H	RBI	2B	3B	HR	BB	SO	BA
TIM THORSEN RF	4	0	1	0	0	0	0	0	0	.289
JACOB BAKER DH	4	0	0	0	0	0	0	0	1	.280
CHICO GOMEZ CF	4	0	1	0	0	0	0	0	1	.288
PETE WARREN 1B	4	0	0	0	0	0	0	0	1	.273
BENJI WASHINGTON SS	3	0	0	0	0	0	0	0	0	.289
TRENT NORRIS LF	4	0	1	0	0	0	0	0	1	.267
LIM CHANG 3B	4	0	2	0	0	0	0	0	2	.283
ALBERT TORRES 2B	3	0	0	0	0	0	0	0	0	.267
CARLOS DIAZ C	3	0	1	0	0	0	0	0	1	.262
PITCHING	IP	H	R	ER	SO	BB	ERA			
ROBERTO COLON (L)	6	7	3	3	4	1	3.34			
MIKE VANDERBERG	1	4	2	2	2	2	3.35			
HIRAM MOLINA	1	2	0	0	1	1	3.88			

INNING	1	2	3	4	5	6	7	8	9	TOTAL
LOS ANGELES	0	0	0	0	0	0	0	0	0	0
CLEVELAND	0	0	0	3	0	0	2	0		5

GAME 133

By SAM LARDNER

The Cleveland Press

CLEVELAND, September 1 — Indians fans said hello again to Ollie Gonzalez, aka Ollie G.

They also said goodbye for now and thank you to Scott Michaels.

It all made for quite a scene Wednesday night at Progressive Field, where the Indians beat the Los Angeles Angels 6–1.

Gonzalez, the venerable lefty, came off the injured list and pitched six-plus innings of five-hit one run ball in his first start since July 19. He got a big hand from the crowd of 37,239 when manager Todd Stein removed him from the game after Gonzalez gave up a single to leadoff hitter Chico Gomez in the top of the seventh.

But things turned extraordinary after the game when the fans refused to leave the ballpark until Michaels came out and did a lap around the warning track. On their feet and chanting, "Scottie, Scottie," the fans saluted Michaels as he went 2-for-5 to extend his hitting streak to 53 games, just three shy of Joe DiMaggio's all-time and seemingly unbreakable record of 56.

If Michaels is going to get there, he'll have to do it on the road as the Indians take off for a three-city road trip to Baltimore, Texas and Chicago.

It's interesting that Michaels will have a chance to tie DiMaggio in Baltimore. That is where Orioles star Cal Ripken Jr. tied and broke another seemingly unbreakable record: Lou Gehrig's streak of 2,130 consecutive games played.

"I never expected anything like that," said Michaels, who needed a push from teammate Angel Rodriguez to take the lap. Rodriguez is the man Michaels supplanted as the Indians' everyday second baseman after Rodriguez got injured in May. "It's pretty wild, especially for a small-town kid like me. I know my parents and girlfriend had tears in their eyes when they saw that. I got a little choked up myself.

"You know, I hadn't even thought of Cal Ripken until you mentioned it. But we've got to get there first. I've got to get the hits, and we have to win the games. This is something, though, I'll always remember, especially when you consider I was hardly playing at the beginning of the season and my career was being called into question."

With the victory, the Indians pulled tantalizingly close to the first-place Minnesota Twins in the American League Central. They now trail the division leaders by just 3.5 games. The Indians are 1.5 games ahead of both Chicago and Boston for the top wild-card spot.

Michaels got the streak drama out of the way with a first-inning single. He singled and scored in the fifth. Each hit brought the crowd to its feet.

The other subplot was Gonzalez, who had not pitched since July 19 because of left-shoulder fatigue. He came off the injured list and gave up five hits and one run. For the rest of the season, Gonzalez will be part of a six-man rotation because of the July trade for Eli Batt.

"I think Eli being here will help us all down the stretch," Gonzalez said. "We've got six quality guys we can run out there every night, plus a damn strong bullpen."

How about the ovation he got?

"Nah, I think they were still cheering for Scottie," he quipped.

The Indians got a two-run double from SS Justin Kestino in the second after a walk to Terry Rovetto and a single by Oliver Reiner. They made it 4–0 in the fifth when Micah Millison and Michaels singled with one out. Terry Rovetto doubled to score Millison and send Michaels to third. He scored on Reiner's sac fly. The Tribe got their last two runs in the seventh on four straight hits by Oliver, Wilson, Kestino and Harper.

The only run off Gonzalez came on a solo homer by Tim Thorsen in the sixth. He reached his pitch limit of 90 in the seventh with the single to Gomez.

Stein gave a chance to reliever Alex Barsky, one of the September call-ups from Class AAA Columbus. Barsky, who had 24 saves at Columbus, retired the next three batters in the seventh before giving way to Geno Milzie and Ivan Zyzna.

"I wouldn't be afraid to throw Barsky out there in the ninth," Stein said. "Ivan has shouldered the workload, so having more viable options is attractive."

About the upcoming road trip, Stein was asked it if could be make or break for the Indians' playoff chances.

"I don't like to use that term," he said. "There's a whole month plus a few days of baseball left. It's going to be a tough trip. Baltimore might be down in the standings, but they'll have a big crowd to see Scottie, and you know how good Texas and Chicago are. Our guys will be up for it."

GAME 133

CLEVELAND INDIANS VS LOS ANGELES ANGELS •SEPTEMBER 1
CLEVELAND 6 / LOS ANGELES 1

CLEVELAND INDIANS										
BATTING	AB	R	H	RBI	2B	3B	HR	BB	SO	BA
RIKKI LABUDDA CF	5	0	0	0	0	0	0	0	1	.272
MICAH MILLISON RF	5	1	2	0	0	0	0	0	0	.279
SCOTT MICHAELS 2B	5	1	2	0	0	0	0	0	1	.386
TERRY ROVETTO 3B	4	1	1	1	0	0	0	1	1	.275
OLIVER REINER 1B	4	1	2	1	1	0	0	0	0	.281
WILSON WHITE LF	5	0	2	0	0	0	0	0	0	.278
JUSTIN KESTINO SS	4	0	2	3	1	0	0	0	1	.278
BERNARD HARPER DH	3	0	1	1	0	0	0	1	0	.259
MORRIS JEROME C	4	0	0	0	0	0	0	0	1	.246
PITCHING	IP	H	R	ER	SO	BB	ERA			
OLLIE GONZALEZ (W)	6	5	1	1	4	1	4.06			
ALEX BARSKY	1	0	0	0	1	0	0.00			
GENO MILZIE	1	0	0	0	0	0	2.30			
IVAN ZYZNA	1	0	0	0	1	0	1.96			
LOS ANGELES ANGELS										
BATTING	AB	R	H	RBI	2B	3B	HR	BB	SO	BA
TIM THORSEN RF	4	1	1	1	0	0	1	0	0	.289
JACOB BAKER DH	4	0	0	0	0	0	0	0	1	278
CHICO GOMEZ CF	4	0	1	0	0	0	0	0	1	.288
PETE WARREN 1B	3	0	0	0	0	0	0	1	0	.271
BENJI WASHINGTON SS	4	0	1	0	0	0	0	0	2	.288
TRENT NORRIS LF	4	0	1	0	0	0	0	0	0	.267
LIM CHANG 3B	4	0	1	0	0	0	0	0	1	.283
ALBERT TORRES 2B	4	0	0	0	0	0	0	0	0	.264
CARLOS DIAZ C	4	0	0	0	0	0	0	0	1	.259
PITCHING	IP	H	R	ER	SO	BB	ERA			
DON ZEGA (L)	4	6	2	2	3	2	3.88			
LEE HICKSON	2.33	4	2	2	1	0	4.06			
DENNY DORMAN	1.67	2	2	2	1	0	4.18			
INNING	1	2	3	4	5	6	7	8	9	TOTAL
LOS ANGELES	0	0	0	0	0	1	0	0	0	1
CLEVELAND	0	2	0	0	2	0	2	0		6

GAME 134

By SAM LARDNER

The Cleveland Press

BALTIMORE, September 3 — There was nothing on the B&O Warehouse — no changing of the numbers — commemorating Scott Michaels' hitting streak as there was for Cal Ripken's consecutive-games streak back in 1995.

That makes perfect sense, as Michaels is a visiting player, one who was virtually unknown to most baseball fans coming into this season.

But given Baltimore's rich baseball history, it wasn't totally out of the question, to hear Orioles manager Ray Rotstin tell it.

"With us being so far out of the race, we did give it some discussion," Rotstin said Friday night after his lowly Birds beat the Indians 3–1 at Camden Yards. "Our job is to stop Michaels, and this is our yard, so we thought against it — all due respect."

The knowledgeable and appreciative Baltimore fans did salute Michaels, who went 2-for-4 to extend his hitting streak to 54 games, just two from Joe DiMaggio's all-time record. Michaels came to the plate with two outs in the first inning and stroked a single on the first pitch he saw from Ofilio Calderon.

That brought the crowd of 45,971 to its feet. More accurate, it kept the folks on their feet as they saluted Michaels with a standing ovation as he came to the plate. Michaels added a single in the sixth and ended his night batting .387 as he takes a long shot aim at .400.

"That was very nice of them," Michaels said. "The loss takes a lot of the juice out of it for me. But given the history of baseball in Baltimore, yeah, it means something special to me."

Before the game, Michaels was besieged by reporters. The Washington Post had two reporters in the clubhouse, and the same national contingent that began following Michaels recently also was there, as was the newspaper from his hometown of Versailles, Indiana.

Michaels also did a sit-down with ESPN, which will televise Sunday night's game nationally, with Michaels having a possible shot at 56. ESPN was there those many years ago for Ripken breaking Lou Gehrig's consecutive-games-played streak.

"As long as it doesn't disrupt my routine, I don't mind," Michaels said. "It's a good thing for baseball, I guess. But I do have to take care of my local people from Versailles. I wish I could give them a big scoop, but you Cleveland guys know how boring I am."

Calderon pretty much bored the Indians to death with his amazing variety of junk. Michaels had two of the only five hits the Indians eked out all night. Calderon went seven innings, with relievers Rodney Davis and Isaac Crawford finishing the job.

In the all-important category of the standings, the Indians are four games behind the first-place Minnesota Twins in the American League Central. They lead both Chicago and Boston by one game for the top wild-card spot.

The only run for the Indians came on Micah Millison's home run, a fly ball that barely cleared the wall down the left-field line in the fourth.

The Orioles got a two-run homer against Eli Batt in the fifth, as Jorge Estrella went deep after Batt walked Kevin Brady. Greg Voight hit a run-scoring double in the sixth. Batt went six innings, giving up six hits.

"No room for error in this park," he said. "It's a lot like pitching in Cincinnati with the Reds. The ball can fly out of here at any time."

Buck Sterling and Lee Hazelton finished up for the Tribe, who have a quick turnaround with a Saturday afternoon game, with a night game to follow Sunday and a Labor Day afternoon game to conclude the holiday weekend.

"This place is going to be rocking all weekend," said manager Todd Stein. "It's kind of cool because it's rocking because of an opposing player. They get caught up in their history here. We're pulling for Scottie, but we are desperate to win these games."

GAME 134

CLEVELAND INDIANS VS BALTIMORE ORIOLES · SEPTEMBER 3
BALTIMORE 3 / CLEVELAND 1

CLEVELAND INDIANS										
BATTING	AB	R	H	RBI	2B	3B	HR	BB	SO	BA
RIKKI LABUDDA CF	4	0	0	0	0	0	0	1	0	.270
MICAH MILLISON RF	4	1	1	1	0	0	0	0	0	.279
SCOTT MICHAELS 2B	4	0	2	0	0	0	0	0	1	.387
TERRY ROVETTO 3B	3	0	0	0	0	0	0	2	0	.273
OLIVER REINER 1B	3	0	0	0	0	0	0	1	0	.279
WILSON WHITE LF	4	0	1	0	0	0	0	0	1	.278
JUSTIN KESTINO SS	3	0	1	0	1	0	0	1	0	.278
BERNARD HARPER DH	4	0	0	0	0	0	0	0	2	.256
MORRIS JEROME C	3	0	0	0	0	0	0	1	2	.244
PITCHING	IP	H	R	ER	SO	BB	ERA			
ELI BATT (L)	6	6	3	3	4	2	3.33			
BUCK STERLING	1	1	0	0	0	0	3.71			
LEE HAZELTON	1	0	0	0	1	0	2.47			

BALTIMORE ORIOLES										
BATTING	AB	R	H	RBI	2B	3B	HR	BB	SO	BA
BARBARO CASTRO SS	3	0	0	0	0	0	0	1	1	.269
KEVIN BRADY CF	4	1	1	0	0	0	0	0	0	.271
JORGE ESTRELLA 3B	4	1	1	2	0	0	1	0	0	.270
JULES PETERSON 1B	3	0	0	0	0	0	0	1	0	.292
ELMER VEGA LF	4	1	1	0	0	0	0	0	0	.274
GREG VOIGHT DH	4	0	2	1	1	0	0	0	0	.287
RODOLFO SANCHEZ CF	4	0	0	0	0	0	0	0	1	.295
WILFREDO MURILLO RF	4	0	1	0	0	0	0	0	1	.245
TERRY SHINER C	4	0	1	0	0	1	0	0	2	.232
PITCHING	IP	H	R	ER	SO	BB	ERA			
OFILIO CALDERON (W)	7	4	1	1	4	4	3.71			
RODNEY DAVIS	1	1	0	0	1	1	3.77			
ISAAC CRAWFORD (S)	1	0	0	0	1	1	2.82			

INNING	1	2	3	4	5	6	7	8	9	TOTAL
CLEVELAND	0	0	0	1	0	0	0	0	0	1
BALTIMORE	0	0	0	0	2	1	0	0		3

GAME 135

By SAM LARDNER
The Cleveland Press

BALTIMORE, September 4 — Oriole Park at Camden Yards showed its true colors Saturday, and so did Scott Michaels.

The Cleveland Indians and the Baltimore Orioles combined for 15 runs and 26 hits in an 8–7 win slugfest for the Indians, more typical of how games are played in this picturesque bandbox than Friday night's 3–1 Orioles win.

Michaels, the Indians' and Major League Baseball's man of the moment, completely stole the show by hitting for the cycle and going 4-for-6, including a ninth-inning two-run homer that lifted the Indians to the victory.

That was quite some way to extend Michaels' hitting streak to 55 games, one short of Joe DiMaggio's record, which for ages was thought to be unbreakable.

What did Michaels do when Indians closer Ivan Zyzna struck out Terry Shiner to end the game and seal the victory? Well, instead of going to the postgame interview room, Michaels went over to the stands next to the Indians dugout and hugged his parents, his girlfriend and his high school baseball, football and basketball coaches, all of whom were flown in by the Indians.

"I had no idea," said Michaels, who appeared floored by the surprise, which general manager J.D. Eisner and manager Todd Stein kept under their hats. "To see this is incredible. These coaches were so instrumental, not only in sports, but in my life. Whoever had the idea to bring them here, well, I can't say thank you enough."

Michaels, 23, was a three-sport star at Versailles High School in Versailles, Ohio, starring in baseball, basketball and football. For those wondering, he was a shooting guard in basketball and a wide receiver in football. But baseball was always his main gig.

"When he was hot, he could shoot the lights out," said Scott's basketball coach Eric Salm.

"Oh, he could get you a first down," said football coach Bill Murphy.

"I'm taking credit for his baseball success," said Versailles High baseball coach Lawrence Fine with a laugh. "That hitting stroke you're seeing, I taught him that."

All kidding aside, Michaels is on the cusp of history. With only one hit in Sunday night's nationally televised game, Michaels will take a seat alongside Joe D, who hit in 56 straight in 1941.

Here is where we stand:

Michaels can tie DiMaggio's streak Sunday night in a nationally televised game on ESPN, one that is expected to draw record ratings.

For the season, Michaels is batting .391, putting him within range of becoming the first .400 hitter in the major leagues since Ted Williams did it with the Red Sox in 1941.

Michaels also has 33 home runs and 122 RBIs, making him the front-runner for the MVP award in the American League. Mo Tanko, of the White Sox, leads the league with 43 home runs and is the only one standing in the way of a potential triple crown.

During the streak, Michaels is 111-for-28 (.466).

"Honestly, I don't know how to explain it, except that it's more fun to talk about this after a win," said Michaels, who was a little late to the postgame podium in the interview room because of the visits with family and coaches. "Sometimes it feels like I'm living in a dream. I mean, who knew? My career almost ended because of a severe shoulder injury, and here I am now. I can thank the trainers for their work with me, and I also think my work ethic — instilled by those high school coaches — has something to do with it, too.

"Let's see what happens tomorrow night. For once, I'm just as eager to see how it goes as you guys are."

Michaels' home run culminated an Indians comeback from a 6–0 deficit after two innings. He crushed a 2–2 slider from Jim Decaster over the left-field wall with Rikki LaBudda on second base. LaBudda opened the ninth with a single and went to second on Micah Millison's groundout. That set the stage for Michaels, who completed the cycle in true fashion, as he singled in the first inning, doubled in the third and tripled in the seventh.

"How do you figure that?" said Indians manager Todd Stein. "Of all thing things going on, he does that. That's some kind of magic. I sure can't explain it, and I'm sure you guys are running out of words for it."

The Orioles chased Indians started Brian Howard after two innings with three runs in the first and three more unearned runs in the second thanks to two errors by Wilson White. But Stein saved praise for long reliever Solly Alvarez, who has excelled in spot-starting and relieving roles this season. He pitched four scoreless innings and allowed Tribe batters to chip away.

Morris Jerome's two-run homer in the fourth cut Baltimore's lead to 6–2. Bernard Harper's three run double in the sixth made it 6–5. Michaels tripled to the gap in right-center in the seventh, and he came home on Terry Rovetto's sacrifice fly to make it a tie game before Kevin Brady made it 7–6 in the bottom of the seventh with a solo homer off Buck Sterling.

Mickey Penney and Geno Milzie held the Birds at bay for an inning apiece, setting the stage for Michaels' ninth-inning heroics. Ivan Zyzna picked up the save by working a 123 bottom of the ninth.

"I don't know, man," Stein said. "What more can happen? Oh, maybe I shouldn't ask that."

CLEVELAND INDIANS VS BALTIMORE ORIOLES • SEPTEMBER 4
CLEVELAND 8 / BALTIMORE 7

CLEVELAND INDIANS										
BATTING	AB	R	H	RBI	2B	3B	HR	BB	SO	BA
RIKKI LABUDDA CF	5	1	2	0	0	0	0	1	0	.271
MICAH MILLISON RF	6	0	2	0	0	0	0	0	0	.280
SCOTT MICHAELS 2B	6	2	4	2	1	1	1	0	0	.391
TERRY ROVETTO 3B	5	1	1	1	0	0	0	0	1	.272
OLIVER REINER 1B	4	1	1	0	0	0	0	1	0	.279
WILSON WHITE LF	5	1	1	0	0	0	0	1	0	.277
JUSTIN KESTINO SS	4	1	1	0	0	0	0	0	2	.278
BERNARD HARPER DH	5	0	2	3	1	0	0	0	1	.258
MORRIS JEROME C	4	1	1	2	0	0	1	1	0	.244
PITCHING	IP	H	R	ER	SO	BB	ERA			
BRIAN HOWARD	2	7	6	3	1	0	5.14			
SOLLY ALVAREZ	4	3	0	0	2	1	2.67			
BUCK STERLING	0.33	1	1	1	0	0	3.89			
MICKEY PENNY	0.67	0	0	0	0	0	3.39			
GENO MILZE (W)	1	1	0	0	1	0	2.26			
IVAN ZYZNA (S)	1	0	0	0	1	0	1.91			
BALTIMORE ORIOLES										
BATTING	AB	R	H	RBI	2B	3B	HR	BB	SO	BA
BARBARO CASTRO SS	5	1	2	2	1	1	0	0	0	.270
KEVIN BRADY CF	5	1	1	2	0	0	1	0	1	.273
JORGE ESTRELLA 3B	4	1	1	0	0	0	0	1	0	.270
JULES PETERSON 1B	5	1	1	0	0	0	0	0	0	.291
ELMER VEGA LF	5	1	2	3	0	0	1	0	1	.275
GREG VOIGHT DH	4	0	0	0	0	0	0	0	0	.284
RODOLFO SANCHEZ CF	4	1	2	0	1	0	0	0	2	.298
WILFREDO MURILLO RF	4	0	0	0	0	0	0	0	0	.243
TERRY SHINER C	4	1	2	0	0	0	0	0	1	.234
PITCHING	IP	H	R	ER	SO	BB	ERA			
RONALDO BUCARDO	5.33	7	5	5	3	3	4.22			
LUIS RAUDEZ	0.67	2	0	0	0	0	3.80			
ANIBAL NOVOA	2	4	1	1	0	1	2.94			
JIM DECASTER (L)	1	2	2	2	1	0	3.60			

INNING	1	2	3	4	5	6	7	8	9	TOTAL
CLEVELAND	0	0	0	2	0	3	1	0	2	8
BALTIMORE	3	3	0	0	0	0	1	0	0	7

GAME 136

By SAM LARDNER
The Cleveland Press

BALTIMORE, September 5 — This wasn't going to be easy, was it?

Getting Joe DiMaggio or the memory of Joe D to move over and make room was never going to be easy.

But Scott Michaels, perhaps the player least prone to drama on the Cleveland Indians, made things as dramatic as they could possibly get Sunday night in his quixotic quest to equal DiMaggio's hitting streak at 56 games.

Saying he did it the hard way might be the understatement of this crazy baseball season that has been anything but understated.

Coming up in the first inning against Baltimore Orioles pitcher Renato Vasquez, Michaels struck out, drawing groans from the 45,980 appreciative baseball fans at Camden Yards, which was electric with excitement.

Those same fans — the vast majority of them rooting for the hometown Birds — booed lustily when Michaels was walked his next three times up, intentionally in the seventh inning.

But everybody got what they came for in the ninth inning. With two outs and Rikki LaBudda on second base, Michaels reached out and lined an opposite-field RBI single to right field to score LaBudda to tie the game at 3–3 and the stadium exploded with applause.

Ignoring the score, the Orioles fans — and friends and family of Michaels — stood and cheered Michaels for certainly more than 56 seconds as he tied DiMaggio's hallowed and seemingly unbreakable mark.

Michaels' hit came against Isaac Crawford, and it hardly seemed to matter to most folks that the Orioles' Jorge Estreva homered in the bottom of the ninth off Lee Hazelton to give the Orioles an anticlimactic 4–3 victory.

After the game, it was all Michaels all the time.

"It was a blur in the ninth inning, and it's a blur now," said Michaels in the Orioles' interview room as he was flanked by his parents, Tom and Jennifer, and his girlfriend, Kristen Williams. "I can't believe any of this. Yeah, I wish we'd have won the game, but the atmosphere here was something special. I'm just glad family and friends were here to share in it."

So, can Michaels make it to 57 on Labor Day?

"Oh, I haven't even thought about it," he said. "Who could have ever dreamed this? Certainly not me. I was a complete non-factor, an afterthought, on this team in April. It took my friend and teammate, Angel Rodriguez, getting hurt for me to get playing time. And I want to thank him for his support. He's been my biggest backer even though he lost his starting job.

"So no, I'm not thinking about 57 or anything like that. Just being mentioned in the same breath as Joe DiMaggio is mind-boggling to me. He was a star in New York, and here I am, a small-town kid from Versailles, Ohio. I got nothing on him."

Michaels posed for photos with the baseball, which featured a "56" written on it. Back in the clubhouse, his teammates gave him the obligatory beer shower.

"That's pretty special," said team leader Terry Rovetto. "We've been sitting here the last several weeks with our mouths open watching this kid. What is he, 23? Yeah, imagine doing that at 23 with all the pressure on you, all the advanced scouting reports and all the media attention on you for the past three weeks or so."

Back in Cleveland, the Indians displayed the No. 56 on the scoreboard and on all outside signs at Progressive Field. Sports Illustrated is planning a commemorative cover juxtaposing DiMaggio and Michaels.

Orioles manager Ray Rotstin said the walks had nothing to do with preventing Michaels from reaching 56 and that the intentional walk was issued because it was a game situation.

"Listen, we're as happy for him as anybody, and we did end up winning the game," Rotstin said. "But he's the hottest hitter on the planet, maybe the entire galaxy, so we didn't want him beating us. We owe that much to the integrity of the game. He got the hit in the end, we won the game, so I think everybody can go home happy."

To a degree.

"We're delighted for Scottie," said Indians manager Todd Stein. "You saw how everybody ran out there to embrace him. And how about Angel securing that ball for him? That's an act of class. In the end, we lost the ballgame, and we've got to come back out here tomorrow afternoon to do it again."

Oriole Park at Camden Yards did not turn out to be Camden's yard, as Indians starter Kenny Camden couldn't hold a 2–0 lead, as he gave up a three-run homer to Greg Voight in the sixth inning. The Indians had gotten on the board in the second on Justin Kestino's two-run double.

"I wish I could have made it a completely satisfying night for Scottie and the team as a whole," Camden said. "But you get a ball up in this place, and it's going to go. That's what happened tonight."

Alex Barsky and Geno Milzie held the O's scoreless in the seventh and eighth. Stein said closer Ivan Zyzna was not available, so he went with Hazelton in the ninth.

The last word went to Michaels, who consoled the young Hazelton in the clubhouse.

"Our guys have pitched their butts off all year," Michaels said. "They have nothing to hang their heads about tonight. In fact, both Wiz (Camden) and Haze came to me afterward to say they wanted to win it for me. I said, 'Don't worry about it. We win it for us' around here. That's how it's been, and that's how it's going to stay with this team."

Somewhere, Joe D was smiling about that sentiment.

CLEVELAND INDIANS VS BALTIMORE ORIOLES · SEPTEMBER 5
BALTIMORE 4 / CLEVELAND 3

CLEVELAND INDIANS										
BATTING	AB	R	H	RBI	2B	3B	HR	BB	SO	BA
RIKKI LABUDDA CF	4	1	1	0	0	0	0	0	0	.271
MICAH MILLISON RF	4	0	0	0	0	0	0	0	0	.277
SCOTT MICHAELS 2B	2	0	1	1	0	0	0	2	0	.391
TERRY ROVETTO 3B	4	0	0	0	0	0	0	0	1	.270
OLIVER REINER 1B	3	1	2	0	0	0	0	1	0	.281
WILSON WHITE LF	4	1	1	0	0	0	0	0	1	.277
JUSTIN KESTINO SS	4	0	2	2	1	0	0	0	1	.280
BERNARD HARPER DH	3	0	0	0	0	0	0	1	0	.256
MORRIS JEROME C	3	0	0	0	0	0	0	0	3	.242
PITCHING	IP	H	R	ER	SO	BB	ERA			
KENNY CAMDEN	2	7	6	3	1	0	4.93			
ALEX BARSKY	4	3	0	0	2	1	0.00			
GENO MILZIE	0.33	1	1	1	0	0	2.40			
LEE HAZELTON (L)	0.67	0	0	0	0	0	2.44			

BALTIMORE ORIOLES										
BATTING	AB	R	H	RBI	2B	3B	HR	BB	SO	BA
BARBARO CASTRO SS	4	0	1	0	1	0	0	0	1	.270
KEVIN BRADY CF	3	0	0	0	0	0	0	1	1	.271
JORGE ESTRELLA 3B	4	1	1	1	0	0	1	0	1	.270
JULES PETERSON 1B	4	1	1	0	0	0	0	0	0	.291
ELMER VEGA LF	4	1	1	0	0	0	0	0	1	.275
GREG VOIGHT DH	4	1	2	3	0	0	1	0	0	.286
RODOLFO SANCHEZ CF	4	0	0	0	1	0	0	0	1	.294
WILFREDO MURILLO RF	3	0	1	0	0	0	0	1	0	.243
TERRY SHINER C	4	0	1	0	0	0	0	0	1	.235
PITCHING	IP	H	R	ER	SO	BB	ERA			
RENATO VASQUEZ	7	5	2	2	4	2	3.93			
RODNEY DAVIS	1	0	0	0	1	1	3.68			
ISAAC CRAWFORD (W)	1	2	1	1	1	1	2.94			

INNING	1	2	3	4	5	6	7	8	9	TOTAL
CLEVELAND	0	2	0	0	0	0	0	0	1	3
BALTIMORE	0	0	0	0	0	3	0	0	1	4

GAME 137

By SAM LARDNER
The Cleveland Press

BALTIMORE, September 6 — Even above the din, the unmistakable crack of the bat was clearly audible.

Scott Michaels connected on a 3–2 pitch from Baltimore Orioles closer Isaac Crawford with two outs and two men on base in the top of the ninth inning Monday.

The ball was scorched.

At worst, it was going to the wall in left-center field for a gapper, a two-run double that would tie the score at 2–2.

At best, the ball would gain elevation and head on a line over the wall for a three-run homer that would put the Indians ahead of the host Orioles 3–2.

But as quickly as the packed house crowd of 45,999 was set to let out a scream, those folks had their collective breath taken from them in an instantaneous gasp as Orioles shortstop Barbaro Castro leaped high into the air and snagged the line drive with a backhand stab of his glove.

Just like that it was over — the game and Michaels' hitting streak in a 2–0 Orioles victory.

It seems silly to say that Michaels will have to "settle" for a 56-game hitting streak, but it's fair to say "the man wuz robbed."

That seemed to be the prevailing sentiment among the throng at Oriole Park. After the crowd got over being stunned — and realizing their

Orioles had actually won the game — the spectators remained on their feet and cheered Michaels, who reluctantly acknowledged the cheers even as the realization hit him that his team had lost and that his chance to break Joe DiMaggio's hitting streak had gone by the wayside by a single leap.

When the Labor Day afternoon game was over, Michaels had gone 0-for-4 with two strikeouts, a fly out to the warning track in left field and the game-ending lineout.

"I'm not pissed about the streak ending," Michaels said in the post-game interview room. "I'm pissed because I thought we had tied the game, or even better.

"To be mentioned with Joe DiMaggio and to share that record with a legendary Hall of Famer is something I'll cherish for the rest of my life. Maybe nobody is supposed to break that record."

In the Orioles locker room, Castro talked of nothing but his own good fortune.

"I just jumped," he said. "The ball got off his bat hot, very hot. I just reacted. When I felt the ball hit my glove, it was almost as if the air went out of the ballpark. I don't think I've ever experienced anything like that feeling. It took the crowd a second or two to decide how they were going to react after being shocked like that. I just hope our fans don't think I'm the bad guy."

So, 56 it is and 56 it will be. Surely, nobody does this again, right?

"I don't know, man," said Indians manager Todd Stein. "Who thought this would or even could happen? I'm never going to say never about anything ever again. I'm happy for Scottie. He never showed any evidence of feeling pressure, and he never made it about himself. It was always about the team. I'm sure it was that way with Joe DiMaggio."

The historic holiday weekend wound up being costly to Stein's club, which lost three of four to the last-place Orioles and fell to 75-62 and to six games behind the first-place Minnesota Twins in the American League Central and into a three-way tie for the two wild-card spots with Chicago and Boston.

By failing to score against Orioles starting pitcher Austin Blackwell and the Baltimore bullpen, the Indians wasted a solid pitching performance by their own starter, Tak Fujimoto, who went seven innings and gave up just four hits, including a two-run homer in the fifth to Kevin Brady.

"I felt I threw the ball pretty well," Fujimoto said through translator Ryuji Sato. "When you have a crowd like this, whether at home or on the road, it gets you into a good rhythm on the mound. My slider wasn't its best, and their hitter (Brady) hit one that stayed up in the zone."

As for Michaels and the streak, he went 112-for-240 (.467) in the 56 games. By going 0-for-4, Michaels saw his season average fall from .391 to .388. Now that talk of "the streak" is over, will the focus now turn to Michaels making a run at the .400 mark?

"Not from me it won't," he said.

And with the streak over, will Stein be tempted to give Michaels a day off? After all, this is the most Michaels has played in any of his three big-league seasons, largely because of injury.

"He'll be in there; we need his bat," Stein said. "I might talk to him and ask if he needs a day, but he didn't play much early in the season. He certainly has shown no signs of fatigue, and he never let on that any pressure was getting to him. He'll be in there tomorrow at Texas."

"Bet on it," Michaels said. "I'm playing."

GAME 137

CLEVELAND INDIANS VS BALTIMORE ORIOLES · SEPTEMBER 6
BALTIMORE 2 / CLEVELAND 0

CLEVELAND INDIANS										
BATTING	**AB**	**R**	**H**	**RBI**	**2B**	**3B**	**HR**	**BB**	**SO**	**BA**
RIKKI LABUDDA CF	4	0	0	0	0	0	0	0	0	.269
MICAH MILLISON RF	3	0	2	0	1	0	0	1	0	.280
SCOTT MICHAELS 2B	4	0	0	0	0	0	0	0	2	.388
TERRY ROVETTO 3B	4	0	1	0	0	0	0	0	1	.270
OLIVER REINER 1B	3	0	0	0	0	0	0	1	0	.280
WILSON WHITE LF	4	0	0	0	0	0	0	0	0	.275
JUSTIN KESTINO SS	4	0	0	0	0	0	0	0	1	.277
BERNARD HARPER DH	3	0	1	0	0	0	0	1	1	.257
ICEBERG PETERS C	3	0	2	0	0	0	0	1	1	.218
LEO TAYLOR PR	0	0	0	0	0	0	0	0	0	.281
PITCHING	**IP**	**H**	**R**	**ER**	**SO**	**BB**	**ERA**			
TAK FUJIMOTO (L)	7	4	2	2	5	2	3.31			
LORRY UNGER	1	1	0	0	0	0	3.83			

BALTIMORE ORIOLES										
BATTING	**AB**	**R**	**H**	**RBI**	**2B**	**3B**	**HR**	**BB**	**SO**	**BA**
BARBARO CASTRO SS	4	1	1	0	0	0	0	0	0	.270
KEVIN BRADY CF	4	1	1	2	0	0	1	0	0	.270
JORGE ESTRELLA 3B	4	0	0	0	0	0	0	0	1	.267
JULES PETERSON 1B	3	0	1	0	0	0	0	1	0	.291
ELMER VEGA LF	4	0	1	0	0	0	0	0	2	.275
GREG VOIGHT DH	3	0	0	0	0	0	0	1	0	.284
RODOLFO SANCHEZ CF	4	0	1	0	1	0	0	0	1	.294
WILFREDO MURILLO RF	4	0	0	0	0	0	0	0	1	.241
TERRY SHINER C	3	0	1	0	0	0	0	0	0	.235
PITCHING	**IP**	**H**	**R**	**ER**	**SO**	**BB**	**ERA**			
AUSTIN BLACKWELL (W)	8	5	0	0	5	3	3.55			
ISAAC CRAWFORD (S)	1	0	0	0	1	1	2.89			

INNING	1	2	3	4	5	6	7	8	9	TOTAL
CLEVELAND	0	0	0	0	0	0	0	0	0	0
BALTIMORE	0	0	0	0	2	0	0	0		2

GAME 138

By SAM LARDNER
The Cleveland Press

ARLINGTON, Texas, September 7 — Things got back to normal, or what passes as normal these days, for the Cleveland Indians at Globe Life Field Tuesday night.

First, the Indians got back to their winning ways, beating the Texas Rangers 6–3 in a battle of postseason hopefuls.

Oh, and Scott Michaels resumed his hitting ways after seeing his hitting streak end at 56 games. Michaels went 3-for-5, including a solo homer in the first inning to get the Indians on their way to their 76th victory of the season against 62 losses.

Of course, "normal" for the Indians always contains a sideshow or two.

Before the game, the National Baseball Hall of Fame and Museum was on hand to take possession of the bat Michaels used to get the hit that tied Joe DiMaggio's record of hitting in 56 consecutive games. The Hall also got Michaels' road jersey, his batting gloves and spikes.

"Since I went 0-fer in the next game, I guess that bat, batting gloves and shoes ran out of luck, so I didn't mind giving them up," Michaels joked. "Maybe they can comp me on a tour of Cooperstown this off-season."

Oh, by the way, the hitting streak might be over, but Michaels raised his season batting average to .390. Even with time in the season running out and the math being daunting, this is going to be a story until it's not, especially considering all the crazy things that have happened this season.

"Hitting .400 is pretty well impossible," Michaels said. "I'm just glad we got back on track and won a game. We can go either way, and not making the postseason isn't an option for us. So that's where my focus is, not on any batting average."

So will Indians manager Todd Stein do anything drastic, such as bat Michaels in the leadoff spot to get him more at-bats if he comes closer to .400?

"Haven't given it any thought," Stein said. "Rikki (LaBudda) has done a fine job there, and you don't want to change things up just to benefit one guy. Scottie would not be for that anyway. You can disrupt the balance and end up hurting your team's chances if you get too cute."

Michaels got a nice hand from the pro-Rangers crowd of 38,898 when he came up in the first inning against Darcy Evans. He promptly cracked a first-pitch fastball and sent it over the wall in left field for his 34th home run and 128th RBI of the season.

The Indians got two more in the second on a run-scoring double by recently recalled Willie Bartlett, who subbed at shortstop for Justin Kestino, who was getting a breather. Bartlett drove in Oliver Reiner, who had singled and went to second on a wild pitch. Morris Jerome knocked in Bartlett with a single.

That staked Indians starting pitcher Lynn Moda to a 3-0 lead. Michaels singled in the fifth and came home on a single by Wilson White.

Moda gave up a pair of runs in the fifth, and he went six innings, giving up five hits. Moda has been a horse for the Indians down the stretch, winning his 15th game.

"It's easy with that run support," Moda said. "Like I said before, it's go time for all of us, and that is true for me more than anybody else."

The Tribe got a pair of runs in the seventh on Bernard Harper's two-run homer. Indians reliever Alex Barsky gave up a run in the seventh, but the usual dependable duo of Geno Milzie and Ivan Zyzna were lights-out again in the eighth and ninth, respectively.

Despite the win, the Indians remained six games behind the Twins for the race for first place in the American League Central. They are tied with the White Sox for the top wild-card spot, one game ahead of Boston.

"This was a big game against a team leading its division," Stein said. "Teams are gunning for us now too. Every game, every series, is going to be a test."

CLEVELAND INDIANS VS TEXAS RANGERS · SEPTEMBER 7
CLEVELAND 6 / TEXAS 3

CLEVELAND INDIANS										
BATTING	AB	R	H	RBI	2B	3B	HR	BB	SO	BA
LEO TAYLOR CF	3	0	1	0	0	0	0	2	0	.283
MICAH MILLISON RF	4	0	0	0	0	0	0	1	0	.277
SCOTT MICHAELS 2B	5	2	3	1	0	0	1	0	0	.390
TERRY ROVETTO 3B	4	0	1	0	0	0	0	0	1	.270
OLIVER REINER 1B	4	1	1	0	0	0	0	1	1	.279
WILSON WHITE LF	4	1	2	1	1	0	0	0	0	.276
WILLIE BARTLETT SS	3	1	1	1	1	0	0	0	1	.286
BERNARD HARPER DH	4	1	1	2	0	0	1	0	1	.257
MORRIS JEROME C	3	0	1	1	0	0	0	0	1	.243
PITCHING	IP	H	R	ER	SO	BB	ERA			
LYNN MODA (W)	6	5	2	2	4	2	3.89			
ALEX BARSKY	1	3	1	1	1	1	1.50			
GENO MILZIE	1	1	0	0	1	1	2.36			
IVAN ZYZNA (S)	1	0	0	0	0	0	1.87			

TEXAS RANGERS										
BATTING	AB	R	H	RBI	2B	3B	HR	BB	SO	BA
ALBERTO RODRIGUEZ SS	4	0	1	0	0	0	0	0	0	.276
RICHIE YOUNG JR 2B	3	0	0	0	0	0	0	1	0	.301
MIGUEL BELTRE 3B	4	1	2	0	0	0	0	0	0	.269
NICK MARSANS 1B	4	1	2	0	0	0	0	0	0	.307
ARTHUR DAHLGREN DH	4	0	0	0	0	0	0	0	2	.282
WILLARD CHANDLER RF	4	0	2	2	1	0	0	0	1	.286
ADRIAN MOLINA CF	3	1	1	0	0	0	0	1	1	.294
RYAN ROSE LF	4	0	0	0	0	0	0	0	2	.282
ROGER BRIDWELL C	3	0	1	1	1	0	0	1	1	.236
PITCHING	IP	H	R	ER	SO	BB	ERA			
DARCY EVANS (L)	4.33	6	3	3	2	2	4.08			
CLEON LEFLOR	1.67	2	1	1	1	1	3.54			
GABE KINDER	2	3	2	2	1	1	3.93			
RUBEN SORIANO	1	0	0	0	1	0	3.69			

INNING	1	2	3	4	5	6	7	8	9	TOTAL
CLEVELAND	1	2	0	0	1	0	2	0	0	6
TEXAS	0	0	0	0	2	0	1	0	0	3

GAME 139

By SAM LARDNER
The Cleveland Press

ARLINGTON, Texas, September 8 — Wednesday night's 4–1 victory for the Indians over the Texas Rangers had the feel of a "statement" game.

The Indians made their own statement by sweeping the short two-game series from the first-place team in the American League West.

Lefty Ollie Gonzalez stated his own claim to being back, as he won his second start since coming off the injured list. Gonzalez went seven innings and gave up six hits and one run. Indians second baseman Scott Michaels extended his new "hitting streak" to two games after having historic streak stopped at a record-tying 56 games.

That didn't come without a statement by Rangers manager Jimmy Degnan, who walked Michaels three times, twice intentionally, after Michaels doubled home a run in the first inning.

"You're damn right we walked him," said Degnan. "He's (freaking) Joe DiMaggio and if he keeps going, he's going to be Ted (freaking) Williams too and hit (freaking) .400. There's no way I'm letting that kid beat us. No (freaking) way."

For his part, Michaels said he didn't mind. By going 1-for-1 with the three walks, saw his batting average go from .390 to .392.

"I take it as a sign of respect," he said. "And you know what? If they walk me, we've got guys coming up who can hurt you. That's what happened tonight. So let them walk me."

The Rangers walked Michaels with two outs in the sixth and Rikki LaBudda on second base. That brought Terry Rovetto to the plate, and he doubled both runners home. Oliver Reiner then singled to give the Indians a 4–0 lead against Cary Simon.

Texas got a solo homer from Miguel Beltre in the bottom of the inning, but Gonzalez struck out Nick Marsans to end the inning and go on to pitch a 1-2-3 seventh.

"Feels good," said Gonzalez, who was on the IL from late July until the first of September with shoulder fatigue. "The time off helped, and with us going to a six-man (rotation), I think it will help us all down the stretch. I can't think of a rotation in this league with as many good arms."

Mickey Penney and Lee Hazelton finished up without incident from the Indians bullpen.

The Indians (77–62) pulled to within five games of the first-place Minnesota Twins in the AL Central. They now lead the White Sox by one for the top wild-card spot, with Boston two games behind.

"We're looking at the division," said manager Todd Stein. "Why not aim high? If there's one thing Scottie's hitting streak showed us is that anything is possible. We're heading to Chicago, and both teams will want to make a statement."

Hmm, there's that word again.

GAME 139

CLEVELAND INDIANS VS TEXAS RANGERS · SEPTEMBER 8
CLEVELAND 4 / TEXAS 1

CLEVELAND INDIANS										
BATTING	AB	R	H	RBI	2B	3B	HR	BB	SO	BA
RIKKI LABUDDA CF	3	1	1	0	0	0	0	1	0	.269
MICAH MILLISON RF	3	1	2	0	0	0	0	1	1	.280
SCOTT MICHAELS 2B	1	1	1	1	1	0	0	3	0	.392
TERRY ROVETTO 3B	4	1	1	2	1	0	0	0	0	.270
OLIVER REINER 1B	4	0	1	1	0	0	0	0	1	.279
WILSON WHITE LF	3	0	0	0	0	0	0	1	0	.275
JUSTIN KESTINO SS	4	0	2	0	1	0	0	0	1	.279
BERNARD HARPER DH	4	0	0	0	0	0	0	0	1	.254
MORRIS JEROME C	4	0	1	0	0	0	0	0	1	.243
PITCHING	IP	H	R	ER	SO	BB	ERA			
OLLIE GONZALEZ (W)	7	6	1	1	4	1	3.90			
MICKEY PENNY	1	1	0	0	0	1	3.52			
LEE HAZELTON (S)	1	0	0	0	1	0	2.38			
TEXAS RANGERS										
BATTING	AB	R	H	RBI	2B	3B	HR	BB	SO	BA
ALBERTO RODRIGUEZ SS	4	0	1	0	1	0	0	0	0	.276
RICHIE YOUNG JR 2B	3	0	0	0	0	0	0	0	0	.299
MIGUEL BELTRE 3B	4	1	1	1	0	0	1	0	0	.269
NICK MARSANS 1B	3	0	1	0	0	0	0	1	0	.307
ARTHUR DAHLGREN DH	4	0	0	0	0	0	0	0	2	.279
WILLARD CHANDLER RF	4	0	1	0	0	0	0	0	0	.286
ADRIAN MOLINA CF	4	0	2	0	0	0	0	0	1	.297
RYAN ROSE LF	3	0	0	0	0	0	0	1	0	.280
ROGER BRIDWELL C	4	0	1	0	1	0	0	0	2	.236
PITCHING	IP	H	R	ER	SO	BB	ERA			
CARY SIMON (L)	5	3	1	1	3	1	3.92			
JOHAN CONCEPCION	1.67	4	3	3	0	2	3.98			
GARY HELMS	1.33	2	0	0	1	2	3.63			
TINO FERNANDEZ	1	0	0	0	1	1	2.93			
INNING	1	2	3	4	5	6	7	8	9	TOTAL
CLEVELAND	1	0	0	0	0	3	0	0	0	4
TEXAS	0	0	0	0	0	1	0	0	0	1

GAME 140

By SAM LARDNER
The Cleveland Press

CHICAGO, September 10 — Pennant-race baseball in all its beauty —
and a bit of its ugliness — was on full display Friday night at Guaranteed
Rate Field.

First, there was the game itself, a 7–3 victory by the Indians over
the White Sox before 35,761 jacked-up fans, many of whom came from
Cleveland.

Next, there was the scoreboard watching. With the Minnesota Twins
losing 4–1 at home to the Angels, the Indians crept to within four games
of the first-place Twins in the American League Central. The Indians now
lead the White Sox and Red Sox by two games for the top wild-card spot.

Finally, there was a bit of edginess to the proceedings. White Sox starting pitcher Mitch Mosel plunked hot-hitting Scott Michaels on the left
thigh with a pitch in the fifth inning with the Tribe leading 4–0. Michaels
hit a solo homer in the first inning and singled in the third on the way to a
2-for-4 night, keeping his batting average at .392.

In the bottom of the fifth, Indians pitcher Eli Batt earned some added
respect from his relatively new teammates as he drilled power-hitting third
baseman Moe Tanko in the back. That brought warnings, but no ejections,
from home-plate umpire John Moss.

"It just got away," pleaded Batt, who convinced absolutely no one. "You
try to pitch inside, especially in this park, and you can miss. It happens."

White Sox manager David Echt was buying that explanation about as much as the media were buying it. "Gimme a (bleeping) break," Echt said. "Batt has pinpoint control, and our guy gets it in the back? That could have been an ejection right there."

What about Michaels getting hit?

"You see how close he stands to the plate?" Echt said. "No wonder he's hitting close to .400 and breaking every (bleeping) record in the book."

The mild-mannered Michaels seemed to take it all in stride. "I don't know; I was just happy to be on base again," he said. "I really didn't have time to think about whether he (Mosel) was throwing at me."

Indians skipper Todd Stein said he was glad cooler heads prevailed in the end. "That could have gotten ugly, but at the same time, we can't even think about being without Scottie," Stein said. "He's the best hitter in the game right now. Not that we threw at Tanko on purpose, but I think the umpires handled it properly."

Michaels got the Indians on the board quickly, with his 35th homer of the season, a drive to left field with two outs in the first. Justin Kestino and Bernard Harper hit back-to-back doubles in the second, with Kestino scoring. Rikki LaBudda then singled home Jerome and stole second base. He came home on Micah Millison's single.

The White Sox made it 4–3 in the sixth on Mike Isenmesser's three-run homer with two outs. Stein brought Alex Barsky in to relieve Batt at that point, and the Indians chased Mosel with two in the seventh on Bernard Harper's double that drove in Wilson White and Oliver Reiner. Kestino added a solo homer in the eighth.

Barsky pitched through the seventh for the Indians, with Geno Milzie and Mickey Penney finishing up.

Stein said he may use Michaels at the DH for at least Saturday's game.

"He's been banged up a little bit, and he went through a lot with that (56-game) hitting streak," the manager said. "Let him catch a breather between at-bats because we sure do need his bat in the lineup."

GAME 140

CLEVELAND INDIANS VS CHICAGO WHITE SOX · SEPTEMBER 10
CLEVELAND 7 / CHICAGO 3

CLEVELAND INDIANS

BATTING	AB	R	H	RBI	2B	3B	HR	BB	SO	BA
RIKKI LABUDDA CF	4	1	2	1	0	0	0	1	0	.271
MICAH MILLISON RF	4	0	1	1	0	0	0	0	1	.280
SCOTT MICHAELS 2B	4	1	2	1	0	0	1	0	1	.392
TERRY ROVETTO 3B	3	0	0	0	0	0	0	1	0	.268
OLIVER REINER 1B	3	1	2	0	0	0	0	1	0	.281
WILSON WHITE LF	3	1	1	0	0	0	0	1	1	.275
JUSTIN KESTINO SS	4	2	2	1	1	0	1	0	0	.281
BERNARD HARPER DH	4	1	2	3	1	0	0	0	0	.257
MORRIS JEROME C	4	0	1	0	0	0	0	0	1	.243

PITCHING	IP	H	R	ER	SO	BB	ERA			
ELI BATT (W)	5	5	3	3	5	1	3.53			
ALEX BARSKY	2	2	0	0	2	0	1.13			
GENO MILZIE	1	1	0	0	0	0	2.32			
MICKEY PENNY	1	0	0	0	1	1	3.46			

CHICAGO WHITE SOX

BATTING	AB	R	H	RBI	2B	3B	HR	BB	SO	BA
MARK ROSE 2B	4	0	2	0	0	0	0	0	1	.304
TRAVIS CAMPBELL SS	4	0	0	0	0	0	0	0	1	.295
MO TANKO 3B	3	1	1	0	1	0	0	1	0	.294
JAY WALLEY LF	4	1	2	0	0	0	0	0	2	.314
MIKE ISENMESSER 1B	4	1	2	3	0	0	1	0	1	.297
JACKIE WINER RF	3	0	0	0	0	0	0	0	0	.279
JASON NAKAMURA DH	4	0	0	0	0	0	0	0	1	.258
VLADIMIR JANAKOWSKI CF	4	0	1	0	0	0	0	0	1	.235
ENRIQUE FUENTES C	3	0	0	0	0	0	0	1	1	/259

PITCHING	IP	H	R	ER	SO	BB	ERA			
MITCH MOSEL (L)	6.67	7	4	4	2	2	3.85			
RANDY ROSELLI	1.33	5	3	3	1	2	4.43			
CARL WOLDMAN	1	1	0	0	1	0	3.16			

INNING	1	2	3	4	5	6	7	8	9	TOTAL
CLEVELAND	1	3	0	0	0	0	2	1	0	7
CHICAGO	0	0	0	0	0	3	0	0	0	3

GAME 141

By SAM LARDNER
The Cleveland Press

CHICAGO, September 11 — Neither Scott Michaels nor the Indians could gain any traction Saturday night. Fortunately for both, no ground was lost in the race for first place in the American League Central, even as the wild-card race tightened a bit.

The Indians fell 6–3 to the White Sox at Guaranteed Rate Field as the Sox showed off their power with three home runs, but with the Minnesota Twins losing at home to the Los Angeles Angels, the Indians remained four games behind the Twins. The White Sox are now a game behind the Indians for the top wild-card spot, with Boston lurking two games back.

As for Michaels, he served as the Indians DH in this game and went 0-for-4. His batting average took a slight dip, from .392 to .389. The man who shocked the baseball world with his 56-game hitting streak to tie the all-time record is still within striking distance of .400 as we head to mid-September.

"I know it's a big deal if I have a 0-fer, but you have to remember that's the norm on more days than not," he said. "That hitting-streak thing really skewed things, including perspective. Let's be real about this. I'm approaching things the same way as I did over those 56 games. I believe that's how I got there in the first place."

First place in the American League Central remains the team's main focus, according to all involved, including Michaels and manager Todd

Stein, whose team fell to 78–63 with one more game remaining on this three-city road trip.

"I know a lot of people say we'd gladly settle for the wild card, especially when you consider that we started this season so poorly," said Stein, who took over as manager 10 games in. "There might be a grain of truth to that, but history tells you that you really want to avoid that wild-card game and win the division. There are so many benefits to finishing first. We've come this far. We might as well go for it, and we are."

Indians starting pitcher Brian Howard, got hit around, giving up four White Sox runs in four innings before Stein removed him in favor of long reliever Solly Alvarez. Howard walked the first two batters in the first inning before Rudy Perrone doubled to make it 2–0. In the third, DH Marty Jay hit a two-run homer. Mo Tanko, who leads the majors with 45 home runs and Jackie Winer hit solo shots in the eighth.

"Steinie did us all a favor by getting me out of there," the veteran Howard said. "The way they were hitting me, it could have been 7–0 or 8–0 right there."

Does the extra rest that comes with using a six-man rotation hurt Howard, a control pitcher who is more effective when he's not as strong?

"Oh, I don't think so," he said. "That would just be excuse making, and I don't do that. We all have a lot of innings under our belt this year, so I think the extra day is more beneficial than anything."

The Indians didn't mount much against Sox starter Jim Zechman or two relievers, picking up single runs in each of the fifth, seventh and ninth innings. Michaels struck out twice, grounded out and flied out. Angel Rodriguez, who played second base with Michaels at DH, singled a home run as did Rikki LaBudda and Morris Jerome. Otherwise, the Indians' big hitters were silent.

"Ah, just forget this one," Stein said. "They're a tough team, especially at home. We'll come back early tomorrow and try to end this trip on a good note."

Still no day off for Michaels?

"Not a chance," Stein said.

GAME 141

CLEVELAND INDIANS VS CHICAGO WHITE SOX • SEPTEMBER 11
CHICAGO 6 / CLEVELAND 3

CLEVELAND INDIANS										
BATTING	**AB**	**R**	**H**	**RBI**	**2B**	**3B**	**HR**	**BB**	**SO**	**BA**
RIKKI LABUDDA CF	4	0	2	1	0	0	0	0	0	.273
MICAH MILLISON RF	4	0	0	0	0	0	0	0	1	.277
SCOTT MICHAELS DH	4	0	0	0	0	0	0	0	2	.389
TERRY ROVETTO 3B	3	0	0	0	0	0	0	1	0	.267
OLIVER REINER 1B	4	0	0	0	0	0	0	0	2	.279
WILSON WHITE LF	3	1	2	0	1	0	0	1	0	.277
JUSTIN KESTINO SS	3	1	1	0	0	0	0	1	0	.281
ANGEL RODRIGUEZ 2B	4	0	1	1	0	0	0	0	1	.244
MORRIS JEROME C	4	1	2	1	1	0	0	0	0	.246
PITCHING	**IP**	**H**	**R**	**ER**	**SO**	**BB**	**ERA**			
BRIAN HOWARD (L)	4	6	4	4	1	3	5.25			
SOLLY ALVAREZ	3	3	0	0	2	2	2.54			
LEE HAZELTON	1	2	2	2	0	0	2.72			

CHICAGO WHITE SOX										
BATTING	**AB**	**R**	**H**	**RBI**	**2B**	**3B**	**HR**	**BB**	**SO**	**BA**
MARK ROSE 2B	4	1	0	0	0	0	0	1	0	.301
TRAVIS CAMPBELL SS	4	1	1	0	0	0	0	1	0	.294
RUDY PERRONE LF	5	0	2	2	1	0	0	0	1	.290
MO TANKO 3B	5	1	2	1	0	0	1	0	0	.296
MIKE ISENMESSER 1B	4	1	1	0	0	0	1	1	0	.297
JACKIE WINER RF	4	1	2	1	0	0	1	0	0	.282
MARTY JAY DH	3	1	2	2	0	0	1	1	0	.263
VLADIMIR JANAKOWSKI CF	4	0	0	0	0	0	0	0	2	.232
ZACK SEARLE C	3	0	1	0	0	0	0	1	0	.242
PITCHING	**IP**	**H**	**R**	**ER**	**SO**	**BB**	**ERA**			
JIM ZECHMAN (W)	6.33	4	2	2	4	1	3.80			
SEAN HITZMAN	1.67	2	0	0	1	1	3.76			
DOUG GORHAM (S)	1	2	1	1	1	1	2.93			

INNING	1	2	3	4	5	6	7	8	9	TOTAL
CLEVELAND	0	0	0	0	1	0	1	0	1	3
CHICAGO	2	0	2	0	0	0	0	2		6

GAME 142

By SAM LARDNER
The Cleveland Press

CHICAGO, September 12 — Maybe it's a good thing that the Indians have stockpiled all those arms for their starting rotation.

It's going to come in handy, for at least a week or so.

Before the Tribe beat the White Sox 9–2 Sunday afternoon at Guaranteed Rate Field, general manager J.D. Eisner called reporters together to tell them that there may have been a good reason for Brian Howard's subpar performance in Saturday's 6–3 loss to the Sox.

It seems Howard told teammates his lower back was hurting during the game. Late Saturday night, he was in so much pain that he called his teammate and buddy, staff ace Lynn Moda, for a ride to a local hospital.

What doctors found was not a back problem, but a kidney stone.

"Of all the things," Eisner said. "The Doc (Howard's nickname) had the presence of mind to go to the hospital. They're going to look at him and hope he can pass it without needing any surgery. It might cost him one start. We're hopeful that's it's only that."

Fortunately for the Indians, the July trade for Eli Batt and the recent activation of Ollie Gonzalez off the injured list gave them a surplus of starting pitching, with manager Todd Stein using a six-man rotation. Even if Howard misses a start, the Indians can go back to a conventional five-man rotation.

In Sunday's series finale, it was the pitching of Kenny Camden and the hitting of Scott Michaels (who else?) that enabled the Indians (79–63) to cruise past their hosts. With the Twins salvaging their finale at home against the Angels, the Indians remained four games behind Minnesota for first place in the American League Central. They lead Chicago by two and Boston by three for the top wild-card spot.

Camden pitched six innings and gave up five hits and one run. With the big lead, Stein gave Lorry Unger two innings of work, with Buck Sterling finishing.

Michaels was the DH again Sunday, and he went 4-for-5, with two doubles, two singles and three runs scored.

That enabled him to raise his batting average from .389 to .393. He has 20 games left to become the first .400 hitter since Ted Williams in 1941. Michaels already made national headlines by hitting in 56 straight games to tie Joe DiMaggio's mark, also set in 1941.

Michaels doubled and scored in the first inning against Wilton Berrios. Terry Rovetto singled Michaels home, and Oliver Reiner homered to give the Indians a 3–0 lead.

The rout was on in the third, as the Indians chased Berrios from the game in favor of Brad Hutchinson. The Tribe scored four runs, with recently recalled Willie Bartlett hitting a two-run triple, scoring Terry Rovetto and Wilson White. Angel Rodriguez's squeeze bunt totally surprised the Sox, and Bartlett scampered home iceberg Peters drove Rodriguez home with a double.

Kieran Catseff came into the game late for White who injured himself sliding into third earlier in the game and hit a two-run homer in the ninth. We'll have to wait to see the extent of the injury.

The Sox got a RBI double from Jackie Winer in the sixth and a solo home run from Rudy Perrone in the eight.

"Overall, it was a good day and a good series for us. We'll have to see how serious the injury to Wilson is," said Stein, whose team took two of three over the weekend.

Things really toughen up, if that's possible in an already tough American League. The Indians finally head home after a three-city road trip but awaiting them will be the Red Sox and Yankees.

"If we make the postseason, we're going to have to face the likes of these teams," Stein said. "Might as well see what we can do against them down the stretch. I know our guys are looking forward to it, and I hope we sell the joint out every night."

GAME 142

CLEVELAND INDIANS VS CHICAGO WHITE SOX · SEPTEMBER 12
CLEVELAND 9 / CHICAGO 2

CLEVELAND INDIANS										
BATTING	AB	R	H	RBI	2B	3B	HR	BB	SO	BA
RIKKI LABUDDA CF	5	0	1	0	0	0	0	0	1	.272
MICAH MILLISON RF	5	0	2	0	0	0	0	0	0	.279
SCOTT MICHAELS DH	5	3	4	0	2	0	0	0	0	.393
TERRY ROVETTO 3B	4	1	2	1	0	0	0	1	0	.268
OLIVER REINER 1B	4	1	1	2	0	0	1	1	0	.279
WILSON WHITE LF	3	1	1	0	1	1	0	0	1	.278
KIERAN CATSEF LF	2	1	1	2	0	0	1	0	0	.253
WILLIE BARTLETT SS	4	1	1	2	0	0	0	1	0	.273
ANGEL RODRIGUEZ 2B	4	1	1	1	0	0	0	0	1	.244
ICEBERG PETERS C	4	0	1	1	1	0	0	0	2	.219
PITCHING	IP	H	R	ER	SO	BB	ERA			
KENNY CAMDEN (W)	6	5	1	1	4	1	4.79			
LORRY UNGER	2	1	1	1	2	0	3.86			
BUCK STERLING	1	0	0	0	0	0	3.80			
CHICAGO WHITE SOX										
BATTING	AB	R	H	RBI	2B	3B	HR	BB	SO	BA
MARK ROSE 2B	4	0	0	0	0	0	0	0	1	.297
TRAVIS CAMPBELL SS	4	0	0	0	0	0	0	0	1	.290
RUDY PERRONE LF	4	1	1	1	0	0	1	0	1	.289
MO TANKO 3B	3	0	1	0	0	0	0	1	0	.296
MIKE ISENMESSER 1B	4	1	1	0	0	0	0	0	0	.296
JACKIE WINER RF	4	0	1	1	1	0	0	0	0	.281
MARTY JAY DH	3	0	2	0	0	0	0	0	0	.267
JAY WALLEY CF	4	0	0	0	0	0	0	0	2	.310
ENRIQUE FUENTES C	3	0	0	0	0	0	0	0	0	.256
ZACK SEARLE PH	1	0	0	0	0	0	0	0	1	.241
PITCHING	IP	H	R	ER	SO	BB	ERA			
WILTON BERRIOS (L)	3	6	3	3	2	1	3.92			
BRAD HUTCHINSON	4	7	4	4	1	1	4.14			
CARL WOLDMAN	1	0	0	0	2	0	2.75			
RANDY ROSELLI	1	2	2	2	0	1	4.76			

INNING	1	2	3	4	5	6	7	8	9	TOTAL
CLEVELAND	3	0	4	0	0	0	0	0	2	9
CHICAGO	0	0	0	0	0	1	0	1	0	2

GAME 143

By SAM LARDNER
The Cleveland Press

CLEVELAND, September 13 — Indians pitcher Tak Fujimoto felt good about being on the right end of a shutout Monday night.

After being on the losing end of a 2–0 decision at Baltimore in his previous start, Fujimoto did his part in a 3–0 blanking of the Boston Red Sox at Progressive Field in a game with massive postseason implications.

And if Indians second baseman Scott Michaels thought his wild media ride ended with the end of his 56-game hitting streak, he thought wrong on a day that was full of news for the Indians as they returned home from their three-city road trip.

Michaels went 2-for-5 against the Red Sox as his batting average ticked up from .393 to .394. The Boston media, which was on hand for the latter parts of "the streak," got in on the fun both pregame and postgame with Michaels. The national contingent is expected to grow again if Michaels makes a serious run at hitting .400.

"I'm starting to get to know some of your names — our beat writers here in Cleveland won't like that," Michaels joked. "I'm just trying to have fun with this. The streak was nice, but more important, it helped the team get into good position to make the playoffs.

"But let me ask one thing: You guys all know my life story by now. Let's talk current events."

Michaels had a pair of singles Monday, one in the fourth inning against Mark Castleberg and one in the sixth off Felix Infante. A sacrifice fly by Fujimoto's personal catcher, Iceberg Peters, put the Indians up 1–0 in the third. Michaels then scored in front of Oliver Reiner's homer in the fourth that gave the Tribe their 3–0 lead. Kieran Catsef, who started for the injured Wilson White, also contributed three hits in the game.

"Wilson's season might have ended, which would be a big loss to the team. He's been so steady the entire season. Guess we'll just have to wait on test results," said Stein.

Fujimoto was in complete command. Manager Todd Stein allowed him to work seven innings for a second straight start, mainly because the Indians have been using a six-man rotation.

That could change in the coming days. Pitcher Brian Howard passed the kidney stone that put him in a Chicago hospital over the weekend, and he's expected to miss one start.

"I really wanted to go back out there for the seventh, and the eighth," Fujimoto said through translator Ryuji Sato. "I felt really fresh out there. But our bullpen has been so good this year that it was hard to argue with the manager."

Alex Barsky pitched the eighth, with Ivan Zyzna earning the save.

The Indians improved to 80–63 and moved within three games of the Minnesota Twins for first place in the American League Central. They remained two ahead of the White Sox for the top wild-card spot and dropped the Red Sox to four back.

"They put a hurtin' on us," said Red Sox manager Billy Stone. "That's a totally different ballclub from what we saw earlier in the season. Give them credit, especially Steinie. He's got them playing good, inspired ball. And what that kid (Michaels) has done, well, you couldn't script it."

And to think there are a few chapters left to be written.

CLEVELAND INDIANS VS BOSTON RED SOX · SEPTEMBER 13
CLEVELAND 3 / BOSTON 0

CLEVELAND INDIANS

BATTING	AB	R	H	RBI	2B	3B	HR	BB	SO	BA
RIKKI LABUDDA CF	5	0	1	0	1	0	0	0	1	.271
MICAH MILLISON RF	3	0	1	0	0	0	0	2	0	.279
SCOTT MICHAELS 2B	5	1	2	0	0	0	0	0	1	.394
TERRY ROVETTO 3B	4	0	1	0	0	0	0	0	1	.268
OLIVER REINER 1B	4	1	1	2	0	0	1	0	1	.279
KIERAN CATSEF LF	4	0	3	0	1	0	0	0	0	.278
JUSTIN KESTINO SS	3	1	1	0	0	0	0	0	0	.282
BERNARD HARPER DH	4	0	0	0	0	0	0	0	2	.254
ICEBERG PETERS C	3	0	0	1	0	0	0	1	0	.214

PITCHING	IP	H	R	ER	SO	BB	ERA			
TAK FUJIMOTO (W)	7	5	0	0	6	1	3.18			
ALEX BARSKY	1	0	0	0	0	0	1.00			
IVAN ZYZNA	1	0	0	0	1	0	1.83			

BOSTON RED SOX

BATTING	AB	R	H	RBI	2B	3B	HR	BB	SO	BA
OMAR PEREZ LF	4	0	0	0	0	0	0	0	0	.294
STU KENNEDY SS	4	0	0	0	0	0	0	0	0	.293
CARLOS BLANCO C	4	0	1	0	0	0	0	0	2	.286
MORGAN LEIFER 1B	3	0	1	0	0	0	0	1	0	.293
TRACE ATTENBERG DH	4	0	0	0	0	0	0	0	1	.277
DESMOND UNDERWOOD 3B	4	0	1	0	1	0	0	0	0	.275
SANTIAGO AVILLA 2B	4	0	1	0	0	0	0	0	1	.279
SALVATORE ESPINOSA RF	3	0	1	0	1	0	0	0	2	.255
VICTOR TRAGGER JR CF	3	0	0	0	0	0	0	0	1	.241

PITCHING	IP	H	R	ER	SO	BB	ERA			
MARK CASTLEBERG (L)	7	8	3	3	6	4	3.80			
FELIX INFANTE	1	2	0	0	0	0	3.14			

INNING	1	2	3	4	5	6	7	8	9	TOTAL
BOSTON	0	0	0	0	0	0	0	0	0	0
CLEVELAND	0	0	1	2	0	0	0	0		3

GAME 144

By SAM LARDNER

The Cleveland Press

CLEVELAND, September 14 — It seems there's just no stopping Scott Michaels or Lynn Moda.

Everybody knows about Michaels.

Moda? He's the nominal ace of the Cleveland Indians' starting rotation, but because of Michaels and his 56-game hitting streak, the veteran pitcher has flown under the radar during the second half of this season.

All the Indians have done is win when Moda has been on the mound lately. Moda went seven innings Tuesday night in a 6–2 victory over the Boston Red Sox at Progressive Field. You have to go all the way back to July 28 to find a game the Tribe lost when Moda started.

"This is the time of year when you expect your ace to step up, and since the all-star break, he's been money," said Indians manager Todd Stein, whose team improved to 81–63 and moved within two games of the faltering Minnesota Twins in the American League Central. The Indians now have a comfortable three-game lead over the White Sox for the top wild-card spot, with the Red Sox now five back.

Stein also announced that Wilson White's regular season is officially over. Test results showed a tear in the meniscus White suffered sliding into third base against the White Sox. "Really too bad for Wilson and the team, he is such an important part of our recent success. We'll miss his steady presence."

Wilson then addressed the crowd with hopes of being back for the playoffs. "I'm a quick healer, and we'll see what happens. You can be sure I'll be traveling with this team the rest of the year."

While Michaels is a shoo-in for MVP and Comeback Player of the Year and maybe Time Magazine Person of the Year, Moda has put his name into the ring for Cy Young consideration.

"I don't think so," he said. "Or at least I haven't paid attention to it. My start to the season was pretty brutal. I'll take American League Central champions for our team. But I've felt pretty good in the second half. We've gotten a little bit of a break here with the six-man (rotation), so I'm feeling pretty fresh."

Moda's drive to the Cy Young pales in comparison to the drive he made over the weekend, when he drove teammate Brian Howard to a Chicago hospital for what turned out to be a kidney stone.

"I suppose we could have called 911 or jumped in a cab, but there was a car-rental desk in the hotel lobby, so we went for it," Moda said. "I was hoping for a sports car, but all they had left were family sedans and mini vans."

On the mound Tuesday, Moda gave up only four hits and one Boston run, an RBI single by Stu Kennedy in the third. Of the 21 outs Moda recorded, 15 were on the ground.

"That's when he's at his best," Stein said. "Modes isn't going to over-power anybody. His bread and butter is keeping the ball on the ground."

Michaels had a "quiet" 2-for-4 night, with a pair of singles and two runs scored. His batting average held at .394, with .400 still there as a possibility. With groundball pitcher Moda on the mound, Stein went with Angel Rodriguez at second base and Michaels serving as DH.

"Angel turned a double play on a ball I don't think I would have even gotten to," Michaels said. "We've got one of the best DH's in the league here in Bernie (Bernard Harper), and he can play first base too, like tonight. I'll leave it to Skip (Stein) to sort it out."

Michaels led off the fourth with a single. He came home on Harper's double, and Justin Kestino drove in Harper with a single.

The Indians wasted no time chasing Red Sox starter Eduardo Suarez with four runs in the bottom of the fifth inning. A single by Kieran Catsef and walks to Justin Kestino and Rodriguez loaded the bases for Morris

Jerome. His double brought home two, and Rikki LaBudda's single drove in two more.

Lorry Unger and Alex Barsky, who gave up a meaningless run in the ninth on a run-scoring groundout by Omar Perez finished up out of the pen for the Indians, who can sweep the series Wednesday and deal a devastating blow to the Red Sox.

"It's certainly there for us," Stein said. "But our approach of not looking past anything has gotten us to this point. They (the Red Sox) are going to be desperate. But we've been in desperation mode all year."

GAME 144

CLEVELAND INDIANS VS BOSTON RED SOX · SEPTEMBER 14
CLEVELAND 6 / BOSTON 2

CLEVELAND INDIANS										
BATTING	AB	R	H	RBI	2B	3B	HR	BB	SO	BA
RIKKI LABUDDA CF	4	0	1	2	0	0	0	0	0	.271
MICAH MILLISON RF	3	0	1	0	0	0	0	1	0	.279
SCOTT MICHAELS 2B	4	1	2	0	0	0	0	0	1	.394
TERRY ROVETTO 3B	3	0	1	0	0	0	0	1	0	.269
BERNARD HARPER 1B	3	1	2	1	1	0	0	0	1	.257
KIERAN CATSEF LF	4	1	1	0	1	0	0	0	0	.277
JUSTIN KESTINO SS	3	1	1	1	0	0	0	1	0	.284
ANGEL RODRIGUEZ 2B	3	1	0	0	0	0	0	1	0	.236
MORRIS JEROME C	4	1	2	2	1	0	0	0	1	.248
PITCHING	IP	H	R	ER	SO	BB	ERA			
LYNN MODA (W)	7	4	1	1	5	1	3.78			
LORRY UNGER	1	1	0	0	0	0	3.77			
ALEX BARSKY	1	1	1	1	0	1	1.80			

BOSTON RED SOX										
BATTING	AB	R	H	RBI	2B	3B	HR	BB	SO	BA
OMAR PEREZ LF	4	0	1	1	0	0	0	0	0	.293
STU KENNEDY SS	4	0	1	1	0	0	0	0	1	.293
CARLOS BLANCO C	3	0	0	0	0	0	0	1	0	.284
MORGAN LEIFER 1B	4	0	0	0	0	0	0	0	0	.291
TRACE ATTENBERG DH	3	0	1	0	0	0	0	0	0	.277
DESMOND UNDERWOOD 3B	4	0	0	0	0	0	0	0	1	.272
SANTIAGO AVILLA 2B	4	0	1	0	0	0	0	0	1	.279
SALVATORE ESPINOSA RF	4	1	1	0	1	0	0	0	1	.255
VICTOR TRAGGER JR CF	3	1	1	0	0	0	0	1	1	.242
PITCHING	IP	H	R	ER	SO	BB	ERA			
EDUARDO SUARDEZ (L)	4.33	7	6	6	3	3	4.08			
EDDIE MYERS	2.67	3	0	0	0	1	3.05			
NICK SPERO	1	1	0	0	0	0	3.64			

INNING	1	2	3	4	5	6	7	8	9	TOTAL
BOSTON	0	0	1	0	0	0	0	0	1	2
CLEVELAND	0	0	0	2	4	0	0	0		6

GAME 145

By SAM LARDNER
The Cleveland Press

CLEVELAND, September 15 –The Boston Red Sox served notice on the Cleveland Indians that they ain't dead yet.

In fact, the Bosox looked very much alive Wednesday night, shellacking the Indians 10–1 at Progressive Field to salvage the finale of this three-game series.

Ollie Gonzalez suffered his first bad outing since coming off the injured list at the beginning of this month. He lasted just 2 and one-third innings, giving up eight hits and six runs.

On the bright side for the Tribe, Scott Michaels went 1-for-3 with a double as his batting average held at .394.

Otherwise it was a pretty forgettable evening. Indians manage Todd Stein got Michaels and a couple of his teammates off their feet late in the game, getting playing time for the likes of Willie Bartlett and Leo Taylor.

"The life went out of this one pretty quick," Stein said. "If could get a couple guys out of there and send them home early, why not? It doesn't get any easier, what with the Yankees coming in here this weekend. You lose one like this and you just shower it off, so to speak. It's not like we lost 21 or in extra innings. Those are the kinds of games eat at you. You just move on from one like this."

Gonzalez gave up a run in the first inning on a homer by Rick Haber. Nothing to worry about, right?

Wrong.

The Red Sox came alive in the third with five runs to chase Gonzalez in favor of Solly Alvarez, who worked the next three innings.

"Sometimes (bleep) happens," Gonzalez said. "And that's what happened tonight. I walked a couple guys, Haber hits a second home run, a couple balls found holes and then (Willard) Washington cranked one. Boom. Three-run homer and I'm out of there. I'm fine. The shoulder is OK, so there are no worries there. It was just a bad game on my part."

Buck Sterling, Mickey Penney and Lee Hazelton followed Alvarez into the game and mopped up. As for Michaels, his double came in the seventh inning, and he scored when Catseff singled him home. That broke up the shutout bid by Red Sox starter Enrique Rodriguez.

The Indians stayed two games behind the Twins for the top spot in the American League West. The White Sox pulled within two for the first wild-card spot, and the Red Sox now are four back.

"We still have a pulse," said Red Sox manager Billy Stone. "I'm glad we don't have to see them (the Indians) again. Let whoever they have left on their schedule deal with them. I can tell you firsthand that they're tough. Goodbye, Cleveland."

CLEVELAND INDIANS VS BOSTON RED SOX · SEPTEMBER 15
BOSTON 10 / CLEVELAND 1

CLEVELAND INDIANS

BATTING	AB	R	H	RBI	2B	3B	HR	BB	SO	BA
RIKKI LABUDDA CF	2	0	1	0	0	0	0	0	0	.272
LEO TAYLOR CF	2	0	0	0	0	0	0	0	0	.277
MICAH MILLISON RF	4	0	1	0	0	0	0	0	0	.279
SCOTT MICHAELS 2B	3	1	1	0	1	0	0	0	0	.394
TERRY ROVETTO 3B	4	0	1	0	0	0	0	0	2	.268
OLIVER REINER 1B	3	0	2	0	1	0	0	1	1	.281
KIERAN CATSEF LF	3	0	1	1	0	0	0	0	0	.279
JUSTIN KESTINO SS	2	0	0	0	0	0	0	0	0	.283
WILLIE BARTLETT SS	2	0	0	0	0	0	0	0	1	.231
BERNARD HARPER DH	3	0	0	0	0	0	0	0	1	.255
MORRIS JEROME C	3	0	1	0	0	0	0	0	1	.249

PITCHING	IP	H	R	ER	SO	BB	ERA			
OLLIE GONZALEZ (L)	2.33	8	6	6	1	2	4.27			
SOLLY ALVAREZ	2.67	4	2	2	1	0	2.71			
BUCK STERLING	2	2	1	1	1	0	3.83			
MICKEY PENNY	1	0	0	0	0	0	3.39			
LEE HAZELTON	1	2	1	1	1	0	2.85			

BOSTON RED SOX

BATTING	AB	R	H	RBI	2B	3B	HR	BB	SO	BA
OMAR PEREZ LF	5	1	1	0	0	0	0	0	0	0.292
STU KENNEDY SS	5	2	3	0	0	1	0	0	0	0.296
CARLOS BLANCO C	4	1	2	3	1	0	0	1	0	0.286
RICK HABER 1B	5	2	3	3	0	0	2	0	1	0.293
TRACE ATTENBERG DH	5	1	1	0	0	0	0	0	2	0.277
DESMOND UNDERWOOD 3B	4	1	1	0	0	0	0	1	0	0.272
WILLARD WASHINGTON 2B	4	2	2	3	1	0	1	0	0	0.281
SALVATORE ESPINOSA RF	4	0	1	0	0	0	0	0	0	0.255
VICTOR TRAGGER JR CF	4	0	2	1	0	0	0	1	1	0.244

PITCHING	IP	H	R	ER	SO	BB	ERA			
ENRIQUE RODRIGUEZ (W)	9	8	1	1	6	1	3.61			

INNING	1	2	3	4	5	6	7	8	9	TOTAL
BOSTON	1	0	5	0	2	0	1	0	1	10
CLEVELAND	0	0	0	0	0	0	1	0	0	1

GAME 146

By SAM LARDNER
The Cleveland Press

CLEVELAND, September 16 — Let's just say it was a big fat zero all the way around for the Indians Thursday night at Progressive Field.

With the high-flying New York Yankees in town and a hint of October cool in the air, the Indians laid a goose egg in a 4–0 loss, their second defeat in a row.

This was a costly one. The Indians (81–65) fell to three games behind the Minnesota Twins for first place in the American League Central. Both the White Sox and Red Sox gained ground in the wild-card race, with the White Sox pulling within one of the Indians for the top wild-card spot and the Red Sox creeping within three.

The Red Sox beat the Indians 10–1 Wednesday, and the loss to the Yankees seems to have gotten the Tribe's attention.

"These teams aren't fooling around," said manager Todd Stein. "Our guys have remained focused most of this second half, and maybe it's good for them to see a couple of teams who traditionally dominate the AL East. The Yankees have a big lead, and the Red Sox want a piece of that wild card. You can safely say that this is the start of our playoffs."

Yankees starting pitcher Greg Sterney turned in a performance worthy of the postseason against the Indians, pitching eight innings of shutout, five-hit ball. Speaking of zero, Sterney held the planet's hottest hitter, Scott

Michaels to a rare 0-fer, as Michaels had no hits in four at-bats, including a pair of strikeouts.

"I would say we had a good scouting report on him, but I'm sure a lot of teams have thought that," said Yankees catcher Rick Steinberg. "Greg just attacked him and just plain beat him on those strikeouts. But we've got to face him three more times, and you're sure not going to hear me say anything bad about him."

Michaels' batting average took a major hit, as it dipped from .394 to .391 as his reluctant quest for .400 continues. It's "reluctant" because Michaels seems weary of the subject after tying Joe DiMaggio's record hitting streak at 56 games.

"There's not really much more I want to say about it," he said. "We've lost a couple games in a row, and I was brutal tonight. So let's just focus on the team."

Indians starting pitcher Eli Batt pitched creditably, giving up three runs and seven hits in six innings. Unfortunately for Batt and the Indians, one of those hits was a three-run homer by Gary Ashcroft in the fourth. The Yanks got a single run off Lorry Unger in the eighth on Vernon Otten's RBI groundout.

"They're the Bronx Bombers for a reason, as I found out," said Batt, a former National Leaguer until coming over from the Reds in July. "One pitch can do you in. That's what happened tonight, but me walking (Willie) Robinson and giving up a single to (Raidel) Medina didn't help. They brought me over here to pitch in a pennant race, and I sure don't want to let them down. I was OK tonight, not great. Either way, I needed to be better, and I will be."

GAME 146

CLEVELAND INDIANS VS NEW YORK YANKEES · SEPTEMBER 16
NEW YORK 4 / CLEVELAND 0

CLEVELAND INDIANS

BATTING	AB	R	H	RBI	2B	3B	HR	BB	SO	BA
RIKKI LABUDDA CF	3	0	1	0	0	0	0	1	0	.272
MICAH MILLISON RF	4	0	1	0	0	0	0	0	0	.279
SCOTT MICHAELS 2B	4	0	0	0	0	0	0	0	2	.391
TERRY ROVETTO 3B	3	0	2	0	0	0	0	1	0	.271
OLIVER REINER 1B	4	0	0	0	0	0	0	0	1	.279
KIERAN CATSEF LF	4	0	0	0	0	0	0	0	2	.267
JUSTIN KESTINO SS	3	0	0	0	0	0	0	1	0	.281
BERNARD HARPER DH	3	0	1	0	1	0	0	0	0	.256
MORRIS JEROME C	3	0	1	0	0	0	0	0	1	.249

PITCHING	IP	H	R	ER	SO	BB	ERA			
ELI BATT (L)	6	6	3	3	3	1	3.63			
LORRY UNGER	2	2	1	1	1	0	3.80			
GENO MILZE	1	0	0	0	0	0	2.29			

NEW YORK YANKEES

BATTING	AB	R	H	RBI	2B	3B	HR	BB	SO	BA
MARK STRANTON CF	4	0	0	0	0	0	0	0	0	.294
WILLIE ROBINSON 3B	3	1	1	0	0	0	0	1	0	.296
RAIDEL MEDINA DH	4	1	1	0	0	0	0	0	0	.286
GARY ASHCROFT LF	4	1	2	3	0	0	1	0	1	.294
RICK STEINBERG C	4	0	1	0	0	0	0	0	1	.279
JAKE KOENIG SS	4	1	2	0	1	0	0	0	1	.276
NICK WRIGHT RF	3	0	0	0	0	0	0	0	0	.277
ORESTES VEGA 1B	4	0	0	0	0	0	0	0	1	.252
LEE LEONARD 2B	3	0	1	1	1	0	0	0	0	.271

PITCHING	IP	H	R	ER	SO	BB	ERA			
GREG STERNEY (W)	8	5	0	0	6	3	3.30			
STEPH PERLOW	1	1	0	0	0	0	3.09			

INNING	1	2	3	4	5	6	7	8	9	TOTAL
NEW YORK	0	0	0	3	0	0	0	1	0	4
CLEVELAND	0	0	0	0	0	0	0	0	0	0

GAME 147

By SAM LARDNER
The Cleveland Press

CLEVELAND, September 17 — The axis on which the Cleveland Indians' world spins righted itself a bit Friday night.

After getting outscored 14–1 in back-to-back losses to the Red Sox and Yankees, Tribe batters pounded out 11 hits Friday night in a 5–3 victory over the Yankees before 37,012 fans at Progressive Field.

The victory assured the Indians of a winning season as they moved to 82–65 and to within two games of the first-place Minnesota Twins in the American League Central. The Indians remained one game ahead of Chicago and three ahead of Boston for the top wild-card spot.

In addition to all of that, Scott Michaels recorded his 198th and 199th hits of the season with a first-inning solo homer. He added a single in the seventh as he went 2-for-4 to raise his batting average to .392.

Michaels has 36 home runs and 131 RBIs. He'll likely win every individual award this season except the Triple Crown, as Chicago's Moe Tanko has 47 home runs to lead the majors.

"This felt good tonight because I got back into a little bit of a rhythm and most importantly, because we won the ballgame," Michaels said. "The rest of that stuff is nice, but look around here and see how much happier everybody is because we won and put ourselves in a better position to win the division."

Michaels' homer got the big crowd into it, and starting pitcher Kenny Camden kept the Yankees at bay for six innings, as he gave up six hits and two runs.

Camden was back on regular four days rest because Brian Howard missed his turn in the rotation after passing a kidney stone last weekend in Chicago. The Indians had been going with a six-man starting rotation.

"I felt ready to go," said Camden, a 32-year-old lefty who maintains he pitches better while a little bit tired anyway. "I'm hoping The Doc (Howard) will be ready to go his next turn, and we'll take it from there. But I've been used to going every five days my whole career, so this was no big deal. That's a hell of a lineup the Yankees have, and I felt we kept them off-balance most of the night."

The only blip Camden faced came in the third inning when Bobby Faulhaber hit a two-run homer to put the Yankees ahead 2–1. But the Indians scored twice against Manuel Acuna in each of the fourth and fifth innings. Micah Millison's two run double in the fourth brought in Morris Jerome and Rikki LaBudda, both of whom singled. In the fifth, Justin Kestino's two-run homer scored Oliver Reiner, who walked. Reliever Alex Barsky gave up a run-scoring single to Vernon Otten in the seventh, but he settled down before giving way to the Indians' dependable duo of Geno Milzie and Ivan Zyzna.

"Pretty much how you draw it up," said manager Todd Stein. "Get six out of the starter and let the pen do its work. Coming from where we came from, being assured of a winning record is nice. It's a big accomplishment and a tribute to the guys, but once they got a taste of winning, they've wanted much more. That's our goal now — to win our division and play deep into October."

Who'd have thought?

GAME 147

CLEVELAND INDIANS VS NEW YORK YANKEES · SEPTEMBER 17
CLEVELAND 5 / NEW YORK 3

CLEVELAND INDIANS										
BATTING	AB	R	H	RBI	2B	3B	HR	BB	SO	BA
RIKKI LABUDDA CF	4	1	1	0	0	0	0	0	0	.272
MICAH MILLISON RF	4	0	1	2	1	0	0	0	1	.279
SCOTT MICHAELS 2B	4	1	2	1	0	0	1	0	0	.392
TERRY ROVETTO 3B	4	0	0	0	0	0	0	0	1	.269
OLIVER REINER 1B	3	1	1	0	0	0	0	1	0	.279
KIERAN CATSEF LF	4	0	0	0	0	0	0	0	2	.255
JUSTIN KESTINO SS	4	1	2	2	1	0	1	0	0	.283
BERNARD HARPER DH	4	0	2	0	1	0	0	0	1	.258
MORRIS JEROME C	3	1	2	0	0	0	0	0	0	.252
PITCHING	IP	H	R	ER	SO	BB	ERA			
KENNY CAMDEN (W)	6	6	2	2	4	1	4.73			
ALEX BARSKY	1	1	1	1	0	1	2.45			
GENO MILZE	1	0	0	0	0	0	2.25			
IVAN ZYZNA (S)	1	0	0	0	1	0	1.79			
NEW YORK YANKEES										
BATTING	AB	R	H	RBI	2B	3B	HR	BB	SO	BA
MARK STRANTON CF	4	0	1	0	1	0	0	0	0	.293
WILLIE ROBINSON 3B	3	0	0	0	0	0	0	0	0	.294
RAIDEL MEDINA DH	4	0	1	0	0	0	0	0	1	.286
GARY ASHCROFT LF	4	0	1	0	0	0	0	0	2	.294
RICK STEINBERG C	3	1	1	0	0	0	0	1	0	.279
JAKE KOENIG SS	3	0	0	0	0	0	0	1	0	.275
BOBBY FAULHABER RF	4	1	1	2	0	0	1	0	1	.277
ORESTES VEGA 1B	4	1	0	0	0	0	0	0	1	.252
LEE LEONARD 2B	3	0	1	1	0	0	0	0	0	.272
PITCHING	IP	H	R	ER	SO	BB	ERA			
MANUAL ACUNA (L)	4.33	6	4	4	3	1	3.63			
STEVE SALINAS	1.67	3	0	0	1	0	3.06			
STEPH PERLOW	1	1	1	1	0	0	3.18			
CARL GREY	1	1	0	0	1	0	3.40			
INNING	1	2	3	4	5	6	7	8	9	TOTAL
NEW YORK	0	0	2	0	0	0	1	0	0	3
CLEVELAND	1	0	0	2	2	0	0	0		5

GAME 148

By SAM LARDNER
The Cleveland Press

CLEVELAND, September 18 — Each starting pitcher for the Indians has taken his turn at being the hard-luck guy or the fortunate one who gets all the run support.

Enter Tak Fujimoto.

The prized free-agent signing out of Japan has been mostly good this season, especially in the second half of the season.

Of late, he's been the guy involved in tight, low-scoring games. It was more of the same on a beautiful Saturday afternoon.

Fujimoto did all he could, but Yankees starter Ty Goodman was just a touch better, and the New Yorkers sneaked out of Progressive Field with a 2–1 victory in what many press-box wags were calling a preview of the American League championship series.

There was an extra layer of drama to this one because of the principal players. More on that in a second.

The loss did not hurt the Indians in the American League Central standings, but it did tighten the wild-card race. The Tribe (82–66) remained two games behind the slumping Minnesota Twins in the AL Central. The White Sox tied the Indians for the top wild-card spot while the Red Sox pulled within two games after being left for dead.

As for Fujimoto, he went seven innings, giving up five hits and two runs, a two-run homer by Makoto Inaba, an old nemesis from both players' glory days in Japan.

"Ahhh, he got me," Fujimoto said through translator Ryuji Sato. "I have faced him many, many times over the years. I usually have his number. But he guessed right today. Perhaps we meet again."

Inaba hit a two-out, two-run homer in the top of the first inning after Fujimoto got two quick outs to start the inning. He then walked Virgil Sandquist on a close pitch. Inaba wasted no time, crushing a first-pitch fastball over the wall in right field.

"I call him 'my friend,'" Inaba said through his own translator. "That's because I think I know him very well — at least on the baseball field. It is true that in Japan, he won many battles against me, but I studied some video of his performances here and picked something up. Don't ask me to tell you what it is because I may see him again next month. But I'm sure this gave the fans back in Japan something to talk about until the postseason, should we meet again."

The Fujimoto-Inaba duel upstaged Indians second baseman Scott Michaels, whose flirtation with the .400 mark took a hit as he went 1-for-5, a harmless single. The hit was Michaels' 200th of the season, but his batting average dipped from .392 to .390. Michaels is going to have to go on quite some tear to become the first .400 hitter since The Splendid Splinter, Ted Williams in 1941.

"Not much to say today, guys," Michaels said. "This is the big leagues, and sometimes, they're going to get you. Both pitchers were on their games today. I just feel bad we couldn't get a couple more runs for Fuji the way he's pitched for us."

The Indians had a couple of chances against Goodman. Michaels grounded into an inning-ending double play in the first inning. Oliver Reiner struck out with two aboard in the sixth just after Terry Rovetto's single knocked in Micah Millison.

Yankees relievers Steph Perlow and Carl Grey shut the door in the final two innings with Grey getting the save, sending the 37,101 fans home disappointed.

"You feel for Tak," said Indians manager Todd Stein. "But we're going to have to get used to these kinds of games. Teams will be playing us tough for the rest of the regular season, and if we do make the postseason, runs are going to be hard to come by. But I'd throw Fuji out there any day against any team."

Perhaps Fujimoto and Inaba shall meet again.

GAME 148

CLEVELAND INDIANS VS NEW YORK YANKEEES · SEPTEMBER 18
NEW YORK 2 / CLEVELAND 1

CLEVELAND INDIANS										
BATTING	AB	R	H	RBI	2B	3B	HR	BB	SO	BA
RIKKI LABUDDA CF	4	0	1	0	0	0	0	1	0	.272
MICAH MILLISON RF	4	1	1	0	1	0	0	1	0	.278
SCOTT MICHAELS 2B	5	0	1	0	0	0	0	0	1	.390
TERRY ROVETTO 3B	4	0	2	1	0	0	0	1	0	.270
OLIVER REINER 1B	4	0	0	0	0	0	0	0	1	.277
KIERAN CATSEF LF	4	0	1	0	0	0	0	0	1	.255
JUSTIN KESTINO SS	4	0	0	0	0	0	0	0	2	.280
BERNARD HARPER DH	4	0	1	0	0	0	0	0	0	.258
ICEBERG PETERS C	3	0	0	0	0	0	0	0	1	.209
MORRIS JEROME C	1	0	0	0	0	0	0	0	0	.252
PITCHING	IP	H	R	ER	SO	BB	ERA			
TAK FUJIMOTO (L)	7	5	2	2	5	1	3.16			
MICKEY PENNY	1	1	0	0	0	1	3.34			
LORRY UNGER	1	0	0	0	1	0	3.72			

NEW YORK YANKEES										
BATTING	AB	R	H	RBI	2B	3B	HR	BB	SO	BA
MARK STRANTON CF	4	0	0	0	0	0	0	0	0	.291
WILLIE ROBINSON 3B	4	0	0	0	0	0	0	0	1	.292
VIRGIL SANDQUIST DH	3	1	2	0	0	0	0	1	0	.288
MAKOTO INABA LF	4	1	1	0	0	0	1	0	1	.293
RICK STEINBERG C	3	0	1	0	0	0	0	0	1	.279
JAKE KOENIG SS	4	0	0	0	0	0	0	0	1	.273
BOBBY FAULHABER RF	3	0	1	0	0	0	0	1	0	.278
ORESTES VEGA 1B	4	0	0	0	0	0	0	0	1	.249
LEE LEONARD 2B	4	0	1	0	0	0	0	0	1	.272
PITCHING	IP	H	R	ER	SO	BB	ERA			
TY GOODMAN (W)	4.33	6	4	4	3	1	3.35			
STEPH PERLOW	1.67	3	0	0	1	0	3.10			
CARL GREY (S)	1	1	1	1	0	0	3.31			

INNING	1	2	3	4	5	6	7	8	9	TOTAL
NEW YORK	2	0	0	0	0	0	0	0	0	2
CLEVELAND	0	0	0	0	0	1	0	0	0	1

GAME 149

By SAM LARDNER
The Cleveland Press

CLEVELAND, September 19 — It was almost a shame to see this Indians-Yankees series end without a rubber game. The two teams gave four sellout crowds all they could want and then some over an eventful weekend.

The Indians saved their best for last Sunday with a walk-off 8–7 victory before an overflow crowd of 37,546 at Progressive Field. That earned them a split of the four-game set.

The man of the moment was none other than Scott Michaels, whose two-run homer in the bottom of the ninth off Yankees closer Pete Snow capped a 3-for-5 day and sent the folks home for their Sunday supper in a delirious mood.

The Yankees had just taken a 7–6 lead in the top half of the inning on a wild pitch by Lee Hazelton. Already emotionally drained, the fans had one more roar left in them when Micah Millison led off the bottom of the ninth inning with a single. Speedy Willie Bartlett pinch ran, but it didn't matter, as Michaels sent a first-pitch offering from Snow over the wall down the left-field line for the game winner.

Stadium security did its best to keep fans off the field — a couple trespassers made it — but there was no sending the fans home without yet another curtain call for Michaels amid thunderous chants of "MVP, MVP."

"What a thrill," he said. "I don't know how many homers I have. I don't know how many RBIs I have. I don't know what my batting average is. The thrill was that we won an important game. I felt like I glided on air around the bases listening to those fans. Can you believe this?"

The entire year for Michaels and the Indians has been hard to believe. And for the record, he has 37 home runs, 133 RBIs and his batting average sits at a tidy .392 with 13 games to go.

More important for the Indians, they are now within one game of the Minnesota Twins for first place in the American League Central. The stubborn Chicago White Sox remain tied with the Indians for the top wild-card spot with the Boston Red Sox falling three games back.

Where do you even start with this one? How about the first inning, when each team scored four runs.

The Yankees jumped on Indians ace Lynn Moda, Terry Rovetto made errors on two consecutive hitters including a botched double play grounder setting the stage for Rodney Rottapel to hit a three-run triple and then steal home. Moda managed to recover and gut out five innings giving up six hits and five runs, only one earned.

"Thanks to my teammates for getting me off the hook," said Moda, who has little to apologize for after shouldering the load down the stretch. "Things just got away from me there. I was probably pissed at myself for the triple and took my eye off him (Rottapel) when he decided to break for home. I threw high and wide and didn't give Mo (catcher Morris Jerome) a chance."

No worries. Moda never mentioned the errors.

Rikki LaBudda led off the bottom of the first against Cameron Swetow with a bunt single before stealing second base, number 33 on the season. After Millison struck out, the Yankees worked carefully to Michaels and he promptly singled to right field. Terry Rovetto made up for the defensive miscues and doubled both runners home. Oliver Reiner singled to drive in Rovetto and went to second on the throw home. Kieran Catsef's single scored Oliver, and just like that, the game was tied.

The Yankees got a solo homer off Moda from Dave Hussey in the fifth before Mickey Penney came in for the sixth and gave up a run. The Indians tied it at 66 in the bottom of the inning on Bernard Harper's two-run homer off Bruce Robinson.

All of that merely set the stage for the late heroics by Michaels.

"I'm running out of things to say about Scottie and this team," said manager Todd Stein. "That was a pretty strong test of character out there today against a damn fine team, and we passed it with flying colors."

The Indians now take off for a three-city road trip to Detroit, Toronto and Kansas City before they finish the regular season at home with four against Toronto.

"I don't want to get too far ahead of things; I'd just like to savor this one for a few minutes," Stein said, taking another long pull of a postgame cold one. "Man, these two teams."

To be continued in October?

"Don't know if my heart could take it," Stein said.

GAME 149

CLEVELAND INDIANS VS NEW YORK YANKEES · SEPTEMBER 19
CLEVELAND 8 / NEW YORK 7

CLEVELAND INDIANS

BATTING	AB	R	H	RBI	2B	3B	HR	BB	SO	BA
RIKKI LABUDDA CF	5	1	2	0	0	0	0	0	0	.273
MICAH MILLISON RF	5	1	2	0	1	0	0	0	0	.279
WILLIE BARTLETT PR	0	0	0	0	0	0	0	0	0	.231
SCOTT MICHAELS 2B	5	2	3	2	0	0	1	0	0	.392
TERRY ROVETTO 3B	4	1	1	2	1	0	0	0	0	.270
OLIVER REINER 1B	5	1	2	1	0	0	0	0	0	.278
KIERAN CATSEF LF	4	0	1	1	0	0	0	0	1	.255
JUSTIN KESTINO SS	4	1	1	0	0	0	0	0	1	.280
BERNARD HARPER DH	4	1	2	2	0	0	1	0	0	.260
MORRIS JEROME C	4	0	0	0	0	0	0	0	1	.249

PITCHING	IP	H	R	ER	SO	BB	ERA			
LYNN MODA	5	6	5	1	4	1	3.72			
MICKEY PENNY	2	2	1	1	1	0	3.38			
ALEX BARSKY	1	0	0	0	1	0	2.25			
LEE HAZELTON (W)	1	3	1	1	0	0	2.98			

NEW YORK YANKEES

BATTING	AB	R	H	RBI	2B	3B	HR	BB	SO	BA
MARK STRANTON CF	5	2	1	0	0	0	0	0	0	.290
WILLIE ROBINSON 3B	4	1	0	0	0	0	0	1	1	.290
MAKOTO INABA LF	5	1	2	1	1	0	0	0	0	.294
RODNEY ROTTAPEL DH	4	1	2	3	0	0	0	0	0	.292
DAVE HUSSEY C	4	1	2	1	0	0	1	0	2	.251
JAKE KOENIG SS	4	1	1	0	0	0	0	0	1	.273
BOBBY FAULHABER RF	4	0	1	0	0	0	0	1	0	.277
ORESTES VEGA 1B	4	0	0	0	0	0	0	0	2	.247
LEE LEONARD 2B	4	0	2	1	1	0	0	0	0	.274

PITCHING	IP	H	R	ER	SO	BB	ERA			
CAMERON SWETOW	5	8	4	4	2	0	3.34			
BRUCE ROBINSON	2	3	2	2	1	0	3.36			
GARY ZIMMERMAN	1	1	0	0	0	0	3.18			
PETE SNOW (L)	0	2	2	2	0	0	2.84			

INNING	1	2	3	4	5	6	7	8	9	TOTAL
NEW YORK	4	0	0	0	1	1	0	0	1	7
CLEVELAND	4	0	0	0	0	2	0	0	2	8

GAME 150

By SAM LARDNER
The Cleveland Press

DETROIT, September 20 — Ollie Gonzalez said he felt a "little more responsible" going out for his start Monday night at Comerica Park.

The Indians' big lefty wasn't ruing the fact that he was injured for much of the second half. But he said he felt he let the team down in his previous start, a 10–1 loss to the Red Sox.

Gonzalez trudged out to the mound Monday and dominated the Tigers, throwing seven innings of four-hit ball in a 6–0 victory before 22,239 fans, many of them from Cleveland.

In fairness, if Gonzalez was responsible for that bad loss, he gets a large share of credit for pitching the Indians into a first-place tie with the Minnesota Twins in the American League Central.

The Tribe improved to 84–66 and gained a share of the top spot in the division for the first time this season. Both the Indians and the Twins will be doing a lot of scoreboard watching as the teams don't face each other again during the regular season.

"I felt kind of bad about that last one," the 26-year-old lefty said. "I let that one get away and damn near killed our bullpen. My mindset tonight was to go out there and pitch as long as I could."

Gonzalez is not too far removed from a bout of left-shoulder fatigue, so manager Todd Stein was mindful of the pitch count. Once the count reached 100 in the seventh and Gonzalez finished with 108, that was it.

"There's no sense in risking it," Stein said. "We're going to need this guy again in the remaining few games and hopefully in the postseason. Lee (Hazelton) and Buck (Sterling) took over out of the pen and gave the other guys a break. We're going to need them, too."

Except for the noise made by the 5,000 or so Indians fans who made the trip from Cleveland, the atmosphere here was decidedly more subdued than what the Indians enjoyed during their four-game weekend series against the Yankees. There's not much for the Tigers to play for, except for pride and spoiling the Indians' chances.

"We ain't layin' down for nobody," drawled Tigers manager Bill Roman. "They just happen to be the hottest team in baseball right now. But they're at our place, and we've got a lot of pride. We'll be heard from this week."

Indians hitting star Scott Michaels was heard from, but just barely, as he went a quiet 1-for-4, a third-inning single. His batting average dipped from .392 to .391.

Michaels got plenty of help from his friends, who hit Tigers starter Mack Mays with three runs in the second inning. With one out, Terry Rovetto walked and went to third on Oliver Reiner's single. Kieran Catsef then used the big outfield to hit a double to the gap in left-center to score both baserunners. Justin Kestino's single drove in Catsef.

Micah Millison hit a solo homer in the third, and Morris Jerome drove in two with a single in the seventh against Detroit reliever Grover Sheard.

"It was kind of nice to win without any drama," Stein said. "Maybe nobody will notice that we sneaked into a tie for first place."

GAME 150

CLEVELAND INDIANS VS DETROIT TIGERS · SEPTEMBER 20
CLEVELAND 6 / DETROIT 0

CLEVELAND INDIANS

BATTING	AB	R	H	RBI	2B	3B	HR	BB	SO	BA
RIKKI LABUDDA CF	4	0	1	0	0	0	0	1	0	.273
MICAH MILLISON RF	4	1	2	1	0	0	1	0	0	.281
SCOTT MICHAELS 2B	4	0	1	0	0	0	0	0	1	.391
TERRY ROVETTO 3B	3	1	1	0	1	0	0	1	1	.270
OLIVER REINER 1B	4	1	2	0	0	0	0	0	0	.280
KIERAN CATSEF LF	4	1	1	2	1	0	0	0	1	.255
JUSTIN KESTINO SS	3	1	1	1	0	0	0	1	0	.280
BERNARD HARPER DH	4	1	1	0	1	0	0	0	1	.260
MORRIS JEROME C	4	0	2	2	0	0	0	0	1	.252

PITCHING	IP	H	R	ER	SO	BB	ERA			
OLLIE GONZALEZ (W)	7	4	0	0	2	1	4.04			
LEE HAZELTON	1	1	0	0	0	0	2.92			
BUCK STERLING	1	0	0	0	0	0	3.75			

DETROIT TIGERS

BATTING	AB	R	H	RBI	2B	3B	HR	BB	SO	BA
RODNEY REYNOLDS 2B	4	0	0	0	0	0	0	0	0	.291
BOBBY BENKERT SS	4	0	1	0	1	0	0	0	0	.293
KYLE CRAMER 3B	3	0	0	0	0	0	0	1	0	.282
FREDDIE DERRING 1B	4	0	1	0	0	0	0	0	0	.290
AARON SCHUTZMAN LF	4	0	2	0	1	0	0	0	0	.279
KRIS WHYTE DH	4	0	0	0	0	0	0	0	1	.270
PORFIRIO FIGUEROA CF	4	0	0	0	0	0	0	0	1	.276
GRANT BERGSTROM RF	3	0	0	0	0	0	0	0	0	.253
RAMON GARCIA C	4	0	1	0	0	0	0	1	0	.242

PITCHING	IP	H	R	ER	SO	BB	ERA			
MACK MAYS (L)	6	7	4	4	4	2	3.58			
GROVER SHEARD	1.67	3	2	2	1	1	4.01			
DAMIEN MOORE	1.33	2	0	0	0	0	3.56			

INNING	1	2	3	4	5	6	7	8	9	TOTAL
CLEVELAND	0	3	1	0	0	0	2	0	0	6
DETROIT	0	0	0	0	0	0	0	0	0	0

GAME 151

By SAM LARDNER
The Cleveland Press

DETROIT, September 21 — The Indians' occupancy of first place, or at least a share of it, lasted all of one day.

The Detroit Tigers helped to evict them from the top floor Tuesday night with a sleepy 4–2 victory over the Tribe at Comerica Park.

Coupled with the Minnesota Twins winning late Tuesday night at Oakland, the Indians are again a game behind the Twins in the American League Central. Here's also how tenuous the Indians' grip on a postseason spot is: They're again tied with the Chicago White Sox for the top wild-card spot, with both teams leading the Boston Red Sox by two games.

In other words, the Indians can find themselves on top when this crazy season is all over, or they could wind up out in the cold altogether.

"This is what we've been preaching," said Indians manager Todd Stein, whose team is 84–67. "There is nothing guaranteed to us, and I know our guys are aware of that. You've heard them say all the right things.

"Even though the Tigers are having a down year, they're not going to give anything to us. We've got to be ready to play against them and all the teams we have left on the schedule."

One of the players with that outlook is second baseman Scott Michaels, he of the 56-game hitting streak and his recent run toward a .400 batting average. That run took a detour Tuesday as he went 0-for-3, dropping his average from .391 to .389.

Stein subbed Michaels out for Angel Rodriguez after the seventh.

"He might be dragging a little bit, and you can hardly blame him," Stein said. "Nobody wants to win more than Scottie, and it eats at him because it doesn't matter what he's doing individually. So it was a good time to get him off his feet for a couple innings. Knowing him, he'll bounce back strong tomorrow."

Rikki LaBudda also got a needed day off with Leo Taylor getting some playing time.

Indians starting pitcher Eli Batt suffered his second straight loss, but his teammates have scored only two runs for him in those games. Batt worked six innings, giving up all four Detroit runs on eight hits. Big Tigers first baseman Freddie Derring hit a two-run homer in the first. Batt gave up single runs in the fourth and fifth.

"I'll get a couple more starts before the season is over, and hopefully I can pick it up," said Batt, who came over in late July from the Reds. "This is what you play the game for. I want a shot at the postseason."

Speaking of pitching, Stein said Brian Howard would start Game 3 of this series Wednesday night. Howard missed his last turn in the rotation after suffering from a kidney stone but was given the OK and green light by team physician Joel Slutsky.

"The Doc tells me he is feeling fine, and he had a good side session the other day," Stein said. "This will get us back to that six-man (rotation), if we chose to do so, for the rest of the season. Of course, that could change. But you want a veteran guy like Doc out there when it's crunch time."

CLEVELAND INDIANS VS DETROIT TIGERS · SEPTEMBER 21
DETROIT 4 / CLEVELAND 2

CLEVELAND INDIANS										
BATTING	**AB**	**R**	**H**	**RBI**	**2B**	**3B**	**HR**	**BB**	**SO**	**BA**
LEO TAYLOR CF	4	0	1	2	0	0	0	0	1	.276
MICAH MILLISON RF	3	0	1	0	0	0	0	1	0	.281
SCOTT MICHAELS 2B	3	0	0	0	0	0	0	1	0	.389
ANGEL RODRIGUEZ 2B	1	0	0	0	0	0	0	0	0	.233
TERRY ROVETTO 3B	4	0	1	0	1	0	0	0	1	.270
OLIVER REINER 1B	4	0	0	0	0	0	0	0	0	.278
KIERAN CATSEF LF	4	0	1	0	0	0	0	0	0	.255
JUSTIN KESTINO SS	3	0	1	0	0	0	0	0	2	.281
BERNARD HARPER DH	4	1	1	0	1	0	0	0	0	.260
MORRIS JEROME C	4	1	1	0	0	0	0	0	1	.252
PITCHING	**IP**	**H**	**R**	**ER**	**SO**	**BB**	**ERA**			
ELI BATT (L)	6	8	4	4	5	1	3.86			
GENO MILZE	1	1	0	0	1	0	2.22			
MICKEY PENNY	1	0	0	0	1	0	3.32			
DETROIT TIGERS										
BATTING	**AB**	**R**	**H**	**RBI**	**2B**	**3B**	**HR**	**BB**	**SO**	**BA**
RODNEY REYNOLDS 2B	4	0	1	0	0	0	0	0	1	.291
BOBBY BENKERT SS	3	2	2	0	0	1	0	1	0	.295
KYLE CRAMER 3B	4	0	1	0	0	0	0	0	0	.282
FREDDIE DERRING 1B	4	1	1	2	0	0	1	0	1	.290
AARON SCHUTZMAN LF	4	1	2	1	1	0	0	0	0	.281
KRIS WHYTE DH	3	0	0	0	0	0	0	0	2	.269
PORFIRIO FIGUEROA CF	4	0	1	1	0	0	0	0	1	.276
GRANT BERGSTROM RF	4	0	1	0	0	0	0	0	0	.253
RAMON GARCIA C	3	0	0	0	0	0	0	0	2	.240
PITCHING	**IP**	**H**	**R**	**ER**	**SO**	**BB**	**ERA**			
SCOTT KREISS (W)	8	6	2	2	6	2	3.23			
SILVIO SEVERING (S)	1	1	0	0	0	0	2.79			

INNING	1	2	3	4	5	6	7	8	9	TOTAL
CLEVELAND	0	0	0	0	2	0	0	0	0	2
DETROIT	2	0	0	1	1	0	0	0		4

GAME 152

By SAM LARDNER
The Cleveland Press

DETROIT, September 22 — Brian Howard might as well have hung out his shingle with this notation on it Wednesday night: "The Doctor is on. The Doctor is on."

The 30-year old Howard showed that his demise was greatly exaggerated as he limited the Detroit Tigers to four hits and one run over seven innings in a 7–1 rout at Comerica Park.

With that victory and the Minnesota Twins' 6–5 loss at Oakland, the Twins (85–67) moved back into a first-place tie in the American League West. The White Sox are lurking a game behind in the best division race in all of baseball.

Howard's performance was, well, just what The Doctor ordered. He missed his last scheduled start after a nasty bout with a kidney stone. That passed, so to speak, and Howard returned and looked like a man on a mission.

He walked nobody, struck out four and allowed no Tigers baserunner past second base.

"I think we're all on a mission," Howard said. "Yeah, I was in some agony there in Chicago with that kidney stone, but once it passed and I rested for a couple days, I was ready to go. No ill effects. No weakness. No lingering pain.

"The other guys in this clubhouse are looking to me as a veteran to take the ball and pitch no matter what. This time of year, nobody is 100 percent physically."

The other bounce-back story of the night was second baseman Scott Michaels. After going 0-for-3 the previous night, Michaels went 2-for-4 (a single and a double) as his batting average held at .389. Michaels scored a pair of runs, coming home in the first on Terry Rovetto's three-run homer off Patrick McCoy. Micah Millison and Michaels each singled and rode home on Rovetto's blast to left-center.

"I kept an eye on Scottie the last couple days, and he might have looked a little gassed, but he'd never admit it," Rovetto said, playing his role as unofficial team captain perfectly. "With all he's done this year and coming out of nowhere to be the leading MVP candidate, it's been a lot to process, I'm sure. But he's handled it like a pro, and we're not here without him."

The Indians got two more in the fourth on Leo Taylor's two-run double. Taylor, who gave Rikki LaBudda a two-day breather in center field, knocked in Justin Kestino and Morris Jerome both singled.

In the ninth, Kieran Catsef tripled to score Micah Millison and Terry Rovetto, both of whom had singled. The Indians got nice mop-up work from Alex Barsky and Solly Alvarez out of the pen.

"This was nice again to get everybody involved," said Stein, whose team has one more left against the Tigers before heading over to Toronto for the weekend. "We'll try to do that the best we can, but the goal is to win games, get into first place and stay there."

CLEVELAND INDIANS VS DETROIT TIGERS · SEPTEMBER 22
CLEVELAND 7 / DETROIT 1

CLEVELAND INDIANS										
BATTING	AB	R	H	RBI	2B	3B	HR	BB	SO	BA
LEO TAYLOR CF	4	0	1	2	1	0	0	0	1	.275
MICAH MILLISON RF	3	2	2	0	0	0	0	1	0	.283
SCOTT MICHAELS 2B	4	1	2	0	1	0	0	0	0	.389
TERRY ROVETTO 3B	4	2	2	3	0	0	1	0	0	.272
OLIVER REINER 1B	3	0	1	0	0	0	0	1	0	.278
KIERAN CATSEF LF	4	0	2	2	1	1	0	0	0	.263
JUSTIN KESTINO SS	3	1	2	0	0	0	0	0	0	.283
BERNARD HARPER DH	4	0	1	0	0	0	0	0	1	.260
MORRIS JEROME C	3	1	1	0	0	0	0	0	1	.252
PITCHING	IP	H	R	ER	SO	BB	ERA			
BRIAN HOWARD (W)	7	5	0	0	4	0	5.01			
ALEX BARSKY	1	3	1	1	0	0	2.77			
SOLLY ALVAREZ	1	0	0	0	1	0	2.67			

DETROIT TIGERS										
BATTING	AB	R	H	RBI	2B	3B	HR	BB	SO	BA
RODNEY REYNOLDS 2B	4	0	2	0	0	0	0	0	0	.292
BOBBY BENKERT SS	4	0	0	0	0	0	0	0	0	.293
KYLE CRAMER 3B	4	0	1	0	0	0	0	0	0	.282
MARLON RIVERS 1B	3	1	1	0	0	0	0	0	2	.290
AARON SCHUTZMAN LF	4	0	1	1	1	0	0	0	0	.280
KRIS WHYTE DH	4	0	1	0	0	0	0	0	0	.269
PORFIRIO FIGUEROA CF	3	0	0	0	0	0	0	0	1	.274
GRANT BERGSTROM RF	3	0	1	0	0	0	0	0	0	.253
RAMON GARCIA C	4	0	1	0	0	0	0	0	2	.240
PITCHING	IP	H	R	ER	SO	BB	ERA			
PATRICK MCCOY (L)	3.67	9	5	5	2	1	3.74			
AARON BRISSETT	3.33	2	0	0	1	1	4.26			
CLAUDE SHOEMAKER	2	3	2	2	1	0	3.76			

INNING	1	2	3	4	5	6	7	8	9	TOTAL
CLEVELAND	3	0	0	2	0	0	0	0	2	7
DETROIT	0	0	0	0	0	0	0	1	0	1

GAME 153

By SAM LARDNER
The Cleveland Press

DETROIT, September 23 — Cleveland Indians, say hello to first place all by yourselves.

The Indians have enjoyed a share of the top spot this month, but they took a half-game lead over the idle Minnesota Twins with a 9–2 pasting of the Detroit Tigers Thursday night.

And hello again, .400 watch for Scott Michaels. The Indians second baseman went 4-for-4 against the Tigers to raise his average from .389 to .394.

"It's been a long road," said Indians manager Todd Stein, whose team is 86–67, a far cry from the 0–6 to start the season and then 2–8 when Stein took over for the fired Dave Mills. "We're not there yet. We've got nine games to play, and the way we feel, we have to win them all. But we'll savor it a little bit on the ride to Toronto. Our guys have earned it."

As for Michaels, things had quieted for him somewhat after he tied Joe DiMaggio's hitting-streak mark at 56 games. The talk of .400 had reared its head from time to time recently, but it also had quieted as he dipped under .390 after being as high as .394 on Sept. 15.

But after he hit three singles and one double (driving in a run) against the Tigers, it's game on again in the hype department.

"Not for me it isn't," he said with a look of resignation. "Like the rest of the guys in here, I'm enjoying being in first place, and that's where we want to stay. I got a little lucky tonight. I hit a couple balls good, but a couple found holes. I guess you need a little luck to hit whatever marks you're talking about. But I had no idea of the number until you guys told me. It's not like I calculate my batting average as I'm running to first base. I'm not that good at math anyway."

Self-deprecating and disarming humor have been Michaels' way of coping with all of the unwanted attention. Things shouldn't be too bad this weekend in Toronto, what with the Maple Leafs garnering all the attention with their training camp in full swing. But all bets will be off after that.

"We know the drill," Stein said. "Scott handled it all well during the hitting streak. I would hope that the press would be focused just as much on the team's comeback story. That's a pretty good one, too. Nobody gave us a chance as recently as midseason. But whatever comes our way, we'll handle it."

Indians batters handled Tigers starting pitcher Austin Wylie, scoring three in the top of the first inning to set the tone. Rikki LaBudda, Micah Millison and Michaels (infield single) all reached to load the bases. Terry Rovetto singled home two, and Oliver Reiner's sac fly scored Michaels.

That gave Indians starter Kenny Camden a cushion from the get-go, and he sailed through six innings, giving up six hits and two runs against a Tigers lineup that looked like it had their air taken out of it.

The Indians busted it open in the fourth, with Michaels' RBI double scoring Millison, who led off with a walk. Terry Rovetto walked, and Oliver Reiner hit a three-run homer to make it 7–0. The Tribe added two more in the sixth on a two-run double by Morris Jerome. The Tigers got a couple runs off Camden in the sixth, but that was it.

Lorry Unger, Alex Barsky and Lee Hazelton finished up out of the pen. Now, the real fun begins.

"We've got Fuji, Modes and Ollie ready to go against the Jays, and we'll see where we go from there with the rotation," Stein said, referring to pitchers Tak Fujimoto, Lynn Moda and Ollie Gonzalez.

And is there any chance Stein would move Michaels up to the leadoff spot to get him more at-bats and a chance at .400?

"I might think about it," the manager said. "But knowing Scottie, he'd see right through it and ask me not to do it because it's not about him. It's about the team for him. Also, I'd hate to break up the chemistry we have with the lineup so I tend to doubt it."

Read that as the door being slightly ajar.

GAME 153

CLEVELAND INDIANS VS DETROIT TIGERS · SEPTEMBER 23
CLEVELAND 9 / DETROIT 2

CLEVELAND INDIANS

BATTING	AB	R	H	RBI	2B	3B	HR	BB	SO	BA
RIKKI LABUDDA CF	5	1	2	0	1	0	0	0	0	.274
MICAH MILLISON RF	4	2	2	0	0	0	0	1	0	.285
SCOTT MICHAELS 2B	4	2	4	1	1	0	0	0	0	.394
TERRY ROVETTO 3B	4	1	2	2	0	0	0	1	0	.274
OLIVER REINER 1B	4	1	2	4	0	0	1	0	1	.280
KIERAN CATSEF LF	3	0	0	0	0	0	0	1	1	.256
JUSTIN KESTINO SS	4	1	1	0	0	0	0	0	1	.283
BERNARD HARPER DH	4	1	1	0	0	0	0	0	1	.260
MORRIS JEROME C	3	0	1	2	1	0	0	0	0	.253

PITCHING	IP	H	R	ER	SO	BB	ERA			
KENNY CAMDEN (W)	6	4	2	2	5	0	4.66			
LORRY UNGER	1	0	0	0	0	1	3.65			
ALEX BARSKY	1	1	0	0	1	0	2.57			
LEE HAZELTON	1	1	0	0	0	0	2.86			

DETROIT TIGERS

BATTING	AB	R	H	RBI	2B	3B	HR	BB	SO	BA
RODNEY REYNOLDS 2B	4	0	1	0	0	0	0	0	1	.292
BOBBY BENKERT SS	4	0	0	0	0	0	0	0	1	.290
KYLE CRAMER 3B	4	1	1	0	0	1	0	0	0	.282
MARLON RIVERS 1B	4	0	1	0	0	0	0	0	1	.290
AARON SCHUTZMAN LF	4	1	1	1	0	0	0	0	0	.280
KRIS WHYTE DH	4	0	0	1	0	0	0	1	0	.267
PORFIRIO FIGUEROA CF	3	0	1	0	0	0	0	0	1	.275
GRANT BERGSTROM RF	4	0	1	0	0	0	0	0	2	.253
RAMON GARCIA C	3	0	0	0	0	0	0	0	0	.239

PITCHING	IP	H	R	ER	SO	BB	ERA			
AUSTIN WYLIE (L)	3.33	9	6	6	3	2	3.80			
GROVER SHEARD	1.67	1	1	1	0	0	4.06			
DAMIEN MOORE	3	4	2	2	1	1	3.71			
AARON BRISSETT	1	1	0	0	0	0	4.17			

INNING	1	2	3	4	5	6	7	8	9	TOTAL
CLEVELAND	3	0	0	4	0	2	0	0	0	9
DETROIT	0	0	0	0	0	2	0	0	0	2

GAME 154

By SAM LARDNER
The Cleveland Press

TORONTO, September 24 — So is this how it's going to be for the next week or so?

If so, buckle up.

The Indians bade farewell Friday night to their few hours in first place with a 4–2 loss to the Toronto Blue Jays at Rogers Centre. Coupled with the Minnesota Twins beating the Chicago White Sox in Minneapolis, the Twins leapfrogged the Indians back into first place by one-half game in the American League Central.

That threw the Indians once again into the wild-card mix. They lead Chicago and Boston by two games for the top spot, with Oakland lurking another game back.

This was a frustrating loss for the Indians. Starter Tak Fujimoto pitched well enough, but errors in the field and the Indians offense leaving 11 runners on base and going 0-for-9 with runners in scoring position combined to doom the Indians on this Ontario night with the retractable roof open.

"Fuji gave us all he had," said Indians manager Todd Stein, whose team is 86–68. "But physical errors are going to happen. I have no problem with that. It's the mental errors that you can get on players about, and we haven't had too many of those. As for the hitting, give their pitchers some credit."

The Indians did get eight hits off Jays starter Dean Pinto, but they left the bases loaded in the first and fourth innings.

It was a rough night for Indians second baseman Scott Michaels. He went 1-for-5 at the plate as his batting average fell from .394 to .392. He also made a key error that allowed two unearned runs to score in the third to enable the Jays to take a 2–0 lead.

Before the game, Stein and general manager J.D. Eisner scotched any notion of Michaels being moved to the leadoff spot to give him more plate appearances and a chance at batting .400.

Michaels had significant input.

"That's putting one guy ahead of the team," Michaels said. "We should be talking about how I cost the team a chance at winning tonight instead of the whole .400 thing. I don't care about that. It was a rough night, and let's leave it at that."

Fujimoto worked five innings. He gave up a two-run homer to first baseman Andy Bell in the fifth, and Stein decided five innings were enough.

"I wanted to go more, but we still have more important games to play," Fujimoto said through translator Ryuji Sato. "I had only 80-some pitches, but that's the manager's decision. We were down 4–0 at that point, and if he wants to save me for one or two more starts, I am fine with that."

The Indians got a ninth-inning two-run homer from Kieran Catsef against Omar Melendez, but it was all too little too late.

"We've got a late-afternoon game tomorrow, and that should be interesting with the shadows if the roof is open again," Stein said. "We've got our ace (Lynn Moda) going, so we like our chances."

When asked about batting Michaels leadoff, Stein waved the question away.

"To be honest, we thought about it, but the player was clearly uncomfortable with it. So that's the end of that story. I might DH him on this (artificial) turf, but that's about the only change we'd make with Scottie. But it was worth some discussion."

GAME 154

CLEVELAND INDIANS VS TORONTO BLUE JAYS · SEPTEMBER 24
TORONTO 4 / CLEVELAND 2

CLEVELAND INDIANS

BATTING	AB	R	H	RBI	2B	3B	HR	BB	SO	BA
RIKKI LABUDDA CF	4	0	1	0	1	0	0	1	0	.274
MICAH MILLISON RF	4	0	0	0	0	0	0	1	0	.283
SCOTT MICHAELS 2B	5	0	1	0	0	0	0	0	1	.392
TERRY ROVETTO 3B	4	1	2	0	1	0	0	1	0	.275
OLIVER REINER 1B	5	0	1	0	0	0	0	0	1	.279
KIERAN CATSEF LF	4	1	1	2	0	0	1	0	2	.256
JUSTIN KESTINO SS	4	0	1	0	0	0	0	0	1	.283
BERNARD HARPER DH	3	0	1	0	0	0	0	1	2	.260
ICEBERG PETERS C	4	0	1	0	0	0	0	0	1	.210

PITCHING	IP	H	R	ER	SO	BB	ERA			
TAK FUJIMOTO (L)	5	6	4	2	3	2	3.17			
MICKEY PENNY	2	3	0	0	1	0	3.22			
BUCK STERLING	1	1	0	0	0	0	3.67			

TORONTO BLUE JAYS

BATTING	AB	R	H	RBI	2B	3B	HR	BB	SO	BA
CARLOS ARNALDO CF	5	0	1	0	0	0	0	0	1	.291
ANDY TENZER 3B	5	1	2	0	0	0	0	0	0	.291
RAMON ORTIZ SS	4	1	1	0	0	0	0	1	0	.281
ANDY BELL 1B	4	1	1	0	0	0	0	0	1	.290
JERMAINE BROWN LF	4	1	2	0	1	0	0	0	1	.282
JEFF STEPHANS DH	4	0	2	2	0	0	1	0	0	.268
JOEL NISSALKE 2B	3	0	1	0	0	0	0	1	0	.275
ROYCE MANFRED RF	4	0	0	0	0	0	0	0	0	.251
JULIAN GOMEZ C	3	0	0	0	0	0	0	0	1	.237

PITCHING	IP	H	R	ER	SO	BB	ERA			
DEAN PINTO (W)	8	8	0	0	6	4	3.90			
OMAR MELENDEZ	1	2	2	2	2	0	3.32			

INNING	1	2	3	4	5	6	7	8	9	TOTAL
CLEVELAND	0	0	0	0	0	0	0	0	2	2
TORONTO	0	0	2	0	2	0	0	0		4

GAME 155

By SAM LARDNER
The Cleveland Press

TORONTO, September 25 — The Phenom and The Ace have been quite the duo down the stretch drive for the Cleveland Indians.

They teamed up again Saturday in a 5–1 victory over the Toronto Blue Jays in a late-Saturday afternoon game at Rogers Centre.

Onetime phenom Scott Michaels paced the offense by going 3 for 5 with a home run as he raised his batting average from .392 to .394 with seven games remaining in the season.

Staff ace Lynn Moda bounced back from last Sunday's five-inning, five-run performance by going eight innings and giving up five hits, no runs, no walks and striking out six. In that last game, Michaels hit a walk-off homer to give the Indians an 8–7 victory over the New York Yankees.

"It's good to have him on my side," joked Moda, who is making his own run at postseason hardware in the form of the Cy Young Award. "What he's done in the second half of this season is something that will never be duplicated. Take that to the bank. A 56-game hitting streak and the possibility of hitting .400 for the season? No way. But he's doing it, and we're all feeding off of it."

Most important for the Indians, the victory enabled them to improve their record to 87 and 68 and pull one-half game ahead of the Minnesota Twins and back into first place in the American League Central. The Twins fell 6–3 at home against the White Sox, who now hold the second wild-card spot behind the Twins.

Michaels hit his 38th home run in the third inning against Victor ("The Opera King") Rossini to break a scoreless tie. Rikki LaBudda led off the inning with a single. After Micah Millison struck out, Michaels, in the DH spot today, launched one that nearly landed in the restaurant beyond the left-field stands, nearly ruining dinner for the patrons out there. Michaels singled in each of his next two at-bats.

"This is a great place to hit, especially with the roof closed," he said. "The ball really jumps here. I hope I didn't bust any plates out there. Being the DH every now and then has helped keep my legs fresh. And with Angel (Rodriguez) at second base, we get a net gain with his defense."

Rodriguez, whom Michaels supplanted in late May when Rodriguez went on the injured list, contributed two sparkling defensive plays and doubled home two runs in the sixth. The Tribe got an insurance run on a solo homer from Millison in the ninth, off of Jamie Shedler. Lee Hazelton worked the ninth and gave up one run on three hits to preserve the win for Moda.

"Scottie has been my biggest backer," Rodriguez said. "If I had to lose my starting job to anybody, I'm glad it was to him. Both on and off the field and personally as well as professionally, he keeps me going. He deserves all the good things that are coming his way."

GAME 155

CLEVELAND INDIANS VS TORONTO BLUE JAYS · SEPTEMBER 25
CLEVELAND 5 / TORONTO 1

CLEVELAND INDIANS										
BATTING	AB	R	H	RBI	2B	3B	HR	BB	SO	BA
RIKKI LABUDDA CF	4	1	1	0	1	0	0	1	0	.274
MICAH MILLISON RF	5	1	1	1	0	0	1	0	1	.282
SCOTT MICHAELS DH	5	1	3	2	0	0	1	0	0	.394
TERRY ROVETTO 3B	4	0	2	0	1	0	0	1	0	.277
OLIVER REINER 1B	4	1	2	0	0	0	0	0	0	.280
KIERAN CATSEF LF	3	1	1	0	0	0	0	1	0	.258
JUSTIN KESTINO SS	4	0	1	0	0	0	0	0	1	.282
ANGEL RODRIGUEZ 2B	4	0	1	2	1	0	0	0	1	.234
MORRIS JEROME C	4	0	0	0	0	0	0	0	2	.251
PITCHING	IP	H	R	ER	SO	BB	ERA			
LYNN MODA (W)	8	6	0	0	6	0	3.56			
LEE HAZELTON	1	3	1	1	0	0	2.98			

TORONTO BLUE JAYS										
BATTING	AB	R	H	RBI	2B	3B	HR	BB	SO	BA
CARLOS ARNALDO CF	4	0	1	0	0	0	0	0	1	.291
ANDY TENZER 3B	4	0	0	0	0	0	0	0	0	.289
RAMON ORTIZ SS	4	0	1	0	0	0	0	0	0	.281
RAYMOND BALKMAN 1B	4	0	2	0	0	0	0	0	0	.291
JERMAINE BROWN LF	4	0	0	0	0	0	0	0	2	.280
JEFF STEPHANS DH	3	1	1	0	1	0	0	0	0	.269
JOEL NISSALKE 2B	4	0	2	1	1	0	0	0	1	.277
ROYCE MANFRED RF	4	0	1	0	0	0	0	0	1	.251
JULIAN GOMEZ C	4	0	0	0	0	0	0	0	1	.235
PITCHING	IP	H	R	ER	SO	BB	ERA			
VICTOR ROSSINI (L)	5.33	7	4	4	4	2	4.22			
MIKE KILCRAN	1.66	2	0	0	1	1	3.28			
BUDDY HARKNESS	1	1	0	0	0	0	3.12			
JAMIE SHEDLER	1	2	1	1	0	0	2.94			

INNING	1	2	3	4	5	6	7	8	9	TOTAL
CLEVELAND	0	0	2	0	0	2	0	0	1	5
TORONTO	0	0	0	0	0	0	0	0	1	1

GAME 156

By SAM LARDNER
The Cleveland Press

TORONTO, September 26 — The final notes of "O Canada" had barely faded away before the Indians began their Sunday onslaught against the helpless Toronto Blue Jays.

Before Jays starting pitcher, Hank O'Brien knew what hit him, the Indians were up 6–0 on the way to a 12–3 victory at Rogers Centre by pounding out 17 hits including three home runs.

The Indians sent nine men to the plate in the first, and don't be surprised if those nine men form a welcoming committee for the Jays when they arrive in Cleveland for a four-game series to end the regular season beginning Thursday.

The victory gave the Indians (88–68) a little "breathing room" at the top of the American League Central. They now lead the Minnesota Twins by 1 and one-half games as the Twins lost 3–1 at home against the White Sox.

The Indians will take Monday off before going to Kansas City while the White Sox and Twins finish their wraparound weekend series in Minneapolis.

Blue Jays manager Paul Morris knows who he likes in the Central.

"My God, this team right here looks like a juggernaut right now," Morris said of the Indians. "They came out in the first inning like a team on a mission, which is what they're on, it seems to me. We're going to have our hands full going into Cleveland to finish the season. Maybe they can start without us."

That's exactly what it looked like beginning at 1:07 p.m. Sunday. Rikki LaBudda led off with a bunt single, and the track meet was underway. Micah Millison walked and Scott Michaels (2-for-6) singled to load the bases. Terry Rovetto singled two home. Oliver Reiner doubled in two more. Later in the inning, Iceberg Peters' two-run homer, his first of the year, ended the onslaught.

The outburst made for a long wait for Indians starting pitcher Ollie Gonzalez. That didn't affect him at all as he went out and to tossed six innings of six-hit three-run ball. All three Toronto runs came in the fifth, and by that time, the Indians had scored four more against Jamie Shedler who gave up back to back home runs to Kieran Catsef and Justin Kestino. The Jays conceded in the ninth when they had outfielder Royce Manfred pitch.

"I'll take it," Gonzalez said of the run support. "It was good to go six and then get out of there. Mickey (Penney) and Buck (Sterling) have been our unsung bullpen guys this year in games like this. They came in and made sure we kept that cushion."

Indians manager Todd Stein got several of his regulars off the field early. Michaels was the DH once again. His "quest" (he refuses to call it that) for .400 took a step backward as his average fell from .394 to .393. He played the whole game, but Stein found time late for Willie Bartlett, Leo Taylor and recent call-ups Steve Skeevers and Sam Traub who were making their major league debuts. Peters got the start behind the plate over No. 1 catcher Morris Jerome.

"We don't get many of these," Stein said. "On this (artificial) turf, it's good to get Scottie his at-bats as the DH, and it's good to get other guys off the field. With tomorrow being an off-day, everybody should be ready to go at Kansas City. It's all in our hands now."

CLEVELAND INDIANS VS TORONTO BLUE JAYS • SEPTEMBER 26
CLEVELAND 12 / TORONTO 3

CLEVELAND INDIANS										
BATTING	AB	R	H	RBI	2B	3B	HR	BB	SO	BA
RIKKI LABUDDA CF	4	1	2	0	0	0	0	1	0	.275
LEO TAYLOR CF	1	0	1	1	0	0	0	1	0	.282
MICAH MILLISON RF	5	1	1	1	0	0	0	0	0	.281
SCOTT MICHAELS DH	6	1	2	0	0	0	0	0	0	.393
TERRY ROVETTO 3B	5	2	2	2	1	0	0	0	1	.278
OLIVER REINER 1B	4	2	2	3	1	0	0	0	1	.282
STEVE SKEEVERS 1B	1	0	0	0	0	0	0	0	0	.000
KIERAN CATSEF LF	4	1	1	2	0	0	1	1	0	.258
WILLIE BARTLETT LF	1	0	0	0	0	0	0	0	1	.214
JUSTIN KESTINO SS	4	2	2	1	0	0	1	1	0	.284
ICEBERG PETERS C	4	1	2	2	0	0	1	0	0	.218
SAM TRAUB C	1	0	0	0	0	0	0	0	1	.000
ANGEL RODRIGUEZ 2B	4	1	2	0	0	0	0	0	0	.245
PITCHING	IP	H	R	ER	SO	BB	ERA			
OLLIE GONZALEZ (W)	6	6	3	3	4	1	4.06			
MICKEY PENNY	2	1	0	0	1	0	3.12			
BUCK STERLING	1	0	0	0	1	0	2.98			

TORONTO BLUE JAYS										
BATTING	AB	R	H	RBI	2B	3B	HR	BB	SO	BA
CARLOS ARNALDO CF	4	1	2	0	0	0	0	0	0	.292
ANDY TENZER 3B	3	0	1	2	0	1	0	1	0	.289
RAMON ORTIZ SS	4	0	0	0	0	0	0	0	1	.279
RAYMOND BALKMAN 1B	4	0	1	0	0	0	0	0	0	.291
JERMAINE BROWN LF	4	0	0	0	0	0	0	0	2	.278
JEFF STEPHANS DH	4	1	2	0	1	0	0	0	0	.270
JOEL NISSALKE 2B	3	0	0	0	0	0	0	0	1	.275
WALLY HUMPFRIES RF	4	1	1	1	0	0	0	0	0	.251
JULIAN GOMEZ C	4	0	0	0	0	0	0	0	1	.232
PITCHING	IP	H	R	ER	SO	BB	ERA			
HANK OBRIEN (L)	5	10	6	6	4	2	4.35			
JAMIE SHEDLER	3	4	4	4	0	1	3.44			
ROYCE MANFRED	1	3	2	2	0	1	18.00			

INNING	1	2	3	4	5	6	7	8	9	TOTAL
CLEVELAND	6	0	0	4	0	0	0	0	2	12
TORONTO	0	0	0	0	3	0	0	0	0	3

GAME 157

By SAM LARDNER
The Cleveland Press

KANSAS CITY, Mo., September 28 — The words "magic number" are now permanent parts of the Cleveland Indians' lexicon.

And there are two such numbers.

First and most important for the Indians, their magic number to win the American League Central is four, following Tuesday night's 6–3 victory over the Kansas City Royals at Kauffman Stadium. That kept the Indians two games ahead of the second-place Minnesota Twins with the five games to play. The Twins beat the Tigers 7–0 at home to keep pace with the suddenly surging Tribe.

The second magic number is .400. Indians second baseman Scott Michaels made a big move toward that number by going 3 for 4 against the Royals to raise his batting average from .393 to .396.

Michaels had three singles, two off starting pitcher Ender Ramos and one in the ninth against Joe Lacher.

"We're delighted for Scottie, but we're not looking at any numbers except for winning one game each day," said Indians manager Todd Stein in perfect manager-speak. "We've won three in row on the road now, and that's put us in a great position. The Twins are showing that they're not going away."

Nestled away in Kansas City, Michaels did not draw the big media crowds he did during his 56-game hitting streak, but that's going to change beginning Thursday, when the Indians return home to open a four-game season-ending series against the Toronto Blue Jays.

There were, of course, a few KC scribes who recalled George Brett's assault on .400 in 1980, when he wound up at .390 and led his team into the World Series.

"Eye of the storm," he said. "And I'm kind of enjoying it. I'm sure it's going to be crazy again this weekend. My family will be there again. Hopefully we're celebrating a division title. Whatever comes in addition to that will be a bonus."

The other story of this game was starting pitcher Eli Batt, who likely made his final start of the regular season. He made it a good one, working seven innings and giving up six hits and two runs. Alex Barsky and Ivan Zyzna finished up with Zyzna getting the save and lowering his ERA to a tiny 1.75.

Indians manager Todd Stein has been going with a six-man rotation for most of September. Brian Howard is lined up for Wednesday's finale of this two-game series. The final two days of the regular season may hinge on when and if the Indians can clinch the division.

"I'll be ready to go anytime, even out of the bullpen starting Thursday," said Batt, who came over from the Reds in a July trade. "I'm just happy to be in this position. I joke that I got traded from fourth place to first place when I came over here. I'm certainly not going to be choosy about when I pitch."

Michaels got things going in the first when he singled to center field with two outs. Terry Rovetto gave the Indians a 2–0 lead with a home run into the fountain waters beyond the center-field wall.

The Royals tied it in the bottom of the second on singles by Derrek Hargrove and Taylor Lawson and two-run double by Truman Greystone.

But that was all Batt gave up. His mates gave him some breathing room in the fourth when Michaels led off with a single. After Rovetto struck out, Oliver Reiner singled Michaels to third. Kieran Catsef hit a sacrifice fly, and Justin Kestino doubled home Reiner.

The Indians added two more in the ninth on Rovetto's single that scored Rikki LaBudda and Michaels against Lacher.

"If we take care of our business, we won't have to worry about the Twins," Stein said. "We've done that against teams we're supposed to be beating. Hopefully the calendar can run out with us on top."

CLEVELAND INDIANS VS KANSAS CITY ROYALS· SEPTEMBER 86
CLEVELAND 6 / KANSAS CITY 3

CLEVELAND INDIANS										
BATTING	AB	R	H	RBI	2B	3B	HR	BB	SO	BA
RIKKI LABUDDA CF	3	1	1	0	0	0	0	1	0	.275
MICAH MILLISON RF	3	0	0	0	0	0	0	1	0	.280
SCOTT MICHAELS 2B	4	3	3	0	0	0	0	0	0	.396
TERRY ROVETTO 3B	4	1	2	4	0	0	1	0	1	.279
OLIVER REINER 1B	3	1	1	0	1	0	0	0	1	.282
KIERAN CATSEF LF	3	0	1	1	0	0	0	0	0	.260
JUSTIN KESTINO SS	4	0	1	1	1	0	0	0	2	.284
BERNARD HARPER DH	4	0	1	0	0	0	0	0	0	.260
MORRIS JEROME C	4	0	1	0	0	0	0	0	0	.251
PITCHING	IP	H	R	ER	SO	BB	ERA			
ELI BATT (W)	7	6	2	2	6	2	3.73			
ALEX BARSKY	1	2	1`	1	0	0	3.00			
IVAN ZYZNA (S)	1	0	0	0	1	0	1.75			

KANSAS CITY ROYALS										
BATTING	AB	R	H	RBI	2B	3B	HR	BB	SO	BA
KYLE MONTGOMERY 2B	3	0	1	0	0	0	0	1	0	.291
NELSON QUARRELS RF	4	0	0	0	0	0	0	0	1	.287
DERREK HARGROVE 3B	4	1	1	0	0	0	0	0	1	.281
TAYLOR LAWSON CF	4	1	1	0	0	0	0	0	0	.291
TRUMAN GREYSTONE DH	4	1	2	2	1	0	0	0	2	.281
MAURICE MORSE RF	4	0	0	0	0	0	0	0	0	.267
WILL GUERRA 1B	4	0	2	1	1	0	0	0	1	.279
DIMITRI DEMOS C	3	0	0	0	0	0	0	1	1	.249
JARED BUCKNER SS	4	0	1	0	0	0	0	0	1	0.235
PITCHING	IP	H	R	ER	SO	BB	ERA			
ENDER RAMOS (L)	6	5	4	4	3	2	4.20			
AARON WESTFALL	2	3	0	0	1	0	3.26			
JOE LACHER	1	3	2	2	0	0	3.49			

INNING	1	2	3	4	5	6	7	8	9	TOTAL
CLEVELAND	2	0	0	2	0	0	0	0	2	6
KANSAS CITY	0	2	0	0	0	0	0	1	0	3

GAME 158

By SAM LARDNER
The Cleveland Press

KANSAS CITY, Mo., September 29 — For the first time with the Cleveland Indians this season, we're seeing something: a killer instinct.

The Indians walked into Kauffman Stadium this week and took it to the last-place team in the American League Central, the Kansas City Royals, at a time when it counted most. After posting a 6–3 victory Tuesday night, the Indians and pitcher Brian Howard shut down and shut out the Royals 7–0 Wednesday night.

That win was especially important with the Minnesota Twins taking care of business at home by beating the Detroit Tigers. The Indians (90–68) reduced their magic number to clinch the AL Central to three as they continue to lead the second-place Twins by two games.

Howard, who just days ago was passing a kidney stone, took the mound Wednesday night and pitched eight innings, giving up six hits while striking out four and walking no one.

Scott Michaels, used as the DH again, went 1-for-4 as his batting average dropped from .396 to .395. If he's going to reach the magic .400 mark, he's going to have to hurry as the Indians have just four games left, all at home against the Toronto Blue Jays beginning Thursday night.

First things first. The Indians succeeded in erasing a day off the schedule even if they did not gain ground on the Twins.

The way they did it impressed manager Todd Stein.

"That's what you call taking care of business," he said. "The Doc (Howard) went out there and dealt. You never would have known he was ill a few days ago. In fact, he never said a word about it or said that he might not be able to go. He just took the ball and went out there like the professional he is. A team can rally around that kind of thing."

For Howard, it was all in a day's, or a night's, work.

"That's what I get paid to do," he said. "We've all seen what Modes (staff ace Lynn Moda) has done down the stretch. The other guys have picked it up, too. And, of course, what Scottie has done and continues to do is beyond belief. So what I did here was no big deal. It was just my small part in helping this team win and get to where it wants to get."

The Indians offense has made a habit recently of jumping on opposing starting pitchers early, and Wednesday was no exception. Leadoff man Rikki LaBudda led off with a hustle double on his blooper to center field. After Micah Millison popped out, Michaels' cued an infield single down the first base line, with LaBudda stopping at third.

Terry Rovetto then hit one over the wall in left to stake the Indians to a 3–0 lead against Madison Behrens. It was Rovetto's second homer in two days.

"They really come at you," said Royals manager Steve Begor. "I can tell you one thing, they're the team nobody is going to want to face in the playoffs if they make it. They have enough momentum to go all the way. And wouldn't that be something? Todd Stein deserves a lot of credit for turning that team around."

From there, Howard coasted. The Indians got a pair in the fifth on a double by Justin Kestino with Rovetto and Reiner on board. Willie Bartlett, who subbed for Catsef in the bottom of the seventh, hit a two-run double in the eighth. Alex Barsky finished up on the mound for the Indians.

"We have a chance to do something special at home," Stein said. "It's going to be sold out all weekend. I know our fans will be into it. It's in our hands now."

GAME 158

CLEVELAND INDIANS VS KANSAS CITY ROYALS • SEPTEMBER 29
CLEVELAND 7 / KANSAS CITY 0

CLEVELAND INDIANS										
BATTING	AB	R	H	RBI	2B	3B	HR	BB	SO	BA
RIKKI LABUDDA CF	5	1	2	0	1	0	0	0	1	.276
MICAH MILLISON RF	4	0	0	0	0	0	0	0	2	.278
SCOTT MICHAELS DH	4	1	1	0	0	0	0	0	0	.395
TERRY ROVETTO 3B	3	2	2	3	0	0	1	1	1	.281
OLIVER REINER 1B	3	2	2	0	0	0	0	1	0	.284
JUSTIN KESTINO SS	3	1	2	2	1	0	0	1	0	.286
KIERAN CATSEF LF	3	0	0	0	0	0	0	0	0	.254
WILLIE BARTLETT LF	1	0	1	2	1	0	0	0	0	.267
MORRIS JEROME C	4	0	0	0	0	0	0	0	1	.248
ANGEL RODRIGUEZ 2B	4	0	1	0	0	0	0	0	1	.245
PITCHING	IP	H	R	ER	SO	BB	ERA			
BRIAN HOWARD (W)	8	6	0	0	4	0	4.77			
ALEX BARSKY	1	0	0	0	0	0	2.81			

KANSAS CITY ROYALS										
BATTING	AB	R	H	RBI	2B	3B	HR	BB	SO	BA
KYLE MONTGOMERY 2B	4	0	0	0	0	0	0	0	0	.289
NELSON QUARRELS RF	4	0	0	0	0	0	0	0	0	.285
DERREK HARGROVE 3B	4	0	1	0	0	0	0	0	1	.281
TAYLOR LAWSON CF	4	0	1	0	0	0	0	0	0	.291
TRUMAN GREYSTONE DH	4	0	1	0	1	0	0	0	1	.281
MAURICE MORSE RF	4	0	1	0	0	0	0	0	0	.267
WILL GUERRA 1B	3	0	2	0	1	0	0	0	1	.281
DIMITRI DEMOS C	3	0	0	0	0	0	0	0	0	.248
JARED BUCKNER SS	3	0	0	0	0	0	0	0	0	.233
PITCHING	IP	H	R	ER	SO	BB	ERA			
MADISON BEHRENS (L)	4.33	6	4	4	4	2	4.24			
GLENN MARCHAND	1.67	2	1	1	1	1	3.43			
JAIR MOSQUERA	2	3	2	2	1	0	3.42			
DERWIN RENTERIA	1	0	0	0	0	0	2.92			

INNING	1	2	3	4	5	6	7	8	9	TOTAL
CLEVELAND	3	0	0	0	2	0	0	2	0	7
KANSAS CITY	0	0	0	0	0	0	0	0	0	0

GAME 159

By SAM LARDNER
The Cleveland Press

CLEVELAND September 30 — If the Indians thought for one minute the Toronto Blue Jays were going to lie down, they thought wrong.

The awakening was a rude and jolting one Thursday night at Progressive Field, where the visiting Blue Jays thrashed the first-place Indians 8–1. So what was supposed to be a celebratory homecoming party for the Tribe has turned into a nervous vigil as the Indians try to complete a season-long comeback and win their division.

With the loss, the Indians dropped to 90 and 69, and with the Twins beating the Tigers, Cleveland's lead in the American League Central shrank to just one game, with each team having three to play.

The Indians' magic number remains three.

"I don't think we took them lightly at all," said Indians manager Todd Stein. "But they did come in here and whup our butts. Give them credit. They have nothing to play for but pride, and they showed a lot of that. We have three more to go, and it's still in our hands I'd rather be one up than one down."

Things got out of hand quickly as the Blue Jays hit the Indians starting pitcher Kenny Camden for three runs in the first inning

Camden didn't help matters by walking two, and Andy Bell made him pay with a bases-clearing double. "That's on me," Camden said. "You walk guys, and you're just asking for trouble. Not a good way to make my final start of the season."

Camden managed to gut out five innings, as he gave up eight hits and four runs. Relievers Lorry Unger and Buck Sterling gave up two runs each.

Meanwhile, Indians batters did nothing with Jays starter Gerry Lurie just three days after an onslaught against Hank O'Brien at Toronto in a 12–4 victory. Lurie worked seven innings, giving up six hits and one run, an RBI groundout off the bat of Morris Jerome in the fifth. Omar Melendez and Mike Kilcran kept the Tribe at bay the rest of the way, keeping the crowd of 37,345 quiet all night.

Indians second baseman Scott Michaels went 1-for-4 as his batting average ticked down from .395 to .394. He's going to have to go some to become the first .400 hitter since Ted Williams in 1941.

"Not a good topic of discussion tonight," Michaels said. "We're trying to win this division, and that's all that matters. If I go 0-fer the rest of the series and we win the division with me contributing in some other way, I'll be just as happy because we're winning. My friends and family will be here for the weekend starting tomorrow, and I want to celebrate going to the postseason with them. The rest of it is all decoration."

CLEVELAND INDIANS VS TORONTO BLUE JAYS • SEPTEMBER 30
TORONTO 8 / CLEVELAND 1

CLEVELAND INDIANS										
BATTING	AB	R	H	RBI	2B	3B	HR	BB	SO	BA
RIKKI LABUDDA CF	3	1	2	0	1	0	0	1	1	.278
MICAH MILLISON RF	3	0	1	0	0	0	0	1	0	.278
SCOTT MICHAELS 2B	4	1	1	0	0	0	0	0	0	.394
TERRY ROVETTO 3B	4	2	0	0	0	0	0	0	1	.279
OLIVER REINER 1B	3	2	0	0	0	0	0	1	1	.282
JUSTIN KESTINO SS	4	1	2	0	1	0	0	0	0	.288
KIERAN CATSEF LF	3	0	1	0	0	0	0	0	0	.255
WILLIE BARTLETT LF	1	0	1	0	0	0	0	0	0	.313
BERNARD HARPER DH	4	0	0	0	0	0	0	0	1	.246
MORRIS JEROME C	4	0	1	1	0	0	0	0	1	.248

PITCHING	IP	H	R	ER	SO	BB	ERA			
KENNY CAMDEN (L)	5	8	4	4	3	2	4.74			
LORRY UNGER	2	2	2	2	1	2	3.86			
BUCK STERLING	2	3	2	2	0	1	3.21			

TORONTO BLUE JAYS										
BATTING	AB	R	H	RBI	2B	3B	HR	BB	SO	BA
CARLOS ARNALDO CF	5	1	2	0	0	0	0	0	0	.292
ANDY TENZER 3B	3	2	2	1	0	0	0	1	0	.293
RAMON ORTIZ SS	2	2	1	1	1	0	0	1	0	.282
ANDY BELL 1B	4	1	3	4	1	0	0	0	0	.293
JERMAINE BROWN LF	4	0	1	1	1	0	0	0	1	.282
JEFF STEPHANS DH	3	1	1	0	0	0	1	1	0	.269
JOEL NISSALKE 2B	4	0	1	1	1	0	0	0	1	.275
ROYCE MANFRED RF	4	0	0	0	0	0	0	1	2	.249
JULIAN GOMEZ C	3	1	2	0	0	0	0	1	0	.240

PITCHING	IP	H	R	ER	SO	BB	ERA			
GERRY LURIE (W)	7	6	1	1	5	2	3.99			
OMAR MELENDEZ	1	1	0	0	0	1	3.32			
MIKE KILCRAN	1	1	0	0	0	0	3.12			

INNING	1	2	3	4	5	6	7	8	9	TOTAL
TORONTO	3	0	1	0	1	1	0	2	0	8
CLEVELAND	0	0	0	0	1	0	0	0	0	1

GAME 160

By SAM LARDNER
The Cleveland Press

CLEVELAND, October 1 — Two players who were questions marks at the beginning of the season and well into it turned in performances worthy of exclamation points Friday night at Progressive Field in a 9–2 victory over the Toronto Blue Jays.

As a result, the Cleveland Indians are on the verge of capturing the American League Central title.

Starting pitcher Tak Fujimoto, the prized free-agent acquisition out of Japan, spent much of the season trying to live up to the hype before he turned it on late in the season. He shut down the pesky Jays on five hits over seven innings to earn the victory.

Second baseman Scott Michaels, the oft-injured onetime phenom came out of oblivion this year to hit in 56 consecutive games and then stage a historical flirtation with .400 that continues into this weekend. He got the Tribe started Friday with a two-run homer, number 39 of the season, in the first inning to start the rout of Jays starting pitcher Armando Ojeda.

With the Minnesota Twins losing 3–1 at Chicago, the Indians (91–69) lead the Twins (89–71) by two games in the Central with each team having two to play. The Indians have clinched a tie for the division title with their magic number being reduced to one.

An Indians victory or a Twins loss Saturday or Sunday will make Cleveland the outright champion in the Central.

"This is what we played for all year, to be in this position," said manager Todd Stein, who took over as interim manager for the fired Dave Mills with the Indians 28 in April. General manager J.D Eisner removed the interim tag recently, giving Stein a well-deserved extension.

"I know a lot of people wrote us off, even at midseason," Stein said. "But our guys never stopped battling, and we kept the faith. We felt coming out of spring training there was plenty of talent on this team. It just took a while for it to jell."

Fujimoto, who has a dazzling array of pitches, found his groove in the second half as he appeared more and more comfortable in foreign surroundings.

"I had pitched for championships in Japan, but nothing like this," he said through translator Ryuji Sato. "To hear the crowd tonight supporting me was a special feeling. They were patient with me all year, and I appreciate that."

Michaels went 2-for-4 to raise his batting average from .394 to .395. He still will have to do some to reach the .400 mark over the final two games of the season.

It is now possible that Stein will move Michaels up to the top spot in the batting order to give him more plate appearances and a chance at becoming the first .400 hitter since Ted Williams in 1941.

Michaels seems amenable to the idea.

"If it's going to help the team, I'm for it," said the humble Michaels, who has resisted the notion to this point. "I just didn't want this to appear about me when we were battling — and still are battling — for a division title. We were in a fight for the wild card until very recently, let alone the division. But if Skip (Stein) feels it gives us a chance to clinch tomorrow, I'll give it a go.

"Just don't expect too many stolen-base attempts."

The Indians scored four times to chase Ojeda in the fourth inning, with backup catcher Iceberg Peters (Fujimoto's unofficial personal catcher) hitting a three-run homer. Rikki LaBudda followed that with a triple and came home on Micah Millison's RBI groundout.

The Indians added single runs in the sixth, seventh and eighth innings with home runs by Oliver Reiner, Justin Kestino and Bernard Harper. Geno Milzie and Lee Hazelton finished up for Fujimoto.

Andy Bell provided the only runs for the Jays with a two-run homer in the fifth.

Saturday's game will feature staff ace Lynn Moda on the mound for the Indians. The game will begin at 4:05 p.m. and be televised nationally by FOX.

"I feel good about our chances with Modes going," Stein said. "He's been our horse down the stretch. I'm sure he'll want to go nine.

"As far as Scottie goes, why not give it a shot up top? He's handled everything thrown at him this year. We're not doing it as a gimmick or anything like that. You want your hottest hitter getting as many ABs as you can. He gets that and so does Rikki, who's done a bang-up job as our spark plug all year. If we do make it (to the postseason), I'd imagine we'd go back to Rikki.

"But let's see what happens."

Indeed, let's see.

GAME 160

CLEVELAND INDIANS VS TORONTO BLUE JAYS • OCTOBER 1
CLEVELAND 9 / TORONTO 2

CLEVELAND INDIANS										
BATTING	AB	R	H	RBI	2B	3B	HR	BB	SO	BA
RIKKI LABUDDA CF	5	1	2	0	1	1	0	0	1	.279
MICAH MILLISON RF	3	1	1	1	0	0	0	2	0	.279
SCOTT MICHAELS 2B	4	1	2	2	0	0	1	1	1	.395
TERRY ROVETTO 3B	3	0	1	0	0	0	0	1	0	.280
OLIVER REINER 1B	4	1	2	1	0	0	1	0	1	.284
JUSTIN KESTINO SS	4	2	2	1	0	0	1	0	0	.289
KIERAN CATSEF LF	4	0	0	1	0	0	0	0	2	.248
BERNARD HARPER DH	3	2	2	0	1	0	1	1	0	.249
ICEBERG PETERS C	4	1	1	3	0	0	1	0	0	.219
PITCHING	IP	H	R	ER	SO	BB	ERA			
TAK FUJIMOTO (W)	7	7	2	2	5	1	3.15			
GENO MILZE	1	1	0	0	1	1	2.18			
LEE HAZELTON	1	0	0	0	0	0	2.92			
TORONTO BLUE JAYS										
BATTING	AB	R	H	RBI	2B	3B	HR	BB	SO	BA
CARLOS ARNALDO CF	4	0	0	0	0	0	0	0	1	.290
ANDY TENZER 3B	4	1	1	0	1	0	0	0	0	.293
RAMON ORTIZ SS	3	0	1	0	0	0	0	1	0	.283
ANDY BELL 1B	3	1	2	2	0	0	1	1	0	.295
JERMAINE BROWN LF	4	0	0	0	0	0	0	0	1	.279
JEFF STEPHANS DH	4	0	2	0	0	0	0	0	0	.270
JOEL NISSALKE 2B	4	0	1	0	1	0	0	0	1	.275
ROYCE MANFRED RF	4	0	1	0	0	0	0	0	1	.249
JULIAN GOMEZ C	3	0	0	0	0	0	0	0	2	.238
PITCHING	IP	H	R	ER	SO	BB	ERA			
ARMANDO OJEDA (L)	3.67	6	3	3	2	3	4.03			
BUDDY HARKNESS	2.33	4	4	4	1	1	3.78			
RICK SANTORI	2	3	2	2	1	0	3.42			
INNING	1	2	3	4	5	6	7	8	9	TOTAL
TORONTO	0	0	0	0	2	0	0	0	0	2
CLEVELAND	2	0	0	4	0	1	1	1		9

GAME 161

By SAM LARDNER
The Cleveland Press

CLEVELAND, October 2 — The clock read 7:07 p.m. when Andy Tenzer's pop fly settled into the glove of Indians second baseman Scott Michaels.

At that moment, the Indians were officially champions of the American League Central by virtue of a 4–0 victory over the Toronto Blue Jays at sold-out Progressive Field. Michaels leaped into the air and was greeted by pitcher Lynn Moda, who spun the rare complete-game shutout. Moda stuck out his glove, and Michaels plopped the ball firmly into the glove's pocket.

The rest of the Indians on the field joined the celebration as did players from the third-base dugout and the bullpen. The Indians didn't need to worry that the Minnesota Twins were losing at Chicago. They took care of business themselves with their 92nd victory of the season against 69 losses.

"How about this group," Moda shouted from inside the champagne-soaked home clubhouse. "We started out poorly. I started out poorly. We battled injuries. And now look at us. Champions of the American League Central. All the credit to the guys in here and to Steinie (manager Todd Stein) and J.D. (general manager Eisner)."

Moda improved to 18–10 with the victory, and after beginning the season 1–3, he's a prime contender for the Cy Young Award.

"That's an ace for you," Stein said as he reveled in the champagne showers. "He hasn't lost a decision since late July. Since then, he put the team on his back and carried us. What a gutsy performance today, too. There was no way I was taking that ball from him. That's OK. I think we'll give Eli (Batt) three innings tomorrow and then go with a bullpen committee. I'll worry about that later. We're all just enjoying this now."

Let's not forget about Michaels. He's back in the running to finish the season with a .400 batting average.

Moved to the leadoff spot Saturday to get more plate appearances, Michaels went 3 for 5 with a double and two runs scored as he raised his average from .395 to .396. He'll bat leadoff again in Sunday's regular-season finale even if many of the other regulars get a much-needed rest after celebrating Saturday night.

"Yeah, I think I'll pace myself tonight," said Michaels, who was nursing a soft drink after having just a sip of two of the bubbly. "Now that we've clinched, I have to admit I'm a little jacked about the possibility of hitting .400. I mean, who wouldn't be? A 56-game hitting streak and the possibility of hitting .400 is something nobody could ever have dreamed of."

Michaels brought the crowd of 37,656 to its feet in the first inning when he laced a single to center field. However, the Indians did not score off Jays starter Dean Pinto in the first, but Michaels' leadoff double in the third turned into a run when he scored on Micah Millison's single. A double by Terry Rovetto, who had a great second half, scored Millison to give the Tribe a 2–0 lead. Michaels singled again in the sixth and rode home on Terry Rovetto's homer, a blast that sent the crowd into a frenzy as the fans called team leader Rovetto out for a curtain call.

"That's something I won't forget," he said. "I joked that they actually wanted Scottie. But he pushed me out of the dugout. To see the fans react like that at the end of the season we've had, it's really special. I hope we can give them a lot more this month."

GAME 161

CLEVELAND INDIANS VS TORONTO BLUE JAYS · OCTOBER 2
CLEVELAND 4 / TORONTO 0

CLEVELAND INDIANS

BATTING	AB	R	H	RBI	2B	3B	HR	BB	SO	BA
SCOTT MICHAELS 2B	5	2	3	0	1	0	0	0	0	.396
MICAH MILLISON RF	3	1	2	1	0	0	0	2	1	.281
TERRY ROVETTO 3B	4	1	2	3	1	0	1	0	0	.281
OLIVER REINER 1B	4	0	0	0	0	0	0	0	2	.282
JUSTIN KESTINO SS	3	0	1	0	0	0	0	1	1	.289
RIKKI LABUDDA CF	4	0	2	0	0	0	0	0	0	.281
KIERAN CATSEF LF	4	0	0	0	0	0	0	0	1	.241
BERNARD HARPER DH	3	0	1	0	1	0	0	1	0	.249
MORRIS JEROME C	4	0	0	0	0	0	0	0	0	.246

PITCHING	IP	H	R	ER	SO	BB	ERA			
LYNN MODA (W)	9	5	0	0	6	0	3.39			

TORONTO BLUE JAYS

BATTING	AB	R	H	RBI	2B	3B	HR	BB	SO	BA
CARLOS ARNALDO CF	4	0	0	0	0	0	0	0	1	.288
ANDY TENZER 3B	4	0	1	0	1	0	0	0	0	.293
RAMON ORTIZ SS	4	0	0	0	0	0	0	0	1	.280
ANDY BELL 1B	4	0	1	0	0	0	0	0	0	.295
JERMAINE BROWN LF	4	0	0	0	0	0	0	0	2	.277
JEFF STEPHANS DH	4	0	1	0	0	0	0	0	0	.270
JOEL NISSALKE 2B	4	0	1	0	1	0	0	0	1	.275
ROYCE MANFRED RF	4	0	1	0	0	0	0	0	1	.249
JULIAN GOMEZ C	3	0	0	0	0	0	0	0	0	.237

PITCHING	IP	H	R	ER	SO	BB	ERA			
DEAN PINTO (L)	6	8	4	4	4	3	3.98			
JAMIE SHEDLER	2	3	0	0	1	1	3.32			

INNING	1	2	3	4	5	6	7	8	9	TOTAL
TORONTO	0	0	0	0	0	0	0	0	0	0
CLEVELAND	0	0	2	0	0	2	0	0		4

GAME 162

By SAM LARDNER
The Cleveland Press

CLEVELAND, October 3 — There was no escaping it, not for the 37,789 Cleveland Indians fans at Progressive Field nor for Scott Michaels.

Each time Michaels stepped to the plate Sunday afternoon; his batting average was there for all to see on the ballpark videoboard.

When he stepped in against Victor (The Opera King) Rossini in the first inning to a standing ovation, the board read .396. After Michaels cracked a single to center field, the average moved to .398.

A third-inning lineout brought both gasps and groans from the crowd, and the number dropped to .397.

The number inched back to .398 after a fifth-inning double down the left-field line.

In the seventh, Michaels' looper to left field dropped in and the board flashed .399.

Of course, Michaels saved his best for last. Stepping to the plate in the bottom of the ninth inning with the Indians down 4–0 and Angel Rodriguez on second base, Michaels fell behind Toronto Blue Jays closer 0 and 2 before teasing the crowd with three straight foul balls, the last of which popped out of the mitt of catcher Rico Espinosa.

On the next pitch, Michaels lofted a fly ball down the left-field line. Jays left fielder Albert Karroll gave chase but the ball cleared the high wall by inches and settled into the first row of the bleachers.

The board flashed ".400, .400, .400!" along with "40 home runs and 140 RBI!"

Rodriguez, whom Michaels supplanted at second base in late May, waited for him at home plate and wrapped him in a bear hug.

It wasn't a walk-off homer — the Indians lost the game 4–2 when Leo Taylor struck out to end the game — but it might as well have been. Michaels' teammates rushed out of the dugout to mob him, and the standing room only crowd stood and screamed for a good five minutes.

At the end of the day, Michaels hit for an even .400 on 230 hits in 575 at bats. He became the first player to reach the .400 mark since Ted Williams hit .406 in 1941, accomplishing something that eluded Hall of Famers Rod Carew, George Brett and Tony Gwynn.

His 56-game hitting streak this season tied the all-time record set by Joe DiMaggio, also set in 1941.

Imagine that: Being named in the same breath as Ted Williams and Joe DiMaggio.

Michaels' individual accomplishments helped enable the Indians to win the American League Central with a record of 92–70 after they started the season 0–6 and 2–8, largely with Michaels on the bench and perhaps contemplating his very future in the game, even at age 23.

To placate a crowd that would not leave the ballpark, Michaels took to a field microphone. His parents, Tom and Jennifer, and his girlfriend, Kristen Williams, were invited to stand on the top step of the dugout.

"You guys rock," he told the throng. "For a kid from Versailles, Ohio, being able to play in this state means so much to me. You guys and the Indians stuck with me all the way, through injuries and slumps. My family is here with me, and I consider all of you my extended family. The best part of all this is not batting .400 or hitting 40 home runs. It's that we have a lot more baseball to play in October!"

The Indians will take on the Texas Rangers on the road in Game 1 of the American League Division Series next Friday with the Yankees hosting the winner of Tuesday's wild-card game between the Twins and White Sox, both of the AL Central.

As for his pitching plans, Indians manager Todd Stein said he may go with Tak Fujimoto in the opener, what with staff ace Lynn Moda having worked Saturday.

"That's the early plan, but we'll see," said Stein. "We lost the game today, but this is Scottie's day. He deserves everything that's happened to him. I've seen him grow up right before my eyes. I can tell you that I never lost faith in him, and neither did this organization."

That sentiment was echoed by general manager J.D. Eisner.

"The only thing holding Scottie back were injuries, especially the shoulder injury," Eisner said. "He showed you why he was a No. 1 pick. Never, ever, did we entertain any offer to trade him, nor were we ever close to releasing him. Now, he's a sure MVP and who knows what else. I'm happy as can be for him and our team."

As for Sunday's game, it was all a blur except for Michaels' moments. Eli Batt got a tune-up start and went three innings, giving up four hits and two runs. Solly Alvarez came in and worked the next four, giving up the other two runs before giving way to Lorry Unger and Buck Sterling.

No one seemed to care.

"We were watching the videoboard along with everybody else," said Rodriguez, Michaels' best buddy on the team. "When I saw him hit that ball in the ninth inning, I was just hoping it had enough to get out. It was so high that I thought maybe their left fielder might catch it at the wall. When I saw it land in the bleachers, I nearly jumped to the sky. And then I looked up and saw that beautiful '400.'

"I had some tough spots this season, but the one guy keeping my spirits up every day was Scott Michaels. I want everybody to know that."

CLEVELAND INDIANS VS TORONTO BLUE JAYS · OCTOBER 3
TORONTO 4 / CLEVELAND 2

CLEVELAND INDIANS										
BATTING	AB	R	H	RBI	2B	3B	HR	BB	SO	BA
SCOTT MICHAELS DH	5	1	4	2	1	0	1	0	0	.400
LEO TAYLOR RF	4	0	0	0	0	0	0	1	1	.271
TERRY ROVETTO 3B	4	0	1	0	0	0	0	1	0	.281
OLIVER REINER 1B	3	0	0	0	0	0	0	0	1	.280
STEVE SKEEVERS 1B	1	0	0	0	0	0	0	0	1	.000
JUSTIN KESTINO SS	1	0	1	0	0	0	0	0	1	.291
WILLIE BARTLETT SS	3	0	0	0	0	0	0	0	1	.222
RIKKI LABUDDA CF	3	0	1	0	0	0	0	0	0	.281
KIERAN CATSEF LF	4	0	0	0	0	0	0	0	0	.235
MORRIS JEROME C	2	0	1	0	0	0	0	0	0	.251
SAM TRAUB C	2	0	0	0	0	0	0	0	1	.000
ANGEL RODRIGUEZ 2B	3	1	1	0	1	0	0	1	0	.248
PITCHING	IP	H	R	ER	SO	BB	ERA			
ELI BATT (L)	3	4	2	2	1	1	3.82			
SOLLY ALVAREZ	4	4	2	2	2	2	2.78			
LORRY UNGER	1	1	0	0	1	0	3.78			
BUCK STERLING	1	1	0	0	1	0	3.15			

TORONTO BLUE JAYS										
BATTING	AB	R	H	RBI	2B	3B	HR	BB	SO	BA
CARLOS ARNALDO CF	4	1	1	0	0	0	0	0	1	.288
ANDY TENZER 3B	4	0	0	0	0	0	0	0	1	.291
RAMON ORTIZ SS	3	1	1	1	0	0	0	1	0	.281
ANDY BELL 1B	4	1	2	1	0	1	0	0	0	.296
JERMAINE BROWN LF	3	1	2	0	0	0	0	1	1	.280
JEFF STEPHANS DH	4	0	1	0	0	0	0	0	1	.270
JOEL NISSALKE 2B	4	0	1	2	1	0	0	0	0	.274
ROYCE MANFRED RF	4	0	1	0	0	0	0	0	1	.249
RICO ESPINOSA C	3	0	1	0	0	0	0	1	0	.242
PITCHING	IP	H	R	ER	SO	BB	ERA			
VICTOR ROSSINI (W)	8	8	2	2	6	4	3.66			
RICK SANTORI	1	1	0	0	0	0	3.35			

INNING	1	2	3	4	5	6	7	8	9	TOTAL
TORONTO	0	0	2	0	2	0	0	0	0	4
CLEVELAND	0	0	0	0	0	0	0	0	2	2

EPILOGUE

November sunshine is something to be savored in the Great Lakes, as it is teasing and fleeting.

But two days after the World Series, downtown Cleveland was bathed in abundant sunshine as the Cleveland Indians and several hundred thousand of their closest friends gathered in Public Square after a citywide parade.

A modern-day philosopher wrote that "no one gets to their heaven without a fight," and the Indians certainly had to fight to get to their World Series heaven.

After the most improbable and historic of regular seasons, the Indians again tempted fate and dodged disaster to capture their first world championship since 1948.

Things began smoothly enough as they polished off the Texas Rangers in four games to win the best-of-five American League Division Series.

In the Championship Series, the Indians got their wished-for regular-season rematch with the New York Yankees, who swept the Chicago White Sox, winners of the wild-card game over the Minnesota Twins.

The Indians and Yankees split a four-game series in mid-September, and the two teams got their rubber game in October as the Indians marched into Yankee Stadium and won Game 7 in convincing fashion, 7–0 on the pitching of Doc Howard and the hitting of Scott Michaels, who had suffered through a mysterious ALCS slump after batting .400 for the season and tying Joe DiMaggio's record-56-game hitting streak.

After going 4-for-24 over the first six games of the series, Michaels hit a two-run homer and a two-run double in Game 7 to silence those who speculated that his magic had run out on the big stage. In fact, Yankees fans at Yankee Stadium taunted Michaels with chants of, "You're no Joe, you're no Joe," in reference to DiMaggio.

As for the World Series, well, perhaps not even seeing was believing.

The Indians took on the Chicago Cubs, who staged their famous comeback against the Indians in 2016, complete with a rain delay that seemed sent from above — if you ask Cubs fans.

Indians fans will tell you that turnabout is indeed fair play. Beginning the Series at Wrigley Field, the Indians were routed 8–1 and 9–3 in the first two games. Coming home for Game 3, the Indians were feeling confident, but starting pitcher Tak Fujimoto was outdueled 2–1 by Dan DeMarte.

Down three games to none, the Indians looked finished. But victories in Games 4 and 5 sent the Series back to Chicago, where the Cubs could clinch the title in front of the Wrigley Field faithful.

Kenny Camden kept the Indians alive in Game 6 by pitching a complete-game four-hitter in a 3–0 victory, with Oliver Reiner's three-run homer in the first inning holding up over nine tense innings.

The Cubs looked to have righted themselves in Game 7, taking a 4–0 lead over Fujimoto, who gave way after the sixth inning to Eli Batt and Geno Milzie. The Indians came within 4–3 in the eighth on a three-run double by Justin Kestino.

In the top of the ninth, Michaels came up with Rikki LaBudda on second base and two outs. With feared Cubs fireballer Andy Anderson on the mound and 41,000 Cubs fans screaming inside the ballpark and outside on the streets around Wrigley Field, Michaels sent a line drive cutting through a cold wind and into the bleachers over the 368-foot marker in left-center.

That kind of shock hadn't hit Wrigley since Game 6 of the National League Championship Series against the Marlins in 2003.

Another surprise was to come.

Indians closer Ivan Zyzna came down with a case of food poisoning, and when the bullpen door in right-center opened, out came ace pitcher Lynn Moda, who started Game 5 in Cleveland to keep the Series alive.

Even though he was going on fumes, Moda got by on guts and guile, inducing a pop out and a groundout before Steve Cook lofted a high fly ball to right field. Unlike Michaels' drive, this one could not overcome the hawk of a north wind, and the ball settled into the glove of Micah Millison on the warning track for the final out.

The Wrigley crowd was so quiet that the Indians players could be heard whooping and hollering all the way into the press box, where Sam Lardner was putting the final touches of his early-edition story for the Cleveland Press.

Cleveland rejoiced as Chicago wept.

"This is for all of Cleveland and for all those years of waiting," said team leader Terry Rovetto as he held up the World Series trophy at the rally. Even Cubs fans could appreciate that sentiment.

The off-season was full of more rejoicing for the Indians. Moda was voted the Cy Young Award winner for the American League, Todd Stein was named Manager of the Year and J.D. Eisner took home Executive of the Year honors.

Indians players voted full playoff money shares to Huron Southworth and J.J. Kulakofski, who were traded to the Reds for Eli Batt (who also got a full share) as well as to former manager Dave Mills, who was fired after just 10 games into the regular season.

Infielder Angel Rodriguez was named the Roberto Clemente Man of the Year for his charitable work benefiting the LGBTQ community.

Sam Lardner was given time off by the Press after the winter meetings, and he holed up in his hideaway on Siesta Key in Sarasota, Florida, no doubt sipping on red wine while watching sunsets over the Gulf of Mexico. But by February, the itch to cover baseball had returned, and Sam packed up and headed across country to Arizona for another spring training.

As for Scott Michaels, well, let's just say he cleaned up in every which way.

Michaels was the unanimous winner of the American League MVP Award as well as Comeback Player of the Year Award after recovering from shoulder surgery and coming out of nowhere to hit .400 and hit 40 home runs.

He also was named the Sporting News Player of the Year and the Sports Illustrated Sports Person of the Year.

So how did he do it? How did he hit .400 and hit in 56 straight games in this era of advanced scouting, shifts and intelligence reports?

As one veteran scout told Sam Lardner, it was a combination of Michaels being a line-drive hitter who makes solid contact and favors the gaps.

"No, I don't see it being done again — unless this kid does it next year," the scout said, perhaps only half-joking.

The kid from Versailles, Ohio, kept it real, though, declining offers to host Saturday Night Live and appearances on most late-night TV shows. He did return to his alma mater, Indiana University, where he was honored before a basketball game. He even sunk a half-court shot, of course he did, during a halftime promotion.

Michaels was eligible for salary arbitration, but the Indians wisely locked him up to a seven-year, $140 million contract, which he said allow him to buy nice places in both Versailles and Bloomington.

And one more thing: Kristen Williams said yes.

Michaels proposed to his longtime sweetheart on New Year's Eve, and the couple plan a late November wedding — after the World Series, of course.

ABOUT THE AUTHORS

Jack Shniderman is a lifelong baseball fan who has spent his entire business career in the retail fashion industry. Prior to his retirement in 2016 he was the president of the Polo Ralph Lauren store in Chicago and also President and owner of The Robert Vance Ltd stores in Chicago and suburbs. He and his wife have two wonderful children and their equally wonderful spouses in addition to five fantastic grandchildren. Raised in Chicago he lives in Northbrook IL and two of his favorite words are "Play Ball".

Bruce Miles has covered sports in the Chicago area for more than four decades. Before retiring in the fall of 2019, he served for 22 years as the beat writer covering the Chicago Cubs for the *Daily Herald* in Arlington Heights, Illinois. He has covered both Chicago baseball teams winning the World Series and has a soft spot for the Cleveland Indians after the Cubs beat them in 2016. A native of Chicago, he lives in the northwest suburbs of Chicago with his family.